Edition

Web 101

Wendy G. Lehnert

University of Massachusetts, Amherst

Richard L. Kopec

St. Edward's University

PEARSON

Addison
Wesley

Boston San Francisco New York
London Toronto Sydney Tokyo Singapore Madrid
Mexico City Munich Paris Cape Town Hong Kong Montreal

Publisher	*Greg Tobin*
Executive Editor	*Michael Hirsch*
Assistant Editor	*Lindsey Triebel*
Associate Managing Editor	*Jeffrey Holcomb*
Senior Production Supervisor	*Marilyn Lloyd*
Senior Marketing Manager	*Michelle Brown*
Marketing Assistant	*Sarah Milmore*
Senior Manufacturing Buyer	*Carol Melville*
Project Management, Text Design, Composition, and Illustrations	*Gillian Hall, The Aardvark Group*
Cover Designer	*Joyce Cosentino Wells*
Cover Image	*Susan Cyr*

Access the latest information about Addison-Wesley titles from our World Wide Web site: http://www.aw-bc.com/computing

Many of the designations used by manufacturers and sellers to distinguish their products are claimed as trademarks. Where those designations appear in this book, and Addison-Wesley was aware of a trademark claim, the designations have been printed in initial caps or all caps.

The programs and applications presented in this book have been included for their instructional value. They have been tested with care, but are not guaranteed for any particular purpose. The publisher does not offer any warranties or representations, nor does it accept any liabilities with respect to the programs or applications.

Library of Congress Cataloging-in-Publication Data

Lehnert, Wendy G.
  Web 101 / Wendy Lehnert, Richard Kopec. -- 3rd ed.
      p. cm.
  Includes index.
  ISBN 0-321-42467-0
  1. World Wide Web. 2. Internet. 3. Computer network resources. I. Kopec, Richard.
II. Title.
  TK5105.888.L435 2002
  025.04--dc22   2006101352

ISBN 0-321-42467-0
4 5 6 7 8 9 10—QGT—11

Preface

This book is for anyone who wants to learn more about the Internet. These pages cover all the basics for those who are just starting out, but they also include more advanced and optional topics for those who want to expand their knowledge in specific directions. At all times, our emphasis is more practical than technical, although we aim for a level of understanding that is more general than the operation of specific software applications.

 ## What's in the Book?

Chapter 1 starts by explaining some basic computer and computer networking concepts as a foundation for all that follows. We develop a working vocabulary in Chapter 1 before moving on to an in-depth tour of the Internet. Chapter 2 surveys important pitfalls and precautions before real hands-on learning begins—we don't want anyone to get into trouble, and there is danger out there. Starting with Chapter 3 on e-mail management, we encourage readers to dive right in and use the Net. E-mail is a good place to start because many people have an e-mail account and are already familiar with at least one e-mail program.

Although the Internet is clearly about computers, computer networks, and computer software, the Internet is also about information, people, and human communication. We cover the social aspects of the Internet such as blogs and social networks (Chapter 4), online search strategies (Chapter 5), software downloads and installations (Chapter 6), e-commerce (Chapter 7), and encryption for the Internet (Chapter 8). To be knowledgeable about the Internet also means being educated about a wide range of contemporary issues, including intellectual property laws, the First Amendment, personal privacy in a digital age, digital wiretapping legislation, self-regulation in American business, and consumer profiling practices. These topics are all introduced and discussed, with advice and guidelines for all Internet users.

No book about the Internet would be complete without an introduction to Web page construction. We cover the basics of Web construction in Chapter

9. Web programming using XHTML and Cascading Style Sheets (CSS) for beginners is in Chapter 10. Chapter 11 concentrates on dynamic elements created through the use of Java applets and CGI. We explain how to find and install existing scripts and applets, and we show what can be done without any knowledge of computer programming.

Where Are All the URLs?

As soon as you put something about the Internet into print, it's out of date. Unfortunately, this is especially true of addresses for Web sites, and this book mentions hundreds of Web sites. Many of the Web sites mentioned throughout this book list an address (URL) for the site, but some do not. Much like mayflies, most URLs live short, tempestuous lives. When a URL dies (stops working), the resource behind it may still be online, but it exists at a new address. We cannot update any dead URLs that appear in these pages, but we can and do update all the URLs at our companion Web site:

`http://www.aw.com/lehnertweb101/`

What's New in the Third Edition?

Like the Internet, itself, any textbook about the Internet needs to change continuously. Unlike the Internet, this is much more difficult to do using print media! In the process of revising the text, we found that the variety and number of Internet applications had increased dramatically since the second edition was published in 2003. In order to keep the size of the book manageable (and affordable), it was necessary to remove some old material to accommodate the new topics. Older and venerable technologies like Web accelerators, Usenet News, and traditional mailing lists were removed or dramatically downsized, and newer applications associated with Web 2.0 technologies like blogs, wikis, and folksonomies were substituted. Links are notorious for becoming obsolete—all links were checked, updated, and, if necessary, removed. Most of the screen shots and text refer to the latest version of Microsoft's browser, Internet Explorer v7, or Mozilla's Firefox v2.

Computer security is an increasingly crucial concern. Chapter 2 includes expanded coverage of security issues including pharming, phishing, smishing, identity theft, laptop security, and firewalls (updated and moved from Chapter 9). A brief description of the Netscape browser v8.1 Security Center is also included here. Chapters 9 and 10 replace Chapters 4 and 5 from the second edition. Chapter 9 is focused on the use of the Mozilla Composer Web page editor to create simple Web pages. Chapter 10 expands on this theme, but goes into more detail, including a review of HTML coding, along with an introduction to CSS. Also included in this chapter is a brief flirtation with forms, form control elements, events, event attributes, and elementary JavaScript to add interactivity to the page. The section on image maps from the previous edition is also included here. Chapter 11 expands on scripting, retaining the XML, Java, and CGI sections from the previous edition, along with entirely new sections on PHP with a worked example and a description of AJAX technologies used to power Web 2.0 applications.

A brief summary of the major changes follows:

Chapter 1. Updated list of TLDs, speed and bottlenecks, browser tips and tricks (with tabbed browsing and phishing filters added), updated/added section on alternate Web browsers (from previous Chapter 9), plus a browser plug-ins section (moved from Chapter 9) in the Above & Beyond section.

Chapter 2. Added phishing and identity theft. Summary of risks and hazards, and firewalls from Chapter 9 previous edition. Updated e-mail viruses. Cookie management updated in the Above & Beyond section.

Chapter 3. Mostly retained intact.

Chapter 4. Replaces previous Chapter 7 (Virtual Communities). Mailing list and Usenet News is dramatically downsized. Blogs, social networks, wikis, and folksonomies plus a section on Google Earth were added.

Chapter 5. Updates previous Chapter 6 (Find What You Want Fast). Searching the invisible Web was added in place of specialized search engines.

Chapter 6. Updates previous Chapter 8 (Software on the Internet). Additions on open source versus proprietary software and file formats. Downsized FTP clients.

Chapter 7. Updates previous Chapter 11 (E-Commerce). Online shopping and auctions is relocated here from Chapter 2.

Chapter 8. Renumbered Chapter 11 (Encryption and Internet) from previous edition; otherwise retained intact.

Chapter 9. Replaces Chapter 4 (Basic Web Page Construction) from previous edition. Uses Mozilla Composer to create Web pages. Includes most of the same topics.

Chapter 10. Replaces Chapter 5 (Advanced Web Page Construction) from previous edition. Adds CSS, expanded coverage for forms, form control elements, events, and event attributes. Retains image maps and rollovers. Introduces JavaScript.

Chapter 11. New chapter, includes CGI, Java, and XML from previous edition, adds AJAX and PHP. Advanced coverage of rollovers and JavaScript from previous edition placed in the Above & Beyond section.

From the 2nd Edition, Chapter 9 (Power Tools for the Internet) was removed. Most of the topics discussed here refer to tools that have been incorporated into all the modern Web browsers. The section on browser plug-ins and alternate Web browsers was moved to Chapter 1 and the firewalls section was moved to Chapter 2.

It's always hard to decide what to keep and what to remove. The publisher has made PDF versions of the deleted material from the previous edition available on the Web. Check our Companion Website at `http://www.aw.com/lehnertweb101`

Software Students Can Use

It is impossible to discuss software without showing examples of specific software packages in action. This is tricky in an educational text because we are not trying to endorse specific products; we just want some concrete examples for good pedagogy. We are also aware that it can be discouraging for students to see software that they cannot afford, and many popular software titles (for example, Web page construction kits) may be out of reach for a large number of students. In an effort to avoid commercial endorsements and pricey software, this book emphasizes the use of freeware (with two or three exceptions where comparable freeware is just not available).

This policy may perplex some instructors and experienced Netizens, who may find themselves wondering why the book showcases an obscure piece of freeware instead of a popular shareware alternative. In all cases, we have tested each of these freeware options and have found them to be largely comparable to their better-known commercial counterparts. Since 40% of all college students have a job and almost 50% take out student loans, it makes sense to help students minimize their computer-related expenses, and software is one place where students can exploit the Internet to great advantage. When it comes to software, high prices and high quality do not always go hand in hand.

Pedagogical Features

Throughout the text, we distinguish notable material using a system of four pedagogical boxes:

Tips. Tips provide useful information of practical value.

TIP: Technical Terms and Casual Usage

Although the term *memory* is correct when discussing RAM, and the term *storage* is correct when discussing long-term storage devices like hard drives, in casual use the term *memory* is often used (incorrectly) to describe both RAM capacity and hard drive capacity. So someone asking you how much memory your computer has may really want to know the size of your hard drive as well as the amount of RAM.

Checklists. Present do-it-yourself software checklists.

CHECKLIST: Get to Know Your Computer

Find out the hardware specs for your home computer:

1. How much RAM do you have?
2. How large is your hard drive?
3. How fast is your CPU?

For Your Information (FYI). Discuss related facts or background material.

FYI: Set Your Own Pace

If you already know a lot about computers, we will help you move through this chapter as quickly as possible. At the start of each section we'll give you a checklist of questions that you can use to assess your knowledge of computers. If you can answer all the questions in the checklist, it's probably safe to skip that section (or perhaps skim it).

Shortcuts. Present faster ways to accomplish tasks.

SHORTCUT: Keyboard Shortcuts

What You Want to Do	What to Type
Press the Back button	Alt + ←
Press the Forward button	Alt + →
Scroll down a little	↓
Scroll up a little	↑

Hands-On Learning

We may steer clear of in-depth software tutorials, but we emphatically stress that there is no substitute for hands-on experience when it comes to software skills. No one can learn about the Internet without getting online and working with Internet software applications. To encourage hands-on experimentation, we include two types of software-related exercises throughout the book: checklists and hands-on exercises.

Checklists. When appropriate, each chapter contains software checklists that enumerate the most important things readers should be able to do with a given piece of software. We do not explain how to do them, just that readers should be able to do them. For readers who have trouble with a software checklist, solutions for all of the most popular software applications are available at `http://www.aw.com/lehnertweb101`. Readers using different software titles can still tackle a software checklist and get the help they need—not from this book, but from this Web site. When the software changes, we will update our checklist solutions with solutions for new software releases or entirely new software packages as needed.

Hands-On Exercises. Additional opportunities for firsthand software experience will be found in exercises at the end of each chapter that have been marked **[HANDS-ON]**. Students will benefit from hands-on exercises whenever they are working with new software skills or a software interface that is unfamiliar to them.

Material at the End of Each Chapter

Things to Remember. Facts, tips, and reminders

Important Concepts. Key terminology and definitions

Where Can I Learn More? URLs for relevant Web sites

Problems and Exercises. Include three special types of questions:

- **[FIND IT ONLINE]** Find the answer on the Web
- **[HANDS-ON]** Gain experience with software
- **[TAKE A STAND]** Present and defend an opinion

 In addition, all exercises that are relatively time-consuming have been marked with a clock icon so students and instructors can plan accordingly. Many tasks on the Internet can be accomplished quickly, but some questions require an in-depth investigation or a careful examination of complicated issues. This book would do a disservice to students if we gave the impression that all questions can be answered with five minutes of effort and Internet access.

Each chapter is divided into two sections: a section containing core topics, followed by a section titled **Above & Beyond** that contains advanced topics. The Above & Beyond topics augment or complement the core chapter material and give students an opportunity to further enrich their understanding of the Internet. At the end of each Above & Beyond section is a second set of exercises, which covers only the material from the Above & Beyond section.

Glossary Terms

Important words and phrases appear boldfaced throughout the text. A glossary of the most important terms is also included at the end of the book for easy reference.

Web Sites to Visit

References to specific Web sites are printed in blue throughout the text. Links for all of these Web sites can be found at `http://www.aw.com/lehnertweb101/`

 # Topics and Chapter Selection

Chapter 1 First Things First

To get off the ground, we introduce the Internet in Chapter 1. Most important, we use this chapter to introduce the core vocabulary used throughout the book. We cover important Internet concepts and practical tips for working with Web browsers. Most of this material should be familiar to seasoned Netizens, but Newbies will find Chapter 1 a prerequisite for everything that follows. To speed more experienced students through this chapter, special mastery checklists are included at the start of each section so students who know the material can skip ahead to the next section. Special optional topics include a brief history of the Internet, an introduction to packet switching, and a discussion of file compression.

Chapter 2 Personal Safety Online

There are some very real dangers online. Many will be discussed throughout the book, but we devote Chapter 2 to the topic of personal safety so the basics of personal safety are all in one place. Chapter 2 will help students steer clear of the most serious mistakes that people make online. Optional topics include intellectual property laws for the Internet, notice and consent policies, how cookies work, safeguards for computers with broadband connections, and a brief history of computer hacking.

Chapter 3 E-Mail Management

Everyone uses e-mail these days, but not everyone has it under control. Chapter 3 begins with the basic operations of any good e-mail program and covers the rules of e-mail Netiquette that everyone should know. We look at different e-mail services (HTTP, POP, IMAP) and discuss the pros and cons of each service. Then we move on to filtering, routing, and some general mail-management tips. Optional topics include spam management, the challenge of managing multiple e-mail accounts, a tutorial on avoiding "raggy" text, and uuencoded mail messages.

Chapter 4 Web 2.0

People are social animals. We grow up in a family, we hang out with friends, and we talk to anyone who will listen. On the Internet, our social selves take on whole new personas. No longer limited to nearby neighbors and face-to-face contact, we can reach out to fellow Netizens across the country or around the world. People tend to look for others with common interests, and the Internet is one huge, never-ending college mixer (minus the bodies and the body language). Once you learn where to look, you can find entire communities of people who share some of your interests and enjoy talking about them. Chapter 4 explores the expanding online world, recently dubbed "Web 2.0," featuring AJAX-powered Web-based applications. Included in this chapter is coverage of Web-based discussion groups, blogs, social networks, RSS feeds, wikis, folksonomies, Google Earth, online chat, and instant messaging. Optional topics include censorship on the Net, privacy safeguards, and the problem of keeping children safe online.

Chapter 5 Find What You Want—Fast!

You might be wasting a lot of time if you keep going back to the same old search engine every time you need to hunt down information on the Net. Chapter 5 presents a systematic approach to online searching. We describe four different types of search tools and explain which tools are best for what types of questions. We show how to use successive query refinement to get the best possible results, and we finish up with a discussion of quality assessment. Optional topics include an introduction to concepts in information retrieval.

Chapter 6 Software on the Internet

Once you learn how to download software from the Internet, you may never visit a software retail outlet again. Excellent software can be obtained (without stealing) for free, and other software is available for a free evaluation—you can give it a test drive on your own computer before you buy. Then if you still want to invest in shrink-wrapped software, you can use search engines to shop around for the best prices. Chapter 6 spells out everything you need to know to find, download, and install software from the Internet. Optional topics include software licenses and the open source software movement.

Chapter 7 E-Commerce

A well-designed e-store makes it easy to shop online, but an educated consumer has to know more than any e-store can be expected to explain. Chapter 7 tells students what they need to know about SSL, digital certificates, certificate authorities, and online auctions. This background will help them understand and assess the level of risk associated with any e-store or auction site on the Web. Optional topics include the rush to establish commercial markets online, the hacker threat, and the resulting consequences for online security.

Chapter 8 Encryption and the Internet

Encryption offers a solution to a lot of problems on the Internet, including system security, private communication, and verifiable authentication for documents, software, and Web sites. Although specific encryption techniques cannot be described in detail to a nontechnical audience, general approaches can be described to a general audience. Chapter 8 explains both private-key and public-key encryption, how digital signatures work, and the difference between strong and weak encryption. Optional topics include PGP, how encryption relates to the culture of the Internet, and encryption as a tool for law enforcement.

Chapter 9 Basic Web Page Construction

Web pages are very easy to create these days and there are a number of very good WYSIWYG editors to make the process easy even for nontechnical people. We cover the use of Composer, a Web page editing application that comes as part of the Mozilla browser Suite courtesy of the Mozilla Foundation. Although the Suite is no longer supported by the foundation, the Mozilla community has adopted the Suite, which has been rechristened as SeaMonkey. We explain how to design and create a basic Web page using the tools provided in Composer, the image files types that can be used on a Web page, creating navigation bars, and publishing Web pages. The basics of copyright law are also presented. With this level of knowledge, students can construct a recreational Web page, spruce up a seller's listing at eBay, or add some pizzazz to an e-mail newsletter. Optional topics include image thumbnails, special image effects, audio files, and how to increase Web page hits.

Chapter 10 Advanced Web Page Construction

Creating Web pages using the Composer Web page is fairly easy to do, but somewhat limiting. While Composer is an extremely useful and capable Web page editor, there are many features that cannot be added directly with Composer, especially the flashy effects that make Web pages attractive. In addition, it's helpful to demystify the process of Web page editors and show that HTML files are nothing more than text files that can be created using a simple text editor. In Chapter 10 we build on the work begun in Chapter 9 by first introducing basic HTML and Web page structure. Students look "under the skin" to see how HTML is used to "markup" a page and control the display of page content. Students are encouraged to create Web pages using a text editor, or edit existing pages to show how simple HTML can be. Then we move on to CSS, describing basic CSS syntax and how CSS is used to gain better control of the appearance of Web page elements. After the presentation of these two topics, we present image maps and then we move on to introduce techniques used to add interactive elements that make for dynamic and sexy Web pages. Included in the last part is presentation of forms and form control elements coupled with elementary scripting using JavaScript to add simple interactive features. Optional topics include layers and Web site maintenance tools.

Chapter 11 Web Pages and Scripting Alternatives

While JavaScript has been specially designed for use on Web pages, there are other alternatives that can be used to add interactive elements to Web pages. In Chapter 11 we explore these other alternatives and how they all work in a similar fashion to achieve effects that can only be done using scripts. We introduce the concept of a CGI script, then apply this to the use of Java applets and data-driven Web pages. We explain the basics of XML and AJAX and show how these tools are used to provide Web 2.0 features. PHP is also introduced along with an application to show how it works. Optional topics include a more advanced treatment of JavaScript to add flashier rollover effects than those presented in the previous chapter.

Chapter Selection for Different Courses

This book was written for students enrolled in a course devoted to the Internet, as well as students in computer-literacy courses or other courses in which the Internet is only part of the curriculum. A curriculum based on all the core sections of this book will easily fill a 15-week course aimed at non–computer science (non-CS) undergraduates. A 15-week curriculum based on both the core and optional sections would be appropriate for an undergraduate (non-CS) honors course. Other combinations of chapters with or without the optional sections can support concentrations, intersession workshops, or independent projects (see below).

- A 15-week course devoted to the Internet: Chapters 1–11 without the Above & Beyond sections
- A 15-week honors course devoted to the Internet: Chapters 1–11 including all optional Above & Beyond sections
- An intensive (6-week) Internet concentration section within a computer-literacy course: Chapters 1–8 without the Above & Beyond sections

- An intensive (3- or 4-week) Internet concentration section in an introductory computer science course: Chapters 1, 2, 4, 9–11 with the Above & Beyond sections
- A workshop or independent project on Web page construction for advanced students: Chapters 9–11 with or without the Above & Beyond sections
- A workshop or independent project on Internet search techniques for advanced students: Chapter 5 with the Above & Beyond section
- A workshop or independent project on practical encryption for advanced students: Chapter 8 with the Above & Beyond section

Note that Chapters 1 and 2 are prerequisite chapters for everyone who is not an advanced student. However, Chapter 1 is easy to cover in a class with students at different levels because it has been designed to help the more experienced students skip over any material they already know. Keep in mind that many students who consider themselves to be very experienced with the Internet may need to review some of the material in Chapter 1 and probably will not know all the material in Chapter 2. Here is a chapter dependency diagram for customizing individual course plans.

1	2	3	4	5	6	7	8	9	10	11
	1	1	1	1	1	1	1	1	1	1
		2	2	2	2	2	2	2	2	2
		3					3			
							4			4
					5		5			
							6			
										9
									9	10
1	2	3	4	5	6	7	8	9	10	11

Each of these chapters requires the chapters listed directly above as prerequisites. Prerequisites highlighted in green are absolute, non-negotiable prerequisites. If you skip the other prerequisites, students can probably get through the material with a little extra help. For more curriculum suggestions, please see the Instructor's Manual (IM).

A Note to the Student

As the Internet evolves, we all have to struggle to keep up, and the first step is a solid foundation. Seemingly mundane activities such as a trip to an e-store can turn into a regrettable undertaking if you don't know how to spot a secure Web server, how to protect personal information from data resellers, or how to expect the unexpected. Other problems creep in over time. For example, e-mail is a breeze until you start getting 100 messages a day. Then you need to get organized and take advantage of specialized tools for e-mail management.

Ignorance of computer security is another pitfall for newcomers to the Internet. Each time you connect to the Internet, you open the door to possible hacker attacks. If you visit a poorly designed e-store, your credit-card number could be stolen. Spend some time at another site, and highly personal or sensitive information could wind up in countless databases. You can break the law by downloading the wrong file, or you could find yourself visited by the FBI or on the receiving end of a lawsuit for speaking candidly about the wrong subject in an online forum.

There is more to understanding the Internet than self-preservation and self-defense. For example, remarkable software is available on the Net—and much of it is free. But you have to know how to find it and how to move it onto your computer. There are some important dos and don'ts when it comes to free software, and all the basics are here. Then when you're ready to take advantage of all the Net has to offer, we'll show you some downloads that can transform your whole Internet experience.

Whether you expect to use the Net personally or professionally, this book will give you the skills you need to make the Net a real asset. No one can say what the Internet will be like 5 or 10 years from now, but the people who are using the Internet today will help shape the Internet of tomorrow. In a very real way, this technology belongs to you and is yours to mould. Every week, some congressional hearing in Washington touches on the Internet in one way or another. Children need to be protected. Consumers need to be protected. Musicians and artists need to be protected. A burgeoning e-commerce needs to be nurtured, and a digital divide between the rich and the poor needs to be crossed. Learn about the Internet today, and you will get the Internet you want tomorrow.

A Note to the Instructor

If you've taught an Internet course before, you know the Internet is not your only moving target. Your students are changing at least as fast as the Net itself, and it is necessary to take their collective pulse two or three times a year. According to a recent survey, 93% of all college students use the Internet and consider it an essential part of their academic and social lives. At least 75% of all college students know how to find and download music from the Net; 73% say they use the Internet to conduct research more often than they use the library; 72% of students check their e-mail every day, and 56% believe that e-mail has been beneficial to their relationships with professors. To stay in contact with friends and relatives, 28% use instant messaging. We are in the business of educating a wired population, and it is our responsibility to provide these students with the guidance and tools they need to use online resources efficiently and effectively. Most students are self-taught when it comes to the Internet, and many are convinced they know everything they need to know. This book was written especially for them.

Supplements

The following resources are available to qualified instructors only. Visit the Addison-Wesley Instructor Resource Center (http://www.aw.com/irc) or send an e-mail to computing@aw.com for information on how to access them.

- **Instructor's Manual**
    - Solutions to many problems and exercises in the book
    - Chapter notes and teaching tips
    - Suggested classroom demonstrations
    - Suggested class projects
    - A checklist of things to do at the start of the semester
    - A sample class syllabus (with variations)

- **PowerPoint Lecture Slides**

- **www.aw.com/lehnertweb101**
    The companion Web site contains a software index, links to software sites, documentation, and tutorials (when available) for all the software mentioned in the book.

Why the Iguana?

I suppose I should say a few words about the iguana. The green iguana is a fitting symbol for everything that is unique and wonderful about the Internet. Iguanas are surprisingly popular in the United States as pets, especially among college students and the 20- or 30-something crowd. Unfortunately, much published misinformation is available to a prospective iguana owner about what constitutes a healthy diet or how an iguana should be housed. Luckily for iguanas, many iguana enthusiasts are active on the Internet and talking to each other. Questions from beginners are being answered in great detail by herpetologists and experienced iguana owners. Thanks to the Internet, this native inhabitant of tropical rain forests now thrives in Arizona, Alaska, and all kinds of intemperate regions. The iguana community is not a place you will find on any map, but it is alive and well on the Internet!

 # Acknowledgments

Updating this text turned out to be a much more labor-intensive task than I had ever imagined—but a most rewarding one. There were many obstacles and delays encountered along the way, but perhaps this was for the best. Microsoft managed to release a new version of Internet Explorer v7 and the Mozilla Foundation released a new version of the Firefox browser before I was too far along so I was able to use them for many of the screenshots and related text in this book. I would like to thank my editor, Michael Hirsch, and the original author, Wendy Lehnert, for giving me the opportunity to revise the Web 101 textbook. I would like to thank my student assistants, Caitlin Cecic and Ruby Ganal for their assistance with proofreading chores as well as link checking and comments on the content. I would also like to thank former student and University employee Anna Stewart for her comments on my writing as well. Finally, I am most grateful to my dean, Charlie Bicak, and all the Addison-Wesley staff (listed in the joint acknowledgement), whose help and support was crucial in the completion of this task.

—Richard Kopec

Many people helped make previous editions of this book possible. First and foremost, I am indebted to my colleagues in the Computer Science Department at the University of Massachusetts who encouraged me to develop an undergraduate course on the Internet. I am also deeply indebted to the many undergraduate students who have taken my course and given me valuable feedback on my choice of topics, exercises, and examples. The enthusiasm and achievements of my students have kept me interested in the challenge of teaching the Internet to non–Computer Science majors in spite of all the work that necessarily accompanies a moving-target curriculum. There are also many individuals behind the scenes who have worked to make my classroom efforts pay off. The Office of Information Technologies (OIT) maintains our public computer labs on campus, provides excellent online software documentation, and keeps the campus online no matter what. The Computer Science Computing Facility (CSCF) is responsible for Internet access from my office, as well as the wired classroom where I teach Problem Solving with the Internet (CmpSci 120). I am also most grateful for the many just-in-time interventions of many remarkable individuals, including the entire CSCF staff and David Fisher, who manages to help me keep it all in perspective. My best defense against inaccuracies and outright errors were my truly excellent reviewers, who were most generous with valuable feedback, corrections, and suggestions. I am most indebted to the following people for their comments.

—Wendy Lehnert

Third Edition Reviewers

Bruce Sculthorpe (Metropolitan State College of Denver), Hossein Bidgoli (California State University, Bakersfield); Jim Chapman (Thomas College), Bruce Hoppe (Boston University), Nicholas R. Howe (Smith College).

Second Edition Reviewers

Hossein Bidgoli (California State University, Bakersfield), Eck Doerry (Northern Arizona University), Robert Franks (Central College), Lenore Horowitz, James Q. Jacobs (Mesa Community College), Edward Medvid (Marymount University), Michael L. Moats (Hillsborough Community College), Gregory B. Newby, Charles Slivinsky (Arizona State University), Ken Wade (Champlain College).

First Edition Reviewers

Jeffrey R. Brown (Montana State University–Great Falls), Janet Brunelle (Old Dominion University), Jack Brzezinski (DePaul University), Peter G. Clote (Boston College), Paul De Palma (Gonzaga University), Michael Gildersleeve (University of New Hampshire), Martin Granier (Western Washington University), Stephanie Ludi (Rochester Institute of Technology), Jayne Valenti Miller (Purdue University), Lori L. Scarlatos (Brooklyn College–CUNY), Scott Tilley (University of California–Riverside).

Their collective expertise and attention to detail improved this manuscript immeasurably. I, alone, must assume responsibility for any errors that have somehow survived the scrutiny of the review process.

Many thanks also to everyone at Addison-Wesley who have supported us in this endeavor. This revision would never have happened without the support and encouragement of Executive Editor Michael Hirsch. Assistant Editor Lindsey Triebel marshaled reviewer feedback, managed the permission of all copyrights, and answered a ton of questions. Maurene Goo and Jean Coston did a masterful job of securing permissions for all the screenshots used in the book. Production Editor Marilyn Lloyd tackled the unenviable job of putting it all together and remaining cool throughout. I am also grateful to Gillian Hall for her great support during the copyedit and composition process. Finally, thanks for Joyce Wells, who designed the book cover, and Susan Cyr, our cover artist, whose fertile imagination produces iguanas who can type and socialize on the Internet.

—Wendy Lehnert and
Richard Kopec (December 2006)

Contents

1 First Things First 1

2 Personal Safety Online   87

3 E-Mail Management 173

Web 2.0   233

5 Find What You Want — Fast!   339

6 Software on the Internet   401

E-Commerce   487

Encryption and the Internet   533

10 Advanced Web Page Construction   679

11 Web Pages and Scripting Alternatives 783

APPENDIX

HTML Tags and Attributes   841

Style Sheets   845

UNIX File Types   849

All about Copyright   851

First Things First

1.1 Taking Charge

As a college student, you have probably spent quite a few hours on the Internet, also called the **Net**, even if you don't own a computer. In 2001, college seniors used the Internet an average of 11 hours a week. Four out of five seniors turned to the Net for news and information, making it their preferred source for news, well ahead of radio or television. It's time to set aside all the hype about how the Internet is changing everything—the ability of the Internet to transform our lives is a given. Now we need to get down to the serious business of really putting the Internet to work for us.

Each of us brings our own set of interests and needs to the Internet. By using Internet resources intelligently, we can be better informed, better connected to others who share our interests, and better able to pursue our goals. However, achieving these benefits doesn't happen automatically. We can easily spend too much time socializing in chat rooms, surfing for entertainment, or exploring online games. In order to make our time online as productive as possible, we must begin by learning about the Internet and software applications for the Internet.

Chapter Goals

- Understand the purpose of your computer's CPU, RAM, and hard drive
- Learn about bits, bytes, kilobytes, megabytes, and gigabytes
- Find out how the Internet is structured and how computers become part of the Internet
- Discover how IP and DNS addresses are used
- Master the basic navigational features of your Web browser
- Learn about other browsers and browser features

Most people do not realize that they have many choices in interacting with the Internet. Surveys show that most Internet users start with one Web browser (typically the one that came with the computer) and never experiment with alternative browsers. Chances are, these people have never thought about all their software options and whether they're working with the software that's best for them. We all have many choices when we go online, and some of these choices will make the difference between a productive Internet experience and an ineffective or frustrating one. An educated Internet user makes informed choices and periodically reviews those choices in order to be as productive as possible online.

The Internet has evolved rapidly during the last decade, and this evolution is likely to continue well into the future. Keeping up with these changes can be distracting. However, we can tame the Net and put it to good use if we get serious about using it wisely. The trick is to figure out when we are using the Net effectively and when we are floundering. Then we can take charge of our expectations and our time in order to maintain the right balance between our online activities and the rest of our lives.

Taking charge means cutting a swath through the astounding number of choices and options that the Net offers. Our lives are shaped by all the choices that we make. We choose our friends, our interests, and our beliefs. We also choose clothes, cars, hairstyles, music, meals, pets, and insurance plans. The list is long and, at times, overwhelming. The Internet can help us make better choices by showing us available options, useful facts, and provocative opinions. The Internet also puts us in touch with a dizzying rate of technological change unparalleled in human history. We are clearly dealing with a transforming technology. The trick is to make sure that we stay in charge of the way the transformation affects our lives.

Much of the challenge before us comes down to plain old time management and the realization that the Internet can be a time sink just as easily as it can be a timesaver. We can conserve and optimize time by making informed selections of Internet software, based on a practical understanding of the Internet and its resources. If you are dealing with large amounts of e-mail, you can take steps to save time and manage those mountains of messages more efficiently (see Section 3.7). If you use a search engine to look for materials for a project (and who doesn't), knowing how search engines work can help you to locate exactly what you are seeking more successfully (see Chapter 5). Of course, when you're still learning it's hard to know what you need to know. That's why it pays to take some time to learn about software options for Internet users.

FYI: Set Your Own Pace

If you already know a lot about computers, we will help you move through this chapter as quickly as possible. At the start of each section we'll give you a checklist of questions that you can use to assess your knowledge of computers. If you can answer all the questions in the checklist, it's probably safe to skip that section (or perhaps skim it).

This book is a good place to start. It will introduce you to the most powerful Internet tools that every Internet user should know about. It will also prepare you to choose your Internet tools wisely regardless of how you intend to use the Internet: for work, pleasure, or both.

Before we start, let's make sure that we're all speaking the same language. Computer jargon is a stumbling block for many Internet newcomers (often called *newbies*) because they haven't yet learned basics. This chapter will help you understand the most commonly used terminology used to describe computers. Computers are typically described in terms of the software they run, how fast they run, and the amount of memory they contain. We will tell you what you need to know about computer software, speed, and memory in the next section.

1.2 Computer Basics

CHECKLIST: Should You Skip This Section?

See how many of the following questions you can answer:

1. What is an example of an operating system? An application program?
2. Will software written for a Macintosh run under Windows? Why or why not?
3. Can you install Windows on a Macintosh computer? Why or why not?
4. What happens to data in RAM when you turn off your computer?

If you can answer these questions, you can probably skip this section and go directly to Section 1.3.

1.2.1 The Operating System and Application Software

The heart of any computer is its operating system. An **operating system (OS)** is a large program that starts whenever you turn on your computer. The most important program running on your computer, the OS is necessary for other programs, called **application software**, to run. An application is a computer program such as Microsoft Excel or Adobe Photoshop. Applications are special-purpose computer programs that address specific computing needs. An application that is valuable to one computer user may be of no use whatsoever to another computer user. If computers were people, software applications would be acquired skills, like the ability to play tennis or speak Swahili. But an OS is something far more fundamental to the computer: an OS is like a computer's nervous system. It recognizes input from the keyboard and mouse, keeps track of files, updates the time display, tells you when you have a problem—it responds to your input and organizes internal resources. Without an OS, your computer cannot perform any of the fundamental tasks that make it useful. If something is wrong with your OS, you are in big trouble.

The world of personal computers has long been divided into two camps based on the OS they run: *Microsoft Windows* or *Apple's Macintosh OS (aka the Mac OS)*. The majority of personal computer users run Windows. However, other OSs are available. For example, *Linux* (a version of *UNIX*) is popular primarily with programmers and experienced computer users, but it is gaining a foothold in both business and home environments as an increasingly popular alternative to Windows. A computer that runs Windows is often called a **PC** (**personal computer**) to distinguish it from a Macintosh computer, called a Mac for short. For simplicity, this book uses the term *personal computer* to mean both PCs and Macs. When it comes to the Internet, PCs and Macs are largely indistinguishable, although software is generally written for one or the other: as a rule, software written for a PC will not run on a Mac (unless that Mac is specially outfitted for the task—see the *FYI: Windows on a Mac?*), and software written for a Mac will not run on a PC. (We will explain why in the next section.) Throughout this book, you will find many examples of Internet software in action. These examples are based on software for PCs,

FYI: Windows on a Mac?

 Current Intel-based Macs can actually run Windows (and Windows applications) instead of the Mac OS, but Apple Computer does not support this feature, so you need to be a sophisticated user to make this happen. Windows applications can also be run using the Mac OS with application software like iEmulator or Parallels Desktop, which allow the user to run Windows in emulation mode (albeit more slowly than on a real PC) in an application window within the Mac OS.

TIP: OS Upgrades and Software Compatibility

 Some OS upgrades are really shifts to a new OS insofar as application software is concerned. Always check to see which of your applications will successfully migrate to the new OS version before you upgrade. For example, Macintosh users who switched from Mac OS 9 to Mac OS X were really switching to a new OS, even though the names "Mac OS 9" and "Mac OS X" suggest a simple OS upgrade. None of the commercial software applications that run under OS 9 can be run under OS X unless they are run in *emulation* mode (aka "Classic" mode), in which OS X executes a program in a window that has the look and feel of Mac OS 9. Using Classic mode, the user can run OS 9 programs, but perhaps more slowly than they would if executed directly by an OS 9 Mac.

but if you have a Mac, don't worry. Whenever you hear about a piece of PC software, there is usually something analogous for Macs. In Chapter 6 we will show you how to find and select software for personal computers (both PCs and Macs).

A newly purchased computer normally comes with an OS already installed. Upgrading to a new version of the same OS is usually straightforward, although you'll want to set aside half a day for the process. Switching to an entirely new OS is a major undertaking because a move to a new OS means acquiring all new application software to replace the old application software that isn't compatible with the new OS. OS updates are frequently released to fix errors (aka bugs) and patch security flaws in the operating system programs.

1.2.2 The Central Processing Unit

The part of the personal computer that performs instructions is the **central processing unit** (**CPU**). The hardware unit that houses the CPU in a personal computer is called a **microprocessor**. (The Pentium D and the G5, formerly used in Macintosh computers, are two examples of microprocessors.) Microprocessors normally contain additional hardware that supports the CPU, but the terms *microprocessor* and *CPU* are often used interchangeably in casual conversation. The CPU is the brain of the computer—it is where most of the computations take place. As a general rule, when comparing two different Windows-based (or two Macintosh) computers to each other, the faster the CPU, the faster the computer. Even though both PCs and Macs now use Intel microprocessors, their operating systems are quite different. Because of the differences in the way their OSs are implemented, Macs and Windows-based computers cannot be directly compared to each other using clock speed. A CPU is characterized by three characteristics:

1. Clock speed
2. Instruction set
3. Word size (the amount of information it can manipulate at one time)

Clock Speed. A CPU's **clock speed** determines how many instructions (simple computer operations) the CPU can execute in a fixed period of time. Clock speed is given in **gigahertz** (**GHz**), a unit that refers to 1 billion cycles per second, where a **cycle** is the smallest unit of time recognized by the computer's internal clock. A CPU running at 2GHz goes through 2 billion processing cycles in 1 second. You may also see descriptions of CPU speed in terms of **MIPS** (1 MIPS = 1 million instructions per second), although this measure is less meaningful because different instructions require a different number of cycles. CPU speeds in personal computers get faster and faster each year. If your computer is three years old, its CPU is probably running at less than a third or even a quarter of the CPU speed of personal computers sold today. Sophisticated new application software often require the fastest available CPUs, so it is sometimes not possible to run new software on an older computer. Unfortunately, there is little you can do to speed up an old CPU. As a result, there is little demand for used computers, unless they are relatively new.

FYI: Moore's Law

Computers double in speed at least every 18 months and do so without any increase in cost.

Instruction Set. A CPU is also distinguished by its instruction set. An **instruction set** (aka **machine instructions**) describes the collection of operations that the CPU can execute. One instruction may negate an integer, while a different instruction adds two integers. Instructions like these are standard fare; other instructions may be specific to a particular microprocessor. As a result, a Motorola CPU runs a different instruction set than does an Intel CPU. At the lowest level, all software operates by executing operations in a specific instruction set. For example, for many years Macs used a Motorola CPU because the Mac OS relied on the Motorola instruction set. (Now Macintosh uses the same Intel CPUs found in many Windows computers, so Windows may now be installed and run directly.) To run Windows, you need an Intel

CPU (or another brand that supports the Intel instruction set) because Windows relies on the Intel instruction set. It is possible to simulate the Intel instruction set on a Motorola CPU and therefore run Windows on an older Mac with a Motorola CPU (see *FYI: Windows on a Mac?*). However, OS simulations on non-native hardware tend to run slowly because the target instruction set has to be simulated by the native instruction set. For this reason, OS simulations are never as satisfactory as an OS running directly on native hardware (the OS is implemented in its instruction set).

Word Size. Computer engineers can achieve significant increases in processor speed by increasing the **word size** (aka the **data width**) of a microprocessor. A larger word size means that a CPU can receive, manipulate, and return more data during each processing cycle. But a larger word size for a microprocessor also means that its instruction set needs to be modified so the instructions can keep up with larger data transfers—it will do no good to hand a CPU a larger block of data if all its instructions are still designed to handle smaller amounts of data. CPU speed, instruction sets, and word size all work together to determine the overall computing power of your computer.

Higher end PCs may also feature the use of dual-core processors. A dual-core processor includes two complete CPUs that can run independent of each other. This allows processing to proceed in a truly parallel fashion rather than having a single processor executing multiple programs by sequentially shifting its resources from one program to another in a rapid (to us) fashion. Theoretically, a dual-core processor should be able to complete twice the number of tasks of a single processor in a given time period, however, some processing time is spent ensuring that the two processors work in a cooperative rather than competitive fashion, so the observed speedup is less.

1.2.3 Memory and Storage

A computer contains different types of memory and internal storage areas, including:

- Random access memory (RAM)
- Long-term storage space

Random Access Memory. The memory that the CPU uses when it executes its machine instructions is **random access memory** (aka **RAM** or **main memory**). RAM is often called **fast memory** because the CPU can write to and read from it very quickly, thereby enabling the CPU to perform its operations as quickly as possible. RAM is also *volatile* memory: when you turn off your computer, all data in RAM is lost. RAM is sometimes described as a computer's version of human short-term memory. The amount of space is limited, and the information it contains doesn't stay there for long. However, it is a crucial gateway to your computer; most of the information going in and out of your computer moves through RAM.

Each program you run on your computer requires some minimal amount of RAM. When running more than one program at a time, your computer allocates a fixed amount of its available RAM to each program. If there is enough RAM to go around, everything works as it should. But if the running programs collectively require more RAM than is available, then the OS resorts to various *memory management strategies*, which may or may not work very well. Your computer might respond very slowly when it is working with less RAM than it needs, and it might crash more often when you try to run too many programs at once. It is usually a good idea to buy as much RAM as you can afford (although all computers have limits on the amount of RAM that can be installed). When you buy a new computer, never settle for the minimal RAM configuration. Research the software you want to run and then ask for at least twice as much RAM as the various software manufacturers say you should have. If you already have a computer that tends to crash when you open too many applications, check to see if your computer has room for more RAM. An ailing computer can often be made healthy with a RAM upgrade.

Long-Term Storage. A different type of hardware is used for long-term data storage. Modern computers contain large hard drives capable of saving all the files your computer needs as well as any data files you create for your personal use. Whereas data in RAM disappears when the power goes off, data saved on the hard drive is stable and persistent. The hard drive can be used to save, for example, computer programs, word processing files, and spreadsheet data, as well as that partially completed tax return. The larger your hard drive, the more files you can save and the more programs you can store on your computer. A lot of RAM can help your computer run faster, but a large hard drive allows you to install more applications, such as office programs and games.

TIP: Technical Terms and Casual Usage

Although the term *memory* is correct when discussing RAM, and the term *storage* is correct when discussing long-term storage devices like hard drives, in casual use the term *memory* is often used (incorrectly) to describe both RAM capacity and hard drive capacity. So someone asking you how much memory your computer has may really want to know the size of your hard drive as well as the amount of RAM.

FYI: Other Bits

If you are interested in computer hardware, there is more to it than RAM and hard drives. Personal computers often contain other types of memory and multiple micro-processors. Most CPUs include their own built-in short-term memory that is faster than RAM (for example, the L1 cache in G5 and Pentium processors). Cache memory is used to store portions of RAM onboard the CPU in order to decrease the time required to fetch needed data and instructions in RAM. If needed data is already available in cache, then the CPU doesn't need to wait a few processing cycles for the data to be located in RAM and sent to it. In addition, most computers also contain a **floating-point unit (FPU)**, a special microprocessor designed to handle floating-point arithmetic, which is crucial for speedy graphics displays. However, for the purposes of this book the most important hardware components are the CPU, RAM, and the hard drive as described in this section.

CHECKLIST: Get to Know Your Computer

Find out the hardware specs for your home computer:

1. How much RAM do you have?
2. How large is your hard drive?
3. How fast is your CPU?

If you don't know the answers, consult the Help feature for your OS and look for information about your system resources. Depending on your OS, you might need to find the answers in a few different places.

 1.3 Units of Memory

CHECKLIST: Should You Skip This Section?

See how many of the following questions you can answer:

1. What is the difference between a bit and a byte?
2. What is the ASCII character set?
3. Is 2,048KB equivalent to 2MB or 2GB?
4. Which consumes more memory, audio files or video files?

If you can answer these questions, you can probably skip this section and go directly to Section 1.4.

As people have become increasingly enamored with the Internet, many applications have surfaced to enhance the online experience. Many of these enable multimedia communication (audio and video) over the Internet. Software designers are always pushing the envelope regarding what applications are able to do on available hardware. In turn, hardware manufacturers labor to produce faster CPUs and larger hard drives at affordable prices. Some leading-edge software applications stress all but the most current and powerful computers, but software manufacturers know that hardware advances will make these products more accessible in a year or two—at least for those users who have access to the latest computers.

To understand how computing limitations can affect your experiences on the Net, you need to understand how files work. A **file** is a collection of electronically recorded information (consisting of either application software or data) that has a name (the **filename**). Almost all the information stored in a computer is stored in files. Thus the file is the building block of everything that we see and hear online. Files are constantly being moved across the Net, and different software applications work with different types of files. The size of a file often determines how long you must wait for an application to do something with that file, so it is important to know how big your files are. Files come in all sizes, from tiny to gigantic. In the next two sections we will explain how file sizes can be described with great precision.

1.3.1 The Bit

The smallest unit of measurement for computer data is called the bit. A **bit** is a memory unit that can hold one of two possible values: 0 or 1. All data inside a computer is represented by *patterns* of bits. A small number of bits can represent small amounts of information; larger amounts of information require more bits. The value of a bit stored in RAM or on your hard drive can be changed by software. When your CPU executes an instruction, it often stores a bit pattern in RAM, performs some manipulation on that pattern, and produces a new bit pattern as the result of the instruction. When you write over old files on your hard drive, you erase old patterns of bits and replace them with new patterns of bits. Media that allow you to save a bit pattern are called **writable** (if you can write to the media just once) or **rewritable** (if you can write over and over again). Media that you cannot overwrite are called **read-only**. For example, some CD-ROMs and DVDs are read-only media: their contents are permanent and cannot be altered. However, you can use a CD burner or a DVD burner to write once, but only once, to a writable CD-ROM or DVD.

FYI: What Is a 64-Bit System?

You may have seen references to a *64-bit system* or *64-bit software*. The number of bits refers to the amount of memory that a CPU can reference by naming specific memory locations (aka **addresses**). The range of addresses that a CPU can reference is called an **address space**. In a 64-bit system, both the OS and the CPU can (theoretically) work with 2^{64} memory locations (this is called a *64-bit address space*) by chunking 64 bits into a single unit that can be moved in and out of the CPU in a single cycle. Video-game consoles have progressed from 8-bit CPUs to 64-bit CPUs (for example, the recently announced Sony Playstation 3 will include a dual-threaded 64-bit IBM PowerPC core, plus 8 additional 64-bit mini-processors, which in fact operate like mini-computers on 128-bit data).

Software described as 64-bit has been programmed to take full advantage of a 64-bit CPU. (Note that both the processor *and* the software must be 64-bit to enjoy the benefits of a 64-bit system.) Windows Professional x64 Edition and Mac OS X (v 10.4) are 64-bit OSs; Windows 3.1 was a 16-bit OS. An application for Windows XP can be either 32-bit or 64-bit, but a 64-bit application will run faster because it can move twice as much information in and out of the CPU in a single cycle. Older Macintosh G5 computers include some 128-bit vector processing storage locations in their CPUs, although they are primarily 64-bit systems.

Yet a third type of CD-ROM and DVD is rewritable, just like a hard drive. Some computer users no longer use floppy disks for file backups because they can burn all their files onto writable or rewritable CD-ROMs, replacing hundreds of floppies with a single CD-ROM. Other examples of rewritable media include compactflash cards (aka flashdrives) and smartmedia cards.

1.3.2 The Byte and Beyond

The next unit of measure for data up from the bit is the byte. A **byte** is a pattern of 8 bits, for example, 00101110. Patterns of bits are used to represent the letters of the English alphabet (among others). It takes only 5 bits to create $32 \ (= 2 \times 2 \times 2 \times 2 \times 2)$ distinct patterns, more than enough to code the letters A through Z. Only 7 bits are required to code both lowercase and uppercase characters, numerical digits, and punctuation marks, with room to spare. The eighth bit is put to good use for error checking, which makes it possible to detect transmission errors when bytes are moved from one computer to another. A byte is quite convenient when you want to represent all the symbols that a keyboard can produce.

The visible characters you can type on a standard keyboard are referred to as **ASCII characters** because they are represented by the **ASCII character code**, which encodes 128 characters. (See Figure 1.1 for a sampling of ASCII character codes.) **ASCII text files** are files that contain only ASCII characters. **Binary files** contain additional characters not found on any keyboard (these files are usually generated by or represent computer programs). The size of a file (for both ASCII and binary files) is measured by the number of bytes needed to represent its contents. For an ASCII text file, this number is roughly equivalent to the number of characters in the file. For example, a page of text that has 60 lines of text and 110 characters per line contains 6,600 characters and consumes 6,600 bytes of memory.

Figure 1.1

ASCII character codes for programmers

	0	1	2	3	4	5	6	7	8	9	A	B	C	D	E	F
0	NUL	SOH	STX	ETX	EOT	ENQ	ACK	BEL	BS	HT	LF	VT	FF	CR	SO	SI
1	DLE	DC1	DC2	DC3	DC4	NAK	SYN	ETB	CAN	EM	SUB	ESC	FS	GS	RS	US
2	SPC	!	"	#	$	%	&	'	(	)	*	+	,	−	.	/
3	0	1	2	3	4	5	6	7	8	9	:	;	<	=	>	?
4	@	A	B	C	D	E	F	G	H	I	J	K	L	M	N	O
5	P	Q	R	S	T	U	V	W	X	Y	Z	[	\	]	^	_
6	'	a	b	c	d	e	f	g	h	i	j	k	l	m	n	o
7	p	q	r	s	t	u	v	w	x	y	z	{	|	}	~	DEL

FYI: Japanese Needs More Than a Byte

The ASCII character code was designed around the Latin alphabet, which has relatively few characters. Non-Latin-based languages like Japanese, which has 1,945 jouyou kanji characters, cannot be encoded using ASCII. To handle the Japanese language and other non-Latin alphabets, a new character coding scheme dubbed **Unicode** was created. The new coding system uses 16 bits to represent an individual character, providing the ability to encode 2^{16} characters, enough for most of the characters used by all languages currently in use around the world. With extensions, Unicode is capable of encoding the characters for every known written language on the planet, past or present.

Kilobytes, Megabytes, and Gigabytes. For easy reference, bytes are grouped into larger units. For example, a **kilobyte** (**KB**) consists of 1,024 bytes. (In casual writing, you might see the abbreviation *K* instead of *KB*.) Although the term *kilo* means 1,000, a kilobyte contains 1,024 bytes rather than 1,000 bytes. Why? Because the arithmetic of computers works with binary (base 2) representations for numbers. Recall that a bit can hold just two values: either a 0 or a 1. Binary numbers are also represented with just 0s and 1s instead of the 10 numerals (0–9) we normally use. Since everything stored in a computer ultimately comes down to collections of bits, binary numbers are the most natural numbers for computers. And just as the number $1,000_{\text{(base 10)}} = 10^3$ is a nice round number in the decimal system, the number 1,024 is a nice round number in base 2 because $1,024_{\text{(base 10)}} = 10,000,000,000_{\text{(base 2)}} = 2^{10}$. When you need only a rough estimate, you can think of a kilobyte as being 1,000 bytes. But when you need to be precise, use 1,024 bytes. For example, a page of text that contains 6,600 bytes consumes approximately 6.6KB (6,600 ÷ 1,000) of memory, or, more precisely, 6.45KB (6,600 ÷ 1,024, rounded to the nearest hundredth).

If you need to deal only with text, you can go far with just kilobytes. For really large numbers of bytes, however, a more convenient unit to work with is the megabyte. A **megabyte** (**MB**) is $2^{20} = 1,024$KB—roughly 1,000KB, if you need only a quick estimate. Therefore 1,000 pages of text with 6,600 characters per page will require 6,445KB (6,600,000 ÷ 1,024) of memory, which is about 6.45MB (6,445 ÷ 1,000, rounded) or, more precisely, 6.29MB (6,445 ÷ 1,024, rounded). Most text files are not this large, but you'll routinely encounter megabytes when referring to RAM. Computers need large amounts of RAM to cope with all the graphics that are commonplace on the Net. Compared to text, graphical images require significantly larger amounts of memory. Whoever said that a picture is worth a thousand words was low-balling the estimate. One thousand words that consist of approximately 5,600 characters require an estimated 5.5KB of memory. For graphics, this would be enough memory for only one black-and-white drawing of, say, Dilbert, or perhaps a small colored arrow on a Web page. Larger images can consume 60KB or more of memory, and a high-resolution photograph, such as the one in Figure 1.2, can eat up as much as 8MB or more if nothing clever has been done to conserve memory. One large photograph is too big for a 1.44MB floppy disk (although that same floppy can hold 200 pages of plain ASCII text)—you'd need at least one CD to store it, and you could only fit about 6 more.

The photograph in Figure 1.2 was taken with a Canon PowerShot S45 digital camera in high-resolution mode (2,272 × 1,704 pixels per picture). The camera produced a JPEG image that consumed 3.7MB of storage space. This is a high level of resolution suitable for printing a high-quality 8-inch × 10-inch

Figure 1.2
Web page authors
work with digital
images.

FYI: Printer Resolution

Printer manufacturers characterize printer resolution in terms of dpi (dots per inch). An image is formed by combining miniscule dots of varying colors in such a way that an image appears. As the dot size gets smaller, the fine details in the printed image become clearer, resulting in higher resolution, so you clearly want to get a printer that has a reasonably high dpi (say about 1200). However, the dpi value only gives you an estimate of the true resolution, which should be reported in terms of lpi (lines per inch). For example, a grayscale image is formed using black ink to form spots of varying sizes placed into a grid of cells in varying patterns known as a halftone grid. Fewer, larger spots create the illusion of black, while smaller, fewer dots create the illusion of grey. The spacing of the cells in the grid, reported as lines per inch, actually determines the resolution. The situation is even trickier when using color. Most color inkjet printers utilize 4–6 different colors of ink. To create colors, the dots must be scattered around randomly, or dithered, in such a way that combination of dots creates the illusion of a different color, like the combination of red and yellow dots to create orange. A 300–600 dpi laser printer can usually print an image at 50–65 lpi resolution. Magazines typically use 133–150 lpi resolution, while your average newspaper is about 85 lpi. The quality of the paper also affects resolution. When using a poor quality paper, the ink spot may spread out, decreasing the effective resolution. Check `http://www.scantips.com/basics03.html` for more details.

photograph on paper. If you are taking pictures just for the Web, you can use lower levels of resolution (for example, $1,152 \times 768$ or 768×512 pixels) because computer monitors display fewer pixels per inch than high-quality printers. A good printer can print as many as 1200 **dpi** (**dots per inch**), but the actual image resolution depends on other factors (see *FYI: Printer Resolution*), and will nearly always be a much lower number. A good computer monitor displays about 72–96 **ppi** (**pixels per inch**—Pixels become "dots" in the context of printer resolution. Even so, many references use dpi when discussing monitor resolution). Lower-resolution settings on your camera allow you to take more pictures before you run out of memory. For example, a 256MB memory card holds about 70 high-resolution ($2,272 \times 1,704$) photographs or 682 low-resolution (768×512) photographs.

As people started working more with graphics on their personal computers, they began to need larger storage devices for handling large files. In 1995, the storage capacity of hard drives for high-end personal computers crossed the line from megabytes to gigabytes. A **gigabyte** (**GB**) is 2^{30} bytes = 1,024MB. At about the same time, floppy disks began to give way to Zip disks (which hold 100MB to 250MB per disk), Jaz disks (1GB to 2GB per disk), writable CD-ROMs (640MB), and now writable DVD disks (4.7GB and up). A format under development is the holographic versatile disk (HVD) with a proposed capacity of 4.7 Terabytes (TB)—4,700GB!

At the time of this writing, entry-level computers are typically configured with 100GB hard drives (give or take 20GB), and high-end computers come with 320GB hard drives (or more). Some people can easily fill 100GB in only a few months; heavy users, in just a few weeks. Where does all that long-term storage go? Figure 1.3 shows a few benchmarks. Microsoft Office 2003 Standard Edition requires 510MB all by itself. A large collection of screen savers could eat up another 100MB, and a family photograph album can easily consume 100MB. But we're still a long way from 100GB. What else can you do with a 100GB hard drive? A photographer or an artist would have no trouble using up that amount of memory. Neither would the average college student.

A Music Revolution. Massive amounts of computer storage in countless dormitory rooms on hundreds of college campuses across the country are consumed by something that was a college preoccupation long before computers became a standard fixture: music. Music is a serious memory hog. For example, a 3-minute music file can require from 3MB to 45MB, depending on how it's stored. To minimize a hefty music file without sacrificing its content, you can use any of the various file compression techniques that are available. (File compression is discussed in more detail in the Above & Beyond section at the end of this chapter.) Without compression, 10GB will store the

Figure 1.3 Where does all the long-term storage go?		
One page of plain ASCII text (54 single-spaced lines, 10pt)		5KB
One color cartoon on a Web page		50KB
One high-resolution photograph		500KB
One floppy disk (high-density/double-sided)		1.44MB
Three minutes of music (compressed MP3 format)		3MB
One medium-sized Web site (text and graphics)		50MB
60 minutes of video (compressed MPEG-4 format)		390MB
One CD-ROM		640MB
A hard drive for a new PC (in the year 2006)		120GB
One DVD		4.7–17GB

FYI: What Is File Compression?

Large files can be stored either in their original format or in a compressed format to save space. Different types of file compression are used for different types of files, such as text, graphics, and audio. You can usually reduce a large file by at least 50 percent, depending on the type of file and the type of compression.

In the case of audio files, for example, the **MP3 (MPEG audio layer 3)** format can be used to reduce audio files by as much as 90–93 percent. Bigger is never better when you're trying to move a large file across the Net.

equivalent of 15 audio CDs. With compression, that same 10GB will store a respectable music library of approximately 200 audio CDs.

You have no doubt heard of Apple's iTunes Music Store—you may even be a customer. iTunes has greatly accelerated the sales rate of digitally recorded music (and so much more). In July 2006, Apple sold its 500,000th song, awarding the lucky customer 10 iPod music players, a gift certificate for 10,000 songs, and 4 tickets to a Coldplay concert to mark the event. So all those GBs may still not be enough!

You can listen to all this digital music on your computer, or you can invest around $200 in an MP3 player designed to play digital audio files wherever you go.

All of this indicates that a music revolution is under way, fueled by digital technology. And where do we get these audio files? At least 75 percent of them come from iTunes via the Internet!

Other ways to fill a 100GB hard drive include storing video files. These files require even more long-term storage space than audio files. For example, a single 9-second MPEG video clip fills 3.2MB. One 90-minute MPEG movie would require almost 2GB of storage space! Currently, few people collect video files from the Internet because they are so memory intensive. However, the introduction of Apple's iMovie HD, with its easy-to-use video editor designed for family use, made personal computers and camcorders a powerful combination. High speed Internet connections are making it possible to download entire movies in reasonable amounts of time. Long-term storage requirements for video and audio files are driving consumer demand for larger hard drives on personal computers. As the cost of large hard drives continues to drop, users will find new ways to use all the long-term storage on their computers.

1.4 The Internet

CHECKLIST: Should You Skip This Section?

See how many of the following questions you can answer:

1. How is the Internet different from a network of computers?
2. What is the difference between hierarchical and heterarchical network architecture?
3. What is a robust network and which type of network architecture is more robust?
4. What is a dynamic route through a network?

If you can answer these questions, you can probably skip this section and go directly to Section 1.5.

Many people think of the Internet as one big network of computers. In fact, the Internet is more than a network of computers. It is actually a network of networks. **Internet** stands for "*inter*networked *net*works." Computer networks were around long before the Internet came into existence. The first computer networks were geographically close to one another, often within a single building. Called **local area networks** (**LANs**), these networks are used by large companies for in-house data processing. Universities use LANs for administrative, educational, and research purposes. Some libraries use LANs to hold their card catalogs. In time, university research LANs and commercial research LANs began to create communication links so that computers in different LANs could share information. Then government networks and corporate networks joined the mix. Eventually, commercial networks were created for the sole purpose of giving consumers access to this rapidly expanding infrastructure, this network of networks and its associated computer-based communications. The Internet now reaches into more than 211 countries, connects more than 300 million computer hosts, and is used by over 880 million people worldwide.

The Internet's structure is largely heterarchical. (The correct word is probably "heterogeneous," but computer scientists insist on saying "heterarchical.") In a **heterarchical network**, the members, or **nodes**, of the network are interconnected randomly, with no node occupying a position of greater importance than any other node. This is done to ensure robust communication. By contrast, some communication networks are designed as a hierarchy.

A **hierarchical network** is organized in the shape of a pyramid and always includes a unique **root node** that is superior to all other nodes. Two nodes that want to exchange data within a hierarchy must use a path that passes through some node that is superior to both. The shortest such path is unique and will always be a part of any path between the same two nodes. In other words, there is always one critical path for getting from one location to another inside a hierarchy (see Figure 1.4).

A **robust network** is a network that can continue to operate even if some parts of the network have been removed or simply fail to work. A hierarchical network is much less robust than a heterarchical network because removing the root node (the single one at the top of the network) from a hierarchy destroys the only communication paths between nodes that are connected to each other within the hierarchy solely through the root. The more nodes that are removed from the top regions of the hierarchy, the more communication is disrupted. In a heterarchy, there are many possible ways to get from one node to another. You may reduce the speed of communication within a heterarchy by removing certain nodes; however, you would have to remove a great many nodes in order to disrupt communications completely.

Figure 1.4

Hierarchies and heterarchies

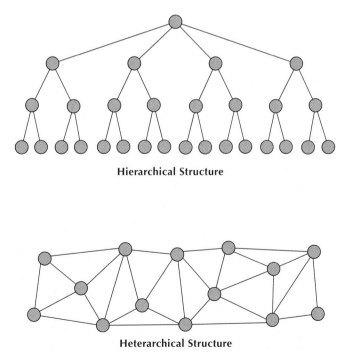

Hierarchical Structure

Heterarchical Structure

The original research that formed the foundation for today's Internet was motivated by concern for robust network communications: if one part of the network failed, the rest should continue to function. This could be accomplished only if more than one way was available for information to get from point A to point B. Network designers decided that the standard means of moving data across the Internet would be **dynamic routing**. A dynamic route is a route that is selected at the time of transmission and based on current network conditions. The ability to select such a route is distributed throughout the network so that no one essential site is responsible for the operation of the entire network. The computers that decide how to route data across the Internet are called **routers**. The Internet has thousands of routers.

1.5 Host Machines and Host Names

CHECKLIST: Should You Skip This Section?

See how many of the following questions you can answer:

1. Explain the difference between an IP address and a DNS address.
2. Where does the host name appear in a DNS address?
3. Give three examples of top-level domain names.

If you can answer these questions, you can probably skip this section and go directly to Section 1.6.

Each computer on the Internet is called an **Internet host** or a **host machine**. Each host machine has a special **Internet Protocol (IP) address** that identifies that host uniquely. IP addresses were never designed for human eyes; they were created by computer programmers for the sake of computer programs. Computers handle numbers well, so each IP address consists of numbers, four integers separated by periods. For example, one host machine at the University of Massachusetts at Amherst has the IP address 128.119.240.41. Some Internet hosts have their own permanent IP addresses, whereas others "borrow" IP addresses for use temporarily. For example, when you connect to the Internet over a telephone line, your home computer is assigned a temporary IP number for the duration of that Internet session.

Although IP addresses are fine for computer communications, most people can't easily remember long strings of numbers. To make life easier for people, most host machines have a symbolic **Domain Name Service (DNS) address** in addition to their IP address. The following are some examples of IP host addresses and their corresponding DNS addresses.

IP Address	DNS Address
128.119.240.41	freya.cs.umass.edu
18.92.0.3	mitvma.mit.edu
66.218.71.63	ns1.yahoo.com

Each DNS address contains a host name followed by a domain name, as illustrated in the following chart.

DNS Address	Host Name	Domain Name
freya.cs.umass.edu	freya	cs.umass.edu
mitvma.mit.edu	mitvma	mit.edu
ns1.yahoo.com	ns1	yahoo.com

Each domain name consists of two parts: the institutional site name and the **Top-Level Domain (TLD) name**. For example, cs.umass is an institutional site name that represents the Department of Computer Science at the University of Massachusetts, and mit represents the Massachusetts Institute of Technology. An example of a TLD name is edu, which refers to an educational site. The TLD name identifies the type of site at which the host machine resides. The main TLD names are as follows:

TLD Name	Type of Site
.aero	A site associated with the aviation industry
.biz	A site associated with a business
.cat*	A site for the Catalan linguistic and cultural community
.com	A commercial organization
.coop	A cooperative or cooperative service organization
.edu	An educational site in the United States
.eu*	European Union site
.gov	A government agency in the United States
.info	An informational site describing people, products, or ideas
.int	For international organizations established by treaty
.jobs*	A site for the international human resources management community
.mil	A military site in the United States
.mobi*	A site associated with mobile optimized Internet content and services
.museum	A museum or professionally affiliated personnel
.name	A noncommercial site associated with a private individual
.net	A network site

`.org`	A nonprofit organization
`.pro*`	A site associated with a professional
`.travel*`	A site oriented to the global travel industry organization

*Active, but not ICANN approved.

Other TLD names identify geographical locations by country, as illustrated in the following partial list.

TLD Name	**Country**
`.au`	Australia
`.ca`	Canada
`.dk`	Denmark
`.fr`	France
`.de`	Germany
`.uk`	Great Britain
`.hk`	Hong Kong
`.hu`	Hungary
`.ie`	Ireland
`.il`	Israel
`.es`	Spain
`.lk`	Sri Lanka

TLD names have been the subject of much discussion in recent years. The original set of domain names quickly became overloaded with more than 28 million domain names registered under `.com`, `.org`, and `.net` TLDs alone. Everyone agreed that a larger set of TLDs was needed, and a nonprofit organization named **ICANN** was created in 1998 to expand and manage the domain name system. ICANN reviewed proposals for new TLDs in 2000, and seven new TLDs were approved out of over 180 proposals. The newest TLDs are `.aero`, `.biz`, `.coop`, `.info`, `.museum`, `.name`, and `.pro`.

ICANN is currently considering the following additional TLDs:

`.asia`	A site for the pan-Asia/Asia Pacific Internet community
`.cym`	A site for the Welsh language community
`.kid`	A site for children
`.kids`	A site intended to deter the spread of pornography to minors
`.mail`	A site for the anti-spam community
`.post`	A site associated with worldwide information and electronic communication services

`.sco`	A site for the Scottish language community (or the nation)
`.tel`	(2 bids being processed) A site associated with the telephone industry
`.xxx`	A site with adult material of a sexual nature

Although each host machine has a unique IP address, some hosts have more than one DNS address. An alternative name for a host machine is an *alias*. Heavily used host machines are often assigned an alias, and a host may have any number of aliases. DNS addresses need to be translated into IP addresses. This essential function in the Internet's operation is handled by **domain name servers** (**DNSs**). If the database used by a DNS is corrupted, all Internet service moving through that server will be affected. DNSs are managed with great care, with many levels of redundancy.

No one polices the aliases that a host machine can use or the selection of DNS names beyond making sure that each DNS address is unique. Anyone can register a host machine under any unclaimed address (although some of the newer TLDs do enforce appropriate restrictions on their registrants). Be cautious about making assumptions based on a host machine's DNS address. For example, Figure 1.5a shows the Web page at the address `http://www.tass.net`. This page looks like it might be the home page for the Russian newspaper *Tass*, but it's not. The actual Web site (in English) for *Tass* is found under the name of the Russian news agency Itar-Tass, which is located at `http://www.itar-tass.com/news.asp`, as shown in Figure 1.5b. One can be reasonably sure, however, that a `.gov` site is truly a government Web site, and `.mil` is a site associated with the military in the United States.

Figure 1.5a

DNSs can't be trusted to tell you where you are.

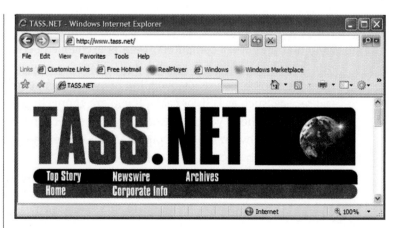

Figure 1.5b
DNSs can't be
trusted to tell you
where you are.

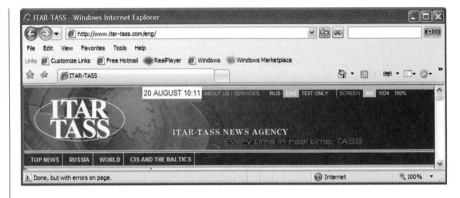

 # **1.6 Speed and Bottlenecks**

CHECKLIST: Should You Skip This Section?

 See how many of the following questions you can answer:

1. Does a computer with a 56K modem really move data at the rate of 56,000 bits per second?
2. How is a file upload different from a file download?
3. What does the term *bandwidth* mean?
4. Does the telephone service to your home use a broadband channel?

If you can answer these questions, you can probably skip this section and go directly to Section 1.7.

When you "go online" you create a communication channel between your computer and other computers. Data is exchanged between computers at a rate described in **bits per second (bps)**. If you're connecting to the Internet from your home, you're likely dialing in over a telephone line or using a special service, such as DSL or cable. If you are connecting from work or a computer lab at school, you might have an Ethernet connection. The actual rate of data flow between any two computers on the Internet will vary, depending on competing traffic.

Even if you are using a high-speed network connection, your Internet connection might act sluggishly. You might be feeling the effects of large file downloads, too much traffic on a specific server, or traffic flow problems on the Net. To find out why your connection is bogged down, you can visit the Bandwidth Place and take a speed test (see Figure 1.6). To find out what's normal for your connection, take the speed test at different times of the day and run the test on a few different days.

For "dial-up" users, the major bottleneck is the computer's modem and the telephone line. A 56K modem is capable of 56,000 bits per second (56.6 kilobits per second, or 56 kbps, or just 56K). However, achieving a true 56K exchange is unlikely because telephone lines rarely can keep up with that rate. A poor-quality telephone line can slow you down to about 20 kbps no matter what your modem can do. The best transmission rate you can hope for with a 56K modem is probably in the range of 40–45 kbps (see Figure 1.7).

Figure 1.6

Test the speed of your Internet connection at the bandwidth place.

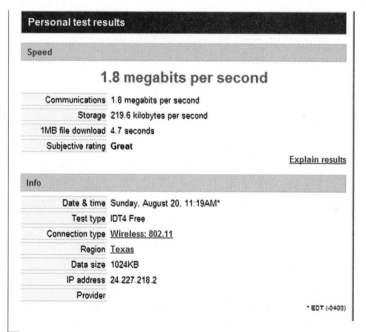

Figure 1.7

Internet connections are described in kilobits/second or bits/second.

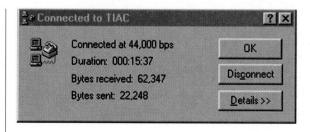

When referring to modems, why does 56K mean 56 × 1,000 bits per second (56 kbps), whereas 56KB (often written as 56K) of memory means 56 × 1,024 bytes? The ambiguity surrounding the letter "K" results because the same symbol is being used to represent both a base-10 (decimal system) kilo (1,000) and a base-2 kilo (1,024). In the context of data transmissions, K always means 1,000. In the context of computer memory, K always means 1,024. You need to know in which context the K is being used. Some authors are careful to use a lowercase "k" for the decimal system version (as in kbps) in an effort to distinguish the two usages. However, you will see Kbps as well as kbps (with both meaning 1,000 bits per second). Further, modem speeds are often described in terms of K (as in a 56K modem), even though what is meant is kbps.

Most authors are careful at least to keep their bits (b) and their bytes (B) straight, although context is useful here, too. Usually, bits (b) describe data transmission rates, whereas bytes (B) describe quantities of computer memory, but file transfers can go either way. For example, the application program WinSCP describes its transfer rate in *kilobytes* per second (kB/s) but it refers to this rate as KB/s(see Figure 1.8). So there is ample room for confusion: sometimes "K" really means "k" and sometimes "b" really means "B." If you're feeling like some poor soul in a Monty Python skit right about now, don't despair. Simply remember that most of the time, K means KB (1,024 bytes), unless you are talking about transmission speeds, in which case K (usually) means kbps (1,000 bits per second) or kBps (1,000 bytes per second). And every so often kbps really means KBps, especially in the context of file transfers. (If this shows up on a test, I hope it's for extra credit.)

The amount of data that can be moved through a digital device during a fixed period of time is determined by the **bandwidth**, the frequency at which

Figure 1.8

File transfers are described in kilobytes/second.

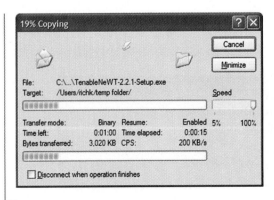

FYI: Downloading and Uploading

The terms *download* and *upload* refer to file transfers across a network. You **download** a file when you move a copy of a file from a computer at a remote location to your local computer. You **upload** a file when you move a copy of a file on your local computer to a computer at a remote location. The terms *local* and *remote* are often used to distinguish computers that are nearby (local) from computers that are far away (remote).

symbols (like bits) may be transmitted through a system. In common use, bandwidth has come to be directly identified with the data transmission rate, however. Regardless of how you interpret this term, the greater the bandwidth, the faster the data exchange. A file in one computer will travel to another computer over various communication channels, ranging from copper telephone wires to optical fiber. **Broadband channels**—that is, high-bandwidth channels—move data at speeds of 200 thousand bits per second or faster. Some broadband connections are capable of speeds of 1 billion bits per second or more, but that doesn't mean you'll see those transmission rates on your home computer. Data transfer on the Internet is ruled by the dictum, "Hurry up and wait." A 1MB file can cross the United States in seconds. However, that same file will hit a major bottleneck when it meets a 56K modem, which can transfer 1MB in, at best, 3 minutes. This is why broadband connections are becoming more and more popular. By April of 2006 over 70 percent of online U.S. homes had broadband Internet service.

1.7 The Client/Server Software Model

CHECKLIST: Should You Skip This Section?

See how many of the following questions you can answer:

1. Is a Web browser an example of a client or a server?
2. Is a keyword search engine on the Web an example of a client or a server?
3. What is an Application Service Provider?
4. What is versionless software?

If you can answer these questions, you can probably skip this section and go directly to Section 1.8.

When you read about Internet software, you will inevitably encounter the terms *client* and *server*. **Clients** and **servers** are Internet hosts that interact with one another when information needs to move across the Net. Any host machine can be programmed to act as either a client or a server, although different software applications are needed to support clients and servers. Client/server interactions underlie all communication on the Internet, and the **client/server model** is a *de facto* standard for network-oriented computing.

As a rule, a client is an information consumer and a server is an information provider. A server acts as a resource for all its clients and provides a service for those clients. For example, a Web server provides information on the Internet by housing publicly accessible Web pages and delivering those pages on demand. A host running a Web browser acts as a client that requests Web pages from Web servers with a single click of a mouse. A server typically interacts with multiple clients at one time (see Figure 1.9). As a result, heavily used

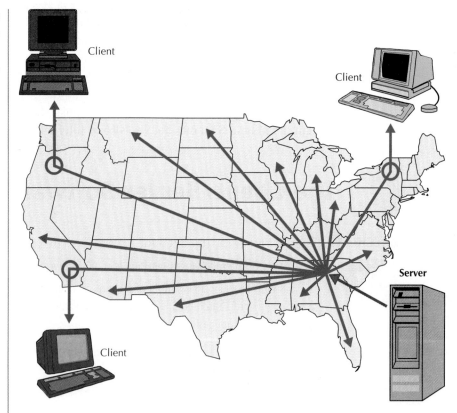

Figure 1.9

One server interacting with many clients

Client

Client

Client

Server

servers are sometimes overwhelmed by client requests. For example, when the Starr Report was initially released on the Internet in 1998, a Cable News Network (CNN) Web server that posted the report handled more than 30,000 client requests per minute—a lot of traffic for a single server. However, even this did not set a record. Some domain name servers routinely receive an average of 42,000 requests per minute.

In client/server interactions, client software interacts with server software so that both the client's host machine and the server's host machine share the total computing load. Clients and servers are designed to form a seamless computing environment. Thus the user typically has no idea which machine is performing which operations, and, indeed, the exact division of labor is irrelevant to the user.

1.7.1 Web-Based Software Hosting

Sometimes proprietary software is made available to the public through the client/server model. For example, a keyword search engine for the Web might reside on a server that can be accessed on demand by many remote clients. This makes it possible for many people to use the server's software without having to install copies of that software on their own individual host machines.

Several companies are currently exploring commercial markets for **Web-based software hosting**. Standard office applications such as spreadsheet and word processing programs are being made available on Web servers by **Application Service Providers** (**ASPs**). Subscribers to an ASP do not need to install software applications on their own computers and do not have to upgrade or patch that software in order to keep it up-to-date. They simply "rent" the applications they need and let the ASP handle everything else.

If a suitable selection of ASP software were available, more of the online computing load would shift from the client side of the client/server equation to the server side. Such a shift would require more-powerful servers while at the same time reducing the amount of computational muscle needed for client machines. The ASP market depends on very fast, reliable Internet connections and is expanding along with broadband Internet access. Worldwide ASP revenues reached $3 billion in 2001 and are on track to top $15 billion by 2006.

The client/server model is a very powerful framework for sharing computational resources over a computer network. By making the computational power of a host available for public use, a software designer can maximize the

FYI: Versionless Software

In 1999, McAfee.com released a suite of services that gives users access to various personal computer utilities via the Web. Called McAfee Clinic, it allows subscribers to scan their local drives for viruses, tune system settings, and rid directories of unneeded files, simply by clicking a few buttons on a Web page. Additional services support online collaborations, a "smart" Web navigation toolbar, and online shopping. Minimal software downloads are required to support the service, and subscribers automatically access the most recent software releases each time they log on. McAfee was one of the first ASPs to pioneer such versionless software. At the time, the McAfee site was the second most-visited software site on the Web (Microsoft was number 1). Currently, Yahoo!, Microsoft, and Google are numbers 1, 2, and 3 in terms of traffic.

number of users (who might also be paying customers) while retaining maximal control over the software.

1.8 The World Wide Web and Web Browsers

CHECKLIST: Should You Skip This Section?

See how many of the following questions you can answer:

1. How is the Web different from the Internet?
2. What makes hypertext different from traditional text?
3. How can you identify the hyperlinks on a Web page?
4. What is a URL?

If you can answer these questions, you can probably skip this section and go directly to Section 1.9.

The **World Wide Web** (aka the **Web**) is the star attraction on the Internet. It has made the Internet widely accessible to millions of people, from children to senior citizens. Many people think that the Web is the same thing as the Internet. This is not true, although the confusion is understandable. The Web is just one of many communications protocols (see the Above & Beyond section at the end of this chapter for more about protocols) that use the Internet. The Web is actually a relative newcomer to the Internet. However, Web browsers do integrate resources from other Internet applications, and this contributes to some confusion about where the Web stops and everything else begins. To clear the confusion we need to look more closely at software applications for the Web. Let's start with Web browsers.

A **Web browser** is a piece of software that enables users to view information on the Web. The essential mechanics of all Web browsers are very simple—learn two or three navigational commands, and you are off and running. Because some Web browsers are integrated with other Internet applications that go beyond Web browsing (for example, e-mail readers, Usenet newsreaders, and FTP clients), it is an excellent starting point for Internet explorations. Even though the Web is not the same as the Internet, many users will find that all their Internet needs can be adequately addressed by using the right Web browser. In this text we will focus on Windows Internet Explorer v7 (aka IE v7; formerly known as Microsoft Internet Explorer), Netscape, and the Mozilla browsers (Firefox, Mozilla, and SeaMonkey).

The Web consists of hypertext interspersed with multimedia elements such as graphics, sound clips, and video clips. **Hypertext** is a dynamic variation on traditional text that makes it easy to digress and view related documents as you wish. A hypertext document contains pointers to other hypertext documents, called **hyperlinks** or **links**, that you click with your mouse. Hyperlinks on a Web page might be underlined, boldfaced, or set in a different color (usually blue) so you can easily see them. Different browsers use different display conventions. Clicking hyperlinks allows you to easily weave through multiple documents according to your interests and preferences. You decide whether you want to digress and visit related documents. In fact, you can jump from document to document and never return to the original at the start of the chain. Figure 1.10 shows a Web page of interest to Internet watchers.

A **Web page** is an online document you view with a Web browser. A Web page may contain any number of words. When a page is long, you can scroll it up and down, typically by pointing to arrows on the scroll bar that runs vertically along the right-hand side of the page. Most documents on the Web contain hyperlinks to other Web pages. The process of reading Web pages and traversing links to more Web pages is called **browsing**. You can browse Web pages casually for entertainment or with a serious goal in mind. Either way, when you don't know beforehand exactly where a link is going to take you, you are browsing. Browsing is an exploratory process. It's a lot like daydreaming: you simply go where your interests lead you. We will elaborate on the details of Web browsers and the browsing process in Section 1.10.

Figure 1.10

The Web is the best place to find facts about the Web.

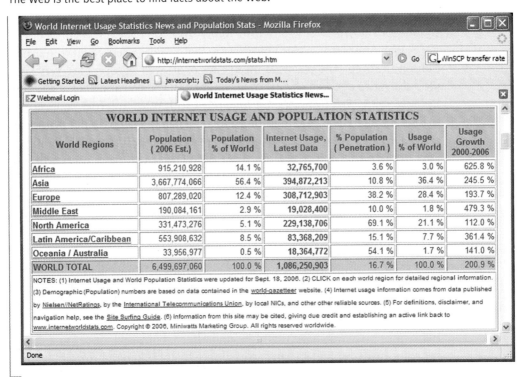

Each Web page is located at a unique global address called a **uniform resource locator** (**URL**). By referencing the URL, you can jump directly to the page at that address no matter where you currently are on the Web. All Web browsers let you jump directly to a URL. In Mozilla for example, you type a URL in a Location text box and press (Enter) or (Return) to jump to the desired page.

 1.9 **How to Get Online**

CHECKLIST: Should You Skip This Section?

 If you already have access to a computer on the Internet, you can skip this section and go directly to Section 1.10.

Before you can do anything online, you must have access to the Internet. Students at colleges and universities can usually obtain an educational account. Check whether your school has an Office of Information Technology or a Computer Services Office that maintains educational accounts for students. If you do not have access to an educational computing facility, you will need to use a commercial **Internet Service Provider** (**ISP**), a company that provides access to the Internet. To find directories of ISPs to help you research the available options, go online at a public library (or a friend's house or your workplace) and visit **The List** (see Figure 1.11). When you work from an educational computing lab, all the software you need to get online will be in place and ready to go. The ISP's staff members can recommend preferred system configurations, including memory requirements. They will set up a personal user identification (**user ID**) and password for you and give you the necessary hardware and software or (if you are using your computer's modem) a telephone number to dial to connect your computer to the Internet.

Figure 1.11

Find an ISP on the Web

Your ISP will also help you obtain and install the software you need if your system does not already have it installed (most do). Many ISPs provide conveniently bundled software that has step-by-step instructions for installation and start-up. If you are fairly new to computers, just follow the ISP's recommendations. It's the ISP's job to get customers up and running as quickly and easily as possible.

When you have difficulties with your Internet software, ask the ISP's technical support staff for assistance. If you are using an ISP, you're paying for technical support as well as other services. If you are a student at a university or college using an educational account, look for a Help Desk service where you first signed up for your account. *Do not* go to your school's Computer Science Department for technical support. These departments are not responsible for campuswide computing facilities; their technical staffs are paid to handle other problems. While it's important to know that you can ask for help when you need it, be sure that you're talking to the right people.

Browser Tips and Tricks

CHECKLIST: Should You Skip This Section?

 See how many of the following questions you can answer:

1. Do you know how to change your browser's default home page?
2. What can you do if your browser gets "stuck" while downloading a Web page?
3. Is a bookmark the same thing as Internet Explorer's Favorites feature?
4. What can you do when a URL for a Web page produces a "404 Not Found" error message?

If you can answer all of these questions, you can skip this section.

Web browsers are very easy to use with only a small amount of instruction. However, some simple tips can make your browsing sessions more productive and less time-consuming. This section focuses on some key browser features and includes specific instructions for Windows Internet Explorer (IE). All of these browser features can be used with other browsers as well—to find out how, pull down the Help menu and go to the Help Index for online documentation. This section discusses the following:

- Select your own default home page.
- Use the Find command.
- Use your history list.
- Use bookmarks.
- Add bookmarks with care.
- Abort a download if you get stuck.
- Turn off graphics.
- Use Tabs.
- Don't let a "404 Not Found" message stop you dead.
- Avoid peak hours.

TIP: IE v7 Does Not Display a Menu Bar by Default

If you're used to the menu and want to insert it, select the Tool icon, then choose Menu Bar (see Figure 1.12). IE will insert a Menu Bar immediately below the Location Bar (see Figure 1.13).

Figure 1.12

Use the Tool icon to add a classic Menu Bar to your browser window.

Figure 1.13

The Menu Bar is displayed immediately below the Location Bar.

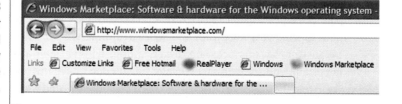

TIP: Shortcut Search Tool

Most Web browsers include an integrated Search tool that sends your query to the default search engine, usually Google. IE puts the Search tool adjacent to the Location Bar at the top of the Web window (see Figure 1.11—"internet statistics" are the search terms used here). Type your search terms here and press ⌶Return⌷. We will learn more about searching in Chapter 5.

1.10.1 Select Your Own Default Home Page

Each time you start your Web browser, you begin from a default home page. Your Web browser probably came configured with a default home page, such as Netscape Navigator's NetCenter or perhaps the MSN Home page. You can change this default Web page to any Web page you want by editing a browser preference setting (see Figure 1.14). To change your default home page in IE (v7 for Windows), follow these steps:

1. Go to the Web page you want to use as your default Web page.
2. From the classic Tools menu *or* using the Tool icon, select Internet Options.
3. Make sure you are on the General tab, and then click the Use Current button.
4. Close the dialog box by clicking OK.

TIP: What If These Instructions Don't Work

If you don't have the correct instructions for your particular browser (or maybe you don't have any instructions at all), don't despair. Some browsers put customization settings under "Preferences" instead of under "Internet Options." Or they may list it on the Edit menu or on the View menu instead of on the Tools menu. Look around— explore your drop-down menus. Then instead of tabs there may be a navigation menu. The button may say "Enter URL" instead of "Use Current." These are all superficial differences in the user interface, and if your interface is designed well, it won't be too hard to find what you're looking for. The most important thing is to know what you should be able to do with your browser. If you know what your browser is capable of, you should be able to figure out how to access various features with a little patience and a willingness to poke around. This book won't explain all the details of how to do everything with the Mozilla browsers, Internet Explorer, and Opera because these interfaces are always a little different and always changing. More important, you shouldn't feel helpless if you don't have instructions in front of you. Try to find the software settings you need on your own, and when all else fails, there's always a Help menu.

Figure 1.14

Pick your own default Web page.

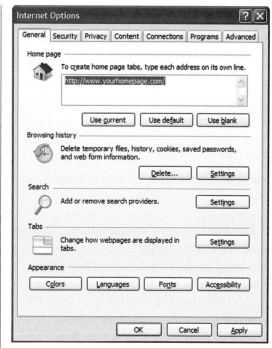

1.10.2 Use the Find Command

If you know exactly where you want to go on a familiar Web page, you can use the Find command to take you there immediately. The Find command lets you enter a text string and go directly to the first instance of that string on the current Web page. Pull down the Edit menu and select Find (or use the keyboard shortcut described on the next page). The Find command is useful on long Web pages when you want to hop to a specific topic. Some browsers also have a Find Next command, which will take you to the next occurrence of your text string.

1.10.3 Use Your History List

You can traverse many links in only a few minutes of browsing. But suppose you want to return to a Web page that you left 20 links ago. How can you find your way back through all those Web pages? Fortunately, all Web browsers make it easy for you to return to earlier pages by keeping track of all the pages you've visited. You can retrace your steps by clicking on the Back button—each click pops you back to the page you were on before the current page. This

SHORTCUT: Keyboard Shortcuts

These shortcuts work for both IE and Netscape Navigator.

What You Want to Do	What to Type
Pop up the dialog box for a Find command	Ctrl + F
Jump to the end of a Web page	End
Jump to the top of a Web page	Home
Open a new browser window	Ctrl + N
Close the current browser window	Ctrl + W

Note: Macintosh users should type the ⌘ key instead of the Ctrl key.

is a little like backtracking by following a trail of breadcrumbs you left along the way. Alternatively, you can ask the browser to pop up its history list. The **history list** is a list of all clickable links to all the pages you've visited recently. To see the history list, select Go To from the View menu (see Figure 1.15). This is especially useful when you've wandered far from familiar territory and you just want to return to an earlier starting page without having to revisit each intermediate page by repeatedly clicking the Back button.

You can summon a more complete version of the history list by using the History button found in the Favorites Center. The Favorites Center is marked by an icon on the toolbar that looks like a star (see Figure 1.16). Click the Favorites Center icon (the orange star at the far left of the icon toolbar) and if not selected, click the History button from the drop-down menu that

Figure 1.15

Web browsers remember where you've been.

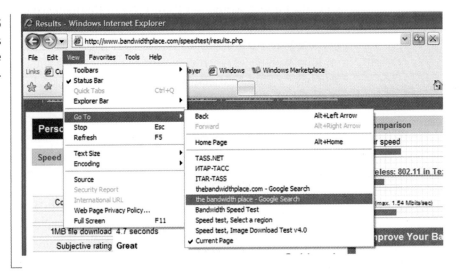

Figure 1.16
IE's history list
remembers sites
you visited last
week.

appears. A navigation menu will appear on the left with clickable links to all the pages you've visited in the last few weeks. Click the calendar and folder icons to see or hide all the pages under each heading. When you are done with the history list, click the History button again and the list will disappear.

You can reorder the list based on date viewed, site visited, or popularity (how many times you visited a site), or today's popularity only (see Figure 1.17).

Figure 1.17
You can reorder
your history list.

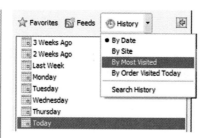

1.10.4 Use Bookmarks

If you spend much time on the Web, you'll find some Web pages that you'll want to revisit regularly. You could keep a list of their URLs and some notes about each one in a text file, or you can take advantage of your browser's *bookmark feature* (Internet Explorer calls them *Favorites*). A **bookmark** is a pointer to a Web page that you expect to revisit. You can add a bookmark whenever you are viewing the page that you want to mark.

Setting up a bookmark in IE takes two steps.

1. Visit the page that you want to mark.
2. From the Favorites menu, select Add to Favorites and then select Add (or type Ctrl+D).

   Or

   Select the Add to Favorites Tool (the plus sign next to the Favorites Center tool—see Figure 1.18)

Once a bookmark has been added, you simply click the bookmark entry whenever you want to return to that particular page. You can organize your bookmarks in folders just like you organize files on your hard drive. A hierarchical structure for your bookmarks is easier to navigate than a flat list without categories and subcategories (see Figure 1.19). IE v7 automatically places bookmarks saved into the Links folder on the Links Toolbar as shown in Figure 1.19. Use the Links folder carefully! You should place only your very frequently used links here!

The bookmark file can grow very quickly and get out of control. You should periodically review your bookmark file to reorganize and weed out entries you no longer use. To do this in IE, follow these steps.

1. From the Favorites menu, select Add to Favorites and then select Organize Favorites.

   Or

   Select the Add to Favorites tool, then select Organize Favorites. A dialog window opens (see Figure 1.20).

Figure 1.18

Add a bookmark.

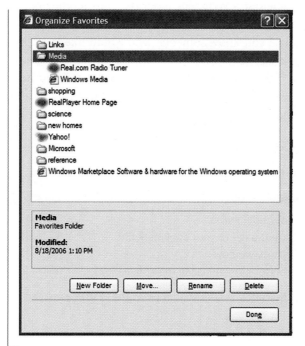

TIP: Live Feeds

IE also has the ability to save a special type of bookmark known as an RSS Feed. This type of bookmark polls its associated site constantly for changes. Updates can be downloaded and viewed later. Read more about RSS feeds in Section 4.4.

2. To move a bookmark to a new location, select it and press Move to Folder.
3. To remove a bookmark (or an entire folder of bookmarks), select it and press Delete.
4. To create a new folder, press Create Folder.

If you collect a lot of bookmarks, your bookmarks will require thoughtful organization. Reorganize your bookmarks whenever a folder gets overloaded, and don't hesitate to prune away long-ignored bookmarks as your information needs change.

1.10.5 Add Bookmarks with Care

You might be tempted to bookmark everything that could ever be of interest to you. Overly impulsive bookmarking tends to produce unwieldy bookmark collections that are very hard to navigate (think of an online packrat). When deciding whether a Web page deserves to be in your bookmark file, consider whether you honestly expect to revisit the page. If you are bookmarking it only because you know someone who would like it or because you wish you had seen it last year when you really needed it, it is probably better to let it pass. And if you really can't pass it up, create a folder just for the borderline bookmarks and then promise to purge that folder once a month before it gets out of hand. Don't let your bookmarks get out of control.

SHORTCUT: Keyboard Shortcuts

These shortcuts work for both IE and Netscape Navigator.

What You Want to Do	What to Type
Organize your bookmarks	Ctrl + B
Add the current page to your bookmark file	Ctrl + D
View the History window	Ctrl + H
Quit the browser session (close the application)	Ctrl + Q

Note: Macintosh users should press the ⌘ key instead of the Ctrl key.

1.10.6 Abort a Download if You Get Stuck

Sometimes your browser might appear to be stuck while downloading a page. If your browser has a status line showing the progress of the download, you will sometimes see it freeze and appear to be dead. Stuck downloads happen for various reasons, and they happen with all browsers. Check your browser for a command button that aborts downloads. In IE, it is the Stop button (⊠ below the title bar). With some browsers, issuing this abort command will make the page mysteriously appear as if it had been waiting for you to ask. With some browsers, the page will sometimes pop up if you click the same link again right after aborting.

1.10.7 Turn Off Graphics

When the Web gets sluggish, you'll find that pages with lots of graphics are always the slowest to load. This is because graphics files are relatively large and consume a fair amount of bandwidth. If you don't have a fast Internet connection, you might find yourself spending too much time waiting for some Web pages. This is no fun if you are accustomed to faster performance or you are in a hurry. You can speed things up by trading in the graphics for faster downloads. Sometimes you don't need to see the graphics; they may be purely cosmetic. Or you might have already seen a page a number of times, and the graphics are no longer important to you.

All browsers enable you to turn off graphics. Because your browser never requests the graphic's file, you don't have to wait for that graphic to appear. When graphics are turned off, a page is displayed with a *placeholder* for each graphic on the page to indicate where the graphic would have been displayed. In IE, follow these steps to turn off graphics.

1. In the Tools menu, select Internet Options.
2. Click the Advanced tab, and scroll down to the Multimedia section.
3. Uncheck the checkbox entitled "Show pictures."

If you decide that you want to see a specific graphic while the graphics are disabled, place your mouse over the missing graphic, click your right mouse button, and select Show Picture from the pop-up menu; IE will download that one graphic file and insert it into the Web page display. Most browsers support graphic file downloads on demand so you can select the graphics you want as needed.

Figure 1.24

Tabs displayed as thumbnails

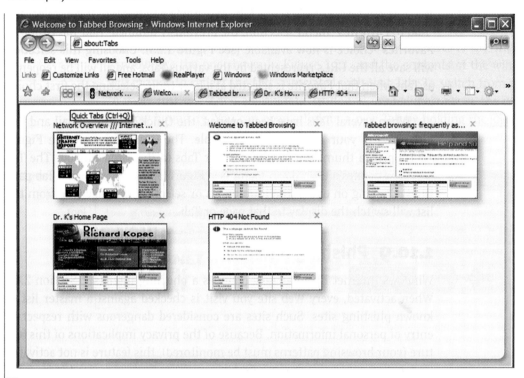

Figure 1.25

Tabs displayed
in a list

Be aware that activating the filter could make your browsing patterns
available to third parties.

Figure 1.26

IE phishing filter

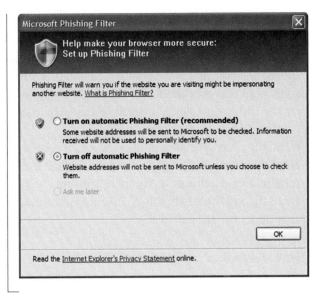

1.10.10 Don't Let a "404 Not Found" Message Stop You Dead

From time to time, everyone sees this error message: "404 Not Found." It means that the requested URL was not found on the specified server. When you see this error, first make sure that the URL is correct. If it is, then the error message appeared for other reasons. For example, the page might have been removed from the server. Or it might have been moved, in which case you might be able to find it at its new location (if you know that new location). Sometimes a site's author will rearrange files and directories, and this creates obsolete URLs. Before you give up all hope of ever seeing the lost page, here are some tricks you can try to retrieve it.

Suppose you try linking to `http://www.lib.unc.edu/launcch/oct96n.htm` and you get the "404 Not Found" error message.

1. Start by examining the URL to see if it looks correct and contains no typos. Look at the diagram of the following URL:

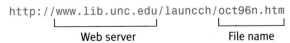

`http://www.lib.unc.edu/launcch/oct96n.htm`

Web server   File name

The first segment gives the name of the Web server, and the last segment is the name of the file in which the page resides. In between are the names of subdirectories (aka folders), in this case `lib` and `launcch`. If this link was bookmarked and previously working, you don't need to worry about the possibility of typing errors. Otherwise, try the URL with `launch` instead of `launcch`, in case there's a typographical error in your typed URL.

2. If the URL is correct, try to backtrack to a related Web page. Sometimes you can find a home page or page index by going to a subdirectory. In this case, try these two subdirectories: the top directory `lib` and the subdirectory `launcch` that resides inside `lib`. To visit these, use these URLs:

   ```
   http://www.lib.unc.edu/launcch/
   http://www.lib.unc.edu/
   ```

   One of these might give you a link or a path to the old Web page. This often works on large institutional sites or a site that houses many Web pages. The contents of large Web sites are periodically reorganized into new subdirectories, thereby causing some URLs to become obsolete.

3. When all else fails, see whether the server has a Web page at the root address, in this case:

   ```
   http://www.unc.edu/
   ```

   With a little luck, you'll find a high-level home page at this address that can point you in the right direction.

1.10.11 Other Useful Browser Features

IE has a few other features that you might find useful in addition to the ones already mentioned. A short list of the most useful ones is presented in Table 1.1.

1.10.12 Avoid Peak Hours

Just as you probably want to avoid rush hour on major highways, you will be wise to avoid peak usage periods on the Internet. In the United States, peak periods are generally the middle of the day and early evenings on weekdays. You can find out when the Internet is congested by monitoring Internet

Table 1.1

Some additional
IE features

Feature	Description
Automatic Update	Tool that checks for product updates, may need to be activated manually or programmed to search periodically
Bookmark Import/Export	Tool that facilitates sharing of bookmarks between different Web browsers, also useful for backup of bookmarks
Bookmark Manager	Permits organization of bookmarks into folders, deletion
Content Advisor	Aka Parental Control, a tool to control access based on content
Cookie Manager	Manages cookies (see Chapter 2, Above & Beyond)
Customizable	Rearranges the order, appearance, and visibility of various tools and Web pages, among other things
Download Manager	Logs downloads, reports progress—some can do more (see the Above & Beyond section at the end of this chapter)
Form Manager	Tool that enables automatic form completion
History Manager	Keeps track of Web pages you've visited; can be edited
Integrated Search	Built-in keyword entry text box linked directly to a search engine, may also be customizable
JavaScript Disable	Permits deactivation of JavaScript programs for security purposes
Password Manager	Keeps track of your passwords, associated with Form Autofill (Form Management)
Pop-up Blocker	Disables those annoying pop-up ads, but it also disables opening windows you do want to see
RSS Feeds	Links to frequently updated content on the Web that is monitored periodically for updates (see Section 4.4)
Security Manager	Keeps track of various aspects related to computer security such as digital certificates and trusted sites (Chapters 7 and 8)

traffic reports (see Figure 1.27). You'll be surprised how much faster your response times can be if you connect during low traffic times.

Figure **1.27**
Slowdowns on the
Internet are
sometimes global.

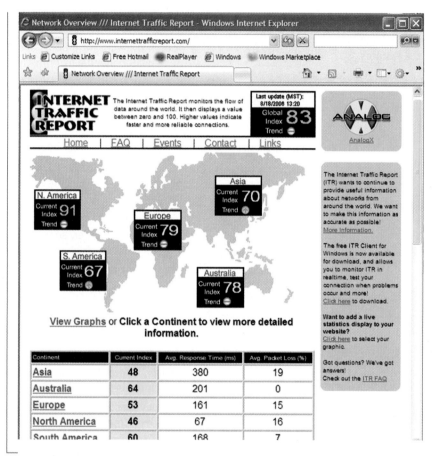

SHORTCUT: Keyboard Shortcuts

These shortcuts work for most browsers.

What You Want to Do	What to Type
Press the Back button	Alt + ←
Press the Forward button	Alt + →
Scroll down a little	↓
Scroll up a little	↑

CHECKLIST: Get to Know Your Browser

1. Change your default home page to something new. When does it make sense to change your default home page?
2. Locate your history list. Does it contain entries for only the current browsing session or also entries from previous browsing sessions? How much control do you have over your history list? (Check your preference settings to see what preferences you can change.)
3. Locate your bookmarks. Add a new bookmark. Create a new folder for just that one bookmark, and move the bookmark into the new folder. Can you add a comment to this bookmark? Delete the new bookmark and the new folder. Where does your browser store your bookmarks? Can you copy your bookmark file as a backup for safekeeping?
4. Try out any five keyboard shortcuts that you choose. Do they all work? Is it hard to remember them? Work with them for a session or two until you can use them easily. Do they save you time?
5. Create a few Tabbed pages. Switch back and forth between them.
6. Locate the update tool in your browser. You may have to hunt for it.

If you don't know how to do everything on this checklist, consult your browser's Help menu. Different browsers have slightly different procedures, but all support these standard features.

Alternate Web Browsers

Most people who use the Web are familiar with the Windows Internet Explorer (IE) browser and its former competitor, the venerable Netscape Navigator. IE comes packaged with every Windows PC sold, and is usually set as the default browser, meaning that this browser will open automatically whenever a browser application is needed to open some file. For the longest time, IE's strongest competitor was the Netscape browser. Shipped with every Macintosh for a time, Netscape was first replaced by Explorer, then by Apple's Safari, currently the default browser for the Mac. Competition between the various browser developers has been great for consumers like us—each company is highly motivated to outdo the other in terms of features and usability.

Since the Netscape–IE browser wars, the browser landscape has expanded to include a few more major browsers, all of which are excellent products.

Adding to the roll-call of browsers we now have Firefox, the Mozilla Suite (now offered as SeaMonkey), Opera, and Safari. Each of these browsers is available for free, or comes packaged with the operating system of the micro-computer. All have similar features and interfaces, so the choice of browser is just a matter of personal preference.

Unless otherwise mentioned, all the Web browsers mentioned here support the following features, although not always as a separate tool or manager. Some may offer more powerful options or are easier to find/use than others.

- Bookmark Import/Export, Management
- Cookie (see Chapter 2, Above & Beyond) , Download, Form Data, History, Password, Security Management (allows the user to view, delete, save, edit or otherwise manage these resources)
- Customizable Toolbars
- Integrated Search (a tool or separate address bar)
- JavaScript (see Chapters 10 and 11), Image Disable
- Keyboard Shortcuts
- Pop-up and Image Blockers
- Tabbed Browsing

Special features of each browser are reviewed briefly below, accompanied by a screen shot of the home page for each. Since the Macintosh user interface incorporates a menu bar for all applications, the Mac OS screen shots include this. The Windows screen shots display only the menu bar if the application provides one.

1.11.1 Firefox

Firefox is available through the same group that distributes the original Mozilla Suite, The Mozilla Foundation. Firefox was developed as a replacement for the "bloated" Mozilla Suite that was bound to the requirements of its corporate sponsor, Netscape Communications Corporation. As a consequence, Firefox has been "slimmed down" and does not include the Usenet news reader (see Section 4.6.3), chat module, integrated mail client or Web page editor found in the Suite. A companion e-mail client, Thunderbird, is also available. Firefox includes a special automatic update feature that downloads and installs browser and **add-on** (see Above & Beyond) updates and security fixes in the background; a phishing filter (see Sections 1.10.9 and 2.4); inline spell-checking for Web forms; and a Session Restore feature that restores windows, tabs, text entered into forms, and in-progress downloads from the last session or after a system crash. Two other special features are RSS Feeds (see Section 4.4) and Live Titles. Users can subscribe to RSS feeds through the Firefox browser as a Live Bookmark, in a standalone RSS Reader, or from a Web service. The Live Titles feature allows users to create bookmarks to Web sites that implement microsummaries (a regularly updated summary of the most important information on a Web page) that provide more relevant and timely information than a static page title (like a stock name and current value). The Live Title displays when a bookmark list is viewed. Firefox meets U.S. government requirements that software be easily accessible for users with physical impairments. All private data can be cleared with a single mouseclick, a feature that is useful when you acquire a new computer. The Netscape browser is now based on Firefox. Firefox is available for both Windows (see Figure 1.28) and Mac OS (see Figure 1.29) at `http://www.mozilla.com/firefox/`.

Figure 1.28

FireFox for Windows

Figure 1.29

FireFox for
Mac OS

1.11.2 Mozilla (v1.7.13) —Now Known as SeaMonkey (v1.0.4)

The Mozilla Suite was developed by the Mozilla Foundation as a totally free, open-source (see Section 6.2) project. It includes not only a Web browser (Navigator), but also an HTML editor (Composer—see Chapter 9), an e-mail and news client, address book, and an IRC client (Chatzilla—see Section 4.6). Consequently, the Mozilla Suite was intended to be an "all in one" Internet package. The Mozilla Suite was also the basis of Netscape versions 6.x and 7.x. Mozilla is used in this text to support Web page development in Chapters 9 and 10. Although no longer being developed by the Mozilla Foundation (the last *official* version is 1.7.13), the Mozilla community continues to support and develop the suite under the name SeaMonkey as of January 30, 2006 (starting at version 1.0). Mozilla supports incremental find (find as you type), custom keywords (bookmark access via entering keywords into the location bar). The Mozilla developers are especially proud of the fact that Mozilla supports all the announced standards then available, including HTML, XML, XHTML, CSS, JavaScript, and others. Mozilla is available for Windows and Linux machines and Macs running Mac OS X. Mozilla can be downloaded from Mozilla at `http://www.mozilla.org/projects/seamonkey/` (SeaMonkey 1.0.4) or `http://www.mozilla.org/products/mozilla1.x/` (Mozilla 1.7.13). Screen shots of the Mozilla Web browser can be seen extensively in Chapters 9 and 10. This is the application we use to create Web pages later in the book using its integrated Web page editor.

1.11.3 Netscape (v8)

The latest version of the Netscape browser is based on the Firefox browser just discussed. Consequently, its feature set is similar to that of Firefox's. Like Internet Explorer, Netscape monitors Web sites and assigns a trust rating designed to warn you about potential phishing Web sites (see Chapter 2). When you visit a questionable site, Netscape generates a warning box to let you know about it. A Security Center collects all the security-related aspects of browsing together into one panel that provides a variety of useful information (see Figure 1.30). Spyware and Adware protection (found in the Security Center) is a very useful feature—you can use this tool to scan memory and the hard drive for surveillance and advertising software. If found, offensive soft-

Figure 1.30

Netscape v8 for Windows showing the Security Center panel

ware is deleted. Separate profiles can be created using Netscape, which allows several different people to use your computer. Each user can create a personalized profile that stores bookmarks and other customizable options. Available profiles are selectable at program launch. RSS feeds are also supported. Netscape version 8 was only available for Windows at the time this section was written. Mac users must use version 7. You can get this browser at http://www.netscape.com.

1.11.4 Opera (v9)

Opera was originally available only as a commercial product, plus a free version that included advertisements. Probably as a result of market forces, beginning with version 8.50 Opera is now available free of charge and completely commercial free. The Opera browser has an especially rich set of features designed to broaden your Web experience. Special features included in Opera include RSS feeds, skins that alter the look and feel of the application, widgets, mouse gestures, thumbnail preview, parental control (content blocking), along with a WYSIWYG (What You See Is What You Get) *rtf* editor, BitTorrent (a peer-to-peer file sharing client, see Section 6.4.1), mail and chat clients. Widgets are small, Web applications that are used to add a variety of different capabilities to your computer, such as games, current weather reports, dictionaries, and the like. Mouse gestures are mouse events (see Section 10.5) that can be programmed via Opera to performs actions like "back" or "forward" without having to click a specific button. The thumbnail feature allows the user to view all open browser pages in one screen for selection. It's also possible to bookmark a whole set of bookmarks, and reopen them all in a group later. In terms of features supported, Opera probably comes closest to the Mozilla Suite in terms of an all-in-one user experience. You can find the latest version of Opera (currently 9.0) for both Windows (see Figure 1.31) and Mac OS (see Figure 1.32) at http://www.opera.com/.

1.11.5 Safari (v2)

Safari (aka **Safari RSS**), is developed by Apple and is the default Web browser installed on all Macintosh computers (see Figure 1.33). Unlike the other browsers discussed here, Safari is only available for the Macintosh. In addition to the usual features listed above, Safari also supports RSS feeds, parental controls, and a "Private Browsing" feature which makes no record of a browsing session when selected, plus the ability to search your bookmarks and

Figure 1.31 Opera for Windows

Figure 1.32 Opera for Mac OS

Figure 1.33

The Safari RSS Web browser

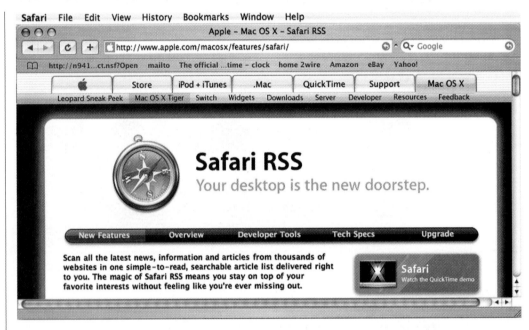

archive and e-mail Web pages. Safari is the first browser to pass the Acid2 test (`http://www.webstandards.org/action/acid2/`), a test page created by the Web Standards Project to find Web page browser display faults. As of this writing, Opera is the only other browser to pass this test. Safari is currently up to version 2.0.4, and is available from Apple (`http://www.apple.com`).

Other Mac-only Web browsers include Camino (`http://www.mozilla.org`), iCab (`http://www.iCab.de/`) and Shiira (`http://shiira.jp/en.php`).

We have only scratched the surface regarding the various similarities and differences between the various Web browsers presented here. Since not all Web pages work correctly on every Web browser, it's probably a good idea to install at least one additional browser on your system. Some people install and use them all.

Things to Remember

- An Internet connection is only as fast as its weakest link.
- Additional RAM might speed up your computer; a larger hard drive will not.
- Each character in the ASCII character set requires one 8-bit byte of memory.
- On average, video files consume more memory than audio files, audio files consume more memory than graphics files, and graphics files consume more memory than text files.
- Computer memory is measured in bytes, kilobytes, megabytes, and gigabytes. Bandwidth is measured in bits per second.
- When your browser displays the error message "404 Not Found," you might still be able to find the missing page.
- You can save time while browsing by using keyboard shortcuts instead of your mouse.

Important Concepts

bandwidth the maximal rate at which symbols may be transmitted over a given communication channel

clients Internet hosts that consume information from the Net

Domain Name Server (DNS) translates host names into IP addresses

Domain Name Service (DNS) address a symbolic name for an Internet host

dynamic routing a strategy for finding the best pathway between two hosts, given current conditions on the Net

heterarchical network a connected structure in which no nodes are more central or more important than any other nodes

hierarchical network a connected structure in which all nodes have a common ancestor (the root node)

host machine a computer connected to the Internet

Internet Protocol (IP) address a numerical name for an Internet host

servers Internet hosts that serve information on the Net

Web browser software for viewing Web pages found on Web servers

Web server a software program on an Internet host that offers Web pages for public consumption

Where Can I Learn More?

Bandwidth Place

http://bandwidthplace.com/speedtest/

Chronology of Personal Computers

http://www.islandnet.com/~kpolsson/comphist/

Cnet's Latest in Browsers

http://www.download.com/2001-2137-0.html

Computer Training 2000

http://computertim.com/

Digital Literacy Checklist: Plug-Ins

http://courses.washington.edu/~hs590a/modules/69/diglit/
    gen-plug.html

Hobb's Internet Timeline

http://www.zakon.org/robert/internet/timeline/

Hobbes' Internet Timeline

http://www.zakon.org/robert/internet/timeline/

How MP3 Files Work

http://www.howstuffworks.com/mp3.html

ICANN for Beginners

http://www.icannwatch.com/icann4beginners.shtml

Internet Errors Explained

http://www.daviestrek.com/computrek/error.htm

Internet Traffic Report

http://www.internettrafficreport.com/

New TLDs

http://www.internic.net/faqs/new-tlds.html

NUA Internet Surveys

http://www.nua.net/surveys/

PC Pitstop

http://www.pcpitstop.com/

Webopedia

http://www.webopedia.com/

Problems and Exercises

1. Explain the difference between a software application and an operating system.

2. Why are used computers, especially computers that are more than three years old, relatively worthless?

3. In 1993 an Intel 486 CPU ran at 40MHz, and in 2002 an Intel P4 processor ran at 2.2GHz. Are these CPU speeds consistent with Moore's Law? You can assume that the cost of a personal computer was constant during this same period.

4. What three CPU features determine the speed of a computer?

5. [FIND IT ONLINE] According to the Environmental Protection Agency, 250 million computers will be retired over the next five years. These unwanted computers constitute an environmental hazard because computers contain large quantities of lead, mercury, and cadmium. IBM, Hewlett-Packard, Dell, and Gateway have all made an effort to help consumers dispose of old computers responsibly. Conduct an online investigation in order to find out how to dispose of an obsolete computer in an environmentally responsible manner.

6. [HANDS-ON] Visit the Bandwidth Place at `http://bandwidthplace .com/speedtest/index.html` and test the speed of your Internet connection. Run the test at least five times on different days and at different times of the day. What is your fastest speed? Your slowest speed? If you run enough tests you may find some patterns. Is there a time of day when your connection is more likely to be fast or slow?

7. Does clicking a link on a Web page begin a file download or a file upload?

8. If *kilo* means 1,000, why doesn't 10KB equal 10,000 bytes? When does "K" mean 1,000, and when does "K" mean something else?

9. If you connect to the Internet with a 56K modem, what is the fastest transmission rate you can hope to have?

10. The screen shot in Figure 1.8 describes the speed of a file transfer as 200 KB/s. Are they referring to 200 kilobits per second or 200 kilobytes per second? Back up your answer with an arithmetic argument [Hint: the screen shot tells you how many bytes have been uploaded and how much time it took.]

11. How does the expression "Hurry up and wait" apply to the Internet?

12. According to a study conducted by Parks Associates in 2001, young adults between the ages of 25 and 34 store an average of 721 MP3 files on their home computers. Estimate the amount of space on a hard drive needed to store a library of 721 MP3s.

13. **[TAKE A STAND]** Different studies come to different conclusions about the effects of the Internet on audio CD sales. Do you think Internet access and MP3 file sharing is hurting the sale of audio CDs, stimulating more CD sales, or having no effect on CD sales at all? Explain your answer and back it up with any hard facts you can find.

14. **[FIND IT ONLINE]** According to the Design Council Web site, "an e-home will be characterized by the seamless interconnection of virtually anything powered by electricity and a host of new services/applications delivered by the Internet." Name three such services that are being built into some new homes today.

15. Is the Internet heterarchical or hierarchical in its overall design? Explain the difference between a heterarchical network and a hierarchical network. Why was the Internet's overall networking design initially adopted?

16. What is dynamic routing, and how is it used on the Internet?

17. If you connect to the Internet over a telephone line, what can you say about your computer's IP address?

18. Match up the items in the left-hand column with their most likely memory requirements in the right-hand column.

    1. One floppy disk   a. 700KB
    2. One sentence   b. 10GB
    3. One small drawing   c. 1 byte
    4. One large photograph   d. 10KB
    5. One DVD disk   e. 4 bytes
    6. 200 audio CDs   f. 640MB
    7. The IE browser   g. 4.7GB
    8. One CD-ROM   h. 65 bytes
    9. 32 bits   i. 1.44MB
    10. The letter "A"   j. 20MB

19. How many bits are needed to represent an alphabet that contains 300 different characters?

20. Explain the difference between an IP address and a DNS address.

21. List six top-level domain names, and explain what they mean.

22. When music is recorded on a CD, a digital recording device samples the sound 44,100 times per second. Each sample is 2 bytes (16 bits) long, and a separate sample is taken for each of the two speakers in a stereo system. Therefore, each second of sound on the CD requires $44{,}100 \times 2 \times 2 = 176{,}400$ bytes of memory. How much memory is this in bits? Determine how many megabytes of memory are needed to store a three-minute song. If you could attain the maximal MP3 file reduction of 93 percent, how much memory would this three-minute song consume as an MP3 file?

23. What does a domain name server do?

24. Which of the following are clients and which are servers?
    a. A Web browser
    b. A Web site where you can access a general search engine
    c. A Web site that tells you the correct time
    d. A program you launch that displays news headlines on your desktop
    e. A Web site that tells you the speed of your Internet connection
    f. A program you launch that tracks stock prices and displays a customized stock ticker for you

25. Who initiates a client/server interaction: the client or the server?

26. How many client requests per second do the busiest Web servers handle?

27. What is an Application Service Provider? Who might want to use one? What advantages does using one offer?

28. Explain the difference between a history list and a bookmark file. When do you use the history list? When do you use a bookmark?

29. [HANDS-ON] Your browser was originally configured with some bookmarks to Web sites that the browser's manufacturer wanted to promote. If you still have these bookmarks on your computer, review them and decide whether you want to keep them. Delete any that are of no interest to you.

 30. [HANDS-ON] If you have already collected a lot of bookmarks, check to see if you have them nicely organized in a hierarchical structure. If not, organize them now. If you haven't created any of your own bookmarks, visit some favorite Web pages and bookmark them. Try to create a good hierarchical structure for them as you add your

bookmarks, but if you don't like this initial structure, go back and reorganize your bookmarks to make it better.

31. What is the first thing you should do when you see a "404 Not Found" error message? What can you try after that?

32. [HANDS-ON] Do you notice different response times when you are on the Net? Which times of day tend to give you the fastest file downloads? Which times are the worst? If you haven't noticed any patterns, try logging on at different times of the day, watch for fast connections and slow connections, and see if you can find any patterns. You might find it useful to keep a log of the times of day and one or two actual download times for each Internet session.

33. [HANDS-ON] Download one of the other browsers listed in Section 1.11. Compare the features you use frequently in your current browser. Which one is better? Use the bookmark import/export feature of your browsers to transfer your bookmarks from one browser to the other. Does either browser allow you to *merge* bookmarks?

34. [HANDS-ON] Download the Opera browser and check out the *widgets*. Review and select a few extra widgets to add to the browser.

35. [GROUP PROJECT] Working as group, download all of the available browsers. Test various features the browsers have in common. Compare and contrast each browser with the other. Select one feature unique to that browser and describe what it does and how it works.

First Things First

A Little History

The Internet can be described in terms of the hardware infrastructure that supports it, the demographics of the people who populate it, and the software that facilitates it. Although it is natural to think of the Internet in terms of computers and communication links between computers, the real force that shapes the Internet is the people who use it. Until the early 1990s, the Internet was used by scientists and academics pursuing long-distance collaborations and scholarly research. Computer science students and professional programmers also used the Internet for more casual communications, and they have been responsible for much of the enabling software. In 1994, widespread distribution of a graphical browser for the Web triggered mainstream America's explosive interest in the Internet. Commercial service providers quickly materialized, offering Internet access to anyone who had a personal computer and a telephone line.

The Internet wasn't discussed by the popular press much before 1990. However, its origins date to 1970, when four computers were first hooked up to each other over telephone lines—connecting the Stanford Research Institute (SRI), the University of California at Los Angeles (UCLA), the University of California at Santa Barbara, and the University of Utah at Salt Lake City. Twenty years of concerted effort by computer scientists and engineers resulted in today's all-purpose global network for high-speed digital communication. That same 20-year period also witnessed the creation and commercialization of personal computers, which made it possible for people to hop on the Internet from the convenience of their own homes.

No one in 1970 could have imagined the Internet of today. There was never a master plan in place to guide all the contributing technologies. However, a sense of limitless possibilities attracted a generation of scientists and technicians to the field of computer science, where innovation is a way of life and nothing stands still for very long. In 1983, what was to become the Internet was a computer science experiment used primarily by scientists; it consisted of only 562 computers. In 1993, it was a global infrastructure with important implications for the business world and telecommunications industries. By then the number of connected computers had grown to over 1.2 million. By 1996, that number exceeded 12 million. Over the last 15 years, the number of computers on the Internet has doubled every 12 to 14 months.

Figure 1.34 shows the growth rate of computers on the Internet.

One critical component underlying today's Internet is the software that supports network communications. In the Internet's early days, network software was not particularly user-friendly. Computer scientists were the only people who used it, and they didn't care about user-friendly interfaces. The software they designed was somewhat difficult to use, although it served its intended user community very well. Two of the earliest Internet applications became standards among computer scientists long before home computers were a commercial concern. **Telnet** was created in 1969, and the **File Transfer Protocol** (**FTP**) was first used in 1971. Both were designed long before anyone began to think about point-and-click user interfaces. However, telnet and FTP are still in use.

Although the Web is the fastest-growing segment of the Internet, the most popular software application on the Internet has always been **e-mail** (electronic mail). More people have access to e-mail than to the Web, and e-mail messages are gradually replacing traditional mail correspondence and telephone conversations for a new generation of workers and private citizens. In 1995 the Internet, for the first time, delivered more mail messages than the United States Postal Service. E-mail software now sports user-friendly interfaces, and Internet communication via e-mail is very easy.

Figure 1.34

Domain name registrations track the growth of the Internet.

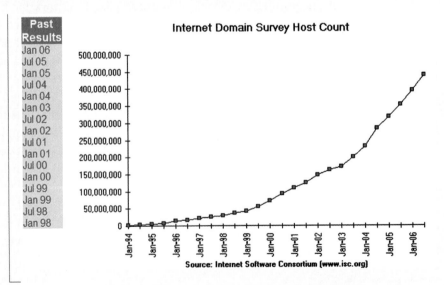

FYI: Telnet and FTP

Telnet allows a user on one host to log on to a computer account on a remote host and work on that remote host as if it were the local machine. Computer scientists with accounts at different universities and research laboratories use telnet to run software on and work on computers that might be thousands of miles away.

FTP makes it possible to move files from one computer account to another, no matter where the computers are located. Files can be both uploaded and downloaded via FTP, but FTP users must have access privileges for the two computers involved in the file transfer. (Read more about FTP in Section 6.10).

However, some people are using e-mail for more than friendly greetings and business correspondence. In recent years, e-mail also has become a highly effective vehicle for spreading *computer viruses*. Viruses and other dangers of going online are discussed in Chapter 2.

How Fast Are Different Internet Connections?

Some readers might be disturbed by the use of the term *speed* to describe the movement of data over the Internet. The speed with which something moves is normally described as a ratio of distance to time, as in "the fastest elevator in the world is in Yokohama and travels at speeds over 40 feet per second." However, people talk about the speed of the Internet in terms of bits per second (bps) or, sometimes, bytes per second (Bps), neither of which have anything to do with distance. Even so, these rates tell how long it takes to view a Web page or download a file, so we naturally think of these ratios as the speed of a data transmission.

If you investigate discussions of speed on the Internet, you might encounter the term *baud rate*. It is often confused with bits per second. The earliest modems ran at 300 **baud**, which meant that the modem could process 300 electrical signals per second. At slow speeds (fewer than 1,200 baud), one bit of data is encoded in one electrical signal, so, for example, 300 baud is the same as 300 bps. However, at higher speeds more than 1 bit might be encoded in each electrical signal. For example, a 4,800-baud modem can transfer data at a rate of 9,600 bps. In fact, a 9,600 bps modem running at only 2,400 baud is possible. Although data transmission rates are usually described in terms of bits per second, you might still see baud rates mentioned in the context of older computer hardware.

The rate of data transmission is often called its **data rate** or **throughput**. High levels of throughput on the Internet are achieved by fast carrier technologies, such as optical fiber, and the use of multiple data channels, called **multiplexing**. Analog telephone lines rely on copper wires (also called **twisted-pair wiring**) to provide **Plain Old Telephone Service (POTS)**. Twisted-pair wires used to support a single channel are limited to 56 kbps, but it is possible to achieve some degree of multiplexing with twisted-pair wiring and thereby raise the throughput to 512 kbps. This is the basis for ISDN and ADSL services available to telephone customers in some areas of the country.

A communication connection that supports many channels is called a **broadband connection**. Broadband technologies are used within ISP networks and for the backbones of the Internet. Figure 1.35 shows a number of communication technologies used to support the Internet.

A cable connection can support up to 52 **megabits per second (Mbps)**. That number describes the rate at which service to *multiple* customers can be delivered. A single personal computer user may not be able to handle more than 10 Mbps. However, throughput rates above 10 Mbps are useful in large corporations or ISP networks. An E5 connection, which relies on optical fiber, can support up to 7,680 simultaneous voice conversations and even more simultaneous Internet connections.

Communication on the Internet tends to be **bursty**, that is, the traffic ebbs and surges. You might be able to see the effects of a heavy surge of traf-

Figure 1.35	POTS	56 Kbps

POTS	56 Kbps
ISDN	64–128 Kbps
IDSL	128 Kbps
T1	1.544 Mbps
Satellite	6 Mbps and up
DSL	512 Kbps–8 Mbps
Ethernet	10 Mbps
Cable modem	512 Kbps–52 Mbps
Wireless (8.02.11)	1–54 Mbps
T3	44.736 Mbps
OC-1	51.84 Mbps
FDDI	100 Mbps
Fast Ethernet	100 Mbps
E5	565.148 Mbps
Gigabit Ethernet	1 Gbps
OC-256	13.271 Gbps

Figure 1.35

Broadband connections are always faster than POTS (Plain Old Telephone Service)

fic on a single download if you are monitoring its transmission rate. During a single download, throughput can slow to a crawl, although it will continue. Internet users are never shut out because of traffic conditions, although limited resources can result in no access at specific locations. For example, a dial-up connection to an ISP is always limited by the number of available telephone lines running into the ISP's servers, and a specific server is limited to the number of simultaneous connections it can support. Occasionally, you'll see a busy signal for a Web server (see Figure 1.36). But when a client encounters a busy server, the client usually keeps trying until it connects, so you will rarely see a server that is too busy to respond for very long.

POTS allocates one dedicated line for each telephone call. As long as there are enough lines to satisfy demand, this system works well. Dedicated lines are not shared, so once you have a call in place, your connection is not affected by how many other users are trying to call in. Internet users, however, do not depend on dedicated lines. On the Internet, many users can share a single channel. This is why busy traffic on the Net can perceptibly affect throughput. But unlike the old telephone party lines, on which people could eavesdrop on each other's conversations, Internet communications are kept distinct and separate through a system called *packet switching*. (Packet switching is explained in an upcoming section.)

Although throughput is growing to meet demand, bottlenecks will always be a problem. High-bandwidth applications such as video-on-demand and full-motion videoconferencing stress current hardware capabilities. Even so, where there's a will there's a way, and clever software can sometimes get us where we want to go even if hardware alone can't do the job. For example, clever software is responsible for the distribution of real-time audio and video clips.

Figure 1.36
A Web server's busy signal

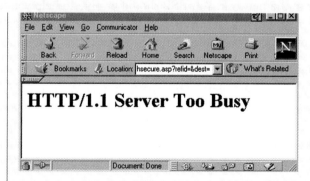

Wireless Internet Connections

WiFi. In our very mobile society, notebook computers are becoming more and more popular, and nearly as powerful as desktop computer systems. In May 2005, the sales of notebook computers exceeded those of desktop units for the first time. Hand in hand with the growing popularity of notebooks is the increasing availability of wireless Internet connectivity that most laptop users will appreciate. Many public places such as airports, hotels, coffee shops (aka Internet cafes) and even municipal organizations now provide wireless access points mostly through WiFi (Wireless Fidelity) technology based on a version of the Institute of Electrical and Electronics Engineers (IEEE) 802.11 standard. Wireless Internet access is also increasingly common on many college campuses. Yahoo (`http://mobile.yahoo.com/wifi`) now provides a place to locate wireless access locations. WiFi connection speeds range from about 11 Mbps and up, depending on the transmission protocol that has been implemented. Most notebook computers now come standard with 802.11 networking hardware to take advantage of wireless connectivity.

WiFi Communications Standards

IEEE Standard Designation	802.11b	802.11g
Maximum Speed	11 Mbps	54 Mbps

Private business and home wireless networks are also fairly common. Most ISPs now offer wireless access as an option when purchasing Internet services. But beware! If you are setting up your own wireless home network, be sure to take advantage of the WEP (wired equivalent privacy), WPA (WiFi Protected Access), or WPA2 security protocols. Although the level of security is debatable, WEP does provide basic encryption protection between your wireless access point and all devices attached to your wireless network. WPA and WPA2 are better. Only devices that know the password (that you specify) can join the network. Your ISP should be able to help you activate a security protocol if you need it. Without some type of access protection, you may end up providing network access to nearby hackers and not know it!

WiMax. A new service, currently dubbed WiMax, will soon be competing with WiFi for your wireless Internet business. WiFi access is currently limited to about 150–300 feet from the wireless transmitter/receiver, more commonly referred to as an access point. Based on the developing 802.16 standard, WiMax promises to extend the range for wireless connections up to 30 miles with data transmission speeds up to 70 Mbps, and also allows connections to be established in moving vehicles. By the time you read this, WiMax products and services should be commercially available, and may possibly supplant the earlier 802.11 wireless standard. In 2005, Sprint and Intel announced a partnership to develop WiMax-based products and services. One can only expect that other cellular phone service providers will soon be following suit.

Bluetooth ®. So what on Earth is Bluetooth? You've probably heard of Bluetooth-enabled devices. Bluetooth is another wireless connection protocol used to create Personal Area Networks (PANs) that connect devices like Personal Digital Assistants (PDAs), mobile phones, laptops, printers, digital cameras and video game consoles over short distances. You may already use a wireless headset with your cell phone. The communications technology it uses is Bluetooth, a peer-to-peer communications protocol. WiFi and WiMax networks require a host to manage the network. With Bluetooth, two devices communicate with each other directly and exchange information over an *ad hoc* Bluetooth PAN—such networks are created "on the fly." On a PAN, cameras can transfer images to your lap, your laptop can transfer phonebook entries to your cell phone, your PDA can synchronize your appointment calendar with its counterpart on your desktop computer. Bluetooth uses the same frequency range for communication as WiFi, but the power is much lower so the range is correspondingly limited. Depending on the power output of the signal, the communication range of a Bluetooth device is 1 meter, 10 meters, or 100 meters with a transfer rate as high as 723 kbps. Proposed enhancements may increase this maximum rate to 2 Mbps. Because Bluetooth uses radio frequency waves, line of sight connections are not necessary, but the walls and other objects may obstruct the signal. WiFi and Bluetooth use different protocols to establish connections, so it is possible, and probable, that both networks exist simultaneously without interfering with each other.

Streaming Media

Audio and video files are extremely bandwidth-intensive. Digital radio broadcasts in real time are hampered by bottlenecks and Internet traffic patterns, yet they are within the reach of users with 28.8 kbps and 56 kbps modems. Even videoconferencing can be attempted, if you don't mind the stop-and-go images that aren't always quite in sync with the audio. These communications are possible today because of streaming media. **Streaming media** is a strategy for playing very large multimedia files in real time while the file is downloading over a bursty Net connection.

Special software is needed to handle streaming media. RealNetworks, the creator of RealPlayer, was a major pioneer in the development of streaming media.

When you download a streaming audio file, your audio player saves the front end of the file in a temporary holding area called a **buffer**. The audio player does not start to play the file until some suitable amount of that file has been saved to the buffer. Once the player has enough data buffered, it begins to play the file while at the same time still downloading and saving more of the file. Buffer space is recycled whenever possible, so room for more data is always available. The hope is that the player will never process its data faster than the Net connection can fill the buffer. If the player does manage to get ahead of the buffer, a break in the song or the video display will occur, and then you'll have to wait for the music or video to restart. However, a large enough buffer can usually smooth out the expected variations in throughput that would interfere with a real-time rendering of the data if no buffers were involved.

Using streaming audio, you can hear, for example, a 60-minute radio show without having to wait for hours to complete a massive download. If your network connection is severely stressed, the quality of the audio playback might not be acceptable (there might be too many breaks in the stream). However, streaming media works well under the right conditions. It enables you to hear and view multimedia materials that would otherwise be beyond the reach of most Internet users.

How Is Data Sent over the Internet?

Two computers can communicate with each other only if they can agree to speak a common language. A common language that computers share is called a **communication protocol**. Different Internet applications use different protocols.

When computer scientists set out to create computer networks, their first challenge was to find a common communication protocol for different types of computers running different OSs. All the computers needed to speak a common language. First, the **Internet Protocol (IP)** was adopted as a universal addressing system for all computers on the Internet. Second, the **Transmission Control Protocol (TCP)** was designed to work closely with IP by preparing the data for the trip from one Internet host to another. All computers on the Internet run these two protocols, called **TCP/IP**, which are available for all computer platforms. These protocols for network communication prevent the Internet from becoming a Tower of Babel (see Figure 1.37).

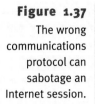

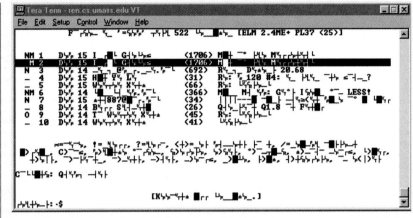

Packets and Packet Switching. At the TCP level, bytes are organized into **packets** before they leave home for a trip on the Net. Once they arrive at their intended destination, TCP is then responsible for unpacking the packets and reconstructing the original file or command. Each Internet host must run TCP in order to send and receive data over the Net. Packets can vary in size, but the average is about 1.5KB. Each is stamped with the IP address of its destination and the IP address of its origin. Before reassembly, packets are examined at the receiving end by error correction techniques to determine whether they are healthy. These techniques, while very effective, are not 100 percent accurate. This means you can still receive a corrupted file over the Internet. If it happens repeatedly with the same file, that file is most likely corrupted on its original host as well.

Fortunately, packets lost or damaged in transit can be resent without the need to resend the entire set of packets that comprise the complete transmission. This feature makes TCP/IP an efficient protocol when large files are sent across poor-quality communication channels, such as noisy telephone lines. No one wants to resend an entire 1MB file just because 1 byte of the file was corrupted.

Internet communications are also expedited by the fact that a single communication channel can carry packets for multiple users. Each packet is stamped with a unique identifier to help the receiving host reassemble the complete transmission. In this way, packets for different jobs can be received at the same time and disentangled without confusion. This system of shared communication channels in combination with TCP/IP is called **packet switching**. Packet switching is responsible for the Internet's robustness and reliability. When demand for a channel exceeds the channel's maximal throughput, packets are set aside in a buffer. If all available buffers become full, any additional packets will be dropped for lack of space. These packets are considered *lost* during transmission. This is no great tragedy, however, since lost packets can always be resent to finish an incomplete data transfer. The transfer will simply take a little longer. This is why traffic loads on the Internet are often described in terms of packet loss. Higher rates of packet loss result in longer transmission times for data transfers.

How Does File Compression Work?

Different types of files require different compression techniques. One technique for compressing text is based on the use of a document-specific dictionary that contains only the words found in that file. Each word in the dictionary is indexed by a number, and the original document is encoded as a list of indices that represent those dictionary entries. For a medium-sized document, the space needed to store the dictionary and the index list will be less than the space needed to store the ASCII-text encoding of the original document. A very long text file that contains many instances of repeated words might be reduced by as much as 50–60 percent of its original size.

The MP3 audio files use a different set of compression techniques. Audio CDs are recorded by sampling data from a recording device 44,100 times per second. Each sound sample is digitized and encoded using 2 bytes (16 bits). Separate sample sets are taken for each speaker in a stereo system. Audio CDs therefore require 1,411,200 ($44,100 \times 16 \times 2$) bits, or about 175KB for each second of sound. A three-minute song therefore consumes about 32MB of space. No one with a 56K modem would want to download music from the Internet if it took two hours to download three minutes of music. This is why MP3 files are so important for the distribution of music over the Internet.

When music is stored using the MP3 format, the original audio file is reduced by a factor of 10 to 14 without a perceivable loss in sound quality. This can mean a huge difference, for example, a 3MB file rather than a 32MB file.

The technique that makes this possible is **perceptual noise shaping**. Characteristics of the human ear are brought into play in order to reduce storage requirements without sacrificing the quality of the recording. For example, some sounds captured on a digital recording might fall outside the range of sounds that people can hear; therefore these frequencies can be omitted without any perceptible loss of sound quality. In addition, under certain conditions, when two sounds are played together one sound might mask the other so that only the one is heard.

Temporal masking due to threshold effects also occur. For example, a loud sound effectively erases softer sounds of the same frequency for a period of 200 milliseconds after the loud sound stops. There is no reason to record sounds that exist but are never perceived by our ears.

Knowledge of human hearing is being exploited whenever music is compressed in an MP3 file. Your dog might be able to hear the difference, but as long as you can't, the MP3 version of your favorite song is fine.

Hypertext: Changing How People Read

The Internet affects interpersonal communication, formal education, and all sorts of long-distance collaborations, not to mention the political process, the economy, and global communication. The multitude of decision points inherent in richly linked hypertext documents and the fast interactive nature of the Web clearly cater to individual interests and varying attention spans. This is likely to have implications not only for how people read but also for how they live their lives in every aspect.

It is not unreasonable to imagine that a generation raised with user-centric technology will be less inclined to wait for answers, less tolerant of information that is deemed irrelevant, and less able to tolerate social situations that do not offer immediate gratification. Once you adapt to e-mail, incoming telephone calls begin to feel obtrusive and unreasonably demanding. Once you become accustomed to finding information on the Web, trips to the library become quaint and tedious.

The next time you pick up a textbook at your campus bookstore, drop by the comparative literature section and see how many of those texts are about cyberspace. Literary scholars are very interested in the impact of the Internet on written communication. Hypertext accelerates attention shifts and can therefore reinforce short attention spans. Readers who are not sufficiently stimulated by the text on a Web page can simply click a link in search of more immediate gratification.

If television was the medium that lulled children into becoming zombie-eyed couch potatoes, the Web is a perfect match for attention deficit disorder. With television, people make decisions about their viewing preferences once an hour. With the Internet, similar decisions can be made about once a minute. If we allow the Internet to replace books and all forms of printed matter, unpredictable consequences will likely result. The choice is ours. It is easy to feel helpless in the face of such a rapidly evolving technology.

Further, the excitement and momentum of such a transformational technology can overwhelm competing concerns. However, we must take a deep breath and conduct our lives with thoughtful deliberation in the face of this ongoing communication revolution. We can still buy books, read novels, and study great literature. We can still pick up the telephone or write a letter on stationery. We can still shop the brick-and mortar stores and seek the advice of close friends over dinner instead of strangers on the Net. None of these low-tech activities get much media attention or create sensations on Wall Street. However, the existence of high-tech options need not make low-tech options obsolete. We simply need to be conscious of our choices and act accordingly.

Applications: Helpers, Plug-Ins, and Add-Ons

An **application** is a program you run on your computer to accomplish specific tasks. You can obtain applications from retail software stores or the Internet (see Chapter 6). The applications you choose to install are what make your computer unique and personal (hence the term *personal computer*). A Web browser is an example of an application that sometimes includes other applications. For example, Web browsers include a Java Virtual Machine (JVM) so you can run Java applets.

Just as you can customize your computer to reflect your general needs and computing activities, you can customize your browser to reflect your Web-browsing needs and activities. For example, you can tell your browser how you want it to handle different types of files found on the Web. If you never want to hear .wav audio files, you won't care if your browser can't handle them. But if .wav files are important to you, you might want your browser to use a specific .wav player whenever it encounters a .wav file on a Web page.

Your browser often uses other applications to view the Web. If you like, you can configure your browser to use the applications you prefer. Helper applications and plug-ins are two ways to enhance the viewing capabilities of your browser. In both cases, you are telling your browser that certain file types should be handled in a certain way. Your browser needs to know which file types require special handling and which application is needed for which file types.

A **helper application** can be any application on your computer. When your browser encounters a file that requires special handling, it looks for an appropriate helper application, launches that application, and then loads the file into the application. If your browser can't handle this on its own, you can always download the file from the Web, save it to some location on your hard drive, launch the appropriate application yourself, and open the downloaded file from inside the desired application. When you configure your browser to use a helper application, your browser does all of this for you automatically. You can always tell when your browser is calling on a helper application because a new application window will open on your desktop.

When you install a **plug-in**, you extend the capabilities of your browser to handle a file type that it wasn't originally designed to handle. When you configure your browser to use a plug-in, any file requiring that plug-in will be displayed inside the browser window, with the plug-in application working as if it were a part of your browser. For example, Macromedia Flash is an application that produces computer animations for the Web. To view these animations, you need a plug-in called Shockwave. If your browser has this plug-in, you can view Web pages that contain Flash animations. If your browser does not have this plug-in, you are out of luck when it comes to Web pages with Flash content. Plug-ins are usually easy to set up because the download and installation processes are normally scripted, that is, automated for you.

Adobe's Acrobat Reader is an example of an application you can add to your browser as either a helper application or a plug-in—but not both! You need Acrobat Reader in order to read multimedia files in PDF format. If you seldom encounter PDF files on the Web, you can always install Acrobat Reader as a regular application, save to disk any PDF files you happen to encounter on the Web, and launch Acrobat Reader manually to open those files. But if you encounter PDF files regularly, you'll save a lot of time if you add Acrobat Reader to your browser as a helper application or a plug-in.

Since helper applications are not scripted to set up appropriate file associations for you, it's important to have detailed instructions when you need to set up a helper application. Sometimes the installation instructions for a helper application are simple. In other cases, they are more involved and should be attempted only by people who have a technical background. Software manufacturers who want to encourage the use of their software in conjunction with Web browsers are wise to release a plug-in so users don't have to go through intimidating and potentially dangerous helper application installations.

Be selective with the plug-ins that you add to your browser; you need only those plug-ins that enhance your experience on the Web. It's fun to see what's available (see, for example, Figure 1.38). However, don't set up all the available plug-ins just because you might need one in the future. Add plug-ins only when you really need them.

A plug-in is software that becomes a part of your browser. It increases your browser's memory requirements and adds to the amount of time needed to launch your browser. So use plug-ins only for frequently encountered file types. Figure 1.39 shows some of the more popular browser plug-ins.

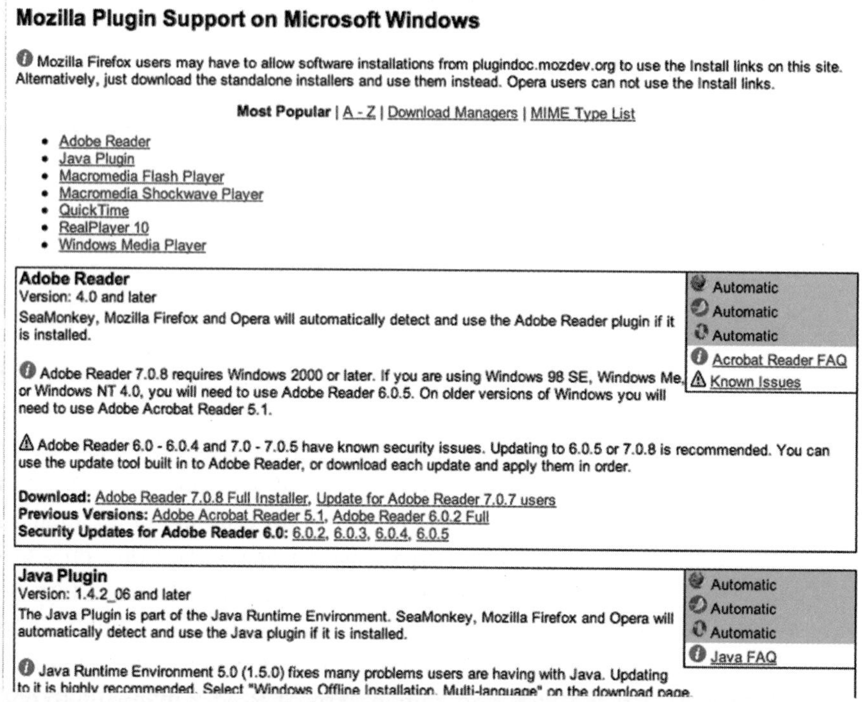

Figure 1.38

A plug-in directory
for Mozilla Firefox

Mozilla Plugin Support on Microsoft Windows

ⓘ Mozilla Firefox users may have to allow software installations from plugindoc.mozdev.org to use the Install links on this site. Alternatively, just download the standalone installers and use them instead. Opera users can not use the Install links.

Most Popular | A - Z | Download Managers | MIME Type List

- Adobe Reader
- Java Plugin
- Macromedia Flash Player
- Macromedia Shockwave Player
- QuickTime
- RealPlayer 10
- Windows Media Player

Adobe Reader
Version: 4.0 and later
SeaMonkey, Mozilla Firefox and Opera will automatically detect and use the Adobe Reader plugin if it is installed.

ⓘ Adobe Reader 7.0.8 requires Windows 2000 or later. If you are using Windows 98 SE, Windows Me, or Windows NT 4.0, you will need to use Adobe Reader 6.0.5. On older versions of Windows you will need to use Adobe Acrobat Reader 5.1.

⚠ Adobe Reader 6.0 - 6.0.4 and 7.0 - 7.0.5 have known security issues. Updating to 6.0.5 or 7.0.8 is recommended. You can use the update tool built in to Adobe Reader, or download each update and apply them in order.

Download: Adobe Reader 7.0.8 Full Installer, Update for Adobe Reader 7.0.7 users
Previous Versions: Adobe Acrobat Reader 5.1, Adobe Reader 6.0.2 Full
Security Updates for Adobe Reader 6.0: 6.0.2, 6.0.3, 6.0.4, 6.0.5

- Automatic
- Automatic
- Automatic
- ⓘ Acrobat Reader FAQ
- ⚠ Known Issues

Java Plugin
Version: 1.4.2_06 and later
The Java Plugin is part of the Java Runtime Environment. SeaMonkey, Mozilla Firefox and Opera will automatically detect and use the Java plugin if it is installed.

ⓘ Java Runtime Environment 5.0 (1.5.0) fixes many problems users are having with Java. Updating to it is highly recommended. Select "Windows Offline Installation, Multi-language" on the download page.

- Automatic
- Automatic
- Automatic
- ⓘ Java FAQ

Figure 1.39

Some popular
browser helper
applications and
plug-ins

Adobe Acrobat Reader	Views, navigates, and prints PDF files.
Quicktime	Displays QuickTime files and other video and audio file formats.
Powerpoint Viewer, Excel Viewer, Word Viewer	View and print Microsoft Office documents without installing the Office suite.
Realplayer	Plays various formats of audio and video files, notably .au, .ra, .ram files. Widely used for streaming audio files.
Shockwave and Flash	Plug-ins for animation and documents produced with Macromedia Director or Flash. Very popular at game sites.
Windows Media Player	Displays popular streaming and local audio and video formats, including ASF, WAV, AVI, MPEG, QuickTime, and more.

FYI: Play It Safe

If you need a plug-in for a specific application and none is available, search the Web for installation instructions that will enable you to set up the application as a helper application. Make sure that the instructions are intended for the browser and OS you use. Be careful if the only instructions you find are confusing in any way. If the instructions look too intimidating, you can always save files to your hard drive and launch the required application independently to open those files. This is not a slick solution, but it's preferable to restoring or reinstalling your system if something goes seriously wrong with a tricky helper application installation.

Your browser will tell you when it doesn't know how to handle a particular file, and this is a good time to decide if you want to add a plug-in. Navigator and IE locate plug-ins on demand with plug-in finders. As soon as you encounter a Web page that requires a plug-in that your browser does not have, the plug-in finder figures out which one you need and offers it to you on the spot (see Figure 1.40).

To see which plug-ins have been added to Navigator v8 or Firefox, select "Extensions" in the Tools menu. To see which plug-ins have been added to IE, select "Manage Add-ons" in the Tools menu (see Figure 1.41).

Helper applications and plug-ins enhance browser viewing capabilities. A third class of browser accessories consists of those available only as browser add-ons. A **browser add-on** is an application that works in conjunction with your Web browser to enhance or complement your browser in some specific way. Browser add-ons can be called from your browser, either automatically or manually when you click a toolbar icon. Some add-ons can be launched

Figure 1.40

IE's plug-in finder pops up when you need a plug-in.

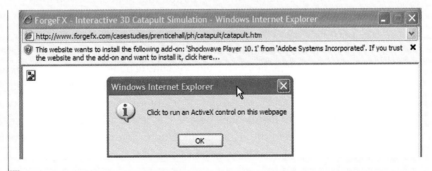

Figure 1.41

The IE v7 Add-on Manager

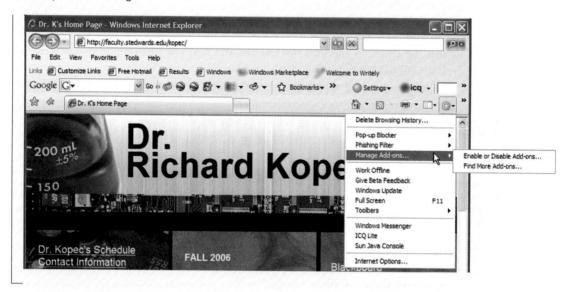

TIP: How to Uninstall Plug-Ins

 Installing plug-ins is usually easy, and there are several ways to remove them. If you are using IE v7, then you can use the "Manage Add-ons" Tool (see Figure 1.41). This tool allows you to enable or disable add-ons of various types. The removal tool appears to need work, though. Other browsers have similar capabilities.

Failing that, if you're a Windows user, look for the plug-in's application under the Change or Remove Programs list in your Control Panel directory. (From the Start menu select the Control Panel.) If the application is listed there, select it and remove it with the Change/Remove button that appears. If you aren't using IE7, then see if plug-in is part of an independent application that comes with its own uninstaller. Look for that, and if you find an uninstaller, use it.

If you're a Macintosh user (or a Windows user who can't locate the application in the Change or Remove Programs control panel), you must resort to deleting the files manually. Each Web browser maintains its own directory of plug-in files, and each plug-in should have its own directory within the plug-in directory. To be safe, search the Web for instructions before you delete any files. Use the keywords "uninstall," "plugin," and the name of the plug-in you want to remove when conducting your search.

independently. An example of a browser add-on is the Alertna TIFF viewer. Alertna allows you to view TIFF files in your browser window and is available as a Netscape-style plug-in or an ActiveX control for IE.

If you are having trouble keeping plug-ins, helper applications, and add-ons straight, see Figure 1.42. But don't despair if you find documentation on the Web that is still confusing to you. Unfortunately, these terms are used a little differently by different browser manufacturers. Figure 1.42 reflects the usage typically seen in conjunction with Navigator. Windows Internet Explorer v7 uses the terms browser helper application, browser extension, and ActiveX control to categorize the types of enhancements that can be added to

Figure 1.42

Keeping it all straight

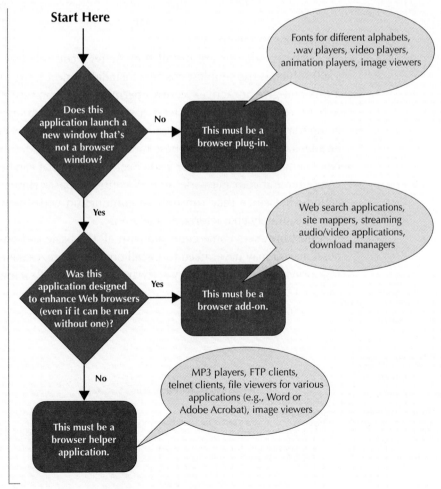

GROWING UP WIRED

Now, the very fabric of my existence is threatened by the Internet. By being exposed to so much information, and so quickly, I seek such stimulation in real life, and find real life to be lacking. Classes drag on, and the simple commutes between classes take a surprising amount of time. . . . I am not afraid of a high-strung, technology-obsessed culture. I welcome it for the same reason everyone younger than me does; it's more exciting than real life.

—Jacob Glazeski, University of Nebraska

the browser. IE describes all these items as "add-ons" that can be accessed from the "Manage Add-ons…" selection in the Tools menu (see Figure 1.41). Browser helper objects are similar to plug-ins, while browser extensions are similar to add-ons. An ActiveX control is a special software module available only for Windows machines that can be used to transform a Web page into an interface that provides totally new capabilities, such as a spreadsheet or a calculator. The concepts are the same—only the jargon shifts around a bit. This book emphasizes Navigator terminology and definitions because they provide more distinctions (although the line between add-ons and helper applications can be fuzzy at times).

Some IE add-ons are installed by ActiveX controls (see Figure 1.41 and 1.43), which is the simplest possible installation procedure. All you do is click a link and give an ActiveX control permission to run (see Figure 1.43). The ActiveX control runs as if it were a standalone application running on your computer, with access to all possible operations. ActiveX controls should not be added indiscriminately—these modules can be used to implement various types of malware (see Chapter 2 and Section 6.4.5) that can be harmful to your computer and your network. ActiveX controls appear similar to helper applications, but since they run only in conjunction with the browser, they are more accurately characterized as add-ons.

Most browsers come equipped with all the basic add-ons needed, so it is possible you may never need to install one. If you do, make note of the warnings provided by your security software (see Chapter 2) if any.

Figure 1.43

You have to decide whom you trust when you run an ActiveX software installation.

Adobe Shockwave player is now installing.

As a part of the installation process, the browser will be restarted.

TIP: Browser Compatibility

Sometimes an Internet application will be available as an add-on or a plug-in for one browser but not all browsers. For example, none of Netscape's plug-ins work with IE 6.0 and above. Most plug-ins are available for several browsers, but be careful to download the correct version for your browser.

Problems and Exercises

Exercises A1, A2, and A3 can be completed using the Internet timeline on the inside of the front cover.

A1. When did the Internet begin? How many computers were connected at that time?

A2. How much time passed between the first ARPANET transmission and the advent of the first commercial ISP? How many hosts were on the Internet when the Internet first became accessible to the general public?

A3. Place the following events on a time line: the first textbook about the Internet, the first e-mail message, the first Apple computer, the first IBM PC, the first telnet transmission, the first version of Netscape Navigator, and the first version of Windows Internet Explorer.

A4. Explain the difference between FTP and telnet.

 A5. [TAKE A STAND] Amazon.com received a patent for 1-Click shopping in 2000, but Apple lost an important lawsuit against Microsoft in 1993 when Apple claimed proprietary rights to the "look and feel" of the desktop interface. Do you think it's right for Amazon to own what amounts to a smart shopping cart if Apple can't own drop-down menus and menu bars? Explain why you think these two legal events make sense (or not).

A6. Explain the difference between a baud rate and bits per second. When are you likely to see references to baud rates?

A7. What is a dedicated communication line? Give an example of a communication medium that uses dedicated lines.

A8. How does streaming media work, and when is it used?

A9. What is TCP/IP, and why is it important for the Internet?

A10. What does it mean to lose a data packet on the Internet? What happens when a packet is lost?

A11. If a small portion of a large file is corrupted during a file transfer over the Internet, does the entire file have to be resent? Explain your answer.

A12. How are text files compressed? Why can larger text files be reduced to a greater extent than smaller text files? Can you think of a way to construct a text file so that it could not be compressed?

A13. How does MP3 compression reduce the size of audio files without hurting the quality of the music?

A14. [FIND IT ONLINE] In 2000, the Motion Picture Association of America (MPAA) sued Eric Corley (and a hacker magazine named *2600* that Corley publishes) for posting the DeCSS code that decrypts DVDs. A federal judge granted a permanent injunction against the defendant and also broadened the ruling to enjoin those acting in concert with *2600*. The MPAA argues that DVDs must be encrypted to protect their intellectual property (movies) from illegal piracy. Who supports the defendant, and what arguments have been set forth in favor of the defense? Who else (other than Corley and *2600*) will be adversely affected by a decision for the plaintiff?

A15. [TAKE A STAND] How do you feel about the MPAA lawsuit against Eric Corley (described in Exercise A14)? How would you decide this case? Explain your reasoning.

A16. Explain the difference between a plug-in and a helper application. Which is generally easier to set up? If an application has a setting for a default browser, does that make it a browser plug-in? Explain why or why not.

A17. Is it necessary to browse directories of available plug-ins for your browser in order to set up the plug-ins you need? Why or why not?

A18. Why would anyone ever want to uninstall a plug-in? Give two possible reasons.

A19. Find out how your browser (if it's not IE, Netscape, or Firefox) manages plug-ins. See if your browser uses terms other than those described here to identify add-ons.

A20. [HANDS-ON] Browser plug-ins can be uninstalled, but when no uninstaller is provided, users must start by finding uninstall instructions for each specific plug-in. For example, instructions for removing the Flash Player are given at `http://www.macromedia.com/cfusion/knowledgebase/index.cfm?id=tn_14157`. Instructions like this often tell you to go to your browser's plug-in directory. Find the plug-in directory on your computer. (Hint: Do a file search with the keyword "plugin.") How many files are in this directory?

A21. **[HANDS-ON]** Find the size of your browser's hard drive cache. All browsers store copies of recently viewed Web pages on the hard drive for quick retrieval if needed again.

A22. If you have a broadband connection, you may not notice much difference in speed between the Web pages that are retrieved from cache and the Web pages that are retrieved from the Web. Does this mean broadband users don't need to use their browser's cache feature? Explain why or why not.

A23. **[HANDS-ON]** Select, download, and install a plug-in for your browser that you would like to try. Test it to make sure it works. Keep a log of your activities so that you can answer the following questions.

    a.   How long did it take to download the plug-in?

    b.   How long did it take to install it?

    c.   Did it work right away?

Describe any difficulties you experienced with this exercise.

Personal Safety Online

2.1 Taking Charge

It might not feel particularly public when you dial into the Internet from the privacy of your own home, but each time you connect, you enter a very public space. This means that your conduct will be visible to—even monitored by—various network administrators and others who may be invisible to you. You have rights as well as responsibilities. To be a good Netizen, you need to act responsibly. And because of aggressive data collection, intrusive advertisers, underhanded business practices, and malicious miscreants, you need to protect your rights.

Being online is not so very different from being offline. When you visit a large city, you plan your trip, tuck your wallet into a safe pocket, obey the law, and use common sense. Going online is much the same. When you log on to the Internet, you need to understand and follow the behavioral codes that are specific to the Net, and you need to minimize your personal risk. The same laws that constrain your behavior in real life still apply when you are on the Internet. However, the extremely public nature of the Internet can amplify and broadcast your actions to a potentially large audience. You can break some rules (the cyberspace equivalent of

Chapter Goals

- Understand the importance of acceptable use policies, passwords, and constant vigilance while online
- Learn why your computer is not secure on the Internet unless you make it secure
- Discover what you can do to protect your computer and personal data while you are online
- Know when your own online activities violate copyright or software piracy laws
- Become aware of privacy issues, and learn what you can do to protect your personal privacy
- Find out how to separate fact from fiction when you see warnings and advice on the Net
- Learn what you can do to protect yourself from identity theft

parking tickets) with little or no consequence. Breaking others (the ones that protect people's rights) might arouse the attention of law enforcement agents. Just as in real life, some actions will have consequences for only you. In any case, it is always wise to anticipate the potential consequences of your actions. Taking the time to read this book will help: we cover everything you need to know to be a good Netizen.

For example, just because some software makes it easy to reproduce an image or distribute a document does not give you the legal or moral right to do so. Many newbies mistakenly assume that they have such rights. Their assumptions are based on unrealistic assumptions about software. Read the licensing agreements that accompany your software. You'll discover that software manufacturers assume no responsibility for any consequences that might arise from the use of their software (see Figure 2.1). Only you can be responsible for your actions. Software doesn't break laws; people break laws.

The virtual world may seem to be a safer place to be than the real world, but the risks and hazards are no less real. The focus of this chapter is on personal safety and security. Common Internet-related personal security issues are presented, along with advice on how to handle them. But because of the pervasive nature of Internet crime and harassment, we also pick up the security thread in Chapter 7 when we discuss risks associated with shopping online and again in Chapter 6 when we talk about downloading software that may be contaminated with spyware and adware. Be sure to read these chapters also!

Acceptable Use Policies

All computer accounts and some public Internet servers are subject to an **acceptable use policy** (**AUP**), a policy that outlines appropriate use of the

Figure 2.1
Software manufacturers assume no liability for their products.

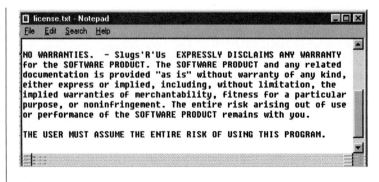

Internet and is enforced by system administrators. Your Internet access privileges can be withdrawn if you violate the rules and restrictions specified by the AUP. You can easily locate examples of AUPs posted on the Web.

The restrictions that pertain to ISP accounts are often called **terms of service (ToS)**. Whenever you open a computer account or join an online discussion group, take the time to locate and read the AUP (or ToS) that governs your use of each facility. University AUPs typically prohibit the use of university resources for commercial profit, any form of academic dishonesty, and ongoing communications with other individuals that are deemed to be harassment. Check your AUP periodically to see if any new restrictions have been added. You are expected to know your AUP and any AUP restrictions that apply to your online activities.

 # Password Security

Your first line of defense against all kinds of mischief and misery is your password, especially the one you use to access the Internet. And even if your computer is safe from thieves and snoopy roommates, you should set a password for your personal computer too—remember that your browser is probably storing all your other passwords for the various controlled access sites you visit. All passwords need to be handled with great care. Someone who steals your laptop or breaks into your university account or ISP account is probably hoping to break into more than only your account. Starting from your account, a digital trespasser might be able to break into other accounts and acquire access privileges normally reserved for system administrators. If you shop on the Internet a lot, and especially if you use one-stop shopping, then you probably have your credit card information stored on your system as well. You must protect your computer passwords not only for your own sake but also for the sake of everyone in your immediate computing environment.

In a secure computing environment, passwords are stored by using special techniques so that no one, including the most powerful system administrator, can retrieve a password for a given account. No system administrator will ever need to know your password for the sake of legitimate system maintenance. Privileged administrators can bypass the usual password protocol if an appropriate circumstance justifies it. So any stranger who asks you for your password is up to no good. No matter what someone tells you, no matter how forceful their argument, don't buy it.

TIP: Report Social Engineering

 Report to a system administrator as soon as possible any request from a stranger for your password. If the request comes to you via e-mail, forward the message to your system postmaster with the Subject: field containing URGENT: PASSWORD THEFT ATTEMPT.

In particular, if you receive an e-mail message from some official-sounding person with an official-looking return address asking for your password, *it's a trick*. Hackers (in this context talented, but bad, guys) who want to break into computer accounts often use elaborate scenarios in an effort to take advantage of the unwary. (Read more about hackers in the Above & Beyond section of this chapter.) This is called **social engineering**. Never give your password to anyone—not even your mother. As soon as you share your password with another person, that person also becomes a potential target for social engineering, and you are no longer in control of your computer account. Your mother (brother, best friend, faithful servant) may have your best interests at heart, but if she is not sufficiently wary and you entrust her with sensitive information, she is just another security risk.

People can also steal passwords without resorting to social engineering. Computer programs can run through a full dictionary of the English language in an effort to "guess" your password. Dictionaries of common names are also used for the same purpose. You can foil these programs by carefully creating passwords that are not words in a dictionary or proper names. Examples of bad passwords are "television" and "Jessica." An example of a good password is "ScAn2go93."

Finally, never use the same password at more than one Web site. A safe, secure password always contains the following elements:

- At least six characters (eight is better)
- Both lowercase and uppercase letters
- At least one numeric character

PASSWORDS AND UNDERWEAR

Passwords are like underwear. Change them often.

Don't share them with anyone.

Not even friends.

—Seen on Usenet

Regardless of how carefully you create your passwords, you should still change them every month or two. Passwords can sometimes be "sniffed out" by software designed to eavesdrop on your Internet communications. Periodic password updates can help protect you in case you're ever "sniffed."

TIP: Tips for Good Password Security

- Never tell anyone your password. Ever.
- Don't write your password where someone can find it.
- Change your password every month or two.
- Don't use the same password in many different places.

2.4 Phishing and Identity Theft

Unscrupulous people (OK, let's face it—thieves!) are always coming up with clever ways to obtain goods and services at somebody else's expense. **Phishing** is one of the more recent methods thieves have developed to deceive unwary people into divulging personal information that can ultimately lead to fraudulent charges made against their accounts. Specifically, *phishing* is a form of online fraud characterized by an *unsolicited* e-mail message from what appears to be a trustworthy source that requests the recipient to "confirm" or "resubmit" confidential information such as bank or credit card account numbers, personal identification numbers (PINs), or passwords.

Most reputable businesses will *never* request such information in an unsolicited e-mail message, so beware. A *phishage* (the *phishers* e-mail) usually contains statements like "You must verify your account in 48 hours or it will be canceled." The phishage may also contain links to your "account," which will open a browser window that appears to be from a reputable business.

A variation involving apparently valid e-mails sent by a trusted employee (maybe even the boss!) of some organization to all other employees in the organization is known as **spear phishing**. These types of attacks are typically directed at the company rather than individual. The goal is to secure a valid user ID and password so that the hacker can gain access to the computer system, which may occur when the user simply clicks on links or opens attachments. Spear phishing can also refer to phishing attacks targeted to very specific groups of people, such as those who use a certain product or web service like eBay.

Shown in Figure 2.2 is an e-mail message that appears to be from PayPal (associated with eBay) requesting account verification. Note that the link URL does not match the listed URL. PayPal also informs me that e-mail from them will be addressed to the user *by name*. Note that this message starts with a generic salutation.

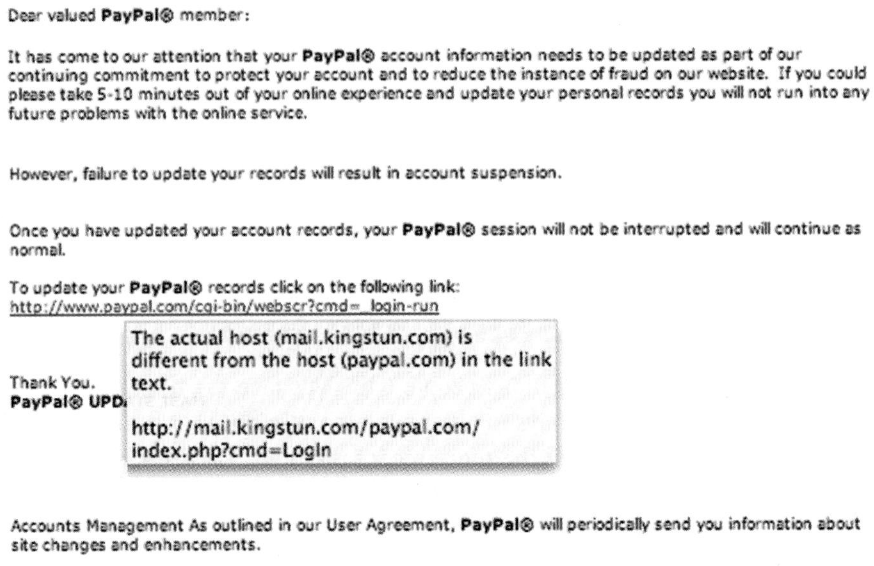

Figure 2.2

Fraudulent e-mail
message
(phishage) show-
ing a warning
message from the
Eudora mail client
(see Chapter 3)

Dear valued **PayPal**® member:

It has come to our attention that your **PayPal**® account information needs to be updated as part of our
continuing commitment to protect your account and to reduce the instance of fraud on our website. If you could
please take 5-10 minutes out of your online experience and update your personal records you will not run into any
future problems with the online service.

However, failure to update your records will result in account suspension.

Once you have updated your account records, your **PayPal**® session will not be interrupted and will continue as
normal.

To update your **PayPal**® records click on the following link:
http://www.paypal.com/cgi-bin/webscr?cmd=_login-run

The actual host (mail.kingstun.com) is
different from the host (paypal.com) in the link
text.

Thank You.
PayPal® UPD

http://mail.kingstun.com/paypal.com/
index.php?cmd=LogIn

Accounts Management As outlined in our User Agreement, **PayPal**® will periodically send you information about
site changes and enhancements.

The account information you enter into the form will be captured by the phisher for immediate and (probably) fraudulent use. It's not always easy to detect when you've been phished, so it's a good idea to review your account statements on a regular basis for unauthorized charges. Even though the account provider may cover most or all of the loss, remember that ultimately, we all pay when this type of theft occurs in the form of higher transaction charges and interest rates. Be sure to report any suspicious activity to the account provider ASAP!

2.4.1 Signs to Look for

How can you tell when you are being phished?

1. Often the phony e-mail message refers to an account you do not have. For example, many people have PayPal accounts to pay for eBay purchases, but many people do not. Phishers target the most popular businesses in their phishages, knowing that you *might* have an account there.

2. Bonafide e-mails from legitimate companies with whom you have accounts usually address their messages to you directly. A generalized salutation like "Dear Valued Customer" is often a clue that the e-mail is from a phisher.

3. If you think the message *is* legitimate, first contact the company involved via a trusted means—phone or previously used e-mail address—that you know to be valid. Confirm that the e-mail and the requested actions are correct.

4. There may be grammatical mistakes and misspellings in the message. Many of these e-mails come from overseas where the command of English is not as good as the requisite computer skills needed to conceal the phisher's true location.

5. Examine the URLs associated with links you are expected to use to "update your account." Placing the cursor over the link (without clicking) should display the URL in the status bar at the bottom of the browser window. The URL will not match that of the business purportedly requesting information (see Figure 2.2). If the status bar is not visible, there may be a browser tool/menu selection provided to display it.

The Federal Trade Commission offers this advice to protect yourself from phishing and related identity theft:

- Don't give out your personal information over the phone, through the mail, or over the Internet unless *you* initiated the contact and *know*—or can *verify*—who you are dealing with.
- *Never* click on links sent in unsolicited e-mail. Instead, type in a Web address you know to be accurate.
- Government agencies and legitimate businesses do not contact people by e-mail or telephone to ask them for—or to confirm—Social Security numbers or other personal information.
- Forward spam that is phishing for information to spam@uce.gov and to the company, bank, or organization impersonated in the phishing e-mail. You also may report phishing e-mail to reportphishing@ antiphishing.org. The Anti-Phishing Working Group—a consortium of ISPs, security vendors, financial institutions, and law enforcement agencies—uses these reports to fight phishing.
- Some additional points to keep in mind are as follows:
  - Be sure to keep your operating system and security software up to date.
  - Monitor sites like sonicwall.com to keep abreast of the latest scams.

When you do provide personal information online, make sure you use a secure and verified site. Most browsers provide some means of identifying

Figure 2.3

Security tab
showing Secure
Web site page
info

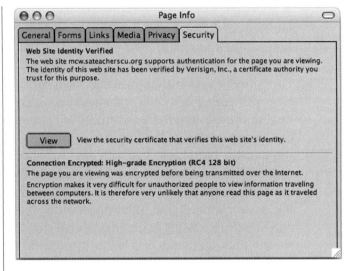

secure sites. For example, in a Mozilla browser window, a lock icon appears in the lower right-hand corner of the window (see Figure 2.3). The icon can be displayed as locked, unlocked, or broken. When locked, it indicates that you are at a secure site, meaning that information you send will be encrypted using the Secure Sockets Layer (SSL) protocol (see Section 7.3). An unlocked icon indicates that the page has been transmitted without encryption. A broken lock icon indicates that although the outermost Web page is encrypted, some or all of the Web page elements within it were not encrypted when transmitted.

If you click on the lock icon in Mozilla, security information related to the page you are viewing will appear in the form of the Security tab from the Page Info window. The top half of the window shows whether the Web site providing the Web page file has been verified. The bottom half of the window indicates whether the page you are viewing was encrypted for transmission over the Internet. Make sure that the Web site name displayed in the upper half of the window matches the Web site in the URL. In Figure 2.3, the Web site name (from the URL) is `http://mcw.sateacherscu.org`.

TIP: Are You Phishing-Savvy?

You can check out your phishing detection skills at this Web site:
`http://www.sonicwall.com/phishing`

TIP: **Phishing Is Not Limited to Computer Users**

McAfee, Inc., has been warning cell phone customers about a new method of attack dubbed **smishing** for "Short Message Service phishing." Some cell phone users received this message in August 2006: "We're confirming you've signed up for our dating service. You will be charged $2/day unless you cancel your order." Included in the message is a URL linked to a Trojan horse. This Trojan horse allows a Web-enabled phone to be inserted into a **bot network** (aka **botnet**) of remotely controlled computers (aka **zombie** computers) that can be used to launch denial of service attacks, install key logging software to steal personal information, and other nefarious activities. Beware of text messages with URLs from unknown (and even known) sources!

TIP: **Pharming**

A new variation of the phishing scheme, called **pharming**, redirects valid URLs typed into a browser to a bogus site that mimics the intended destination. Antivirus and spyware removal software cannot protect users from such attacks. Instead special antipharming tools are needed. Users should make sure that only secure Web connections (HTTPS—see Chapter 7) are used and only accept valid public key certificates (see Chapter 8). Expired certificates and certificates from unknown organizations should be rejected.

2.4.2 Identity Theft

Identity theft is a closely related activity that may or may not involve the Internet (but frequently does). The Identity Theft and Assumption Deterrence Act of 1998 defines identity theft as the illegal use of someone's means of identification, which includes something like a credit card. If someone finds your lost card and uses it, then you have been a victim of identity theft. Typically, the thieves capture personal information such as Social Security numbers, phone numbers, addresses, date/place of birth, driver's license numbers, mother's maiden names, and so on. This information can be used to open accounts in your name and subsequently used to make fraudulent purchases. Fortunately, federal law caps personal liability in such cases at $50, and even that is typically waived by the creditor.

Identity theft can occur without any action on your part. In May 2006, the home of a Veteran's Administration (VA) employee was burglarized. Among other things, the thieves stole the employee's laptop computer, leading to the loss of personal information about more than 17.5 million veterans and active duty personnel (originally it was believed to have contained 26.5 million records), plus an undisclosed number of current members of the armed forces. (The stolen laptop was recovered a few weeks later and the records appeared to have been untouched.) The University of Texas computer system was hacked in April 2006 and personal data on some 197,000 people associated with the business school was accessed and presumably copied. A hacker accessed records of a mobile telephone service provider in Bellevue, Washington, obtaining personal information on 16.8 million customers. In May 2006, the Texas Guaranteed Student Loan Corporation announced that a piece of equipment containing the names and Social Security numbers of 1.3 million borrowers had been "lost."

Since so much consumer information is recorded in computer databases that can be accessed via Internet, nobody is immune. There are some things you can do. Like phishing expeditions, the best way to guard against identity theft is to monitor your account records for suspicious activity. Safeguard your personal information, especially when providing personal information online. Make sure the Web site you are using is verified and pages are encrypted. Encrypted pages use HTTPS protocol rather than the default HTTP protocol for nonsecure pages. You can check this simply by examining the URL of the page you are visiting.

Watch for signs of identity theft—late or missing bills, receiving credit cards you didn't apply for, being denied credit or offered less favorable terms for no apparent reason, or being contacted by debt collectors or others about purchases you didn't make. If you think you have been the victim of a phisher or identity theft, you can take the following action:

1. Contact any of the three major credit bureaus and have a fraud alert placed in your file. Once confirmed by the credit bureau, the other two bureaus will be notified. Once you place a fraud alert in your file, you are entitled to a free copy of your credit report. If you ask, only the last four digits of your Social Security number will appear in your credit reports. The three major credit bureaus are Equifax, (800) 525-6285 or `http://www.equifax.com`; Experian, (888) 397-3742 or `http://www.experian.com`; and TransUnion, (800) 680-7289 or `http://www.transunion.com`.

2. Close accounts that have been compromised. Use the ID Theft Affidavit to contest new unauthorized accounts (from `http://www.consumer.gov/idtheft/pdf/affidavit.pdf`).

TIP: Closely Related to Identity Theft Is Pretexting

Pretexting is the practice of acquiring personal information under false pretenses, typically via a phone call to some organization or business from someone impersonating the person whose personal data is being sought—maybe you! This information (phone numbers, account numbers, Social Security numbers, etc.) is sold to someone else who may use it to obtain credit in your name, steal from you, sue you, or investigate you. Some information is a matter of public record, such as whether you own a home or pay real estate taxes, and other publicly accessible information—it is legal to collect this type of information. It is illegal to collect most other information when doing so under false pretenses. Pretexting is at the heart of a scandal involving the board of directors of the Hewlett-Packard Company. Private investigators for the company claiming to be board directors and members of the press tricked phone companies into providing lists of personal calls. Pretexting often occurs in conjunction with **spoofing**, the use of electronic devices to show false phone numbers on caller ID systems.

3. File a report with your local law enforcement office or the police in the community where the identity theft occurred (if known). Get the report number, or better yet a copy, and provide this information to creditors and others who may require proof of the crime.

4. File your complaint with the Federal Trade Commission at `https://rn.ftc.gov/pls/dod/cis1.widtpubl$.startup? Z_ORG_CODE=PU06Z_CHK=0`

5. Contact relevant government agencies to cancel and replace any stolen drivers' licenses or other identification documents and to flag your file appropriately.

6. Consult your financial institution about handling the effects on bank or brokerage accounts.

2.5 Viruses, Trojan Horses, and Worms

Computer security experts worry about software that can be used maliciously to put computer users at risk. Over the years, experts have found it useful to distinguish different classes of software that are often associated with security problems. Mainstream news outlets tend to call all such software "computer

TIP: Is Your Front Door Open?

As soon as you connect your home computer to the Internet, financial records and other personal information stored on your computer become potential targets of cyberattacks. All computers are at some risk if appropriate steps have not been taken to limit access to them. Computers operating over broadband connections are especially susceptible to attack.

Failure to take steps to secure your computer and its most sensitive files is like leaving the front door of your home wide open.

viruses." However, many fast-spreading troublemakers are actually worms, and one of the most insidious forms of software attack is called a Trojan horse.

A **virus** is a computer program with the ability to replicate itself via files that move from one computer to another. Some viruses are relatively benign, doing nothing more than leaving the equivalent of their initials on a file somewhere. Others are extremely destructive, capable of destroying files or even entire file systems.

A **Trojan horse** is a program that slips into a system under the guise of another program. To qualify as a Trojan horse, the program must do something undocumented that the user would not approve of. Deception is a key characteristic of all Trojan horses. You think that you've installed one program, but you end up getting more than you expected. Some Trojan horses are designed to record every key you hit, including the credit card account number you use when shopping online. Your keystrokes might be monitored by the program's author in real time, or they might be saved to a log file that the program can send back to its author at a later time. Other Trojan horses allow a stranger to take control of your computer and issue commands remotely. If this is done cleverly, sensitive files can be uploaded to a remote host without your knowledge.

A **worm** is very similar to a virus but differs in its reproductive habits. Whereas viruses can be spread via file downloads, shared disks, or other media and require a host program in order to propagate, a worm depends only on active network connections. Worms also exploit weaknesses in existing software and thrive when many different hosts run the same software. Sophisticated worms can have multiple parts, or segments, running on different machines, doing different things, and communicating with each other over a network. Some are programmed to act maliciously, while others are merely resource hogs that pull down entire networks by tying up too much memory or too many CPU cycles.

The cost of computer viruses and security breaches to businesses worldwide is notoriously difficult to estimate. The Love Bug virus was estimated at $8.7 billion in lost productivity and cleanup costs in 2000. Code Red, Nimda, and Sircam may have cost as much as $15 billion in 2001.

If you can't remember how these three methods of cyberattack differ from each other, just remember that everyone who uses computers is vulnerable to attack and must take precautions. To protect your system, follow the simple precautions listed here. Once you know the ropes, good computer security doesn't have to take a lot of your time.

- **Use antivirus software.** Your antivirus software should contain a virus scanner with a memory-resident option running in the background that checks every new file that enters your computer no matter where it comes from (flash drive, DVD/CD-ROM drive, or Internet download). You should also configure the software to scan all files when you open or execute them (see Figure 2.4). Check all the

Figure 2.4

Your virus scanner should always be running in the background.

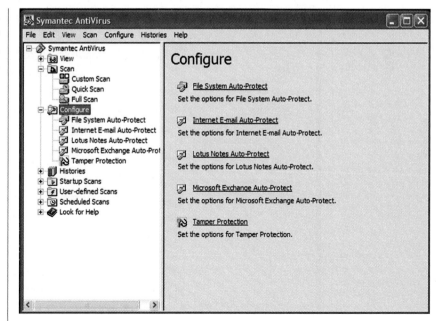

options in your antivirus software and make sure you have it configured to check e-mail (see Figure 2.5). This option may not be the
default setting.

- **Update your antivirus software regularly.** Antivirus software depends
  on data files for descriptions of known viruses. Since new viruses are
  created every day, it is important to keep these data files up-to-date.
  Everyone should update their antivirus software *at least* every two
  weeks. Daily updates are even better. People who are especially active
  online and who install a lot of software, use instant messaging, or
  engage in peer-to-peer file sharing should update twice a week. Your
  software can probably be configured to run software updates automatically (see Figure 2.6). For example, Norton has a LiveUpdate utility that makes it easy to keep your time-sensitive files up-to-date (see
  Figure 2.7).

- **Keep bootable disks out of your drive unless you are actively working with the files on the disk.** Boot sector viruses hide on bootable
  disks. They are triggered when your machine checks to see whether it
  should run its start-up sequence from the removable disk drive,
  which routinely happens whenever you start or restart your computer

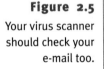

Figure 2.5

Your virus scanner
should check your
e-mail too.

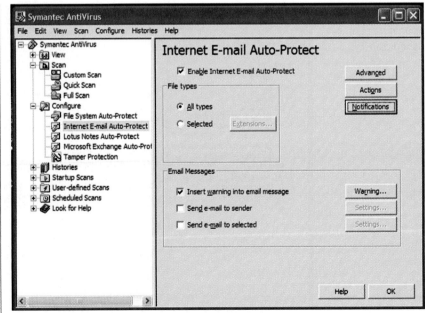

Figure 2.6

Virus protection software requires frequent updates.

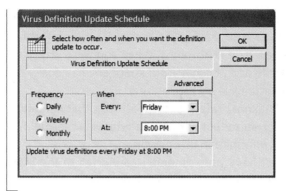

Figure 2.7

Automatic software updates are convenient.

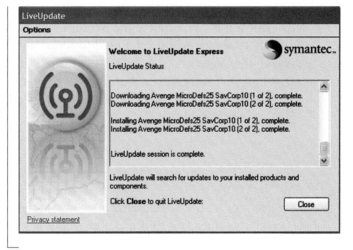

with a disk in the drive. If the disk's boot sector is infected, its virus will kick into action.

- **If, for some reason, you need to work without a virus scanner running continuously in the background, you must remember to manually scan each file before opening or executing it.** Don't take someone else's word that a file is safe. Always check for yourself.

- **Install a firewall on your home computer** (see Section 2.8). This is the only way to protect yourself from hacker intrusions (see Section 2.7). Firewalls are especially important if you have a broadband connection, but they are important for all computers with Internet access.

- **Do not download files offered to you in chat rooms or personal Web pages.** Viruses and Trojan horses are often passed along to unsuspecting people in chat rooms. When you were little you were taught never to accept candy from strangers: be equally suspicious of files from strangers on the Internet.
- **For maximal safety, encrypt all files that contain sensitive information or store them offline on removable media.** See Chapter 8 for more information on encryption.
- **Do not leave your computer connected to the Internet any longer than necessary.** A computer connected to the Internet via a 56K modem is not an attractive target for unauthorized file access. It is easier to break into systems that have faster Net connections. However, even a computer on a phone line can still be compromised, especially if it is connected to the Net for long intervals of time. Disconnect whenever you don't need to access online resources. In general, the longer you stay online, the easier it is for someone to break into your system over your Internet connection. The amount of time you spend connected to the Net is a greater risk factor than the speed of your Net connection.

FYI: Viruses Are Big Business

Symantec and McAfee are two major players in the world of antivirus software. They watch for new viruses around the clock and track reports of virus outbreaks all over the world (see Figure 2.8). Antivirus software often comes preinstalled on new computers. It is an absolute necessity. You might have heard that Macs are safe from viruses and therefore don't need antivirus software. This is partly true because most viruses "in the wild" are designed to attack Windows installations. However, no operating system is immune to virus attacks, and some viruses are platform-independent—they can attack any running software application regardless of the operating system.

The most common platform-independent viruses are called *macro viruses*. A **macro** is a small computer program that runs in response to a specific combination of keystrokes or clicks on a particular icon; some macros are set to run automatically whenever someone opens the document. A **macro virus** is a virus written inside a macro, which typically executes as soon as the document containing the macro is opened. Of all virus incidents reported in 1997, 80 percent were the work of macro viruses.

Figure 2.8
Computer viruses
are monitored
worldwide.

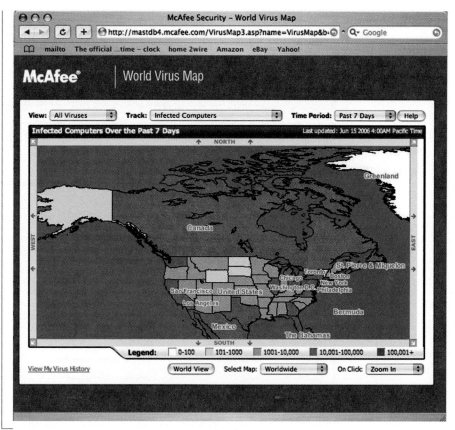

If you have installed a memory-resident virus scanner on your machine, you can determine whether your scanner is working correctly by testing what it does when it finds a virus. Do this by introducing a harmless test virus called EICAR. You can download files containing the EICAR test virus from http://www.eicar.org/anti_virus_test_file.htm.

Scroll down to the bottom of this page and you'll see four clickable links for file download (see Figure 2.9). A good antivirus program will be able to detect EICAR in each of these downloads. When you click one of these file names, a copy of the file is downloaded to your computer. If your virus scanner is running in the background, it should recognize the EICAR virus and display a virus alert (see Figure 2.10).

Under certain circumstances, when file sharing is turned on, sensitive files on your hard drive can be made publicly available to anyone on the Internet. Although this function can be useful on a local area network where

Figure 2.9

Visit
www.eicar.com
to test your virus
scanner.

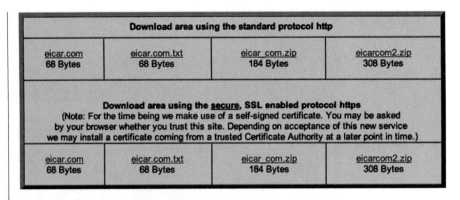

Figure 2.10

A virus scanner
passes the EICAR
virus test.

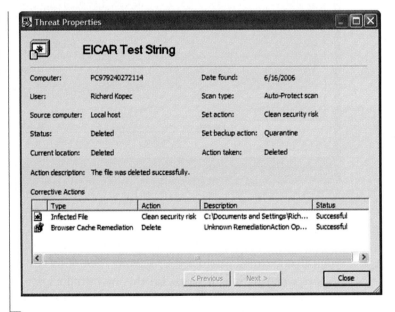

the users sharing files are coworkers or colleagues, it is a dangerous feature on the Internet, where hackers and irresponsible tricksters abound. On a personal computer that runs Windows, you can protect yourself from a relatively trivial attack by ensuring that the File and Printer Sharing setting is turned off. Follow these steps.

1. From the Start menu, select the Control Panel.
2. Select the Security Center.

3. Select "Manage security settings for:" Windows Firewall.
4. Make sure the "File and Printer Sharing" checkbox is not checked (see Figure 2.11).

TIP: Antivirus Software Facts

- Good commercial antivirus software watches for Trojan horses and worms, as well as viruses.
- Multiple virus scanners can interfere with one another. Don't install more than one.
- No virus scanner can guarantee 100% safety, but keeping your scanner up-to-date will minimize your risk.
- Don't take unnecessary chances. Avoid suspicious files from unknown sources.

Figure 2.11

Turn off file and printer sharing for better security.

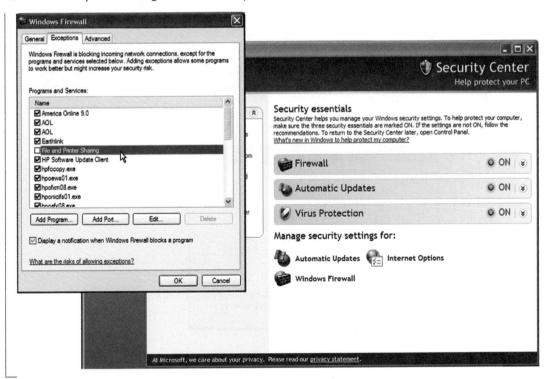

2.6 E-Mail Viruses

E-mail is currently the number-one source of computer viruses, but you can avoid e-mail viruses with proper precautions. The most common villain is the e-mail attachment. Attachments cause problems because they are not always just data files. Some e-mail attachments contain *scripts*. A **script** is a small computer program written in a scripting language such as Microsoft's Visual Basic (VB), and script-based attacks typically target computers running Windows. Other e-mail attachments may contain macros. Your first line of defense against viruses is antiviral software such as Symantec or MacAfee. Make sure that your antiviral software has been configured to automatically check e-mail messages. Be aware that your software can guard you against only known viruses and other malware. The bad guys are constantly looking for and finding new ways to penetrate your defenses and attack your computer in some way. That's why it's so important to keep your antiviral software up to date. The best way to do so is to set your software to update itself automatically on a daily basis (if not more frequently).

When you elect to open an attachment, most computers will ask you if you want to open or save the file (see Figure 2.12). Of course, if you're really paranoid, you might want to contact the person who sent you the e-mail for confirmation if the message includes an attachment you weren't expecting before you open it. Remember that a common way to spread mayhem in the cyberworld is to send infected messages that appear to be from friends of the recipient. Select Save rather than Open so the file will be scanned by your antiviral software.

Figure 2.12

Most e-mail clients will warn you before opening attachments.

2.6.1 Macro Viruses

For many years, macros in Microsoft Word documents were the single greatest source of computer viruses. Opening a Word file that comes to your mailbox from an unknown party is definitely asking for trouble. But it is not enough to know and trust the person who sends you the attachment. Word users are often infected themselves, passing macro viruses to friends and coworkers without realizing it. Many macro viruses are relatively subtle and can easily go unnoticed; they can migrate freely within a large population of uninformed e-mail users.

Macro viruses, which primarily affect Word users, spread rapidly for two reasons.

1. Microsoft's domination of the office application market results in many users (potential victims) who share documents in a common format.
2. Microsoft decided to allow powerful programming instructions, in the form of macros, to be embedded within documents. Other software manufacturers that support macro capabilities store their macros in separate files, for example, Corel WordPerfect and Lotus WordPro. However, 90 percent of all home computers run Windows, and a large percentage of them run Word. (Word is also available for the Mac, where it enjoys a substantial user community as well.)

FYI: The Melissa Virus

In March 1999, a fast-spreading new MS Word macro virus called Melissa first appeared. It used the e-mail address books of its victims to send copies of itself to more potential victims. The virus attached an infected document named list.doc to an e-mail message bearing the subject line "Important Message From <sender>," where <sender> was the name of the inadvertent sender. The message body read, "Here is that document you asked for . . . don't show anyone else ;-)." The Melissa virus was the first e-mail attachment virus designed to exploit the user's e-mail address book in order to propagate itself. Trusting recipients recognized the return address on the Melissa mail and let down their guard, just as Melissa's author intended. The message was not what it appeared to be, even though it did come from the indicated source.

TIP: Avoid Macro Viruses by Using RTF

The **Rich Text Format (RTF)** is an ASCII text alternative to Word's usual .doc file format. Any Word document can be saved in RTF format, but Word macros cannot be saved in RTF files. To create an RTF file, select Save As from the File menu, and then look at the pull-down menu next to the "Save as type" box. Select Rich Text Format (`*.rtf`) from the pull-down menu and save your Word document. To reopen an RTF file inside Word, go to the File menu, select Open, and navigate your way to the RTF file.

If everyone saved Word files in RTF format and avoided Word macros altogether, macro viruses in Word documents would go away. Unfortunately, files that contain graphics are much larger in RTF format than in Word's .doc format. So reserve the RTF format for documents that contain only text or mostly text.

FYI: How Word Macro Viruses Infect a Computer

Word templates allow users to customize various settings for different types of documents. A number of predefined templates for business letters, faxes, professional résumés, and other document types are available. To see these templates, select File and then New; then click the various tabs in the pop-up window. Most people who use Word rely on its default template, normal.dot, for most documents. Word uses this template when you create a new document using [Ctrl] + [N] or the new document icon.

Recall that a crucial feature of macros is that they can be set up to run automatically whenever a document is opened. Anyone can create a Word macro by recording a sequence of Word commands using Word's macro recorder. Programmers who know VB can create Word macros that are not limited to operations available as Word commands. User-defined macros are associated with specific templates. A Word document moved from one computer to another takes its template with it, along with any macros associated with that template. When you open a Word file whose template is new to your system, Word installs the new template for you. This usually means overwriting an existing template file to make new macros available to you.

Macro viruses most often are passed to new systems by their overwriting of the normal.dot template. A macro virus in the normal.dot template will be attached to all your Word files that use normal.dot, both new and old. If you pass on a Word file that uses this template to someone else, it will overwrite that person's version of normal.dot—and the macro virus will have claimed another computer. The normal.dot template is the foundation template for all other Word templates, so you can't stop a macro virus by using a different template for your Word documents.

FYI: Deception and Trickery

A little social engineering and an ignorant user population are all it takes to unleash a malevolent computer virus. Hackers have fooled people into clicking e-mail attachments by disguising file extensions or using misleading file icons. Fooled by a persuasive message body, too many people have fallen for e-mail attachments that supposedly fix software bugs, claim to protect people from viruses, or appear to be innocuous communications from friends. In reality, some of these attachments destroy files on hard drives, send user and passwords out onto the Net, or replicate worms using e-mail addresses in a mail client's address book.

Word's widespread popularity, combined with the routine use of e-mail attachments for document distribution by largely naive newbies, enabled a highly successful class of computer viruses to flourish. We can blame the people who create the viruses, the people who make questionable software design decisions, or the users who embrace sophisticated software without adequate training or preparation. In fact, a macro virus needs all three of these groups to create widespread chaos.

Standard virus protection measures are largely effective against macro viruses. As long as you save your file to disk and make sure it has been scanned before you open it, you will be safe from any known macro virus.

Unfortunately, a computer programmer can easily take an existing macro virus and alter it so that virus scanners will no longer recognize it. Cautious and savvy users can protect themselves simply by refusing to open any documents that contain macros. If you use Word 2003, you can set an option so that Word will warn you whenever you attempt to open a document that contains a macro and then give you the opportunity to disable that macro (see Figure 2.13). To set up the macro alert, use the following steps:

1. Select Tools, Options, and then the Security tab.
2. Press the "Macro Security . . ." button (see Figure 2.14).
3. Make sure the "High" (default) or "Very High" radio button is selected. Lesser levels of protection are not recommended by Microsoft (see Figure 2.15).

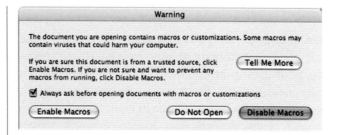

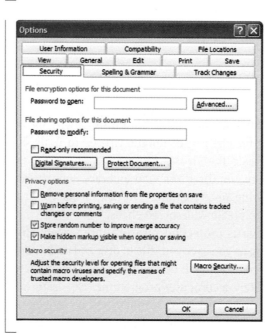

TIP: What to Do When You Receive an E-Mail Attachment

1. If you receive an unsolicited e-mail attachment from an unknown person, delete it without opening it.
2. If you receive an e-mail attachment accompanied by an empty message body, delete it without opening it. Even if you recognize the return address, the absence of a message is very suspicious (or, given the potential dangers associated with e-mail attachments, very rude).
3. If you receive an unexpected e-mail attachment from someone you know and the message body looks generic, contact the sender before you open it to make sure that person really did send the attachment to you.
4. Once you do decide to open any e-mail attachment, scan it with antivirus software first (if your software does not do this automatically as most now do), even if you have confirmed its authorship and you trust the source.
5. Disable all macros before opening any Microsoft Office document.

Note: If you deal with a lot of e-mail and you find this too tedious, just tell your friends and coworkers that you have found it necessary to ignore all e-mail attachments in the name of system security. This will alert others to the potential dangers and give everyone an opportunity to learn about safe e-mail practices. In fact, it's not really necessary to abandon e-mail attachments altogether—people just have to know how to send and receive them safely.

TIP: What to Do When You Send an E-Mail Attachment

Whenever possible, avoid using attachments in outgoing e-mail. But if you must attach a file to an e-mail message, be considerate of your recipient.

- Include a personalized message body that only you could send. If your message body looks too generic, your recipient will be (should be) suspicious.
- Describe the purpose and content of your attachment in the message body.
- If the file you are attaching is a Word file that contains no graphics, save it as an RTF file. A knowledgeable recipient will know that RTF files are safer than .doc files.

2.6.2 Script Attacks

Although attachments are the primary source of e-mail risk, e-mail clients that render message bodies into Web-like page displays (complete with clickable links and graphics) can also be susceptible to malicious attacks. This happens if the content of a message body is allowed to trigger scripts.

In 2000, two new e-mail attachment attacks targeted users of Outlook and Outlook Express. The LoveLetter and NewLove viruses (technically speaking, these were worms, not viruses) were spread in VB scripts passed along as e-mail attachments. Each script deleted files from the target host and then sent itself on to new targets, using addresses in the Outlook address book. Users who knew to scan all e-mail attachments before opening them and to keep their antivirus software up-to-date should have been safe. However, the LoveLetter virus spread very quickly and the damage it caused was not immediately obvious, so the antivirus protection software companies were slow to catch it and alert their customers. The effects of the NewLove virus were more immediately obvious, which kept it from spreading too far too fast.

2.6.3 Blended Threats

During 2001, script attacks, worms, Trojan horses, and viruses all began to mix together to enable a new class of "blended threat" attacks. Worms like Code Red, Sircam, and Nimda exploited combinations of Web servers, operating system vulnerabilities, script vulnerabilities, and reckless recipients of e-mail attachments in order to propagate at remarkable speeds. In some cases, no response on the part of the recipient was even necessary—it was enough to simply receive an infected message in your e-mail inbox. Peter Tippett of *InfoSecurity Magazine* observed, "When the Form boot-sector virus was released in 1989, it took nearly a year to become pervasive. The Concept Macro virus, first seen in 1995, took about three months to fully make the rounds. LoveLetter took only about one day, while Code Red needed roughly 90 minutes. Nimda took less than 30 minutes." When a worm can infect millions of Internet users within a matter of hours or minutes, a defense based on virus scanners alone is no longer adequate. Stronger defenses are needed

TIP: Microsoft and Security Patches

If you use Outlook or Outlook Express, be on the lookout for software patches and system upgrades whenever a new security hole is discovered. Patches and upgrades for all Microsoft products are available from the Microsoft Windows Update Center at `http://update.microsoft.com/windowsupdate/v6/default.aspx?in=en-us`. Alternatively, if you want to avoid having to deal with frequent software updates, shop around for a different e-mail client.

at all contributing points of vulnerability: server software, operating systems, scripting languages, and any programs with easy Internet access.

Because blended threats are more sophisticated and very difficult to stop in a timely fashion, we will undoubtedly see more of them. Nimda spread across the Net in record time by exploiting e-mail, JavaScript, open network shares, and vulnerable Web servers. Although less nimble, W32/Klez surfaced in 2002 and is believed to be the most pervasive computer virus ever seen. The most effective version of Klez appeared in April 2002. One month later, the Klez virus was showing up in 1 in every 300 e-mails sent, which amounts to 20,000 e-mail messages a day. Klez propagated by selecting random names from e-mail address books, but the virus is especially hard for virus scanners to identify because it uses a large number of different subject headers, message bodies, and attachment names. W32/Klez is a blended threat, spreading via e-mail and open network shares. When spread via e-mail, W32/Klez attempts to exploit a vulnerability that can cause a Windows system to be infected by simply reading or previewing the message. In addition, W32/Klez disables antivirus products on the affected host and is also capable of corrupting files.

Blended threats can be addressed only by better computer security all around. In many cases, critical solutions lie in the hands of software manufacturers and system administrators. But home computer users can do their part by installing firewalls (see Section 2.8) to block Internet access for all unauthorized (that is, all unrecognized) executables. That way, even an infected user can stop the spread of the virus. It would also help to have more software diversity among Internet users. When 97% of the world is running

TIP: **Is ICF Enough?**

If you are running XP, Service Pack 2 (SP2) includes the Internet Connection Firewall (ICF) which is activated by default. You can still install a personal firewall on top of ICF, and it is a good idea to do so. ICF gives you some protection, which is certainly better than nothing, but it doesn't block any outbound traffic. Thus your computer could still be used as a drone in a distributed denial of service attack, and it could still be used to propagate worms if you are ever infected with something like the Klez virus. ICF does not interfere with other firewalls; it was designed to work with them rather than compete with them. So there is no good reason to stop with ICF if you want to maximize your online security. Beware that some ISPs do not allow Windows clients to use ICF. In this case, you should contact your ISP for security recommendations.

the same e-mail client and the same operating system, vulnerabilities in those products are irresistible targets for virus authors. This is one case where "safety in numbers" does not hold—there is much more safety in diversity when it comes to computer viruses and blended threats.

2.6.4 Internet Scams

If you bother to actually read your SPAM—beware! The famous saying "There's a sucker born every minute" dates from 1869. (It was never actually said by the famous P. T. Barnum. Someone named David Hannum said it, but that's another story.) Since the advent of the Internet, it might be more accurate to say, "There are 1,000 suckers born every minute." Scam artists are nothing new. The Internet has simply made it easier than ever for them to reach a huge pool of potential pigeons. The Internet Fraud site has compiled a complete index of commonly encountered Internet frauds and scams. You can also read the Internet ScamBusters newsletter or research classic scams in the ScamBusters archive of back issues.

If something sounds too good to be true, it probably is—and if you saw it on the Internet, you can be sure it's too good to be true. Here are some tips for avoiding scams on the Net:

- Beware of get-rich-quick offers, especially if they show up in your e-mail inbox as unsolicited e-mail messages.
- Don't trust an operation just because it has a slick-looking Web site.
- Be wary of anyone who pressures you to respond fast.
- Never send cash. When buying something from a private individual over the Net, try to arrange for a cash on delivery (COD) payment to protect yourself. Any operation that lists only a P.O. box address could disappear tomorrow without a trace. If you must send someone a check or money order, don't spend more than you are prepared to lose.

Further, watch out for any e-mail offer that promises you any of the following:

- Money by pulling in additional "investors"
- Money by stuffing envelopes at home
- Money playing the currency exchange markets
- Free goods once you pay a membership fee
- Miracle health cures and diet formulas
- Your credit record repaired for a fee

- Insider investment advice for a fee
- Free cable service by using a descrambler (these are illegal)
- Guaranteed loans or credit
- Vacations as a prize

Con artists and criminals have greater reach and more opportunities than ever before. As more people go online, the potential audience for scams and rip-offs grows as well. A scam artist can set up shop in cyberspace and then quickly vanish to stay clear of the law. However, law enforcement agencies are getting wise to online crime. If you believe that a scam artist or fraudulent business has victimized you or you become aware of any suspicious communications or criminal activities, contact the National Fraud Information Center. This agency may not be able to resolve your complaint, but it will forward your report to a relevant law enforcement agency that can initiate an investigation.

2.7 Hacker Attacks and Intrusions

Hacker intrusions are less common than computer viruses, but they can be far more devastating to your computer, your psyche, and your legal defense fund. Large companies monitor their computers for evidence of intrusions, and full-time security personnel are responsible for keeping hackers from gaining access to sensitive files. Home computers are easier targets and are therefore attractive to entry-level hackers and adolescents. Some young people experiment with hacker tools because they are simply curious; they do not understand that they are engaged in illegal activities. The hacker phenomenon will be discussed in more detail in the Above & Beyond sections of both this chapter and Chapter 7. For now, you need to know only two things. First, it does not take much effort or much expertise to break into a computer that is not protected (that's the bad news). Second, you do not need to be a security professional to protect your home computer from hacker attacks and intrusions (that's the good news).

A variety of hacker tools and utilities are freely available on the Internet. Moreover, many of these tools have been designed so that anyone can take advantage of them. You don't have to be a programmer (or even very smart) to use a beginning hacker's toolset. Some programs designed for hackers even come with point-and-click interfaces (see Figure 2.16). But remember—just because it's easy doesn't make it right. Breaking into another computer on the

Figure 2.16

This Trojan horse invites hackers to sit down at your computer keyboard.

TIP: If You Are Curious . . . Be Warned!

Just in case anyone reading this decides to delve into the world of computer hacking, please take heed. It may be all too easy to use the tools of the hackers, but it still takes intelligence and considerable know-how to avoid getting caught. Hacking is illegal, and anyone who plays around with hacker software will attract the attention of system administrators, security professionals, and law enforcement personnel. If you are seriously curious about networks and network security, consider taking some computer science courses. There will always be plenty of jobs for security professionals, and the pay is quite good.

TIP: Who Is at Risk?

Everyone with a live Internet connection is a potential target, but some targets are more attractive than others. Computers with poor Internet security are more attractive than computers with good security. Computers that are online 24/7 are more attractive than computers that are not online for extended periods of time. Computers with broadband connections are more attractive than computers with telephone modems. As a rule, most Windows users do not bother to download and install all the security patches released by Microsoft, so this makes most computers running Windows attractive targets. People who use chat clients, instant messenger clients, and peer-to-peer file sharing are at greater risk than people who don't. People who download a lot of games or other software from random Web sites are at greater risk than people who are more cautious with their software installations. As usual, you have to weigh risks against benefits. If you want to engage in risky behaviors, it is even more important to take appropriate security precautions.

Internet is illegal under both state and federal laws, punishable by both fines and jail sentences.

If your computer is vulnerable to attack, a hacker can effectively take control of your computer from a remote location. This means that some random person out there on the Internet can create files on your hard drive, delete files, change existing files, run programs, move files back and forth across the Internet, read anything on your hard drive, install new software, run software, and do all this without your knowledge. That same person can do things that are more visible to you, such as changing your wallpaper, taking charge of your mouse's cursor, or shutting down your application software. It is also easy to crash a computer from a remote location.

Why would a hacker go after you when there are so many other targets? Hackers rarely target people personally. But they often target easy victims just to see what they can find. If you have any passwords or credit card numbers stored on your computer, they are at risk. Did you ever tell your browser to remember a password or credit card number for a specific Web site? That information is probably at risk, depending on which browser you use. Do you have personal e-mail or financial statements stored on your computer? Income tax returns? Suppose you're clean and nothing of any value (financially or personally) is stored on your computer. A hacker may still be interested for the sake of plotting additional hacker attacks from your computer. Hackers always work from remote computers belonging to unsuspecting innocents—for the same reason a criminal makes all phone calls from pay phones. Your personal computer could be set up as a "drone" in a distributed attack on Yahoo! or a government server. When the dirty work is traced to your computer, law enforcement officials would have a right to seize your hard drive. You'll be innocent of any wrongdoing, but it could take weeks or months to sort it all out.

 # 2.8 Firewalls

Exactly what can you do to protect yourself from hackers? The answer is simple: install a firewall. A **firewall** is software that monitors all attempts to move bytes over the Internet in either direction and notifies you when such movement is attempted. It acts as a protective boundary between your computer and the outside world. Just as an antivirus program protects your computer from computer viruses, a firewall program protects your computer from hackers and unwanted intruders. You can purchase a firewall, or you may be able to find good ones for free. If you run Windows XP, you have a firewall already built into XP, the Internet Connection Firewall (ICF).

Firewalls previously were used only by large corporations, but no longer. Anyone with a computer connected to the Internet can set up a firewall to prevent a Trojan horse from sending sensitive files on the hard drive to a remote host (see Section 2.5) or to stop spyware from "phoning home" (see Section 6.7).

Firewall software usually includes additional features as well, such as antiphishing, spam control, and parental blocking. Windows users can try a freeware firewall called ZoneAlarm. When an outgoing transmission is attempted, the firewall asks the user to give permission to the application in question (see Figure 2.17). When an incoming transmission is attempted, the firewall alerts the user (see Figure 2.18).

ZoneAlarm keeps track of how you answer its various alerts in order to customize a detailed security policy for your host (see Figure 2.19). You can reset these application-specific settings at any time.

To get you started, ZoneAlarm offers some basic default policies that are easy to put into effect. You can select one of three security levels for your LAN and a different level for the Internet at large (see Figure 2.20). If you aren't sure which defaults to take, ZoneAlarm recommends a medium level of security for the LAN and a high level for the Internet. These default settings will keep you safe while ZoneAlarm collects additional preferences from your responses to ZoneAlarm alert boxes.

Figure 2.17

Applications need permission to access the Net when ZoneAlarm is running.

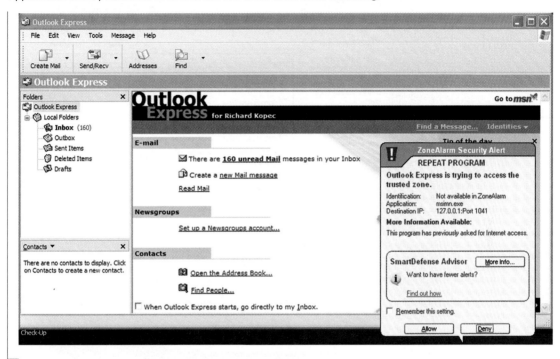

Figure 2.18

ZoneAlarm blocks unauthorized communications.

The program's control panel includes a dynamic display that shows all uploading and downloading activities (see Figure 2.21). In this way, you

Figure 2.19

You can change ZoneAlarm's permission settings at any time.

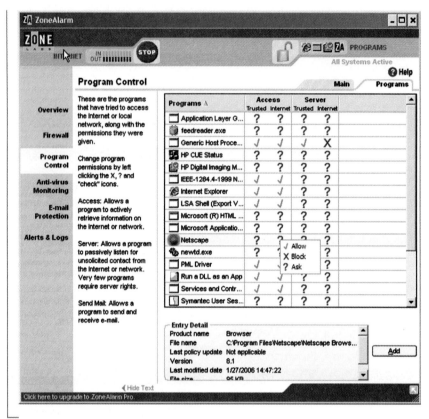

Figure 2.20

Blanket default settings make it easy to get started.

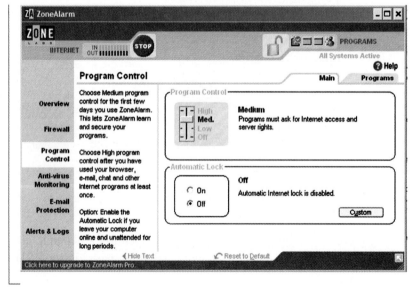

always know when data is moving into or out of your computer and the application that is responsible for the traffic. In case of an emergency, clicking the Stop button shuts down all Internet activity as soon as possible.

Another very popular firewall for Windows is Norton Internet Security by Symantec. Norton makes it easy to customize permissions for specific

TIP: Which Firewall Is Best?

As with all software decisions, it pays to read software reviews and do a little research. A firewall is a complicated piece of software, and some firewalls cause software conflicts or system instability on some computers. If you experience difficulties after installing one firewall, it may pay to try a different one.

TIP: Rootkits

Another tool in the hacker's arsenal is the **rootkit**, a set of software tools that can conceal running processes, files, or system data. A rootkit can be used by hackers to gain undetected remote access to your computer, allowing complete control over the system and its resources—in effect turning your computer into a zombie. The most famous example of a rootkit was perpetrated not by a rogue programmer, but by Sony BMG in 2005. When a Sony music CD with Extended Copy Protection (XCP) or MediaMax 5.0 software was played on a Windows PC, a rootkit was surreptitiously installed that interfered with the way the operating system processed CDs as a way to prevent unauthorized copies. Unfortunately, this rootkit opened large security holes that were immediately exploited by several worms and viruses. To make matters worse, after the outcry that occurred when the rootkit was discovered, Sony released a software utility purported to remove the rootkit. Instead, it merely uncloaked hidden files created by the rootkit and installed *additional, unremoveable* software! And the rootkit remained! Eventually, Sony was forced to release a "new and improved" removal tool to excise it completely. All CDs with the XCP or MediaMax software were recalled and replaced. Rootkits are especially hard to remove because they insert themselves directly into the operating system, and by their very nature they cannot be detected in a system so infected—another uninfected computer must be used. If detected, the most reliable way to remove a rootkit is to reinstall the operating system from scratch.

Internet applications, just like ZoneAlarm, but Norton's firewall also asks you for permission to run ActiveX controls and applets. And when it detects hacker intrusions, Norton's firewall often identifies the type of software being run or a specific Trojan attack. Norton supplies a bit more detail about its monitoring activities than ZoneAlarm does. If you find these details interesting, you'll be very happy with Norton Internet Security.

One additional way you can minimize your risk is simply to turn your computer off when you are not using it. If you connect to the Internet using a cable or DSL modem, the connection is always on. If your computer is always on too, then your chances of invasion are much greater.

 # Protecting Your Privacy

Sometimes people don't appreciate what they have until it's gone. Privacy is like that. Consumer data have always been valuable for marketing purposes, but the Internet has created opportunities for data collection on a scale never before encountered. Imagine a man following you around all day, taking notes. He jots down which television shows you watch and how many times you leave the room while the television is on. He pays attention to how much time you spend on the telephone and to whom you talk. He follows you when you go shopping, recording which stores you visit, how much time you spend looking at specific items, and which items you purchased. He notes which magazines and newspapers you read, as well as exactly which articles catch your eye. He knows when you wake up and when you go to bed. He does this every day—and then he sells this information to anyone who wants it!

This level of surveillance might seem an unthinkable invasion of privacy, but this is what can happen each time you take your Web browser for a spin. Any Web page can be programmed to collect information about, for example, when you visited the page and how many times, which links you clicked on the page, and how long it took before you clicked them. A federal law passed in 2002, the Online Personal Privacy Act (S. 2201), does impose some limits on what kinds of personal information can be collected online and under what circumstances, but it's up to each of us to know our rights and protect ourselves if we want to keep our private lives private.

Never fill out a form on a Web page that asks for personal information unless that information is required for a credit card transaction (for example, your home address is needed for shipping purposes). Under no circumstances should you divulge your Social Security number, age, income, or other sensitive information. This information is used only for profiling purposes and should not be required by any company, online or offline.

Before you complete a site's form as part of a credit card transaction, check the site's **privacy policy** (see *Tip: Privacy Policies*). As a rule, companies can collect and sell your personal data if you have not instructed them otherwise. So read the policy to find out if the company plans to sell or distribute your personal information to third parties or business partners. If so, and if you object, look for a checkbox where you can opt out of the data distributions. Companies are required by law to give you this option. In fact, it is prudent to explicitly opt out of any data-sharing possibilities regardless of what a privacy policy may say. Note also that companies are required by law to divulge computer records and data upon receipt of a court order or warrant, in which case they do not need to obtain your permission before releasing your personal data to a law enforcement, national security, or regulatory agency.

Sometimes a company will offer you a customized service of some sort in exchange for information about your interests and other background information. This is a big feature for portal sites and online news delivery services. You might feel that a personalized Web page is exactly what you need, and in such cases, collecting personal information might be necessary. For example, to receive a regional weather report, you must reveal where you live. However, be aware that the same information needed to customize a service for you can also be used by banner advertisers, junk e-mail operations, and direct mail companies if the site chooses to sell that information. Check for a privacy policy and opt out of any corporate data transfers before you give away your personal information. Once it goes up for grabs, you will not be able to recall it.

Two federal laws have been passed to protect privacy on the Internet: the Children's Online Privacy Protection Act of 1998, which applies to data collection from children under 13 years of age, and the Online Personal Privacy

TIP: Privacy Policies

A responsible e-commerce site points to its privacy policy via a link at the bottom of its home page. Some sites display a TRUSTe icon that you can click to see the site's privacy policy (see Figure 4.76). If a company does not make it easy to find its privacy policy, assume the worst. Sites that take your privacy seriously will go out of their way to reassure you that your data are safe.

Act of 2002, which applies to everyone. You can study more about privacy safeguards by visiting the Privacy Rights Clearinghouse's Internet Privacy Resources at `http://www.privacyrights.org/netprivacy.htm` and by reading more about privacy in the Above & Beyond section of Chapter 4. You do need to protect your personal information; no one else will do it for you.

 # Libel and Lawsuits

Libel is any written or pictorial statement that damages a person or an organization. Posting libelous statements on the Net can result in legal actions against the poster. Some large corporations monitor Web pages and online discussions in public forums in an effort to discover potentially damaging statements about corporate services or products. Libel is not a criminal offense, so you can't be sent to jail for it. However, you can be sued for damages in civil court.

Statements about a company's products or services could be considered libelous if they result in lost revenues for the company. The Internet offers ample opportunity for people to make damaging misrepresentations that could have widespread negative consequences. *A person who disseminates information deemed harmful to a company can be the target of a lawsuit even if the information is accurate.* If the claims can be verified, the lawsuit will fail, but the ensuing legal process can be very costly and time-consuming. Most people do not want to risk a lawsuit even if they know their defense is solid.

Statements about individuals can also be considered libelous under certain conditions, although individuals are less likely to initiate lawsuits, and if the person libeled is a public figure, no lawsuit is likely. In 1988, the U.S. Supreme Court held that public figures can be publicly ridiculed, even if that ridicule borders on libel. For example, Bill Gates, the founder and former CEO of Microsoft, is considered to be a public figure and therefore a safe target. If Bill Gates won a civil suit each time someone said something nasty about him on the Internet, he could probably collect enough money to buy out all his company's shareholders. However, care should be taken regarding people who are less famous. In a libel dispute, a private individual who has not opted for public life has stronger rights than does a public figure.

Information is difficult to contain on the Internet. All digital communication can be easily reproduced and distributed without your permission, so you can't be sure that a private e-mail communication will remain private.

Before you send anything out onto the Internet, ask yourself how you would feel if your message turned up on the front page of the local newspaper. If that thought makes you sweat, reconsider posting your message. Any online communication can be easily transformed into a very public document, either by its intended recipient or by someone who has broken system security and covertly intercepted your outgoing e-mail.

2.11 Threats and Harassment

Children used to scream "I'm going to kill you!" on playgrounds and school-yards all over the country with total impunity. However, that was before grade school children started carrying handguns—and following through on their threats. Our society takes threats of deadly force more seriously these days.

Threats posted to chat rooms or contained in e-mail messages are likely to arouse serious attention. There is no such thing as a casual threat on the Internet, even when said in jest and between close friends. Online stalking and hate mail incidents are a reality. One chilling Web site detailed the emotional breakdown of a teenage boy who eventually carried out his murderous fantasies about a 15-year-old girl who had spurned his advances.

The Internet fosters online attacks in which anonymity and geographical distance can turn some seemingly normal people into raving lunatics who engage in flame wars. A **flame** is an e-mail or newsgroup message in which the writer attacks another person with uninhibited hostility. A **flame war** is an exchange of flames between two or more participants. It can be very easy to write off any online display of rage. Who can say when the rage is pathological and when it's just another flame? This makes many people nervous since it's impossible to know much about the people behind the words in an Internet communication.

Regardless of the social climate, U.S. criminal laws make issuing threats on or off the Internet illegal. Anyone who threatens the President of the United States will be investigated by the Secret Service and can be both fined and jailed for the offense (18 USC Sec. 871). Any threat of kidnapping or causing bodily harm that crosses state lines can be punished with a $250,000 fine and five years in jail (18 USC Sec. 875). How do state lines apply to the Net? A packet moving through an out-of-state server might qualify even if it contains an e-mail message that has a source address and destination address in the same state. For example, packets traveling between two locations in Massachusetts often move through New York.

Consider as an example the 18-year-old Florida student who made threatening remarks to a student in an Internet chat room in December 1999 (see Figure 2.22). The second student attended Columbine High School in Littleton, Colorado. Those threats resulted in Columbine High School's closing down for two days while the FBI investigated the threat and tracked down the author. (Recall that in April 1999 two Columbine students, Eric Harris and Dylan Klebold, killed 12 fellow students and a teacher at their school before killing themselves.) Once identified, the Florida youth publicly apologized for his chat room fantasy play. No firearms were found in his possession, and there was no evidence that he intended to carry out his threats. His words were nevertheless a felony offense worthy of an FBI investigation and subsequent arrest under the Interstate Communications statute.

Figure 2.22

Chat session that triggered an FBI investigation

Soup81: Listen, I can't tell you who I am because you know me. . . . Do me a favor, don't go to school tomorrow.

Student: Why?

Soup81: Please, I trust in you and confide in you.

Student: I have to go. I can't miss school.

Soup81: I need to finish what begun and if you go I don't want blood on your hands.

Student: Please don't do this. You are really scaring me.

Soup81: There is nothing to be scared about, just don't go to school and don't tell anyone. If anyone finds out, you'll be the first to go.

Student: Please don't do this.

Soup81: *Time* magazine has brought more chaos and I need to strengthen this. This is what they wanted and people need to know what is really going on here. Don't go to school.

Student: What am I going to tell my parents when they wonder why I didn't go to school?

Soup81: Pretend you're sick! But don't tell anyone because you and only one person knows now. I had to tell someone before the big day.

Student: Well, what about my two best friends?

Soup81: It was nice to know you. I only wish I could tell you who I really was and to let you know how much I liked you. But I'm a nobody, and soon everyone will know who I am. Goodbye. Good to evil and evil to good.

Student: Please don't do this. You are really scaring me.

Harassment in the workplace is another potential trouble area for Internet users. Title VII of the 1964 Civil Rights Act changed the workplace dramatically. Since Title VII, you can't hang up a *Penthouse* calendar in your office, and you can't make a racist joke with impunity. Similarly, offensive materials available on the Internet have no business in the workplace. If an employee is looking at a Web page that contains sexually (or religiously or racially) offensive material, and a coworker happens to see it while walking by, the employer could be cited for harassment. An employee who receives an e-mail that contains religiously, sexually, or racially offensive jokes and forwards the e-mail to the whole department could be the target of a lawsuit.

Companies have become increasingly vigilant about Title VII infractions because they are legally liable if an employee chooses to initiate a lawsuit based on a civil rights violation in the workplace. In an effort to avoid lawsuits, many companies have installed pornography filters on their Web browsers and mail monitors on their e-mail servers. Employees are subject to stringent AUPs (see Section 2.2) and can be terminated for noncompliance. Free speech in the workplace takes a back seat to Title VII, and employees need to understand that some workplace restrictions may have been put into place to comply with Title VII. (See Section 2.13 for more on the rights of employees in the workplace.)

It is often said that e-mail communications are more like postcards than letters: Anyone can read the writing on a postcard that is in transit. In fact, it's safer to think of e-mail in the workplace like posting a notice on a billboard. Not only is your e-mail very visible to anyone who wants to look, but you can be fairly sure that someone *is* looking regularly. Similarly, your employer might be keeping a log of all your browser activities in an effort to maintain a proper workplace environment. If you want to exercise your First Amendment rights on the Internet, do it on your own time, from your own personal computer, using a commercial ISP. When it comes to the workplace, you are subject to a different set of behavioral codes than the ones that apply after hours (see also Section 2.13).

Students are similarly constrained by the AUPs of their educational institutions, although colleges and universities are somewhat more reluctant to enforce rules that could interfere with the free expression of ideas. Schools can nevertheless be fined for Title VII violations and must therefore walk a fine line regarding offensive material in student e-mails and graphical displays on computers in public areas.

2.12 Software Piracy and Copyright Infringements

Software piracy is the willful reproduction or distribution of one or more copies of a computer program that prohibits such reproductions or distributions. Pirating software titles with a total retail value of more than $1,000 is a criminal offense punishable by a jail term and a fine. Newcomers to the Internet often mistakenly think that copyright violations can be prosecuted only if the materials being distributed are sold for profit. This is not true; the person performing the piracy need not profit from the action to be found guilty of software piracy (see the Above & Beyond section later in this chapter for more details). The seriousness of a copyright violation is measured by how much the copyright owner's potential income has been harmed.

When you purchase commercial software, you do not become the owner of that software. Rather, you purchase licensee rights to the software. Software licenses grant you only the right to use the software subject to specific restrictions. It is your responsibility to understand the applicable licensing restrictions of the commercial software you use. For more information about software piracy and answers to commonly asked questions, visit Microsoft's Anti-Piracy Web site.

Be especially careful about software distributed over the Internet. Legitimate software is always accompanied by a licensing agreement, even when distributed for free. If you obtain any software that does not come with a licensing agreement, discard the software.

In August 1999, a 22-year-old University of Oregon senior became the first person convicted under the 1997 No Electronic Theft (NET) Act for software piracy and other copyright violations on the Internet. This student used his

FYI: Software Piracy Is Big Business

According to a December 2005 report from the Business Software Alliance:

- In 2004, $90 billion worth of software was installed worldwide, but only $59 billion was actually spent purchasing it.
- 21% of all business software used in the United States in 2001 was pirated software. Worldwide, the piracy rate is 35%.
- 90% of the software sold via online auctions is sold illegally, costing the industry more than $13 billion in lost revenues annually.

university computer account to publicly post on the Web a large number of MP3 files, as well as software applications, games, and movies. Under the law, acts of software piracy are either felonies or misdemeanors, depending on the value of the materials distributed. A felony conviction is punishable by up to three years in prison and a $250,000 fine.

While the U.S. Justice Department is poised to make Internet piracy a law enforcement priority under NET, the Recording Industry Association of America (RIAA) is taking matters into its own hands when it comes to illegal MP3 file distributions. RIAA is a trade association whose members create, manufacture, or distribute approximately 90% of all audio recordings produced in the United States. The Anti-Piracy division of the RIAA investigates the illegal production and distribution of these recordings. According to the RIAA, increased access to CD-R (compact disc–recordable) drives is responsible for the surge in the number of illegal audio CDs being created. The RIAA reports that nearly 1.7 million counterfeit audio CDs were seized by law enforcement agents in 2000. This was an increase of 79% over CD seizures during 1999.

The RIAA is presumably looking for the big fish—the people who run large MP3 distribution sites on the Web or who manufacture CDs on order. However, anyone who downloads illegal MP3s from the Internet is also engaging in a criminal activity. The RIAA could stage a well-publicized prosecution of a lowly individual just to make a point.

The routine distribution of illegal MP3 files on the Internet presents an ethical dilemma for college students. Some universities are stepping in to protect themselves when copyright infringements are brought to their attention. For example, in 1999, university officials at Carnegie Mellon University shut down the Internet access accounts of 71 students who posted music files and other copyrighted material on the campus computer system.

All forms of intellectual property (text, images, sound clips) are protected by law and all Internet users should understand how these laws apply to them. Students must be especially careful not to misrepresent materials found on

FYI: The RIAA Fights Back

The RIAA is taking aggressive steps to curb the illegal sales of pirated music CDs. For example, RIAA's Operation Clean Streets was launched in April 2000 to halt the distribution of unauthorized sound recordings on the streets of New York City. In the first eight months, Operation Clean Streets led to the seizure of roughly 600,000 illegal audio CDs and 1,035 arrests.

FYI: When Is It Against the Law to Copy a Music File?

Some music files on the Internet are freely available from artists and record companies looking for maximal exposure. Downloading these files for personal use is legal. Other music, however, typically music recorded by major record companies, cannot be downloaded from the Internet without violating copyright protections. Commercial MP3 sites are careful to post only legal MP3 files for public downloads. Other sites, usually private sites run by students or hackers, post MP3 files illegally. If you download an audio file that is being distributed illegally, you are guilty of copyright infringement.

Your legal status is somewhat more complicated if you have purchased the music in question on a CD (however, bootlegged CDs are not legitimate). The Copyright Act of 1971 prohibits anyone but the copyright owner from making a copy of a recording. However, the Audio Home Recording Act of 1992 protects consumers from lawsuits by record companies when they make copies of personal recordings for their own use. Under this act, people may copy cassette tapes and CDs onto computer files as long as the original source material was acquired legally and the copies are made for personal use only. Is it illegal to download a file from an Internet site if you have a legal right to create the file on your own through other means? The courts have not yet had an opportunity to rule on this issue. The RIAA is not likely to prosecute anyone who legitimately paid for the right to enjoy a piece of music produced and distributed by RIAA member companies. The RIAA is more concerned with blatant copyright infringements since those activities pose a serious threat to the recording industry.

FYI: When Is It Plagiarism?

Copyright violations occur when you reproduce a substantial subset of a written work verbatim. If you paraphrase a work, you are not guilty of a copyright violation, but you could be guilty of plagiarism. **Plagiarism** is the presentation of the ideas of a published work in one's own words but without proper attribution. Although plagiarism is not punishable by law, all educational institutions recognize it as a form of academic dishonesty and prohibit it by a code of ethics for all professional writers. For example, Mike Barnicle, a veteran columnist for the *Boston Globe*, resigned after someone noticed that he had plagiarized excerpts from the book *Mind Droppings* by George Carlin in one of his columns. College students who plagiarize published materials for course assignments are at the mercy of their professors, who are usually free to flunk them.

FYI: Converting CD Tracks to MP3 Files

The 1992 Audio Home Recording Act gives you the legal right to convert CD tracks to MP3 files as long as you are the legitimate owner of the CD you want to copy. Converting the tracks requires the right software. You need a CD ripper to copy the tracks into a .wav file format and an MP3 converter to translate the .wav file into an MP3 file. (You can find more details, extensive tutorials, and pointers to relevant software on the Internet.) Note that this is legal only when you use these copies for your own personal use. The Audio Home Recording Act does not give you the right to distribute ripped audio files to friends, relatives, or strangers visiting a Web site.

the Internet as their own. Web page authors must also be careful about possible copyright infringements on their Web sites. Copyright law for Web page authors is covered in Appendix D.

Pornography and Other Lapses in Good Taste

For those who enjoy off-color jokes or have an interest in "blue" material (pornography), the Internet might appear to be a haven in which anything goes. This is not quite true. The FBI has launched many successful sting operations on the Internet to trap child pornography rings.

The First Amendment protects against the censorship of pornography and the prosecution of those who create or distribute pornography. These protections also extend to pornography on the Internet. As a result, attempts to outlaw "bad" language online have so far been unsuccessful. For example, the Communications Decency Act of 1996 was overturned by the U.S. Supreme Court in 1998 for violating the First Amendment. Although the First Amendment does limit the powers of government, exclusions do apply. For example, pornography involving adults is generally protected (as long as it doesn't cross a mysterious line that separates the merely pornographic from the genuinely obscene), but owning or distributing child pornography in the United States is a felony.

Chances are, your proclivities are more mainstream. Who hasn't passed along a raunchy joke or made a sexist statement (in jest, if not in earnest), perhaps in an e-mail message to a friend or relative from work? Be aware that personal e-mail on a company computer is less private than a personal tele-

WORKPLACE RULES

Computer communications must be consistent with conventional standards of ethical and proper conduct, behavior, and manners, and are not to be used to create, forward or display any offensive or disruptive messages, including photographs, graphics and audio materials.

—From a policy document for employees of *The New York Times*

phone call on an office telephone. *Employers cannot legally monitor personal calls on company telephones, but they can monitor e-mail messages that pass through company computers.* If company policy prohibits offensive materials on office computers, a raunchy joke or a sexist statement could cost you your job. The First Amendment affords you no protection in such situations.

Your employer determines your rights and freedoms in the workplace. Even though *The New York Times* allows its employees "reasonable" personal use of company e-mail, its management fired 22 workers in 1999 for sending offensive e-mail messages. The *Times* justified the firings as necessary in order to minimize its legal liability in the face of potential harassment lawsuits.

When it comes to offensive materials in the workplace, legal liability is the bottom line. In 1995, offensive e-mail played a key role in a case involving a subsidiary of Chevron Corporation. An e-mail message entitled "25 reasons beer is better than women" was used as supporting evidence in a sexual harassment claim that cost the company a $2.2 million settlement. Given this legal climate, some companies use sophisticated software to spy on employee e-mail. Although employees might feel that they deserve more privacy in the workplace, the courts generally find that companies are justified in monitoring the use of their computer equipment. The right to free expression is squaring off against the right to a harassment-free workplace—and free expression is losing. If you must be off-color, save it for after work hours and keep it out of your office e-mail. Note that if the computer in your home is

FYI: When Your Personal Computer Is Not

In 1998 the dean of the Harvard Divinity School resigned from his post "for conduct unbecoming a dean." Apparently, he had a healthy collection of explicit pornography on his personal computer—equipment that was actually the property of Harvard University. When he asked university technical support personnel to transfer his files to a larger hard drive, the collection was discovered and brought to the attention of Harvard's president.

Although the dean had done nothing illegal, his resignation was accepted presumably to minimize public embarrassment for Harvard. He still holds a tenured faculty position at the university.

owned by your employer, you should treat it as you would any computer in the office. The same company policies apply at 2:00 A.M. in your own bedroom if the computer you are using is company property.

Search engines make finding adult content online easy, and all sorts of kinky characters can be found in chat rooms devoted to pornography. Indulge if you must, but if you want to stay out of trouble you need to understand what lines you can and cannot cross.

Hoaxes and Legends

The Internet is a source of valuable information and, unfortunately, much misinformation. This section discusses the long-standing tradition of Internet hoaxes and urban legends that never fail to snare innocent new victims year after year.

These warnings typically tell you to never read anything with a specific Subject: field content (such as Good Times or Pen Pal Greetings) and to be sure to pass this warning along to everyone you know. Such warnings are hoaxes. You cannot get a computer virus from reading a plain text e-mail message. The bogus virus warnings tend to come and go and come again whenever enough collective ignorance is available to breathe life into them one more time. This problem will go away only when everyone becomes educated about the Internet. If you see such a virus warning, you can check whether it is a known hoax by visiting the Computer Virus Myths Web site.

Whatever you do, don't forward the message to all your friends and coworkers. If there is a real virus on the loose, leave it to the professionals in technical support to distribute appropriate warnings.

The Internet is particularly effective at propagating misinformation designed to alarm people and generate panic among the uninitiated. Once you start getting e-mail, you might begin to see earnest computer virus alerts and chain letters that promise to turn your life into a living hell (or heaven on Earth) if you don't (or do) send the letter to other people. These notices always ask you to pass the information along to all your friends, relatives, and

TIP: Don't Be Naive

You can't believe everything you read, especially if you read it on the Internet.

coworkers. Since there are always enough newbies on the Net who helpfully comply out of ignorance and goodwill, the Net will probably never be rid of these things.

Although the Internet is a fertile breeding ground for frauds, scams, and misinformation, some information on the Net is not necessarily malicious—it's just false. If you see something on the Net that sounds not quite right, visit the Urban Legends and Folklore Web site and conduct a keyword search for the item. If it's an Internet classic, you'll find it there. In time, you'll learn to spot an Internet hoax a mile away.

 # Laptops and Wireless Networks

Wireless networks and laptops go together like peanut butter and jelly. One of the most attractive aspects of mobile computing is, well, the mobility! Wireless networks are sprouting like weeds. The network installed at MIT not only gets you online, it also tracks how many people are logged on at any given time and can even identify users. In 2004 Hermiston, Oregon, became the world's largest wireless "hot spot," a wireless cloud that covers over 700 square miles (probably by the time you read this Hermiston will no longer hold that title). In 2005, Mauritius, a tropical island off the east coast of Africa, announced plans to turn the entire island into one gigantic hot spot (about 788 square miles worth of "heat"). An April 2006 survey by MuniWireless (http://muniwireless.com/municipal/1227) found 59 region/citywide networks covering 24 states, with an additional 121 planned deployments in these and an additional nine states.

Many wireless networks are free and insecure, such as the networks often found in Internet cafes and other public establishments that do not require accounts and passwords to join. Be careful when joining an unprotected network—wireless communications can be intercepted and decoded by computer programs known as **packet sniffers.** When using your laptop over an unsecured network, do not send confidential information unless you are using a

TIP: Free Wireless on the Horizon?

 Many of the municipal networks are free, causing some distress to commercial ISPs. Lawmakers are getting into the act. Bills have been introduced in legislatures around the country both supporting and opposing these free networks. Stay tuned.

secure transmission protocol (in a browser address bar you will see HTTPS instead of HTTP). Read more about secure connections in Chapters 7 and 8. Not sure if the connection is secure? From the Start menu select "Connect To" and select "Show All Connections." Select your network on the window that appears. In the Details panel on the lower left-hand side of the window you will see "Encryption: Enabled" if the network connection is secure. Even if there is a packet sniffer at work, all your communications will be encrypted and therefore secure.

When joining a wireless network, keep these safety tips in mind:

1. Use encryption for communication. The two main encryption schemes are WiFi Protected Access (WPA) and Wired Equivalent Privacy (WEP). Of the two, WPA is stronger. Use it if available. How will you know? When you come in range of a wireless network, the communication software installed on most laptops will cause a screen to appear automatically asking for an access key to join a selected network, which you must acquire from the wireless provider.
2. Make sure your antivirus and antispyware software is up-to-date and active (see Sections 2.5 and 6.7).
3. Make sure your firewall is on (see Section 2.8).
4. Use a Virtual Private Network (VPN) when connecting to your institution's network. Ask the IT staff how to do this. They will be happy to help!
5. Disable File and Printer Sharing (see Section 2.5 and Figure 2.11).
6. Keep your folders private. By default, Windows XP makes all user folders private, meaning that they can be accessed only by the owner of the folder. Don't change this setting! Right-click on the folder icon and select "Sharing and Security" from the drop-down menu that appears. If the folder is set up for sharing, disable it!
7. Password protect your files. If you have really sensitive information on your laptop, you may wish to separately secure individual files to make sure that only you can view them. Chapter 8 talks about methods for securing individual files via encryption.

TIP: Need a Hot Spot?

Go to http://www.wi-fihotspotlist.com/ to find one.

8. Ask the ISP what security measures are in place at the site. If the answer is none, then consider using another hot spot or avoid transmitting any sensitive information.

If you are establishing your own wireless network, then consult OnGuardOnline.gov for practical tips to help guard against Internet fraud, secure your computer, and protect your personal information.

 # 2.16 Summary of Computer Software-Based Risks and Nuisances

Like the real world, the cyberworld has its share of safety risks and nuisances. We have mentioned several in this chapter including viruses, worms, phishing, and spam. Unfortunately, there are more hazards we have yet to discuss. Chapter 3 covers e-mail and how to filter spam and other undesirable posts. In Chapter 4 we will talk more about the social side of the Internet and the risks associated with participation. Chapter 6 focuses on software on the Internet including spyware, adware, and more about antivirus protection. Chapter 7 is concerned with online shopping and how to minimize your risks as a shopper. Chapter 8 reviews encryption and encryption tools you can use to store and transmit files securely.

It's always helpful to collect useful safety information together, so Table 2.1 summarizes topics presented in this chapter plus additional safety information appearing in later chapters.

FYI: Netscape's Security Center

Version 7 of the Netscape browser includes a Security Center (see Figure 2.23) to help guard against attacks. The Security Center panel opens when you click its name just below the menu in the title bar (see Figure 2.24). You can see if the site you are at has been verified (see Chapters 7 and 8, SSL Certification), the state of the pop-up blocker for the current site, information about ID theft and spyware protection, and if your browser is up to date. Figure 2.24 shows that ID theft and spyware protection is not effective. You can fix this by selecting the Spyware Protection tab to open up the Spyware Panel (see Figure 2.25) and selecting the "Run Full Scan" button. This will cause the security tools to examine all files on your hard drive for any known malware. Infected files will be deleted, and the Security Center Panel will give you the green light (see Figure 2.26).

Table 2.1

Summary of Online Risks and Hazards

Risk/Hazard	Danger Level	Description
AdWare	Low	Software that automatically downloads, displays, or plays commercial advertisements **Solution:** Adware removal tool, firewall **Reference:** Section 6.7
Pharming	High	Hacker attack that redirects valid URLs to bogus sites enabling capture of sensitive information **Solution:** Secure connection (HTTPS); accept only valid public key certificates **Reference:** Section 7.3 and Chapter 8
Phishing Spear Phishing	High	E-mails from apparently trustworthy sources requesting personal information for purposes of identity theft **Solution:** Phish filter, firewall **Reference:** Section 2.4 **Cost:** $630 million*
Rootkit	Very high	Software tools that become integrated with the operating system software, proving the ability to hide running programs and files. Can be detected only by another, uninfected computer. **Solution:** Reinstallation of OS (may require professional help), firewall **Reference:** Section 2.7
Spam	Low	Unsolicited e-mail sent for commercial purposes **Solution:** Spam filter, firewall **Reference:** Chapter 3 Above & Beyond, Section 2.8
Spyware	High	Software that takes control of a computer without the knowledge or permission of the owner, monitoring and reporting on user activity **Solution:** Spyware removal tool, firewall **Reference:** Sections 2.8, 6.7 **Cost:** $2.6 billion*
Trojan Horse	High	Malicious software disguised as or embedded within another apparently harmless application, allowing remotely controlled access for nefarious purposes **Solution:** Antivirus tool, firewall **Reference:** Sections 2.5, 2.8, 6.5
Virus	High	Self-replicating software that inserts itself into other computer files, potentially destroying files in the process or worse **Solution:** Antivirus tool, firewall **Reference:** Sections 2.5, 2.8, 6.5 **Damage:** $5.2 billion*
Worm	High	Self-replicating, stand-alone program that sends copies of itself over the network, potentially "jamming" it **Solution:** Antivirus tool, firewall **Reference:** Sections 2.5, 2.8, 6.5

*Consumer Reports, September 2006.

Figure 2.23

Netscape v7
Security Center
tool

Figure 2.24

Netscape Security
Center panel

Figure 2.25

Netscape can
scan your files for
spyware.

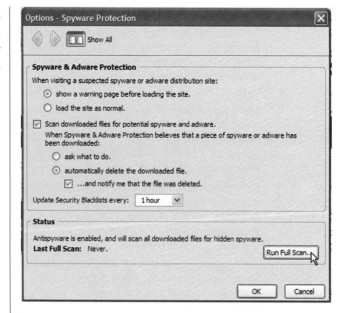

Figure 2.26
A happy Security
Center

Things to Remember

- Read the terms of all AUPs that apply to you.
- Never tell anyone your passwords.
- Change your passwords periodically.
- E-mail is not private, and chat room participants can be traced.
- Do not offer personal information on a site before reviewing the site's privacy policy, and look for opt-out checkboxes.
- Handle e-mail attachments with care.
- Keep your antivirus software up-to-date and keep it running in the background.
- Turn off File and Printer Sharing.
- Do not give out credit card account information on a nonsecure Web page.
- Assume all computers in a workplace are being monitored for offensive materials.
- Just because something is easy to do doesn't make it legal.
- It is your responsibility to know the laws that pertain to your activities (both online and offline).
- Add an additional firewall to supplement (or replace Windows ICF).
- Be wary about providing confidential information using insecure channels.
- Firewalls are easy to install, but it's important to customize the access privileges you need.

Important Concepts

acceptable use policy (aup) usage restrictions for computer accounts, Internet access accounts, and many other Internet-related services.

copyright infringement unauthorized distribution of material protected by copyright restrictions.

e-mail virus although called a virus, these are technically worms spread by e-mail attachments or scripts associated with HTML-enabled e-mail.

Firewall software application that protects your computer from hacker attacks and intruders.

Harassment offensive, unwanted, and unavoidable communications or content, usually characterized by multiple or habitual incidents.

identity theft using personal information to open credit card or other accounts for the purpose of identity theft.

libel damaging statements about a company or individual.

password security your first and most powerful line of defense against hackers.

pharming variation of phishing that redirects a valid URL to a look-alike web site designed to capture confidential information you would use to access the genuine site.

phish, phishing, spear phishing fraudulent e-mail messages that appear to come from trusted sources requesting confidential information to facilitate identity theft.

pretexting non-Internet means of phishing.

script a small computer program written in a scripting language such as Microsoft's Visual Basic.

secure Web page Web page where it is safe to enter sensitive data such as credit card account numbers.

smish, smishing instant messaging version of phish.

software piracy unauthorized distribution of commercial software.

spoofing using an electronic device to display a false phone number on a caller ID system

terms of service (ToS) same as **acceptable use policy**.

Trojan horse unauthorized code, often designed to enable remote control over a computer at a later date.

virus potentially destructive code hidden inside a host program and distributed to a large number of computers.

worm potentially destructive code that depends on networked communications and commonly used software in order to propagate.

zombie computer that is being controlled by a hacker using another computer without the owner's knowledge or permission, usually used to launch Internet attacks. (See Distributed Denial-of-Service Attacks in the Above & Beyond section of this chapter for more details.)

Where Can I Learn More?

Another Phine Kettle of Phish: Identity Theft Prevention
http://www.infotoday.com/SEARCHER/nov05/ebbinghouse.shtml

Anti-Phishing Working Group
http://www.antiphishing.org/index.html

Antivirus Research-Scientific Papers
http://researchweb.watson.ibm.com/antivirus/SciPapers.htm

Building "Synergistic" AV
http://www.infosecuritymag.com/2002/may/synergisticav.shtml

Burning Your Own CDs—the Facts and the Fiction
http://www.computermusic.co.uk/tutorial/cds/cdmain.asp

Business Software Alliance
http://www.bsa.org/

CD Burning Basics
http://hotwired.lycos.com/webmonkey/00/38/
   index4a.html?tw=multimedia

Center for Democracy and Technology
http://www.cdt.org/

Computer Virus Myths
http://www.Vmyths.com

Cost of Data Loss
http://www.ontrack.com/datarecovery/cost.asp

Dollar Diddling and the Billion-Dollar Viruses
http://online.securityfocus.com/columnists/78

Electronic Frontier Foundation
http://www.eff.org/

Electronic Privacy Information Center
http://www.epic.org/

Federal Trade Commission: Your National Resource About ID Theft
http://www.consumer.gov/idtheft/
File and Printer Sharing (NetBIOS) Fact and Fiction
http://cable-dsl.home.att.net/netbios.htm
First Amendment Cyber-Tribune
http://w3.trib.com/FACT/
https://www.paypal.com/us/cgi-bin/webscr?cmd=xpt/cps/
    general/IdentityTheftProtect-outside
PayPal—Identity Protection Resources
https://www.paypal.com/us/cgi-bin/webscr?cmd=xpt/cps/
    general/IdentityTheftProtect-outside
People for Internet Responsibility (PFIR)
http://www.pfir.org/
Phishing Examples
http://www.mailfrontier.com/docs/field_guide.pdf
Privacy Net
http://privacy.net/
Privacy Rights Clearinghouse
http://www.privacyrights.org/
Urban Legends and Folklore
http://urbanlegends.about.com/index.htm
Why You Need a Firewall
http://www.cisco.com/univercd/cc/td/doc/product/iaabu/
    centri4/user/scf4ch2.htm
Widespread Virus Myths
http://www.stiller.com/myths.htm

Problems and Exercises

1. What is an acceptable use policy (AUP)? Find the AUP for your Internet access account, and study it carefully. Have you ever violated the terms of your AUP without realizing it at the time? Are there any restrictions you do not understand or to which you object?

2. Explain how a computer virus, a Trojan horse, and a worm differ from each other.

3. The Melissa virus used an innovative strategy for tricking people into opening e-mail attachments. How did Melissa fool users?

4. What is an RTF file? Can an RTF file contain a macro virus? Should Microsoft make RTF the default file format for Word? Explain why or why not.

5. Suppose you know and trust someone who sends you a Word file in an e-mail attachment. Can you be sure he or she isn't sending you a file containing a macro virus? Why or why not?

6. What is normal.dot? Explain how normal.dot is used to spread macro viruses.

7. Explain how HTML-enabled e-mail clients can spread worms without the use of e-mail attachments.

8. Explain why it is difficult for antivirus software to recognize the Klez virus.

9. Your roommate says she doesn't need to install a personal firewall because she's running Windows XP. Is she right? Why or why not?

10. [HANDS-ON] Visit Gibson Research at `http://grc.com/default.htm` and scroll down to ShieldsUP! Click the Shields UP! Link and run both the Test My Shields test and the Probe My Ports test. What vulnerabilities did these tests reveal? Note: Anyone who is not running a firewall will fail at least one of these security checks. This is a good site to visit after you've installed a firewall—it will show you if your firewall is working properly. If the Shields test determined that file sharing is enabled, either turn it off or limit it to a specific file directory. To turn off file sharing under Windows, go to the Network Control Panel, then click the File and Print Sharing button. Make sure no boxes are checked to allow access by others. To turn file sharing off on a Mac, go to the File Sharing control panel and make sure it says File Sharing off.

11. [FIND IT ONLINE] Visit the University of Virginia's Security Best Practices page at `http://www.itc.virginia.edu/security/vulnerabilities.html` and find out which three security vulnerabilities are common to all users and all operating systems.

12. [TAKE A STAND] All operating systems exhibit security vulnerabilities that require ongoing patches and system updates. System administrators take responsibility for these maintenance tasks when computers are used in the workplace, but home computers are relatively vulnerable because home computer users often have no understanding of

online security and proper precautions. Who should assume responsibility for the online security of home computers? Computer manufacturers? Software manufacturers? ISPs? Everyone who owns a home computer? How would you go about fixing the problem of Internet security for recreational or casual computer users?

13. If you care about keeping personal data private, what should you do before you enter any personal information on a Web page?

14. **[FIND IT ONLINE]** The Online Personal Privacy Act of 2002 distinguishes two kinds of personally identifiable information (PII): sensitive PII and nonsensitive PII. How are these two types of PII treated differently under the law? Give seven examples of sensitive PII.

15. **[HANDS-ON]** Visit `http://privacy.net/` and click the link that says *Analyzer at Network-Tools.com/analyze*. The site will show you how much information your computer is willing to reveal when you visit a Web page that asks for this information. Did it detect your operating system correctly? Do you think a Web page really needs to know your operating system? Why or why not?

16. When can someone be sued for libel? Why is it relatively safe to criticize a politician?

17. Is it safe to criticize a person or company in a personal e-mail message to a friend? Is it safer to make the same statements in a personal telephone call? A written letter? How about posting the statements on a Web site if you don't give out the URL to anyone? Discuss the relative risks and worst-case scenarios in each of these situations.

18. What is the maximal penalty for making a threat of bodily harm that crosses state lines?

19. Which law makes a business liable for harassment in the workplace? What steps are companies taking to protect themselves against harassment lawsuits?

20. What is the legal definition of software piracy? Do you have to profit from your activities to be guilty of software piracy?

21. **[HANDS-ON]** Select one of the software applications on your computer and read its licensing agreement. Are you allowed to install the software on more than one computer? Are you allowed to resell the software under any circumstances? Do you think the restrictions of the licensing agreement are reasonable? Why or why not?

22. When is it legal for a private individual to make a copy of an audio CD? Is it illegal to make copies of audio CDs by using a CD-R drive?

23. What is the Recording Industry Association of America, and what is it doing to combat the illegal distribution of MP3 files?

24. Explain the difference between plagiarism and copyright infringement.

25. Does the First Amendment give you the right to download pornography? Can your employer legally override your First Amendment rights in its AUP? Can your employer legally monitor all your online activities? Can employers censor objectionable Web sites on workplace computers?

26. **[FIND IT ONLINE]** Browse one of the online archives of Urban Legends, and pick out the funniest or most improbable urban legend you can find. Do you think this rumor caused anyone any damage, or was it completely harmless? Are most of the urban legends you saw harmless bits of folklore? Did you see any that looked like they might have been dangerous?

27. Visit `http://www.sonicwall.com/phishing/` and check out your phish detection skills. How did you score?

28. **[HANDS-ON]** Install a firewall, and live with it for a week. How distracting are its pop-up alerts? Did it detect any unexpected intruders during this time?

29. Explain why it might be a good idea to run Ad-aware (see Chapter 6) whenever you install a new Web browser. (Hint: What additional software is sometimes bundled with a Web browser?)

Personal Safety Online

No Electronic Theft Act of 1997

Software piracy is a serious threat to the software industry. Intellectual property laws never anticipated the unprecedented ease with which software can be duplicated and distributed over the Internet. New laws are often motivated by specific incidents, and every so often someone seems to deliberately challenge the establishment in order to force a change.

That seemed to be the case when in 1994 a 21-year-old MIT student, David LaMacchia, set up a public server on the Internet and invited people to post their favorite software for public distribution. LaMacchia made no effort to commercialize his server or benefit from its software archive financially. He merely gave people a place where they could freely upload and download all sorts of software. Much of the software that people posted was subject to copyright restrictions, and the people who traded these files were breaking the law. However, it seemed silly to go after the people who used the site without going after LaMacchia for facilitating software piracy on an international scale. The tricky part was finding a law that LaMacchia had broken. He was not guilty of software piracy himself, even though he clearly encouraged it. Moreover, it seemed that he had found a legal loophole in existing copyright law. That is, as long as he did not benefit from the activities on his server, his actions did not fall under any of the criminal statutes for copyright violations. LaMacchia's actions were thought to have cost software copyright owners more than $1 million in losses.

Eventually, LaMacchia was indicted by a grand jury for wire fraud under the wire fraud statute (18 USC Sec. 1343) enacted in 1952 to protect consumers from false advertising on radio and television. It was never intended to apply to copyright infringements, and it certainly didn't anticipate computer-mediated communications. LaMacchia filed for a dismissal of the case, and the judge agreed. Lawmakers soon thereafter went to work on new legislation to make sure something like this could never happen again. Most important, industry proponents wanted to close what had come to be called the LaMacchia Loophole, the loophole in copyright laws that protects software distributors from prosecution for copyright infringements as long as they do not profit from their actions.

Three years after LaMacchia's case was dismissed, in December 1997, President Clinton signed into law the No Electronic Theft (NET) Act. NET makes it illegal to reproduce or distribute copyrighted works, such as software programs and musical recordings, even if the defendant derives no financial gain. Reproducing or distributing one or more copies of a copyrighted work with a value of more than $1,000 and up to $2,500 is a misdemeanor that can result in up to one year in prison and a fine of up to $100,000. Reproducing or distributing ten or more copies of a copyrighted work that have a total value of more than $2,500 is a felony, punishable by up to three years in prison and a fine of up to $250,000.

Digital Millennium Copyright Act of 1998

While software manufacturers have been struggling with the problem of software piracy over computer networks since the 1980s, the publishing and entertainment industries began to grasp the magnitude of their potential losses only after the Internet went mainstream in the 1990s. Publishers and movie studios want to capitalize on the Internet, but they also need to protect their lawful intellectual properties from unauthorized online distribution.

Although NET was a step in the right direction, copyright violations on the Internet are still notoriously difficult to enforce. If networks and online services won't share the responsibility for enforcing copyright restrictions, copyright owners will face a major uphill battle. Who should be liable when a copyright infringement shows up on a Web site or a mailing list? Should the managers of the server be held responsible, as well as the author of the Web page or e-mail message? Should liability extend to the author's ISP and the network service behind the ISP? How far should liability extend, and who should police copyright infringements?

The policing question is a crucial concern for ISPs and system administrators. With countless people posting personal home pages on millions of Web servers, the task of checking all those sites for copyright infringements would drive commercial ISPs out of business and force universities to shut down all student Web sites. This is not a viable scenario for a technology that is transforming everything from education to economic prosperity.

Any new law designed to strengthen the enforcement of copyright restrictions on the Internet must also limit the liability of the service providers. Furthermore, system administrators need to assume some responsibility for Web sites that contain copyright infringements. The Digital Millennium Copyright Act (DMCA) was designed to balance the responsibility of service providers and copyright owners.

tion about you. For example, suppose that the last time you visited a particular site, you spent all your time on two particular pages. A cookie can record this information so that on your next visit to that site, the server might greet you with a page display that makes it especially easy for you to navigate to those pages again.

Cookies allow Web servers to create a profile about you and your prior activities. Parts of this profile might have been collected with your assistance (for example, you have to tell it your name if you want a personal greeting). Other parts might be deduced from your past interactions with the server.

How can you tell if you have cookies on your hard drive? Search your hard drive for a file whose file name includes the string "cookie." It might be called cookies.txt or MagicCookie. Once you've located a cookie file, open it—it's just a text file that contains separate cookies from different Web sites.

Here's an example of a short cookie file that has eight cookies from eight different Web sites. The names of the sites are given first, so you can always tell which sites dropped their cookies into the file.

```
.realaudio.com        TRUE / FALSE   946684740    uid        2062544869497233244
.timecast.com         TRUE / FALSE   946684740    uid        20618930869497239997
.dailybriefing.com    TRUE / FALSE   946684740    dbprofile  1040|fdotx
.abcnews.com          TRUE / FALSE   1500192813   SWID       711D5932-01DBCF9-080009DC93B5
.pathfinder.com       TRUE / FALSE   2051222400   PFUID      cc47f22035221ff33f41000ffff9d
.hotbot.com           TRUE / FALSE   937396800    ink        IU0TiDPvAC5874DFB49F09E6BCA7A
.boston.com           TRUE / FALSE   946684799    BGEP       206.119.237.14:24463877899644
.geocities.com        FALSE/ FALSE   941580297    GeoId      20413652878508297662
```

Cookies can make your time on the Web more personal. For example, Amazon.com tracks the books you browse when you visit its pages so that the company can offer recommendations the next time you visit its site. The more time you spend looking at books, the better these recommendations are likely to be. *The New York Times* on the Web is free but requires visitors to register with a name and a password. Once you've registered, a cookie is installed that checks for your name and password each time you return to the site. This way you can enter the site automatically without having to enter your name or password, as though the site were unrestricted. This is particularly convenient for people who visit a lot of password-protected Web sites and want to streamline the sign-in process.

Cookies are also used to target potential customers with banner ads. ZDNet.com generates cookies for any mouse clicks that reveal an interest in specific technologies. The next time you visit ZDNet.com, these cookies can be used to show you an ad about a product that reflects your interests. Some people like targeted advertising: If you have to see an ad, it's better to see one that might actually interest you. Other people object to the data collection practices that underlie targeted advertisements: It's just creepy to have Web pages watching you and recording information about you.

Cookies can provide useful services. Maybe you want to hear about products and promotions you might find interesting. At the same time, you might also want to be reassured that your personal information is not being sold to information brokers and marketing companies. At the very least, you might want to be informed if a Web site is going to put a cookie on your hard drive. This is why people take the time to configure their cookies with a cookie manager. A **cookie manager** is a software application that gives you control over your cookies. You decide which Web sites can record information about you and which ones cannot. More important, you can restrict the use of third-party cookies, the kind used to create user profiles for data brokers.

Earlier versions of IE did not give users much real control over their cookies. Simple preference settings gave you a choice of accepting all cookies, rejecting all cookies, or asking for explicit permission for all cookies. This level of cookie management is perhaps better than nothing, but not by much. What people really need is the ability to set cookie controls for specific Web sites and to have the controls in place for each new browsing session (no one wants to reset all the controls each time they restart their browser). IE 7.0 incorporates a nicely designed cookie manager that is easy to use and a good place to start if you are new to cookie managers.

To see the cookie manager, go to the View menu and select Privacy Report. You will see a pop-up window that looks something like the one in Figure 2.27, but it probably has fewer or no site entries. This display shows

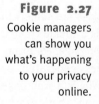

Figure 2.27
Cookie managers can show you what's happening to your privacy online.

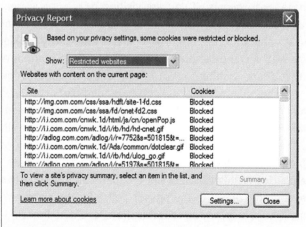

you which cookies were blocked by the browser when you opened up the current Web page. If you want to see all the servers responsible for all the cookies on your current Web page, change the pull-down menu setting from "Restricted Web sites" to "All Web sites."

You can control cookies in two ways. First, you can set a general cookie policy for all Web sites. If you click the Settings button, you will see your current policy setting. If you haven't changed this setting before, you should be on the default setting, called Medium (see Figure 2.28). There are seven general policies, and you can see each of them by sliding the vertical control up and down. You can turn off all cookies (without destroying them) by selecting the most conservative policy, called Block All Cookies (see Figure 2.29), but this is probably not the setting you really want.

Chances are, you've been surfing the Web, accumulating cookies left and right, and some of these cookies are worth keeping. Others are probably of no use to you whatsoever. The trick is to separate the wheat from the chaff. Unfortunately, MSIE's general policy settings apply only to new cookies—not old ones. Thus you have to delete all your old cookie files and start over again with a stricter cookie policy in place if you want to disable all the existing cookies that may not meet your privacy criteria. Deleting all your cookies means having to reregister at personalized Web sites, so think carefully before you delete all your cookies. Alternatively, you can keep your existing cookies and settle for blocking only new cookies. This won't stop any user profiling already in place, but it does keep the Web just the way you like it.

FYI: First- and Third-Party Cookies

A **first-party cookie** is a cookie created by the Web server that hosts the current Web page. For example, if you are visiting `http://www.weather.com`, cookies generated by weather.com are first-party cookies. First-party cookies are subject to the privacy policy for the current Web site. A **third-party cookie** is a cookie created by some Web server other than the one that hosts the current Web page. For example, if you are visiting `http://www.weather.com`, cookies generated by `http://amch.questionmarket.com` are third-party cookies. Why is a Web page at weather.com handing you cookies from amch.questionmarket.com? That's exactly what worries a lot of people—no one can be sure what's really going on in these cases. The cookie could be instrumental to an online survey, targeted advertising, user profiling, all three, or something else altogether. That's why some general cookie policies distinguish between first-party and third-party cookies: Third-party cookies are not subject to the privacy policy for the current Web site, and, unbeknownst to you, they may be collecting data for a data broker.

Figure 2.28

You decide how much privacy you want.

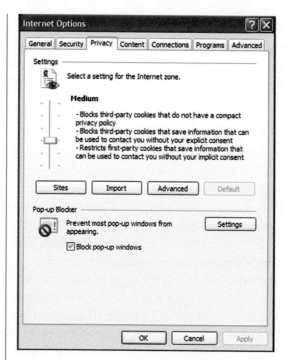

Figure 2.29

Block all cookies for maximal privacy.

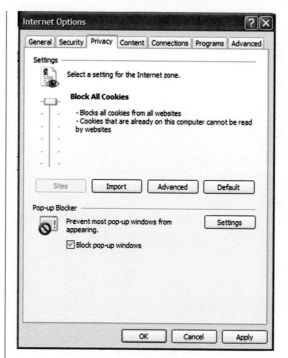

TIP: Seeing the Effects of New Settings

 If you are fine-tuning the cookie setting for a Web site, and you are moving from a more restrictive setting to a less restrictive setting, you will have to reload the Web page to see any effects. Changes to your cookie settings don't swing into action until the next time the Web page is downloaded.

We recommend changing your general setting to High (see Figure 2.30). For sites where this general policy is not what you want, you can fine-tune your cookie manager by identifying specific domains that should be allowed or blocked as you see fit. For example, if you know that doubleclick.com is a site that enables targeted advertising and you don't want targeted advertising, you can explicitly block all cookies from doubleclick.com by going to the Privacy Settings window (select Internet Options from the Tools menu and then go to the Privacy tab) and clicking the Sites button. This will give you a pop-up window where you can enter the name of a specific domain and specify whether you want to allow or block all cookies from that domain (see Figure 2.31). The directives you enter here will always override your general policy setting (unless you have selected the highest setting, Block All Cookies; that setting ignores all site-specific overrides).

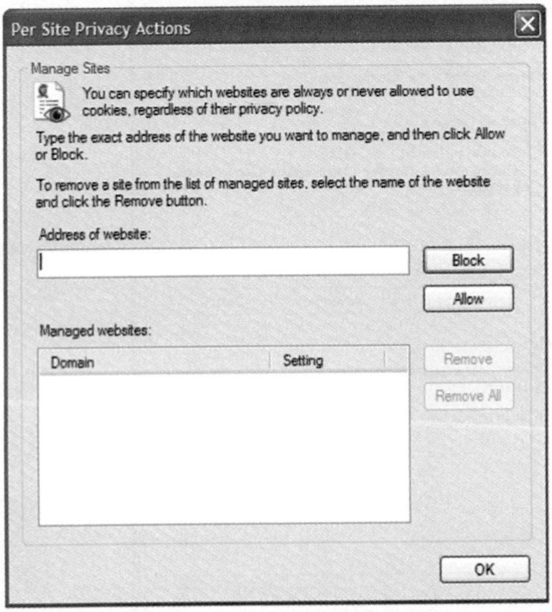

Figure 2.30

A High privacy setting can be overridden for exceptions.

Per Site Privacy Actions ☒

Manage Sites

You can specify which websites are always or never allowed to use cookies, regardless of their privacy policy.

Type the exact address of the website you want to manage, and then click Allow or Block.

To remove a site from the list of managed sites, select the name of the website and click the Remove button.

Address of website:

| | Block |
| | Allow |

Managed websites:

| Domain | Setting | | Remove |
| | | | Remove All |

OK

Figure 2.31

You can pick and choose the sites you trust.

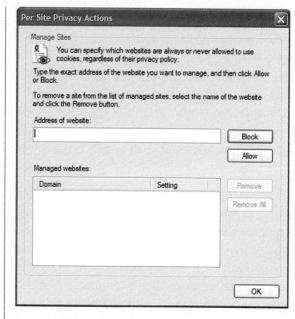

If you find that the High setting is too restrictive (too many Web sites aren't functioning properly), you can drop down to the next highest setting and see if that one fits you better. If you lower the setting, you could be sacrificing some of your privacy to indulge your desire for convenience. Any Web site that isn't working properly on the High setting can be made to work with appropriate site-specific overrides. The High setting maximizes your privacy; lower settings cater to convenience. It's up to you to decide how much time you want to invest in maintaining personal privacy online.

A cookie can be read only by a server from the domain of the Web site responsible for the cookie. So a cookie created by one Web server at Yahoo.com can be read only by other servers at Yahoo.com. It would nevertheless be reassuring to know that personal information stays within the confines of the site that collected it and is not being sold to marketers and

SHORTCUT: MSIE Privacy Reports

If any cookies have been blocked on the current Web page, you will see an icon containing an eye and a red minus sign at the bottom of your browser window. Double-click on this icon to see the Privacy Report for that Web page.

FYI: Cookies Can Be Useful

Cookies make the following things possible:

- Online shopping carts for e-commerce sites
- Automatic logons to restricted sites (for example, Web-based discussion groups and e-mail accounts)
- Personalized Web portals that show you customized information you care about

If you disable all cookies, you won't be able to use any of these features.

third-party vendors. The controversy over cookies arises from concerns about user profiling, consumer consent, and privacy violations.

E-commerce sites have begun to address consumer privacy concerns in response to pending legislation and consumer demands. For example, the Online Privacy Protection Act of 2005 (pending Congressional approval at the time of this writing) requires that e-commerce provide a way for visitors to opt out of data resale operations. Although these policies will protect data collected by in-house Web servers, most commercial data collection is done by ad servers, and few consumers understand how ad servers operate, let alone how to track them down in order to opt out of their notice-and-consent options. Ad servers and their privacy policies still worry privacy advocates, especially since the general public is largely unaware of the fact that banner ads can collect data even if you never click them.

When you visit a page at Yahoo.com, you might view a banner ad from a third-party ad server such as DoubleClick. (DoubleClick is the largest supplier of banner ads on the Web.) Banner ads from ad servers are often paired with cookies. If you accept a cookie from an ad server, the cookie can be accessed and read by the server whenever new material (such as another banner ad) is downloaded from that ad server or any other server in the same domain. None of this is explained to the user, and few users take the time to learn about cookies and how ad servers use them.

Proponents of user profiling often argue that no identifying information is associated with the data collected by cookies. That is, the cookie ID numbers that make it possible to collect user profiles don't reveal user names, addresses, or other information. However, Web forms can capture personal identifiers and pass them along to third-party data brokers, with or without the use of cookies. Even if you have never given your e-mail address to a Web site via a Web form, it may still be part of your user profile as a result of HTML-enabled e-mail.

If you read your e-mail with an HTML-enhanced e-mail client, your user profiles have probably already been connected to your e-mail address. Here's how it works.

It begins when you open a piece of mail from a mail spammer. If that message contains a 1×1–pixel GIF image located on ad servers, you've just handed your e-mail address over to the ad server. Suppose that the spammer is an outfit named Spam-O-Rama and the company that runs the ad server is named Tracker. Before Spam-O-Rama sends out one of its mailings to 30 million e-mail addresses, it sells 1 pixel of space in its message body to Tracker. This means that Tracker can insert a URL to its ad server in the e-mail message. This is all the space Tracker needs because Tracker will insert an invisible GIF from its ad server. Each time Spam-O-Rama sends out this e-mail message, the URL for Tracker's GIF can be modified to include the e-mail address of the current recipient, much like URLs can be modified to include keywords from search engine queries. Then, when the recipient opens this message with an HTML-enabled e-mail client, the GIF file is downloaded and the recipient's e-mail address is sent back to Tracker's ad server. When the URL request arrives at Tracker's ad server, the server extracts the address from the URL and launches a script to collect more information from the recipient's Web browser. (The recipient's HTML-enabled e-mail client is running a Web browser to read this message.) The script asks the browser for any cookies from Tracker's domain. Any cookies that the browser finds are then sent back to Tracker, and the cookies' ID numbers are connected to the recently obtained e-mail address. If a user profile is available for an ID number, then the e-mail address can now be added to the profile (see Figure 2.32).

A 1-pixel banner ad is sometimes called a **Web bug**. Web bugs don't threaten your system security, but they are a blatant violation of your privacy. You can foil Web bugs by doing any of the following.

1. Never open any mail that looks like spam.
2. Set up ad filters for all the big ad server operations.
3. Set up cookie filters for the big ad server operations.

Turn off the graphics for your browser (see Section 1.10.7) when you read your e-mail messages. If that 1-pixel GIF image is never downloaded from the ad server, it cannot send your e-mail address back to the server.

If you are curious about Web bugs and would like to see some real ones in action, you can install an MSIE add-on called Bugnosis, which is available at `http://www.bugnosis.org/`. When Bugnosis is enabled, it generates a Web bug report whenever you visit a Web page containing Web bugs (see

Figure 2.32

Invisible banner ads collect profiling data.

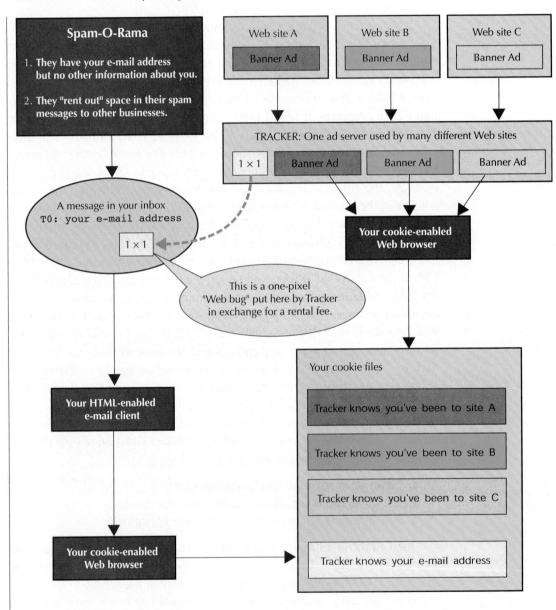

Figure 2.33). But be prepared to disable it once the novelty wears off: there are a lot of Web bugs out there.

As mentioned, some cookies are useful, but others are nothing but a threat to your privacy. Happily, there's a solution to the cookie problem. All the popular browsers provide cookie management capabilities. Opera and Firefox even arrange them into folders to make them easier to find and also to help you determine common cookie sources. Using these built-in cookie managers, you can view, delete, block and otherwise manage your cookies. Take

Figure 2.33

Bugnosis is a web bug detector.

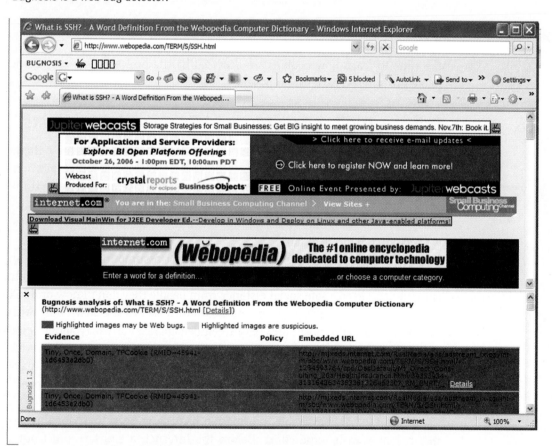

A **proxy server** is a piece of software that retrieves and delivers documents on demand. When a Web browser is instructed to go through a proxy server, every document moves through the proxy server before it's delivered to the browser. A server programmed to filter ads from Web pages removes all ads before passing the pages to a browser.

A proxy server can be located on a local host or on a remote host (for example, it could be an ISP server or it could be part of a firewall if you're working in a business environment). Proxy servers can also be used for purposes other than ad filtering. For example, sometimes Web pages are cached on a proxy server so that everyone in a LAN can benefit from a large cache of shared pages. (This works much like your browser's personal cache, but this cache is shared by a community of users.)

the time to learn how cookies are accessed by the browsers you use. Some make this process easier than others.

Privacy, Digital Records, and Commercial Interests

Some concepts are so entrenched in our culture that we rarely examine them. As long as our lungs are full of air, we don't have to think about respiration. As long as our supremacy in the food chain is secure, we don't have to think about predators. As long as life moves along in a predictable fashion, we try not to dwell on potential catastrophes. Then, when the unexpected happens, we cope first and reflect later.

The concept of privacy has been a dormant assumption in the lives of most Americans. Most people know the difference between public and private activities and keep a safe social distance from people they don't know or don't want to know. In addition, everyone has information they share only with trusted friends, and most don't have to elude paparazzi or worry about being the next hot item in the tabloids. So they drop the shades at night and feel safe from the eyes of the world. As social causes go, privacy issues have yet to make much of a dent in the collective consciousness, although the Internet is beginning to sensitize people to privacy violations.

A lot of publicly available information has always been there for the taking, but only with some effort. Before the Internet, a court record from a divorce proceeding was public, but it was available only if you visited the courthouse at which it was stored. Copies of old newspapers usually were available on microfiche, but to view them you had to travel to the newspaper's offices or to a regional library and spend time in front of a microfiche reader. Private investigators doing background checks knew their way around all the public resources, as well as a few backdoor tricks of the trade. Whatever sources they traditionally used, the job always involved some amount of footwork. Hence, obtaining information that was technically free demanded a high price in terms of time and energy.

The Internet is changing many of the hidden costs associated with free information. When a court places its records online, no one needs to travel to the courthouse to see them. With telephone listings for the entire United States available online, you can research a hundred cities as easily as one. The Internet isn't giving people anything they couldn't get before; it simply makes many information-gathering tasks much easier. In a legal sense, nothing has changed with respect to the availability of information. In a practical sense, nothing will ever be the same. More than just the work of private investigators is facilitated. People who previously never would have taken the time to learn about the resources that a public library offers are now surfing Web information resources. Amateurs are barging in where only professionals used to tread.

Computer technologies are also altering the line between transient information and archival information. Articles in newspapers and magazines used to have a limited shelf life. A 10-year-old newspaper article could easily vanish and be gone forever. Now, as more newspapers put their contents online, newspaper stories become part of the permanent record. Anyone can create a massive digital library for anything online, hook it up to a search engine, and post it on the Web—and the world has instant access to an archival resource. Items that used to fade and die natural deaths can now have the technological equivalent of eternal life.

Digital records also make it easier for people to assemble information from disparate sources. Pulling up an instant profile of someone who is active online takes less than a minute—give the name to a Web search engine and you'll be rewarded with hits from Web pages, Usenet newsgroups, and mailing list archives. All the legwork of looking in different places and all the brainwork of figuring out where to look in the first place has been solved by the indexing capability of a search engine that operates almost instantaneously.

When it comes to personal data, the whole is always greater than the sum of the pieces. No one piece might be particularly threatening or worrisome by itself. However, when a hundred pieces of information can be pulled together, a bigger picture begins to emerge. Big Brother hasn't materialized as the result of a massive totalitarian government, but it might now emerge from what amounts to technological serendipity. Nobody planned it this way. Like so many things on the Internet, forces were simply set into motion, and now the consequences require careful consideration. People are accustomed to thinking about degrees of privacy. Absolute privacy is difficult to attain, but relative privacy might be a reasonable goal. For example, most e-mail messages are read and discarded or sometimes just discarded without even being read. A message posted to a mailing list is public relative to that list but private with respect to the world at large. Even when mailing lists are archived, the business of locating and searching a mailing list archive may not be easy. As long as the convenience factor is low, mailing list participants enjoy some degree of privacy. However, the use of computers often makes formerly difficult tasks effortless. All of those difficult-to-read mailing list archives now can be placed on Web pages, where they are much easier to find with the right search engine. Before you know it, search engines are pointing to messages sent seven years ago. Archives that were relatively private in 1990 are suddenly popping up in search engine hit lists for the entire world to see. If it's digital, the potential for public distribution is unimaginable.

You need to consider whether the Internet's benefits outweigh the possible indignities of reduced privacy. For some people, the ability to communicate freely and openly on a global scale is well worth it. For others, any loss of privacy is an unsettling prospect.

Broadband Risks and Remedies

Anyone who spends a lot of time on the Internet over a telephone line would welcome a broadband connection such as cable modem or DSL. The difference in speed is significant and very visible to a Web surfer. However, broadband connections to the Internet introduce additional, invisible security risks that are not likely to be discussed in the ISP's promotional material. Cable modems are not just fast; they can also be left connected all the time without additional charges to the user. For people tired of waiting for dial-up connections whenever they want to get online, constant connectivity might sound very convenient. However, fast Internet connections are also more attractive to computer hackers, and connections that are active 24 hours a day are very desirable as platforms for remote-controlled operations.

Some Internet users don't worry about hackers and computer security. They assume that hackers and other perpetrators of cyberattacks would not be interested in them. However, hackers don't always break into systems simply

FYI: Distributed Denial-of-Service Attacks

In February 2000, **denial-of-service attacks** were aimed at large, highly visible Web sites for three days. Yahoo, Amazon.com, CNN, eBay, eTrade, and ZDNet were among the sites targeted. During the attacks, each site experienced crippling numbers of packet requests for a period of about three hours. Nothing was stolen, but users were largely shut out of these sites during the attacks due to overloaded servers (hence, "denial of service"). The attacks were accomplished by hackers doing nothing more than sending unusually large numbers of packets to the targeted servers. To avoid detection, the packets were sent from many zombie hosts that were called into action after the hackers installed appropriate remote control software on each zombie. The remote controls could have been installed via a Trojan horse months before the actual attack. Once enough zombies had been properly prepared to respond, one or more hackers could then mount a coordinated attack at any time by sending simultaneous commands to all the zombie computers. Any computer with a continuous high-speed connection to the Internet is a perfect candidate to be a zombie for a distributed denial-of-service attack.

to, say, steal credit card account numbers. Sometimes they break in to acquire a base from which to conduct illegal activities by turning your computer into a zombie under their control. This extra level of indirection affords the hacker some protection from the law. However, it can cause the innocent bystander significant grief if the FBI decides to seize his or her computer in order to secure evidence.

Hackers and Script Kiddies

Hackers

The general public has become accustomed to images of computer **hackers** created by Hollywood and fueled by the mainstream media. Kevin Mitnick has been portrayed as a brilliant arch villain, and 14-year-old kids who leave electronic graffiti on government Web sites are often portrayed as computer geniuses. Whereas all this might be fodder for exciting stories (remember how the media primed us for Y2K catastrophes?), the facts behind the stories are generally more mundane.

Once upon a time, students who loved computers did whatever it took to get a few hours alone with a coveted mainframe. Before 1970, most computers did not have time-sharing capabilities, so only one program could be run at a time. Time with the computer was highly prized. Hands-on learning began when the routine work of the day was done. This meant that the people who were most passionate about computers tended to be up late at night to get some time with the machine. Few schools taught computer programming, and no textbooks about computers existed. People who wanted to learn about computers had to study arcane technical manuals and pick up what they could from friends and contacts. There was no Internet to facilitate student-to-student communications, so computer geeks tended to cluster in favorable environments such as high-powered research universities. This is how the culture of the computer hacker was born.

Circa 1970, the term hacker described a self-taught expert who had extensive first-hand knowledge of one or two computers. Computers at the time were rather primitive, and programmers worked with low-level programming languages designed for a specific CPU and its particular instruction set. By today's standards, these computers were ludicrously limited by their minuscule amounts of memory and slothlike clock speeds. However, the drawbacks only made it all the more important for programmers to understand how to push a given machine to the limit. Tricks and secrets were shared over late-night snacks. Hackers tended to hang with their own, united by curiosity and a passion for computers. Being a hacker back then was not glamorous. Rather, a love for computers was nothing to brag about at a time when hippies were cool, the military-industrial complex was evil, and technology was something that a lot of young people were trying to live without (albeit not very successfully).

FYI: The First Personal Computers

The first personal computers were sold as kits for home hobbyists who had a background in electronics. In March 1974, the Scelbi Computer Consulting Company of Milford, Connecticut, started advertising the Scelbi, a computer built around the Intel 8008 microprocessor. The Scelbi came with 1KB of RAM and sold for $565. An additional 15K of memory was available for $2,760. The 8008 had a clock speed of 200 KHz.

In January 1975, *Popular Electronics* ran a cover story describing the Altair computer. The computer revolution was off and running. The Altair was the brainchild of a company named MITS (Micro Instrumentation Telemetry Systems), which was originally in the electronic calculator business. The Altair contained an Intel 8080 microprocessor and 256 bytes of RAM, all for just $400. It had to be assembled, however, and it came with no software, but it was a hit, in part because of the exposure it got in *Popular Electronics*.

It was a few more years before the concept of a personal computer sparked the public imagination. The political protest "Power to the People" (fade to a video clip of student demonstrators in the 1960s chanting with raised fists on high) took on a technological meaning a decade later. The year 1975 saw the beginning of the end of the monopoly of IBM mainframes. Computers became available to a rising proletariat class, and computer access was no longer restricted to the ruling class of Fortune 500 data processing departments.

In 1975, no commercial software was available for personal computers; computer owners were expected to write their own. The advent of the personal computer and the nascent hacker culture was a marriage made in heaven. With no commercial software market in sight, the task of writing software for the first personal computers fell into the able hands of hackers. Programs were freely shared, published in photocopied newsletters (the Internet was not a public resource at that time), and subjected to endless rounds of revisions by anyone who saw a way to contribute an improvement. This was the beginning of the "open source" software movement, which eventually produced the Linux OS. Professional programmers had "real" jobs working on "serious" computers. The evolution of the personal computer was left to a grassroots campaign consisting of students and random computer aficionados. Apple Computer grew out of this culture and maintains its countercultural David versus Goliath image even today.

The momentum of the growing personal computer industry began to bring new elements to the mix, and people began to look for ways to make money (enter Bill Gates). Hippie chic was on the wane, and maturing baby boomers decided that economic stability might not be such a bad thing after all. The hacker culture nevertheless thrived and preserved its traditional activities: tinkering, experimenting, and unconstrained inquiry. Primitive modems were added to personal computers in the 1980s, thereby prompting computer bulletin board systems (BBSs) to spring up in every major U.S. city.

Combine the anarchistic tendencies of phone phreaks (see *FYI: Phone Phreaks*) with the passionate dedication of hackers, and you have a cultural

FYI: The Origins of Commercial Software

Two young programmers, Paul Allen and Bill Gates, wrote a version of the BASIC programming language for the Altair computer. Paul Allen was subsequently given a job as the Director of Software for MITS (in charge of a department of one). Bill Gates, who had not yet dropped out of Harvard, worked for MITS part-time before moving on to found Microsoft in 1975.

FYI: Hacking Is a Felony

Under the Computer Fraud and Abuse Act, a hacker in the United States faces a max-imum penalty of 10 years in jail and a fine of $250,000, or in some cases, twice the dollar loss to the victim. But the Anti-Terrorism Act of 2001 expands these penalties for cyberterrorists, so that hackers who are prosecuted for acts of terrorism can now be sentenced to life in prison without parole.

heritage in which knowledge is power, open communication is a life force, and all authority must be questioned. Today's hackers are portrayed in the media as criminals who wreak havoc for fun or terrorists who are bent on under-mining national security. In fact, hackers come in various types and colors.

A *black-hat hacker* engages in criminal activities with no remorse or mis-givings. This type of hacker breaks into a computer and steals sensitive data

FYI: Phone Phreaks

When telephones first started to use touch-tone dialing in the 1960s, a new counter-cultural element surfaced in short order: they were the **phone phreaks** and they delighted in playing games with the telephone company. At that time, AT&T was a powerful monopoly and a politically attractive target for countercultural disdain. Ripping off the telephone company was both an act of civil disobedience and a protest against the Vietnam War (for this to make sense, you probably had to be there). Within this peculiar zeitgeist, a small but significant segment of the 1960s counterculture used plastic toy whistles and homemade "blue boxes" to trick AT&T's switching circuits into giving away free telephone calls. It was a political statement, it was radical, and it was harmless (big, faceless corporations were thought to be invincible).

The phone phreak ethos was based on a worldview that held that "the estab-lishment" was evil, people who worked within the establishment were robotic morons, and one's ability to get around the establishment was evidence of political commitment. Much about our world and the politics of disenfranchised youth has changed since the 1960s, but some things never seem to change. We still live in a predominantly anti-intellectual culture in which bright youngsters are frequently ostracized and too often spend their adolescent years feeling exceptionally angry, alienated, and isolated (see Figure 2.34). There will always be bright teenagers who take refuge in technological brave new worlds. They think that if you are not happy with your current world, it makes sense to position yourself on the brink of change and contribute to the next new thing, whatever that might be.

Figure 2.34

A hacker explains why

```
Written on January 8, 1986
=.-.=.-.=.-.=.-.=.-.=.-.=.-.=.-.=.-.=.-.=.-.=.-.=.-.=.-.=.-.=.-.=.-.=.-.=.-.=
```
Another one got caught today, it's all over the papers. "Teenager Arrested in Computer Crime Scandal," "Hacker Arrested after Bank Tampering"...

Damn kids. They're all alike.

But did you, in your three-piece psychology and 1950's technobrain, ever take a look behind the eyes of the hacker? Did you ever wonder what made him tick, what forces shaped him, what may have molded him?

I am a hacker, enter my world.... Mine is a world that begins with school.... I'm smarter than most of the other kids, this crap they teach us bores me....

Damn underachievers. They're all alike.

I'm in junior high or high school. I've listened to teachers explain for the fifteenth time how to reduce a fraction. I understand it. "No, Ms. Smith, I didn't show my work. I did it in my head...."

Damn kid. Probably copied it. They're all alike.

I made a discovery today. I found a computer. Wait a second, this is cool. It does what I want it to. If it makes a mistake, it's because I screwed it up. Not because it doesn't like me...,

Or feels threatened by me...

Or thinks I'm a smart ass...

Or doesn't like teaching and shouldn't be here...

Damn kid. All he does is play games. They're all alike.

And then it happened ... a door opened to a world ... rushing through the phone line like heroin through an addict's veins, an electronic pulse is sent out, a refuge from the day-to-day incompetencies is sought ... a board is found.

"This is it ... this is where I belong...."

I know everyone here ... even if I've never met them, never talked to them, may never hear from them again.... I know you all....

Damn kid. Tying up the phone line again. They're all alike....

You bet your ass we're all alike ... we've been spoon-fed baby food at school when we hungered for steak ... the bits of meat that you did let slip through were prechewed and tasteless. We've been dominated by sadists or ignored by the apathetic. The few that had something to teach found us willing pupils, but those few are like drops of water in the desert.

This is our world now ... the world of the electron and the switch, the beauty of the baud. We make use of a service already existing without paying for what could be dirt-cheap if it wasn't run by profiteering gluttons, and you call us criminals. We explore ... and you call us criminals. We seek after knowledge ... and you call us criminals. We exist without skin color, without nationality, without religious bias ... and you call us criminals. You build atomic bombs, you wage wars, you murder, cheat, and lie to us and try to make us believe it's for our own good, yet we're the criminals.

Yes, I am a criminal. My crime is that of curiosity. My crime is that of judging people by what they say and think, not what they look like. My crime is that of outsmarting you, something that you will never forgive me for.

I am a hacker, and this is my manifesto. You may stop this individual, but you can't stop us all ... after all, we're all alike.

+++The Mentor+++

and then often reports the theft to the violated party in an extortion attempt. An example is a 19-year-old Russian who demanded $100,000 from CD Universe in exchange for 30,000 stolen customer records. A *white-hat hacker* breaks into a computer only when invited to do so to identify security holes. Government laboratories started this tradition in the 1970s with the use of tiger teams. A *tiger team* is a group of white-hat hackers who are invited to do their worst and then discuss the outcome afterward. This practice is a respected and effective way to strengthen system security in the never-ending struggle to stay on top of what the black-hat hackers know. Finally, there are gray-hat hackers. A *gray-hat hacker* hacks only when provoked by some "great" social injustice. For example, a gray-hat hacker might cripple a Web server run by a hate group or an oppressive government or perform the periodic defacement of Web pages on .gov Web sites.

Script Kiddies

During the 1990s, a new breed of troublemaker developed, the **script kiddie**. Unlike the original hackers who cultivated knowledge and worked to understand as much as they could about CPUs and OSs, script kiddies are only superficially interested in computers. They are interested primarily in determining what they can get away with and who will be impressed. Most of the so-called 14-year-old computer geniuses are only script kiddies. Someone told them where to find a piece of software that can be used to crack passwords and another piece of software that can crash a remote host, and that's how the 14-year-olds crack passwords and crash systems.

Script kiddies can do a lot of seemingly impressive things with only a superficial knowledge of computers and no knowledge of computer programming. They share their knowledge, such as it is, much like other kids bargain for trading cards, rarely digging deep in order to understand the tools they

---

FYI: How Hard Is It to Attack Another Computer on the Internet?

How difficult it is to attack another computer on the Net depends on how much security is in place on the target host. UNIX hosts managed by computer professionals are relatively difficult to disrupt. Hosts running Windows, however, often are very vulnerable, most often when OS upgrades and software patches are not being installed to address known security problems. If a computer open to attack is connected to the Net, anyone on the Internet can send it a "hostile" packet that will cause it to crash. All you need is the IP address of the target host and the right program (which is easy to find on the Web once you know what to look for).

use. Like many adolescents, script kiddies enjoy the fact that they can create havoc for adults. They generally have no sense of the seriousness of the damage they inflict.

Anyone who knows how to download software can fire off hostile packets without understanding exactly what is happening and why it works. The user being attacked will know only that the computer crashed for some unknown reason (not an unusual event for Windows users). A casual user has no way to know that the system was shot down by a sniper somewhere on the Net.

From one perspective, computers and computer networks are property, and property owners have a right to protect their possessions. Unauthorized computer access and unauthorized network utilization are the electronic versions of breaking and entering. These computer crimes are punishable by law. Another perspective is that of an explorer on a quest for knowledge. From this perspective, computers and computer networks create a virtual space that begs to be explored and investigated, and a property owner who cannot protect his or her own property deserves the results because private property within this space should be protected by impenetrable boundaries. Computer security is a game of wits in which superior knowledge always wins.

If the Internet is a new frontier, the hackers are its cowboys. Some hackers are idealistic people who deeply distrust authority and are passionate defenders of freedom in cyberspace. Others are career criminals and terrorists driven by darker forces. On the one hand, anyone who gains unauthorized access to a computer is a criminal in the eyes of the law. On the other hand, Internet technology is forcing us to reexamine our legal system, our concept of ownership, and our ability to control valuable resources in a digital world. For better or for worse, hackers are forcing us to confront these uncharted territories and challenge our understanding of life in a digital world.

Problems and Exercises

A1. Why was David LaMacchia indicted for wire fraud in 1994 and what law was created in 1997 in response to the "LaMacchia Loophole"? What is illegal under this 1997 law?

A2. How does the Digital Millennium Copyright Act protect both ISPs and copyright holders when a copyright dispute targets material on a Web site? Explain the role of the DMCA agent.

A3. Name three corporations that are especially aggressive about protecting their trademarks from unauthorized use.

A4. What is a notice and consent policy?

A5. If you delete your cookie files, how will your browsing sessions be affected? Do you frequent any Web sites at which cookies are a welcome convenience? Describe one, and explain why you like the way the site uses cookies. What preference settings does your browser offer for cookie management?

A6. [TAKE A STAND] Many people are initially shocked and annoyed when they discover that their Web browser is storing information about them in files and delivering those files to Web servers on demand. How do you feel about the concept of cookies? Are they a fundamental invasion of personal privacy or a useful device for personalized services?

A7. [HANDS-ON] If you are running IE under Windows, change your general cookie policy setting to High and then spend some time browsing new Web sites. Do you see any problems with any of the Web pages? Visit a new e-store site and see if you can add an item to your shopping cart (you don't have to complete the transaction). If not, see if you can fine-tune your cookie settings to make the shopping cart work without lowering the High policy setting.

A8. [HANDS-ON] Find all the cookies on your hard drive. If you are running MSIE, begin by selecting Internet Options from the Tools menu. Then, on the General tab, click Settings and then click View Files. The folder that appears contains all your cookies. To see them easily use the Details option under the View menu and click on the Name header to sort all the files alphabetically. The cookie files all begin Cookie:default. How many cookies do you have? What is the oldest expiration date? (Scroll to the right if the Expires column is not visible.) One way to clean up your old cookies is by examining these files and deleting the ones with domains you don't recognize. You might remove a "good" cookie by accident, but this is certainly preferable to wiping the slate clean and starting again from scratch.

A9. Some information is technically free but nevertheless requires substantial time and know-how. How is the Internet changing the balance of relative privacy? Do you have to be active online to be affected by this change? Explain your answer.

A10. Explain how a denial-of-service attack works. Is it more advantageous to recruit "zombies" with fast Internet connections or 24/7 availability?

A11. Explain the difference between a script kiddie and a serious hacker. Is it possible to crack a password or crash a remote host without knowing anything about computer programming? Why do you think adult hackers like to recruit minors and encourage them to engage in hacking activities?

A12. [FIND IT ONLINE] If you have space on a Web server through your school or a commercial ISP, find out who is the DMCA agent responsible for materials posted on that server. How hard was it to identify this person?

A13. [FIND IT ONLINE] Conduct a search on the Internet for issues of the online newsletter *Phrack*. When was *Phrack* started, and how long did it run? Do you think the authors of *Phrack* were breaking the law by distributing the information they did? The First Amendment protects publishers from censorship by the government, but it does not protect publishers from lawsuits. Do you think anyone has a right to sue the publishers of *Phrack*? If so, on what grounds?

A14. [TAKE A STAND] In 2000 the RIAA sued mp3.com after mp3.com established an online service called BeamIt. BeamIt was a client/server service that allowed CD owners to "beam" their CDs to an mp3.com server for future access online. Anyone with a BeamIt account could then download their music from the Net at any time from any location, making it possible to hear an entire CD library at, say, work even if all the CDs were at home. The music tracks were never actually uploaded to the mp3.com server: they already had a large library of popular CDs on hand at the server's end. The process of beaming was just an examination of an audio CD in a CD-ROM player to determine which CD was being beamed. If the CD was one in the server's library, it was "beamed up" to the user's account and then made available to that user online. BeamIt accounts were password protected, so random people couldn't access the BeamIt library. Why do you suppose the RIAA didn't like BeamIt? Was there some obvious way for people to steal or "borrow" music that didn't belong to them using BeamIt? Do you think that people who legitimately own an audio CD should have the right to access that CD from an online library? Would you side with the RIAA or with mp3.com on the question of BeamIt?

A15. [TAKE A STAND] Script kiddies would not be able to operate if stronger actions were taken to stop the people who make tools for

stronger actions were taken to stop the people who make tools for hackers and distribute them freely. Pornography is not given to children even though it enjoys First Amendment protection. Why can't destructive software be treated the same way? That is, all "malware" could be tagged with an X rating and laws would prevent its distribution to minors. Explore this issue on the Net, and make a case for or against the concept of such X-rated software.

A16. **[TAKE A STAND]** People who want to protect their privacy online first have to educate themselves about things like cookies, spyware, and Web bugs, and then they have to spend time installing and tuning special software to combat these technologies (for example, cookie managers, Ad-aware, and Bugnosis). Do you think this much burden should be placed on members of the general public to defend their rights to privacy? How do you think privacy rights should be protected? Is this a problem best addressed by passing laws, or is this a problem best handled by technological counterstrikes (software designed to protect Internet users)?

A17. Name five kinds of information that a cookie can contain using information your browser routinely hands off to Web servers.

A18. If you allow the Web server foo23.little.com to place a cookie on your hard drive, will you be able to see what is stored inside the cookie? Who will be able to retrieve the contents of that cookie?

A19. In May 2000 a major security problem was discovered that affected all users of IE working on the Windows platform. Because of a problem with IE, cookies could be returned to Web servers outside the domains that created the cookies. You can read more about the problem at http://www.peacefire.org/security/iecookies/. Explain how this security hole could have been exploited by someone who wanted to steal a credit card account number.

A20. **[TAKE A STAND]** How do you feel about user profiling? Do consumers need to be protected by industry regulations or should people be responsible for protecting themselves? Research the Online Personal Privacy Act and find out why some privacy watchdogs are against this legislation. Do you think privacy rights are important to most people? Do privacy issues concern you?

E-Mail Management

3.1 Taking Charge

E-mail is here to stay, and a lot of people have a love-hate relationship with it. E-mail has become an indispensable tool for business communication and a speedy, inexpensive alternative to *snail mail* (physical mail). People of all ages use it to stay in touch with friends and relatives. Virtual communities blossom via e-mail, and virtual relationships transcend geography because of e-mail (see Chapter 4).

However, e-mail also has a dark side. As convenient as it is, it can still be time-consuming, and there is no escape from it if your workplace requires frequent e-mail contact. Indeed, e-mail has undermined the concept of "normal working hours" for those who check their workplace e-mail from home. A message that begs for an urgent reply might be difficult to set aside, no matter when you read it. Moreover, it is downright impossible to estimate how much time you'll need to deal with a pile of new e-mail. While 10 mail messages might look like something that should require no more than 15 minutes of your time, if just 1 of those messages compels you to investigate a URL or compose a thoughtful reply, those 15 minutes can easily expand into 30 minutes or more. This

Chapter Goals

- Become familiar with the basic operations of your e-mail client
- Understand the basic differences among the SMTP, HTTP, POP, and IMAP mail protocols
- Learn how the MIME protocol and HTML-enabled e-mail clients have changed e-mail
- Find out how to augment your primary e-mail service with a Web-based e-mail account
- Learn to use e-mail filters to save time and combat information overload

can mean the difference between a pot of boiling water and a very hot but empty pot that is beginning to crackle because you let all the water boil away. (I have ruined a lot of cookware because of e-mail.) It also can make you late for an appointment, a dinner date, or a class if you were silly enough to check your e-mail just before you had to go somewhere. If you are reading e-mail a few times a day, you might have noticed how your e-mail habit can rob you of those little blocks of time that you used to have for other things (taking a water cooler break, playing a quick game of fetch with the dog, or enjoying a quiet moment of contemplation). Everyone seems to feel pressed for time these days, and e-mail might be one reason why.

If you have just started to use e-mail and you are getting only 10 or 20 messages a week, you probably don't have much of an e-mail problem. The challenges mount with increasing numbers of e-mail in your mailbox. More and more people receive at least 100 messages a day, and that's when you really need to look at the amount of time you are spending with e-mail. You might not be at this level now, but there's a good chance you will join the "100 Club" sometime in the near future. Even if you are not yet flooded with e-mail, but you do need to check your e-mail once a day, you will find useful information in this chapter.

E-mail is a compelling siren that claims our time and can lure us away from lots of little things we used to do. It can become an addiction, especially when it masquerades as a work requirement or an enjoyable social activity. The activities we drop in order to accommodate an e-mail habit might not seem important enough to mourn. However, if a large number of these "unimportant" activities are abandoned with little or no thought, the long-term effects of an e-mail habit might creep up in unexpected ways. Many people who telecommute or augment their normal workday with "overtime" e-mail sessions begin to resent their work. When no clean division exists between working hours and personal time, the feeling of being constantly "on call" can be very stressful for some people (not to mention their families). The ubiquitous availability of e-mail access seems like a wonderful convenience at first, but it can result in "e-mail burnout" when people let the technology run them—instead of the other way around.

As compulsive behaviors go, an e-mail habit is relatively easy to modify and manage. If you want to spend less time on e-mail (or perhaps just more time on other things), it's really not that difficult. You just need to understand your options. This chapter describes time-saving software options, along with software tips to help you manage your e-mail more productively.

3.2 Basic E-Mail Client Operations

Before learning about e-mail management strategies, you need to understand the basic functions of an e-mail client. If you have been using e-mail for a year or more, you probably know everything in this section; simply skim the next few pages to make sure. If you are new to e-mail, this is the place to start. Read this section carefully, and do the e-mail checklist exercises to make sure you have these operations under control. Each e-mail client works a little differently, but all support the same basic e-mail operations. If you aren't sure how to do something with your specific e-mail client, browse the resources in the Where Can I Learn More? section later in this chapter to find tutorials and online help.

If you do consult a tutorial for your e-mail client, don't worry about all the preference settings right now. Many advanced features are available, but you don't have to understand them all at first. Your software comes preconfigured with default preference settings; these will be fine while you are learning.

3.2.1 Anatomy of an E-Mail Message

An e-mail message is very similar to an office memo, sharing the following characteristics:

- E-mail messages are usually fairly short.
- Each message usually addresses a single topic.
- Most messages rely on plain text (no graphics or fancy fonts), although this is changing.
- Messages are usually written in an informal style.
- Some messages are replies to previous messages.
- Messages can be sent to one person or to many people.
- Messages can be forwarded to many other people.
- E-mail is often timely.
- A reckless e-mail message might someday come back to haunt you.

Although these are typical features of e-mail messages, you can push the technology in different directions. You could send an entire book manuscript to someone via e-mail (although there are better ways, like ftp clients—see Section 6.7, to send large documents). You can send files through e-mail that are not text files (for example, photographs). You can also have an e-mail discussion with someone about all sorts of highly personal matters, despite the fact that e-mail is neither secure nor truly private. (See Chapter 8 to learn how encryption can make your e-mail private.)

Each e-mail message contains two parts:

- The header
- The message body

The header contains addressing information, such as who sent the message and who should receive it, the time the message was sent, and a subject line describing the content of the message. Figure 3.1 shows a short e-mail message.

The first four lines of the message are part of the header, and the rest is the message body. When you create an e-mail message, the mail program automatically fills in the From: and Date: fields of the header. You complete the To: and Subject: fields.

You must complete the To: field, but you can leave the Subject: field blank. You can even leave the message body empty and still have a legitimate e-mail message. However, if you don't fill in the To: field, your message will have no place to go.

When completing the To: field, you must specify an e-mail address. A valid **e-mail address** consists of a **user ID** and a **host address** separated by the @ character. If the address contains any typographical errors, your message

Figure 3.1

A typical e-mail message

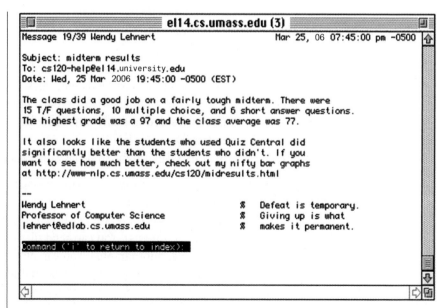

SHORTCUT: Shortcuts for E-Mail Addresses

If you send a lot of e-mail to the same person, most mail programs will let you refer to that person's full e-mail address by using a shortcut abbreviation, or a **nickname**. Check your mail client for an address book feature. When an e-mail address is very long or hard to remember, put it in your address book and assign a nickname for that entry. Then you need to remember only the nickname. Whenever you enter the nickname in a mail header, your mail client will automatically substitute the full e-mail address.

A system based on the first name followed by the last initial is easy to remember. If the names of two people overlap, you can always add the second letter from the last name to distinguish them. Whatever system you use, use it consistently. Nicknames can save you a lot of time, but only if you can get the address you need on the first try.

will usually be returned to you along with an error message. However, a typographical error might send your mail to a legitimate address—just not the one you intended. In that case, no error message will alert you. If the accidental recipient does not respond, you may never know that something went wrong. So be careful when you complete the To: field.

Here are some examples of valid e-mail addresses.

User ID	Host Address	E-Mail Address
ajones	apple.orchard.com	ajones@apple.orchard.com
deadbug	antfarm.net	deadbug@antfarm.net
kgranite	context.wccm.org	kgranite@context.wccm.org

If you don't know the address of the person you want to contact, you'll have to track it down. Many online directories can help you find e-mail addresses. You can take a guess, but only if you don't care that your mail might go to a wrong person. Some user IDs are not particularly formulaic. For example, if you know that Dave Brown is an AOL subscriber, you will have only the host address, aol.com. It would be impossible to guess a user ID like DRBMC986 or BossMan10.

Although you type in only a few header fields when you send e-mail, the header that your mail software uses is a bit more involved. Figure 3.1 showed only a short version of the full mail header. Figure 3.2 shows a full e-mail header.

The header in this message contains routing information and various time stamps that indicate when the message was received by different hosts

Figure 3.2

A full e-mail
header

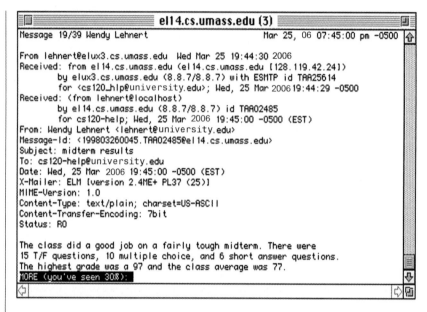

```
┌────────────────────────────────────────────────────────────────────┐
│ ▣ ▤▤▤▤▤▤▤▤▤▤▤ el14.cs.umass.edu (3) ▤▤▤▤▤▤▤▤▤▤▤ ⬜ │
├────────────────────────────────────────────────────────────────────┤
│ Message 19/39 Wendy Lehnert            Mar 25, 06 07:45:00 pm -0500 ⬆ │
│                                                                      │
│ From lehnert@elux3.cs.umass.edu  Wed Mar 25 19:44:30 2006            │
│ Received: from el14.cs.umass.edu (el14.cs.umass.edu [128.119.42.24]) │
│          by elux3.cs.umass.edu (8.8.7/8.8.7) with ESMTP id TAA25614  │
│          for <cs120_hlp@university.edu>; Wed, 25 Mar 2006 19:44:29 -0500│
│ Received: (from lehnert@localhost)                                   │
│          by el14.cs.umass.edu (8.8.7/8.8.7) id TAA02485             │
│          for cs120-help; Wed, 25 Mar 2006 19:45:00 -0500 (EST)      │
│ From: Wendy Lehnert <lehnert@university.edu>                         │
│ Message-Id: <199803260045.TAA02485@el14.cs.umass.edu>               │
│ Subject: midterm results                                            │
│ To: cs120-help@university.edu                                       │
│ Date: Wed, 25 Mar 2006 19:45:00 -0500 (EST)                         │
│ X-Mailer: ELM [version 2.4ME+ PL37 (25)]                            │
│ MIME-Version: 1.0                                                   │
│ Content-Type: text/plain; charset=US-ASCII                          │
│ Content-Transfer-Encoding: 7bit                                     │
│ Status: RO                                                          │
│                                                                      │
│ The class did a good job on a fairly tough midterm. There were      │
│ 15 T/F questions, 10 multiple choice, and 6 short answer questions. │
│ The highest grade was a 97 and the class average was 77.            │
│ MORE (you've seen 30%):                                             │
│ ◁                                                              ▷ ▣ │
└────────────────────────────────────────────────────────────────────┘
```

along the route from your machine to the recipient's (note the different Received: fields). Most users don't need to see this information, so most mailers hide it. However, it should always be available on request because sometimes the full version is useful.

Each e-mail message you receive is stored in a plain text file. The full header appears at the top of the file, and the message body follows. Your mail program is responsible for scanning this file and deciding how much of it you probably want to see. Don't confuse a mail message with the way the mail

SHORTCUT: How to Create a Distribution List

If you send e-mail to the same group of people regularly (for example, all members of the same committee), you can use the address book feature to create a mail distribution list. To do this, follow these steps.

1. Create a new address book entry.
2. Enter the list of e-mail addresses, separated by blanks or commas.
3. Give the list a nickname.
4. Use the nickname as you would any other address book entry.

A distribution list will save you from a lot of tedious typing and possible typographical errors.

message is being displayed. There might be more to your mail than meets the eye.

Other address fields are available to use when you send an e-mail message. The most commonly used optional field is Cc: (carbon copy). When you put an e-mail address in this field, a copy of your message is sent to that person. Some people always Cc: themselves so they can have copies of all the messages they send. This is called a *self-Cc:*. Some mailers give you a switch you can set to make self-Cc: copies automatically. If a message is intended primarily for one person but would also be useful to other people, use the Cc: field for the other addresses. However, if your message is intended for more than one person, all of whom are equally important as recipients, put their addresses in the To: field.

The Bcc: field is similar to Cc: but is a *blind* carbon copy. When you include an address in this field, the message is sent to that recipient, but that recipient's address is not visible in the header received by other recipients. Use Bcc: when you want to preserve someone's privacy or not broadcast their e-mail address.

3.2.2 What to Expect from Your E-Mail Client

Many different **e-mail clients** (aka *mailers*) are available, and their operations and features are all quite similar. Once you've seen one mail client, you'll know what to expect from another. This means that you don't have to worry too much about which mailer to adopt. Moreover, if you ever need to switch mail clients, you won't have to learn how to work with the new one from scratch. A few basic commands are enough to make you operational. If you're accustomed to some special features in your former mailer, you should be able to find equivalent features in your new mailer.

All mailers will enable you to:

- Send a message that you have written to yourself
- Read any message that has been sent to you
- Reply to any message that has been sent to you
- Forward a message to a third party
- Save or delete messages sent to you
- Scan the Subject: and From: fields of all your new mail

A good e-mail client also supports other features, such as:

- The ability to sort mail and save it in different locations
- The ability to tag unread mail messages for easy identification

- An address book to hold frequently used e-mail addresses
- A reply option that allows you to edit the original message
- A customizable mail filter that sorts and routes incoming mail
- The ability to include a signature automatically

If you're working on a Windows-based personal computer or a Mac and have Internet access through an ISP or university, the Eudora mail program is a popular option. It includes many advanced features and has an intuitive interface. However, you also can manage your mail with the mail clients bundled with the Opera, Mozilla, and IE Web browsers. The mail client that comes with IE is called Outlook Express.

A good mail program will give you the most commonly used commands in convenient toolbar buttons and pull-down menus. In addition, good mailers make it easy to find information under the Help menu in case you can't remember all the details of their operation.

3.2.3 Viewing Your Inbox

Typically the first thing people do when they open their mailers is to check for new mail. New mail waits for you in your inbox and piles up until you do something with it. The **inbox** is very much like a mailbox, and many mailers take you directly to the inbox at startup. Others might require you to load the inbox in order to see your new mail.

The inbox displays a list of mail messages, with a single descriptive line for each mail message. This line displays the Subject: and From: fields so you can see what each message is about and who sent it to you. Most inboxes also show the message's date of arrival. Figure 3.3 shows the inbox for Microsoft Outlook Express, with a list of message headers in the top half of the display window and a selected message body (aka a *preview*) in the bottom half.

Each message in the inbox display is given a header line that indicates the following information:

- The subject header for the message
- Whether the user has marked the message for deletion
- Whether the message has been read
- The name of the author
- The date received

In most inbox displays, a message listed without an icon or marker next to it usually means that the message has been read. All the messages in Figure

Figure 3.3

Outlook Express' inbox and preview pane

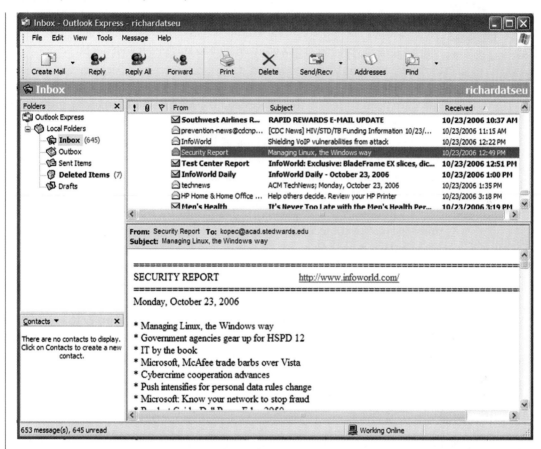

TIP: Which Mailer?

If spelling is a challenge for you, look for a mailer with a spelling checker. If you expect to handle a lot of e-mail, look for a mailer that offers automated filtering and routing. For some users, a single crucial feature might be enough to decide which mailer to use. For example, most modern mailers recognize URLs inside mail message bodies. If someone sends a URL in a mail message, the mailer will recognize it as a hyperlink, underline it in the display, and make it an operational hot link that you can click if you want to visit the Web page right then. For people who get a lot of Web pointers in their mail, this might be the most wonderful feature in the world. For others, it might not matter. Only you can decide what features are important to you.

TIP: Warning—Does Your Inbox Have a Quota?

If you use a university account for your e-mail, it probably has an inbox quota. If you exceed this quota, any new incoming messages may be lost (without any warnings going back to the authors of the lost messages). Find out what your quota is and make sure you visit your inbox often enough to stay under your quota.

3.3 have been sorted by their dates and times. You can change the preference setting if you prefer to have messages sorted by another criterion, such as the senders' names, the subject headers, or the lengths of the messages. A subject header or a sender's name that is too long is truncated (shortened) in the display; however, you can resize these fields within the fixed dimensions of the message header display window to show more information. Keep space limitations in mind when you write your own subject headers. If you give a mail message a long subject header, only the first few words may be visible in the recipient's inbox display.

The sender's entry may show either the return e-mail address of the sender or the actual name of the sender. Whenever you send mail, your From: field is filled with both your e-mail address and an *alias* (an alternative identifier) for yourself. Most mail programs give you an opportunity to enter your full name in one of your configuration or preference settings. Whatever you enter becomes your e-mail alias, which will be added automatically to the From: field (along with your return address) whenever you send mail. Other

TIP: What's Your Name?

Use your real name when you configure your mail client. People who use obviously fictitious names to hide their identities give the impression of being 12 years old. People who use believable names that are not theirs will look like crooks to ISP administrators if questionable activities are detected. People cast first impressions on the Internet, just as in real life. Make sure yours is a good one.

CHECKLIST: E-Mail Checklist 1

Study your mailer's documentation to be sure you know how to do the following.

1. View your inbox and identify all your new mail.
2. Distinguish read messages from unread messages.
3. Navigate multiple pages in a large inbox (both forward and backward).

mail programs that receive your mail often display aliases in addition to or in place of e-mail addresses. You can specify any alias you want, but most people use their real names.

Sometimes your inbox contains more messages than your screen can display in one window. In that case, you can scroll to the next block of messages and move back and forth across different segments of your inbox. Be sure to view all the headers in your inbox so you can see everything that's in there.

3.2.4 Viewing Individual E-Mail Messages

When you view your inbox, you see only a short header for each mail message. To see the body of a message, click the message header to open the message. You'll then see a screen display that contains an abbreviated version of the full message header followed by the message body. A very long message body won't fit in a single screen display. However, you can navigate both forward and backward by using the vertical scroll bar on the right border of the window. Some mailers let you use keyboard commands for navigation (for example, the Spacebar scrolls messages down in Outlook and Outlook Express).

All mailers offer many options you can set, along with many advanced commands you might find useful. Start by learning the settings and commands you need to complete the e-mail checklists in this chapter. Whenever you need to learn a new command, use your Help menu selection.

3.2.5 Sending a New E-Mail Message

All mailers have a command that puts you in a mode for creating and sending a mail message. Look for a New Message command in a pull-down menu or a special "new message" icon on a toolbar. Once in that mode, you enter information in the To: field, the Subject: field, and, optionally, the Cc: field. The mailer will fill in the From: field automatically. You will probably be given a

CHECKLIST: E-Mail Checklist 2

Study your mailer's documentation to be sure you know how to do the following.

1. Select a specific message in your inbox.
2. Open a single mail message in order to view its message body.
3. Page forward and backward through a long message body.
4. Exit a mail message display and return to the inbox.
5. Display the long version of a message header.

TIP: What Can You Send?

Some mailers can display text in different fonts or with special effects such as color. Outlook and Outlook Express make it easy to create messages with these features. When composing a new message, you can use the toolbar that appears in the new message window offering access to such text effects as boldface, colors, italics, and indented lists.

You also can create hyperlinks or insert graphics from files. Some mailers, such as Outlook and Outlook Express, can do this in a message body and even create operational hyperlinks. This makes the message body resemble a Web page. A mailer that can do this is called an *HTML-enabled mail client*. HTML-enabled mail is fun when you want to send someone a colorful greeting or a photograph. Just be aware that the person receiving your mail may not be using an HTML-enabled mail client; in that case, all the graphics and special text effects will be lost. Many people choose for various reasons to use mailers that are not HTML-enabled. Most e-mail clients are HTML-enabled by default.

window display where you can enter all the necessary information by clicking the field you want to complete. If you don't want to put something in a given field, press the ⌈Return⌉ or ⌈Enter⌉ key to leave it blank. Remember, the only field that you must complete is the To: field, but it is normally poor netiquette (see Section 3.4) to leave the subject body empty. If you're new to sending messages, you can experiment by sending a message to yourself. Simply put your own user ID in the To: field, and the mail will be sent to you.

In most mailers, a blank window is reserved for the message body. Type the text for your message body, then review it to be sure it says what you think it says. All mailers are designed to make the most basic operations highly intuitive, so editing an e-mail message isn't likely to require much beyond the most basic editing commands. If you have a spell checker, use it (especially if you are a poor speller). When you're satisfied with your message, click the Send button. As a rule, you should limit the text in your message body to 50KB (which is roughly 10 times more text than most people want to see in a mail message anyway). Some mail servers reject mail messages that are too large.

TIP: Do You Have a Sent Mail Folder?

Some mailers automatically save copies of all outgoing mail to a Sent Mail (or Sent Items) Folder. Check to see if you have such a folder. This is a useful feature, but the messages do pile up and you will want to clean out the oldest ones from time to time.

SHORTCUT: Outlook and Outlook Express Support Keyboard Shortcuts

Open a message	`Ctrl` + `Shift` + `M`
Open the address book	`Ctrl` + `Shift` + `B`
Open an appointment	`Ctrl` + `Shift` + `A`
Open a contact	`Ctrl` + `Shift` + `C`
Open a meeting request	`Ctrl` + `Shift` + `Q`
Open a task	`Ctrl` + `Shift` + `K`
Make the Find a Contact box active	`F11`
Open the inbox	`Ctrl` + `Shift` + `I`
Open the outbox	`Ctrl` + `Shift` + `O`
Check for new mail	`F5` or `Ctrl` + `M`
Open the Advanced Find box	`Ctrl` + `Shift` + `F`
Mark as read	`Ctrl` + `Q`
Delete	`Ctrl` + `D`
Delete word	`Ctrl` + `Backspace`
Select all	`Ctrl` + `A`
Copy	`Ctrl` + `C`
Paste	`Ctrl` + `V`
Undo	`Ctrl` + `Z`
Print	`Ctrl` + `P`
Scroll down the message preview	`Spacebar`
Jump to the top of the message preview	`Shift` + `Spacebar`
Move to the next message	`↓`
Move to the previous message	`↑`

All mailers also allow you to scrap the message if you decide you don't want to send it. Simply close the window that contains your message without saving or sending it.

3.2.6 Using Signatures

Another time-saver is the **signature file** (aka **sig file**). People who send a lot of e-mail often append a signature file to the end of the message body. A sig file identifies the sender in some way. It personalizes your e-mail and saves you the tedious task of retyping the same identifying lines for each message. For business communications, it should contain your name, title, organization, mailing address, telephone number, fax number, and e-mail address. For casual e-mail, it could include a name and e-mail address, with perhaps a favorite quotation to add a little personality to an e-mail message. Figure 3.4 shows some sig files I have used.

Some mailers automatically add your sig file to the end of your message body, whereas others add it only on command. You might or might not be able to see your sig file at the end of your outgoing mail message. If you can't, that doesn't mean it isn't being included in your outgoing messages (send yourself a test message to see). Some mailers also let you set up and select from multiple sig files to convey different online personas. You might want to use a straightforward signature until you've been online for a while and have seen a lot of different signatures.

Some people will see your signature repeatedly. An unobtrusive sig file wears well after repeated exposures. Extremely lengthy signatures become annoying after a few encounters. Generally, keep your sig file to no more than four lines. By using all the available horizontal space, you can pack a lot of information into those four lines.

Figure 3.4

Sample signature files

```
| Prof. Wendy Lehnert          Office hours: Mon. 11-12 and Wed 2:30-3:30
| lehnert@elux3.cs.umass.edu   LGRC A327 (the lowrise)
| (413) 545-3639               http://www-edlab.cs.umass.edu/cs120/
| ICQ #4909018                 http://www-nlp.cs.umass.edu/aw/home.html



| Prof. Wendy Lehnert     Get my public PGP key from:                     |
| lehnert@cs.umass.edu    http://pgp5.ai.mit.edu/pks-commands-beta.html   |



--
Wendy Lehnert                    %
Professor of Computer Science    %   "640K ought to be enough for anybody."
University of Massachusetts      %
lehnert@edlab.cs.umass.edu       %                        -Bill Gates, 1981



        Wendy Lehnert, dachshund owner and member of the world famous
                    Dachshund Underground Railroad
                    ( - We Go The Extra Lengths - )
           http://www.geocities.com/Heartland/Prairie/5370/index.html
```

TIP: Message Body Dos and Don'ts

Beginners often make some common mistakes regarding their e-mail. Because you're reading this book, you can avoid the most common newbie errors:

- Avoid inserting carriage returns into your message body. If you must insert them, limit the width of each line to no more than 72 characters—but 65 characters is better. (See the Above & Beyond section on raggy text for more details.)
- Keep your sig file short and sweet: use no more than four lines.
- Always include a signature in the message body that contains your full name and return e-mail address.
- Reread the complete message body before sending your mail. Be sure that it says what you think it says, and correct any errors. Careless errors can be embarrassing, especially if the message goes to many people. Be extra careful when people are relying on you for accurate information.

3.2.7 Importing Text into Messages

Importing text from an existing file into an e-mail message body is often useful. If the text fragment is small, you can easily insert it into your message body by using copy-and-paste techniques (but see the Above & Beyond section for a discussion of raggy text that can result from this operation). Text insertion comes in handy when you want to set up stock replies to frequently encountered requests or situations. You essentially create a form letter in a file and then when you need to send it to someone, you insert it into your message body, change it here and there as needed, and you're done. Form letters are most often needed in work environments, but you might find them useful for certain casual communication as well.

3.2.8 The Importance of Good Writing

Practice sending e-mail to a friend until you feel comfortable and confident about your mailer. Once you have the hang of it, the mechanics of sending e-mail will be second nature and you can concentrate on content.

Be aware that on the Internet, you are what you type. A message filled with misspelled words and ungrammatical sentences does not reflect well on the sender. The quality of your writing is particularly important when you're writing to people who have no other contact with you. Some people take creative liberties with e-mail, devising their own quirky writing styles. While this

CHECKLIST: E-Mail Checklist 3

Study your mailer's documentation to be sure you know how to do the following.

1. Set up an address book entry with a nickname for someone.
2. Begin a new message.
3. Enter information in the message header and the message body.
4. Change the message header and message body as needed.
5. Cancel a message before you send it.
6. Run the spell checker (if the mailer offers one).
7. Set up a sig file (if your mailer supports that feature).
8. Insert text from a file into a message body.
9. Send a message after you've completed the message body.

might be appropriate in some contexts, it will not be appreciated in the business world. Think about who you're writing to, how busy that person is, how well you know that person, and the point of your message. Each message you send takes time to read. Try not to waste anyone's time. Think carefully about what you write. We'll cover more rules of e-mail netiquette in Section 3.4.

3.2.9 Replying to and Forwarding E-Mail Messages

Many e-mail conversations begin when someone replies to a message. By using the Reply command, you can conduct one-on-one discussions in a series of replies to previous messages, as well as conversations involving a large group of people.

Before replying to anyone, first be sure that you understand the difference between two variations on the Reply command: the **sender-only reply** and the **group reply** (sometimes called **reply-to-all**). In the first case, your message is sent only to the original author of the current message. In the second case, your message is sent to the original author as well as everyone the author included in the To: and Cc: fields. The first type of reply is private; the second type might be very public. Sometimes you will want to use a group reply, but you'll probably use the sender-only reply most of the time.

One of the most helpful features of mailers is the inclusion of the original mail message in the reply message body. All the better mailers give you the option of either including in your message body the original message to which you are replying or starting from scratch with an empty message body.

If you include the original message in your reply, you don't have to preserve it all. You can keep only the parts you need to make your reply coherent. Just use your editor to delete anything that doesn't need to be seen again. This courtesy is greatly appreciated if your reply is going to many people who have already seen the original. No one wants to scroll through a long message they've already read.

Each mailer uses a convention for distinguishing the text of an original message from the text you add in the reply. Indentations and special characters such as the ">" character are often used (see Figure 3.5).

A reply to a reply shows two levels of indentation, a reply to that shows three levels, and so on. You can make a dialog more readable by using blank lines to separate different speakers. Use your editor freely.

When you reply to a message, your mailer may or may not include your sig file automatically. Your mailer might have a preference setting to control this default. If all your e-mail replies go to people who already know you, it makes sense to forgo a sig file; friends and colleagues don't need to see your signature repeatedly. In addition, many people who have been using e-mail since its beginning tend not to use sig files because they grew up in an e-mail culture in which messages were never sent to strangers. Sig files make more sense when your mail is going to people who don't know you.

Figure 3.5

An e-mail reply with an indented original message

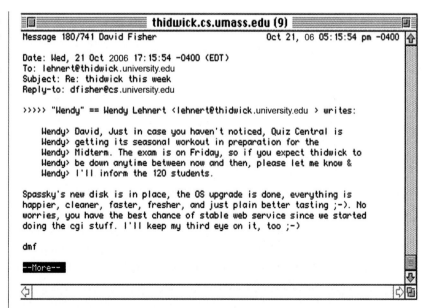

TIP: E-Mail Reply Dos and Don'ts

Here are some more mistakes that beginners make that are easy to avoid:

- Know the difference between the sender-only reply and the group reply. If you use the group reply for a message intended for the original sender only, you might embarrass yourself by broadcasting something unintentionally.

- If you get into a lengthy dialog with someone, take the time to replace the subject in the Subject: field with a new subject when the original no longer describes the topic of your conversation. It's easy to keep the original subject throughout, but after a lengthy exchange, your mailbox will contain many messages that have the same subject. If you ever need to return to one of these messages, you won't know where to look.

- If you find yourself responding emotionally to a piece of e-mail, cool off a bit before replying, especially if you feel angry. Although your feelings might be justified, take some time to think about what you want to say before responding.

- Be selective when you include text from the original message in your reply. Don't duplicate the original message in its entirety unless it is absolutely necessary. However, do include enough content so your reply will make sense to someone who can't remember the message that preceded yours.

Forwarding e-mail is like replying to e-mail, except that you send the message to a third party. Most mailers will let you edit the message body when you forward a message, a useful feature when you want to insert your own comments or remove a more personal portion of the original message. You can forward anything to anyone; however, be aware that you might be dealing with sensitive information or information given to you in confidence. Betraying a confidence can hurt someone who trusted you, as well as make you look untrustworthy. Just because a program makes something easy to do doesn't necessarily make doing it a good idea.

CHECKLIST: E-Mail Checklist 4

Study your mailer's documentation to be sure you know how to do the following.

1. Send a reply only to the original author of the current message.
2. Send a group reply to everyone associated with the current message.
3. Include the text of the current message in your reply.
4. Reply by using a blank message body (no old text included).
5. Change the subject header for your reply.
6. Forward a message to a third party with or without your comments.

MIME Attachments and HTML-Enabled Mailers

Once upon a time all mailers expected to see plain ASCII text in their message bodies, and life was simple. No one had to worry about e-mail viruses (although some bogus virus warnings tried to convince the uninitiated otherwise), and no one had to spend much time beautifying their messages, because there's only so much that can be done with plain ASCII text. However, people are rarely happy with what they have, and so it was with e-mail. Why be limited to plain ASCII text? Wouldn't it be nice to be able to send binary files?

For a long time, users got around the text-only message body constraint by converting binary files into ASCII-encoded binary files (see the Above & Beyond section). These converted files could then be inserted into plain ASCII text message bodies and sent via e-mail. Mailers needed to make no changes to handle these files, although extra work was required to encode the file before sending it and to decode it after receipt. It worked well enough, but it was a little clumsy.

As more people began using e-mail, demand grew for more sophisticated e-mail programs. E-mail software programmers decided to make the software smarter about handling binary files by having it do all the encoding and decoding automatically. The process wasn't that difficult to automate, and it would save everyone a lot of time. But to do this, a new protocol was needed.

3.3.1 The MIME Protocol

To transfer binary files via e-mail, a special mail protocol was created in 1991: the **Multipurpose Internet Mail Extension** (**MIME**). Today, the MIME protocol is a globally recognized standard. If you have ever sent or received an **e-mail attachment**, you have used MIME. Thanks to MIME, modern mailers now make sending any file as a mail attachment easy to do. You either click a toolbar button for adding an attachment (often marked by a paper-clip icon) or select an "add attachment" command in a pull-down menu. Then you use a dialog box to navigate your way to the local file you want to include as an attachment, select the file, and return to your message (see Figure 3.6). You can add more than one attachment to a single message, and you can include a file in any file format.

Figure 3.6

Including a file in
a message as a
MIME attachment

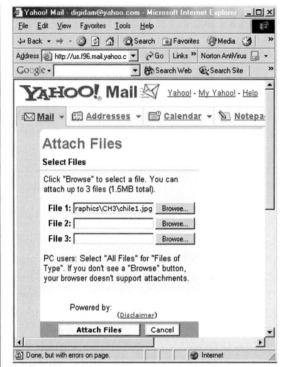

Reproduced with permission of Yahoo! Inc. © 2006 by Yahoo! Inc.
YAHOO! and the YAHOO! logo are trademarks of Yahoo! Inc.

MIME is clearly an improvement over the old way of doing e-mail, although new users need to be aware of possible dangers whenever they receive an e-mail attachment (see Section 2.6).

3.3.2 HTML-Enabled Mailers

Soon after MIME was created, the Internet began to attract the general public. Commercial software vendors saw an opportunity to make the Internet as user-friendly as possible, and e-mail was one popular application in which improvements could be made. The result was the HTML-enabled mailer. Suppose you want to send a hyperlink to someone. If you send it in a plain ASCII text message body, the recipient will have to copy and paste it into a browser window. Sending a clickable hyperlink would be better. Then the recipient only needs to click the link in order to go automatically to the referenced Web page. Embedded hyperlinks inside a message body are fast, convenient, and easy to understand.

TIP: Before You Send That Attachment, Read This!

As explained in Section 2.6, people receiving e-mail attachments must protect themselves from e-mail viruses. You should never send an e-mail attachment unnecessarily. There is almost always some way around sending e-mail attachments. An attachment that is a plain text file can be inserted directly into the message body by using copy-and-paste techniques. You can save a Word file in RTF format and then copy and paste the resulting text into the message body. Instead of sending photographs as attachments, you can post them on a Web site for public photo albums and send your friends the URL pointing to your album.

However, if you absolutely must send an attachment, be careful to include some personal information in the message body so your recipient will know the message really is from you (rather than some devious e-mail worm that appropriated your mailer after infecting your computer). Always identify the attachment by name, format, and file size. Also avoid attaching very large files (greater than 500KB–1MB) unless you have cleared the transfer with your recipient beforehand. People who must manage their mail over a phone line are slowed down waiting for large attachments to download. Also note that some mail servers reject attachments that are too large: The size limits vary depending on the server, but a limit of 2MB per file is very generous.

The first HTML-enabled mailers were programmed to recognize URLs and render them as clickable hyperlinks, as they would be on a Web page. Navigator's mailer sent its URLs to Navigator, and Microsoft's mailer sent its links to Explorer. A few independent mailers (for example, Eudora) let the user decide which browser to use in a preference setting.

Clickable hyperlinks were only the first step. If a mailer could recognize a URL, why not have it render entire Web pages like a Web browser would? Web pages are simply ASCII text files, so a Web page could be sent as an e-mail message body without any alterations to existing mail protocols. All that was needed were mailers that could make message bodies look like Web pages. Then e-mail could be as flashy and as much fun as a Web page (see Figure 3.7).

Of course, most people don't want to have to author Web pages in order to send a simple e-mail message to a friend. Moreover, for most people, plain old ASCII text is perfectly adequate. However, advertisers were quick to jump on the idea of HTML-enabled e-mail. This new form of e-mail meant the difference between sending out a black-and-white typed paragraph and sending out a slick color brochure. In addition, Web-based e-mail and free e-mail services on the Web had begun to catch on. If you're already using your Web

Figure 3.7

HTML-enabled mail messages look like Web pages.

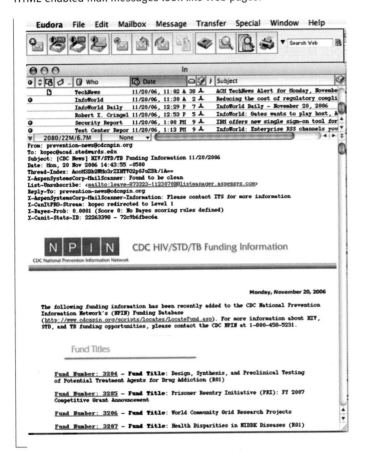

browser to read mail on the Web, why not see some mail that looks like it belongs on the Web? Users who simply want to send a picture to a friend need not create an HTML file or post the picture on a Web server. They can just send the picture as a MIME attachment and trust the receiving mailer to handle the attachment appropriately. Because of the prevalence of infected attachments, some Web-based e-mail accounts (see Section 3.8) will ask the user what to do with the attachment before it's actually downloaded. Others will display the image in the body of the message. The Eudora mail client displays the image in the body of the message (see Figure 3.8).

HTML-enabled mailers do entail some risk. Some mailers run executable scripts in order to render HTML-enhanced mail messages more effectively.

Figure 3.8

Web-based mail
displaying a
graphical MIME
attachment

Richard Kopec, 10/27/06 10:36 AM -0500, New pictures

New pictures

Date: Fri, 27 Oct 2006 10:36:44 -0500
To: kopec@stedwards.edu
From: Richard Kopec <kopec@stedwards.edu>
Subject: New pictures
X-CanItPRO-Stream: kopec redirected to Level 1

Hi there!

The new pics are attached!

Richard
--
Richard L. Kopec, Ph.D.
Professor, Computer Science & Chemistry

http://faculty.stedwards.edu/kopec

08-26-06_1517.jpg

TIP: Can I Protect Myself from Malicious E-Mail Scripts?

If you use Outlook or Outlook Express and you are worried about scripting viruses, you can turn off the Windows Scripting Host option and you will be safe. It is also a good idea to install any security patches released by the software manufacturers of your Internet applications. Most security breaches could be avoided if everyone kept their software up-to-date in order to prevent known problems. You can visit the Microsoft Download Center (www.microsoft.com/downloads/) to find all the available security patches for Microsoft products. Always go back to the original manufacturer's site for any software upgrades, updates, or patches. And, of course, there's always the anti-virus software you've installed on your computer. It should be configured to review all incoming mail.

This in turn enables a new breed of e-mail virus based on malicious scripts embedded in e-mail messages. The BubbleBoy virus, which surfaced in 1999, was the first scripting virus. It attacked Outlook and Outlook Express users and was more theoretical than real. BubbleBoy nonetheless demonstrated that these two particular mail clients could be tricked into running malicious code even when it was reading only a plain-text message body. Microsoft solved the BubbleBoy problem by releasing a software patch for that particular type of attack. However, there is always a possibility of new scripting viruses, and users of Outlook and Outlook Express should be careful to install critical security patches from the Microsoft Update Center as they become available (see Section 2.6).

 # E-Mail Netiquette and Netspeak

Good e-mail etiquette, or **netiquette**, is all about respect. Good netiquette shows respect for people whom you don't know and might never get to know all that well despite long-standing, online conversations. This is especially important because the Internet encourages interactive communication between strangers on such a grand scale. We have never experienced such a global range in other public forums, where the reality of physical distance limits our reach and binds us to geographically limited communities.

Whenever you send e-mail, remember the following netiquette guidelines:

- Keep your messages short and to the point.
- Watch your grammar and spelling.
- Be careful with humor; avoid sarcasm.
- Use uppercase words sparingly. UPPERCASE TEXT YELLS AT THE RECIPIENT.
- Never leave the Subject: field blank.
- Include your name and e-mail address in the message body (for example, in your sig file).

If you are new to e-mail, you have probably not experienced its mixed blessings. Some people deal with 100 or more e-mail messages every day. They are understandably annoyed by any message that wastes their time, especially if the person writing the message doesn't use good netiquette. Online conversations are not the same as face-to-face or even telephone conversations. When you talk online, no body language cues or vocal intonations are available to help the recipient interpret your message. If you are inexperienced with online dialogs, you might not realize how important and useful all this "unspoken" communication is. For example, much well-intentioned humor falls flat on the Internet. Or worse, such humor may be completely misinterpreted and end up making someone feel hurt or angry. If you're in the habit of speaking sarcastically, temper that tendency until you have a good feel for how your written words come across to people. What you intend is not always what others perceive.

3.4.1 Emoticons

Some people express themselves by using **emoticons**—combinations of keyboard characters that represent emotions. The most commonly seen emoticon is the **smiley**, shown as :-) or ☺. A smiley might seem unnecessarily cutesy and perhaps a little annoying :-(if you aren't used to it, but it can be useful :-o. A smiley explicitly tells the reader when something is being said in jest or when something shouldn't be taken seriously <grin>.

Messages with smileys are written by people who want to ensure that no one misunderstands :-{ the spirit of their words. I don't think I've ever seen someone take offense >:-(at a statement punctuated by a smiley. It's the equivalent of a smile and a wink ;-) or a friendly laugh accompanied by a pat on the back. It works well among people who don't know each other well :-}. In general, emoticons allow people to insert some personality {ll:-) into their writing without fear =:-o of being misinterpreted. See Table 3.1 for a list of commonly used emoticons and the emotions they convey.

Table 3.1

Common emoticons

Emotion	Character Representation	Graphical Representation
Happy, satisfied, joking	☺	☺
Winking, exaggerating	;-)	
Sad, unsatisfied	:-(	☹
Crying	:'-(	
Confused	%-(	
Apathetic	:-l	☺
Shocked, unbelieving	:-o	
Ohmigosh!	8-o	

3.4.2 Flames and Flame Wars

If you find yourself in an emotional exchange, it's best to cool down before responding. An angry e-mail message is called a **flame**, and people who write them are flaming (see Section 2.11). Flaming is not polite, and if you ever get flamed, you might feel hurt or downright abused. The Internet seems to encourage some people to indulge their pent-up rage by subjecting innocent bystanders to verbal abuse. Two people trading flames are engaged in a *flame war*. This behavior seems to be peculiar to the Internet; it probably wouldn't occur in a face-to-face interaction.

Flames can be contagious. Emotional heat has a way of generating more heat, unless someone is willing to cool off and break the cycle. If a message angers you, wait awhile before responding. You might have misinterpreted what was written, and a flame war usually isn't worth the elevated blood pressure. Sometimes the best reply is no reply. If you care about good working relationships, you can't be too careful with your online communications. If you're angry or upset about something involving a friend or coworker, deal with it face-to-face. E-mail is not a suitable medium for everything.

 # SMTP and Mail Servers

The client-server software model discussed in Section 1.7 is also the foundation for all e-mail service. The mailer that you use to read and send e-mail is an e-mail client that depends on an **e-mail server** each time you launch it to read or send mail. In fact, it depends on two separate servers: one to send outgoing mail and one to read incoming mail. If one host machine is responsible for mail going in both directions, one piece of software handles the outgoing mail and different software handles the incoming mail. Thus e-mail involves two separate programs, depending on the direction in which the mail is headed.

When you install and configure a new mailer, you need to know the names of the servers responsible for outgoing mail and incoming mail. Whether you configure your client with a setup wizard or do it yourself with preference settings, you will need to know the names of your outgoing and incoming mail servers. Figure 3.9 shows the preference settings for an Outlook Express mail account. This pop-up window is found by going to the Tools menu, selecting Accounts, and looking for the Properties of a specific mail account. You can find all server information by clicking on the Servers tab. If you are managing your mail through a commercial ISP, you should be

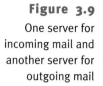

Figure 3.9

One server for incoming mail and another server for outgoing mail

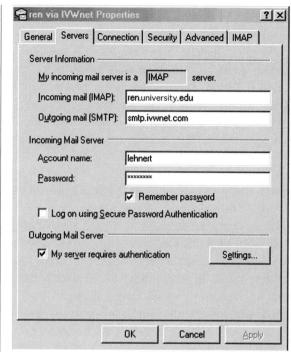

able to find the names of your two mail servers in the ISP's online documentation. The rest of this section discusses outgoing mail. Section 3.6 deals with three different types of servers for incoming mail.

Mail is sent over the Internet by using the **Simple Mail Transfer Protocol (SMTP)**. One of the oldest Internet protocols, SMTP is the universal standard for moving mail over the Net. To send e-mail, you need access to an SMTP server, the e-mail address of your intended recipient, and a mailer. When you sign up for Internet access, you are given access to an SMTP server, using an account you can activate with a user ID and password.

A mailer sending a mail message to a specified address contacts your SMTP server, which passes the DNS address to a domain name server for verification and translation into an IP address. If an outgoing message bounces back to you with a "host unknown" error message, the DNS name server could not locate the host name in its directory of known DNS addresses. If all goes well with the domain name server, an IP address is returned for your intended recipient, and the mail message is prepared for transport over the Net using TCP/IP.

TIP: ISPs and School or Workplace Internet Access

If you have access to the Internet through your school or place of work, you probably have a mail account associated with that Internet computer account. But suppose you live too far away from school or work to dial in to that facility without long-distance charges. Then you need an account with a commercial ISP to get you online without long-distance phone calls. Alternatively, you may just want broadband access from your home, which is another reason to get an ISP account. Either way, you can use a commercial ISP to access the Internet from home while still handling your e-mail via your e-mail account at school or work.

To make this work, don't use the ISP's mail server for incoming mail—use the name of the incoming mail server for your school or workplace. That way you'll have direct access to all incoming mail addressed to you at school or work when you're at home. In some cases, your commercial ISP will also let you use an outgoing mail server at school or work, but many ISPs now prohibit "third-party" SMTP access. If you get error messages about unauthorized server access when you try to send mail through a third-party SMTP server, switch over to the SMTP server for your ISP. That's how I set up the account shown in Figure 3.9. Incoming mail is received through a server (ren.cs.umass.edu) at the University of Massachusetts, and outgoing mail is processed by a commercial ISP server (smtp.ivwnet.com) in Seattle, Washington. Everyone who receives e-mail from me sees my return address at UMass, but when I send mail from my home in Massachusetts, that mail is always routed through Seattle. My outgoing mail is a little slow sometimes, but never enough to be a problem.

The receiving mail server at the destination saves the message in an inbox for the specified recipient. At that point, SMTP is done with the message. Another server steps in to negotiate the final delivery to the recipient's mail client. This is where things get a bit more complicated.

3.6   HTTP, POP, and IMAP

Different kinds of mail servers are designed to deliver incoming messages to mail clients. If you are setting up a new mail account, note that not all mailers are compatible with all mail servers. If you are shopping around for a mailer, first check to find out the type of incoming mail service you have since that will constrain your choice. Currently, the three most popular e-mail protocols for incoming mail are:

1. Hypertext Transfer Protocol (HTTP mail)
2. Post Office Protocol 3 (POP mail)
3. Internet Message Access Protocol (IMAP mail)

3.6.1 Hypertext Transfer Protocol

Hypertext Transfer Protocol (HTTP) should be familiar to you as the Web protocol, because it is used to specify URLs for Web browsers. Web pages and HTTP can also act as gateways to e-mail servers at Web sites that provide Web-based e-mail services (see Section 3.8). In such cases, your Web browser steps in and takes the place of a mailer because the Web site is set up as an interface to the appropriate e-mail servers. Web-based e-mail is always HTML-enabled.

3.6.2 Post Office Protocol 3 and Internet Message Access Protocol

Although Web-based mail has some nice features, people who rely on e-mail for business or other crucial communications opt for either a POP or IMAP mail service. Note, however, that the choice might not be yours—most ISPs offer one service or the other but not both (see Figure 3.10).

Some mailers can handle both POP and IMAP servers, but you need to know which service you want to use when you install your mailer (see Figure 3.11).

Post Office Protocol (POP) 3. If you had an ISP account before 1999, you were probably using a **Post Office Protocol (POP)** mail server. Both Communicator and Internet Explorer came with POP mailers, and Eudora was a popular POP mailer for both Windows-based personal computers and Macs.

POP was designed to support offline mail management, which made great sense when people had to pay for connect time by the hour. Users are in **offline mode** when they work without an active Internet connection. In a POP mail service, the server is basically a drop box in which mail is temporarily stored until the client connects and asks for it. The server then forwards all the accumulated mail to the client on the local host, and clears its temporary store to make room for more mail. The user downloads the mail, disconnects from the Net, and then deals with the e-mail locally and offline. After reading the messages, the user can delete them or store them in a local folder. Messages and replies to messages are written while offline and then sent all at

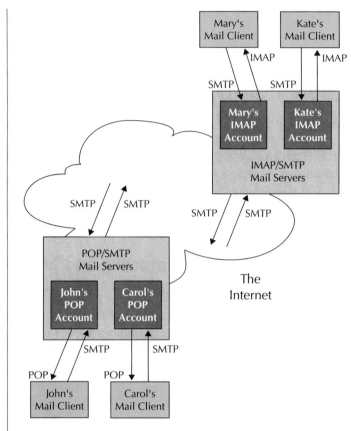

once the next time the user gets online. Thus the most time-consuming work is completed offline, reserving the Internet connection for brief mail uploads and downloads. All saved mail is stored on the local host, thereby freeing up the server to accept new mail.

Anyone who has had to access their e-mail from multiple locations understands a major drawback with POP mail. Suppose you have computers both at work and at home and you want to read your e-mail at both locations. Now suppose you download 20 messages to the office machine so you can catch up on the day's mail before you go home. But then you never do get around to reading the last 10 before you leave the office. You'd like to read them at home later, but your home computer cannot access them because they have already been removed from the mail server by your office computer. To get at the mail from your home, you need a connection between your home computer and

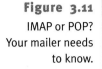

Figure 3.11
IMAP or POP?
Your mailer needs
to know.

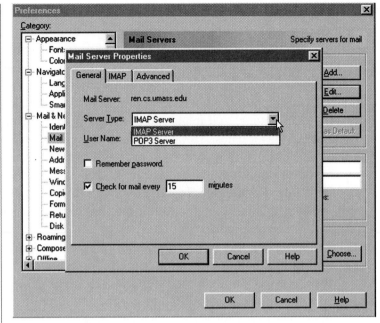

your office computer so you can transfer a mail folder from your office machine to your home machine. This is cumbersome, but it can be done. Copying a mail folder enables you to read those messages, but now you have copies of the same mail messages in two places. If you want to save one message and delete the others, you have to figure out where to save the message that you want to keep (on the home machine or the office machine?). You also have to delete all the other messages twice because you have copies of everything in two places now.

This is tedious and time-consuming, not to mention risky because it's easy to make mistakes. (For example, thinking you had saved an important message on one machine, you delete it on the other but then discover you just deleted your last copy of the message.) POP servers can be instructed to download mail without deleting it, but having multiple copies of every message in multiple computers complicates mail management. Coordinating offline mail in multiple locations is difficult—especially for people who have high volumes of mail and urgent communication requirements. This offline model for e-mail dominated the Internet throughout the 1990s. Increasingly, however, it is being replaced by IMAP, a newer, more powerful e-mail service.

Internet Message Access Protocol (IMAP). An alternative to offline mail management is "online" mail management. In online mode, the mail client interacts with the mail server seamlessly. The user manipulates mail and mail folders as if they were local, but everything stays on the server. Instead of downloading all the mail messages in a single block, the user can start by downloading just the mail headers. Some mail can be deleted on the basis of the header alone, so it might not be necessary to download all the mail messages to the local host. However, if the user wants to read a message or search a mail folder for a keyword in the message bodies, then some or all of the mail messages can be downloaded as needed. This is how the IMAP model works. With **Internet Message Access Protocol (IMAP)**, the client and the server work together more interactively in an effort to make mail management more flexible and negotiable.

Depending on how the client is configured, an IMAP mail program can work online, offline, or in a "disconnected" mode. In disconnected mode, the client connects to the server, creates a local cache of selected messages, and goes offline. The user then has an opportunity to go through the mail, delete some messages, write some replies, and maybe compose some new messages. At any time the client can reconnect with the server to send off new mail or purge a message marked for deletion. When the client and server reconnect, the client automatically resynchronizes its local cache with the server. All mail folders and all mail are left on the IMAP server at all times, making it easier to work with the same mail store from different locations.

IMAP client options are more flexible than POP options because an IMAP client can work in online, offline, or disconnected modes. A POP client works only in offline mode. This can make the preference settings for an IMAP client more complicated, but it is not necessary to master all the settings to work with an IMAP server. If you ever need to switch from a POP server to an IMAP server, just remember that the POP server gave you a "store-and-forward" service. The IMAP server allows you to store messages on the server and manage mail folders on the server through your IMAP client. All the familiar mail operations are still available, but you are working with messages that remain on your mail server until you explicitly (1) mark them for deletion and then (2) purge your deleted messages. You do not need to store mail on a local host, and you do not need to download all your unread messages in order to read just one. You also don't need to worry about when you are in online mode, offline mode, or disconnected mode. Just select the basic mail operations you need to perform and let the client negotiate the client-server communications. You can just concentrate on your mail, and your IMAP client will take care of everything else.

 # Filtering and Routing

People who receive a lot of e-mail find it useful to organize their mail in mail folders. A **mail folder** is like a file folder for correspondence. Storing mail messages in a system of mail folders makes it easier to find specific messages and to move large blocks of mail into long-term archives (or the trash) when the time comes to weed out the current folders. It takes some thinking and experimentation to come up with a set of folders that work well—no two people can hope to use the exact same system. If 90 percent of your mail comes from the same 20 people, you might want to create a folder for each person. If you just want to separate your personal mail, your business mail, and your mailing lists, you could begin with three folders for those three categories. And if your mail is difficult to categorize, you could create a new mail folder once a month in order to store monthly archives chronologically.

Once you settle on a good system of mail folders, you might find it convenient to move mail into certain folders automatically by using a mail client that supports filtering and routing. With e-mail **filtering**, the mailer recognizes specific messages based on keywords in their subject headers, fields, or message bodies. With e-mail **routing**, the mailer directs e-mail to a specific folder or subdirectory. Filtering and routing are usually combined to help people manage large volumes of e-mail: messages are automatically sorted and routed to assigned folders. Some folders are for important messages for daily review, and other folders hold less urgent mail for review once a week. Many people rely heavily on mail filters and cannot imagine life without them. It is about as close as most of us will ever get to having a personal secretary who faithfully sorts our mail, 7 days a week, 24 hours a day.

If your mail client supports mail filters, it is easy to create any number of filter rules for your own needs. Each filter rule should try to identify mail messages that belong in a particular mail folder, filter them out of the incoming mail stream, and then route them to the appropriate folder. For example, it is usually easy to write a filter rule that routes e-mail from a mailing list to a folder for that mailing list.

Figure 3.12 shows an Outlook Express filter rule designed to trap messages about mortgage rates. It consists of a condition (match a word in the

Figure 3.12

A filter rule in
Outlook Express

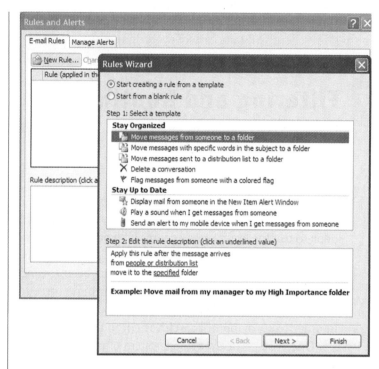

Figure 3.12

A filter rule in
Outlook Express

subject header) and an action (move it to a folder named "spam"). To create a rule like this, go to the Tools menu and select Rules and Alerts. This will display a tabbed window in which you can select options for the type of conditions and actions that you want for your rule (select E-Mail Rules). When you select a condition and an action, text lines appear automatically in the Rule Description box (see Figure 3.13). If you click the links in those lines, you'll get new pop-up windows where you can specify which word to match (see Figure 3.14) and which folder to send it to (see Figure 3.15). The rule depicted in these screen shots traps any message with the word "mortgage" in the sub-

Figure 3.13

Edit the condition
and action using
these links.

Figure 3.14

Specify the condition

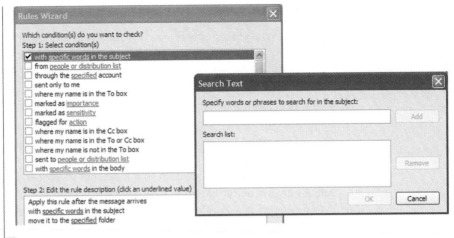

Figure 3.15

Specify the action.

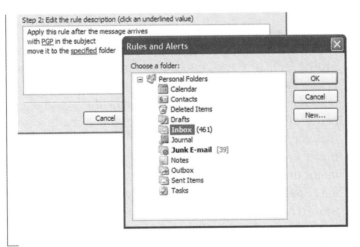

ject header and moves that message to a folder named "spam" for probable disposal at some later time.

When you see how easy it is to create filter rules, you might be tempted to create filters for everything you can think to trap and route to a folder. It's fine to experiment with lots of filter rules. If one turns out to be a bad idea, you can always delete it. Just watch out for the "out of sight, out of mind" pitfall. When mail is automatically routed to a mail folder, it's very easy to forget about it—totally. So when you first start routing mail into mail folders, remind yourself to take a look at all those folders at least once a week. Then

TIP: Routing Messages to Folders Is Safer than Automatically Deleting Them

If you feel certain that any message with the word "mortgage" in the subject header is something you don't need to see, you could create a filter rule that would automatically delete all such messages. While this may be tempting, it is very difficult to come up with filter rules that can root out annoying commercial messages and other time-wasters with 100 percent accuracy. A lot of mail messages about mortgages are commercial messages from companies that want to sell you a mortgage. But you may also have a friend in the process of buying her first home who decides to ask you something about mortgage rates. If a filter rule catches that message and deletes it, you'll never see the message from your friend or even know she sent it. For this reason, it's always better to route unwanted mail into a folder where you can review it before deleting it. A legitimate message that gets automatically routed out of your inbox might not be seen as quickly as it would have without your filter rule in place, but it doesn't have to be lost forever if you are watching your mail folders.

decide if and how you are going to pay attention to those folders. If anything urgent could be routed into a folder, it's important to check the folder at least once a day.

When used correctly, automatic mail filters can help you stay focused and be less distracted by a constant barrage of e-mail. You might even discover that you can drop an entire mailing list that doesn't really interest you that much anymore, now that you aren't seeing the messages all the time. Or you might find out that you just don't want to set aside a dedicated block of time for a specific interest—that interest was actually just an excuse for avoiding work-related messages. If you want to improve your time management, try some automated mail filters; you might be surprised by what you learn.

TIP: Be More Productive with Your E-Mail Management

Automatic mail filters can teach you a lot about how you spend your time and how you might spend your time differently. If you aren't constantly watching over your inbox for new mail, you can better control the time you spend on your mail. Set a time each day to handle work-related mail that's been routed into work folders. Then schedule a block of time once or twice a week for recreational folders. For example, you might spend an hour twice a week for recreational mailing lists after handling more important messages.

3.8 Web-Based E-Mail Accounts

Every major portal on the Web offers free Web-based e-mail in order to maximize repeat visits to the site. These services are usually subsidized by banner ads, and they give advertisers many opportunities to grab your attention at least once a day or, at worst (if you check your mail infrequently), maybe once a week. It is easy to register for these services—you just have to think of a user ID no one else has picked first and provide another e-mail address to verify your identity. Some sites require additional personal information; some don't. Once you've signed up, your account is password protected.

Web-based e-mail has some very nice features. Because you read it with a Web browser, it is always HTML-enabled (see Figure 3.16). Web-based e-mail

Figure 3.16

A Web-based e-mail account

TIP: Cookies and Web-Based E-Mail

Some Web-based e-mail services work only when cookies are enabled in your browser. If you have disabled cookies, you might need to manually enable them each time you visit your Web-based e-mail account. If this becomes annoying, you can use a cookie manager and set it to enable cookies at your mail site. (See the Above & Beyond section in Chapter 2 for an introduction to cookies.)

accounts often support filtering and routing capabilities, and when they do, the process of rule creation tends to be fast and easy. Some of the big portal-related mail services offer an instant messaging client (see Section 4.7.3) that can monitor your mail account and alert you when a new mail message arrives. Others allow you to consolidate incoming mail from multiple POP accounts so you can read all your POP mail in one place. There is usually an inbox quota, but the larger sites will increase your quota for a monthly subscription fee. Different services offer different features, so it pays to look around and to watch for new features.

Unfortunately, the quality of service can also vary, and you might need to shop around for a service you can trust. Some of the most popular mail services struggle to keep up with a rapidly expanding subscriber population. As a result, their servers might be overloaded from time to time. Hotmail has been known to refuse to accept e-mail for hours at a time when the system load is high. Many Web-based mail servers are stable, but most experience periodic difficulties (see Figure 3.17). If you need the most reliable mail service possible, it is best to look for a POP or IMAP mail account instead of an HTTP mail account.

If you already have a POP or IMAP mail account, you might want to experiment with a few Web-based mail accounts to help you segregate certain kinds of e-mail for better mail handling. For example, you could reserve one Web account for commercial transactions. Then all the e-mail receipts and follow-up messages for online purchases will stay in one place and never get tangled up with other types of e-mail. You could use another Web account for mailing lists and newsletters—any material that does not require immediate attention or fast responses. By reserving entire mail accounts for different types of e-mail, you are really just filtering and routing e-mail on a large scale. Just try not to set up too many separate Web accounts. The added overhead of having to visit multiple mail accounts might overwhelm any advantage associated with heavily segregated mail. If you push it too hard, excessive mail filtering might generate new problems for you. Only you can know when the cost-

Figure 3.17

HTTP servers experience more downtime than IMAP or POP servers.

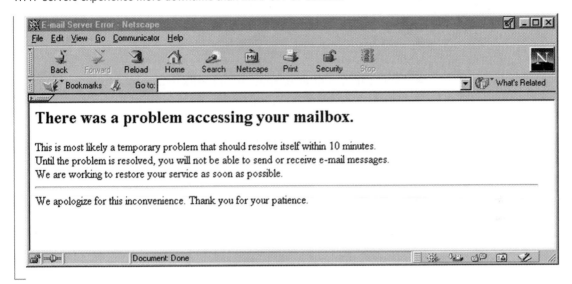

benefit ratio of multiple mail accounts has crossed a line (see the Above & Beyond section for this chapter).

Things to Remember

- Avoid sending files larger than 1MB in an e-mail message body.
- Avoid mail attachments larger than 1MB unless your recipient has given you prior approval.
- Student mail accounts and Web-based mail accounts usually have restrictive quotas—know your quota.
- Clean out your Sent Mail folder periodically.
- Avoid signature files that are more than four lines long.
- Don't send mail in HTML format unless you know your recipient's mail client is HTML-enabled.
- When you configure a mail client you will need the names of both your outgoing (SMTP) mail server and your incoming (POP or IMAP) mail server.

- POP mail accounts are good for offline mail management.
- IMAP mail accounts support offline, online, and disconnected mail management.
- Free Web-based mail accounts may not be as reliable as POP and IMAP accounts.
- Don't set up a filter to route mail into a mail folder and then forget about it.
- Filter rules that automatically delete mail messages are dangerous.
- Web-based e-mail accounts may require a cookie-enabled Web browser.

Important Concepts

e-mail client software that can transfer e-mail messages between a local host and a remote e-mail server, as well as display and compose messages on the local host

e-mail server software that can send e-mail messages to and receive e-mail messages from other e-mail servers, as well as hold incoming messages for local e-mail clients

emoticons a symbolic system for expressing simple emotions using graphic characters or ASCII text

filtering a way to recognize specific messages based on keywords in their Subject: fields, From: fields, or message bodies

flame an uninhibited display of anger or aggression online

HTTP a Web-based e-mail protocol

imap an e-mail protocol that stores incoming mail on a mail server

netiquette standard rules of courtesy for online communication

pop an e-mail protocol that stores incoming mail on a local host

routing a way to direct mail to a specific folder or subdirectory for later viewing

SMTP the protocol for moving outgoing e-mail over the Internet

Where Can I Learn More?

E-Mail Filters—How Netscape Messenger Can Help Keep You Sane!
```
http://www.education.purdue.edu/edit/emailstuff/messenger/
    filters/welcome.html
```

Fight Spam on the Internet
http://spam.abuse.net/

Free E-Mail Guide
http://freemailguide.com/

Harness E-Mail: How It Works
http://www.learnthenet.com/english/html/20how.htm

Mail Filtering Frequently Asked Questions
http://www.hwg.org/resources/faqs/filterFAQ.html

Netlingo
http://www.netlingo.com

Spam-Tracking 101 (for Newbies)
http://www.cv.nrao.edu/~pmurphy/spam/
    bill_mattocks_lesson_101.html

The Core Rules of Netiquette
http://www.albion.com/netiquette/corerules.html

Things Worth Knowing about E-Mail
http://www.ualberta.ca/~pletendr/e-netiquette.html

UM E-Mail Client Feature Matrix
http://www.mcsr.olemiss.edu/bookshelf/doc/email/
    email_table.html

Using IMAP instead of POP3
http://www.email.calpoly.edu/documentation/oracle/
    imap_pop.html

Problems and Exercises

1. Name two header fields that are completed for you automatically when you send an e-mail message.

2. What does a signature file contain? What is a good length for a signature file?

3. What is the difference between the Cc: field and the Bcc: field?

4. Why is it a bad idea to compose long Subject: fields?

5. What are emoticons, and why are they useful?

6. Explain the difference between a group reply and a single author reply.

7. **[HANDS-ON]** If your mail client has a toolbar, examine its icons. Explain what each one does. Are there any that you don't understand? If so, consult your online Help documentation or other software documentation.

8. **[HANDS-ON]** If your mail client has pull-down menus, look to see how many commands are under each one. How many of these do you use regularly? How many do you use rarely? How many have you never used? How many do you understand and how many are a mystery to you? Do you think you might be more productive if you learned more about what your mail client can do for you? Why or why not?

9. When you include the original message in an e-mail reply, should you always include the original message in its entirety? Explain your answer.

10. **[HANDS-ON]** Check to see if your mail client has preference settings for how it flags text from an original message when you compose a reply to that message. If it does, change the character used to flag that text to a ^. This will make your e-mail messages more distinctive when you engage in group discussions.

11. If you exchange a series of e-mail messages with someone by using the Reply command, what should you remember to do every so often?

12. What is an HTML-enabled mail client?

13. **[HANDS-ON]** Find a Web page that contains some graphics and send it to yourself via e-mail (go to the File menu and look for a Send command). View the Web page with your mail client. Do you see the same Web page that your browser saw? Try it again with two more Web pages (pick different kinds of pages). Can you make any conclusions about mailing Web pages from this? Do you think different mail clients might behave differently?

14. When is it a bad idea to send an HTML-enhanced mail message to someone? Can you ever know what mail client someone is using when he or she reads your mail? Is it always safe to send HTML-enhanced mail to recipients who have Web-based mail accounts such as Yahoo.com or Hotmail.com addresses?

15. **[HANDS-ON]** Look at the preference settings for your mail client to check the format of your outgoing mail messages (the two most commonly encountered choices are plain text and HTML). Send yourself a test message in HTML format and then send yourself another test message in plain text format. How do these two test messages look different when you view them as a mail recipient? Which format is the better one to use?

16. **[FIND IT ONLINE]** If an e-mail address is important for business reasons, it is not a good idea to abandon that address for any reason. But people who have an e-mail address affiliated with an ISP can feel trapped by their ISP because changing ISPs means dropping an old e-mail address. Why don't ISPs offer e-mail forwarding services to customers who want to switch? Are there any solutions for people who want to switch without disrupting their business?

17. **[HANDS-ON]** Create a signature file that your e-mail client will automatically add to the end of any message body you create. Send yourself a test message to make sure the signature file is being added. Why is it a bad idea to include very long signatures?

18. **[FIND IT ONLINE]** A signature file is a good place to add a little personality to your e-mail messages. Some signature files include favorite quotes, pointers to recommended Web sites, political sound bites, or random epigrams. Visit `http://www.coolsig.com/` for a collection of signature files found on the Net. Pick out five sigs you like. Do you like one enough to use it yourself?

19. Explain the main difference between an IMAP mail service and a POP mail service. Which is more powerful? Which was designed to minimize connect time? Which is better for people who need to work with their mail from multiple locations? Which would you want if your hard drive was very full but you still needed to save a lot of new mail?

20. What is the MIME protocol used for?

21. **[FIND IT ONLINE]** Suppose that you have a Web-based mail account that opens and displays graphical file attachments automatically. Do you need to worry about macro viruses on this account? Explain your answer.

22. Is an HTTP mail account more like a POP mail account or an IMAP mail account? Think about where the mail messages are stored, and then explain your answer.

23. **[FIND IT ONLINE]** Visit `http://www.netlingo.com/emailsh.cfm` and find definitions for the following Netspeak terms in its e-mail glossary: AFAIK, CMIIW, CUL, IAC, IKALOPLT, IMHO, OTOH, ROTFL, and TIA.

24. **[FIND IT ONLINE]** Before we had MIME attachments, the closest thing to graphics in an e-mail message was ASCII art. Visit Joan Stark's Development of (ASCII) Art Web site

E-Mail Management

Spam: Trouble in Paradise

Sooner or later, everyone who uses e-mail encounters Internet abuse. It is important to understand what constitutes Internet abuse so that you don't inadvertently contribute to it yourself. It is also good to know how to respond to it when it happens to you. The most common form of Net abuse via e-mail involves unsolicited messages. These are typically commercial advertisements. However, they can also be political calls for action, religious sermons, philosophical manifestos, or the ravings of someone who is angry about something.

WHY IS IT CALLED SPAM?

The term *spam* comes from an old Monty Python sketch. The connection to digital spam is self-evident.

Scene: A cafe. One table is occupied by a group of Vikings wearing horned helmets. A man and his wife enter.

Man: You sit here, dear.

Wife: All right.

Man: (to Waitress) Morning!

Waitress: Morning!

Man: Well, what've you got?

Waitress: Well, there's egg and bacon; egg sausage and bacon; egg and spam; egg bacon and spam; egg bacon sausage and spam; spam bacon sausage and spam; spam egg spam spam bacon and spam; spam sausage spam spam bacon spam tomato and spam. . .

Vikings: (starting to chant) Spam spam spam spam. . .

Waitress: . . .spam spam spam egg and spam; spam spam spam spam spam spam baked beans spam spam spam. . .

—from *Monty Python's Previous Record*

If you are affiliated with a commercial interest, never broadcast unsolicited product announcements or advertisements via e-mail. Unsolicited e-mail sent to a large number of people is called **spam** and is a classic form of Internet abuse. It is all right, for example, to compile a list of friends and acquaintances and then tell them you've changed jobs and now have a new Internet address. Just don't try to sell anything at the same time. You can tell people what your new company does, and you can even include a URL pointer to a corporate Web page. Just keep the chest-thumping to a minimum lest anyone think you are plugging your new employer.

If you are new to the Internet, you won't see much mail spam right away. After you've been online awhile, you will begin to see spam from time to time. The longer you are online, the more you're likely to see. How much you get depends on how visible your e-mail address is, who has collected it, who has sold it, and who has bought it.

Since the Internet is not policed by any legal authority, we do not have precise definitions of Internet abuse. There are clear-cut cases of Internet abuse, and there are borderline cases that will strike some people, but not everyone, as a form

16. **[FIND IT ONLINE]** If an e-mail address is important for business reasons, it is not a good idea to abandon that address for any reason. But people who have an e-mail address affiliated with an ISP can feel trapped by their ISP because changing ISPs means dropping an old e-mail address. Why don't ISPs offer e-mail forwarding services to customers who want to switch? Are there any solutions for people who want to switch without disrupting their business?

17. **[HANDS-ON]** Create a signature file that your e-mail client will automatically add to the end of any message body you create. Send yourself a test message to make sure the signature file is being added. Why is it a bad idea to include very long signatures?

18. **[FIND IT ONLINE]** A signature file is a good place to add a little personality to your e-mail messages. Some signature files include favorite quotes, pointers to recommended Web sites, political sound bites, or random epigrams. Visit `http://www.coolsig.com/` for a collection of signature files found on the Net. Pick out five sigs you like. Do you like one enough to use it yourself?

19. Explain the main difference between an IMAP mail service and a POP mail service. Which is more powerful? Which was designed to minimize connect time? Which is better for people who need to work with their mail from multiple locations? Which would you want if your hard drive was very full but you still needed to save a lot of new mail?

20. What is the MIME protocol used for?

21. **[FIND IT ONLINE]** Suppose that you have a Web-based mail account that opens and displays graphical file attachments automatically. Do you need to worry about macro viruses on this account? Explain your answer.

22. Is an HTTP mail account more like a POP mail account or an IMAP mail account? Think about where the mail messages are stored, and then explain your answer.

23. **[FIND IT ONLINE]** Visit `http://www.netlingo.com/emailsh.cfm` and find definitions for the following Netspeak terms in its e-mail glossary: AFAIK, CMIIW, CUL, IAC, IKALOPLT, IMHO, OTOH, ROTFL, and TIA.

24. **[FIND IT ONLINE]** Before we had MIME attachments, the closest thing to graphics in an e-mail message was ASCII art. Visit Joan Stark's Development of (ASCII) Art Web site

(`http://www.geocities.com/joan_stark/textasciihistory.txt`),
and find out when typewriter art was first documented.

25. **[HANDS-ON]** Send yourself an e-mail message. Does your mailer
default to a full header display or a short header display? If it defaults
to a short header, how many lines are in the header display? Can you
find a command that will show you the full header display? How
many lines are in the full header? Look at another mail message in
your inbox, and check its short and long header displays. Do the
short headers for these two messages have the same number of lines?
Do the full headers have the same number of lines?

26. **[HANDS-ON]** Visit Planet PDF (`http://www.planetpdf.com/`
`mainpage.asp?menuid=98&WebPageID=603`) and send yourself a postcard. What did you have to do to view your postcard? Several postcard
services on the Web work like this. Why don't they use e-mail attachments instead?

27. **[HANDS-ON]** If your mail client supports filters and you have never
worked with them, create a rule that routes any messages sent by you
to a special folder. Test your rule to make sure it is working correctly.

28. **[HANDS-ON]** Monitor your e-mail habits for one week. How much
time do you spend on e-mail each day? How many times a day do you
check your e-mail? How much of your e-mail is work-related (or
school-related), and how much is personal? Try to answer that question both in terms of quantity (how many messages fall into each category) and time (how much time you spend on each category).

29. **[HANDS-ON]** (Do Exercise 28 before attempting this one.) Given your
e-mail usage patterns, try to think of something you can do to reduce
the amount of time you spend on e-mail. This could involve some
reorganization with respect to multiple e-mail accounts or perhaps
the use of mail filters for routing some messages into special folders.
Alternatively, you might try a purely behavioral adjustment (for
example, reducing the number of times you check your mail each
day). Try out your new regime for one week, tracking the amount of
time you spend on e-mail. Were you able to reduce it? How much
time was it in terms of a percentage drop? Do you think you are any
less productive or responsive than you were before? If so, explain.

30. **[TAKE A STAND]** Do you think e-mail can be addictive? Who would you guess is at high risk? Do you know any people whom you would characterize as addicted to e-mail? Do you think this is a serious problem for some people?

31. **[TAKE A STAND]** Have you ever received an offensive e-mail message from a stranger? Do you think offensive e-mail is fundamentally different from offensive books, catalogs, or movies? Explain why or why not.

32. **[HANDS-ON]** Start a Web-based mail account at Hotmail.com and start another one at Yahoo.com. (If you already have an account at one of these sites, use the one you already have.) Monitor these two accounts for one week and note any differences in the amount of incoming mail and the type of incoming mail you receive. Given your observations, would you recommend one site over the other? Explain why or why not.

E-Mail Management

Spam: Trouble in Paradise

Sooner or later, everyone who uses e-mail encounters Internet abuse. It is important to understand what constitutes Internet abuse so that you don't inadvertently contribute to it yourself. It is also good to know how to respond to it when it happens to you. The most common form of Net abuse via e-mail involves unsolicited messages. These are typically commercial advertisements. However, they can also be political calls for action, religious sermons, philosophical manifestos, or the ravings of someone who is angry about something.

If you are affiliated with a commercial interest, never broadcast unsolicited product announcements or advertisements via e-mail. Unsolicited e-mail sent to a large number of people is called **spam** and is a classic form of Internet abuse. It is all right, for example, to compile a list of friends and acquaintances and then tell them you've changed jobs and now have a new Internet address. Just don't try to sell anything at the same time. You can tell people what your new company does, and you can even include a URL pointer to a corporate Web page. Just keep the chest-thumping to a minimum lest anyone think you are plugging your new employer.

If you are new to the Internet, you won't see much mail spam right away. After you've been online awhile, you will begin to see spam from time to time. The longer you are online, the more you're likely to see. How much you get depends on how visible your e-mail address is, who has collected it, who has sold it, and who has bought it.

Since the Internet is not policed by any legal authority, we do not have precise definitions of Internet abuse. There are clear-cut cases of Internet abuse, and there are borderline cases that will strike some people, but not everyone, as a form

---

WHY IS IT CALLED SPAM?

The term *spam* comes from an old Monty Python sketch. The connection to digital spam is self-evident.

Scene: A cafe. One table is occupied by a group of Vikings wearing horned helmets. A man and his wife enter.

Man: You sit here, dear.

Wife: All right.

Man: (to Waitress) Morning!

Waitress: Morning!

Man: Well, what've you got?

Waitress: Well, there's egg and bacon; egg sausage and bacon; egg and spam; egg bacon and spam; egg bacon sausage and spam; spam bacon sausage and spam; spam egg spam spam bacon and spam; spam sausage spam spam bacon spam tomato and spam. . .

Vikings: (starting to chant) Spam spam spam spam. . .

Waitress: . . .spam spam spam egg and spam; spam spam spam spam spam spam baked beans spam spam spam. . .

—from *Monty Python's Previous Record*

FYI: How Much Spam Is There?

According to a study by IDC, email is expected to reach 84 billion messages in 2006, with 33 billion of which will be spam! This number is predicted to grow to 2.7 trillion in 2007 according to an eMarketer analyst. The future looks good to the spammers!

of abuse. Here's an example of the latter. Suppose you send a very short message to a very large list of "acquaintances" announcing your move to a new company. The message includes a corporate URL in the message body but nothing remotely personal about you as anyone more than a corporate contact. If this goes out to people who don't recognize your name, it is probably Internet abuse. An even trickier example is the case of sig files. What if you insert a brief plug for your freelance services in your sig file just in case someone might be interested? If the sig file is no more than four lines, chances are no one will object. However, some people might consider even that to be tacky.

All of these prohibitions apply primarily to commercial interests, although politics and religion are not far behind. No one wants to get unsolicited e-mail from an unknown individual about a favorite political cause (no matter how worthy) or one's latest transcendental experience (no matter how profound). If you study a few hundred sig files, you will find that most Netizens stick to "tag lines" (witty quotations) or opinionated proclamations of a purely technical nature. Responsible people try to err on the side of caution when it comes to proper netiquette.

TIP: It Is ILLEGAL to Send Spam!

One of the more notorious spammers, rated the fourth-worst spammer in the world by Spamhaus Project at the time, was successfully prosecuted by the state of Texas and Microsoft Corp for using misleading subject lines and not indicating that their messages were advertisements, in violation of the Controlling the Assault of Non-Solicited Pornography and Marketing (CAN-SPAM) Act passed by Congress in 2003. In an agreement reached in May 2006, the spammer was fined $1 million and agreed to never again send out false, misleading, or unsolicited commercial e-mails. He also lost most of his assets and will now be using his skills to help companies fight spam. In this spammer's heyday in 2004, as many as 25 million e-mail messages were sent *every day*. The lawsuit that was subsequently filed sought $500 million in damages.

How *Not* to Fight Back Against Spam

If you get spammed, don't bother replying to the original sender for the sake of speaking your mind. An angry reply to the sender will have no effect whatsoever. Chances are the originating account was terminated or abandoned right after the spamming event (the people who do these things are no fools). Alternatively, the account in question might have been broken into by the spammer, in which case you will only be victimizing another innocent victim. And finally, it is relatively easy to forge (aka *spoof*) a mail header, so the information in a From: slot could be a totally fictitious address or, in some cases, a legitimate address that has nothing to do with the actual origin of the message.

A demonstration of this last scenario came to light in 2002 in the form of the Klez virus (see Section 2.6.3). Klez is an e-mail worm that infects Outlook and Outlook Express users, but nevertheless manages to victimize people who are not infected with the virus and who may not even be running either of the vulnerable Outlook mail clients. The W32.Klez variant of Klez contains its own spam engine that pulls addresses out of the Outlook address book, sends out a variety of spam to those addresses, and hides its tracks by filling the From: slot with another random address it got from the address book. This results in millions of spam messages being attributed to hundreds of thousands of innocent people who simply had the bad luck to be in the address book of someone infected with Klez. It happened to me: Figure 3.18 shows a list of incoming mail messages sent to me (almost all spam), including two Klez messages supposedly sent to me *by* me about life insurance.

It's unsettling to get angry e-mail messages from people accusing you of being a spammer. In some cases, the reputation of an otherwise innocent business has been irreparably harmed when pornographic spam appears to be coming from them. Lawsuits for libel and defamation have been filed as a

Figure 3.18

I don't really send messages to myself about life insurance.

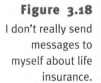

!	0	?	↓	From	Subject	Received	
				marketalert@www.com	OTCBB: IVIP A Company On the Ris...	6/14/2002 8:26 AM	
				industrynews200220...	(ADV) OTCBB: IVIP A Com...	6/13/2002 9:12 PM	
				industrynews20022002@...	(ADV) OTCBB: XCNT Company On...	6/12/2002 11:14 PM	
	0			**Netsurfer Digest**	**Netsurfer Digest: Vol. 08, #23**	**6/15/2002 1:25 PM**	
				NYTimes.com News Alert	NYTimes.com News Alert: Andersen ...	6/15/2002 11:55 AM	
				lehnert@university.edu	**Best Life Insurance, Lowest ...**	**6/15/2002 6:52 AM**	
				lehnert@university.edu	**Lowest Cost Life Insurance Q...**	**6/15/2002 4:28 AM**	
				Sales Heads	**SalesHeads Newsletter**	**6/14/2002 6:51 PM**	
				NYTimes.com News ...	**NYTimes.com News Alert: Am...**	**6/14/2002 6:02 PM**	

TIP: Don't Believe the From: Header

 Be careful whom you accuse of being a spammer. A company in Australia sued an individual it claimed was responsible for putting the company on a public blacklist of spammers, thereby causing the company 20 days of lost income due to an interruption in Internet connectivity. The defendant is being sued for $137,500 (Australian) and must cover his legal expenses, win or lose. If you want to point a finger at a spammer, be prepared for possible litigation.

result of Klez, although the individual responsible for Klez may never be identified.

It is also a bad idea to trust any piece of spam that tells you its senders will remove you from their mailing list. Sometimes they tell you to send an e-mail reply, and sometimes they tell you to click a link (see Figure 3.19).

Figure 3.19
Clicking on this link doesn't really remove you from any mailing lists.

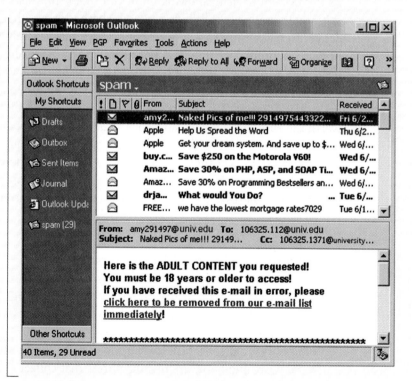

How to Fight Back Against Spam

Everyone becomes a **spam magnet** sooner or later. You can consider adopting a response to spam based on how much spam is finding you and how tolerant or intolerant you feel. Because of its prevalence, your ISP is probably already filtering the most obvious spam, but even the best filters cannot catch everything. Additional measures are up to you.

Stage 1 Spam Defense

This is the simplest response—it involves nothing more than your Delete button. Once you learn to recognize spam on the basis of the mail header alone, you can just delete it when you see it and get on with your life. This is a good solution when the amount of spam you receive is not great. When more spam starts piling up in your inbox, you will probably move on to the next stage.

Stage 2 Spam Defense

As the amount of spam showing up in your inbox increases, you'll find yourself wondering how it all finds you and whether or not there are things you can do to make yourself a less visible target. Unfortunately, it's very hard to become invisible once you're a known target. You basically need to start all over again with a new online identity and a lot of know-how about how to stay invisible. On the other hand, there are certainly things you can do to make yourself a bit less visible, and those things will result in a bit less spam. So it's worth the effort even if you can't hope to get back to a totally pristine inbox.

If you want to decrease your visibility, you need to know all the ways the e-mail harvesters find their e-mail addresses. An **e-mail harvester** is a computer program that explores public resources on the Internet and collects active e-mail addresses. Here are some places where the harvesters obtain e-mail addresses:

- Internet service providers
- Unconcealed mailing list subscribers
- Unconcealed authors of Usenet newsgroup articles
- Unconcealed participants of chat rooms and message boards
- E-mail addresses posted on personal Web pages or in online directories
- E-stores that collect the e-mail addresses of their customers
- Software and hardware manufacturers that collect e-mail addresses from product registrations
- Web sites that offer games and prizes in exchange for e-mail addresses

- Web sites that require user registrations
- Domain name registrations that make all their point-of-contact e-mail addresses public
- Address directories in e-mail clients that are open to attacks
- Replies to spam messages when they invite you to tell them to remove you from their list
- Web bugs activated by HTML-enabled mail clients (see the Above & Beyond section in Chapter 1)
- Browsers that are configured to reveal your e-mail address to inquisitive Web servers
- Cookies that store your e-mail address and reveal it on request
- Trojans, worms, and viruses that search your hard drive for e-mail addresses

As a rule, if you are ever asked to give your e-mail address, there is an excellent chance that an e-mail harvester will be picking it up sometime later. Consult `http://spam.abuse.net/` and `http://spam.abuse.net/userhelp/` for ideas on how to conceal your e-mail address from harvesters. In the meantime, to hold the spammers at bay, you can (1) avoid all Web sites and mailing lists that cannot be trusted to protect your privacy, and (2) learn how to hide your true identity everywhere else.

In the end, there will always be some things over which you have absolutely no control. For example, you cannot hope to ask everyone with whom you exchange e-mail to keep your address out of their address books just in case they get infected with an e-mail virus that contains an address harvester. This is why the serious stealth wizards (folks at Stage 5) use the services of an anonymizer whenever they connect to the Internet. An **anonymizer** is a service that shields your true identity behind a protective curtain while giving you a working alias for all your online communications. You can obtain a similar level of protection by using disposable e-mail addresses for all online communications.

Stage 3 Spam Defense

You may arrive at Stage 3 on a day when you are feeling a little stressed out and grumpy to begin with—and then you receive your thousandth piece of spam. That's when you finally vow to actually *do* something about all that junk in your inbox. Now is the time to set up a mail filter to route likely spam messages into a mail folder where they can sit until you get around to deleting them. It takes about an hour to set up a dozen obvious spam rules. After that, you can spend an hour each week or each month fine-tuning your rules and adding to them.

If you are not interested in designing your own spam filter rules, you might want to look into software designed to stop spam. There are also online services that will help you deal with spam for a monthly fee. For pointers to lots of online resources, visit a good Web site dedicated to the problem of spam (see Figure 3.20).

Stage 4 Spam Defense

This is the stage where your thoughts turn to retaliation. Why should hard-working folks have to educate themselves about the workings of address harvesters and then spend time tuning and retuning filter rules just because the get-rich-quick crowd has discovered the Internet? Spam is similar to the tele-marketers who call at dinnertime. No one wants to hear from these people, and the whole thing gets really annoying after a while. Why can't we just shut them down?

Figure 3.20

If you want to fight spam, learn all you can.

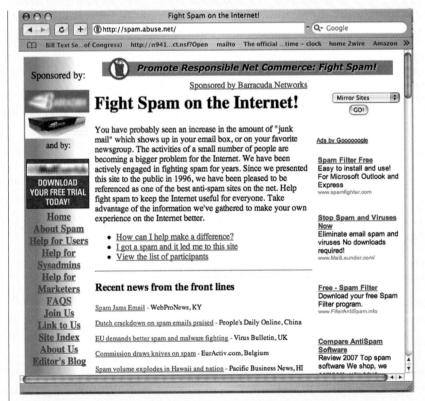

There are steps you can take to change the world if you want to consider the big picture. Some of these take more time than others, but if you feel passionately opposed to spam, you may decide that this is time well spent. For example, you can:

- Report spam incidents to the system administrator for your Internet access account.
- Boycott companies that generate spam.
- Boycott companies that do not respect customer privacy.
- Boycott ISPs that do not take steps to thwart spammers.
- Use existing laws on spam regulation to sue operations that are not in compliance.
- Join CAUCE (`http://www.cauce.org/`) and participate in political letter-writing campaigns.
- Look for opportunities to educate others about spam—bone up on all the antispam arguments.

For more details about these ideas, consult `http://spam.abuse.net/userhelp/`. Do not hesitate to inform technical support when you receive spam. Most administrators are every bit as annoyed by spam as the rest of us—and many are trying to take what steps they can to combat it at their level. Plus, technical support people are in a better position to report incidents of network abuse to appropriate carriers and gateway services.

Stage 5 Spam Defense

At this point you are thinking about reinventing yourself with a new Internet identity, knowing now all the things you wish you had known the first time you went online. You are looking into anonymizers (if you aren't already using one), and you have developed a healthy cynicism about everything you see online. If a service offers to remove your e-mail address from the spammers' mailing lists, you don't need to be told this is a ruse—you can figure that out for yourself. You may think you've been spending altogether too much time trying to outsmart the spammers, but at least you know the score and how to play the game.

Managing Multiple E-Mail Accounts

With so many personal computers in offices, homes, and the now almost ubiquitous wireless connections in hotel rooms, many people are not just wired into the Net but wired two and three times over. As you saw in Section 3.6, some mail clients make this easier than others. Now the same person may try not only to access the same mail account from multiple computers but also to deal with multiple e-mail accounts on multiple computers. These are two separate problems, but they both require some careful planning on the part of the user.

It might seem that the natural solution to multiple e-mail accounts is to consolidate those accounts into one hefty inbox, and to some extent that's right. You can find mail clients that will assist in this strategy. For example, Outlook Express will allow you to set up input from multiple POP or IMAP servers (see Figure 3.21), but it won't let you mix both POP and IMAP servers on the same installation.

If you are consolidating multiple POP accounts, proceed with caution. POP mail accounts do not give you a lot of control over what gets downloaded—if you have 500 mail messages on the server, you may have to download 500 messages in order to find the one or two that require an urgent response. This is about the worst e-mail nightmare anyone can imagine, and perhaps the strongest argument you can muster against consolidating POP mail accounts. If you are dealing with a lot of traffic on POP mail servers, try to stay on top of it so you never have to deal with huge backlogs. Alternatively, look for a POP mail client that lets you pick and choose your downloads based on message headers.

The consolidation of multiple IMAP accounts is a completely different story. On an IMAP server you have a lot of control over what gets read, what gets ignored, and what gets set aside. If you have multiple IMAP accounts, consolidation is an excellent strategy. There will still be times when the mail piles up, but that's when you really need the sort of control that IMAP has to offer.

Figure 3.21

Mail clients support multiple e-mail accounts.

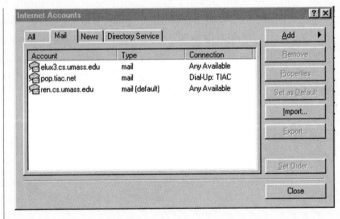

If you research available freeware and shareware on the Net, you might be able to find additional mail management tools that will meet your needs. For example, alarm systems can be very useful when you are expecting a specific mail message and you want to grab it as quickly as possible.

Sometimes it pays to use e-mail alternatives. Consider the teacher who fields the same questions from lots of different students via e-mail. Reading all that mail and sending the same replies out to everyone is extremely inefficient. If it is possible to consolidate all or most of those communications in a real-time chat room, one question can be answered for 10 different people for the same amount of effort needed to answer it for one person. Sometimes you need to consolidate your mail, but with an eye toward reducing it or handling it more efficiently. With a little creativity, you might be able to find the perfect combination of e-mail and some other medium. If the teacher asks students to send in questions via e-mail prior to a scheduled chat room session, those questions can then be answered and discussed interactively as chat topics, and the teacher can make the chat time as productive as possible with some advanced preparation.

If you find yourself drowning in e-mail, you can segregate it by categorizing it, filtering it, and routing it to different mail folders or different e-mail accounts. The ongoing segregation of your e-mail can all be automated with the right software. However, sooner or later, you still have to look at it and figure out what to do with it all. That's when it pays to consolidate, but consolidate with as much control as possible over the client-server interactions. Watch for new ideas in the area of mail management and experiment with any new tools that sound useful to you.

Conquering Raggy Text

One thing a good mail editor can do for you is wrap text from one line to the next so that you don't need to press [Return] or [Enter] unless you want to start a new paragraph. When you insert your own returns at the end of each line, people reading your mail might see **raggy text**—text that wraps around to the next line and then abruptly halts after an inch or two, only to continue on the next line where it wraps around again, and then halts, and so on (see Figure 3.22). Raggy text is very difficult to read and will annoy people who are trying to read your mail. You can inadvertently create raggy text if you use copy-and-paste operations to insert text from some other document into your message body. If you do see raggy text after a copy-and-paste operation, fix it before

Subject: Martin Gardner on Fuzzy Math
   Date: Wed, 9 Sep 1998 02:26:12 -0500 (CDT)
   From: Wayne Bishop <wbishop@univ.edu>
Reply-To: amte@univ.edu>
      To: Multiple recipients of list <amte@univ.edu>

Martin Gardner, "The New New Math," _New York Review of Books_, Sept. 24,
1998,
pp. 9-12.

Gardner is the former mathematical puzzle editor of _Scientific American_
and a
prolific writer on science and math topics. The Cover headline is "The Fuzzy
New Math."

The article includes a detailed criticism of the textbook _Focus on
Algebra: An
Integrated Approach_, also known as "Rainforest Algebra."

An excerpt from Gardner's article:

"I seldom agree with the conservative political views of Lynne Cheney, but
when
she criticized extreme aspects of the new new math on the Op-Ed page of _The
New York Times_ on August 11, 1997, I found myself cheering."

****

sending it off. Or prevent it in the first place by controlling line lengths in the source document with appropriate preference settings.

You can prevent raggy text very simply: Never add your own line returns. Let your client wrap long lines for you automatically, and press [Return] or [Enter] only if you want to start a new paragraph. Unfortunately, some people are prone to adding an occasional carriage return out of force of habit. If you can't break this habit, make sure your line length is limited to 72 characters or less (some people prefer 65 characters so replies and nested replies don't turn raggy). Check your mail client to see if you can set a maximum line length for your outgoing mail (see Figure 3.23).

Uuencoded Mail

Attachments clearly make e-mail more versatile. Most people today use MIME attachments to move binary files through the mail. However, you might someday run into an old technique that people used to move binary files before the advent of MIME. UNIX users have long had access to a tool called **uuencode**, which turns a binary file into an ASCII-based version suitable for

Figure 3.23

Use the right preference setting to avoid raggy text.

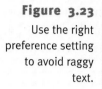

Figure 3.23

Use the right preference setting to avoid raggy text.

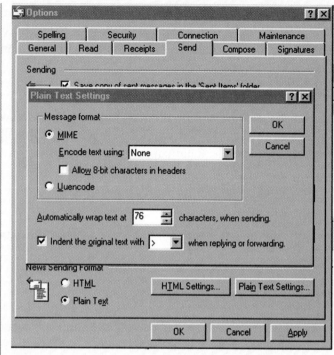

e-mail and Usenet (we will introduce Usenet in Section 4.6.3). Uuencoding is still around, and you will find tools for creating and reading uuencoded files in many file utilities. Uuencoded files are still used in Usenet newsgroups whenever someone wants to post a graphics file. Figure 3.24 shows an example of some uuencoded text. You can always recognize a uuencoded file by the way it begins. The string `"begin 666"` followed by a lot of random characters always signals a uuencoded file.

The uuencoded part of the sig file in Figure 3.24 is

```
"begin 666 foo B22!C86XG="!B96QI979E('EO=2!D96-09&5D ('1H:7,A"@'
end"
```

Figure 3.24

Uuencoded text in a signature file

```
--
XXXXXXXXXX EMT-P, K5ZC, PP-ASEL | Never ascribe to malice that which can
XXXXXX@oac.hsc.uth.tmc.edu       | adequately be explained by stupidity.
    "begin 666 foo B22!C86XG="!B96QI979E('EO=2!D96-09&5D('1H:7,A"@' end"
                -- XXXXXXXXXXX
```

To see what this fragment means, you have to run it through uudecode. Most uuencoded files are considerably longer than this sample one, so not much can be expected from the small sample fragment given here. Uudecoded, it reads:

```
"I can't believe you decoded this!"
```

Typical geek humor. By the way, if you want to decode this yourself, be aware that the string will have to be broken into three lines in order to be readable by uudecode. Reformat it to look like this:

```
"begin 666 foo
B22!C86XG="!B96QI979E('E0=2!D96-O9&5D('1H:7,A"@'
end"
```

After running this through uudecode, look for the output in a file named foo.

Problems and Exercises

A1. If you receive spam and you want to complain about that, what should you do? Why is it a bad idea to reply to the sender?

A2. Describe three ways that spammers cover their tracks so they are hard to trace.

A3. Explain how the Klez virus has created a lot of spam-related confusion. What is a good lesson for everyone to learn from Klez?

A4. [FIND IT ONLINE] An e-mail filter is only as good as its rules. Procmail is an e-mail client (favored by computer programmers) with a highly configurable filtering capability. Visit `http://petemoss.com/spam/spamstats.html` to see Procmail spam and filtering statistics collected by one user at Concordia University. What percentage of his incoming mail is spam? What is his best spam filtering rate?

A5. [FIND IT ONLINE] Visit `http://spam.abuse.net/goodsites/` to see a list of ISPs that have taken active steps to eliminate spamming activities on their facilities. If you use an ISP, check to see if yours is listed here. Are Hotmail and AOL included in this list?

A6. [FIND IT ONLINE] Visit `http://www.spamlaws.com/us.shtml` to get the latest updates on antispam laws. Are there any federal laws in the United States that address the spam problem? How many states have passed laws that regulate spam? Is your state one of them? If so, what are the penalties for a spam violation?

A7. **[FIND IT ONLINE]** Visit `http://www.cmsconnect.com/Marketing/spamcalc.htm` and see how much spam is costing businesses with this Cost of Spam calculator. Make up some feasible parameters for a fictitious company and see how many days of business productivity are lost each year because of spam. Record your results along with the input parameters that produced them.

A8. Explain what causes raggy text. How can you make sure your e-mail messages don't look raggy to your recipients?

A9. Explain what a uuencoded file is. What protocol effectively replaced uuencoded files in e-mail communications?

A10. **[FIND IT ONLINE]** Investigate a "stealth e-mail" service like the one found at `http://www.stealthemailservice.com/`. Do you think that you might want to use this service yourself? Do you think this service is a good idea? Explain your answers.

A11. **[FIND IT ONLINE]** Visit CAUCE (`http://www.cauce.org/`) and find out what the Electronic Mail Preference Service (e-MPS) is. Why is CAUCE opposed to e-MPS?

A12. **[FIND IT ONLINE]** Visit CAUCE (`http://www.cauce.org/`) and find out how an antispam law that doesn't carry criminal penalties can still be upheld in the courts and act as an effective deterrent against spammers. (Hint: Look in the Frequently Asked Questions section.)

A13. **[FIND IT ONLINE]** Visit Junkbusters (`http://www.junkbusters.com/ht/en/junkemail.html`) and find out why some people believe that the United States might already have a law that makes spam illegal. What law are they talking about, and when was it passed?

A14. **[HANDS-ON]** Monitor all your e-mail (over multiple accounts if need be), and count the number of times you are spammed during a one-week period. If you are filtering incoming e-mail to reduce your spam exposure, trap the filtered messages so that you can count them. How long have you been online? Do you think that the amount of spam you are receiving is increasing? Decreasing? Holding steady? If you are part of a class in which everyone is collecting this data, form a task force to collect all the data and post it on a scatter-plot graph (track the amount of spam on the y-axis and the amount of time online on the x-axis). See if any patterns to the data are evident.

A15. **[FIND IT ONLINE]** "Reverse filtering" has been proposed as a solution to spam. Find out what reverse filtering is, and think about applying it to your own mail. Do you think it would work? Why or why not?

Web 2.0

4.1 Getting Started

People are social beings. We are drawn to each other and form communities, share experiences, and enjoy meals together. The electronic era has spawned yet another way for people to socialize—the World Wide Web via the Internet. Computer scientists first used computer networks in the 1970s to transfer files and enable remote access to powerful computers. At that time, no one anticipated affordable personal computers, the Internet, or the ever-increasing numbers and variety of users who would come to rely on these technologies. A survey conducted in 2003 by the Pew Internet & American Life Project found that more than 53 million American adults have used the Internet to blog, communicate, post images, share files, or contribute content. It's likely that soon every American will be using the Internet as an integral part of daily life.

E-mail remains the most popular Internet application, but other activities, like instant messaging (IM), blogging, and podcasting, are rapidly increasing in popularity. Thanks to the increasing availability and popularity of broadband connections, the ubiquity of the personal computer with ever more powerful dual core microprocessors, and the open

Chapter Goals

- Learn how to blog and find blogs
- Learn how to find and participate in social networks
- Learn about RSS and podcasting
- Learn about wikis and folksonomies
- Learn about discussion groups
- Learn about chat rooms and instant messaging
- Explore the psychology of chat rooms
- Learn about Google Earth

source philosophy (see Section 6.2), Web sites have morphed from primarily static applications to highly dynamic, people-oriented, participatory services that form a complete virtual community.

The World Wide Web is now much more than the original 1990s collection of Web pages linked via the Internet. It is a highly interactive virtual world characterized by its key dependence on human beings interacting with each other in collaborative ways to produce a whole that is truly greater than the sum of its parts. There is a part for everyone to play in this new virtual world, from the most accomplished hacker (the good ones!) to the least technically adept user. All you need is a computer with a browser and Internet access. This new people-centric Web world has been named **Web 2.0**, a term coined by Dale Dougherty and promoted by O'Reilly Media and MediaLive International. Web 2.0 applications are typically created using asynchronous JavaScript and XML (eXtensible Markup Language)—known as **AJAX** applications (see Section 11.6). JavaScript is a scripting language used in computer programming; XML (see Section 11.5) is a markup language similar to HTML (Hypertext Markup Language) used to describe data. We will learn more about JavaScript and HTML in Chapter 10.

Web 2.0 services, including social networking (MySpace, Facebook, YouTube), Weblogs (blogs), syndication (RSS/Atom feeds), wikis (Wikipedia), and folksonomies (del.icio.us) are highly interactive and people oriented. In every case, people like you and me are the vital ingredient necessary for success. For example, consider Wikipedia, an online encyclopedia that you may have used when researching a class paper. The content on Wikipedia is contributed by its users—the Wikipedia staff primarily administers the site and maintains the computer hardware!

You may already write a blog. Countless people keep logs on topics ranging from their daily activities to critical comments about current world events. Often news appears in a blog before it reaches the more traditional news sources. Blogs are found at numerous Web sites, but they are also published; the posted content can be displayed in contexts other than the original source. New content can be forwarded automatically to interested readers via RSS/Atom feeds.

You have certainly used Google to search the Web. It's also probable that you had trouble finding what you were looking for. The del.icio.us Web site was created to allow people to **tag** and post their bookmarks for viewing by the world. In effect, people can organize data and make it available for others. Can't find what you're looking for on Google? Try a keyword search at del.icio.us—there's a good chance that someone who thinks like you has already researched your topic, assembled relevant bookmarks, tagged them the way you would tag them, and posted them. People establish the categories and assign the tags, thereby creating a **folksonomy**—contrasted with a taxonomy, which is a more formal organizational scheme.

All these examples feature the one indispensable component that makes them work: you. The Internet, the Web, and the associated hardware and software is nothing more than a series of circuits and wires. People are the key ingredient that drive Web 2.0, a **Living Web**, as it were, where we can live our lives virtually, and well, really. We can make real connections on the Web: We can meet, date, and even marry people we initially encounter in the virtual world.

Many Web 2.0 sites offer several services simultaneously. MySpace is a social networking site, but it also provides a blogging service. Flickr is primarily a photo-sharing Web site, but it also serves as a **social network** and blogging site—and you can publish and subscribe too. Google Earth provides 3D images of the planet, but you can also get driving directions and participate in associated **online forums** (aka **discussion groups** and **message boards**).

This chapter focuses primarily on presenting an overview of representative Web 2.0 services, together with a few more venerable communications applications: Usenet news, mailing lists, discussion groups, and chat. We conclude the chapter with a presentation of Google Earth, a new technology that fits with the Web 2.0 philosophy in many respects, although the data used to create the images is assembled by professionals. Google Earth is highly interactive and people friendly, allowing people to annotate existing data by creating placemark files.

4.1.1 Virtual Communities, Privacy, and Personal Safety

A **virtual community** is a group of people, usually brought together by a shared interest, who maintain ongoing group communications online. New digital communication technologies are often tested by virtual communities,

TIP: Faster Is Better

Web 2.0 services are typically characterized by the dependence on graphical user interfaces (GUIs) and network connections. To enjoy the Web 2.0 experience fully, you must have broadband access plus a computer with a fast processor, sizable memory, and separate video RAM and video processor.

Figure 4.2
Your blog has
been created!

Figure 4.2
Your blog has
been created!

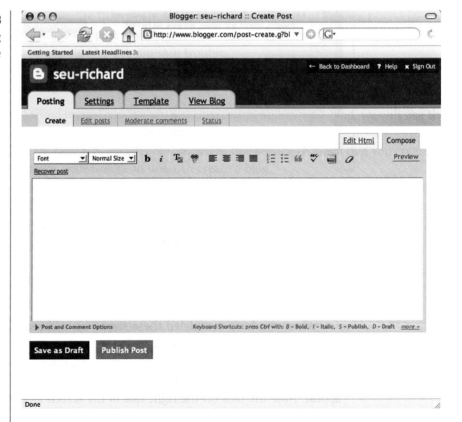

Figure 4.3
Compose a blog
message

already researched your topic, assembled relevant bookmarks, tagged them the way you would tag them, and posted them. People establish the categories and assign the tags, thereby creating a **folksonomy**—contrasted with a taxonomy, which is a more formal organizational scheme.

All these examples feature the one indispensable component that makes them work: you. The Internet, the Web, and the associated hardware and software is nothing more than a series of circuits and wires. People are the key ingredient that drive Web 2.0, a **Living Web**, as it were, where we can live our lives virtually, and well, really. We can make real connections on the Web: We can meet, date, and even marry people we initially encounter in the virtual world.

Many Web 2.0 sites offer several services simultaneously. MySpace is a social networking site, but it also provides a blogging service. Flickr is primarily a photo-sharing Web site, but it also serves as a **social network** and blogging site—and you can publish and subscribe too. Google Earth provides 3D images of the planet, but you can also get driving directions and participate in associated **online forums** (aka **discussion groups** and **message boards**).

This chapter focuses primarily on presenting an overview of representative Web 2.0 services, together with a few more venerable communications applications: Usenet news, mailing lists, discussion groups, and chat. We conclude the chapter with a presentation of Google Earth, a new technology that fits with the Web 2.0 philosophy in many respects, although the data used to create the images is assembled by professionals. Google Earth is highly interactive and people friendly, allowing people to annotate existing data by creating placemark files.

4.1.1 Virtual Communities, Privacy, and Personal Safety

A **virtual community** is a group of people, usually brought together by a shared interest, who maintain ongoing group communications online. New digital communication technologies are often tested by virtual communities,

TIP: Faster Is Better

Web 2.0 services are typically characterized by the dependence on graphical user interfaces (GUIs) and network connections. To enjoy the Web 2.0 experience fully, you must have broadband access plus a computer with a fast processor, sizable memory, and separate video RAM and video processor.

whose participants are looking for new and better ways to communicate online.

Some people are reluctant to participate in virtual communities because of privacy concerns. For example, if you join a support group for incest survivors or AIDS patients, you will want to know how private your sensitive communications are. Some virtual communities are more private than others, but none can guarantee absolute privacy. If a law enforcement agency wants access to your online communications and the hosting service has an archive containing those communications, you should assume that the hosting service, if asked to surrender the archive, will cooperate. Furthermore, archives and log files could be posted on public Web pages in the future. It's possible that someone active in an online community might someday become famous or notorious, thereby making archives with communications from that person of great public or historical interest. Graduate students in 2100 will undoubtedly study online archives from 2000 for information about cultural beliefs, social mores, linguistic usage, and anything else deemed worthy of academic study.

Anonymous Remailers. If you are concerned about personal privacy when participating in a virtual community, use an **anonymous remailer**, an e-mail account (owned and operated outside of the United States, if you want to be safe from subpoenas) that safeguards your real identity. It is akin to a Swiss bank account for online communications. It is the only safeguard that can fully protect you from the unpredictability of other community members, investigations by law enforcement agencies, data collection on behalf of corporate interests, and the vulnerability of poorly secured servers. Some anonymous remailers are free; others charge a fee.

If you are concerned about your privacy in virtual communities, but you are not ready for an anonymous remailer, you should at least understand how visible your communications are to corporate data collection operations, your current or prospective boss, and the person you just started dating (if he or she is a typical Internet user), among others. Throughout this chapter, a privacy assessment for each virtual community is described along with the steps you can take to protect your privacy. These assessments are not based on empirical data; they merely reflect technological facts. No one can guarantee that an online communication is absolutely secure because it's impossible to guarantee that only the intended virtual community will see it. However, you do have some control over your level of risk. This chapter explains what safeguards are available to minimize that risk.

TIP: Be Careful

If you enter into a personal relationship with someone online, remember that deceptions are easily accomplished on the Internet, and some people assume online personas that have nothing to do with their real-life personalities. Don't give out your real name, address, telephone number, place of work, or any collection of facts that would make it possible to deduce such unique identifiers. Be exceedingly careful about physically meeting someone you know only from the Internet. Any such meeting should take place in a public location in the presence of friends who understand what is happening and are prepared to watch out for you. No one under 18 should arrange to meet with an online acquaintance without parental knowledge: Children are easy prey for adults with ulterior motives.

Originally, personal communications were dominated by parties who know each other: friends, relatives, colleagues, and acquaintances. With the advent of the Internet, strangers routinely exchange e-mail messages, respond to public queries, and chat. Online, social ties are not restricted to people who know each other in real life, and social contacts are no longer constrained by geographical proximity, economic class, age, educational level, or social mores. This is liberating for many people, yet it carries risks. It's been said that "on the Internet, nobody knows you're a dog."

4.2 Blogs

Weblogs, most commonly referred to as **blogs**, are the online equivalent of a diary or personal journal. A blog is implemented as a Web page that can be used to post text, images, sound files, video files, and links to other Web pages or blogs—virtually anything that can be rendered digitally. They differ from a typical Web page in the sense that usually they are not created using a Web page editor (see Chapter 9). Usually blogging tools are made available over the Internet via a browser interface by a blog service provider, such as Blogger. (`http://www.blogger.com`). The blogger (you) only needs to add content. The blog service provider takes care of the details, such as general formatting, posting, and dating. Typically, the provider also provides the ability to collect, date, and post comments from readers.

Blogs have been around in some form since 1994, although they hit the mainstream of American consciousness about 2004. According to Wikipedia, the first blog (then known as an online diary or journal) was created by

Justin Hall, a Swarthmore student, in 1994. Since Technorati (http://technorati.com) began tracking the **blogosphere** in March 2003, the number of blogs has increased from a few thousand to over 57 million as of October 2006. At this rate, 175,000 new blogs are created daily—more than two every second! The size of the blogosphere doubles approximately every six months. Over 19.4 million bloggers continue to post messages to their blogs after three months. As of June 2006, the primary language of the blogosphere is English (at 39 percent), but this number changes constantly. Occasionally swapping places with English is Japanese (at 31 percent).

Blogs have had a significant impact on American culture, especially in politics. In 2002 bloggers reported on comments made by then U.S. Senate Majority Leader Trent Lott at a retirement party honoring fellow senator Strom Thurmond. Initially ignored by the more circumspect mainstream media, the racist nature of the comments made their way into the public sphere, ultimately resulting in the resignation of Senator Lott as majority leader. In 2006 bloggers were the first to post "inappropriate" instant messages and e-mails sent by Congressman Mark Foley to congressional pages. Foley resigned from office shortly thereafter.

There are blog search engines, blog monitoring services, and numerous blog service providers and specialized blogging tools. You can find blogs on just about every subject imaginable. You can create your own blog, place comments in other blogs, surf blogs, and create links to blogs. You can form your own blogging group, localizing posts to group members only.

Blogs can be helpful and harmful to a career. Since September 2005, Scott McNulty, a systems administrator, maintains a blog on personal and technical topics at http://blankbaby.typepad.com. Based largely on the blog content, McNulty was promoted to systems programmer, proving clearly that McNulty knows his business.

Others are not so fortunate. For example, a Boston University instructor was fired for blogging about an attractive student, a flight attendant was fired for posting her "sexy" pictures in uniform, and a nanny lost her job for being too chatty about her employers. Employers may pass on an otherwise quali-

TIP: Web Log = We Blog = Blog

Jorn Barger coined the term **Weblog** in 1997. Peter Merholz is responsible for the term blog. He took the word "Weblog" and rewrote it as "we blog" in a personal blog in mid 1999.

TIP: The Bloggers Will Get You!

In 2006 two U.S. senators placed a "secret hold" on legislation intended to create an online, searchable database listing all government spending. The mystery sparked a campaign by bloggers to find the culprits. Within days, the secret was out: The senators from Alaska (Ted Stevens) and West Virginia (Robert Byrd) placed the hold so they'd have more time to review the legislation. Without the database, it is nearly impossible for interested parties to find out exactly how federal funds are being spent. These senators are known as the most skilled providers of federal funding in the U.S. Senate.

fied applicant based on a blog that uses obscenities and name calling deemed by the employer as indicative of poor journalistic judgment.

4.2.1 Creating a Blog

Before you create a blog, it's important to consider the content and your audience. And it's important to keep your personal safety in mind. As you make your blogging plans, note the following simple rules about blogs and blogging:

- Blog anonymously. Use an alias rather than your real name (although most blog service providers will want to keep a record of your true identity somewhere). One suggestion is to establish your blog at Invisiblog (`http://invisiblog.com/`). Not only is your true identity concealed from your readers, but also it's concealed from the service provider as well. The Electronic Freedom Foundation (EFF) (`http://eee.eff.org/bloggers/`) has even more sophisticated ways to conceal your identity.
- Limit your audience. Many blog services provide ways to control who can access your blog. Depending on the nature and purpose of your blog, you may want to control access to it.
- Don't write anything that you might regret later. Blogs can be *very* public—they're usually open to the world. If you are writing negative comments about your job or employer (which you may want to avoid altogether), keep your comments as general as possible. If you are too specific, you may inadvertently give yourself away—and lose your job. Even though you may live in a free speech country, private employers can fire you based on what you write about them. There is no legal protection in this case. Since the blog is electronically recorded, it's

also very easy to copy. Comments made in the heat of passion may come back to haunt you days (or even years) later. Remember that electronically recorded information lingers somewhere, long after you've deleted the original entry. Consult the Electronic Freedom Foundation (EFF) for more information about the legal aspects associated with blogging.

- Be especially careful with your grammar. If your blog is accessible to the world, the world in turn will be forming its opinion of you based solely on what you write and how you write it. You should always be conscious of your grammar. If your service does not have a grammar checker, compose and check your post in a word processor application, and then paste it into your blog.
- Never put confidential information into your blog. That's why it's confidential! Revealing company trade secrets could be grounds for losing your job.
- Do not post any material that is unlawful, harassing, libelous, abusive, threatening, or harmful in any way. (Most blog service providers require this constraint as part of their Terms of Service.)
- Do not post any material that encourages criminal activity. This could also get you into trouble.
- Read and observe the Terms of Service posted by your blog service provider.

To demonstrate the process of creating and using a blog, we will use the blogging service (Blogger) supported and owned by Google (http://www.blogger.com). Access to this service requires that you create an account with Google in order to create a blog.

When you first visit Blogger, a welcome screen similar to that shown in Figure 4.1 will appear. Creating a blog is very simple—simply follow the instructions shown on the Web pages that appear as you step through the process. There are three steps:

1. All bloggers must first create an account. Review the Terms of Service before you continue.

Blogger doubles as a social networking site (see Section 4.3). As of April 2006, Blogger had over 18 million registered users.

Figure 4.1
Blogger, a Google company

2. Once you have created an account, you must select a name for your blog. Click the Check Availability link to ensure the name has not already been taken. If it has, then Blogger will suggest available names.

3. Select a Skin to set the cosmetic appearance of the page onto which your posts will be placed. This template can always be changed later.

When you have completed these steps, you will see the successful completion screen shown in Figure 4.2.

Now you are ready to post your first message. Click the Start Posting arrow to create your first message. The composition screen shown in Figure 4.3 will appear. Note the tabs on the right side of the screen labeled "Edit Html" and

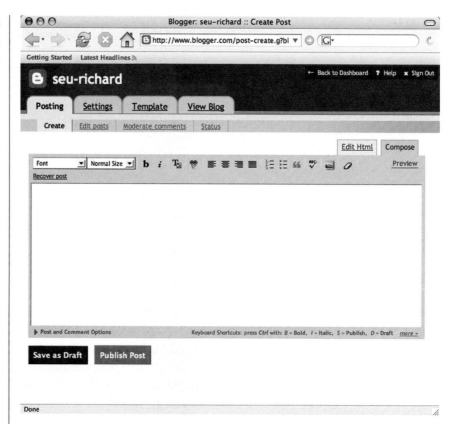

"Compose." The Compose tab provides a what-you-see-is-what-you-get (WYSI-WYG—"whizzy-wig") view of your post. An array of tools is provided above the white text entry area. This is similar to what is provided by the Mozilla Web page Composer feature, which we will explore in Chapter 9.

Like most software applications, these tools are best learned by use. Create a post in your blog, make sure it's grammatically correct and appropriate for a blog, and then press the orange Publish Post button. That's it! You're a blogger! See Figure 4.4 for a screenshot of this post.

Once you have created your blog, a URL is also created to go directly to it. The URL will be the blog name you select, followed by blogspot.com. The one created here can be found at `http://seu-richard.blogspot.com/`.

Figure 4.4

The first post to the blog; click "0 comments" to add a comment

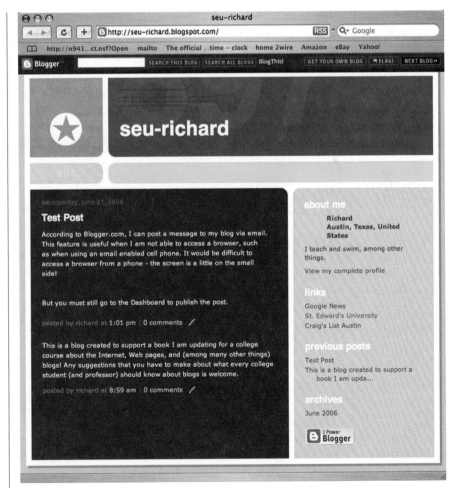

There are links found on the right side of the page (under "links" see Figure 4.4). You must edit the template to insert links, which means you must learn a little bit about HTML and Web page structure. We will defer this topic until Chapter 10. If you can't wait, when you first create your blog there are links named Edit Me. When you click these links, a page with instructions will appear telling you how to insert your links in place of or in addition to the default ones inserted by Blogger. (Or you can skip ahead to Chapter 10 where links are discussed in the HTML section.)

By default, Blogger allows only registered users to post replies to your blog, which can be done by clicking where it says "0 comments" (see Figure 4.4). The comment screen is shown in Figure 4.5.

When you return to your blog (return to Blogger), you will log in using the account name and password you created when you originally visited the site. On completion of the login process, you will be presented with the Dashboard screen shown in Figure 4.6. You can create a new post by pressing the green plus sign (+) in the Blog window.

Figure 4.5

Posting a comment to a blog

Figure 4.6

The Blogger
Dashboard

You can control the appearance of your blog and certain administrative properties, including who can post, links, archive features, and e-mail postings (as opposed to browser-based postings). You can also add members to your blog and limit access to them only. Click the Change Settings button and then the Settings-Comments tab to designate who is able to post to your blog: Only Registered Users, Anyone, or Only Members of this Blog (see Figure 4.7). By default, only registered users (Blogger users) are allowed to post. There is a comment moderation switch on this page, as shown in Figure 4.8. When comments are moderated you can review comments before they appear on your blog. You choose if the comments should be posted or deleted. Note that when making changes in your settings, the blog must be republished to take effect. A message will appear reminding you of this when you make a change (see Figure 4.9).

Figure 4.7
Selecting who can comment

Figure 4.8
Moderating comments

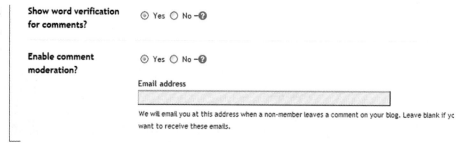

Figure 4.9
Changes to your blog require republishing (the dark blue button).

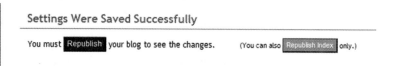

We've only scratched the surface of the blogosphere in this section. Blogger and its peers provide many options to assist you in the development of your blog. Check them out—they're free!

Social Networking

We all have social networks of some sort—families, relatives, classmates, colleagues, and friends. Unless you've been living on Mars, you are probably aware that the social networking scene has expanded to include online social networks. Like real social networks, virtual social networks are formed around common interests, experiences, or friends. Like blogs, social networks require a service provider to supply the technical framework in which people can meet, talk, and share media. Social network providers typically provide blogging capabilities as well.

As of April 2006, the largest social network is hosted at MySpace (`http://www.myspace.com`) (see Figure 4.10). With over 38 million members, it's far ahead of its closest competitor, Blogger (see Section 4.2), which has over 18 million members. In February 2004, the Pew Internet & American Life Project reported that 27 percent of U.S. adults read them and 7 percent contribute to them, numbers that continue to increase. The top 10 social network sites are listed in Table 4.1.

The major feature of a social network is the **profile** you create when you first join the network. Your profile lists personal information such as your

Figure 4.10

MySpace join screen

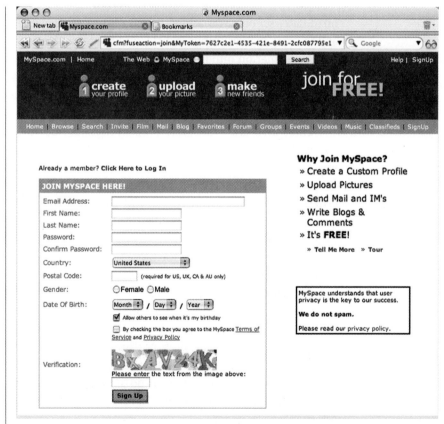

Service	URL	Users (Millions)
MySpace	http://www.myspace.com/	38,359
Blogger	http://www.blogger.com/	18,508
Classmates Online	http://www.classmates.com/	12,865
YouTube	http://www.youtube.com/	12,505
MSN Groups	http://groups.msn.com/	10,570
AOL Hometown	http://hometown.aol.com/	9,590
Yahoo! Groups	http://groups.yahoo.com/	9,165
MSN Spaces	http://spaces.msn.com/	7,165
Six Apart/Type Pad	http://www.sixapart.com/ http://www.typepad.com/	6,711
Xanga.com	http://www.xanga.com/	6,631

birth date, schools you attend or have attended, degrees you hold, interests, and favorite movies, songs, artists, and hobbies. Most sites convert your personal information into links that display pages of links to other members who listed the same interests in their profile. All social network services provide a means for you to search for (see Figure 4.11) and invite people to become your "friends" and add them to your friend space.

These links and other search capabilities provide ways to meet people who you would not otherwise meet. Often, the social network services provide a way for you to move your "real" networks to the virtual world. Figure 4.11 shows a simple search for the purpose of meeting people. Based on selected criteria, 10 members were found. Not shown in the figure is a link for each person who matched the specified criteria. One of the members found is Noodles, who describes herself as "a fun luving girl, can swim like an otter and there is nothing that pleases me more than not sharing my toys." She goes on to say "O and I have a tattoo, just rub my belly to see it."

But Noodles is a dog—just my luck!

Like anything else, there's a downside to the Internet. There is no such thing as an Internet police force, or any other type of policing agency. There is nothing to stop people from posting inaccurate and misleading information. There is no way to verify that the posted member picture matches the person who posted it and there is no simple way to verify the age of a member. So it's important to be on guard at all times. People you meet on the Internet are strangers!

Figure 4.11

Searching for
friends in
MySpace

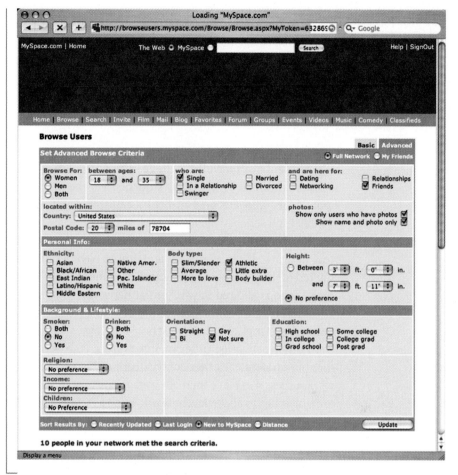

TIP: Politicians in Cyberspace

The popularity of social networking sites has now become part of the campaign trail. The 2006 Democratic candidate for governor of California "adopted" the profile created for him in MySpace by an enthusiastic volunteer. The candidate proceeded to use his personal page to post position papers and other announcements. He also used the site to gather information on issues of interest to the public. MySpace is considering creating a section just for politicians and activists. YouTube has also been used to circulate television announcements and parodies associated with campaign events, although no formal political options are being considered. Facebook is reviewing reduced rates for campaigns and advocacy groups, letting them create miniprofiles.

TIP: Six Degrees of Separation

In 1967 psychologist Stanley Milgram found that two random U.S. citizens were connected to each other by, at most, six degrees of separation (acquaintances). Subsequent studies conducted at Ohio State University and Columbia University showed that a maximum of five to seven degrees of separation are sufficient for connecting any two people on the Internet.

Students, especially college students, are probably familiar with Facebook. Aimed primarily at students, Facebook membership is limited to individuals who are on Facebook's registered network list, which includes 22,000 high schools, 2,500 colleges, and 1,000 work networks. You must have a valid school e-mail account or college alumni account to be a member of this network. High school students must have a school e-mail address or be invited to join by another student at the school. In this way, your school determines who is allowed in your initial network.

Facebook limits the availability of your profile to other members in your network (your classmates and school employees) and friends that you approve from other networks. Other members from your school can access your profile, but students at other schools cannot because they are not in your network, unless you place them on your friends list. Facebook also provides a way for a member to add a new network, such as when a high school student graduates and goes on to college or when a college student transfers to a new school.

Like MySpace, Facebook uses the information in your profile (see Figure 4.12) to help you connect with others who share similar interests. Based on the information you submit, Facebook converts the information into links that display one or more pages of other members who provide similar information.

Although Facebook's network limitation can provide some degree of security lacking in MySpace, it's not foolproof. But because you must have a valid network e-mail and you must be able to reply to messages to this address from Facebook to confirm your registration, there is at least some degree of assurance that the member is indeed a fellow student or a school employee. And since records of account owners are undoubtedly kept by the institution, the true owner of the e-mail can probably be found and confirmed (or arrested if necessary!).

An interesting feature of Facebook is Pulse (see Figure 4.13). Facebook tracks locally emerging trends compared to the entire Facebook community

Figure 4.12

The basic Facebook member profile screen

facebook   home search browse invite help logout
Edit My Profile

Basic Contact Personal Education Work Summer Plans Courses Picture

Note: To edit your school status, year or geography, go to the Networks page in My Account.

Sex:	Male
Interested In:	☐ Men ☐ Women
Relationship Status:	It's Complicated with...
Looking For:	☐ Friendship ☐ Dating ☐ A Relationship ☐ Random Play ☐ Whatever I can get
Residence:	
Room:	
Birthday:	Month: Day: Year:
Hometown:	
State:	Select State: United States

Save Changes   Cancel

by listing the top 10 recording artists, movies, television programs, books, and hometowns based on information entered in member profiles.

The growth in social networks is astounding. Facebook was created by a Harvard student in February 2004 and grew to more than 7.5 million people in two years. It is ranked as the seventh most visited site in the United States by comScore (April 2006). MySpace was launched in its current form (it had an earlier identity as a file-sharing service) in July 2003. MySpace reported over 87 million users as of June 2006!

TIP: Videos and Social Networking

If you're into videos, you might want to check out YouTube (http://www.youtube.com). YouTube is a social networking site for people who want to watch and share videos worldwide. If a picture is worth 1,000 words, then a video must be millions! But be careful what you post – three men posing as police officers questioned a teenage boy about a fictitious robbery and posted a video of the event in YouTube. When the teen later learned of the post, the authorities were notified and one of the pranksters was arraigned on various charges, including impersonating a police officer.

Figure 4.13
Facebook Pulse—
current trends of
students at
St. Edward's
University and
all Facebook
members

With such rapid growth, social networking has also suffered its own peculiar sort of growing pains, especially affecting teens. In June 2006, a 16-year-old teen from Michigan tricked her parents into providing a passport and plane tickets to the Middle East so she could meet a West Bank man she met on MySpace. She had been communicating with the man, described as a 25-year-old from Jericho, for about three months. U.S. officials in Jordan intercepted and persuaded her to return home safely.

A group of boys in California created a fictitious 15-year-old girl persona on MySpace to cheer up a friend who had broken up with his girlfriend. Soon, another MySpace member began sending messages to the girl, including his picture. The messages included sexually suggestive comments, and eventually a meeting in a public park was suggested. When the man arrived for the tryst, the police confronted him and he was arrested.

Not all these meetings end positively. In April 2006, a 14-year-old Texas girl met a 19-year-old boy on MySpace. After several weeks of sending messages to each other, they arranged a date. The boy picked her up after school, treated her to a burger and a movie, and then took her to an apartment complex parking lot where he sexually assaulted her. Consequently, the girl's parents filed a $30 million lawsuit against MySpace.

Although these examples feature MySpace (popularity is not without its own problems!), similar problems happen in all social networks. The Federal Trade Commission (`http://www.ftc.gov/bcp/edu/pubs/consumer/tech/tec14.htm`) offers the following recommendations for young users (and older ones too):

- **Learn how members may contact each other.** Member-posted content can be limited to members only, selected members, or anybody. Find out if it's possible to limit access and how to do this for sites that are wide open by default.
- **Keep some control over the information you post.** Some profile forms can be quite detailed. If you don't feel comfortable about sharing some of the information requested, then don't provide it. Also consider restricting access to the most personal posts to select family members and friends.
- **Don't post critical information.** Never post information like Social Security numbers, driver's license numbers, phone numbers, addresses, full names, bank account, or credit card numbers, or other information that is unique to you. And don't post this type of information about others! Be cautious about posting information that could help someone locate you, such as your school, your work, or places you hang out.
- **Select a login/account name that provides some degree of anonymity.** A user name like HazelParkJanie (after Hazel Park, Michigan, population ~19,000) might make it easy for someone to find you. Avoid using your real name (if it's unique), your age, or your hometown.
- **Once posted, this information cannot be recalled.** Even if you delete the information at a later date, it can still exist on some computer somewhere. So consider carefully before posting.
- **Consider not posting your photo.** A picture is probably worth more than 1,000 words, especially if someone is searching for you. Even worse, with today's photo editing tools, you might find your head

convincingly patched onto a somewhat compromising photographic tableau!

- **Flirting with strangers online could have serious consequences.** Because some people lie about who they really are, you never really know who you're dealing with, as demonstrated in the preceding paragraphs.
- **Be wary if a new online friend wants to meet you in person.** Before you decide to meet someone, do some research. Ask whether any of your friends know the person, and see what background you can dig up through online searches. If you decide to meet the person, be smart about it. Meet in a public place, during the day, and bring friends you trust. Tell an adult, a responsible sibling, or a close friend where you're going, and when you expect to return.
- **Trust your gut if you have suspicions.** If you feel threatened by someone or uncomfortable because of something said online, tell someone you trust and report it to the police and the social networking site. You could end up preventing someone else from becoming a victim.

Coincidentally, MySpace implemented new restrictions on how adults and younger users can interact. Children under 14 years old have always been prohibited from creating accounts. Previously, full profiles of members 14–15 years old were viewable by approved (by the profile owner) "friends" only. Anybody could search the profiles and make such a request to the owner of the profile.

The new rules prevent members over 17 years old from requesting to be on a younger member's list unless they know the full name or e-mail address of the youth. All users are still able to view partial profiles of younger members and all users have the option of making only partial profiles available to other members. There is no doubt that other social network services will make similar changes.

Regrettably, there is no way for any provider to guarantee the age of a member, so these new rules will not eliminate the possibility of fraud or worse. Your personal safety is your responsibility!

 # 4.4 RSS

If you have or read a blog and maintain a profile on MySpace or Facebook, then you probably spend time visiting various Web sites and perusing Web pages to see what's new. If you visit many pages, then you might want to learn about RSS feeds. An **RSS feed** (aka **channel**) is basically a URL to a location on a Web server (more precisely an **RSS server**) that displays a time-stamped list of short titles and/or summaries of newly posted content (such as articles or blog entries), including a link to the source, which can be polled periodically for updates by an **RSS client**. The document provided by the server is usually written in **XML**, a markup language used to facilitate computer-to-computer communication. In other words, once you **subscribe** to that feed from an RSS server, the RSS client can locate and display lists of updates to content that you want to follow. Often, the RSS client will generate an audible and/or visual alert (mine chirps!) to let you know that an RSS feed has been updated.

The acronym RSS has more than one interpretation. The current interpretation is "Really Simple Syndication," which reflects the fact that a Web site or blog is considered "syndicated" when the author makes it available for "publication," much like the way an advice column (Dear Abby, Ann Landers) appears simultaneously in newspapers all over the country. Once the source is "published" on an RSS server, anyone can subscribe to the feed, so the feed is now syndicated. RSS feeds can be used to syndicate any type of content that can be recorded digitally, including text, video, and audio. When the RSS feed is audio only, sometimes it is referred to as **podcasting**, in reference to the use of **iPods** to listen to the broadcasts. (Originally, the iPod could play audio files only—newer iPods can also display video, but the name podcast persists.)

The technology was originally developed by Netscape in 1999. At that time Netscape defined RSS as "RDF (Resource Description Framework) Site Summary." Shortly after, RSS was redefined to mean "Rich Site Summary." The current definition—Really Simple Syndication—was proposed in 2002. The constant reinterpretation of the acronym reflects the immaturity of the technology and jockeying between different groups determined to publish a definitive standard. To make matters more complicated, a third standard for syndication of Internet content, known as **Atom**, has been proposed and adopted by the Internet Engineering Task Force (IETF).

4.4.1 RSS Aggregators

Fortunately, regardless of how the RSS standard battle and the meaning of its acronym turn out, it's not that hard to take advantage of the technology. As you might have surmised, there are two basic requirements to make it possible to subscribe to an RSS feed: an RSS server to provide the RSS feed (over which you have no control) and an RSS client (which you can control) presumably running on your home computer. The RSS client is also known as an **aggregator** or an **RSS reader** because it can manage RSS feeds from multiple sources, providing access to all of them through a single consistent interface. An aggregator can be implemented in the following ways:

- Via an online aggregator service such as Bloglines, My Yahoo!, or NewsGator Online
- With a Web browser that supports RSS feeds (currently, Internet Explorer v7+, Firefox v1.5+, Netscape v8+, and Opera v9+ support RSS feeds)
- With a stand-alone program such as NewsReader or FeedDemon
- Via an add-on such as NewsGator's E-mail Edition, which adds RSS capability to Outlook Express, Eudora, or any POP3 e-mail client

Feedreader, a stand-alone aggregator, is shown in Figure 4.14. The complete text of the article referenced in the headline is displayed on the right side of the Feedreader screen, shown in Figure 4.15. The RSS subscription list for

Figure 4.14

The Feedreader stand-alone RSS client

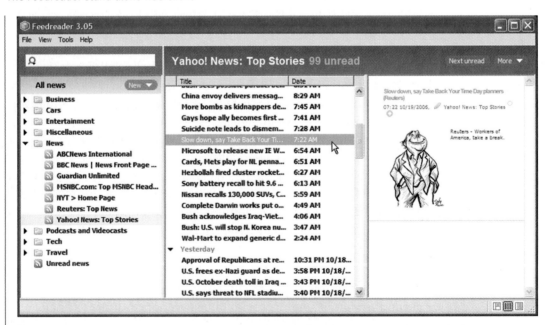

Figure 4.15

The full text of the selected displays when the headline is selected

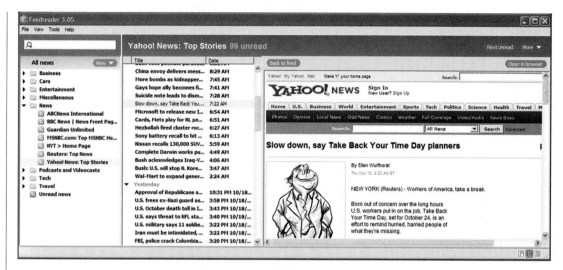

IE (v7), which now includes a built-in RSS aggregator, is shown in Figure 4.16. The NewsGator free online RSS client is shown in Figure 4.17. Figure 4.18 displays a list and icons for some popular RSS clients.

4.4.2 Finding RSS Feeds

So where do you find feeds? One way is to go to a site that maintains a directory of RSS feeds, such as Syndic8 (http://www.syndic8.com/), NewsIsFree.com (http://newsisfree.com), Feedster.com, (http://www.feedster.com/feedfinder.php/), or Blogstreet (http://blogstreet.com/). Most of the news service Web sites provide the capability to subscribe. Figure 4.19 shows a drop-down list of the RSS feeds found at MSNBC displayed by the Firefox browser. Although the list of articles looks like a simple bookmark list, in fact, it is updated periodically as content of the MSNBC site changes in real time.

Web pages that provide RSS feeds to which you can subscribe are easily identified by the orange RSS icon located adjacent to the URL (Firefox—

Figure 4.16

IE v7 RSS feed list

Figure 4.17

NewsGator online RSS client

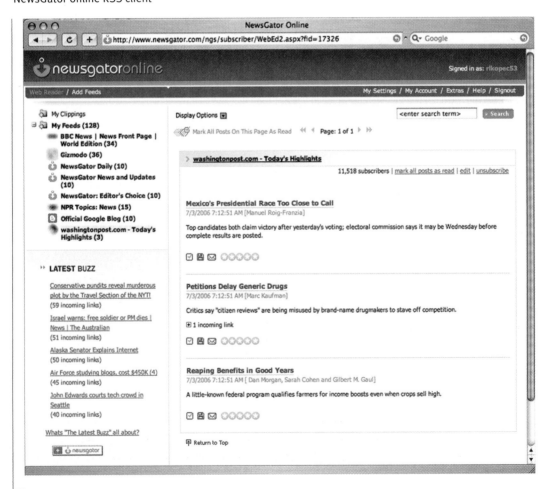

Figure 4.18

Several popular RSS and feed-reading clients (as displayed by a site using FeedBurner's service platform for feed management)

Reproduced with permission of Yahoo! Inc. © 2006 by Yahoo! Inc. YAHOO! and the YAHOO! logo are trademarks of Yahoo! Inc.

Figure 4.19

RSS feeds from MSNBC

TIP: Older Browsers Can Display Feeds

If you are using an older browser that does not directly support RSS feeds, you can still use it to display RSS feeds with an add-on like AmphetaDesk (http://www.disobey.com/amphetadesk). AmphetaDesk adds a subscribing/polling module to your browser that displays the subscribed feeds.

Figure 4.20(a), Opera—Figure 4.20(b), or on the toolbar above the browser window (IE v7—Figure 4.20(c). Netscape uses a different icon (Figure 4.20(d), while Safari uses the RSS (Figure 4.20(e). Because of the confusion in standards mentioned above, you may also see RSS , XML , or even RDF . You may also see variations of the XML icon such as these: ■ (AmphetaDesk) and ■ (Radio UserLand). In any case, it's usually just a matter of clicking the icon to subscribe to that feed if you are planning to use one of these browsers to view RSS feeds. RSS feeds are becoming more and more common on Web pages that you may frequent. Look for one of the icons described above to see if your favorite Web site includes an RSS feed.

How does it work? We'll step you through the process using Feedreader and IE v7. Once you have downloaded and installed Feedreader (http://www.feedreader.com) you are ready to go. To add a feed, first you must navigate to the RSS source you wish to add to your list of channels from your browser—the free version of Feedreader does not support direct searches for available RSS channels. Once you find a source of RSS channels you wish to add (as determined by the symbols shown above), click the symbol, then copy the associated URL (in this case to MSNBC top headlines) into the text entry box at the top of the Feedreader window, as shown in Figure 4.21(a). The URL will end with .rss, .rdf, .xml, or .atom. Note that you need to determine which of these formats your aggregator can handle. Once the URL has been added, click the OK button to subscribe.

Once you have subscribed to the feed, its name will appear in the list of RSS feeds on the left side of the window, as shown in Figure 4.21(b).

When a new article is posted on any of your RSS feeds, Feedreader will signal the event visually, as shown in Figure 4.22 and audibly, with a chirp. Figure 4.22 shows the pop-up window that appears briefly when a new article is posted on one of the subscribed RSS feeds. They can be annoying if you subscribe to many feeds, so Feedreader allows you to turn them off from the Tool→Options menu.

Don't get carried away with RSS feed subscriptions! Remember that regardless of which method you select to access RSS feeds, the associated application will be polling the RSS servers at regular intervals and probably downloading content. This activity usually occurs in the background, but it still steals CPU cycles from your computer. If you are doing something else when this happens (for example, using your word processor), you may notice a distinct slowdown, or even a momentary freeze in response. The more feeds you have, the longer it will take to poll all of them for updates.

Figure 4.20

RSS icons displayed in various Web browsers

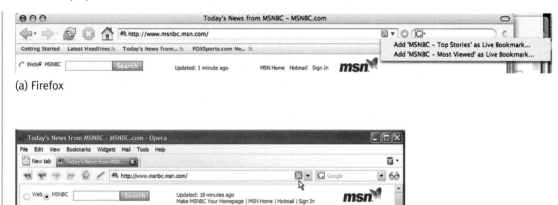

(a) Firefox

(b) Opera

(c) IE v7 (Windows only)

(d) Netscape v8 (Windows only)

(e) Safari (Macintosh only)

Figure 4.21

Adding an RSS
feed to
Feedreader

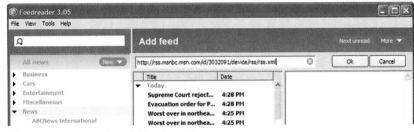

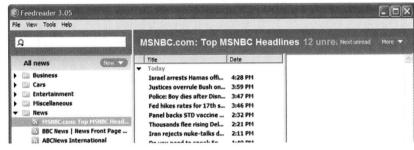

(a) Enter the URL in the Add feed text box

(b) MSNBC appears in the list of subscribed feeds

Figure 4.22

A Feedreader
pop-up window
announcing a
new post

TIP: Live Bookmarks and Live Titles

The Firefox browser (v1.5+) supports RSS subscriptions via Live Bookmarks. Feeds in your subscription list will appear as bookmarks in Firefox, which displays a list of item titles when the bookmark is selected. Figure 4.23 shows the dialog box that appears when the RSS icon to the right of the URL is clicked. The resulting bookmark can be displayed on the toolbar above the Firefox browser window. When selected, a drop-down list showing article headlines appears for selection, as shown in Figure 4.24. Firefox also supports "Live Titles"—sort of like an RSS feed for page titles. When viewing your bookmark list, the bookmark name can summarize page info dynamically. When changes are made to the page content, a summary of those changes will appear along with the page title, but only if the Web site supports this feature and the page includes it.

Figure 4.23

Adding a live bookmark using Firefox

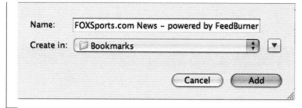

Figure 4.24

Item headlines displayed in Firefox Bookmarks appearing on the toolbar above the browser window

Even though most of the mainstream browsers now support feeds directly, if you are heavily subscribed you might want to consider a standalone RSS reader anyway. You can always close the reader when you don't need it and continue with "normal" browsing.

4.4.3 Podcasting

Another related mechanism for syndication of electronically authored materials is podcasting, originally interpreted as a means to publish audio files. Named after the phenomenally successful Apple iPod, a podcast can be made from any multimedia file, usually in an MP3 format, which allows distribution of songs, interviews, personal audio blogs, and retransmission of regularly syndicated radio and television broadcasts. The term podcast itself can refer to the content or the method of distribution via an RSS feed, so one can subscribe to regularly published podcasts. Figure 4.25 shows some of the podcasts available from Podcast Alley (http://www.podcastalley.com). Podcasts can be downloaded via subscription or individually from a list of choices, then transferred to and played on an MP3 player at any time.

Podcasts are similar to Webcasts, except that podcasts can be downloaded automatically once subscribed and viewed whenever it's convenient. A **Webcast** is usually a real-time (live) or pre-recorded video or audio feed that you must

Figure 4.25

The Podcast Alley Directory

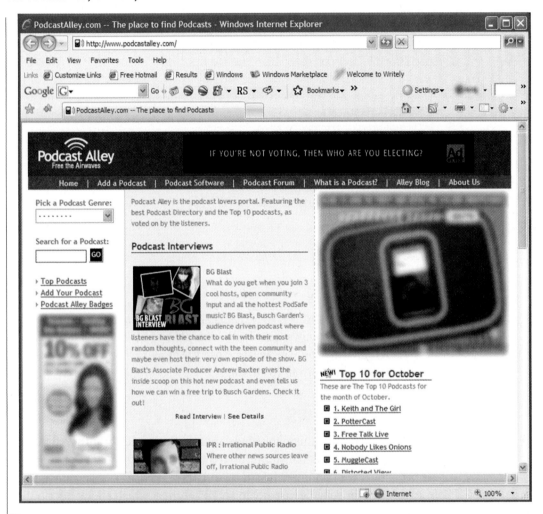

actively seek, and it typically involves a regularly scheduled broadcast that uses streaming media technology to distribute content (often live) to multiple destinations simultaneously. Webcasts are produced by major news organizations, numerous radio stations, and private individuals. Because **streaming technology** (a file transmission protocol designed to view media files as they are being transmitted) can make it difficult to record files delivered this way, Webcasts are intended to be viewed only once, when they are broadcast, not later. However, many Webcasts may also be recorded and subsequently made available as podcasts, and many podcasts may also be made available as Webcasts. The difference between the two terms is blurring rapidly.

Video files containing your favorite television programs are becoming available as podcasts. Once bandwidth issues have been resolved, it's likely that you will be able to subscribe to movies in this fashion.

To listen to or view podcasts, you can use the audio file capabilities of your personal computer or you can transfer the downloaded files from your computer to an MP3 player (like the iPod). Apple's iTunes software, which is available for both Windows and Mac users, makes this process very simple. Figure 4.26 shows the window for the Apple iTunes Store, which facilitates access to podcasts. To play a podcast, select it and use the controls shown at the top of the iTunes window, as shown in Figure 4.27.

Figure 4.26

The Apple iTunes list of podcasts

Figure 4.27

Two subscribed podcasts; use the control at the top of the window to play the selected podcast

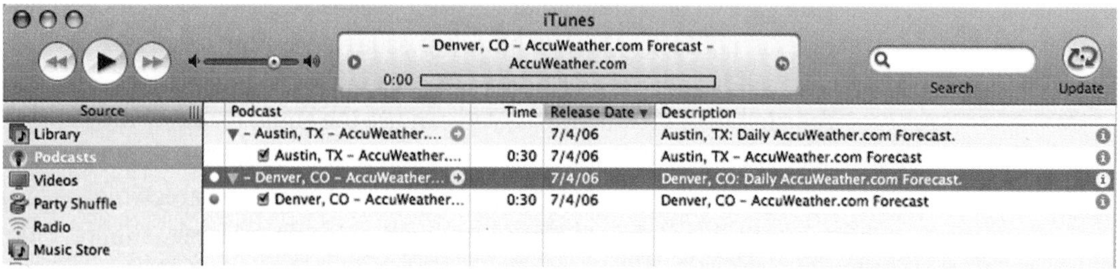

To create a podcast, all you need is a computer equipped with a microphone and audio recording software such as Audacity (PC), GarageBand, or Quicktime Pro. Once the audio files are created, they must be published on a server that allows RSS feeds. Once published, you can add your podcast to the iTunes podcast listing using the tools provided, as shown in Figure 4.28.

Podcasting has grown dramatically since it was first introduced in 2004. At that time a Google search on podcasts (see Chapter 5) turned up 24 hits. Five days later there were 2,750, and in three weeks the number was over 100,000. On July 4, 2006, a Google search reported 422,000,000 hits, including links to 28,800 podcast sites!

4.5 Wikis and Folksonomies

Another aspect of Web 2.0 is the use of a server, a data management system, and a Web interface to collect, organize, and store data. A wiki or a folksonomy can be created with these tools. The former focuses on collecting information on a specific topic or theme (for example, cooking recipes) and the latter focuses on tagging existing data using informal classification schemes as opposed to formal classification rules (a **taxonomy**). But the lines are blurry—a wiki site necessarily organizes its content while a folksonomy might also store the data it's categorizing. We will look at each of the variants. Both wikis and folksonomies make it possible for people to work together on collaborative projects.

4.5.1 Wikis

A true Web 2.0 phenomenon is the wiki. Simply put, a **wiki** is server software that provides the capability to create and edit Web page content using any

Figure 4.28

Submitting your podcast to the iTunes directory

Web browser. Typically it uses a database to store, organize and retrieve content on demand. But in a larger context, a wiki is a social network of countless individuals, each contributing their own unique piece to a larger whole.

The most obvious example of a wiki is **Wikipedia**, an online encyclopedia (see Figure 4.29). Any visitor to the site (`http://www.wikipedia.org`) can contribute. The result, according to creator Jimmy Wales, is "an effort to create and distribute a multilingual free encyclopedia of the highest possible quality to every single person on the planet in their own language." With regard to content, Wikipedia relies on the trustworthiness of its contributors. When one contributor posts incorrect or objectionable content, another contributor can correct it. Consistent with Web 2.0 philosophy, information is constantly being added and updated, resulting in an amazingly current

Figure 4.29

Wikipedia, the free online encyclopedia

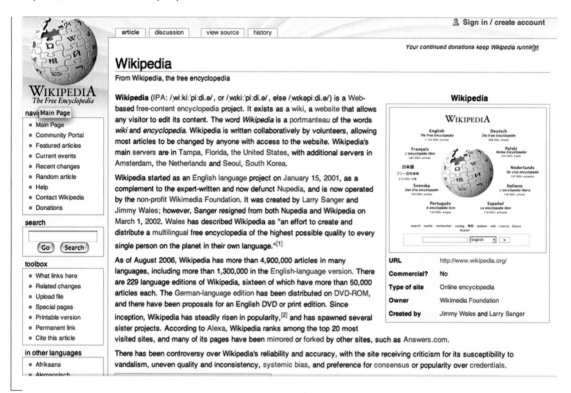

source. Critics have pointed out the uneven quality and consistency, a preference for consensus or popularity over professional credentials, and cultural bias on the part of the contributors. For these reasons, when doing research, readers should not rely solely on Wikipedia.

Wikipedia claims to be the largest and most used encyclopedia in the world. Other online encyclopedias include Stanford Encyclopedia of Philosophy (http://plato.stanford.edu/), and **h2g2** (http://www.bbc.co.uk/dna/h2g2/)—named after *The Hitchhiker's Guide to the Galaxy* by Douglas Adams (see Figures 4.30 and 4.31). As you might guess from its name, the Stanford encyclopedia is more narrowly focused on philosophy.

Like Wikipedia, the h2g2 encyclopedia is more expansive, but it also includes some more offbeat topics such as "How to Hypnotise a Chicken." The site is owned by the British Broadcasting Corporation (BBC), and is based in

Figure 4.30

Home page of the
Stanford
Encyclopedia of
Philosophy

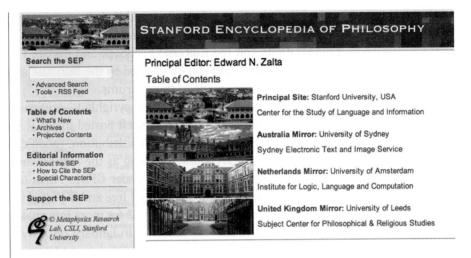

Figure 4.31

Home page of
h2g2

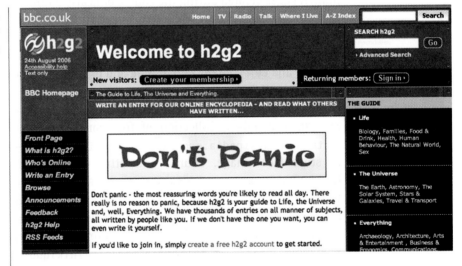

the United Kingdom. The mission of the site is to be a guide to life, the galaxy, and, well, everything! The tone of the entries is generally humorous and well written. Unlike Wikipedia, every entry on h2g2 goes through an in-house editing process. After a period of collaboration, entry content is "locked" and becomes part of the official edited guide. This makes the entries more reliable because vandals cannot change the content—but neither can anyone else, even if the edits are constructive. Each entry also includes a discussion group (`http://docs.google.com`), an online word processor and spreadsheet tool that facilitates the collaborative development of text and spreadsheet documents by a group of people. To access this service via your Web browser, first you must register by entering an e-mail address and password. Once you reply to the confirmation e-mail message, you're ready to go.

New documents are created by selecting the New Document or New Spreadsheet link in the Google Docs window (see Figure 4.34). When you create and open a document, the browser window displays like any word processor (see Figure 4.35) with menus and toolbars that provide all the functions you would expect in a word processor, including cut, copy, paste, print, and spell check. Likewise, if you create and open a spreadsheet, the browser window displays like a spreadsheet program (see Figure 4.36), including sort, formulas, and separate sheets as in all spreadsheet applications. In both cases, the difference is that the document is maintained remotely from your computer.

Google Docs & Spreadsheets permits you to add other people as readers (aka viewers) or contributors (aka collaborators). When you have collabora-

Figure 4.34

Google Docs & Spreadsheets Web site

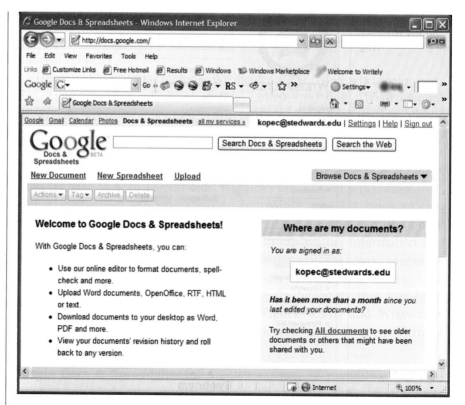

Figure 4.35
Google Docs &
Spreadsheets
word processor
window

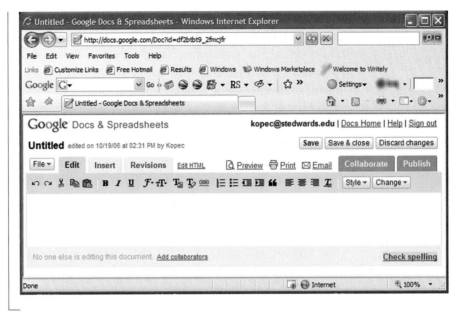

Figure 4.36
Google Docs &
Spreadsheet
spreadsheet
window

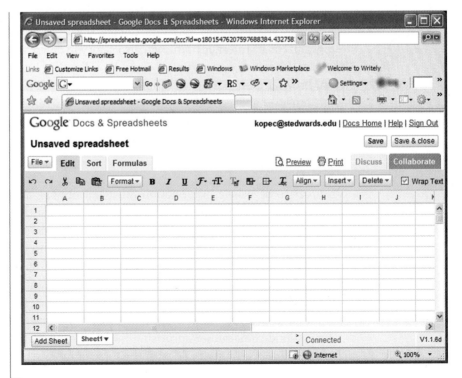

tors, Google Docs & Spreadsheets informs you if they are actively editing the document. When two collaborators change the same section of text or spreadsheet cell at the same time, Google Docs & Spreadsheets detects this. One user will be notified and a fix will be requested. You can publish your document, in effect creating a blog made available via an RSS feed. Documents can also be tagged (see Section 4.5.2) so that you can find and organize files to support RSS feeds by topic. You can upload and download documents into Google Docs & Spreadsheets, and insert images as well as text. Other cool features include the ability to revert to a previous version of your document and compare the latest version of your document with a previous one to find the changes.

Google spreadsheets provide nearly all the basic functions of a spreadsheet (like Microsoft Excel) with the added capability of a sharing function that lets you and selected others have access to view and/or edit the spreadsheet file over the Web. Changes are made in real-time, so simultaneous viewers see the same numbers after every change. The only downside is that the program does not (yet) provide tools for creating graphs or pie charts and the like, nor can they be published, although by the time you read this, such features may be available.

To use these Google tools, a broadband Internet connection is highly desirable, otherwise you may find Google Docs & Spreadsheets to be a bit sluggish. Heavy Internet traffic will also slow you down a bit too. Google Docs & Spreadsheets does not run on every browser. Check the Web site to see if your browser is supported. In order for Google Docs & Spreadsheets to work, you must enable cookies and JavaScript. Currently, Google Docs & Spreadsheets accounts are free.

4.5.2 Folksonomies

In order to be usable, information must not only be accessible, but also it must be searchable, which implies some way to organize and categorize the data. Search engines use applications known as spiders (aka spider bots) to examine Web pages, extract keywords, and use them to form an index of keywords. Based on the keywords you enter, the search engine returns pages featuring that word, but not necessarily the pages you want. The problem is that spiders do not understand the purpose of the page, they simply look for words on the page that are suitable for categorizing that page in an index. This is why you find some rather surprising hits when you do a search—pages that have absolutely nothing to do with the topic of interest!

The best way to organize Web-accessible information is to have somebody actually read the page, and then associate it with only those keywords that truly characterize the topic of the page—a process known as **tagging**. No organization in the world has the resources to do such a thing, even if it were possible—there are billions of pages posted on the Web. No one could possibly read them all. But there are billions of people in the world. If everybody tagged only a few Web pages, and then reported their results to a central database, it would be possible to index far more Web pages correctly than any spider can do!

Furthermore, the data can be organized in a more flexible fashion than that dictated by formal classification schemes. While the latter classification scheme is certainly necessary and helpful, not everybody is knowledgeable about all the various ways that information can be organized. In practice, we tend to use more idiosyncratic terms to classify information and organize our important papers. When the information is classified according to an informal taxonomy, we have what is known as a folksonomy.

The best example of a folksonomy can be found at del.icio.us (that's the complete URL—no "www" or ".com"). del.icio.us allows people to upload their bookmarks, tag them, and make them available for others to use. Not everybody thinks alike, but some people do. Wouldn't it be nice to access a set of bookmarks from someone who thinks like you? del.icio.us provides this exact service. Figure 4.37 shows a screenshot of a del.icio.us search for "asteroids." Figure 4.38 shows the results of a Google search for "folksonomy." Recently Yahoo! launched a new folksonomy service that allows users to tag their bookmarks like del.icio.us does. Check it out at `http://myweb2.search.yahoo.com/`.

Another popular folksonomy is Flickr (`http://www.flickr.com`). Flickr was originally established as a photo sharing Web site. It was purchased by Yahoo! so Yahoo! members can become Flickr members simply by entering their Yahoo! account information into the login screen. Others can sign up for free accounts on Flickr. Registered members (registration is free) can browse and upload photos; visitors can search the photo library. Photos can be marked public or private and private photos can be shared selectively with other members.

FYI: Cool Domain Names

The URL del.icio.us is an example of a **domain hack**—an unconventional name formed by a clever use of letters to form a common word or phrase.

Figure 4.37
del.icio.us results
for "asteroids"

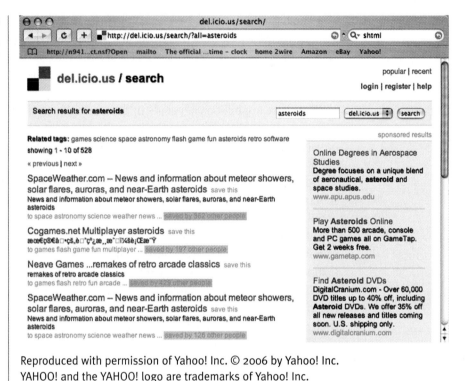

Reproduced with permission of Yahoo! Inc. © 2006 by Yahoo! Inc.
YAHOO! and the YAHOO! logo are trademarks of Yahoo! Inc.

Figure 4.38
Google results for
"folksonomy"

Flickr members tag their photos, allowing Flickr to organize the photos in the library according to keywords suggested by the members. Users can search for photos by entering keywords into the search box provided (see Figure 4.39). Photos tagged with the keywords you use will be located and displayed in list format. Figure 4.39 shows the results of a Flickr search on "Jupiter."

Flickr is more than just a photo sharing Web site—it's also a social network. When you register with Flickr you can create a profile that collects personal information, which can be used to help you establish a social network with other Flickr members, participate in discussion groups (see Section 4.6), and even create a blog. Photos posted on Flickr are not free. If you wish to use a photo, you must contact the member who posted the photo to secure the

Figure 4.39 Flickr, a photo folksonomy

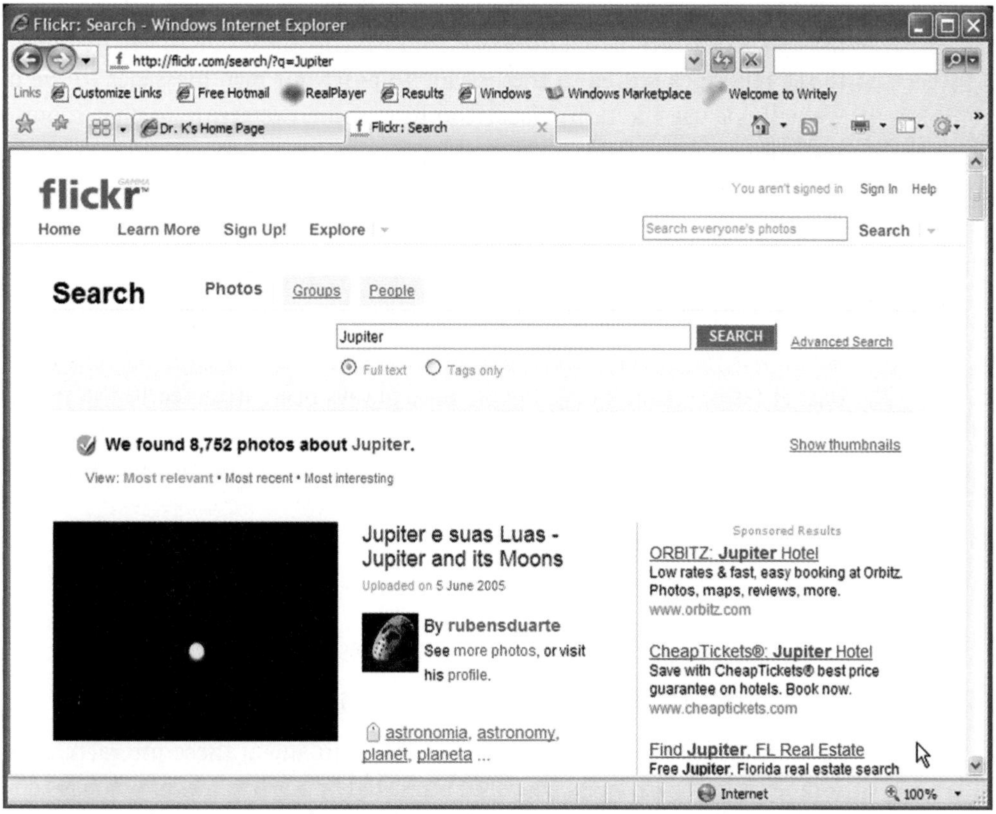

necessary permission for use. In some cases, fair use may apply, and permission may not be required, but the source and contributor should always be cited. See Appendix D for more information about copyright guidelines.

 # Discussion Groups

A discussion group can be a message board (see Section 4.6.1) or a Web-based **mailing list** (see Section 4.6.2). The terms message board and forum are used interchangeably, but message boards should not be confused with Web-based mailing lists. A message board (or **forum**) is a Web site where people can read messages, post messages, reply to messages, and track discussion threads. Many message boards allow the general public to view posts on the forum, but you must register and log in if you want to post your own messages. Some message boards allow anyone to post messages, but registered members have additional privileges and conveniences. A Web-based mailing list is a mailing list that has a Web-based interface. You have to subscribe to the mailing list to see messages posted to the list and to post your own messages to the list. We will *not* use the term discussion group when referring to chat rooms or instant messaging (see Section 4.7).

4.6.1 Message Boards

It didn't take long for someone to coin a new marketing dictum for the Internet: "If you let 'em talk, they will come." Thus the Web-based message board was born. Its historical roots are in the 1980s BBS movement and Usenet (see Section 4.6.3). People have always been attracted to the Internet equivalent of the office water cooler. With the advent of the Web and the widespread use of Java-enabled browsers, new opportunities for ongoing discussion groups have emerged.

Examples of message boards include the following:

- Voting polls
- Opinion surveys
- Topical discussion boards
- Product review forums (see Figure 4.40)

Anyone is free to jump in and sound off in any of these interactive environments, but each message board is created by a group owner who lays down the discussion topics and the rules of conduct. Web portal sites experiment with all sorts of Web-based discussion groups. If you want to register a com-

Figure 4.40 Epinions' product review forum

plaint or post a good word about something that sparks your interest, undoubtedly there is a discussion group that will welcome your opinions.

Many message boards are related to the content of a specific Web site. A commercial site promoting a product might have a message board where users can look for advice and ask questions about the product. A recreational site might have a message board where visitors can share tips and offer help to newcomers. The best way to get a feel for message boards is to visit a few. The sites we explore in this section are representative of many online communities you can find on the Web.

On the Internet people are drawn together by common interests and goals, a natural desire to mingle and socialize, or possibly, for darker purposes. Feel free to explore these communities to see what you can find, but watch your step because some virtual neighborhoods are safer than others.

If you know where to go, often you can get the expert advice you need for free. The trick is to find the right Web-based forum where people gather to ask questions and share their expertise. Setting aside the question of how to find such a place, let's look at MacFixIt Forums, a site where people go to troubleshoot Macintosh problems (see Figure 4.41).

Registered users have more privileges at MacFixIt (http://www.macfixit.com), but for every registered user, there are at least five unregistered visitors perusing the forums for useful information.

There is a lot of interaction at this site, so in order to keep communications efficient and useful, the site is divided into separate forums where people can talk about various problems they are experiencing with their Macintosh computers. (Yes, even Macs have problems.) Individual forums address hardware problems, multimedia problems, and Internet-related problems, among others (see Figure 4.42). This particular site is useful to technicians and software specialists who are grappling with unusually difficult

Figure 4.41
This forum shows you what registered users are doing.

Figure 4.42

Active sites keep discussions organized with multiple message boards.

Hardware Troubleshooting (Any OS)	Threads	Posts	Last post	Moderator
Desktop Macs Covers Power Macs, Cubes and iMacs and related problems.	5654	21215	08/18/02 12:54 PM	David Knuth, Ilene Hoffman, Lee, Voyager
Portable Macs Covers PowerBooks and iBooks hardware problems.	3555	13713	08/18/02 10:29 AM	darkstranger, David Knuth, Ilene Hoffman
Printers Covers problems with printing and printers.	1653	5448	08/18/02 03:27 AM	darkstranger, Ilene Hoffman
Peripherals, Cards, Monitors, etc. Troubleshooting displays, scanners, drives, PCI/AGP cards and any other hardware not covered in other categories. Use Internet Related Help for modem problems.	2317	6337	08/18/02 01:00 PM	darkstranger, Lee

Multimedia Troubleshooting (Any OS)	Threads	Posts	Last post	Moderator
Apple - i - Products Troubleshoot iDisk, iDVD, iMovie, iPhoto, iPod and iTunes here. Old threads will be moved here.	124	446	08/17/02 05:20 PM	Ilene Hoffman
CD, CD-RW, DVD Solve all those CD burning and buying questions - hardware and software here. Includes Toast, etc. This area under reorganization, patience please.	1922	5929	08/18/02 10:21 AM	darkstranger, Ilene Hoffman, Lee
Music and Audio MP3s, sound converstion and Pro Audio. (If the trouble involves burning a CD, DVD, etc. use this forum: CD, CD-RW, DVD.)	53	245	08/14/02 10:41 AM	Lee
Video, Movies and Photography If you shoot with a camera (digital or analog), edit it, republish it, or offload it to your Mac, ask your questions here!	60	202	08/15/02 06:45 PM	Ilene Hoffman
Other Multimedia QuickTime and other multimedia matters. (Use CD/CDRW for burning issues.) This area is under reorganization, posts are being moved as time permits.	1635	4337	08/16/02 06:42 PM	Ilene Hoffman, Lee

Internet or Cross-Platform Troubleshooting (Any OS)	Threads	Posts	Last post	Moderator
Internet Related Help Internet issues: From getting online, web browsers, setting up a web site, email questions, modems, DSL, Cable, etc.	5573	20512	08/18/02 11:12 AM	darkstranger, P.A.M. Borys
PDA including Palm, Visor, etc. For troubleshooting Mac-to-Palm Organizer, Visor, and even Newton issues.	974	3017	08/17/02 07:28 PM	David Knuth, P.A.M. Borys

problems, but it is also appropriate for casual computer users who are willing to take the time to find the right forum to post a query. Everyone is treated with respect and consideration. Only registered users have posting privileges, but there is no registration fee. The site is completely free and open to the public. When it comes to computers and computer problems, the Internet is the best resource around.

Sending a post to the MacFixIt Forums is easy. You can flag your post with an appropriate posting icon (note, chat, exclamation, file, idea, link, question, ribbon, trophy), and you can insert appropriate smileys by clicking them. You can also preview your post before submitting it so you'll know exactly how it will look on the forum before it appears there (see Figure 4.43).

When you benefit from the kindness of strangers on a message board like this, follow up with an outcome report so others can benefit from your problem-solving experiences (successful or otherwise). Message boards like these are usually archived and indexed by a site-specific search engine so

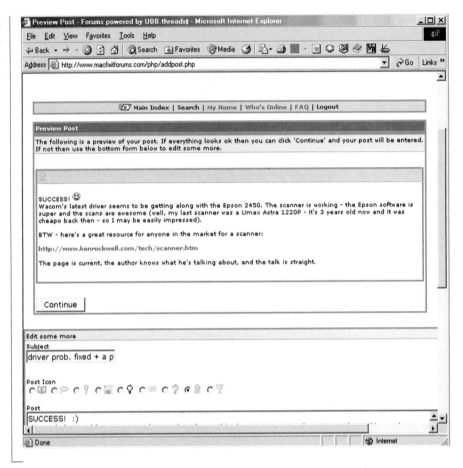

Figure 4.43

Preview your
message before
you post it.

TIP: Posting to a Message Board

If you are having trouble posting a message to a forum, the problem is probably due
to one of the following:

- You aren't registered at the site or you are registered but you haven't
  logged in
- Your browser does not have cookies enabled for the site (most message
  boards require cookies)
- Your firewall is blocking incoming communications from the site (see Figure
  4.44)

Each of these can be easily remedied. Just remember, if you reset your cookie
preferences you will have to reload the Web page that requires the cookie in order for
the change to kick in. And if you have to turn off your firewall to submit a post, turn
it back on right away.

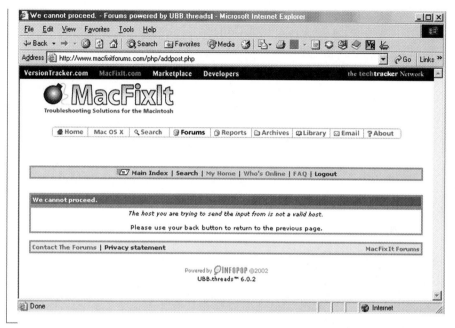

Figure 4.44
Turn off your firewall if you see an error like this one.

visitors can search the archives to see if their particular problem has already been encountered and discussed by others. There is no good reason to initiate a conversation about a problem if that particular problem has already been discussed and solved by others.

If you are inexperienced dealing with technical problems, you may need to consult with someone who will ask a lot of questions before arriving at a plan of action. Getting to that point can require a lot of hand-holding, which is sometimes best accomplished by phone. Technical forums tend to run well when the participants are somewhere beyond the newbie stage. But don't let that stop you from asking for help if you have a problem that looks appropri-

TIP: Asking for Help

Even experts get stuck from time to time. Computer experts often figure out tough problems on their own (techies love a good puzzle), but they won't hesitate to ask fellow experts for help when it's important to get it fixed and get it fixed fast. People who are pressed for time are usually comfortable asking others for help. I've had experts hold my hand pretty tightly when I've wandered off into deep waters. (Try fixing a computer that has been rendered totally useless by a Subseven Trojan.) Everyone who works with computers has to ask for help sooner or later. The people who never figure this out tend to hate computers.

ate for a particular group. Just make sure you are talking to the right forum, be prepared to describe your problem thoroughly, be polite, and above all, be patient.

The **MacFixIt Forums** are a great resource for Mac users and technical support professionals alike. Other message boards are far less ambitious in scope but nevertheless admirable for what they accomplish in other ways.

Braingle (http://www.braingle.com) is an example of a site that uses message boards in a very narrow way for a very limited purpose but with very good effect. Each day a new puzzle is posted at Braingle for anyone who wants to solve it (see Figure 4.45). If you are registered at the site you can cast a vote

Figure 4.45

Some message boards focus on user feedback.

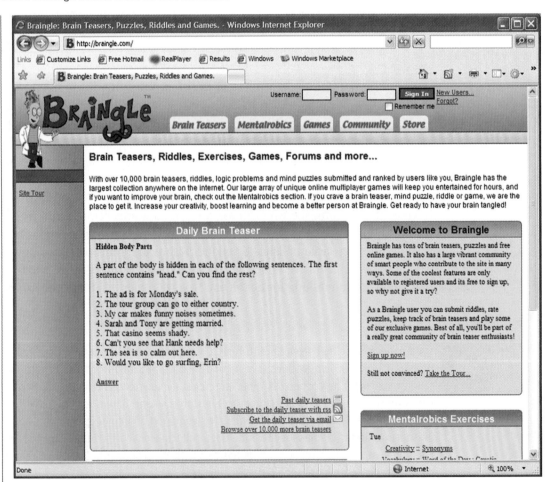

for the puzzle's level of difficulty and another vote for how much fun it was. You can also comment on the puzzle (see Figure 4.46) or suggest a puzzle yourself. Anyone can browse the puzzle archives, organized by puzzle type, popularity, and level of difficulty. Braingle is simple and primarily recreational, but it is a nice resource for teachers or anyone who wants some puzzles on hand for amusement and entertainment.

The two sites we visited (MacFixIt and Braingle) support relatively narrow communities with clearly defined interests. You can also find generic sites that support a large collection of message boards on a wide variety of topics. For example, Yahoo! Message Boards includes forms on hundreds of discussion topics (see Figure 4.47).

Message boards at very large popular sites like Yahoo! can be magnets for irrelevant posts, flame wars, spam, and porn, even though these behaviors are prohibited by the terms of service. It is difficult to police a large online community, and online communities seem to be less susceptible to disruptive behaviors when they are not too large or too unwieldy. Yahoo! is one of the most popular sites on the Web, which makes it feel more like New York City than a friendly little town off the beaten track. When you look for online communities, don't expect to find what you're looking for in five minutes. It may take weeks or months to find a group you truly want to join.

Figure 4.46
Registered users usually have more privileges.

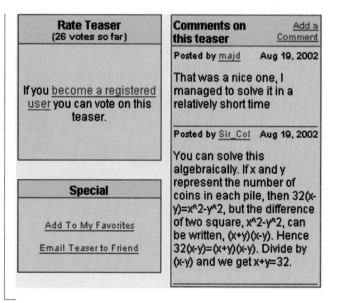

Figure 4.47

The directory of forums at Yahoo! Message Boards

TIP: Truth, Lies, and Misinformation

When looking for information from a message board, be careful. People who post to message boards might misrepresent themselves and/or their institutional affiliation and might post false information, either deliberately or out of ignorance. Always verify important information with at least one independent source before acting on it.

Be especially careful about anyone who offers you financial, technical, medical, or legal advice (for example, regarding investments, computer troubleshooting, personal health, medical treatment, or possible litigation). Suggestions posted to message boards can be informed and on target, or they can be completely off base. Be wary about what you read on message boards, especially if you are new to the topic.

When you participate in a message board, you do not need to identify yourself. As a rule, it's better not to use your real name. Most people use a temporary handle (alias) or, in the case of Yahoo!, their Yahoo! logon ID. Handles protect you to some extent and are certainly better than using your real name. But you should not confuse the use of a handle with true anonymity. Site administrators generally protect the privacy of their registered members (always read the privacy policies for details). However, you should assume your identity will be relinquished to law enforcement agents in response to a court order or a subpoena. If you are comfortable with a site's privacy policy, you trust the site to follow through on that policy, and you do not anticipate legal prosecution; it's enough to use a handle when you post to a message board and keep your identity to yourself.

4.6.2 Web-Based Mailing Lists

Web-based mailing lists are a technological hybrid. They grew out of original mailing lists, which relied on e-mail for all communication (see Section 4.6.3). But they take advantage of the Web in order to make the participation on the mailing list as easy as possible.

When you subscribe to a Web-based mailing list, you'll be asked to set your delivery preferences. You can change these preferences at any time if you want to experiment with other options. You can have messages sent to your e-mail account or you can view the messages on the Web. You might also be able to set preferences that determine how visible you are on the list. Such privacy safeguards can be important if you want to join, say, a mailing list that addresses a serious medical condition or other personal problems. Most people don't want to join a discussion group if it means sacrificing personal privacy regarding sensitive topics.

Most Web-based mailing lists are open to the public; some restrict membership according to rules that the list manager deems appropriate. For example, a mailing list for a specific college course might be limited to students registered for that course. As with any mailing list, you must be a member of the list in order to post messages.

If you want to run your own discussion group, it is very easy to create a Web-based mailing list if you use a site like **Yahoo! Groups** (`http://groups.yahoo.com`). Note that Yahoo! Groups and **Yahoo! Message Boards** (`http://messages.yahoo.com`) are two different things. Yahoo! Message Boards are created by site administrators; members are not allowed to create new ones. But at Yahoo! Groups, any member can create a new mailing list on any topic. If you want to start your own mailing list, first check to see if there is an established mailing list on your proposed topic. It is easy to start a mailing list, but it is not as easy to attract a critical mass of subscribers. Mailing lists that don't have enough subscribers tend to be pretty dead.

Yahoo! Groups is not the only site that will let you start your own mailing list. Free mailing list services include the following:

Yahoo! Groups	`http://groups.yahoo.com/`
bravenet	`http://www.bravenet.com/webtools/elist/`
zinester	`http://www.zinester.com/`

But before you set up your own mailing list, subscribe to a few mailing lists maintained by some different hosting services in order to see which service you like best. If you want lots of people to find your mailing list, it helps to pick a hosting site that is very popular and easy to search (see Figure 4.48).

It's easy to confuse Web-based mailing lists with message boards, but they are different types of discussion groups. You can always tell them apart if you know what to look for (Figure 4.49).

Figure 4.48

Yahoo! Groups is a directory of Yahoo!-sponsored mailing lists.

Reproduced with permission of Yahoo! Inc. © 2006 by Yahoo! Inc.
YAHOO! and the YAHOO! logo are trademarks of Yahoo! Inc.

Figure 4.49

Message boards
versus Web-based
mailing lists

Features	Message Boards	Web-Based Mailing Lists
Mail delivery option	No	Yes
Digest option	No	Yes
Thread-tracking option	Sometimes	No
Anyone can post messages	Sometimes	No
Posting privileges based on a site login	Usually	No
Posting privileges based on a subscription	No	Yes
Create your own discussion group at a hosting site	No	Yes
Consistently fast response times (less than 30 minutes)	Sometimes	Rarely

FYI: Web-Based Discussion Group Privacy

The amount of privacy associated with a Web-based discussion group depends primarily on whether the Web site maintains a searchable archive. Remember the following when joining a Web-based discussion group:

- Use an anonymous remailer to keep your identity maximally safe
- Use a handle to keep your identity relatively safe
- Look for privacy preference settings at Web-based mailing lists (don't assume the default settings are configured to protect your identity)
- Remember that your identity will always be available to law enforcement agents via a court order (unless you use an anonymous remailer)
- If a discussion group is open to the public and maintains a searchable archive, anyone can view your messages
- If a discussion group is not open to the public but maintains a searchable archive, your messages are somewhat safe (however, any group member or infiltrator can copy an archive and "liberate" all the archived messages for public access)

4.6.3 Usenet

Usenet is a distributed online **bulletin board** system that began at Duke University in 1979. Usenet is one of the oldest online message boards in existence. The articles that users post into Usenet are organized into categories (lots of categories!) dubbed **newsgroups**. Usenet users can post messages that can be read by anybody with online access. Like the Web-based discussion groups, you can start new topics (a thread), or you can add comments to an existing thread. Originally, you needed special software to access Usenet (**news client** software). Today, a news client is built in to the Mozilla and Opera (PC only) Web browsers or you can get standalone news clients such as GrabIt (`http://www.shemes.com/`), MesNews (`http://www.shemes.com/`), or Xnews (`http://en.wikipedia.org/wiki/Xnews`), all for Windows. For the Mac, you can try MT-NewsWatcher (`http://www.smfr.org/mtnw/`), a shareware program, or free Mozilla Thunderbird, which is also available for the PC.

The news client keeps track of which articles you have read and which you have not read. To do this, it is necessary to subscribe to the newsgroup using your e-mail address as a user name, but the subscription is usually free, and you do not need to register. In order to subscribe to Usenet, you need access to a news server, a special program that keeps track of the various message boards and their posts. Typically, the name of the news client will be something like *news.yourcollege.edu*. You need this information to successfully subscribe to Usenet. Call your IT help line to get enrollment information for your news server.

An easier way to access Usenet is by viewing the Usenet archives through your browser. Yahoo! and Google Groups allow access to the newsgroups in

FYI: Anything That Old Can't Be Very Good, Can It?

Usenet has been around since 1979, yet less than 5 percent of the online population visits Usenet. If it's that old and it's not more popular, it can't be very good, right? Wrong! Usenet is one of the most valuable resources on the Internet. Sometimes it's good to have a low profile, especially if that small percentage of Internet users represents the "cream of the crop." One reviewer for this book asked me not to talk about Usenet, lest word gets out and Usenet gets ruined. So we'll just call this our little secret. I'm sure my *Web 101* readers are the sort of people Usenet users want on Usenet. Just be careful not to tell anyone else. . . .

TIP: Google Groups and Yahoo! Groups

Please don't confuse **Google Groups** (`http://groups.google.com/`) and Yahoo! Groups (`http://groups.yahoo.com/`). Google Groups is a gateway to the Usenet newsgroups; Yahoo! Groups is a directory of Yahoo!-sponsored mailing lists. They are two very different types of sites.

TIP: Usenet as a Search Tool

If you are thinking of buying a VW Jetta and you want to talk to some Jetta owners, you can find them on Usenet. If you want to know what kind of wood to use for a pool deck, you may find the answer waiting for you in a Usenet archive. If you are looking for a great clearinghouse on a specific topic, you may find a pointer to it in a Usenet post (like the MacFixIt Forums shown in Section 4.6.1). Usenet is an excellent source of generally reliable information and informed opinions on a remarkable range of topics, although it has its share of less than useful posts too.

this way. Google Groups provides access to archives of newsgroup posts back to 1981. You can also get access to the archives at `http://newsone.net`.

You do not need to join Google Groups to read posts, but you must be a member to create your own group, access restricted groups, or post messages to existing groups. Help is provided at `http://groups.google.com/` to teach you how to make use of the facilities provided by Google Groups.

Usenet is not as popular as it was when it was the only game in town. Today, besides Usenet, users have a wide variety of information sources to choose from, including blogs, Web forums, and social networks.

Spend some time at Usenet; I think you'll be impressed. But remember that people turn to Usenet for serious information. Quality content drives the Usenet newsgroups, although Usenet also has its share of junk. If you are more interested in online socializing or just hanging out, you'll be happier in a **real-time** chat session—our next topic.

4.6.4 Mailing Lists

Another impressive Internet service is an **electronic mailing list** developed in 1986 for the BitNet network. A mailing list is a list of e-mail accounts and user names that is used to distribute topically oriented e-mail messages to large numbers of e-mail account holders who have subscribed to the list. To create an Internet-based mailing list, you need a mail server, known as a **listserv**, to maintain the list and manage messages, plus an e-mail client (like Eudora) to send and receive messages. Some listservs also maintain message archives, so it's possible for new users to scan previous messages on the listserv.

Mailing lists are organized by topic, like Usenet news, and you must subscribe to them as well. Users can subscribe, unsubscribe, read, and post using only their e-mail client, but more often, mailing lists support Web-based enrollment to simplify the process. The primary difference between an entirely Web-based discussion list and a traditional mailing list is that the latter "pushes" all the messages addressed to the list to you automatically (whether you want them or not). With a Web-based list, you must actively visit the list and select the messages you want to read.

Traditional e-mail client-based listservs are not as popular as they once were. Listservs have largely been superceded by more interactive forms of online communication like blogs and Web-based forums. You can find a searchable list of listservs at `http://www.lsoft.com/lists/listref.html`. Enrollment instructions are provided as well.

 # 4.7 Internet Relay Chat, Web-Based Chat, and Instant Messaging

Internet relay chat (IRC), Web-based chat, and instant messaging (IM) are three highly popular online applications offered by many large Web portals in an effort to draw people to their sites. They differ from e-mail, message boards, and Usenet in that they offer real-time communication, with response times limited only by participants' typing speeds.

Online chat is not as fast as spoken conversation, but it's certainly a step in that direction and can be quite useful if you need a fast response. There has been at least one incident where someone communicated an urgent medical emergency to an online chat partner. The partner then notified appropriate authorities, who were able to intervene quickly. If you think that you're having a heart attack, you're better off in a chat room than a Usenet newsgroup (although a call to 911 is still your best option).

FYI: Some Different IRC Networks

Search the Web using the keyword "IRC" to find IRC tutorials and IRC-related Web sites. Then visit some IRC networks to discover whether any interest you.

Here are a few IRC networks to get you started. It doesn't matter which you visit first. Note: All IRC clients are compatible with all IRC networks.

- **Efnet** (`http://www.irchelp.org/irchelp/networks/servers/efnet.html`)—the best-known and largest IRC network
- **Undernet** (`http://servers.undernet.org/`)—designed to fix problems at EFnet
- **IRCnet** (`http://www.irchelp.org/irchelp/networks/servers/ircnet.html`)—the oldest IRC network; has many European channels

IRC and IM are two separate Internet applications, although they share some features that make them look very similar. Newbies tend to know about IM (especially if they're teenagers), whereas it takes an old-timer (someone who was online before 1996) to know about IRC. We'll start with IRC because it's the oldest application of the three covered in this section.

4.7.1 Internet Relay Chat

Internet Relay Chat (IRC) predates the Web and relies on a system of IRC servers that share common chat channels, much like the Usenet news servers that share common newsgroups. Users can connect to a local IRC server with an IRC client and tune into any of the available channels. IRC servers are open to the Internet public, unlike the Usenet news servers that restrict news access to some fixed set of Internet domains. IRC is also structured differently from Usenet. Unlike Usenet, which has only one Usenet network that all the Usenet servers share, IRC networks operate their own sets of chat channels. The Net offers many free IRC clients, which are well documented.

To try IRC, download an IRC client and then review the basic commands before you go online. Working with IRC initially might look difficult, but you need only a few commands in order to start chatting. Your IRC client might give you a choice of servers when you first connect; you can pick any of them.

TIP: Children and Chat

Adult chat channels are not for minors. Unless the chat room is policed, participants are free to indulge in adult conversation, including X-rated language and explicit (albeit text-based) sexual encounters. In addition, IRC attracts pedophiles looking for children to befriend and pursue.

Children should be allowed to participate only in family-friendly chat rooms policed by adults who keep the content clean and the language proper. Any child who goes online should know not to reveal identifying information such as last name, address, telephone number, school, and hometown. When an online relationship crosses over into real-world contact, criminal intent can be the motive of the seemingly sincere chat buddy. Some children who have revealed personal information during chat sessions have been subsequently abducted, assaulted, and, in some cases, murdered. Such tragic events have always been a nightmare for concerned parents.

Parents teach their children not to talk to strangers and not to wander off too far from home. They must apply analogous precautions to online encounters. Internet chat with a friend or relative is one thing, but when a child or teenager starts chatting with strangers, serious risks arise.

To keep your identity safe, you must use an anonymous remailer. Although IRC channels don't maintain public archives, nothing will prevent someone from creating a searchable archive for IRC, much like the Google Groups archive for Usenet. In fact, ChatScan does just that for both IRC and some Web-based chat rooms. It helps people locate ongoing conversations in real time, so it probably maintains more of an IRC "snapshot" than a cumulative archive. In any case, IRC could be archived, just like Usenet, and extensive IRC chat logs could easily be created by law enforcement agencies.

Once online, you'll see a list of available channels, with some channels listing the current topics of discussion. The names of the channels are relatively stable, but the topics can change daily or hourly. In a very active channel, the discussion might look confusing because probably many different discussions are going on at once. Any number of people can join a discussion, and some like to monitor multiple chat channels at the same time.

If you want a private conversation with a friend, you can create your own channel and set it up so that others can join by invitation only. This is a great way to save on long-distance telephone calls. IRC is popular among teenagers as a place to meet new people and develop virtual relationships.

4.7.2 Web-Based Chat

IRC clients are fine, but why bother with IRC if you can chat online using only your Web browser? If you have a JavaScript-enabled Web browser, you can participate in thousands of Web-based chat sessions. Often called live chats or chat rooms, these watering holes might or might not have supervisors (most do not) and might or might not focus on a particular topic. Some Web-based chat sessions are scheduled in advance and feature a special guest (see Figure 4.50). Others are always available for anyone who wants to drop in.

No single directory of all the Web-based chat rooms or special events is available. Individual sites that support many chat activities have their own directories and might also maintain an archive of chat sessions with public persons such as celebrities, authors, and athletes. Online chat can be fun, but if you're serious about getting answers to specific questions, you'll get better results from an active message board or a Usenet newsgroup.

Chatting online is a social activity, and it often attracts teenagers and preteens who want a relatively safe (in the sense that nobody knows you) place to

Figure 4.50

Some sites schedule live chats with special guests.

	Tuesday, March 14 - 6:30PM PT gazoontite.com presents ... Managing Pet Allergies with Anton Dotson MD, and Kathryn Schrader, DVM
	Wednesday, March 15 - 5:00PM PT Chat with Mike Keenan Stanley Cup-winning coach Mike Keenan shares NHL insights.
	Wednesday, March 15 - 5:00PM PT Chat with a Columnist Chat with a columnist attending the Erma Bombeck Conference.

TIP: Where Are the Best Chat Rooms?

The best chat rooms are usually found on topic-specific Web sites, where people share a common passion. For example, chat rooms to discuss role-playing games are rather central to online role-playing and tend to attract people who really want to talk about various aspects of one particular game. As a rule, any site with a participatory activity (for example, sites where you can play chess) maintains relatively purposeful chat rooms. Chat rooms where foreign languages are spoken by non-native speakers are wonderful for people trying to learn a foreign language. (There are even chat rooms where you can practice your Latin.) The worst chat rooms are the ones where people just go "to chat." Those places attract a lot of unfortunate souls who have nothing better to do than to visit a chat room to kill time, and that's obvious.

socialize. And just as with any public space where people gather to socialize, all kinds of people can show up and act unpredictably. This is, undoubtedly, part of the allure. Sites also exist where you can set up your own private chat room for personal conversations.

Web-based chat is so popular that some people set up chat capabilities on their personal Web pages. Some of the IRC networks offer Web-based access to their servers so that newcomers can check out the action without downloading an IRC client. In addition, a few commercial Web sites support live chat for real-time customer service and online help. For example, you can access online help from Time-Warner Cable Company. After you provide some contact information, a Road Runner Technical Chat window will open, allowing you to send queries to a tech support representative (see Figure 4.51).

Many teenagers use chat rooms and instant messaging (see Section 4.7.3) as an alternative to telephone calls. Parents are understandably worried about pedophiles preying on children, but most teens spend most of their time chatting online with their friends about school, their plans for

Figure 4.51

Time-Warner Cable offers chat-based support.

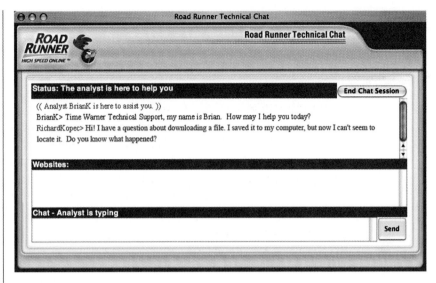

Friday night, and anyone who's not online. Typing is slower than talking, but you can fit many people in a chat room. It's also a less stressful activity than a phone call when two people are still in the getting-to-know-you phase of a relationship. College students use chat rooms as an alternative to expensive long-distance phone calls.

As with all forms of online communication, nothing is private in a chat room. If you bad-mouth someone, your words can be saved and passed along to that individual. In the opinion of some school principals, trashing a fellow student in a chat room is a form of verbal harassment (even though the offending party never meant for those words to get back to the victim). Students have been suspended from school for making cruel statements about other students in chat rooms.

FYI: Locating Chat Rooms

The Web offers many chat directories and chat-related sites. These sites may not point you to the best chat rooms around (see *Tip: Where Are the Best Chat Rooms?*), but at least you can get started with one of the following:

- **Yahoo! Chat** (`http://messenger.yahoo.com/chat.php`)—live chat events, a large number of public chat rooms, and voice chat
- **MSN Chat** (`http://groups.msn.com/ChatCentral/Gateway/chat1.msnw/`)—pick your room based on a city, an age group, or a favorite sport

To keep your identity safe, you must use an anonymous remailer. Most Web-based chat rooms ask you to use a handle. Therefore, many people think that their identities are secure. However, many Web sites keep a log of all chat room conversations, along with records that make it possible to trace the handles that people use, either via e-mail addresses or IP addresses.

So-called "private" chat rooms offer no additional privacy as far as these monitoring activities are concerned. Chat rooms are sometimes monitored by the FBI looking for pedophiles and child pornography operations; the SEC looking for fraudulent stock market manipulations; and large corporations looking for libelous statements (see Section 2.11) or the unlawful distribution of proprietary information.

4.7.3 Instant Messaging

Over 50 million people use an **instant messaging (IM)** client for real-time chat. IM is another variation on real-time chat that combines elements of both IRC and Web-based chat, yet offers some features not found elsewhere. IM is user friendly for newcomers who have little or no experience on the Net.

IM is similar to IRC in that you need to download and install an IM client. It differs from IRC in that each IM network was originally compatible only with its proprietary IM client (and that's how the owners of the most popular IM clients originally wanted it). For example, if you have installed AOL's Instant Messenger (AIM), which has 45 million users, you weren't originally able to talk to people on ICQ's network (**ICQ** stands for I Seek You).

IRC was part of the precommercial Internet, but IM is thoroughly commercial. Although no formal industry standards exist to enable interconnected communications across different IM networks, the major providers have now adopted a *defacto* standard and have signed agreements amongst themselves to allow users in different networks to cross-communicate. If you are using an obscure network (the big three are AOL, Microsoft, and Yahoo!), you may still have trouble sending messages to users in different networks.

All IM clients give you access to many public chat rooms; however, that is not their most popular feature (the generic chat rooms run by the chat client vendors are not very focused). IM clients also support private chat between pairs of people, and this is where most IM communication happens. Chat rooms filled with many strangers tend to be chaotic (see Figure 4.52). Silliness is the norm, and thoughtful communication is difficult to sustain. People who are experienced with online chat tend to split off from the crowd

Figure 4.52
Silliness is the
norm in many
chat rooms.

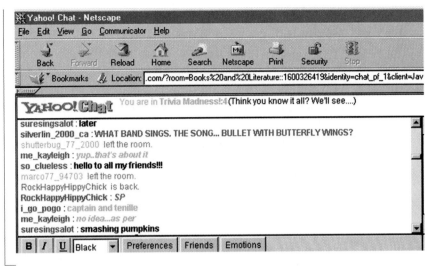

for more manageable conversations. The original IRC servers supported private conversations for this reason, so there's nothing new about IM—it's basically an old idea repackaged for a point-and-click audience.

Any two people who have registered with the same IM network can page each other and set up a private chat session (for example, to exchange pleasantries, communicate details of travel arrangements, or negotiate a restaurant for dinner). IM paging is faster than e-mail but requires that both parties be online at the same time.

If you visit a chat room and meet someone who seems friendly, you might initiate a private conversation with that person. Even in this more workable environment, however, conversations via keyboard are a little awkward. People can't type as fast as they can talk, so these real-time interactions favor short statements, telegraphic writing, and rapid responses. Worse, you can't see what your partner is typing until that person hits the Return or Enter key, so there are periodic pauses when nothing is happening on the screen and

TIP: How to Start a Private Conversation

In AIM, you send the other party an instant message that includes an invitation to talk. The other person can use the same window in which the invitation appears to reply (new text can be added to the window in the frame on the bottom), and you can hold a conversation there. In ICQ, when you send an invitation to chat, a special chat window opens in which you can converse. Each client works a little differently, but they all do more or less the same things.

both of you may be typing something just to keep the conversation going. This can result in questions and answers that overlap and are mixed up—much like having different conversational threads ongoing with the same person (something that doesn't happen with other communication media). Figure 4.53 shows an IM conversation with AIM in which some questions and answers show up out of order, even though both parties are trying to be polite and respond to all questions.

If you want, you can turn your computer into a telephone. Simply install a microphone and use voice chat. Many software packages enable free long-distance telephone calls over the Internet by using voice-enabled chat servers or special telephony servers. The jump from real-time chat to voice chat is not technically difficult. Once you have the IM software in place, you use a microphone instead of a keyboard and modify the chat software to handle audio files as well as text files. You'll have a plausible imitation of a telephone (although bandwidth bottlenecks and Net congestion can cause some breaks and lags).

If you find yourself spending a lot of time with real-time chat and IM, consider investigating some of the more sophisticated chat clients such as ICQ. ICQ is a full-featured client that offers a vast selection of online communities and many nice extras. For example, to contact people who are not currently online, you can drop notes into their message boxes for them to see when they come online. This resembles sending e-mail, except that you don't need to start a mail client and you don't need an e-mail address. ICQ also supports two chat modes for those who want to experiment with different options. In IRC-

Figure 4.53

Two people can have more than one thread going when messages cross.

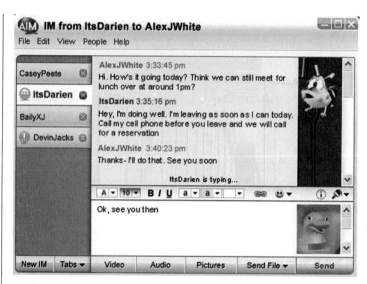

TIP: Getting Started with Live Chat

The following are some tips for engaging in live chat:

- Begin by using one of the simpler chat clients, such as AIM
- Try talking in an IM window instead of a chat room—it's less confusing
- Keep your questions and answers short; don't say too much at once
- Ask lots of questions to keep the conversation going
- Don't be offended if your partner decides to leave abruptly (life is short)
- Learn how to insert emoticons to make up for the absence of vocal intonations and body language

mode chat, no text appears until the user hits the [Return] or [Enter] key. In split-mode chat, each letter appears as it's typed. When two people chat using split-mode chat, the online conversations are more like real conversations.

ICQ is a good place to hook up with people who share very specific interests. For example, if you want to learn about Internet telephony and voice chat, you can join a chat group devoted to that topic and be informed whenever another member of that group is online. You can also register your own interests in terms of a fixed set of categories so that others with similar interests can find you, even if they don't know you (see Figure 4.54).

If you're concerned about your privacy, don't reveal personal information when you set up a chat client or register at Web-based chat sites. Chat rooms are the venue of choice for pedophiles, stalkers, and other potentially dangerous individuals. The anonymity and fast-paced atmosphere of a chat room gives some people license to indulge aspects of their personality that normally might be suppressed. Always consider your personal safety.

IM clients are designed to track people online. If you're running AIM and other people running AIM add you to their Buddy List, they will be informed each time you connect and disconnect to the Net. They can also know when you're online but idle. This might not strike you as a serious invasion of pri-

FYI: IM Clients

AIM is the leading IM client, followed by MSN Messenger, Yahoo! Messenger, and ICQ. ICQ is popular among techies and is somewhat more complicated and less easy to use than the other three. AIM is a good choice for beginners.

AIM (`http://www.aol.com/`)
MSN Messenger (`http://messenger.msn.com/`)
Yahoo! Messenger (`http://pager.yahoo.com`)
ICQ (`http://www.icq.com/`)

Figure 4.54
ICQ ActiveList
helps people
meet people.

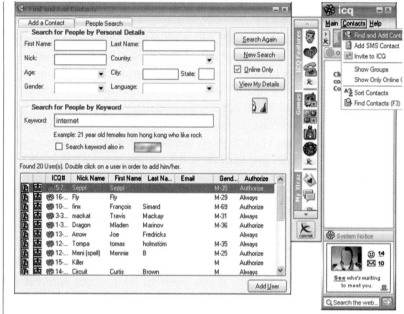

vacy, especially if the person tracking you is a close friend. But it's not wise to have your movements watched by strangers, especially if you reveal patterns and routines that might tell someone when you're normally at home and when you aren't. If someone learns something about your lifestyle, where you live, and when your home is empty, you've set yourself up for a possible attack or burglary. When it comes to online chat with strangers, expect the worst and proceed with caution.

Administrators for chat networks understand the potential risks of their enterprises and try to give users appropriate tools for personal safety (see Figure 4.55). Unfortunately, few newbies take the time to learn everything about the software they use, and most service providers don't assume responsibility for the education of their account holders.

For example, not all AOL subscribers realize that their online comings and goings can be tracked by anyone who knows their AOL user ID, which happens to be the same user ID used for AOL's e-mail addresses. To disable this rather controversial feature, you need to change the AIM access setting from its default option (which makes you visible to everyone) to a more secure option (which makes you visible to no one or only to people whom you select). First launch AIM, and then, from the File menu, select My Options, Edit Preferences, and the Control tab (see Figure 4.56).

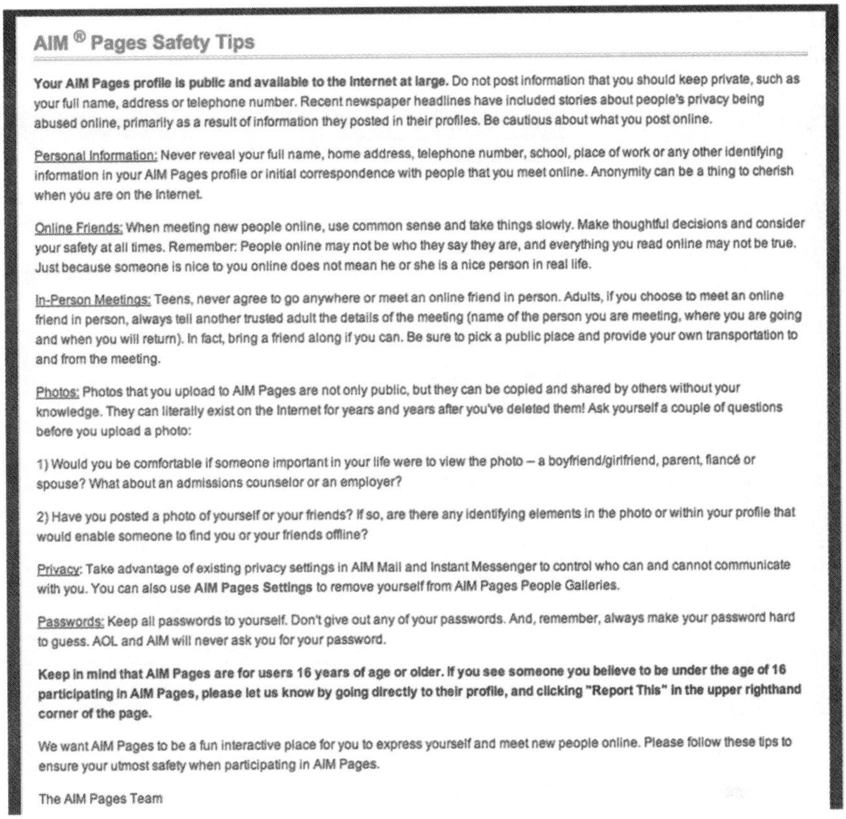

Figure 4.55

Personal privacy
options for AIM
users

AIM ® Pages Safety Tips

Your AIM Pages profile is public and available to the Internet at large. Do not post information that you should keep private, such as your full name, address or telephone number. Recent newspaper headlines have included stories about people's privacy being abused online, primarily as a result of information they posted in their profiles. Be cautious about what you post online.

Personal Information: Never reveal your full name, home address, telephone number, school, place of work or any other identifying information in your AIM Pages profile or initial correspondence with people that you meet online. Anonymity can be a thing to cherish when you are on the Internet.

Online Friends: When meeting new people online, use common sense and take things slowly. Make thoughtful decisions and consider your safety at all times. Remember: People online may not be who they say they are, and everything you read online may not be true. Just because someone is nice to you online does not mean he or she is a nice person in real life.

In-Person Meetings: Teens, never agree to go anywhere or meet an online friend in person. Adults, if you choose to meet an online friend in person, always tell another trusted adult the details of the meeting (name of the person you are meeting, where you are going and when you will return). In fact, bring a friend along if you can. Be sure to pick a public place and provide your own transportation to and from the meeting.

Photos: Photos that you upload to AIM Pages are not only public, but they can be copied and shared by others without your knowledge. They can literally exist on the Internet for years and years after you've deleted them! Ask yourself a couple of questions before you upload a photo:

1) Would you be comfortable if someone important in your life were to view the photo – a boyfriend/girlfriend, parent, fiancé or spouse? What about an admissions counselor or an employer?

2) Have you posted a photo of yourself or your friends? If so, are there any identifying elements in the photo or within your profile that would enable someone to find you or your friends offline?

Privacy: Take advantage of existing privacy settings in AIM Mail and Instant Messenger to control who can and cannot communicate with you. You can also use AIM Pages Settings to remove yourself from AIM Pages People Galleries.

Passwords: Keep all passwords to yourself. Don't give out any of your passwords. And, remember, always make your password hard to guess. AOL and AIM will never ask you for your password.

Keep in mind that AIM Pages are for users 16 years of age or older. If you see someone you believe to be under the age of 16 participating in AIM Pages, please let us know by going directly to their profile, and clicking "Report This" in the upper righthand corner of the page.

We want AIM Pages to be a fun interactive place for you to express yourself and meet new people online. Please follow these tips to ensure your utmost safety when participating in AIM Pages.

The AIM Pages Team

System security is another risky aspect of IM clients. If you have AIM installed on your computer and some malicious individual tampers with the settings, he or she might open the door for unlimited file transfers onto your machine. A worse scenario is leaving your computer online and unattended with an IM client running. This is like leaving your front door wide open and then going away for a week. As mentioned earlier in the book, it's never a good idea to keep a live Internet connection unattended for long periods of time.

Some people who get involved with online chat become addicted to it. They spend so much time chatting with people that it interferes with more important activities and responsibilities. Psychologists are studying this phenomenon in an effort to understand who is at risk and to devise ways to spot and help such online addicts (see Section 4.8). If you think you might be addicted, don't wait for the self-help books on Internet addiction to appear. You can visit the alt.irc.recovery newsgroup on Usenet and determine whether the technology that got you into trouble can help you get out of it.

Figure 4.56

Setting AIM privacy options

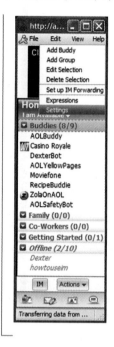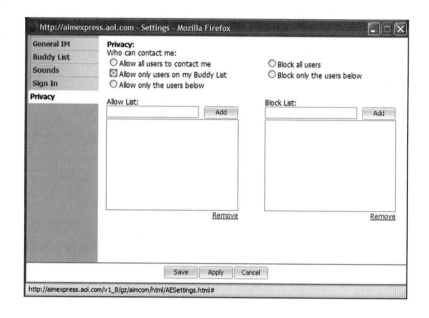

FYI: IM Privacy

 To keep your identity safe, you must use an anonymous remailer. Your privacy can be safeguarded with the right security and preference settings. Always hide your e-mail address and your IP address.

A poorly configured IM client represents a serious security risk that can, in turn, result in a major invasion of your privacy. For example, some IM clients support file sharing, which is a very powerful feature. However, it can also open your entire hard drive to total strangers if you don't manage your preference settings carefully. Whenever you install a new IM client, take some time to learn about your preferences before you go live.

 # 4.8 The Psychology of Chat Rooms

People often behave differently online than they do in real life. Shy, introverted people become uninhibited and gregarious. People who are courteous and polite become hostile and abusive. Men pretend to be women, and women pretend to be men. Nowhere are these transformations more common than in chat rooms. Interestingly, chat rooms are also the most popular online activity for people who are pathologically dependent on the Internet.

Real-time interactive communication, along with online anonymity, is a powerful combination. Anonymity gives people license to experiment with different online personalities, fantasy lifestyles, and erotic relationships. When this freedom allows people to release repressed rage, to fantasize a life better than the one they have, or simply to take a mental vacation from the daily grind, the Internet can become an irresistible and sometimes uncontrollable habit.

Even psychologically stable individuals can regress into antisocial behavior on the Internet. People who are perfectly reasonable in real life have been known to launch flame wars. Both men and women who would never be sexually aggressive in any other setting find it easy (and fun) to hit on people online. Online communities invite people to indulge themselves in behaviors that would be censured in the real world. When people interact online, the experience may feel more like a video game than a conversation with a real person. It is easy to forget that real people are behind the words that appear on a computer monitor—responses are disembodied, and real people begin to resemble characters in a video game. It follows that if the people you meet online aren't real people, then no serious consequences will result from your actions (unless perhaps your actions violate an acceptable use policy (AUP)).

Some chat rooms try to impose a social order by adopting strict AUPs. Others seem to condone an anything goes attitude whereby people can

FYI: When Does the Internet Become a Problem?

In one study, a group of Internet addicts were asked with which Internet applications they spent the most time. The results reveal that the most compelling applications involve interactive communication in real time—chat and fantasy chat. The least compelling applications involved no human interactions—the Web and FTP. Here are the results of the study.

Feature	Percentage of Time Spent
Chat	35
Fantasy chat	28
Newsgroups	15
E-mail	13
Web	7
Other (for example, FTP)	2

indulge themselves in impulsive or antisocial behaviors without fear. A strong desire to play out fantasies and escape real life might be one component of a compulsive Internet personality.

At the same time, the Internet encourages emotional bonding and emotionally intimate relationships that are free from the traditional requirements of shared experiences. Two people can enter into a purely verbal relationship unencumbered by the complications of physical chemistry, body language, and the slower rituals of real-life socialization.

A relationship based on nothing but an exchange of words is a peculiar animal. Emotionally rich fantasies about the other person can be encouraged and nurtured even as deep personal truths are revealed and souls are bared. Participants in long-time cyber relationships often fear the possibility of a face-to-face meeting, especially if they have shared their innermost beliefs, desires, hopes, and dreams. People instinctively seem to understand how much interpersonal give-and-take is missing from a relationship made of nothing but words. The eyes see no face, and the ears hear no voice. No gestures are seen, no facial expressions are read, no intonations are interpreted, and no eye contact is made. Any or all of these missing components can contradict an ideal person constructed from words and expectations. A simple exchange of photographs could easily jar some ideal mental image, however vague, that exists only in the mind's eye.

The computer keyboard fosters a paradoxical type of intimacy. People can dive into an exchange of personal information about themselves on a first meeting and feel perfectly comfortable revealing all sorts of things, with the exception of a real name. Many people find it easy to open up and share intimate details about themselves as long as these online revelations are safely separated from real life. However, the level of trust in an online relationship is very delicate and could be threatened by a partner who wants to cross the line to a real-life meeting. Even when no lies have been told and no facts have been twisted, the difference between an online relationship and a real-life relationship might be far too threatening to contemplate.

People who insist on anonymity behind a pseudonym or a P.O. box number are often viewed with suspicion. Anonymous letters to the editor are tolerated for the sake of free expression, but in most contexts, anonymity is perceived as a dark, vaguely threatening shadow of a person with something to hide. People withholding their true identities tilt the playing field in their direction. They know who you are, but you can't know who they are. From the perspective of the mystery person, there might be something thrilling about the act of secrecy. For example, before the advent of caller ID for telephone

TIP: Some Fantasy Games Are Not Cool, Even in a Chat Room

Any online talk about murder or mayhem might prompt someone to save the transcript to a file and report it to system administrators and the police. An ISP can consult its log files to determine who was in which chat rooms when and then release all such information to law enforcement authorities. If a transcript of an online chat session is deemed admissible as evidence in a court of law, someone's "harmless" fantasy game could result in a prison sentence or a fine. The so-called fantasy defense has been tested in court, without success.

In addition, the FBI has conducted a number of successful chat room sting operations in order to catch pedophiles trying to contact minors or to trade child pornography.

If you want to joke around about sex with children, doing away with your spouse, or pulling off a Rambo-style massacre at the local post office, don't do it with strangers in a public chat room. You could get more of a reaction than you expect.

calls, mischievous children delighted in making prank telephone calls. Even children know that some things can be done only when your identity is safely hidden.

However, in a chat room setting, anonymity is not only accepted but also it's expected. People are allowed and encouraged to identify themselves by online handles. This acceptance of anonymity suggests that some rules of social conduct might also be suspended. For many people, this freedom can translate into regressive behavior or dishonesty. For people with serious psychological problems, the absence of social censure in a chat room can open doors that might be better left closed. It's doubtful that chat rooms transform normal, well-adjusted people into pedophiles or misogynists, but they certainly can bring nascent tendencies to the surface. A sociopath would be hard-pressed to come up with a more comfortable place to hang out than an Internet chat room.

On the brighter side, some online communities offer heart-felt support and understanding to participants. Online friendships quickly blossom among people who share a passion for some common interest. For members of groups organized around personal problems or health concerns, daily conversation and member updates provide a foundation of support that is difficult to obtain elsewhere. A sensitive health problem might be easier to discuss online than face-to-face, and a good online support group will be a source of caring conversation and constant encouragement. More serious communications seem to thrive on e-mail-based mailing lists, where there's a stronger sense of a stable and controlled community. Newcomers are always welcome, but disruptive behavior is not tolerated by the list owner.

Online communication provides a safe haven for the expression of inner thoughts and suppressed emotions. The resulting sense of freedom can either manifest itself irresponsibly (when people misrepresent their real personas) or lead to a genuine sense of community (when people are honest about who they are). To witness a virtual community rally on behalf of a community member, subscribe to a mailing list for dog owners and watch what happens when someone reports the passing of a beloved canine companion. (Conduct a Web search for "Rainbow Bridge" to get a sense of the emotional intensity associated with these communications. Rainbow Bridge is a description of "dog heaven" that is frequently passed along in mailing lists to console fellow members at times of bereavement. Variations on Rainbow Bridge have been written for other pets as well, including, most remarkably, goldfish.) The Internet can be a gentle, compassionate place or one in which idiocy reigns supreme. In this respect, life online is not very different from life in the real world.

 # Google Earth

If you are a Google user (and who isn't!), you may have heard of Earth viewer software named Google Earth (see Figure 4.57) that can be downloaded free at `http://earth.google.com/`. The Google Earth software is capable of displaying patchwork images of the Earth's surface with resolution of at least 15 meters/pixel. Google Earth offers a variety of features for viewing, searching, and sharing information about the Earth and the various points of interest on its surface. Packaged as a complete Internet experience, a Google Earth community has also been formed to allow users to interact in a Web 2.0 fashion.

The Google Earth control panel is visible in the upper-right side of Figure 4.57. Using these controls, you can zoom in and out and rotate the globe to view it from any angle. The cursor can also be used to accomplish these actions by selecting and dragging (to move), double-clicking (zoom in), and right double-clicking (zoom out). As you zoom in to the planet, the resolution increases, and city names and topographical features begin to appear if checked in the Layers panel on the lower-left side of the screen (see Figures 4.57–4.59).

Figure 4.59 shows an image of the Massachusetts State House in Boston as seen from above. In the lower portion of the image you can see people and a car. As you can see, the resolution of select major cities like Boston, London,

Figure 4.57

Google Earth (v 4.0.1693)

Viewing angle control

Zoom in (+)/out (−)

Orientation/ Direction control

Figure 4.58

In Google Earth city names and topographical features appear when you zoom in.

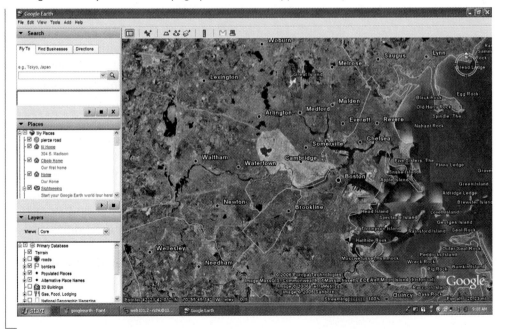

Figure 4.59

A near-maximum resolution image of the Massachusetts State House in Boston.
Notice the car and the people in the mid- and lower-right section of the image.

and New York is high. Cambridge, Massachusetts (see Figure 4.60), and Fulton County, New York, have the highest resolution at six inches per pixel. The viewing perspective can also be changed and some cities can be viewed with a 3D Building perspective. Select this option in the Layers panel on the lower-left and use the tilt slider (the top slider in the viewing controls) to alter the viewing angle. Figure 4.61 shows Detroit viewed from across the Detroit River after using the tilt slider to lower the viewing angle.

With Google Earth you may be able to locate aerial views of your home, your place of business, and certainly large geographic features like the Grand Canyon. Google Earth can also insert labels marking points of interest in the displayed image. You can cause labels to appear for highways, populated areas, gas, food, lodging, shopping, geographic features, and parks and recreation areas. Figure 4.62 shows a view of historic Boston showing highways and parks and recreation areas. Various labels and other display features can be turned on and off using the Layers control panel, as shown in Figure 4.63.

Figure 4.60
University Hall, Harvard University, Cambridge, Massachusetts; notice the U.S. flag and the students gathered in front of the building.

Figure 4.61
Downtown Detroit, as viewed from across the Detroit River with 3D Buildings selected

Figure 4.62

Historic Boston showing highways, and parks and recreation areas viewed from above

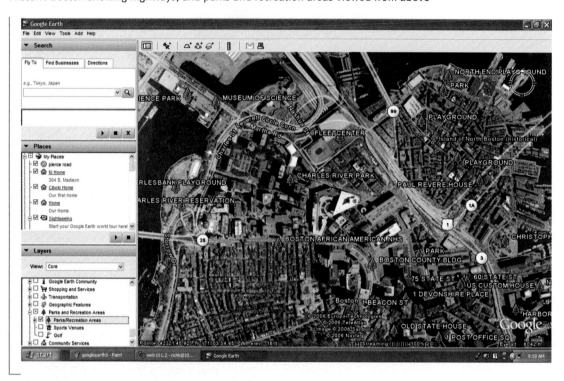

Figure 4.63

The Layers control panel; checked items will change the displayed image by inserting/ removing labels and other topological features

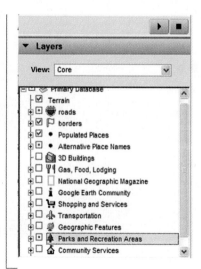

You can also use Google Earth to get travel information using the Search panel and Directions tab in the upper-left corner of the window. Figure 4.64 shows the directions from Cambridge, MA to Boston, MA. If you select the Play Tour button in the Places panel, you can "fly" the route you searched for from the Search panel. You can also save these directions into the Places panel for later reference. To save, right-click in the Search panel and select Save to My Places. (You can also use the File menu to do this.) You may want to double check your route using another mapping site, though. Google Earth does not always choose the most direct route. For example, when traveling from Detroit to Chicago, Google Earth sends the motorist to the Interstate 80/90 Tollway, rather than Interstate 94 as suggested by MapQuest.

There are a number of predefined points of interest, **placemarks**, in the Places panel, including the Grand Canyon. Double-click the Colorado River View in the panel and the display will shift to the view shown in Figure 4.65. You can make your own placemark by navigating to a place of interest and

Figure 4.64

Google Earth directions from Cambridge, MA to Boston, MA

Figure 4.65

View of the Grand Canyon, Colorado River placemark

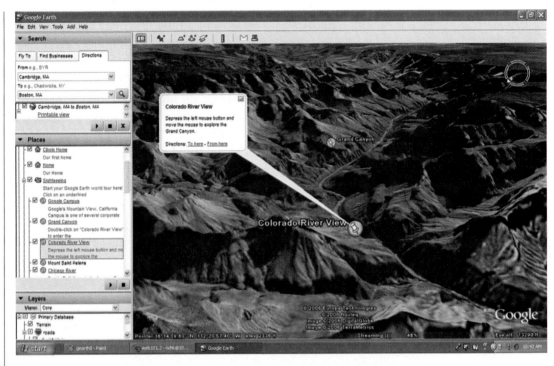

clicking on the Add Placemark tool (looks like a pushpin) on the toolbar below the menu bar. (See Section 4.9.1 for more details).

Consistent with Web 2.0 philosophy, a Google Earth community facilitates sharing of tours, points of interest, and other related information (it's also a social network and discussion group). If you have inserted a placemark that you wish to share with others on the network, then right-click ([Ctrl]-click on a Mac) and choose Share/Post. Figure 4.59 shows such a placemark—the **i** next to Hart Plaza. Figure 4.66 shows a Worldwide Panorama placemark of a suburban marketplace located near Athens, Greece, posted by Yiorgos Teo. Selecting a posted placemark opens a balloon with information about that placemark, as shown in the figure. Be prepared to wait a few months before your placemark appears on a Google Earth image. It takes Google some time to incorporate user placemarks into its database.

Placemarks may have links to Web pages or other posted information about that placemark. Clicking on the link shown in Figure 4.66 causes a new

Figure 4.66

A Worldwide Panorama placemark in Athens, Greece

panel to appear in the lower portion of the Google Earth window showing additional information (see Figure 4.67). You can also cause this panel to open up in a separate browser window by clicking on the New Window tool located immediately to the left of the Close Window tool (the X) on the toolbar located just below the Google Earth 3D panel. You must join the Google Earth community before you can post files—but it's free.

Joining Google Earth puts you in contact with users around the globe. You can read and post messages in the various forums. Figure 4.68 shows the discussion forums available when this text was written. For example, archaeologists have used Google Earth to locate potential sites for examination and study. This work is posted in the Education forum category, as shown in Figure 4.69.

TIP: HTML Isn't the Only Markup Langauge

Keyhole Markup Language (KML) is a markup language used by Google for modeling and storing geographic features (placemarks) for display in Google Earth and Google Maps. KML is an XML grammar (see Section 11.5) that has many similarities with HTML that we will study in Chapter 10. As you might guess, KML files usually have a `.kml` extension. KML can also be stored in a `.kmz` file—a zipped version of a KML file. You can learn more about KML and how it can be used in Google Earth at `http://earth.google.com/kml/`.

Figure 4.67

Image of suburban Athens marketplace posted in the Google
Earth Community Showcase, Worldwide Panoramas

Figure 4.68

Google Earth Community discussion groups

Category	Forums	Topics	Posts
News Google Earth News	2	72 (72)	117 (117)
Earth See and share locations of interest to others around the earth	15	270580 (272544)	418308 (420249)
Other Planets Exploring our solar system	1	94 (97)	425 (428)
Discovery Club Placemark collections by seasoned explorers	4	1265 (1266)	5009 (5012)
Education Information for Students and Educators using Google Earth in the Classroom	3	8844 (8846)	10714 (10748)
Support Resources for both new and experienced users	9	9326 (2218)	39493 (8085)
Archive Retired Databases	2	1163	5335
Members' Open Area Places of interest to only a few and discussions that are off-topic from all other forums	3	7119 (1)	20049 (3)

Figure 4.69

Google Earth Community Education forum post

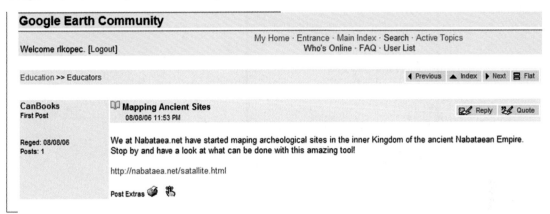

Google Earth is heavily graphics and processor intensive, so you'll want to make sure that your computer system *at least* meets the minimum configuration parameters specified by Google. You can learn more about Google Earth by consulting the user guide at http://earth.google.com/ userguide/v4/ug_kml.html.

4.9.1 Creating a Google Earth Tour

A Google Earth Tour is a collection of placemarks placed into a folder that you create in the Places panel that Google Earth will "fly" to in sequence when triggered. To create a tour, you will need Google Earth and a list of the places you wish to insert into your tour. To start your tour, first you must create and name the folder you will use to store your placemarks. Do this by selecting My Places in the Places panel, and then choosing Folder from the Add menu at the top of the screen. A dialog box will appear asking you to name the folder and provide a description of the tour you will be creating (see Figure 4.70). Click OK and the folder will be placed into the Places panel.

Now you're ready to create your tour by navigating to the places you wish to visit on your tour and creating a placemark for each location. Google Earth will automatically insert placemarks that you create into the folder selected in the Places panel, so make sure the desired folder is selected first as shown in Figure 4.71. Google Earth puts every new placemark at the top of the folder. When you play a tour, places are visited in top-down order as listed, so you

Figure 4.70

Create a New
Folder in Places

Figure 4.71

A new folder
appears in the
Places panel

may wish to enter your tour in reverse order (last location to visit first, first location to visit last). Otherwise you will need to drag the placemarks around in the folder until they appear in the order you wish to visit them.

To create a placemark, navigate to a location you want to include in your tour, and then use the placemark tool, as shown in Figure 4.72 to insert a placemark. You may need to use the mouse to drag the placemark around until it appears exactly where you want it. Enter the necessary information in the dialog box that appears (see Figure 4.73) and click the OK button to insert it. The placemark will be stored in the selected folder in the Places panel, as shown in Figure 4.74. Repeat this process for each location you want to visit.

Now you're ready to play the tour. Make sure that the check box appearing immediately to the left of your tour folder is checked, and that all other folder check boxes in the Place panel are *not* checked. (Otherwise all locations

Figure 4.72
The Google Earth
placemark tool

Figure 4.73
A placemark
dialog box

Figure 4.74
The new place-
mark appears in
the myTour folder

in the checked folders will be visited!) Then press the Play button at the bottom of the Places panel (the arrow pointing to the right in Figure 4.74). Google Earth will immediately move the display to your first placemark, pause

Figure 4.75

A Google Earth tour can be saved as a stand-alone file.

a few seconds, and then fly to the next placemark, continuing until all the placemarks have been visited. Viewers of your tour can pause, continue the tour, or stop it altogether.

You can also save the tour into a stand-alone file and send it your friends, or post it in a Google Earth Community forum for the world to see. To save a tour, again make sure that the folder to be saved is selected, and then right-click it or select "Save As..." from the File menu. The file will be saved onto your hard drive as a `.kmz` file (see Figure 4.75).

Things to Remember

- Be careful what you post in a blog or podcast
- Be sensitive to personal safety guidelines when participating in a social network
- Don't get carried away with too many RSS subscriptions—it might bog down your computer
- Consider using a stand-alone RSS client
- Contribute your fair share to wikis and folksonomies you use
- Google Earth can be used to preview a route you plan to travel
- When you join a new mailing list, lurk for a while before you post
- Find out if a mailing list is archived for public consumption before you post sensitive information to the list

- Always use a handle when you sign on for any type of online chat session
- Be careful giving out personal information to strangers during chat sessions
- Locate and understand all available privacy settings before you use an IM client
- Never post sensitive information to a blog, social network forum, group, or chat room unless you're comfortable with the possibility of its being archived and released to the public
- If you do something illegal in a chat room, your identity can be traced

Important Concepts

AJAX use of asynchronous JavaScript, CSS, and XML to implement Web applications

anonymous remailer an e-mail account designed to protect the identity of its owner

blogs online journals, also known as Weblogs

folksonomy a Web accessible database with content organized by its users

instant messaging (IM) a private communication channel between people who use the same IM client software; typically used by people who know each other and want to stay in close touch

mailing list a discussion forum in which subscribers post messages via e-mail

message boards discussion forums on the Web that normally require you to register with the Web site if you want to post messages

newsreader client software for reading and posting messages to Usenet newsgroups

online forums, discussion groups, message boards, bulletin boards online methods of communication typically using a Web browser

podcasting a multimedia file playing on mobile devices (iPods) or computers

profile a collection of personal information describing an Internet service account holder suitable for posting on the Internet

real-time chat a public communication channel whereby people gather in a chat room to exchange typed messages in real time

RSS client (aka aggregator or RSS Reader) manages and displays RSS feeds from a variety of sources

RSS feed a data format used for servers providing frequently updated content

RSS server a program able to provide content in the form of an RSS feed

social network an online community where people with common interests can meet, share files, and find information

spambot a program designed to collect e-mail addresses from the Internet in order to form mailing lists for unsolicited mail (spam)

streaming technology transmission protocol that allows media to be viewed/heard as it is being transmitted

Usenet a discussion forum within the Usenet hierarchy in which anyone can drop in to ask questions or post messages

virtual community a group of people, usually brought together by some shared interest, who maintain ongoing group communications online

Web 2.0 the latest buzzword in the computer industry that usually refers to applications built using AJAX techniques

Webcast a real-time multimedia broadcast transmitted over the Internet using streaming technology

wiki a Web site that allows visitors to add, modify, or remove content associated with a unifying theme

Wikipedia an online encyclopedia where content is contributed by the users

Where Can I Learn More?

Blogs

Blog software comparison chart
http://www.ojr.org/ojr/images/blog_software_comparison.cfm

Legal guide for bloggers
http://www.eff.org/bloggers/lg/

Blog Search Engines

Blogdigger `http://www.blogdigger.com/`
Bloglines `http://www.bloglines.com/`
Feedster `http://www.feedster.com/`
Google Blog Search `http://blogsearch.google.com/`

Social Networking

Find one

`http://socialsoftware.weblogsinc.com/2005/02/14/`
   `home-of-the-social-networking-services-meta-list/`
`http://en.wikipedia.org/wiki/`
   `List_of_social_networking_websites`
`https://www.quickbase.com/db/9f72vfgx?a=q&qid=1`

History

`http://en.wikipedia.org/wiki/Social_networking`

Podcast Sources

`http://www.podcast.net/`
`http://www.podcastalley.com/`
`http://www.ipodder.org/`
`http://audio.weblogs.com/`
`http://www.allpodcasts.com/Directory/`

How to Make Your Own Podcast

`http://www.makezine.com/blog/archive/2005/07/`
   `how_to_make_enh.html`
`http://weblogs.elearning.ubc.ca/audio/archives/011746.php`
`http://reelreviewsradio.com/archives/2004/12/27/`
   `podcast-about-the-podcast/#more-131`
`http://www.apple.com/quicktime/tutorials/videopodcasts.html`
`http://www.apple.com/quicktime/tutorials/podcasting.html`
`http://www.engadget.com/2004/10/05/`
   `engadget-podcast-001-10-05-2004-how-to-podcasting-get/`
   (Mac/PC/Linux—free)
`http://radio.about.com/od/podcastin1/a/aa030805a.htm` (PC)

Audio Processing Software for PC (Audacity)

`http://audacity.sourceforge.net/`

All about RSS

http://www.faganfinder.com/search/rss.shtml

http://developer.mozilla.org/en/docs/RSS

http://www.howstuffworks.com/rss-feeds.htm

http://publisher.yahoo.com/rss/RSS_whitePaper1004.pdf

http://www.computerworld.com/
    action/article.do?command=viewArticleBasicarticleId=93544

Firefox and Live Bookmarks

http://johnbokma.com/firefox/rss-and-live-bookmarks.html

RSS Subscription Sites

http://www.syndic8.com/

http://www.newsisfree.com/sources/power/

http://www.newsgator.com/

Wikis

About wikis

http://computer.howstuffworks.com/wiki.htm

Compare wikis

http://www.wikimatrix.org/

Google Earth

http://earth.google.com

Google Earth Community

http://bbs.keyhole.com

Mailing Lists

http://www.ifla.org/I/training/listserv/lists.htm

Usenet News

http://www.ibiblio.org/usenet-i/usenet-help.html

Wiki science

http://en.wikibooks.org/wiki/Wiki_Science

E-Mail Discussion Groups/Lists/Resources

Essays: virtual communities

http://netculture.about.com/library/weekly/msub16.htm

IRC networks and server lists

http://www.irchelp.org/irchelp/networks/

Privacy toolbox

http://www.privacy.getnetwise.org/"GetNitWise"

Problems and Exercises

1. What is a Web 2.0 application? What are the characteristic features of a Web 2.0 application?

2. What does the acronym AJAX stand for? What is AJAX used for?

3. What is a blog?

4. What does it mean to publish a blog?

5. What can you do in a social network that would be difficult to do otherwise?

6. What is a Live Bookmark? How does it differ from an ordinary bookmark?

7. What tools are required to publish a blog?

8. What is the characteristic feature of a wiki? What key ingredient is necessary for a successful wiki?

9. What is a tag? Who creates tags? What gets tagged?

10. What is stored in a `.kml` or `.kmz` file? What is the difference between these file formats?

11. [HANDS-ON] Start a blog at Blogger (`http://www.blogger.com`). Publish your blog and invite your classmates to comment.

12. [HANDS-ON] Join a social network. Find out what's currently popular in the network.

13. [HANDS-ON] Subscribe to an RSS feed using your feed-enabled browser. Does it signal you when new posts appear? How does it do so?

14. [HANDS-ON] Install Feedreader onto your computer. Subscribe to a few RSS feeds. How does Feedreader compare to your RSS-enabled browser?

15. [HANDS-ON] Join Google Docs and use this service to write your next group report. Enter all your group members as collaborators.

 16. [HANDS-ON] Join Google Docs and use this service to create a spreadsheet for your group. Have all the group members log on to the spreadsheet and test the response times and update features of the spreadsheet application. Write a group report of your experience using a Google Docs document.

17. [HANDS-ON] Search Flickr for a picture of a sonic boom. It's spectacular!

18. [HANDS-ON] Use Google Earth to find your home. Insert a placemark into My Places.

19. [HANDS-ON] Install Google Earth. If you live in a large city, use Google Earth to create a tour of your favorite places in the city. If you live in a city limited to lower resolution images (objects with dimensions smaller than 15 meters), create a tour of nearby cities.

20. [HANDS-ON] Use Google Earth to find directions from the U.S. Capitol to the National Cathedral. Save these directions as a tour and e-mail it to yourself. Confirm that you can play this tour in Google Earth.

21. [HANDS-ON] Use Google Earth to set up a tour of the locations of the Seven Wonders of the Ancient World.

22. Compare and contrast a site-specific discussion group on the Web with a commercial chat room at a large portal site like Yahoo!. Give at least one difference and two similarities.

23. [FIND IT ONLINE] What makes the MacFixIt Forums so successful? There is no registration fee and the quality of the technical support is, by all accounts, superb. Who pays for this site?

24. What three things should you check if you are having trouble posting an article to a Web-based forum?

25. Are some newsgroups easier to create than others? Explain.

26. Which of the following are organized into one *comprehensive* directory?
    a. All the e-mail-based mailing lists
    b. All the Web-based mailing lists
    c. All the Usenet newsgroups
    d. All the IRC channels
    e. All the Web-based chat rooms
    f. All the live chat events on the Web
    g. All IM users

27. [FIND IT ONLINE] Using one of the resources described in this chapter, find a site where K–12 teachers can find lesson plans on the subject of plastics.

28. [FIND IT ONLINE] Using one of the resources described in this chapter, find a clearinghouse for Internal Revenue Service rulings and tax-related information.

29. If a chat room's AUP prohibits foul language and cybersex, does that mean a monitor will be present to police the chat room? What can happen to you if you violate the AUP?

30. Are conversations in a private chat room really private? Explain your answer.

31. Compare and contrast IRC with Web-based chat. Give at least four differences and two similarities.

32. In general, does more Net abuse occur on Usenet newsgroups or on mailing lists? Explain your answer.

33. Can people be banned from Usenet newsgroups? Can people be banned from mailing lists?

34. [FIND IT ONLINE] Can people with different IM clients talk to each other? Can people with different IRC clients talk to each other? Can people with different Web browsers talk to each other if they use the same Web-page chat site? Which of these scenarios benefits from an industry standard to ensure software compatibility?

35. ICQ supports both IRC-mode chat and split-mode chat. Decide which of these two modes consumes more bandwidth. Explain your reasoning.

36. The file transfer feature in AIM is convenient when friends want to exchange photographs or audio files. Users can set preference settings for this feature to allow incoming file transfers by (a) anyone, (b) anyone on a specified Buddy List, (c) people specifically listed in the preference settings, or (d) no one. Which options seem reasonable to you? Are you completely safe if you select option (d)? Can you imagine scenarios in which option (a) would make sense? Do you think options (b) or (c) could be regrettable choices? Explain your answers.

37. [TAKE A STAND] Do you think a school has a legal right to establish codes of conduct for children in chat rooms when the chat room has no connection with the school? Visit the Student Press Law Center at http://www.splc.org/ to see if you can find support for your position.

38. **[FIND IT ONLINE]** Find two court cases in which the defendant pled the "fantasy defense" in response to child endangerment or kidnapping charges. What were the circumstances of the two cases? What were the outcomes? Has anyone who used the fantasy defense been acquitted?

Web 2.0

Censorship and the Spam

If your goal is to send an ad to as many people as possible as cheaply as possible, Usenet probably looks like a gift from God. However, it might become tedious to send out the same ad to 30,000 newsgroups manually. So thoughtful programmers have written spambots, which conveniently automate the process. A **spambot** is a program that enables you to post a message to thousands of Usenet newsgroups in only a few seconds. Of course, this is Internet abuse, so you'll want to cover your tracks if you choose this path. Many states have passed laws to regulate spam, but this is still very murky legal territory.

Usenet articles have an interesting property that makes them very different from e-mail messages. Unlike e-mail, a message that has been posted to a newsgroup can be canceled via a Cancel command. The Cancel command originally was intended to be used only by the author of an article, in the event that the author noticed an egregious error after the article was posted. A news server won't honor a Cancel command unless it's convinced that it comes from the same person who posted the article. An accepted Cancel command gets distributed to all the other news servers until the article has been removed from all of Usenet.

FYI: Famous Moments in the History of Spam

In 1994 two attorneys, Laurence A. Canter and Martha S. Siegal, became infamous for hawking their immigration green card services on more than 7,000 newsgroups. Although Usenet spamming was not unusual, the popular press picked up on this incident, probably because the perpetrators were attorneys who openly identified themselves and publicly argued that their activities were perfectly legal. They claimed that the Internet had outgrown its insular academic origins and was now open territory for commercial advertisements.

Given the absence of laws and regulations regarding the Internet, Netizens were naive to think that voluntary Netiquette would be an adequate mechanism for regulating behavior on the Internet. This affront to the Net culture symbolized a turning point for the Internet. Some people even predicted its imminent death. Others decided to fight fire with fire (see the Cancelbots section).

In 1995 members of the Church of Scientology canceled Usenet articles posted by people who were critical of Scientology. The Scientologists argued that their actions were justified because the canceled posts contained copyrighted material used without permission.

Are copyright violations a valid reason for unauthorized cancellations? Who has the right to evaluate a possible copyright violation? Many people felt that the church was practicing censorship. Censorship is a very real danger on Usenet, and you don't have to be in a position of authority to act as a censor.

However, with a little trickery, a person can fool a news server into thinking that the Cancel command is coming from the original author of an article.

This means that anyone can, in principle, cancel someone's Usenet article. Unauthorized Usenet cancellations normally represent a serious breach of Netiquette and are dealt with very harshly by system administrators.

Cancelbots

Third-party article cancellations are not strictly a "bug" in newsreader software. Third-party cancellations are also a "feature" because they offer a technical solution to spam. Someone so inclined can monitor a newsgroup for spam and issue an unauthorized cancellation to kill any offending articles from all of Usenet. Although this is a controversial practice, most Usenet users approve of this solution. Worries about censorship and freedom of speech tend to fade when one is confronted with too many unwanted advertisements and diatribes about gun control or abortion.

Programs called **cancelbots** have been designed to detect spam, not on the basis of content but on the basis of multiple postings. If the same article has been cross-posted too many times (for example, 15 is often used as the trigger number), a cancelbot will recognize it as spam and issue a Cancel command.

One famous cancelbot operated anonymously for a time under the name "Cancelmoose." Cancelmoose acted with the utmost sensitivity for the rights of all Internet users. Whenever a spam was canceled, Cancelmoose issued a notice explaining the action and included full copies of the spam message. Therefore, users could not claim that their right to see spam had been violated.

Now the spam was neatly bundled inside identifiable notices from Cancelmoose. If you had a kill file, you could add Cancelmoose to your kill file and never see the spam again. In addition, local administrators had the option of overriding Cancelmoose and refusing to allow cancellations originating from Cancelmoose. So each news server could make its own policy decision with respect to Cancelmoose's actions and support Cancelmoose or not. The war between the spambots and cancelbots is one arena in which the culture of the Internet has taken matters into its own technological hands.

Privacy Safeguards

The Usenet community was struggling with questions of online privacy long before the Web was born, and some of its solutions work for the Web as well. In general, you should assume that anything you put online will always be online, so think before you post. This is true for Web pages as well as Usenet articles and archived e-mail messages. In particular, be careful where you post your e-mail address, lest it be picked up by an address harvester, a program that searches the Web and Usenet for e-mail addresses. Once yours has been harvested, you can become a spam magnet. The more visible your e-mail address, the more spam you'll get. Spambots were first active on Usenet, so Usenet message authors were the first to figure out how to fool them.

Spoofing Your E-Mail Address to Fool Spambots

The trick to fooling spambots is to post your e-mail address in a way that makes your correct e-mail address obvious to a human being but useless to spambots. Address harvesters are designed to collect addresses without human intervention. No person ever reviews the list of addresses that an address harvester generates in order to remove or correct invalid addresses. Some lists contain millions of addresses—if a person had to review each entry, the cost of doing business would be prohibitive. Therefore, it's easy to trick the address harvester into accepting an address that won't work.

Suppose your real e-mail address is

```
bob544@ucs.madison.edu
```

You could use a variation on your real address when you put your address on the Web, Usenet, or a mailing list. The following examples are some possibilities, all involving adding extra, irrelevant characters. People who understand the trick will know to delete the extra characters in order to arrive at your valid e-mail address.

```
bob544NOSPAM@ucs.madison.edu
bob544SPAM-ME-NOT@ucs.madison.edu
```

```
bob544SPAMMERS-DIE@ucs.madison.edu
bob544REMOVE-THIS@ucs.madison.edu
```

To ensure that your e-mail recipients can figure out what to do, you can explain it near the address, like this:

```
bob544NOSPAM@ucs.madison.edu
(To e-mail me, remove NOSPAM from the address above.)
```

By doing this, everyone but the spammers win. The spambot is not smart enough to read the instructions, but people are (you hope). You'll see this trick used often on Usenet, where the user population is relatively savvy about online privacy. It's less common on the Web, so explanations are probably needed more often on a Web page.

Note that you cannot use this trick with mailto: links in an HTML page. If you alter an e-mail address inside a mailto: link, people will end up trying to send mail to an invalid address when they click the link.

Using X-No-Archive to Keep Your Articles Out of the Google Groups Archive

Another insider's trick is available if you want to post articles to Usenet but not have them archived by Google Groups. Before you post an article to a Usenet newsgroup, add an extra header line before the Subject: field as follows:

```
X-No-Archive: Yes
```

Some newsreaders make doing this easier than others. If you have trouble figuring out how to add this extra header line, consult `http://www.helwithwindows.com/"HelpWithWindows"` for instructions. If you still can't do this, you can add this line as the first line of the message body. In the article's body, it will be a little more distracting, but the archiving software will still recognize it.

Using Anonymizers

If you want to interact with people on the Internet but require absolute anonymity, don't trust your ISP to keep your identity safe. Services called anonymizers will "launder" your identity for you, thereby making it impossible for anyone to find out who you are. Anonymizers can protect you when you surf the Web and can give you anonymous e-mail service. Anonymizer products and services vary and might become more popular as Internet users become more aware of privacy risks online. For more information, do an online search using the keyword "anonymizer."

Using TRUSTe to Achieve Privacy

If you're concerned about personal privacy, locate privacy policies each time you interact with a Web site that is new to you, use a cookie manager to disable profiling software (see Chapter 2: Above & Beyond), and take steps to minimize spam. However, if you want to take these steps, but you don't want to spend a lot of time doing it, be on the lookout for shortcuts.

One helpful shortcut is to click the **TRUSTe privacy icon** (see Figure 4.76), which connects you with a site's privacy policy. Many consumers are reassured to see the TRUSTe icon and assume that when a site has TRUSTe certification, their privacy is adequately protected. However, you should always review a site's privacy policy, even if the TRUSTe icon is present. Some privacy advocates fear that the TRUSTe "stamp of approval" does not represent a sufficiently stringent standard for consumer privacy.

Privacy awareness and safeguards will grow as people better understand the potentially intrusive capabilities of the Internet. To stay current about available options and developments, visit the **Electronic Privacy Information Center (EPIC)**, a clearinghouse for all Internet-related privacy concerns.

Protecting Children

Children who use the Internet need to be protected from adult content and other objectionable materials. They need protection not only from pornography sites (although they are certainly something to worry about) but also hate group sites, those that glorify violence, and those filled with disturbing images. Some steps have been taken to make the Web a safer place for children, but parental guidance will always be needed.

In 2002 81 percent of all teenagers used e-mail to communicate with friends and relatives, and 70 percent also used IM clients. In one survey 86 percent of teenage girls said they were able to visit chat rooms without parental knowledge, and 30 percent reported that they had been sexually harassed in a chat room. Another survey of children in Ireland found that 86 percent of the children who use chat rooms had been asked for face-to-face

Figure 4.76
The TRUSTe icon connects you to a Web site's privacy policy.

meetings. Schools supervise their students online. Dangerous encounters are more likely to happen in the home, where Internet access is frequently unsupervised.

Child Safety on the Web

Many parents rely on Web browser content filters to protect their children from unacceptable Web fare. Commercial software packages designed to block out objectionable Web pages do a good job, but they are far from perfect. Often these packages block sites that should not be blocked, and they miss some sites that most parents would want blocked. However, who can say for sure which materials are objectionable for all families? This is the problem. Some parents are more protective than others. It's difficult to create software filters according to everyone's needs. However, Web filters, although not perfect, are a step in the right direction for protecting children from unacceptable Web content.

In addition to the usual concerns about inappropriate content, many adults are offended by commercial sites that exploit children in various ways. Before 1998 many sites were designed specifically for children, who were prompted by marketers to give up all sorts of personal information in order to play a game or participate in a contest. The Children's Online Privacy Protection Act was passed in 1998 in an effort to stem commercial exploitation of children. This law requires commercial sites aimed at children under 13 years old to obtain verifiable parental consent before a child can send private information over the Web. The law has had the intended effect, although unfortunately, teenagers are not covered. Additional legislation will be required to protect them.

TIP: Making the Web Safe for Children

Parental guidance is made easier if you and your family establish and follow a few rules. The following are some suggested rules for making the Web safe for children:

- Set up a Web portal for family use, and use a child-friendly preference setting for all Web searches
- Install a Web filter that satisfies your personal requirements
- Instruct children never to submit a form on the Web without first obtaining parental permission
- Keep the computer in a visible, central location where parents can easily see what is on the screen
- Don't set up a computer with a Net connection in a child's room

Parents concerned about personal privacy must discuss the dos and don'ts of Web questionnaires with all children in the household. A child who is inclined to answer online surveys can be an unwitting threat to family privacy and must be taught to resist the temptation to offer personal or family information online.

Child Safety in Chat Rooms

Web browsing is only one online activity for which children must be supervised. Rules for online chat must also be specified. Because there are so many Web-based chat rooms, children can easily stumble into the wrong ones if no rules are in place. Parents must see for themselves what goes on in order to decide what to allow.

The simplest solution is to prohibit all online chat. This might be a reasonable rule since chat has little educational value. However, some children have friends who want to talk online. A blanket prohibition then becomes harder to enforce.

Each family must work out its own solutions. However, regardless of the policies adopted, parents should supervise their children's behavior in case the temptations to engage in chat or to visit unacceptable Web sites is more than they can handle.

Ideally, restrictions on Internet access will be established when a child is very young, when a child doesn't mind having a parent sitting close during a chat session. As a child gets older, it should be easier for a parent to step back and offer some privacy. The privacy question is more delicate for teenagers—

TIP: Making Chat Safe for Children

The following are some suggestions for making online chat safe for children:

- Use IM software, and set its privacy options for maximal safety
- Make the IM client visible only to people on their Buddy Lists
- Accept instant messages only from people on their Buddy Lists
- Require that children ask for permission before adding someone to their Buddy Lists
- Require that children not enter public chat rooms that have not been preapproved by a parent
- Require that children not accept invitations to private chat rooms from people not on their Buddy Lists
- Capture log sessions of children's online chat sessions for periodic review
- Tell children that you're keeping a record of all online chat sessions

a family must negotiate a proper balance between safety and privacy. If good habits have already been established, parents will find it easier to trust their teenagers to exercise good judgment. However, parents should not hesitate to monitor online sessions if they have any reason to be concerned about online activities.

Problems and Exercises

A1. What is a spambot, and what is an address harvester? How do they work together?

A2. What is a cancelbot? How do cancelbots recognize spam on Usenet?

A3. Explain why the cancelbot approach works well for Usenet servers but doesn't work for e-mail servers.

 A4. [TAKE A STAND] Do you think the Church of Scientology was justified when it censored certain Usenet articles that were critical of Scientology? Explain your reasoning. Go online to find more details about this incident before you take a position.

A5. Explain how Usenet message authors foil spambots. Does this technique work on Web pages?

A6. How does the Children's Online Privacy Protection Act protect children on the Internet? What group of children is protected?

A7. [FIND IT ONLINE] Visit SafeKids at `http://www.safekids.com/`, and find out why a Massachusetts teenager was prohibited from using IM by a court of law.

A8. [FIND IT ONLINE] Visit Google Groups `http://groups.yahoo.com/`, and search its Usenet archives for articles in which people have posted bogus e-mail addresses in order to fool spambots. List five such e-mail addresses. (Hint: Conduct an author search with the keyword "spam.")

A9. [FIND IT ONLINE] Read "The Truth about TRUSTe and Your Privacy" at `http://www.e-commercealert.com/article47.html`, and explain how the TRUSTe icon at a Web site might mislead consumers. Who created TRUSTe in the first place? Has TRUSTe ever revoked its seal from a Web site in response to a privacy violation?

A10. [FIND IT ONLINE] Visit Wired News `http://www.wired.com`, and search for an article about TRUSTe's investigation of RealNetworks' data-collection practices. What was the outcome of the investigation?

What other major Web sites has TRUSTe investigated? What fundamental limitation applies to the TRUSTe seal of approval?

A11. **[FIND IT ONLINE]** Visit Wired News `http://www.wired.com`, and search for articles about privacy issues raised by Toysmart.com. Is anyone protecting consumer privacy when an e-commerce company files for bankruptcy and sells its assets? Is it legal for an e-commerce company to toss its privacy policy aside under extraordinary circumstances or at times of severe financial pressure? Explain your answers.

A12. **[FIND IT ONLINE]** Go the Library of Congress search site (`http://thomas.loc.gov/`) and find the current status of the Online Privacy Protection Act. Do some research and see when the bill was first filed (you can search previous sessions of Congress).

Find What You Want — Fast!

5.1 Taking Charge

Search engines and meta search engines have become ubiquitous in recent years. People who use Google (the Web's most popular search engine) can be remarkably successful even if they've never read anything about search engines or techniques for online searches. Indeed, you may be wondering if you should skip this whole chapter. It's true that search engines have been designed to be user-friendly for the largest possible audience of users, striving to be effective no matter who types in a **query**. But some queries are harder than others, and some users are more demanding than others. If you haven't done a lot on online searching, you may have never encountered a difficult search. So let's start by convincing everyone that some online searches can be challenging. See how many of the following questions you can answer on the basis of an online search.

1. Find out why zebras have never been domesticated. Is it impossible to train a zebra, is it just too much trouble, or is there some other reason?
2. When did forks first become commonplace eating utensils in North America?

Chapter Goals

- Find out how to analyze your information needs in order to select appropriate tools for the job
- Learn how to search subject trees and clearinghouses for useful information and resources
- Discover how to use successive query refinement when you visit a general search engine
- Explore how and when to select a new query mode
- Find out about advanced search features and specialized search engines
- Find out how to assess the credibility of information on the Web

3. List the 20 largest cities in New York state, ranked from largest to smallest, along with their populations.

If you can't answer all three questions (or if you can, but it took more than an hour), this chapter will give you some strategies for making your online searches more efficient and effective. There are powerful search tools at your disposal, but you have to use them. We'll show you some practical tips and tricks for finding what you want—fast.

Your ability to quickly find what you need has little to do with mastering arcane search techniques or being privy to insider search engine tricks. The key lies in your advance preparations: You need some familiarity with the available resources, and you need a thoughtful analysis of your information needs. If you take some time to think about your search, you'll be rewarded accordingly. Begin by analyzing your information needs, selecting appropriate search strategies, and experimenting with queries. If you expect to get what you want with your first query, you'll almost certainly be disappointed.

When you first begin to work with search engines, it pays to consult online documentation, located under the Help or Search Tips link. If online searching is an important part of your daily routine, you can stay up-to-date on search engine advances by visiting **Search Engine Watch** (see Figure 5.1) periodically or by subscribing to that service's free monthly newsletter, which offers timely articles, reviews, and performance evaluations.

Each time you start a Web search, begin by deciding which of the following question types you have.

- A **Voyager question** is an open-ended, exploratory question. You're curious about something and simply want to see what's out there. You might have some general expectations about the subject, but you're largely ignorant and willing to be educated. This type of question derives its name from the *Voyager* space probe. If the topic of interest were the solar system, you would send out the *Voyager* space probe to collect as much data as possible, just to see what would come back. Voyager questions tend to cover a lot of ground and require time for exploration.
- A **Deep Thought question** is also open-ended but is more focused and goal-oriented than a Voyager question. It might have many possible answers. This type of question derives its name from *The Hitchhiker's Guide to the Galaxy* by Douglas Adams. In the book, a computer named Deep Thought sets out to learn the meaning of life. This is a good example of an open-ended quest with a specific goal. The search

Figure 5.1

Search Engine
Watch home page

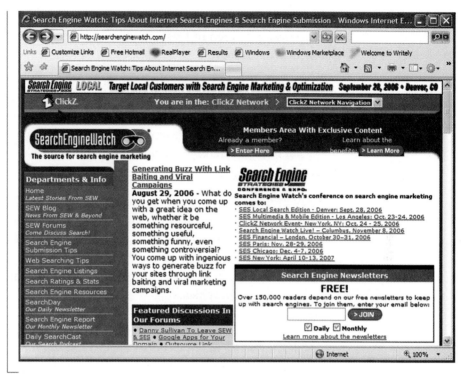

for an answer could go on for quite a while because it's difficult to know when you have the right answer. Most people quit when they're too tired to continue or, in the case of the Deep Thought computer, after 7.5 million years. Whenever you want to collect multiple hypotheses, opinions, or perspectives on an issue, you are asking a Deep Thought question, which is often philosophical, political, or academic in nature.

- A **Joe Friday question** is very specific and characterized by the expectation that there will be a simple, straightforward answer. This type of question derives its name from the 1950s weekly television show *Dragnet*. On the show, actor Jack Webb played a police detective named Joe Friday—a dry, businesslike soul who was famous for the line "The facts, ma'am. Just the facts." With a Joe Friday question, you'll know the answer when you see it, and there will be no point in looking any further. Questions that ask about names, dates, locations, and other verifiable facts are examples of Joe Friday questions. Once you know how to handle them, most Joe Friday questions can be answered on the Net in a minute or two.

As you explore the various search strategies available on the Web, it will become clear that each of these question types is best handled by a specific type of Internet resource.

- Voyager and Deep Thought questions require input from multiple documents. Once you've found the right resource, browsing is an integral part of the exploratory process.
- Joe Friday questions require facts. Facts are facts; their context does not require extensive examination.

Four types of Web resources are available to help you to find the answers to questions.

1. A **subject tree** is a hierarchically organized category of topics with lists of Web sites and online documents relevant to each topic. By navigating the hierarchy, you can find information sources for questions about specific topics. Subject trees are also called **directories** and **topic hierarchies**.

2. A **clearinghouse** is a collection of Web sites and online documents about a specific topic. The topic might be broad, in which case the clearinghouse might be either divided into subtopics or organized hierarchically, like a subject tree. However, a clearinghouse is always more narrow in its focus than a subject tree.

3. A **general search engine** is a search engine that indexes a large collection of Web pages via keywords. A general search engine relies on an automated Web spider (see the Above & Beyond section at the end of this chapter) to create a database of documents. Spiders are not restricted to specific topics, and they index more Web resources than do subject trees. These databases are very big, and it is sometimes difficult to formulate effective keyword search queries.

4. A **specialized search engine** is like a general search engine, except that it is limited to Web pages that feature a specific topic. It is harder to create a specialized search engine than to create a general search engine. While a general search engine relies on an automated Web spider to create its database, a specialized search engine relies on a collection of documents handpicked by people familiar with the topic.

Many questions are best tackled by asking more questions. Each time one question leads you to another question, identify the new question type and go to a resource that's right for that question.

TIP: Different Resources for Different Question Types

Once you know the type of question you want to ask, you can select an appropriate resource on the Web.

Type of Question	Resource
Voyager	Subject tree or clearinghouse
Deep Thought	Subject tree or specialized search engine
Joe Friday	Subject tree or general search engine

Note that many Joe Friday questions turn out to be Deep Thought questions once you've dredged up some information. This typically happens with historical events, where opinions and facts often intertwine. For example, suppose you thought there was a straightforward answer to the question "Who invented the telescope?" You might start with a general search engine because you think you have a Joe Friday question. However, when conflicting answers begin to come up, you can shift into Deep Thought mode and look for a specialized search engine on inventions or inventors in order to get a fuller picture. When you find competing answers to a seemingly straightforward question, keep looking until you're satisfied that you've gathered all the information you want.

TIP: Not So Fast

With Voyager and Deep Thought questions, don't expect to find all the information you need at one site. Depending on the topic, you might need hours or even days of careful exploration before you'd be satisfied. With a Joe Friday question, answers come faster. Even so, you shouldn't stop at the first answer. If you're not confident about the credibility of a source (see Section 5.6), check a second site (and maybe even a third) to make sure you're getting reliable information.

5.2 More about Subject Trees and Clearinghouses

A subject tree is actually a browsing aid. All subject trees require some exploration. Yahoo! is the Web's oldest, largest, and most popular subject tree. Other trees include About and the Open Directory Project. These three subject trees are discussed in more detail in the next three subsections. Following those subsections is more information about clearinghouses.

5.2.1 Yahoo!

When you browse a subject tree, you start from the root of the tree and branch out to more specific topics, moving at each decision point in new directions. For example, suppose you want to send a letter to Elton John and you need his fan mail e-mail address. You can use **Yahoo!** to answer this Joe Friday question. On the Yahoo! home page (see Figure 5.2), you need to find a branch of the tree that will start you in the right direction. In this case, the branch is the Entertainment branch:

Entertainment → Music → Artists → By Genre → Rock and Pop → John, Elton

The Elton John category contains a number of fan-related links you can explore to find an official address for fan mail (see Figure 5.3).

A good subject tree will make it easy to get where you want to go. Yahoo!'s subject tree, growing since its inception in 1994, now organizes over 1.5 million documents. Each document is added to Yahoo! by people who first check

Figure 5.2

Yahoo's subject tree

Reproduced with permission of Yahoo! Inc. © 2006 by Yahoo! Inc.
YAHOO! and the YAHOO! logo are trademarks of Yahoo! Inc.

Figure 5.3

Elton John branch
of Yahoo!

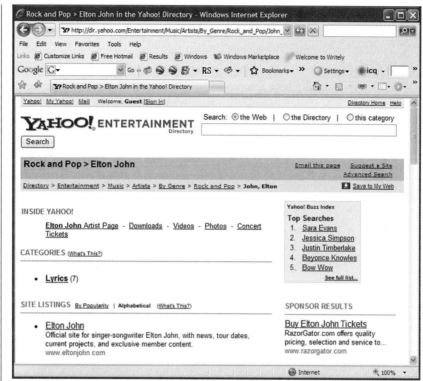

Reproduced with permission of Yahoo! Inc. © 2006 by Yahoo! Inc.
YAHOO! and the YAHOO! logo are trademarks of Yahoo! Inc.

the document for its content and proper position in the tree structure. This keeps the documents well organized; however, it does not mean that every document has been subjected to quality control for content. It is relatively easy to glance at a document to see what it's about, but editorial control requires knowledgeable reviewers and is far more time-consuming.

Although a lot of effort goes into maintaining a subject tree's organization, subject trees are not immune to organizational problems. It is difficult to design a comprehensive hierarchy in a way that seems perfectly intuitive to everyone. Different subject trees use different categories and subtree structures. Although there's no one best hierarchy, some subject trees are probably easier to navigate than others.

Another difficulty is that it's often impossible to store everything that's relevant to a single topic under a single location in the tree. For example, if you're interested in weaving, which keyword should you look under—"art," "textiles," or "crafts"? Depending on exactly what you want to know, you might find relevant documents under any of these keywords. This makes it difficult to know when you've exhausted all the possibilities in a subject tree. Happily, the larger subject trees are equipped with search engines to help you cover all the bases. When you use a search engine for a subject tree, you're conducting a site search. A **site search** is a search in which hits are restricted to Web pages within the current Web site.

By contrast, a search engine that has a subject tree is a completely different animal. Examples include AltaVista, Google, and Excite. A search engine with a subject tree returns hits from a large database of documents that includes but is not restricted to the documents in its subject tree. In this case, the search engine is the main attraction; the subject tree is an extra feature.

A subject tree with a search engine lets you see how many branches might hold relevant documents. For example, suppose you want to assemble a long list of different types of clocks. This is a Deep Thought question (it has a focus but it's open-ended), and a subject tree is a good place to start. However, you'll definitely want to use the search engine for the subject tree.

When you query Yahoo!'s search engine, the results come back in two parts: category matches and site matches. Each Yahoo! category is a location in the tree where you can examine more subcategories or jump directly into relevant documents. Documents are always represented by URLs for Web pages (which are not part of the Yahoo! Web site). As an example, go to Yahoo! and enter the query "clocks" (see Figure 5.4).

The first group of hits is category matches. A category match shows all the places in the subject tree where you can examine a branch that has something to do with clocks. In this example, we get back a list of all the category titles that contain the keyword "clocks." There are 10 different categories on the Yahoo! tree that have something to do with clocks (see Figure 5.5). The site matches appear after the category matches. At Yahoo!, a site match is a list of relevant Web pages found inside Yahoo!'s subject tree.

Examine the category matches for the keyword "clocks." Notice that the clock categories include one devoted to humor about VCR clocks, one for

FYI: Subject Trees with Search Engines versus Search Engines with Subject Trees

A subject tree that has a search engine (for example, Yahoo!) allows you to conduct a search that is restricted to the subject tree's categories and documents. The main attraction is the subject tree; the search engine exists to enhance the subject tree. Sometimes a search engine for a subject tree gives you the choice of searching the tree or searching the Web. If you choose to search the Web, you'll leave the subject tree and move to a general search engine.

Figure 5.4
Keyword search of Yahoo!'s subject tree

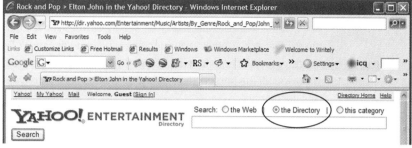

Reproduced with permission of Yahoo! Inc. © 2006 by Yahoo! Inc.
YAHOO! and the YAHOO! logo are trademarks of Yahoo! Inc.

Figure 5.5
Yahoo!'s 12 sub-trees for the keyword "clocks"

Reproduced with permission of Yahoo! Inc. © 2006 by Yahoo! Inc.
YAHOO! and the YAHOO! logo are trademarks of Yahoo! Inc.

housewares and clocks, one for B2B (business-to-business) clocks, and one about national debt clocks. Click the housewares and clocks link, and take a closer look (see Figure 5.6). Notice that now there are five subcategories

TIP: Keywords for Site Searches

When you conduct a site search at a subject tree, you're searching for categories in the subject tree as well as for documents. For a Voyager or Deep Thought question, the category hits are more important than the document hits because the categories show you all the perspectives you should consider before you start digging into specific documents.

To yield a good list of category hits, follow these tips:

- Use only one keyword instead of a list of keywords.
- Choose a keyword that is simple and obvious.
- If you can think of different keywords, investigate them one at a time.

Some keywords will open worlds of information, but others will return nothing. You might need to try a few keywords before you find the right ones.

under Sales and Repair that might be of interest: Antique@, Business to Business@, Cuckoo Clocks (13), Repair (7), and Watches@. Because we are dealing with a subject hierarchy, each of these subcategories corresponds to a branch within the tree structure of the hierarchy.

Two of the categories list a number in parentheses, and three are followed by "@". Each numbered category is a branch within the current subtree, and the number tells you how many document hits are stored in that particular part of the tree. The @ character tags indicate cross-listed categories found somewhere outside the current subtree. Those categories are listed because they are strongly associated with the current category. Both the subtree categories and the cross-listed categories give you opportunities to explore relevant parts of the subject tree.

A large subject tree is a great way to explore open-ended questions because someone else has already figured out what categories relate to a concept and what associations should be made between categories that reside in different parts of the tree. In the clock example, you may not need to examine all the document hits, but you do need to explore the category matches to see how many different kinds of clocks you can find.

TIP: Follow Up on a Category Search in a Subject Tree with Some Browsing

Subject trees are designed to facilitate browsing. Start with a category search to find relevant locations within the tree. The resulting category matches are all possible starting points for browsing expeditions. Don't rush into the site matches before you've scoped out all the category matches. You can miss a lot of information if you narrow your search too quickly.

Figure 5.6

Five more sub-trees

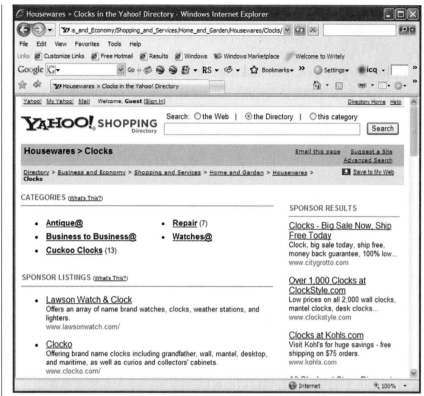

Reproduced with permission of Yahoo! Inc. © 2006 by Yahoo! Inc.
YAHOO! and the YAHOO! logo are trademarks of Yahoo! Inc.

CHECKLIST: Subject Tree Exercise 1: Create a List of Clocks

1. Search Yahoo! and create a list of different types of clocks. Work on this search for 15 minutes.
2. How many types of clocks did you find?
3. Do you think you've exhausted all that Yahoo! has to offer for this exercise?

Although hierarchical organizations are powerful devices for information retrieval, don't let the logic of categories and subcategories lull you into mindlessness. You may still need to think about your search strategies for subject trees. Recall the Deep Thought computer in *The Hitchhiker's Guide to the Galaxy*. When asked to explain the meaning of life, Deep Thought worked for 7.5 million years and produced the answer "42." Douglas Adams has many fans, and they have naturally pondered this answer in an effort to

TIP: Try a Web encyclopedia

In some cases, you might find what you're looking for in an encyclopedia. You're probably familiar with wikipedia (see Section 4.5). Like the web, wikipedia is also searchable in ways similar to the way you use a Web search engine. You might also try h2g2 if you're searching for something "unusual". The h2g2 wiki (also in section 4.5) site is named after *The Hitchiker's Guide to the Galaxy*. Like the book, it too tries to explain "everything," like "How to survive being swallowed by a whale" ! It's searchable too. Check it out at `http://www.bbc.co.uk/dna/h2g2/`.

understand its deeper meaning. Some have set out to answer such questions as "What role does the number 42 play in the lives of all dogs?" Subject Tree Exercise 2 asks you to work on that question at Yahoo! It is a Deep Thought question because there may be more than one "correct" answer.

Given the question "What role does the number 42 play in the lives of all dogs?", you might be hard-pressed to find useful keywords for a search query. Specific numbers tend to be bad keywords (many search engines ignore numbers). When I conducted a keyword search at Yahoo! on the keyword "dogs," I found 226 category matches and 5,540 site matches. My keyword search on "42" yielded four category matches and 151 site matches. None of the category matches looked promising, and no one wants to wade through long lists of site matches. Searching with the query "dogs 42" gave me site matches, but they did not look as if they had anything to say about the role of the number 42 in the lives of dogs (see Figure 5.7).

What can you do to answer the question? You could try to guess at some plausible answers and work backward from them. But this might take a long time. Maybe you need to think more about the query. Maybe you can think of additional keywords by using associative thinking.

Let's consider the larger context in which this question was originally posed. Where did this question come from? What motivated it? If you can answer these additional questions, you'll have some new leads you can use at Yahoo! For example, the only people who would ever ask this peculiar

CHECKLIST: Subject Tree Exercise 2: Role of the Number 42 in the
         Lives of All Dogs

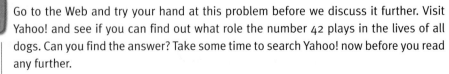

Go to the Web and try your hand at this problem before we discuss it further. Visit Yahoo! and see if you can find out what role the number 42 plays in the lives of all dogs. Can you find the answer? Take some time to search Yahoo! now before you read any further.

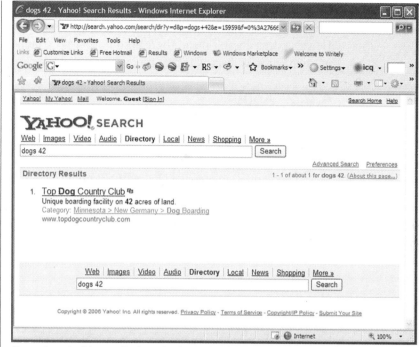

question are probably Douglas Adams fans. So search Yahoo! to see what is available under "Douglas Adams." Yahoo! has an entire category devoted to Douglas Adams, as well as 35 site matches that mention his name. Once you've made the Douglas Adams connection, you're just a couple of links away from the answer. See if you can find it. (This is Exercise 14 in the Problems and Exercises section.)

TIP: Associative Thinking

When you think about keywords and categories, sometimes you really have to think. *Don't just fixate on the words in the immediate question.* Ask yourself questions:

- Who would care about the answer to this question?
- What sort of people might be talking about this topic?
- Are there any organizations that might post the information I want?

Try to associate a query with people or organizations; those connections can be the breakthrough you need. This type of thinking is called associative thinking, and it can be a powerful search strategy.

The Yahoo! subject tree contains over 1.5 million documents and over 150,000 categories. Yahoo! is a major Web portal that has a loyal following. However, this doesn't mean there aren't other good subject trees. The following two sections discuss two of them: About and the Open Directory Project.

5.2.2 About

If you need solid, reliable information on a serious topic, check out About (originally called the Mining Company). This is a subject tree that supports over 700 major topic sites, each with its own hierarchical subject tree (see Figure 5.8) and each managed by an About guide, who is an expert in that subject area. About displays category matches and document hits, although the document hits at About are always overview pages written by the About guides. These overviews also contain pointers to hand-picked Web sites and documents, so the About guides do take you to reliable Web resources.

Figure 5.8

About: Subject tree managed by experts in 700 fields

About does not point to as many Web pages as Yahoo! However, all the pages it does index have been reviewed by an expert in the field who polices Web page content for reliability and accuracy. The About enterprise is very similar to an encyclopedia in its scope and operation. As such, it's a good subject tree for introductory articles and short tutorials. Documents found at About can be trusted to contain high-quality information.

5.2.3 Open Directory Project

Another subject tree with a strong following is run by Lycos.com: the Open Directory Project. Lycos was one of the first search engines with a subject tree. Now, in an aggressive quest to outperform Yahoo!, Lycos is concentrating on its Open Directory Project. This subject tree emphasizes practical know-how more than academic expertise, as its home page illustrates (see Figure 5.9), so it might not actually be competing with Yahoo! head-on. The

Figure 5.9
Open Directory Project home page

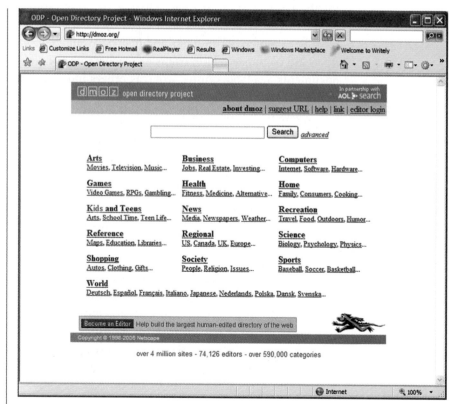

Open Directory Project uses a system of category matches and document hits much like Yahoo!, including the @ tag for cross-listed categories.

The Open Directory Project is unique in that it uses 22,000 volunteers who act as editors in specific content areas, and the directory contains over 230,000 categories. Time will tell if a system of volunteers can maintain the quality control that Lycos cultivated in its early years (under the name "Lycos Guides") with paid staffers. In any event, the Open Directory Project is a resource worth bookmarking.

5.2.4 Clearinghouses

Some of your questions will be general and easily satisfied, whereas others might be more sophisticated and harder to answer. As your information needs shift from casual questions to more demanding questions, you'll need to find new Web resources. This is where clearinghouses come into play.

Recall that a clearinghouse is a large collection of resources or documents about a specific topic. On the Internet, some clearinghouses are maintained by researchers subsidized by federal funding. Others are compiled by commercial interests and may be available to paid subscribers only. A few are compiled by librarians or teachers. Some clearinghouses focus on documents available online, whereas others index documents available only in hard copy.

Always be on the lookout for clearinghouses that address your interests. Each is organized in its own way and supports its own search tools, so you need to learn about them on a case-by-case basis. Some are slick professional sites, whereas others are minimal lists of plain text and hyperlinks. Figure 5.10 shows the home page for the **Environmental Law Net**, a clearinghouse devoted to environmental laws, regulations, enforcement, and pending court cases. Figure 5.11 shows a small portion of a clearinghouse for computer security professionals. (You have to visit this page to get a real sense of just how extensive this particular clearinghouse is.)

A good clearinghouse is a powerful research tool because it is comprehensive in scope while maintaining high standards for document quality. When you use a good clearinghouse, 90% of the hard work has been done for you. All you need to do is peruse the offerings to locate the specific information you want. Figure 5.12 shows one of the specialized resources available at the Environmental Law Net clearinghouse, a collection of pointers to environmental court cases indexed by states.

Figure 5.10

Clearinghouse about environmental law

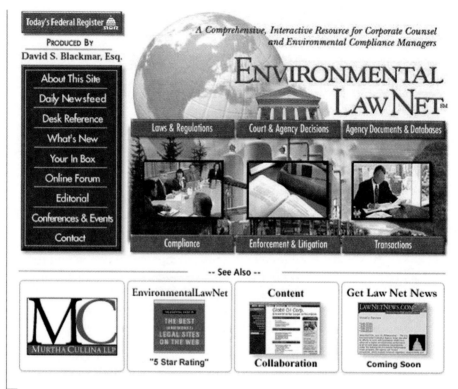

One way to find good clearinghouses is at a clearinghouse index. There are a number worth trying:

- The Reference Desk `http://www.martindalecenter.com`
- The Internet Public Library (IPL) `http://www.ipl.org/`
- BIOTN (see the alphabetized subject index)
  `http://library.sau.edu/bestinfo`
- Netsurfer Science (all science)
  `http://www.netsurf.com/nss/search.html`
- Netsurfer Digest (all sorts of things)
  `http://www.netsurf.com/nsd/search.html`
- Internet Scout Project (academic/educational)
  `http://www.scout.cs.wisc.edu/`
- Ready Reference
  `http://www.ipl.org/div/subject/browse/ref00.00.00`

Figure 5.11

Infosyssec.com is a clearinghouse for computer security professionals.

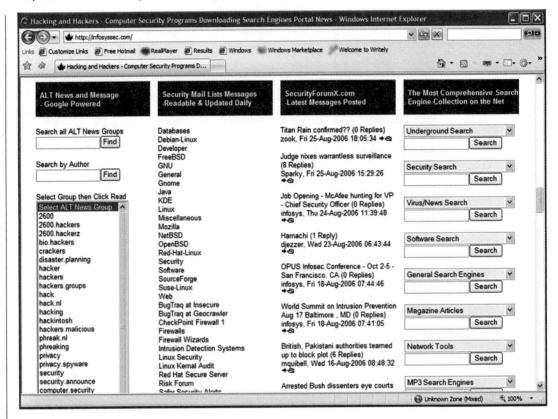

TIP: How to Find Clearinghouses

There are thousands of online clearinghouses. Whenever you need to conduct in-depth research, first check to see if a relevant clearinghouse can help you. Go to any general search engine, and conduct a keyword search that includes the word "clearinghouse."

Always investigate pointers to clearinghouses that might be useful to you. Clearinghouses are great bookmark entries because they give you fast access to many links via a single URL. If you spend most of your time online focus-

Figure 5.12

Index of environ-
mental law court
cases

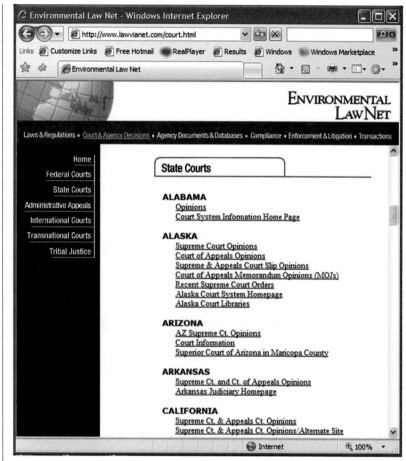

ing on one topic, you might want to set your browser's default home page to an appropriate clearinghouse page so that you can hit the ground running each time you go online.

5.3 General Search Engines and Meta Search Engines

A great deal can be said about search engines. We could talk about concepts in information retrieval and explore the manner in which search engines compile databases of documents and index those documents for retrieval. We could investigate the tricky business of ranking documents so that the best ones appear at the top of the hit list. We'll look at these and other behind-the-scenes aspects of search engines in the Above & Beyond section at the end of this chapter.

For now, we will concentrate on purely practical advice. Remember that general search engines are not always the best place to go for an online search. As a rule, general search engines are best for Joe Friday questions; open-ended questions are better handled by subject trees and clearinghouses.

5.3.1 Some Ground Rules

Before you start using a general search engine, here are some ground rules.

Know Your Search Engine. Suppose you're visiting a search engine for the first time. Before initiating a search, you should review the information at any link called Search Tips or Help (see Figure 5.13) to learn how the engine oper-

Figure 5.13

The Google search engine makes it easy to learn the ropes.

ates and what it offers. Different search engines support different features, and it pays to know how each one works. We will look at a number of search options in more detail. In the meantime, here is a sampling of some things you can control if you know how.

- Return pages only if they contain all the keywords in your query.
- Return pages containing at least one but not necessarily all of your keywords.
- Automatically look for morphological variations on your keywords. For example, you enter the keyword "book" and the search engine looks for both "book" and "books."
- Look for variations on a keyword only if you enter the keyword with a wildcard (*) character, as in "book*."
- Automatically add synonyms to your query. For example, you enter the keyword "law" and the search engine looks for "legislation."
- Control the number of hits displayed on each page returned.

You need to know exactly what a search engine is doing with your queries or you'll never be able to fine-tune your queries for the best possible results.

Never Look beyond the First 20 to 30 Hits for Any Given Query. Most search engines are proud to announce how many hits were found, assuming that you will be pleased to know that the one document you really want might (or might not) be somewhere in a list of 1.2 million documents. In fact, a good query will display the hits you most want at the top of the hit list. A bad query is not worth more than a quick glance at the top 10 hits. If the top 10 hits are off-base, don't waste time looking any further in the hit list. If the top 10 hits look good, you might want to look at the next 10 or 20, but no more. If you need to see additional hits, enter a different query.

Experiment with Different Keywords in Different Queries. Conducting a keyword search is like learning a musical instrument: the more you work at it, the better the results. Start out with an initial query based on the best keywords you can think of. Examine the hits that come back, and then adjust your original query, broadening it to bring in more hits or narrowing it to bring in fewer hits. Each new query should benefit from the feedback resulting from the preceding queries through a process of **successive query refinement**. No one, no matter how experienced, can nail a search with just one query. Each search offers you a new learning curve, and some queries are easier to refine than others.

Don't Expect the First Query You Try to Be Your Last. No matter how experienced you become with keyword searches, the process will always require adjustments and refinement. Even the experts try one or two preliminary queries before they expect anything very useful to materialize. Don't waste time trying to perfect your first-pass queries; let feedback from the search engine and successive query refinement help you out.

5.3.2 Getting Started

Understanding the general process of working with search engines is important, but experience with concrete examples is also very instructive. So let's take a look at some specific queries and specific search engines. For a Joe Friday query about a mainstream topic (that is, something that many people ask about), **Ask.com** is a good place to start, and it's one of the simplest search engines available.

For example, suppose you want to know who invented the telescope. You type the question you want answered and then see what comes back. Unlike other search engines, Ask.com doesn't return hits. Instead, it shows you a set of questions for which it already has answers. Some of these questions will be on target; others will not. With luck, at least one of them will be relevant. Figure 5.14 shows the hit list returned by Ask.com in response to the query "Who invented the telescope?" Some of these hits appear to be quite relevant, but if we can't find what we need here, we review some questions and answers to the right deleted here under "Narrow Your Search" that Ask.com has already anticipated and look for relevant matches there (on the far right side of Figure 5.14).

Ask.com has a database of over 7 million hand-crafted questions and answers. When it analyzes a query, it tries to match the query to one of its question/answer (Q/A) entries. The matching process is not perfect, so Ask.com returns a few of its best matches for your inspection. For the telescope question, we can see that the keyword "telescope" figured heavily in the matching process and took us in some directions we didn't want.

Ask.com is a wonderful search engine for beginners. Queries can be entered as English questions, the Teoma search engine has a rapidly expanding document database, and it's easy to see whether the predefined Q/A items are relevant. Ask.com also has a special search page for children. Unfortunately, no one search engine can be expected to work on all queries, so it is sometimes necessary to visit more than one search engine. For example, suppose you need a ranked list of California's 20 largest cities. Although

Figure 5.14

Ask.com processes questions in English.

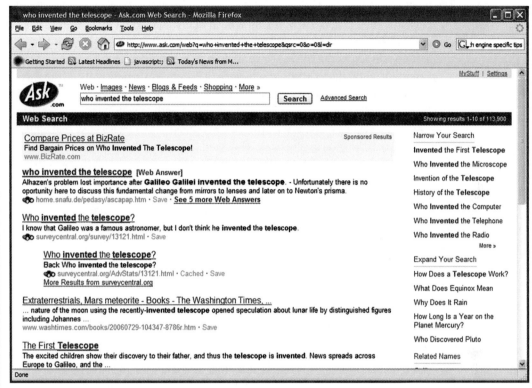

the information seems mainstream, Ask.com has (at this writing) trouble producing a document that contains this information.

Most search engines will have trouble producing a list of California cities ranked by population. You might be able to find alphabetically ranked lists of cities in California, along with their populations, from which you could derive

FYI: Ask.com and Teoma Search

When Ask.com (formery known as AskJeeves) returns a hit list of Web pages in response to a query, it is processing your query with the Teoma search engine (`http://www.teoma.com`). Ask.com purchased Teoma in 2001 and added it to the Ask.com Web site in 2002. Teoma's technology and the original Ask.com database are fully independent: if one doesn't work, the other might still come through for you.

TIP: Not All Keywords Are Equal

When you create a query for a search engine, concentrate on nouns. Search engines don't understand English, even if they encourage users to post a query "in plain English." They extract keywords from each query and ignore other words, typically prepositions, conjunctions, and articles. Word proximity is usually taken into consideration, so don't enter your keywords in a random order, and if a noun phrase is important, enter those words in sequence. It is not easy to anticipate all the ways an author might talk about your topic, but descriptive nouns are more reliable indices than descriptive verbs. If you have an important verb in your query, try replacing it with an analogous noun, even if the query ends up sounding less like real English.

CHECKLIST: Search Engine Exercise 1: Who Invented the Telescope?

1. In Ask.com, enter the query "Who invented the telescope?" (do not include the quotes). Examine both the Teoma hit list and the predefined Q/A items.
2. Which items look promising enough to examine?
3. Can you answer the question from the results of this one query at Ask.com?

TIP: Different Search Engines—Different Documents

If you can't find what you want at one search engine, you may be able to find it at a different one. Experiments have shown that different search engines do not have as much overlap in their document databases as you might expect. Many documents are available at one or two search engines, but not all search engines. For more details, see `http://notess.com/search/stats/overlap.shtml`.

the list you want. However, it takes time to do this by hand, and you might make a mistake. When a query comes up dry, you have two choices:

1. Try a different search engine.
2. Try a different query.

Strategies for option 1 are discussed next. Those for option 2 are discussed in Section 5.4.

Selecting a good search engine for a specific search problem is perhaps one of the most difficult challenges in online searching. None covers the entire Web, so it is sometimes necessary to experiment with at least three or four of the better-known search engines.

5.3.3 Meta Search Engines

Tapping into multiple search engines is repetitive and tedious, as well as largely mechanical. But that's actually good news. For every repetitive and mechanical computer activity, someone has probably written software to automate it. The automated approach to multiple Web searches is the meta search engine. A **meta search engine** is an engine that sends a query to several different search engines and then returns some number of the top hits found by each. With a meta search engine, you type in your query once, press Enter, and then sift through the returned hits.

Many meta search engines are available on the Web, and they have improved significantly in recent years. The better ones are careful not to swamp you with too many hits or with duplicate copies of the same hits. An especially powerful technique you will find in some meta search engines is **clustering**. Instead of presenting you with one long hit list, the hits are clustered for easier navigation. At some meta search engines, you can use clustering to filter in (keep) a category of hits or filter out (remove) a category of hits. We will look at an example of this shortly. A good meta search engine leverages your time and reduces your effort, thereby enabling you to streamline your Web searches.

If you give a good query to a good meta search engine, you'll probably find what you're looking for. For example, suppose that we use **Infonetware** to track down the list of California cities mentioned earlier. We'll begin with a simple query: "California cities population" (see Figure 5.15). Fire up your browser and follow along if you like; your results probably won't be identical to our screen shots, but you should be able to get to the same target document in any case.

CHECKLIST: Search Engine Exercise 2: Find a Ranked List
of California's 20 Largest Cities

Before you read further, try to find a list of California's 20 largest cities. Enter the keywords "California cities populations" at two or three different search engines and see what comes back. If you have no favorite search engines (yet), select some from this list:

Ask.com	`http://ask.com/`
FAST Search	`http://www.alltheweb.com/`
Google	`http://www.google.com/`
HotBot	`http://www.hotbot.com/Default.asp`
Lycos	`http://www.lycos.com/`

Figure 5.15

InfoNetWare is a meta search engine.

FYI: The Web Offers Many Good Meta Search Engines

Here are some good meta search engines to investigate:

Brainboost	`http://www.brainboost.com`
DogPile	`http://www.dogpile.com`
Excite	`http://excite.com`
InfoGrid	`http://www.infogrid.com`
Infonetware RealTerm Search	`http://www.infonetware.com`
Ixquick	`http://www.ixquick.com/`
Kartoo	`http://www.kartoo.com`
Mamma	`http://mamma.com`
Metacrawler	`http://metacrawler.com`
ProFusion	`http://www.profusion.com`
qbSearch	`http://www.qbsearch.com`
Query Server	`http://www.queryserver.com/web.htm`
SurfWax	`http://www.surfwax.com`
Vivisimo	`http://vivisimo.com/`
Webcrawler	`http://www.webcrawler.com`

Find a list of search engines at `http:www.interq.or.jp/japan/se-inoue/e_search.htm`

Infonetware processes the query and returns a list of hits in one frame and a list of categories in a second frame (see Figure 5.16). If we're lucky, we might find a good hit in this initial hit list. Unfortunately, the hit lists returned by meta search engines are a little different from the hit lists returned by search engines. When you are reviewing a hit list from a search

Figure 5.16

Each query generates a list of topics as well as a document hit list.

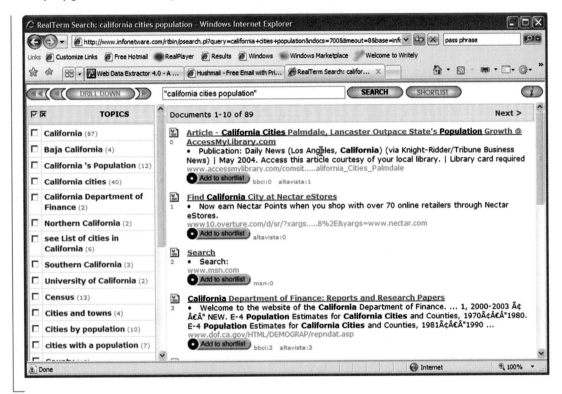

engine, it's generally wise to go no deeper than 20 or 30 hits. But hit lists from meta search engines are harder to rank—a good document is more likely to be hiding much deeper inside these lists. So the best meta search engines are designed to help us navigate these longer hit lists by identifying different categories of hits within the hit list. This is how the list of categories on the left side of Figure 5.16 can help us.

Begin by examining the initial list of hits shown on the right side of the figure. The hit list contains 89 documents, and hit four, "California Department of Finance: Reports and Research Papers," looks promising. Unfortunately, a visit to this site shows that we can request data for specific cities and counties by name, but there is no ranked list of cities here. Nothing else jumps out as a good candidate at the top of this list, so let's take advantage of the categories on the left. This list of categories was dynamically generated by Infonetware based on an examination of the 89 documents in the hit list. Infonetware analyzes document titles and abstracts to arrive at semantic categories for groups of documents. The number in parentheses next to each category tells us how many documents are in that category. The documents are not mutually exclusive: some documents may be in more than one category.

We can use the categories to reduce the length of our hit list and zero in on the best hits. There are two ways to focus the hit list. We can eliminate hits by focusing on a desired category and removing any documents that aren't in that category (this is called **filtering in**), or we can eliminate hits by identifying an undesirable category and removing all documents that are part of that category (this is called **filtering out**). Filtering in categories reduces the list faster but is riskier. We'll try that first. Then if that doesn't work, we can always come back to this page and move more slowly by filtering out some categories.

To filter in some hits, we look for categories on the left that sound right on target. It's generally best to pick just one or two that aren't too small. Let's try "California Cities." We click on the checkbox for this category and a green

Figure 5.17

Use the topics to filter the hit list.

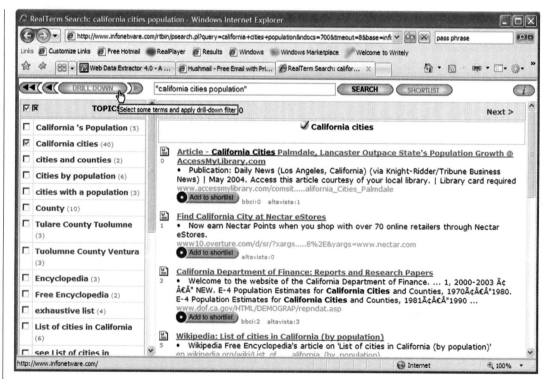

checkmark appears. This means we are going to reduce the hit list to the 40 documents in this one category. To see this reduced list, we click the Drill Down button. Now we see three or four promising hits right at the top of the list (see Figure 5.17). Taking the time to examine them, we find a page of demographic reports from the California Department of Finance (see Figure 5.18). This turns out to be a broken link, but we can go to the home page of the California Department of Finance using the technique we learned in Section 1.10.10 to go to the root address. Bingo! But there is one small wrinkle: the document is an .xls file, which is the format for Microsoft Excel documents. If you have Microsoft Excel installed on your computer, you will have no trouble reading it. At the left we see a link for "Demographic Information." With a little hunting we find population lists for all California cities by county (Figure 5.19). If you are using Windows XP, an Explorer window will open displaying the file. Otherwise, you will need to find and install an Excel viewer to see the contents of this file.

Figure 5.18

Perusing a hit list document with potentially relevant links

Figure 5.19

Windows Explorer view of California census data

http://www.dof.ca.gov/HTML/DEMOGRAP/SDC/documents/table2.xls - Windows Internet Explorer

	A	B	C	D	E	F	G	H	I	J	K	L	M	N
1						California Department of Finance, Demographic Reseach Unit								
2						California State Census Data Center								
3						Census 2000 PL94-171								
4														
5						Table Two								
6						Population by Race/Ethnicity								
7						Incorporated Cities by County								
8														
9														
10		Total							American				Pacific	
11	County/City	Population	White	%	Hispanic	%	Black	%	Indian	%	Asian	%	Islander	%
82	Fresno	799,407	317,522	39.7	351,636	44.0	40,291	5.0	6,223	0.8	63,029	7.9	682	0.1
83	Clovis	68,468	46,186	67.4	13,876	20.3	1,207	1.8	679	1.0	4,322	6.3	75	0.1
84	Coalinga	11,668	5,056	43.3	5,811	49.9	259	2.2	116	1.0	186	1.6	21	0.2
85	Firebaugh	5,743	565	9.8	5,026	87.5	61	1.1	17	0.3	38	0.7	0	0.0
86	Fowler	3,979	948	23.8	2,677	67.3	67	1.7	19	0.5	209	5.3	1	0.0
87	Fresno	427,652	159,473	37.3	170,520	39.9	34,357	8.0	3,259	0.8	47,136	11.0	427	0.1
88	Huron	6,306	65	1.0	6,197	98.3	5	0.1	9	0.1	23	0.4	0	0.0
89	Kerman	8,551	2,070	24.2	5,552	64.9	24	0.3	26	0.3	699	8.2	1	0.0
90	Kingsburg	9,199	5,505	59.9	3,166	34.4	25	0.3	38	0.4	246	2.7	3	0.0
91	Mendota	7,890	248	3.1	7,468	94.7	38	0.5	32	0.4	57	0.7	0	0.0
92	Orange Cove	7,722	526	6.9	6,996	90.6	15	0.2	46	0.6	103	1.3	0	0.0
93	Parlier	11,145	190	1.7	10,807	96.9	9	0.1	18	0.2	74	0.7	1	0.0

CHECKLIST: **Meta Search Engine Exercise 1: Find a Ranked List of Florida's 20 Largest Cities**

1. Use Infonetware and the keywords "Florida cities populations" to obtain a ranked list of Florida's 20 largest cities.
2. Did you use any filters?
3. Try this exercise for one or two other states and see if the search process is comparable for different states. Can you find the 20 largest cities in New York state? (Give up if this takes more time than you can afford to spend— we will see a better technique for this particular type of query in Section 5.5.)

Try this exercise with some of the other meta search engines listed earlier. There is more variation in meta search engines than in search engines. Look for speed, ease of use, and, of course, good results. Once you find a meta search engine you like, you may find it replacing your favorite search engine.

TIP: Meta Search Engines Work Best with Simple Queries

When you formulate a query for a meta search engine, keep it simple. List a few descriptive keywords, and don't try to use advanced search features (see Section 5.4). The meta search engine won't be able to adjust your query for each search engine it consults, so you have to give it a query that will work at all of them.

In this case we were able to zero in on a good hit by filtering in just one relevant category. When you can't find a good category for filtering in, go back to the original hit list and look for categories you can filter out. Checking a category box twice produces a red X for that category, which means that all documents in that category will be removed from the hit list. Then use the Drill Down button to generate the reduced hit list.

If you took the time to do Search Engine Exercise 2, you'll appreciate how quick and easy Infonetware can be. A well-designed meta search engine often outperforms the best search engines, especially when it allows you to filter your hit lists. Recall that different search engines index different sets of documents. Meta search engines give you the best possible document coverage by querying multiple search engines.

TIP: Searching and Browsing Go Together

The information you need might be one or two links away from an item on a search engine's hit list. If you see a document that's not exactly on target, check to see whether it contains any links that look promising.

Also, it's important that you stay on track and not get distracted by interesting but irrelevant hyperlinks. Carefully focused browsing can get you where you need to go when you're hot on the trail of an elusive Web page.

CHECKLIST: Meta Search Engine Exercise 2: Find a Ranked List
of the Most Popular Cars

1. Find a ranked list of the most popular cars in the United States. Try to find the most up-to-date data possible.
2. Were you successful? Which meta search engines did you try? Which one got you to the answer? How many different queries did you try? What were they? Which one succeeded? Did you use filters?

Some meta search engines are packaged as application software to be installed on your personal computer. These search engines are also called client-side search software. Three popular packages are **WebFerret**, **Copernic 2000**, and **BullsEye 2**. If you do a lot of online searching, you may want to look into these options.

5.4 Tools of the Trade

Remember, don't expect to get the best hits on your first try. No matter how skilled you become with Internet searches, each new search problem will require some experimentation. Through a process of systematic trial and error, you'll modify and fine-tune your queries to get increasingly better hits. The process of moving from an initial experimental query to a final successful query is called successive query refinement. Query refinement addresses the fine-tuning of a query in three different ways: (1) narrowing, (2) broadening, and (3) redirecting. You need to narrow a query when you are getting many hits that are in the right ballpark but not quite on target. You need to broaden a query when you are getting one or two good hits but they don't adequately address your needs. Redirection is helpful when you aren't getting anything that looks remotely useful. Different tools are useful for different types of query refinement.

With experience, you can become skilled at successive query refinement. Let's look at some powerful search tools that can help you with query refinement.

5.4.1 Exact Phrase Matching

Exact phrase matching is a simple but powerful device that is probably supported by every search engine on the Web. Exact phrase matching allows you to quote a phrase so that it will be treated as if it were a single keyword. Documents that contain the exact phrase will be ranked more highly on a hit list than documents that don't. If you want your hits to contain an exact

TIP: Check the Documentation

Not all search engines support all search tools. If you want to use a device described here, check first to make sure your search engine offers it.

phrase, put double quotes at the start and end of your phrase (for example, "New York"). Without the quotation marks, the two keywords "New" and "York" would be treated as independent keywords with no expectation that they need be next to one another or even close by. Check the documentation for each search engine you use to find out if the exact phrase matching is case sensitive (uppercase and lowercase characters do not match one another) or case insensitive (no distinction is made between uppercase and lowercase characters). Some search engines are normally case insensitive except for exact phrases, which are case sensitive.

Exact phrase matching is useful for narrowing a query or redirecting a query. For example, suppose you are looking for a chocolate mousse recipe. If your query contains the two keywords "chocolate" and "mousse," you could end up with a recipe for vanilla mousse with chocolate sauce. Any such hits would be eliminated with the exact phrase "chocolate mousse," thereby narrowing your query.

Exact phrase matching is especially useful with proper names, although care must be taken when the name of a person could include a middle initial (or not). "Martin Luther King" is a safe bet, but "Martin King" or "Martin L. King" are conceivable variations. Names of people are also complicated by the possibility of nicknames or initials in place of full names.

There are some specific situations when exact phrase matching is especially effective. For example, compound noun phrases (for example, "wisdom tooth") are better off as exact phrases, as are technical terms (for example, "luxated patella"). If you are looking for a literary work and you happen to know a portion of the work verbatim, you may be able to locate the work by the one exact phrase. For example, a document about the life of an early mathematician named Hypatia can be retrieved on the basis of the exact phrase "murdered her with tiles." At the time of this writing, this particular phrase produces a hit list of only two distinct documents at each of the largest search engines. Just be careful to make sure you have the exact quotation. If you are not 100% correct, the query will fail.

5.4.2 Title Searches

Most people never use this simple and extremely powerful search technique. Many document databases created for search engines pay attention to special parts of a Web page so that keywords found in special places can be tagged with distinguishing markers. For example, some keywords in a document index are tagged as special because they were found in the title of the Web page, while

the Web are legitimate and can be trusted. Others are less reliable. You must learn to evaluate all online information before you reference it or use it for your own purposes.

Your evaluation should focus on the Web page content. Don't be influenced by the look and feel of a page. Beautiful graphics and careful text formatting mean that the author cares about the attractiveness of the page. However, that doesn't guarantee the credibility of the information. If the graphics don't contribute to the information on the page, you might find it helpful to turn them off in order to concentrate on the written content.

The Internet is a *content-neutral medium*. That is, it distributes falsehoods and fantasies as easily as facts and truth. It encourages people to produce pages on anything and everything, and the line between fact and fiction can be twisted in many subtle ways. A delusional author might report wishful thinking or hallucinogenic experiences as fact. If the departure from reality is subtle and believable, assessing credibility with absolute certainty could be impossible. Conspiracy theories thrive on the Internet because conspiracy buffs can easily hook up with one another and find strength in numbers. Always use common sense when assessing information credibility on the Web. If the topic you're researching involves conspiracy theories or controversial political scandals, everything you find should be treated with extreme caution.

You can complete a good content evaluation with the help of a credibility checklist. Many checklist criteria apply to the evaluation of traditional print documents; others are specific to Web documents. You can find several useful checklists for Web page assessment on the Web. The following sections discuss some of the most common criteria used to assess Web page credibility.

5.6.1 Author Credibility

A page is useless for research purposes if it fails to clearly identify its author, as well as offer additional information about the author either in the current document or via hyperlinks to other documents. The author's institutional affiliation and job title should be available, as well as a telephone number and complete mailing address. An author's e-mail address that ends in `.gov` or `.edu` is evidence of a legitimate institutional affiliation. However, remember that college students and staff members (as well as faculty) have `.edu` addresses. Look for a short professional biography on an associated Web page.

The author of the Web page should make it clear whether he or she is the original author of the material in question. Look for a copyright statement. If there is some doubt about the copyright statement or there is no copyright statement, contact the author to double-check the material's originality. A legitimate author is normally happy to verify authorship.

Try to verify that the author is who he or she claims to be. If someone is identified as a biology professor at Home State University, go to the home page for the university and look for a list of the faculty in the biology department or in a general university directory. Most universities and colleges maintain a faculty/staff directory on the Web. Corporate environments might or might not have online employee directories. However, a telephone call to corporate headquarters will tell you if someone is employed by the company.

Author credibility is normally not a concern if the work has been published by a respected journal or magazine or if you've located a published citation to the work in question in such a journal or magazine. You can double-check anything that someone claims to have published by going to the publication's home page and locating a table of contents that contains the article in question. It is increasingly common for magazines and journals to maintain Web sites where you can see at least a table of contents, if not an entire article. Checking will protect you from a fraudulent publication claim.

After you've verified the author's identity, investigate whether the author is qualified to write on the topic. A university professor might not be an expert in an area unrelated to his or her professional specialty. The title "professor" does not automatically confer expertise in all areas, so always do a background check on the author. Look for additional evidence of scholarly activities in that area. The existence of only a single, isolated paper is more questionable than are a dozen papers in the same area. If the author has published other papers in the area but the article in question has not been published, a certain amount of credibility can be assumed from the other publications.

When the author is a writer for a news organization, it's best to verify reported facts independently. If the article mentions a published source for its information, go to the original source document and check it yourself. If no additional sources are cited, look for independent corroborating reports.

5.6.2 Accurate Writing and Documentation

If an article is poorly written and has grammatical errors and misspellings, its content might be sloppy as well. Serious writing takes time and effort. If you sense that the article was written casually and quickly, it's probably not a good source. In addition, check whether the author cites other sources. Are the citations complete? If they are hyperlinks to other online sources, are the links operational and up-to-date? An accurate information source will include correct attributions where needed and disclaimers when information or conclusions are questionable.

If the resource has been published, is the online version identical to the printed version or is it a shorter version? Some magazines post partial versions of their printed articles. The Web site should state clearly whether the article is complete or partial.

5.6.3 Objectivity

If an article's author is affiliated with a commercial entity, try to separate informational content from advertising. This is not always easy. Some pages are carefully designed to make it clear where promotion stops and objective information starts. If no effort has been made to do this and the article is unpublished, you should be concerned about its objectivity.

Scientists working in private industry publish their legitimate research to establish credibility within the scientific establishment. Scientific papers are subjected to a process of peer review to maintain quality control within the sciences. Evaluating the objectivity of writers outside the scientific establishment is difficult. However, articles in respected publications are good indicators of objective writing.

Many authors provide information online as a public service. Sometimes authors and their work are supported by or are otherwise affiliated with nonprofit organizations; objectivity can be a problem if these organizations have their own political agendas. If you cite information distributed by an advocacy group, do your own fact checking with independent sources and try to corroborate the information.

5.6.4 Stability of Web Pages

The Web is a dynamic medium, with new information popping up every day. Pages also disappear every day. You can't know whether a page will still be on the Web next year or even next month. This is a problem for people doing scholarly research. However, here are some guidelines that can help you assess a page's stability.

- Does the page include a date? When was it last revised?
- Is it part of a larger site that has other dated materials?
- Do other Web sites refer to the work at this address?
- Is the page part of an institutional resource?

A heavily cited work might appear at multiple Web sites. If you cite an online source, always cite the original URL rather than a copy at a mirror site.

The original site usually will be associated with the author or the author's home institution, and it is presumably the most stable site.

No matter how hard you try to select stable Web pages, it's impossible to know how long a Web page will either be available or be available at its current URL. Sometimes a Web site designer rearranges a Web site, especially if it's growing. This means that old URLs might become obsolete but that the pages are still available under new URLs. One study found that the lifetime of the average URL is only 75 days. Presumably, this figure is low because a large number of experimental pages created by newcomers to the Web have since ceased to exist, along with Web pages that have moved to new URLs. Regardless, this is a sobering statistic.

5.6.5 Fraudulent Web Pages

Constructing a Web site in another person's name in order to misrepresent the person is easy. Although it's unlikely that the academic community would do this, bogus Web sites for political candidates were found during both the 1996 and 2000 presidential campaigns. Bogus home pages often are created as parodies of the real thing. If you find material on a page that is blatantly off-beat, contradictory, or surprising in any way, there is always the possibility that the page was maliciously crafted for the sake of deceiving the unwary.

Things to Remember

- Use different resources to find different kinds of information.
- Subject trees and clearinghouses are good sources for answers to open-ended questions.
- General search engines are good sources for fact-based answers to specific questions.
- Yahoo! is not the only subject tree.
- Google is not the only search engine.
- When you visit a search engine for the first time, read the online documentation.

- Use successive query refinement to develop effective search engine queries.
- Select keywords because you expect to see them in your target documents.
- Think carefully about your keywords—look for associative connections to people and organizations.
- Don't bother looking beyond the first 20 to 30 hits in a hit list.
- Use Boolean queries when you have unusual keywords or distinctive combinations of keywords.
- Different search engines index different documents. If you are having trouble finding something, try a meta search engine or a specialized search engine.
- Add the keyword "database" to your searches to access the Invisible Web.

Important Concepts

Boolean query a query format based on logical operators

clearinghouse an exhaustive collection of online resources for a specific topic

Invisible Web (aka Deep Web) Web pages and content that are not indexed by a search engine

meta-search engine an engine that sends a query to several different search engines and then returns some number of the top hits found by each

query a list of keywords given to a search engine

search engine a query-driven interface to a document database indexed for keyword retrieval

subject tree a hierarchically arranged collection of topic categories and Web page resources

Where Can I Learn More?

Boolean Searching
http://www.searchenginewatch.com/facts/boolean.html

Evaluating Web Resources
http://www2.widener.edu/Academics/Libraries/
   Wolfgram-Memorial-Library/Evaluate_Web_Pages/659/
Invisible Web
http://websearch.about.com/od/invisibleweb/a/
   invisible_web.htm
Meta Search Engine Reviews
http://searchenginewatch.com/showPage.html?page=2156241
Metacrawlers or Meta Search Engines
http://searchenginewatch.com/links/article.php/2156241
Search Engine Showdown
http://www.searchengineshowdown.com/
Search Engine Watch
http://searchenginewatch.com/
Search Features Chart
http://searchenginewatch.com/facts/assistance.html
Sites for Special Searches
http://www.suite101.com/reference/search_engine_reviews
Searchenginez
http://searchenginez.com/
Tool Kit for the Expert Web Searcher
http://www.lita.org/committe/toptech/toolkit.htm

Problems and Exercises

1. Describe and contrast three general types of questions. Why is it useful to categorize your information needs before you conduct a search on the Web? Which question type is best served by general search engines?

2. How does a clearinghouse differ from a subject tree?

3. What distinguishing features differentiate Yahoo!, Google, the Open Directory Project, About, and Ask.com?

4. Organize your list of clocks from Subject Tree Exercise 1 in a hierarchical tree. Don't look at Yahoo!'s hierarchy or try to reconstruct its hierarchy—work out your own. Was it easy to build a tree structure for your list, or did you need to start over a few times? Was this a straightforward exercise or a difficult one? Explain your answers.

5. Explain the difference between a category match and a site match at Yahoo!

6. Suppose you've tried several queries at one general search engine and you're not receiving any good hits. What two options do you have at this point?

7. How does a meta search engine differ from a search engine?

8. Suppose a teacher has collected some essays and one looks as if it hasn't been written by the student who handed it in. How can the teacher check to see if the paper was taken from a Web site?

9. What will happen if you enter a Boolean query in an input box not set up for Boolean queries?

10. What tag should you use at Google to conduct a title search?

11. If an article on the Web has a .edu address, is it necessarily more trustworthy than an article at a .com address? Explain your answer.

12. What is a content-neutral medium? Can you think of three communications media that are content-neutral?

13. [FIND IT ONLINE] Which search engine accesses a larger database of documents, the one at Yahoo! or the one at Excite? Explain your answer. (For the purposes of this question, ignore the fact that Yahoo!'s search pages give you the option of conducting a general search of the Web if you're not satisfied with the hits returned by Yahoo!)

14. [FIND IT ONLINE] The connection between dogs and the number 42 was discussed in Section 5.2.1. Go to Yahoo!, and, beginning with a search for Douglas Adams fan sites, track down the answer to the question, "What role does the number 42 play in the lives of all dogs?"

15. [FIND IT ONLINE] Find the exact date of the denial-of-service attacks on Yahoo! and CNN that happened sometime between February 1, 2000, and March 1, 2000. First use the advanced search option at AltaVista (http://www.altavista.com/). Then do the search again by using an advanced site search at CNN (http://search.cnn.com/pages/search.jsp). Which resource made it easier to find the answers? Describe your experience with this exercise at both sites.

16. [FIND IT ONLINE] Suppose you want to track down all the Web pages you can find that cite Wendy Lehnert. To ensure that you don't miss anything, look for all the possible name variations: Wendy Lehnert,

W. Lehnert, Wendy G. Lehnert, W. G. Lehnert, and Wendy Grace Lehnert. Create a Boolean query that will cover all these variations as simply as possible. (Hint: Find a search engine that supports the NEAR logical operator and read the documentation for the use of NEAR. Formulate a Boolean query that uses NEAR for this exercise.) What query did you use?

17. **[FIND IT ONLINE]** Experiment with Boolean queries to find informational pages about browser cookies. Keep a log of all queries you try. Don't stop until the top 10 hits on your hit list are all general pages about browser cookies; eliminate all false hits associated with recipes, food retailers, and so on. How many queries did you use to find your answers? Which search engine did you use? Did you use any advanced search features in addition to a Boolean query? Describe the reasoning that led you to a good hit list. Hand in a copy of your final hit list (copy and paste it into a word processing document) with your other answers.

18. **[FIND IT ONLINE]** Who was the first famous woman mathematician? For what was she famous?

19. **[FIND IT ONLINE]** Who was the first U.S. president to be born in a hospital?

20. **[FIND IT ONLINE]** The green iguana is said to have a third eye. Investigate. How is the third eye used? How does it work? Is it unique to green iguanas?

21. **[FIND IT ONLINE]** Suppose you hear a song on the radio that you want to track down. You didn't catch the name of it on the radio, and the only part of the lyrics you can remember is one line from the refrain: ". . . thinking about eter-nity. . . ." Find out the name of the song, the artist who sings it, and the name of a CD that contains the song.

22. **[FIND IT ONLINE]** Find a searchable Web site (one that has its own site search facility) devoted to the subject of tigers. How did you find it? How hard was it to find the site? List the URL for the site you found.

23. **[FIND IT ONLINE]** After swimming in chlorinated water, a person's blonde hair sometimes acquires a greenish tint. Find out everything you can about this problem: what causes it, how to fix it, and how to prevent it. Look for different explanations and solutions. For each piece of information you find, rate its credibility on a scale of 1 to 10. Explain the reasoning behind your ratings.

24. **[FIND IT ONLINE]** Chapter 9 will explain how to add a link to a Web page for an audio clip. If the user clicks the link, the audio clip plays. Find out how to add an audio clip to a Web page so that the music starts playing as soon as the Web page is displayed. How did you find this information?

25. **[FIND IT ONLINE]** A lot of people know about MP3 files. However, few know about MIDI files. Find out how MIDI files differ from MP3 files. When would it make sense to put a MIDI file instead of an MP3 file on a Web page?

26. **[FIND IT ONLINE]** You can conduct a search at Google to find all the Web pages that contain links pointing to a specific URL. Find out how to do this and see how many pages have links to your browser's default Web page.

27. **[FIND IT ONLINE]** There are three general modes for making digital television work interactively: single mode, simultaneous mode, and pause mode. Describe these three modes, and identify any companies that have developed working technologies along these lines.

28. **[FIND IT ONLINE]** David Kline estimates that 75% of all corporate wealth is in intellectual property or patents. Who is David Kline? How many U.S. patents were granted to Internet companies in 1995? In 1998? In 2001? Can business models and processes be patented? Back up your answers with specific sources and details.

29. **[FIND IT ONLINE]** Can a U.S. public high school legally suspend or otherwise punish one of its students for publishing a satirical or unofficial home page for the school? Assume that the page is produced without the use of school resources. Argue yes or no by citing specific lawsuits concerning censorship by high schools. How did you find your information?

30. **[FIND IT ONLINE]** Go to `http://www.thomas.gov/` and find how many bills have been filed in the current Congress by your local representative. How many of these bills have been passed?

Find What You Want—Fast!

Information Retrieval Concepts

Information retrieval (**IR**) is the branch of computer science that deals with finding information in large text databases. IR existed as an academic endeavor for decades, but general interest in it has increased since the birth of the Web. A Web search engine is an IR system dressed up with a user-friendly interface. Beneath the interface is a computer program that has no understanding of human language and no ability to comprehend your information needs. IR systems work by using the keywords in your input query to attempt to locate documents that contain the keywords.

A search engine query can be a single keyword, a grammatical sentence, or a group of words tossed together in random order. For most search engines, the grammatical construction of a query is irrelevant. The most important information lies in the specific keywords of the query. Keywords index the document database. It's your job to distinguish between effective and ineffective indexes when you compose a query. Generally, you can't know beforehand which queries are best, so experimentation and feedback are the keys to a successful query. There is a method to the madness, but you'll still need to feel your way through the process each time.

Fast response times from query engines are possible because all the documents in a search engine's database have been indexed. Document indexing is managed behind the scenes by processes that have nothing to do with you or your search engine interactions. It goes on continually as new URLs are added to the database. The better engines work to eliminate obsolete URLs from their databases as quickly as possible. So any Web database that you tap into today isn't likely to be the same one you'll tap into tomorrow. It won't be terribly different. However, it *will* be different.

The Web is one massive, moving target, so humans can't hope to examine each new Web page in order to identify good indexes for that page. Web search engines must create and update their document databases automatically by using Web spiders. A **Web spider** is a computer program that examines Web pages, collecting URLs from the old Web pages that lead to new Web pages, examining the new Web pages for more URLs, which in turn lead to more Web pages, and so on. The Web spider is responsible only for finding new Web pages. As it traverses hyperlinks from page to page, it keeps a list of all the pages it has visited. This list of URLs for each page is returned to the search engine, with any URLs for Web pages not known to the search engine's database added to the document database. Each new page must be processed for its keyword before the page's URL is added to the database. Different indexing methods are used to index the document. The large search engines run Web spiders constantly in an effort to index as much of the Web as possible.

The entire process of collecting new Web pages, indexing them, and adding them to a document database is totally automated. Human intervention at any step along the way would only slow the process. A Web spider can't pass judgment on the quality of a document, but it can process documents faster than people can. When we tackle the Web, we are dealing with terabytes of text (1 **terabyte** = 1,024 gigabytes). Web spiders are the only way we can hope to stay on top of this much text.

Search Engine Indexing Methods

Some search engines explain their text indexing methods online. Specific online newsletters and subscription services are dedicated to tracking this information and summarizing it for conscientious Web masters who want to make their Web pages as visible as possible. Indexing for any specific search engine cannot be described in detail here. Rather, this section describes the most commonly encountered methods so that you'll get some idea of how it's done.

Because search engines evolve, a change in indexing methods can result in a skewed database in which older documents are indexed with one method and newer documents with another. Online documentation sometimes describes only the most current indexing method. This makes it difficult to know whether a search engine's database has been indexed consistently throughout.

For retrieval purposes, the most important question is whether a database is indexing most of its documents with selective-text indexing or with full-text indexing. The answer to this question has important implications for query design and search engine selection.

Selective-Text Indexing

Indexing that does not treat all text as equal is called **selective-text indexing**. The title of a document is very important, as is the document's first paragraph and its hyperlinks. Thus a good set of indexes can be created on the basis of only those components; the rest of the document can be ignored. Each word in the title is added to the database and associated with its parent URL. Similarly, each of the first, say, 100 to 200 words might be added to the database, along with each word that is part of a hyperlink. When the same word is found in a few thousand other Web page titles, all those URLs are also indexed under that one word. Thus a single word can index hundreds or thousands of Web pages.

Additional database entries are added to capture word adjacencies, which are needed to match exact phrases. The database is probably also organized in a way that makes it easy to find frequency counts for each URL index. The **frequency count** for a single word is the number of times the word appears in a document. Frequency counts are often helpful in ranking retrieved documents.

Different search engines might invoke different text selection methods. For example, one might index words found in bulleted lists or in text headers. Web pages make it easy for a computer to identify selected text because selected text can be found by looking for specific HTML tags. If you know exactly how a given search engine looks for its document indexes, you can design your Web pages with special attention to the text elements used to index the document. Professional Web page designers try to consider this to make their pages more visible to the most popular search engines. (See How to Increase Your Web Page Hit Counts in the Above & Beyond section in Chapter 4.)

Full-Text Indexing

Indexing that allows no text to go to waste—all text in a document is scanned for indexing terms—is **full-text indexing**. It takes more time to index a document in this manner, and the resulting database is much larger than one that uses selective-text indexing. Until 1995, the computational load associated with full-text indexing was too demanding for most search engines. Since then, the most powerful host machines have had enough memory and speed to make compiling a full-text document database viable.

Although a full-text database is thought to be more powerful than a selective-text database, it seldom abandons the utility of selected text. Even in a full-text database, some terms are still identifiable as selected text. Thus a full-text database doesn't necessarily treat all words as equals. Terms from the title or the first 50 words of the document can be tagged as such and weighted more heavily. Some search engines also permit searches on selective subsets of all the available text so that you can decide whether it's better to conduct your search on the full-text database or a selective-text subset. At times, it's advantageous to work with the smaller set of indexes associated with selected text.

Search engines that use full-text indexing typically stop indexing very large documents after a certain point. If a Web page is larger than 50KB, anything after the first 50KB is probably never indexed. This can be a problem for some huge archive files that contain hundreds of archived articles.

Ignored Words

All search engines have a list of words they ignore. For example, articles, conjunctions, and prepositions appear in too many documents to be of any use as document indexes. Also, some nouns (for example, "people" and "Internet") are ignored because they appear in too many documents.

AltaVista shows you term counts for each keyword in your query so that you can see how often each appears in AltaVista's full-text database. It also shows you which keywords were ignored when its database was constructed (it marks them "ignored"). If a preposition or some other word is crucial for your query and your search engine is ignoring it, try to reword your query without the preposition or other ignored words.

Document Rankings

In the world of IR, few things are black and white. Documents can be strongly connected to a query or only mildly connected to it. A document that contains all the keywords in a query clears the qualifying hurdles with room to spare. However, what about a document that contains only one query keyword? Should a hit for it be returned? What if a document contains multiple instances of the query's keywords? Does a higher frequency count make a document a stronger hit?

Term counts and term frequency counts can reflect an intuitive sense of strong hits and weak hits. However, it's difficult to know how all the hits should be ranked. Is a keyword that appears in the title of a document better than the same keyword seen a hundred times in the document body? Although it might be impossible to answer this question, some judgment calls must be made one way or another. As a rule, no one wants to look past the first 20 to 30 items in a hit list no matter how long the list. So some method of ranking relevant documents is needed to put the best possible candidates at the top of the list. If a Web search engine does everything else right but gets its document rankings wrong, it is useless.

Sometimes a search engine returns a highly ranked document that makes no sense and you can't understand why it was picked up. When this happens, the search engine might have been responding to **hidden text** on the Web page, text that is not displayed by Web browsers but is used by search engines. This happens when a Web page designer has specified a list of keywords (using the META tag) that is included for search engine indexing purposes only.

Intelligent Concept Extraction

Some search engines offer a fuzzy query option that tries to identify underlying concepts in your query. For example, the phrase "senior citizens" refers to a concept that is semantically close to other words and phrases such as "retired people," "grandparents," and "the elderly." Most search engines require you to think of all these variations and add them to your query to get full coverage from the query. A few search engines, however, perform **intelligent concept extraction**, a method of searching that automatically augments your query with synonyms and related terms.

Intelligent concept extraction attempts to rewrite the original query in words that capture its underlying concepts. This is a great feature for those who can't think of all the different ways a concept might be expressed (or don't want to bother doing so). If, however, you have a very specific need and you don't want to see any variations on your terms, you should avoid any search engines that use intelligent concept extraction. When a search engine supports intelligent concept extraction, it is probably not a feature that can be turned off.

If you're not finding enough hits, you might try intelligent concept extraction to see whether a broader interpretation of your needs can locate more documents. Documents will still be ranked with exact matches first, so you should easily see any documents that contain your specific keywords. In addition, you might be surprised at how many more relevant documents you can find when you make appropriate keyword substitutions.

The **Excite** search engine uses intelligent concept extraction. This feature may become more common as search engines try to be more helpful and intelligent.

Relevance Feedback

Rarely can you create the perfect query on the first try. Most people who work extensively with search engines try some exploratory queries before they settle on the query they really want to use. Successive query refinement is one way to explore a search space and zero in on a good query. It requires you to generate a sequence of queries that are increasingly focused. Sometimes this works well, and sometimes it doesn't. So IR researchers have tried to automate much of the effort associated with successive query refinement. The most successful strategy for this automated query refinement is called relevance feedback.

Relevance feedback is the process of identifying reliably useful keywords on the basis of good representative documents. It is a form of successive query refinement in which the search engine tries to meet you halfway. In classic relevance feedback, you issue an initial query and then review the resulting hits. If a hit is on target, you flag it as a good hit; otherwise, you don't flag it. Once you've flagged a few good hits, the relevance feedback engine goes to work and examines the affected documents in an effort to identify words or phrases that best characterize those hits. If it finds the same word or phrase in all the good hits, that word or phrase becomes a useful keyword or keywords.

The beauty of relevance feedback is in the use of only a few good example documents. Once you've identified such documents, you automatically generate keywords that should lead to more good documents. You don't have to think about the keywords to use or how to construct a good query because that is done automatically. Relevance feedback can be a very effective and painless way to home in on the documents you want.

Many search engines support a simple form of relevance feedback. When you see a document that is close to the type of document you want, look for a link named "More Like This" or "Similar Pages." Clicking this link triggers the relevance feedback feature, which will take you from that document to similar documents. If one of the similar documents is also on target, you can ask for more documents like it. Each time you select a document and ask for more like it, the search engine uses that document as a source of additional relevance feedback. If you select a chain of documents linked by relevance feedback, the search engine uses all the documents in that chain each time it searches for additional similar documents. You never see the enhanced queries generated by relevance feedback, so the entire process seems vaguely magical.

Problems and Exercises

A1. [FIND IT ONLINE] The largest search engines brag about how many documents they index, but how accurate are those claims? Visit `http://www.searchengineshowdown.com/stats/sizeest.shtml` and find out if any of these claims are inflated. How much of Google's claimed database is actually being used? When does HotBot fail to use its entire database?

A2. What is relevance feedback, and when is it useful?

A3. Does relevance feedback work better with fiction or with nonfiction? Explain your answer.

A4. [TAKE A STAND] If you haven't already done so, answer the question about zebras posed at the start of this chapter by querying Google and using Google's "similar pages" feature. Then visit the Extractor Demo at `http://139.142.234.8/on_line_demo.html` and see if it can help you locate additional documents you didn't find when using Google's similar pages. Do you think Extractor is a valuable search tool or is it no better than Google's relevance feedback?

A5. What is intelligent concept extraction, and when should you avoid it?

A6. [TAKE A STAND] Most of the major search engines accept "paid placements" from commercial businesses. Visit `http://searchenginewatch.com/resources/article.php/2156561` and `http://www.pcworld.com/features/article/0,aid,97431,00.asp` to read about this practice. What impact is this likely to have on the general public? Are search engines doing anything to protect their integrity as information providers? Are there any legal issues surrounding paid placements? How do you feel about paid placements?

A7. To conduct an exact phrase search for an entire sentence, would you expect better success at a search engine that uses full-text indexing or one that uses selective-text indexing? Explain your answer.

A8. [FIND IT ONLINE] Explain the difference between full-text indexing and selective-text indexing. Which one does Yahoo!'s search engine use? If you aren't sure, pick a lengthy document in Yahoo!'s database, extract an exact phrase from a paragraph somewhere inside the document, and query Yahoo! with that exact phrase to determine whether it can retrieve the document for you. Try this a few times to see if your results are consistent.

A9. [**FIND IT ONLINE**] AllTheWeb and Google both index .pdf files (readable via Adobe's Acrobat reader), but Google reportedly stops indexing its .pdf documents after about 120KB (about 35 pages into a document). You can verify this for yourself by visiting both Google and AllTheWeb and searching for the exact phrase "truck struck the cherry picker basket." See if you can find a .pdf document in AllTheWeb's hit list that does not appear in Google's hit list. Can you test for the presence of this document in Google's database? How? Is it there?

A10. [**FIND IT ONLINE**] Google's hit lists sometimes contain Web pages that Google's spider has never visited: These are Google's unindexed URLs. Visit `http://www.searchengineshowdown.com/features/google/unindexed.shtml` and find out how Google is able to do this. How do you know when you see an unindexed URL in a hit list?

A11. [**FIND IT ONLINE**] The sites `http://www.findarticles.com/` and `http://www.magportal.com/` index full-text articles from a variety of magazines. Visit one of these sites and see if you can find an article about the information technology challenges facing researchers who study biodiversity. How hard would it be to zero in on this particular article at a general search engine? Try it and see.

A12. [**FIND IT ONLINE**] Do any general search engines index the entire Web? If not, what percentage of the Web do the largest search engines cover? Get the most current information available.

A13. [**FIND IT ONLINE**] The most successful search engines use clustering when they compile their hit lists. Visit `http://www.searchenginewatch.com` and learn more about clustering. What is Google's policy on clustering?

A14. [**TAKE A STAND**] Some people believe that the next big improvement in search capabilities will result not from improvements to search engines but from improvements to the documents we put on the Web. Visit `http://www.searchenginewatch.com/searchday/article.php/2160191` to find out about "The Language of the Semantic Web." Who stands to benefit the most from the Semantic Web if it comes to pass? What effect would it have on today's "anyone can put up a Web page" ethos? Are there pros and cons? Do you think this is a good idea?

Software on the Internet

6.1 Taking Charge

You may think of your computer primarily as a piece of equipment on which to run a word processor, launch a browser, and read e-mail. That's what many people do with their computers most of the time. How you use your computer can be the result of a conscious decision or a mindless habit. If you understand your options and make a thoughtful decision about how to spend your computer time, no one can tell you that you aren't using your computer to its full advantage. However, if you haven't investigated your computer's full potential, you can't say that you've made an informed decision. The power of your computer lies in the software it can run. Most people don't need to know about all the software in the world. Everyone, however, should know about the software that can make his or her life more productive, informed, and enjoyable.

Internet access makes investigating your computer's full potential easy. On the Net, you can find thousands of software-related recommendations, reviews, documentation, tutorials, and discussion groups, not to mention software itself. Once you learn how easy it is to download software from the Internet onto your own computer, you might never

Chapter Goals

- Know what to expect when you download software from the Internet
- Learn to configure antivirus software and ensure it scans new files
- Become familiar with five different software installation scenarios
- Know which file utility to use when you need to open a file archive
- Locate reputable software on the Internet through clearinghouses
- Learn how to navigate FTP servers and download files from them
- Find out how to keep your computer in good working order as you add software to your system
- Learn the proper procedure for removing unwanted software from your system
- Find many software reviews
- Learn the difference between open source and proprietary software
- Learn about the file formats

shop at a retail software store again. Software sold in a retail store is more expensive to produce and distribute than software distributed over the Net. As a result, the same software is often available through both distribution channels, with the retail version being more expensive. For the extra money, you get your software on a CD-ROM plus some printed documentation that you hope you won't have to read. In addition, the software on the CD-ROM might not be the latest version available. However, you can check the manufacturer's Web site for the latest software updates, since most manufacturers that distribute software on CD-ROMs also have Web sites where they distribute their software.

At the manufacturer's Web site, you can probably download the complete software package—or at least a limited version for a free trial. In the latter case, you can try the software on your own computer for a specified period of time at no charge, during which time you can decide if it's what you want. By doing the same with competing products from other manufacturers, you can do some serious comparison shopping. Once you've tried all the free samples, you can decide which one is right for you and purchase a software license online.

Software distribution Web sites encourage ongoing communication between manufacturers and customers and offer streamlined customer support. Online you might be able to find manufacturers' software patches you can install to fix any bugs in the software. New software releases or updates might become available to registered users over the Web, often before the shrink-wrapped versions make it into retail stores. If you are uncomfortable not having a printed user's manual, be aware that online documentation and help files are usually at least as good as the printed versions. In addition, you'll probably find a searchable help feature easier to work with than the index of a large user's manual. It's easier for manufacturers to make corrections and additions on a Web site than in a printed manual. The manufacturer might also support an online technical support discussion group in which users can discuss software problems with each other as well as the company's technical support personnel. Another welcome feature is technical support via e-mail, for users who don't like to be put on hold when they call for help.

When you purchase a software license for software obtained from the Web, you might be given a special URL from which you download the registered version of the software. Alternatively, if you have a free-trial version, you might be given a registration key that will unlock the registered version, which is already on your computer, hiding inside the free-trial version. Commercial software distributed as a free-trial version along with a (usually superior) paid version is called **shareware**. Some shareware is programmed to shut itself down when the trial period expires. Other shareware shows you a reminder window each time you launch the software during the trial period, reminding you to register (see Figure 6.1). This type of shareware is sometimes called **nagware** (if it nags you to buy it), special edition software, or limited edition software. Some shareware vendors rely on the honor system alone. Paying for the product is left entirely up to the user.

A manufacturer that withholds features from its free-trial version hopes that you'll like what you see well enough to pay for the registered version. A free-trial version purposely crippled by having some features omitted is still usable. In fact, it might be missing only one key feature, which is either a big time-saver or some obviously desirable feature that the manufacturer expects everyone to want. Alternatively, in the free-trial version you might have to endure banner ads from commercial sponsors. When you purchase the registered version, the banner ads go away.

Manufacturers who rely on "nag screens" hope that you'll buy the full version if you're reminded often enough (at every possible opportunity). Some nagware allows you to continue using the software after the free-trial expiration date has passed, although the program keeps reminding you that you've passed the deadline and you really should pay for the software. You can ignore these reminders, but sooner or later, guilt might set in or you might simply

Figure 6.1

A shareware registration reminder

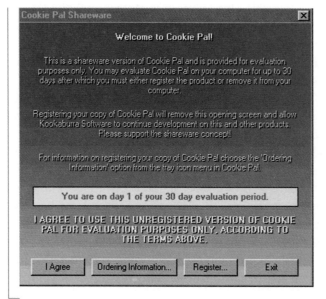

get tired of seeing the nag screen, so eventually you give in and buy the shareware. Shareware that self-destructs (refuses to launch) when the free-trial period is over is perhaps more effective at making people pay for the software. Making shareware that self-destructs is not unreasonable from the manufacturers' point of view—they are simply protecting their inventories from shoplifters. How many retailers are willing to let you take an item home at no charge so that you can decide whether you like it and want to keep it?

Newbies are often surprised to discover how much software is provided on the Web at no charge. It might be natural to assume that such software, called **freeware**, must not be very good simply because it's free. This is not necessarily true. Some freeware is as good as any commercial counterpart, and it may be distributed at no charge for many different reasons. For example, a manufacturer who wants to increase traffic on its official Web site might offer a modest piece of freeware as an incentive to visit. Sometimes, however, the software is not modest. For example, during the Browser Wars of the mid-1990s, Microsoft and Netscape offered their browsers at no charge, for noncommercial use, in bids to establish market dominance. This high-profile competition worked so well that many casual Internet users didn't realize other browsers were (and still are) available (for example, the Opera Web browser, described in Section 1.11).

Other reasons for giving away software include the case in which a freelance programmer who is reworking a piece of software wants to obtain feedback and suggestions during its development (or beta) phase from as many users as possible. Or a novice programmer might find it gratifying to see other people using his or her creation, even if no money is involved.

Some programmers distribute freeware as an act of guerrilla warfare against old-order economic forces. For example, the author of the Napster program, which facilitated MP3 distribution over the Net, claimed that Napster's file-sharing technology was protected by the Audio Home Recording Act of 1992 and did not harm commercial sales of CDs. Recall from Chapter 2 that the trade association Recording Industry Association of America (RIAA) filed lawsuits against MP3-related Web sites to stop illegal MP3 file distributions. Many Napster advocates consider these lawsuits as doomed efforts by the RIAA to control the distribution channels for commercial music. In situations such as this, the expression "computer revolution" is more than a metaphor for social upheaval. Entire industries can rise and fall when new technologies become freely available over the Internet.

Finally, there's long-standing support within the academic community for **open source software**—software whose code is willingly shared publicly so that other programmers can offer their improvements. This is done in a communal effort to create superior software. Linux is an example of open source software that has gained considerable momentum in recent years as an alternative operating system (OS) to Windows. One notable advantage of Linux systems is the large set of freeware that is included with Linux or available elsewhere. For example, Open Office offers office suite features comparable to those available in Microsoft Office. There are numerous other free packages available for Linux systems that compete directly with Windows counterparts.

Although it is not (yet) as easy to use as Windows, Linux does have one advantage that makes it the OS of choice for programmers: almost all the application software developed for Linux is open source. If you value excellence in software design, open source software often rivals the best software produced by leading software companies. In open source software, user-friendly interfaces are typically not a priority (open source interfaces are usually written by programmers for other programmers), so it might not be easy to use. However, more consumer-oriented open source products are becoming available to the general public. For example, Netscape Navigator did not begin as open source software, but it "went open" in 1998 in an effort to encourage software developers to incorporate Netscape client technologies into their own products. Mozilla 1.0, the first open source spin-off from Netscape, was released in 2002.

By taking advantage of what the Web offers, you can explore an exciting world of commercial software, shareware, and freeware on your home computer. The right software makes a significant difference between a computer that works really well for you and one that isn't doing everything it could. The Web makes it easy and fun to explore the possibilities. If you own your own computer and you haven't been sampling software on the Web, you're missing out on a big part of what it has to offer. This chapter covers everything you need to know about file formats, **software downloads** and safe installation practices. If you're new to software downloads, you'll be surprised how easy the process is. More experienced readers might want to skim this chapter for tips and tricks that can make the experience smoother and faster.

Open Source versus Proprietary Software versus Freeware

If you are a typical computer user, you probably use the Microsoft Office Suite (Word, Excel, PowerPoint) as part of your regular routine. You probably also use Internet Explorer, Mozilla Firefox, or other browsers to surf the Web and perform routine tasks. Most likely you paid for the former and got the latter software free. The Microsoft Office Suite is an example of **proprietary software**—software that is protected by a patent or trademark, and may not be modified or distributed for free or sold for profit. Your browser, on the other hand, may be the result of an open source project, such as the Mozilla browsers and other software provided by the Mozilla Foundation (http://www.mozilla.org/), or a hybrid of the two, like Apple's Safari browser, which includes WebCore and JavaScriptCore, open source products released under the GNU Lesser Public License. Open source software includes any software whose executable *and* source code is freely available for examination, modification, distribution, and use.

Open source products are often available for free, but they are *not* in the public domain. Open source software is **copylefted**: a general way to make intellectual property like a computer program free and that requires all modified and extended versions of the original work to be free as well. If a user wishes to modify and redistribute the software, a license must be secured. Such a license is usually granted only if the modified product including source code is freely available, modifiable, and distributable without restriction. This license does not *require* that the product is free of charge, however most open source products *are* free. Recently, the term **FLOSS** (aka **free-libre/open source software**) has been used in place of the original acronym **OSS** when referring to open source software products.

Don't confuse open source software with freeware. Freeware includes only the *executable* code. Often freeware is proprietary software that is distributed free alongside more sophisticated versions that must be purchased.

TIP: Source Code versus Executable Code

Software application **source code** is the software product in its original form: a (usually large) set of computer instructions written in some programming language. When you purchase or download application software, you are getting a translated (or **compiled**) version of the source code in the form of machine-language instructions, usually called **executable code**. Computers cannot understand application programs written in source code. A **compiler** is needed to translate the source code into a form that the computer can read directly. Since each microprocessor has its own set of machine language instructions (see Section 1.2.2), source code must be compiled for each different processor (and operating system) that will use that application. When you acquire software, you must ensure that the version you are getting has been compiled specifically for your processor and operating system.

Often the free version includes advertisements as an integral part of the product—so you must suffer through the commercials! The source code is generally *not* available for examination, modification, and redistribution. Eudora, an e-mail client for the PC and the Mac, is an example of freeware that comes with ever-changing advertisements. There are many other examples found throughout the text. FLOSS may be freeware, but freeware does not always fit the FLOSS criteria.

6.2.1 Advantages and Disadvantages

To a large extent, the choice between open source and proprietary software largely depends on what is available and your level of computer skill. Most of the personal computers are running the Windows operating system, and most use proprietary Microsoft products such as Windows Internet Explorer, Office Suite, and other familiar products. But there are comparable open source software applications. Table 6.1 lists a few of the open source products available for PCs and Macs. There are many free software applications that are not listed because they are not FLOSS. An example of this is the Eudora mail client that is available free for both the PC and the Mac.

The major advantage promoted by the vendors of proprietary software is assistance with the product. Typically vendors put some effort into developing user-friendly documentation that can be searched for topics of interest. Many maintain online chat rooms, message boards, e-mail centers, and/or toll-free telephone support for their clients. The down side is that these products are *not* free and upgrades usually incur an additional charge. And telephone support (typically) expires after a fixed period. Users are often *forced* to purchase upgrades when they acquire a new machine, a new operating system, or an operating system upgrade. Also it may be necessary to purchase additional telephone support if you still need it after the free support period expires. And since this market is profit driven, the vendor may want to ensure a continued revenue stream by dribbling out upgrades according to a vendor-driven agenda.

On the other hand, freeware may not be supported at all. Some freeware products are written strictly for fun by lone developers. Once the project is completed, they move on to other things, leaving the unsupported product to slowly sink into the sea of obsolescence. These products can range from very good to nonfunctional. Some freeware products become reincarnated as polished commercial versions, as was the case with Everest Home, a free system diagnostics, system information, and benchmarking tool for PCs. It is now available for purchase as Everest Corporate and Ultimate Edition versions.

Table 6.1 Selected examples of FLOSS products for PCs and Macs

Category	Product	URL	Windows	Mac
Audio Editor	Audacity	`http://audacity.sourceforge.net/`	✓	✓
	Streamripper	`http://streamripper.sourceforge.net/`	✓	1
Compression/Zip	7-Zip	`http://www.7-zip.org/`	✓	
Drawing Programs	Dia	`http://www.gnome.org/projects/dia/`	✓	
E-mail	Mozilla	`http://www.mozilla.org`	✓	✓
	Phoneix Mail	`http://phxmail.sourceforge.net/index.html`	✓	
	Thunderbird	`http://www.mozilla.org`	✓	✓
FTP	Cyberduck	`http://cyberduck.ch/`		✓
	Filezilla	`http://filezilla.sourceforge.net/`	✓	
Image Editor	GIMP	`http://www.gimp.org/windows/`	✓	
	GIMPShop	`http://www.apple.com/downloads/macosx/unix_open_source/gimpshop.html`		✓
	Seashore	`http://seashore.sourceforge.net/index.php`		✓
Internet Radio	Juice	`http://juicereceiver.sourceforge.net/index.php`	✓	✓
Instant Messaging	Adium	`http://www.opensourcemac.org/`		✓
	Exodus	`http://exodus.jabberstudio.org/`	✓	
	Miranda ICQ	`http://www.miranda-im.org/`	✓	
Internet Voice Chat	Colloquy	`http://colloquy.info/downloads.html`		✓
	Speak Freely	`http://www.speakfreely.org/`	✓	
Internet TV	Democracy Player	`http://www.getdemocracy.com/`	✓	✓
Media Player	CoolPlayer	`http://coolplayer.sourceforge.net/`	✓	
	Zinf	`http://www.zinf.org/`	✓	
Productivity Software	OpenOffice	`http://www.openoffice.org/`	✓	✓
	NeoOffice	`http://www.macupdate.com/info.php/id/15797`		✓
RSS Client	RSSOwl	`http://www.opensourcemac.org/`		✓
	Vienna	`http://www.opensourcemac.org/`		✓
Software Library Package	Winlibre	`http://www.winlibre.com/en/`	✓	
Video Capture/ Conversion	Dscaler	`http://www.dscaler.org/`	✓	
	VirtualDub	`http://www.virtualdub.org/`	✓	
Web Browser	Camino	`http://www.caminobrowser.org`		✓
	Firefox	`http://www.mozilla.org`	✓	✓
	Mozilla	`http://www.mozilla.org/products/mozilla1.x/`	✓	✓
	Netscape	`http://browser.netscape.com/ns8/`	✓	2

[1]Macintosh version no longer supported
[2]Version 8 only available for Windows, Macs use v 7.2

Open source software is *usually* free, including upgrades—which is a major advantage. It's hard for someone to sell a product that can be acquired for free elsewhere, which is often the case with FLOSS. But support can be a problem. Typically, FLOSS is developed by organized groups of people who are passionate programmers, but dispassionate writers. Consequently, documentation quality can vary widely from excellent to nonexistent. Getting a live body on the phone is even more difficult, but may be available for a fee. The Mozilla Foundation provides newsgroups, message boards, guidebooks, and online chat for their products, but you must pay for telephone support. However, open source products are typically very dynamic. Information is continuously gathered from users to drive the upgrade process in a continuous, unscheduled, client-driven fashion. True open source projects can be very professional, especially those sponsored by open source organizations such as the Mozilla Foundation, Sourceforge, OpenOffice.org, and the Open Source Development Labs.

Interested in a FLOSS product but are unsure whether to try it? Generally, a product with a high version number suggests that it's popular (enough people have used it to drive further development), mature (the product has many "bells and whistles"), and reliable (it would not have lasted long enough to rise to a high version level). Be aware, however, that the version number is not always a true indicator of stability. SeaMonkey is the new name of the venerable Mozilla Suite, which was up to version 1.7.13 before it was regenerated as SeaMonkey v 1.0.4.

Alpha versions, the first release of a new version, may intentionally be incomplete and should probably be avoided unless you are the adventurous type and can deal with computer crashes. **Beta** versions are more mature products, but still under development. You might want to avoid these also. (Be aware that open source software may be in *perpetual beta*—because it's under continuous development and may never be *finished*!)

TIP: Contribute Your Fair Share

Open source products are usually free, but in most cases, a great deal of effort went into the production of the software. Users are encouraged to contribute their fair share as well. Whenever you obtain and use a FLOSS product, be sure to participate in the ongoing development process by sending bug reports and suggestions for improvements and new features to the core developers. In this way you will become a supporting member of the open source community.

Read more about open source and proprietary software in the Above & Beyond Section of this chapter.

Beta versions may also be incompletely implemented. Look for a version that is listed as stable. Read the reviews from clients. Then select and try one of the FLOSS products listed in Table 6.1 and decide for yourself.

 # File Formats

If you're going to be a knowledgeable computer user, then you need to know about the various file formats you may be working with in the course of your Internet experience. Every software application that has the ability to create documents needs to be able to store the file data (information that you entered into the document in some fashion plus some **meta-data** that describes the data itself, such as the name of the file, when it was created, and how the data is recorded). Meta-data is usually stored in a **file header**, followed by the data itself. Additionally, often the file will have a **file extension**, characters appended to the filename preceded by a period, which further identifies the software application that created it, the format used, or both.

For example, a file with the extension .doc refers to a file created by Microsoft Word. Word also has the ability to create a **rich text format** file that has the .rtf extension. Rich text format is a generic text file format that supports common text styles (like font, family, bold, and italicized text). An rtf file can be successfully opened, with formatting intact, by several different applications. This format was created to facilitate text file sharing among several users who are using different word processors. For example, although many applications can successfully read an rtf file, fewer applications are able to read WordPerfect documents because WordPerfect uses a proprietary file format that most other word processors cannot decipher.

Adding an extension to a file does not change the format associated with a file. For example, adding .txt to a file does not make it a generic text file. (But it may allow you to open this file using a text editor.) The application itself determines the format, which is often selectable by the user when saving the file. Figure 6.2 shows the file formats available in Microsoft Word. Sometimes the operating system uses the file extension to decide which application to use when the file is opened by double-clicking. If the file format is not consistent with the extension, then the OS may not be able to open the file. In this case, you might be able to open the file via the File-Open command from within the application.

More and more users are taking advantage of the power of spreadsheets and sharing those files with others. There are several different spreadsheet applications on the market, each with its own particular file format, so two

Figure 6.2

Figure 6.2

File formats
available in
Microsoft Word
for the Macintosh

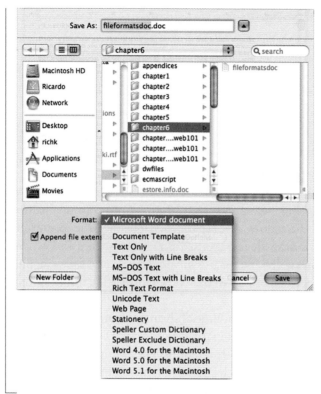

TIP: Notepad and Cross-Platform Text File Sharing

When sharing text files between a PC and Macintosh or LINUX machines be aware that Windows text applications use DOS text formatting conventions that insert two ASCII control characters (see the purple characters in Figure 1.1) at the end of each line: a carriage return (CR) and a line feed (LF). The Mac uses only the CR and LINUX uses only the LF to mark the end of a line. When reading Mac text files on a Windows machine, the text may be displayed as a single long line. When viewing a Windows text file on a LINUX box, you will see a ^M at the end of each line. Most modern text editors are smart enough to convert text files appropriately. Unfortunately, Notepad, the text processor distributed with Windows, does not. This is only a problem if you share files that have been recorded onto a CD, DVD, or floppy disk. FTP clients like WinSCP (PC) or Fetch (Mac) are aware of this issue and make the proper substitutions automatically. This is why the application wants to know the file type you are transferring because this is an issue only for text files. Word is also aware of this and gives you a choice of text file formats (see Figure 6.2).

TIP: Don't Change Those File Extensions!

Avoid changing the assigned file format extension. In some cases you *may* not be able to open the file until you change the extension back to the correct value. (I experienced this myself.) In most cases, it's best to use the application-assigned file extension.

generic spreadsheet files formats have been promoted to facilitate file sharing: CSV and TAB. CSV files use a comma and TAB files use a tab character to separate the values in individual cells, hence the acronym and file extension: comma separated values (`.csv`) and tab separated values (`.tab`). When **importing** a generic spreadsheet file into your application you may be asked how the values are separated. Hopefully the file extension will correctly describe the file format used. You may also be asked which format to use when **exporting** the file for use on a different spreadsheet application. Only the cell values will be saved in the file; all formatting information is usually lost when files are *exported*.

Table 6.2 shows some of the more common file formats that you are likely to encounter, by category. Be aware that the file extensions listed in the table may have other interpretations. For example, FILExt lists 11 different entries for ASP! A more complete list maintained by FILExt, the File Extension Source, can be found at `http://filext.com/`. Consult Appendix C for some common UNIX file extensions.

Table 6.2

Common file extensions

Category	Extension	Associated Application	Description
Applications			
	`.class`	Java interpreter	Java class file
	`.dll`	Windows OS	Dynamic link library
	`.exe`[1]	Windows OS	DOS executable file
	`.jar`	Java interpreter	Java class archive
	`.js`	Web browser, JavaScript interpreter	JavaScript program file
	`.war`	Java interpreter	Archive of Java Web applications
Archived and Compressed			
	`.bin`	Stuffit	Macintosh binary file
	`.gzip, .gz`	Gunzip, others	GNU free software file compression program, "zipped"

(continued)

Table 6.2 *(continued)*

Common file extensions

Category	Extension	Associated Application	Description
Archived and Compressed (continued)			
	`.sea`	Mac OS X	Self-extracting archive, Macintosh
	`.sit`	Stuffit	Cross platform compressed file format
	`.tar`	UNIX, Linux	Tape archive, archive file format
	`.tar.gz`	UNIX, Linux	Zipped archive files
	`.zip`	PKZIP, UnZip, WinZip, WinUnZip	Compressed file format
Audio			
	`.aiff`	Audio player/recorder	Audio interchange file format, Apple
	`.au`	Audio player/recorder	Audio file format, Sun Microsystems
	`.mp3`	Audio player/recorder	Moving picture experts group audio compression format, lossy
	`.ra`	Audio player/recorder, RealProducer	RealAudio, audio, compressed, streaming
	`.ram`	RealPlayer	Real Audio Meta Data, link to RealAudio, RealMedia, RealVideo files on Web pages
	`.rm`	Video player/recorded, RealProducer	RealMedia, audio and video, compressed, streaming
	`.swa`	Shockwave	Shockwave audio file
	`.wav`	Audio player/recorder, RealProducer	Waveform audio format, Microsoft and IBM
	`.wma`	Windows Media Player, others	Windows media audio file, lossy
Graphics			
	`.bmp`	Image editors/viewers and browsers, Windows	Bit map image
	`.gif`	Image editors/viewers and browsers	CompuServe's graphic interchange format
	`.jpg`, `.jpeg`	Image editors/viewers and browsers	Lossy photographic file format proposed by the joint photographic expert group
	`.mng`	Animated image editors/ viewers and browsers	Multiple network graphic, animated version of `.png`
	`.pict`	Image editors/viewers,	Apple image file format
	`.png`	Image editors/viewers and browsers	Portable network graphic, lossless image file format
	`.psd`	Adobe Photoshop	

(continued)

Table 6.2 *(continued)*

Common file extentions

Category	Extension	Associated Application	Description
Graphics (continued)			
	`.tif, .tiff`	Image editors/viewers	Tagged image file format, lossy or lossless
Page Description Language			
	`.css`	Web browser	Cascading style sheet, Web page formatting
	`.pcl`	Printers	Printer control language
	`.pdf`	Adobe Acrobat, Adobe Reader	Portable document format
	`.ps`	Adobe	Postscript, desktop publishing language
Spreadsheet			
	`.123`	Lotus 123	Lotus spreadsheet file
	`.csv`	Spreadsheet application	Comma separated values, generic format
	`.qpw`	Quattro	Quattro spreadsheet
	`.tab`	Spreadsheet application	Tab separated values, generic format
	`.wks`	Microsoft Works	Works spreadsheet
	`.xlk`	Microsoft Excel	Excel backup spreadsheet
	`.xls`	Microsoft Excel	Excel spreadsheet
	`.xlt`	Microsoft Excel	Excel spreadsheet template
Video			
	`.aaf`	Video editor/player	Advanced authoring format
	`.avi`	Windows Media Player	Audio video interleave, Microsoft
	`.mov`	Quicktime	Apple Quicktime video format
	`.mpeg, .mpg, .mpe`	Video editor/player	Moving picture experts group video and compression format, lossy
	`.mp4`	Sony PlayStation Portable, Apple iPod	Moving picture experts group video and compression format, lossy
	`.rv`	RealPlayer	Real video
Web Associated			
	`.asp`	Web browser/server	Microsoft active server page, dynamically generated Web pages
	`.cfm`	Web browser/Cold Fusion server	Cold Fusion, dynamically generated Web pages
	`.cgi`	Web browser/CGI server	Common gateway interface, links Web page to server application

(continued)

Table 6.2 *(continued)*

Common file extentions

Category	Extension	Associated Application	Description
Web Associated (continued)			
	`.html`, `.htm`	Web browser	Hypertext markup language for Web pages
	`.jsp`	Web browser/Java server	Java server pages, dynamically generated Web pages
	`.kml`	Google Earth	Keyhole markup language for modeling and storing geographic features
	`.kmz`	Google Earth	A compressed `.kml` file
	`.php`	Web browser/PHP server	Hypertext preprocessor, server-side application software
	`.shtml`	Web browser	HTML file that has server-side include commands
	`.xhtml`	Web browser	Extensible hypertext markup language, a stricter version of HTML based on XML
	`.xml`	XML based application	Extensible markup language, a more rigorous grammar
Word Processor			
	`.asc`	Notepad, Wordpad, TextEdit, word processor	Generic text document with no formatting
	`.cwk`	ClarisWorks	ClarisWorks text document with formatting
	`.doc`	Microsoft Word	Word text document with formatting
	`.docx`	Microsoft Word	XML-based Word 2007 text document with formatting
	`.dot`	Microsoft Word	Word template
	`.dotx`	Microsoft Word	XML-based Word 2007 template
	`.rft`	Word processor	Rich text format text document with formatting
	`.txt`	Notepad, Wordpad, TextEdit, word processor	Generic text document with no formatting
	`.wpd`	WordPerfect	WordPerfect text document with formatting
	`.wps`	Microsoft Works	Microsoft Works text document with formatting

[1]May also be a PC self-extracting archive (aka installer)

6.4   Trouble-Free Downloads

Programmers have made the process of downloading software easy. Most software available on the Internet can be found on the Web, in which case your browser can usually handle the download for you. For large amounts of downloading, you might find it useful to have a download manager or an **FTP client**. FTP clients are discussed in more detail later in this chapter.

You need to ensure that the software you download from the Internet doesn't contain malicious code and has not been tampered with by anyone along the way. You can do this by going to trusted sources for software such as `http://download.cnet.com` and `http://www.tucows.com`. Generally,

TIP: Picking a Reputable Site for Software Downloads

To download software from the Internet, go to the Web site of a reputable commercial software manufacturer or a large, well-known software clearinghouse. Never download an executable file from someone's personal home page, a link in an e-mail message, a link in a newsgroup article, or a link in a chat room, chat channel, or instant messaging session.

FYI: Selecting the Right Software File for Your Computer

Generally, different OSs cannot run the same computer programs. Each requires its own set of executable code. (Java-based applications are the exception. As long as the Java Virtual Machine (JVM) is installed, a Java program can be run on any machine.) Much software is available for Windows-based personal computers or for the Macintosh but not for both. If the software you want is not available for your OS, you'll need to search for something similar that will work on your OS. Popular software is often available for different OSs, so make sure you download the version that's correct for your OS (see Figure 6.3). If you download the wrong version, you won't be able to install or run it on your computer. Most Web sites make it easy for you to pick the right version. Some Web sites will automatically direct you to the correct download page.

All software downloads on the Web are available via clickable hyperlinks. A link can point to a software file as easily as to an HTML file. The browser decides what to do with a link that points to a given file type; if it doesn't know, it'll ask you (see Figure 6.4). Browsers recognize file types by their file extensions. The most commonly used extensions for Windows software are `.exe` and `.zip`; for Macintosh software, `.bin` and `.sea`. Table 6.2 contains a longer list of file extensions associated with software files.

Figure 6.3 Different operating systems require different software.

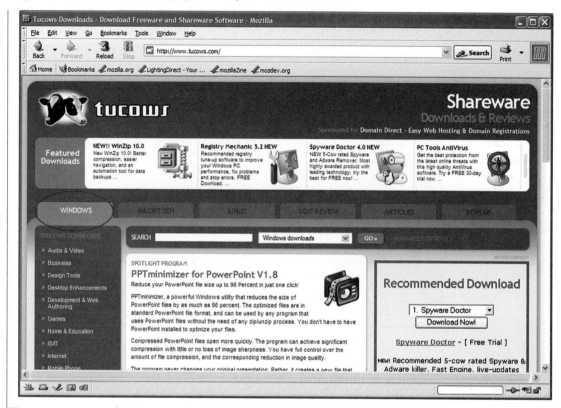

Figure 6.4
Save is the safest
option.

when you download commercial software you should go to the source—the original software manufacturer—if only to ensure that you download the most recent version. Using the source minimizes but does not eliminate the possibility of downloading an infected file. You still must take care to protect your computer from viruses no matter from which site you download.

Sometimes you might be given a choice between saving the program to disk and running it from its current location (see Figure 6.5). Again, the safest

Figure 6.5

Save the file to disk so your antivirus software can scan it before running the program.

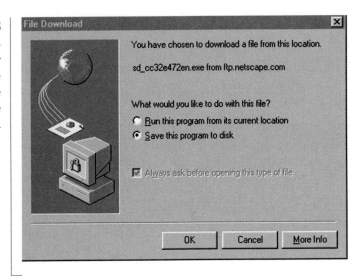

TIP: Saving Executable Files Safely

When your browser encounters a file that is not an HTML file or an image file, it checks a list of known file extensions to determine whether it knows how to open the file by using software already available on your computer. This is a good idea for data files such as PDF and MP3 but not for executable files.

All executable files should be scanned for viruses before you run them. Your browser might be configured to notify you when it encounters executable files and to let you decide how to handle the file (see Figure 6.4). Always elect to save it to your hard disk. This way, you'll be able to scan the file for viruses before you run it.

In addition, if when you're downloading an executable file type you are offered a check box that says, "Always ask before opening this type of file," be sure to check the box. By doing this you ensure that you always see your browser's current preference setting regarding executable files that are downloaded. You want to be sure that the browser is not set to run the file automatically before you've scanned it, keeping in mind that preference settings can be reset without your knowledge. Unwanted changes to preference settings are most likely to occur when other people have access to your computer, but they can also take place during abnormal shutdowns or when your browser is experiencing difficulties. Being extra careful with all software downloads safeguards against hackers and malicious code.

option is to save the program to disk. By the way, you can't really run the program from its current location, which is on the server. "Run this program from its current location" means that you download it to a temporary file in your browser's cache, and it will be run there. If you know and trust the file in question (because you've downloaded and scanned it before), choosing to run the program from its current location will save you from having to delete the executable later. However, most of the time you shouldn't trust the file. By saving it to disk, you ensure that your **antivirus software** has a chance to scan it for viruses before anything gets run.

Whenever you elect to save an executable file to disk, you're prompted for the location in which to save it (see Figure 6.6). Either accept the default location suggested by your browser or select any other location on your hard drive (or flash drive). It doesn't matter where you put the file as long as you know where it is for later execution; however, you might want to create a special folder for each download and save to that location. Downloaded files often have nondescriptive names. If you choose the folder name wisely, you have a better chance of finding downloaded software whenever you may need it.

Once you have selected a location for your download, the download will begin. Your browser will show you how the download is progressing by displaying a status bar. Figure 6.7 shows how Navigator tracks its file downloads. IE has a download manager that enables multiple downloads to be started and tracked simultaneously. Although it's useful to see these progress reports for large downloads, you don't need to drop everything to watch the download. You can run other applications, including your browser, while the download continues in the background. Note: Don't terminate your Internet connection or shutdown your computer until the download is completed.

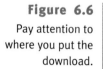

Figure 6.6

Pay attention to where you put the download.

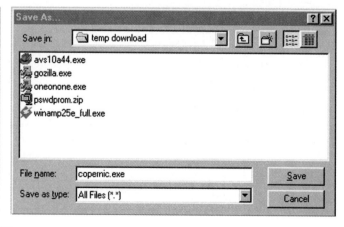

Figure 6.7
Navigator's
download
progress report

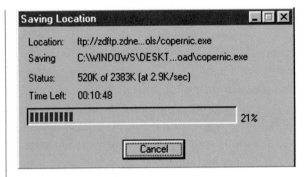

After the download or insertion of shrink wrap software media scan the file for viruses (don't assume that shrink wrap software is virus-free). Assuming that you have antivirus software on your computer, make sure you understand how it operates. Most antivirus utilities can be configured to scan all new files automatically as soon as they are on your hard drive; others must be manually invoked. Figure 6.8 shows how to check Norton's AntiVirus software to make sure it will automatically scan all new files as soon as they are added to your computer.

Recall that you cannot catch a computer virus simply by downloading an executable file, even if that file is infected. You must run an executable file in order to activate a virus. Antivirus software that automatically intercepts and

Figure 6.8
Auto-protect
scans all
downloads
automatically.

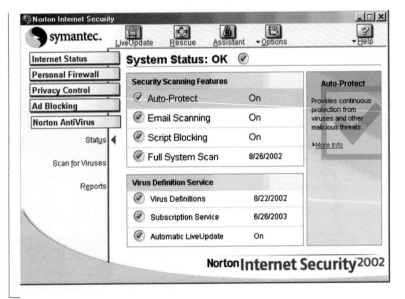

TIP: Scanning for Viruses after a Download

As soon as the file has been downloaded, scan it for viruses if your anti-virus software has not been configured to do this automatically. Never double-click an executable file until it has been scanned with antivirus software.

Also remember to keep your antivirus software up-to-date. If you don't update your virus data files at least once a week as a matter of routine, be sure to update whenever you download new software (*before* you download). Antivirus software that doesn't know about the latest viruses can't protect your computer.

scans all new files that arrive onto your hard drive will protect you in case you forget to scan the file yourself. Remember to ensure that the antivirus software is running in the background whenever you download executables from the Internet. Once the download has been scanned and deemed safe to open, you can install your software.

6.4.1 BitTorrent

Most files that you download from the Internet use either the FTP or HTTP protocols. But there is another protocol known generically as peer-to-peer (P2P) protocol. A **P2P protocol** differs from the now traditional client/server protocol by using the participants in the P2P network as both clients and servers simultaneously. A P2P network doesn't have a single centralized server managing a bunch of files for its clients, but rather peers (your computer for example) that can simultaneously upload and download popular files to other peers. Hence the name peer-to-peer—computers share files directly with each other as equals, or peers, in the network. This works because it balances the file transfer load between the uploading and downloading bandwidth. In a traditional file transfer arrangement (FTP and HTTP), the *upload* bandwidth for the client is often underutilized.

Since the peers themselves provide all the resources (bandwidth, computing power, and files), the capacity of the network is not fixed as it would be in a traditional client/server network. This is because P2P networks are formed in *ad hoc* fashion since the peers come and go as users join and quit the network. As the number of peers in the network changes, so does the capacity.

A particular implementation of the P2P protocol is BitTorrent. Instead of a server, a BitTorrent network has a tracker that coordinates the file transfers between peer machines. The tracker keeps track of where all the various pieces of file can be found on the various peers, issuing instructions to the BitTorrent software on the peer to upload selected portions of a file requested by another peer. In this way, no single peer has sole responsibility for transferring the entire file, even it has the only available copy. Instead, several peers that have the file (or at least some parts of it) can upload the file to the requesting peer. In return, each peer that wants a file can get it collectively from its other peers in the network. Once a peer receives portions of the file, it can also become a server for that file. When a peer is sending a file, it's known as a *seed* (aka *seeder*). A peer receiving a file is known as a *downloader* (aka *peer*—but we'll use the term downloader). As you might guess, if a file is being transferred by several peers simultaneously, the downloader will probably acquire the file more quickly than it would if only a single server had sole responsibility for servicing all file requests. Of course, since the network is *ad hoc* you may find that there are currently no seeds available for a particular file you are seeking—you may wait hours, or even days (assuming that you keep your BitTorrent software running all that time) before you get the file you are seeking.

Since the network is an *ad hoc* network, the peers change dynamically as the participants launch and close their P2P software. Once your computer receives a complete copy of some file, then it can become a seed for the other nodes on the network. Users that always close their BitTorrent software after downloading a file (so they can't serve as seeds) are known as *leeches*.

There are several ways to get BitTorrent software for your computer (try the source: `http://www.bittorrent.com/`), but probably the easiest way is to use the Opera browser (see Section 1.11). Opera has BitTorrent software built into it, so when you go to a BitTorrent site and download a file, all the work is done entirely in a browser window (see Figure 6.9). As you can see in Figure

Figure 6.9

The Opera browser includes built-in BitTorrent software.

...	Name	Size	Progress	Time
○	StreetBike.mp4	7.7 MB	35.8%	0:53

From	StreetBike.mp4
To	/Users/richk/Desktop/StreetBike.mp4
Size	7.7 MB (8051872 bytes)
Transferred	2.8 MB (2899968 bytes) / 0 B
Connections	Seeds: 1, Peers: 3 (Total seeds/peers: 1/3)
Active transfers (In/Out)	1 / 0

6.9, the number of seeds is shown in the download window. Before you select a file to download, check first to see how many seeds there are. As you might guess, more is better. If there are no seeds currently available, then you're out of luck, for the moment at least. Also note that it may take a few minutes for the download to begin. The tracker has to do a lot of "housekeeping" before it can begin the download. Subsequent downloads will begin more quickly.

The BitTorrent tracker has no knowledge of the nature of the file being transferred. It simply coordinates transfers. Because of this, BitTorrent networks are often used to share copyrighted material, a violation of copyright law. But so far, the tracker site has not been held liable—it's only providing a coordination service, not the files themselves. The files to be shared are provided by the peers in the network. Some college campuses have shut down the BitTorrent network access for this reason, and also because it can consume a great deal of the available bandwidth (thus slowing everybody else down). So you may find that your BitTorrent software will not work. Numerous providers of copyrighted digital content are seeking to shut down BitTorrent trackers in various ways, with some success. It will be interesting to see how this all plays out in the courts and Congress.

Other popular P2P implementations include Napster, Gnutella, KaZaA and Freenet. Usenet News also relies on a P2P protocol to propagate articles through the network (see Section 4.6.3 for more information about Usenet News).

Antivirus Protection

Computer viruses are a fact of life. Recall that viruses are spread via executable files, documents that contain macros, and scripts read by script-enabled e-mail clients (see Section 2.6). Because software consists of executable files, viruses are a possibility in downloaded software. If you don't have antivirus software on a Windows computer, don't download software from the Internet. On a Macintosh computer, even though you're much less likely to pick up a virus from downloaded software, don't forgo antivirus software. Most viruses are designed to attack Windows-based personal computers, rather than Macs, primarily because 90 percent of personal computers run Windows. If someone wants to create a virus that will bring the world to a halt, it makes sense to target the Windows OS. However, recall from Chapter 2 that macro viruses are platform-independent—they will infect a Mac as readily as a Windows-based personal computer. Thus, antivirus software for a

Mac is a good idea for anyone who exchanges Word or Excel documents with other people.

Suppose you want to minimize the risk of contracting a virus and you have antivirus software on your computer. You need to explore its configuration to understand how it works. Some antivirus software must be run manually on individual files or file folders whenever you want to scan for viruses. Others can be set to run in the background, where they'll intercept all incoming files and scan them automatically. An automatic scanner that runs in the background is especially convenient for people who download a lot of software.

You also need to ensure that your antivirus preference settings are set to check all incoming files, not only executable files (see Figure 6.10). This will protect you against macro viruses. Note that some scanners can be configured to open a **file archive** (a single file that contains the (usually) compressed contents of several other files) and scan its contents as well; others can't scan an archive unless you open the archive. However, all scanners will check any files

Figure 6.10

Check your antivirus software's preference settings.

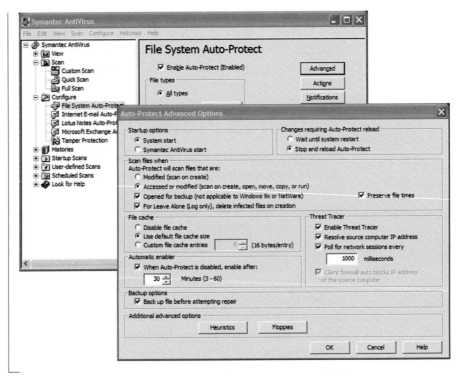

TIP: Make Sure Your Antivirus Software Is Running in the Background

Even if you have antivirus software running in the background, always double-check to ensure that it is running before you begin a software download and installation. Although background scanning is wonderful so that you don't have to run manual scans yourself, the software must be active in order to protect you. It's easy to forget about a background scanner. The software won't tell you when a scan turns up nothing; it will make its presence known only when it detects a virus. Although this is generally what you want, don't forget about your antivirus software altogether. Symantec's AntiVirus software can place an icon in the system tray (at the bottom-right side of your monitor) to reassure you that it is running in the background (see Figure 6.10).

being copied onto your hard drive, including files extracted from a file archive (as well as files created by a software installer). Thus, even if you don't trigger a virus warning when you download a software file archive, you can trigger a warning when files are being extracted from an archive. One way or another, your antivirus software can protect you when you download file archives (as long as you have it turned on).

Consider also having your antivirus software configured to test as many incoming files as possible. The CPU load is negligible, and you need to worry about macro viruses in data files as well as executable files.

Most antivirus software allows you to scan specific files or folders on demand. (McAfee's ActiveShield is an exception. To scan a specific folder by using ActiveShield, you must go to the Web-based McAfee Clinic site and request a scan using IE and an active Internet connection.) If possible, configure your file archive utility to launch your antivirus software from inside the archive program. Figure 6.11 shows how to tell the archive utility ZipCentral where to find antivirus software. Figure 6.12 shows how to launch antivirus software from inside ZipCentral.

When you do this you can scan some or all of the files inside the archive on demand, before they are extracted from the archive. This isn't necessary if your scanner is running in the background, ready to pounce on any infected files as soon as they are extracted from the archive. However, some people find it reassuring to scan file archives manually before they proceed with an installation. A manual file scan always reports its results, regardless of whether a virus is found. It never hurts to run an automatic scan *and* a manual scan on the same files.

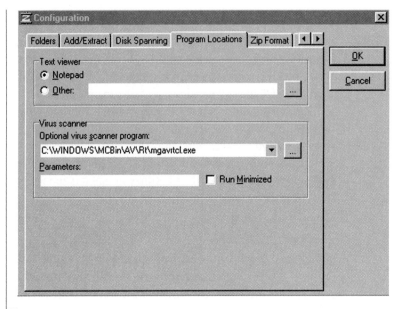

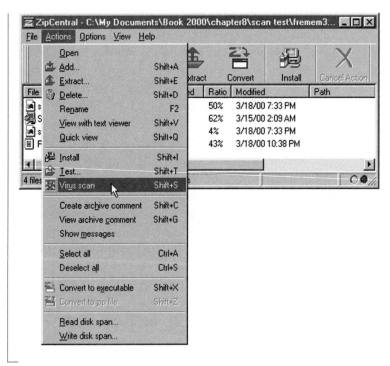

TIP: You Can Get a Virus from Mobile Devices

Viruses don't always come with software installs or e-mail attachments—you may get one from a networked device like your mobile phone or MP3 player. In October 2006, Apple reported that some of its popular iPod players contained a virus that infects only Windows systems when connected. Up-to-date antivirus software should catch the problem.

 # Installation Tips

Software installations are usually simple, but if you're inexperienced and don't know what to expect, you might encounter a few stumbling blocks. This section describes the five standard installation scenarios you are likely to encounter when downloading software from the Internet.

1. Executable installers (most commonly used for large commercial programs)
2. Ready-to-go executables (most commonly used for small noncommercial programs)
3. Zipped file archives (most commonly used for small noncommercial programs)
4. Self-extracting archives (similar to a zipped archive but require no extra software)
5. ActiveX installers (not seen on Macs since they require IE on a Windows system)

Note that although the file extensions for Windows differ from those for the Mac, the general installation steps we give in the following sections are the same for either OS. The Web site from which you obtain your download will not explain which installation scenario applies. However, with a little experience you'll recognize the different installation scenarios and the usual procedures associated with them.

6.6.1 Executable Installers

If your download is an `.exe` file (or a `.sea` file for a Mac), you've probably downloaded an installer. An **installer** is a setup utility used whenever a computer program requires multiple files in order to operate. If the file's icon includes an arrow pointing downward or a picture of a box and a floppy disk in front of a computer (see Figure 6.13), the file is an installer. An installer

Figure 6.13

An installer icon

might include one file that contains the executable code, additional data files (for example, help files), and some graphics files (for animations or ad banners). To install these manually, you would have to follow detailed instructions on where to save all the different files; you probably would have to edit at least a few of them as well. Manual installations are time-consuming and error-prone. Bundling complex software inside an installer that can do all the busywork for you is a much better arrangement. An installer needs to be run only once; then you can discard it (or perhaps save it in case you need to reinstall the software).

Some people like to save installers (in a specific folder for easy locating) so they can recreate their computing environment when they upgrade to a new computer. If you have plenty of space on your hard drive, consider doing this.

Figure 6.14 shows the first screen of an installer for a Windows program named Go!Zilla. If you download a lot of software, you'll see the same installer

Figure 6.14

Read and follow the installer's instructions.

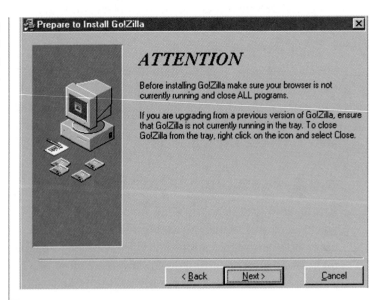

TIP: When to Turn Off Your Antivirus Software

In some cases, new software will not run properly if you install it while other programs are running on your machine. Most installers will remind you to shut down other programs before proceeding with an installation. Sometimes an installer will ask you to turn off your antivirus software before you begin the installation. This might sound suspicious, but it is a legitimate requirement; in many cases, an installer cannot perform properly while antivirus software is running in the background. However, whenever you turn off your antivirus software, proceed with caution. If the downloaded software is a popular brand and you obtained it from a well-known site, you can safely turn off your antivirus software and continue the installation. (Be sure to turn it back on as soon as the installation is over.) As a precaution, you can run a complete scan of your entire hard drive right after the installation.

However, if the downloaded software is obscure or seems suspicious in any way (for example, it's not available in any of the big software archives), reconsider installing it. Turning off your antivirus software involves some risk, even if you do a full disk scan afterward. A malicious installer could construct an infected executable, launch it, and delete it before you have a chance to detect it. This is not a standard virus delivery method, but it's possible.

utilities used for different downloads. Each installation looks a little different, but all ask the same types of questions and perform the same types of actions.

Sometimes a program is simple enough to require only one program file: in this case, no installer is needed. This is a *ready-to-go executable* and is less common than an installer download (see Section 6.6.2). If you aren't sure which kind of download you have, simply double-click the file's name and see what happens. If it's the actual program and you decide to keep it, move it to an appropriate directory for long-term storage. No other installation is needed.

If you are dealing with a program that came with an installer, note that most installers will ask you a few questions so you can control certain aspects of the installation. The first question is likely about where you want to put the executable program file(s). The installer will make a suggestion about this location, but you can override it if you prefer to store the program in a different location (see Figure 6.15). Remember that Windows shortcuts and Mac aliases enable you to access the same program from many locations on your computer, so the location of the program files might not be important. If you don't care, take the installer's suggestion.

Figure 6.15

Telling the
installer where to
save a program

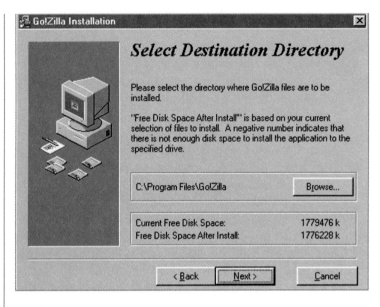

TIP: Selecting a Location on Your Hard Drive for Your New Program

If you like to categorize your computer programs and store them according to your own system, you can tell the installer where to put a new program. Otherwise, the installer will use a default location (which is fine). If you aren't sure what to do, go with the installer's suggestion.

Although it doesn't really matter where you put a program, once you've installed it, don't move any of its files. Program files often need to know the location of other support files, and these locations are recorded at the time of installation. If you move any program files around, their old locations cease to be valid, and the entire program may fail to perform correctly the next time you try to run it. If you ever need to move a program to another directory, uninstall the software (see Section 6.11.1) and then reinstall it at the new location.

Usually installers display a copy of the software's licensing agreement and will not complete the installation if you don't agree to the terms of the license. By clicking the "I agree" option, you enter into a legally binding contract. Always read a contract before you sign it. These agreements are sometimes long and tedious, but you still should read them because they are legitimate contracts, even though you aren't signing your name to a piece of paper.

TIP: When to Leave the Installer's Settings Alone

The installer might ask other questions about the installation before installing the program (see Figure 6.16). The more complicated the program, the more questions the installer will ask. For example, you might be asked if you want a standard installation or a custom installation. The standard installation will be the installer's default setting, but you can opt for a custom installation if you understand the software well enough to take more control over the installation process (custom installations always involve more decisions). Custom installations can be more problem prone than standard installations. If you have problems after a custom install, you might want to remove the software and then reinstall it using the standard method.

An installer generally explains why it needs the input, but sometimes you might not be certain how to respond. In this case, you can read the help files that the installer offers to try to make sense of the question or you can accept the installer's suggested default setting (the default setting is almost always the right one anyway).

Figure 6.16
Some installers ask a lot of questions.

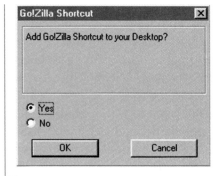

You might also find, buried inside these agreements, important information about known software incompatibilities. When you add new software to your computer, you should learn everything you can about the new software. Often computer programs depend on shared resources in order to operate properly. Because of this, various computer programs can interact with each

TIP: Read Everything the Installer Has to Say

Most installations are short and sweet. However, if an installer gives you something to read, it's wise to read it (see Figure 6.17). You may find that you're also agreeing to install spyware and/or adware (see Section 6.7).

Figure 6.17

An installer might
have important
information for
you.

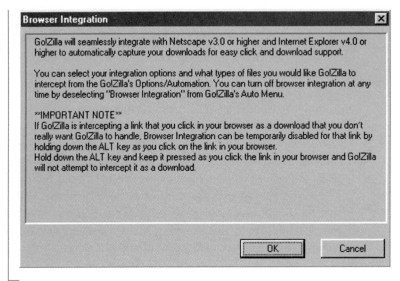

other in unexpected ways, even if they aren't running at the same time. You might find that your system starts crashing a lot after you've installed a new program, even if the new program isn't running at the time of the crash. This problem is discussed in Section 6.11. Meanwhile, remember to read all the information your installer offers.

Software downloads often come with a README file, which you may be prompted to read after installation ends (see Figure 6.18). The **README file**, typically written by the software's author or manufacturer, is a text file that contains information, usually late-breaking, that the user needs but that is not included in the software's official documentation. Read these files since they can contain useful information about problems with the program or ways to avoid known bugs. *If you have a problem with a particular program, always check the README file before contacting the manufacturer's technical support staff for assistance.* You can solve many problems by consulting the README file.

FYI: Always Read the README File

README files are a software tradition. When the author (or manufacturer) of a computer program discovers a problem with the program, the README file can alert users to the problem. In this way, anyone who purchases the most recent version of the software will be up-to-date on all the known bugs and possible fixes. Of course, this works only when the user downloading the software reads the README file.

Figure 6.18

README files contain timely information.

The last screen the installer displays informs you that the installation is complete. An installer might automatically put a shortcut to its program on your desktop (this practice is common on Windows-based PCs). You can delete the shortcut if you don't want it. In addition, it might automatically add its program name to your Start menu (another Windows tradition). You can remove this as well if you don't want it. Both practices are designed to make it easy for you to find the program when you want to launch it. If you delete these conveniences, you can still run the program, as long as you know where it's located on your hard drive (remember when the installer asked you where to save your program?). If you can't remember where the installer put it, do a search for a file with the name of the program.

6.6.2 Ready-to-Go Executables

If a computer program is simple enough, it won't need auxiliary files—the entire program can be stored in a single file and will not require a complicated installation process. In this case, you might be downloading an executable file that is the actual program you're looking for—this is a **ready-to-go executable**. You only need to decide where you want to store the program file for safekeeping. It won't matter where you put it. Unlike files for programs installed through the use of an executable installer, you can move the program file at any time if you decide to rearrange your directories.

A ready-to-go executable won't come with a README file, so be sure to check the programmer's Web site for recent news and announcements. If you need help operating the software or setting its user preferences, check the program for a Help menu. If the program lacks sufficient documentation, check the programmer's Web site for additional information. You might find all sorts of useful resources on the site, such as a user's manual, the most recent README file, and other timely communications from the programmer. Programmers who distribute their programs over the Web are relying more on the Web as their primary means of communication with their users.

A ready-to-go executable is usually an .exe file for a Windows-based PC or a .bin file for the Mac. Sometimes it is compressed for faster downloads, in which case you might see a .zip extension for a Windows-based machine or a .sit extension for the Mac. You might also see an ASCII-encoded executable (.uue for Windows or .hqx for the Mac). These formats are much less common now that the Web is the major vehicle for online software distribution. If you're having difficulty with a file that won't open when you double-click its name, see Section 6.8 for a discussion of useful file utilities.

6.6.3 Zipped File Archives

A **zipped file archive** is a file that contains other files. It's like a file folder. You can open the archive to see what's inside, if you have the right file utility. Otherwise, you can't do anything with a zipped file archive. File archives have a .zip file extension under Windows or a .sit extension on a Mac. If your system has the appropriate file utility application associated with the archive's file extension, you should be able to open the archive by double-clicking the file's name. Once you've opened the archive, look for a README file (see Figure 6.19). If there is one, open it; typically it will explain the contents of

Figure 6.19
ZipCentral looks inside a zipped file archive.

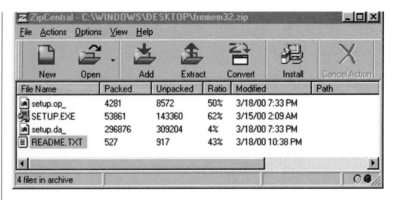

the archive and tell you what to do next. Some archive files contain a ready-to-go executable along with documentation files and data files needed to run the program. Others contain an installer.

For FreeMem Professional, the README file explains what you need to know before you run the installer (see Figure 6.20). Each program's README file will contain different instructions, so look for each README file and read it carefully before proceeding with the installation.

6.6.4 Self-Extracting Archives

Some downloads are self-extracting archives. A **self-extracting archive** is an archive file, similar to the zipped archives discussed in the previous section, but you don't need a special file utility to open a self-extracting archive. It has an .exe extension under Windows or an .sea extension on a Mac. Because .exe extensions are also used for executable installers and ready-to-go executables, it's difficult to know when an .exe file is a self-extracting archive.

Figure 6.20

When there's no installer, installation instructions may be in the README file.

When you double-click a self-extracting archive, it expands and creates a second .exe file, which is usually the executable program. Additional files might be created when you expand the archive, so watch for documentation files (look for a README file).

A self-extracting archive places its archive files in the current subdirectory (the same directory that contains the self-extracting archive file) or creates a new subdirectory for the expanded archive. It won't hide the archive in some other directory far from the original download. You can expand the original self-extracting archive as often as needed. The archive is not altered or exhausted when you expand it.

6.6.5 ActiveX Installers

Another installation scenario relies on **ActiveX**, a Microsoft product distributed with IE (versions 3.0 and higher). If you're not running IE on a Windows system, you cannot install software that uses an ActiveX installer. For example, ActiveX software does not run on Macs.

ActiveX installations are designed to make the software download process as simple as possible. With an ActiveX installation, you only need to click a link on a Web page and you're done. The installation process is fully automated, and you won't be asked any questions, like where to put the files. McAfee's Clinic (see Figure 6.21) is an example of a **software installation** that relies on ActiveX.

ActiveX controls can create or remove files on your hard drive and run executable files on your computer. Web programming languages (for example, JavaScript and Java) impose some restrictions on what their programs can do, for the sake of preserving your system security. ActiveX has no such restrictions. You must be very careful with ActiveX installations; you must trust the site that offers an ActiveX installer. If a deceptive Web site tricks you into running a malicious ActiveX installer, you conceivably could lose every file on your hard drive. Moreover, the script could be programmed to run at some future date, thereby making it impossible to connect the destructive executable with its source on the Web. It could search for personal information in the data files of applications such as Quicken and send those files out on the Internet to someone unknown to you without your permission. It could hunt down your e-mail address and ship it off to countless spamming operations. It could steal your credit card account number (if you store it on your computer without first encrypting it). It could steal passwords to restricted Web sites (if you store them on your computer without first encrypting them).

Figure 6.21

McAfee clinic uses an ActiveX installer.

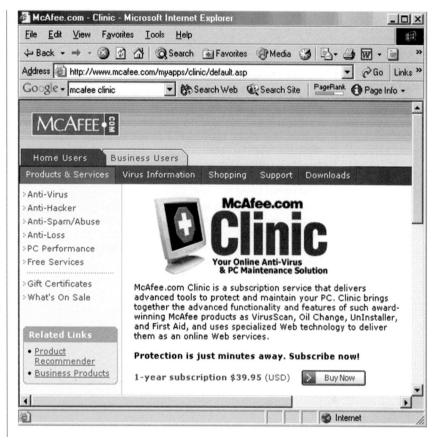

Because the destructive potential of malicious ActiveX controls is so great, special safeguards are used when ActiveX controls are built into Web pages.

Microsoft understands the risks inherent in ActiveX. It attempts to protect users from malicious ActiveX downloads by using a mechanism called Authenticode that enables a system developer (such as Microsoft) to place a digital signature on any original ActiveX utilities. In this case, the digital signature identifies the person or organization behind the software. Your browser will check this signature before continuing with the download. Then if your browser does not recognize a digital signature as the mark of a trusted software source, it will inform you of the situation and ask if you still want to run the software anyway. Chapter 8 discusses the technology of digital signatures and their application to software downloads. For now, it's enough to understand that your browser might issue a warning (see Figure 6.22) if appropriate ActiveX safeguards have not been put in place.

Figure 6.22

Digital signatures protect consumers from malicious ActiveX installations

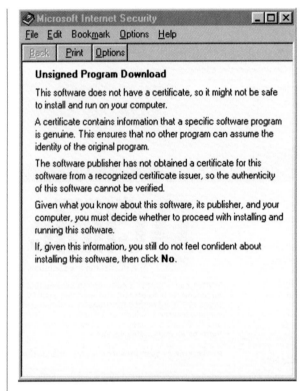

Unsigned Program Download

This software does not have a certificate, so it might not be safe to install and run on your computer.

A certificate contains information that a specific software program is genuine. This ensures that no other program can assume the identity of the original program.

The software publisher has not obtained a certificate for this software from a recognized certificate issuer, so the authenticity of this software cannot be verified.

Given what you know about this software, its publisher, and your computer, you must decide whether to proceed with installing and running this software.

If, given this information, you still do not feel confident about installing this software, then click **No**.

TIP: ActiveX Programs Download and Install in One Step—Is This Safe?

You cannot scan an ActiveX installer for viruses because an ActiveX installer runs automatically after downloading. ActiveX installers are very risky because you must take someone else's word that the executable is safe. Many security experts advise turning off ActiveX altogether and simply avoiding sites that require it.

A signature verification failure might or might not mean that the software in question is risky. If you trust the source (and you're confident that the download site is what it says it is), you can opt to continue with the download. But to be as safe as possible, you should reject any software that cannot be authenticated with an Authenticode signature. Figure 6.23 warns about a program file that does not contain an Authenticode signature—its authorship can't be verified. The URL suggests that the files come from Microsoft's Web site, but the Microsoft Web page might have been hacked and the download might not be Microsoft's. Figure 6.24 shows a successful Authenticode verification.

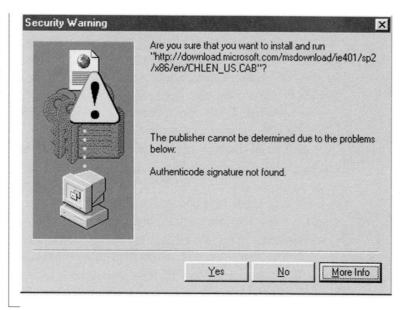

Figure 6.23

This program file was never signed—you don't know where it comes from.

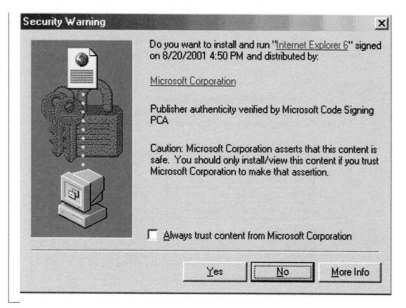

Figure 6.24

This program file was signed—you must still decide if you trust it.

Critics of the Authenticode system point out that a verified signature is only as good as the source of the signature. If you trust the source to distribute software that does what it says it does and nothing more, then a digital signature will give you peace of mind. However, some software manufacturers might embed functionality in their software that they consider to be benign but that you might disagree with (if you knew what it was doing). For example, in 1999 millions of people downloaded the popular freeware version of RealPlayer 7.0, a streaming audio player. Apparently few people who installed RealPlayer questioned what Comet Cursor was, although it was listed as a feature in two of three download options (see Figure 6.25). Even if users had taken the time to track down the **Comet Systems** site, they still would not have discovered the true purpose of this cursor-tracking application. It was tracking user browsing behavior and sending this information to Comet Systems for inclusion in a Web-tracking database. Comet Systems neglected to inform its consumers about this aspect of the Comet Cursor until a news reporter broke the story, raised questions about online privacy, and forced Comet Systems to explain what it was doing. In this case, a digital signature check for RealPlayer would have made no difference because the manufacturers of RealPlayer and Comet Cursor distributed software without fully disclosing exactly what it was doing. Is it conceivable that RealPlayer's manufacturer didn't fully understand the actual capabilities of the Comet Cursor? Would you trust the company more or less if it claimed ignorance?

Trusting your system security to a commercial software manufacturer is a risky business, no matter how much you might like its product. Even

Figure 6.25

The comet cursor was bundled with RealPlayer.

Select your Free RealPlayer 7 Basic
Based on your connection speed, we have selected a download size for you. To change your selection, check the button next to the one you want.

Features Include:	Complete (7.4 MB)	Standard (7.0 MB)	Minimal (3.4 MB)
Plays all Real content	✓	✓	✓
NEW! Take5 showcase	✓	✓	✓
NEW! Over 100 Radio Stations	✓	✓	✓
Support for MP3	✓	✓	✓
AutoUpdate	✓	✓	✓
Built-in Help	✓	✓	
RealJukebox Basic	✓	✓	
Comet Cursor	✓	✓	
Additional Playback Formats	All	Some	
Est. download time (56k)	18 min.	17 min.	8 min.
Make Your Selection	⌀	●	⌀

| Download FREE RealPlayer 7 Basic beta |

Microsoft has been sabotaged, including by its own programmers (to find out more, do a Web search with the query "Microsoft security risk FrontPage 98 extensions"). Malicious programmers can make mischief anywhere.

If you're worried about the security risks inherent in ActiveX, don't use IE as your Web browser and avoid all software that depends on ActiveX. Alternatively, trade in your Windows-based PC for a Mac (IE on a Mac can't run ActiveX) or install Linux alongside Windows to create a dual-boot machine. Use Linux for network tasks and Windows when you must use a Windows application. Alternatively, avoid IE entirely and use a different browser for Web work. If you aren't sure how much you should worry about all of this, remember that whereas many things are possible on the Internet, relatively few worst-case scenarios actually materialize. Moreover, the chances of the worst case happening to you probably are fewer than the chances of your being struck by lightning. However, here are some simple, common-sense precautions you can take (which could save you from total disaster if you happen to be very unlucky).

- Periodically back up your hard drive or the most important files on your hard drive (catastrophic hardware failures can happen without warning)
- Encrypt your most sensitive data files or store them offline (on floppies, flash drives, or other media)
- Don't download software from obscure Web sites

In the future, you'll see more variations on software installations, including ASP services, which minimize the need for full application downloads. Although using utilities such as ActiveX involves security risks, these same tools can be used to good advantage.

 # Spyware and Adware

In the last section we discussed the bundling of the Comet Cursor with RealPlayer 7.0. This software was downloaded and installed by millions of people before word went out about what the Comet Cursor was doing behind the scenes. Ever since the Comet Cursor incident in 1999, savvy computer users have been less trusting of Internet software. Although software like the Comet Cursor is not, strictly speaking, malicious, it does represent a violation of trust. Computer users have a right to know what a piece of software is designed to do.

Unfortunately, the number of software installations containing unannounced and undocumented features has increased since 1999. But so has consumer awareness. Software that "phones home" to report on your activities is called **spyware** (also known as *E.T. applications* in honor of the extraterrestrial), and you can decide what you want to do about it. If you want to protect your privacy online, or you simply dislike the idea of hidden software capabilities, you can protect yourself from spyware by taking a couple of simple precautions. It doesn't take much time, and it's very easy.

Before you install new software on your computer (especially freeware, shareware, or peer-to-peer file-sharing software), visit the SpyChecker Web site (`http://www.spychecker.com/`) and find out if the software in question is known to contain spyware (see Figure 6.26). SpyChecker maintains a list of useful software tools that have been validated to be malware free. You can search this category (see Figure 6.27) manually or you can use the search box at the bottom of the home page to search for a specific title.

Figure 6.26

Check for spyware before you download new software.

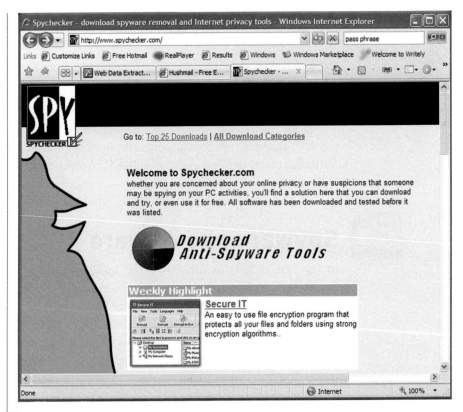

Figure 6.27
SpyChecker has
hundreds of
spyware titles in
its database.

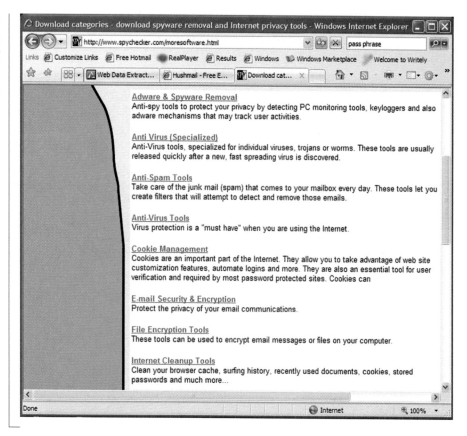

FYI: Spyware and Full Disclosure

Companies that distribute spyware may not be engaged in deceptive business practices if they disclose the full nature of the software in their software license or privacy
policy. When there is no intent to deceive consumers, the software should really not
be called spyware, but this distinction will be lost on anyone who does not read his
or her software licenses carefully. *Caveat emptor!*

Software that only displays ads is called **adware**, and the ads are often used
as a shareware registration incentive. You are welcome to run adware applications for free as long as you are willing to view the advertisements each time
you launch the application. Users who pay for and register the software get a
registered version of the software without the ads. Unfortunately, the registered software could still contain spyware, even if the ads are gone, so it's
really spyware in disguise.

Most people learn about spyware after they've been on the Internet for a while and have installed Internet applications on their computers. If you are concerned about the possibility of spyware on your computer, you can download Ad-aware, a utility designed to detect and remove spyware. Ad-aware scans your hard drive looking for spyware (see Figure 6.28), much like antivirus software scans your hard drive looking for viruses. When the scan is complete, you get a report (see Figure 6.29), and you can ask Ad-aware to remove any items it found.

Figure 6.28
Ad-aware finds spyware on your computer.

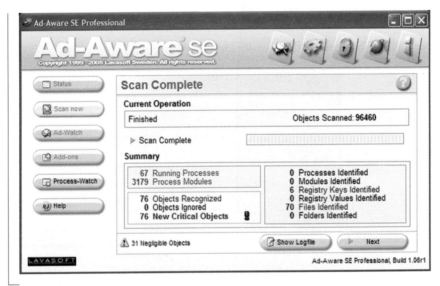

Figure 6.29
Ad-aware

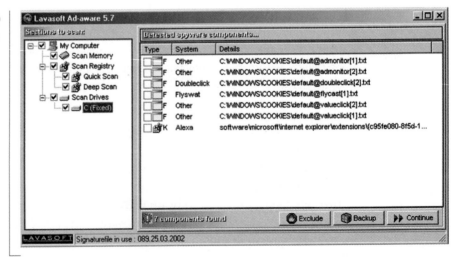

TIP: What if Ad-aware Makes a Mistake?

When Ad-aware finds spyware, you should always run an Ad-aware Backup (use the Backup button) before allowing Ad-aware to remove any files. This will protect you in case Ad-aware mistakenly identifies a benign file as a spyware file, and it may be important for certain software uninstallers (some software won't uninstall properly if the spyware has been removed). Once you have completed this backup, you can safely remove any files Ad-aware has flagged; if you need them later, you can always recover any files that Ad-aware removed.

If you're not sure about the nature of some object identified by Ad-aware as a possible threat, you can right-click it to open a window that describes it. Figure 6.30 shows the window that appears describing a tracking cookie. The amount of spyware is substantial, and the makers of Ad-aware acknowledge that they could easily miss some titles because it is hard to keep up with all of

Figure 6.30

Ad aware finds tracking cookies.

them. But using Ad-aware is better than not using Ad-aware, and you can trust it to know about the most popular software titles, which are the ones you are most likely to install yourself.

The SpyChecker Web site and the Ad-aware software utility are two important privacy tools for people who want to enjoy Internet applications with some peace of mind. Whenever computer technology creates widespread problems for people, there is usually more computer technology available to combat it.

When you install new software, often you will be required to endorse an End User License Agreement (EULA) that contains all the required disclosures, including the license agreement and privacy statement. Many companies guilty of installing adware/spyware surreptitiously will bury disclosure of these installs deep in the fine print—you might have to read quite a large amount of text before you find the passage that mentions these additional and unwanted packages. How many times have you immediately clicked OK on the EULA button without reading the fine print? Malware purveyors can then claim the legal right to spy on your every online move.

Often the user *knowingly* installs adware (perhaps even spyware too) as a way to acquire software for free. Eudora, for example, has a free version that displays ads along with your e-mail. To make things worse, some companies that deal in adware have sued other companies that provide antiadware/spyware tools, claiming that the users have given permission to install these components!

The 109th Congress is getting into the act too. The Spyblock (Software Principles Yielding Better Levels of Consumer Knowledge) Act prohibits spyware, outlaws the installation of adware programs without a computer user's explicit permission, prohibits hackers from remotely taking over a computer, outlaws programs that hijack Web browsers, and protects antispyware software companies from being sued by companies whose software they remove. The Securely Protect Yourself Against Cyber Trespass Act (aka Spy Act) prohibits remote control of computers by hackers, browser hijacks, the collecting of personal information using keyloggers, and Web advertising that users cannot deactivate "without undue effort." The Internet Spyware Prevention

FYI: Kazaa Complications

Kazaa had a spyware component that caused some difficulties for Ad-aware users. If you removed Kazaa's spyware with Ad-aware, you could not uninstall Kazaa afterward. This shows why it is important always to make Ad-aware backups in case you need to recover any spyware files later.

Act (aka I-Spy Act) covers these concerns and specifies a five-year jail term for spyware users or hackers who take over a computer remotely. None of these laws has yet been passed (as of August 2006). Check the following Web site to see the current status of these bills: `http://thomas.loc.gov/bss/109search.html`.

In the meantime, the Anti-Spyware Coalition (ASC) offers these tips to help protect against adware-spyware problems:

- Use and keep your security programs (antivirals, antispyware, and so on) up-to-date.
- Download programs only from Web sites that you trust.
- Read the fine print attached to any downloadable software before you download it—you may be giving permission for the installation of adware/spyware utilities!
- Avoid being tricked into clicking on the close button inside a pop-up dialog box or window—they may contain code that installs malware. Use the window close button in the title bar instead.
- Be wary of "free" programs—they often harbor adware/spyware.

 # File Download Utilities

If you expect to download a lot of software from the Internet, eventually you'll need a **file archive utility** if your system does not already include one (most do) to open a zipped file archive. Three of the most widely used utilities are described as follows:

- **WinZip** (Windows shareware)

  `http://www.winzip.com/tucows/`

  For Windows, the most popular archive utility is the shareware WinZip. You can try it at no charge for 21 days. After that if you elect to keep it, you need to register and pay for it. WinZip has won numerous software awards, including ZDNet's "Download of the Millennium."

  Don't confuse WinZip with WinZip Self-Extractor. You don't need Self-Extractor unless you want to distribute your own software over the Internet. The WinZip Web site contains excellent documentation, including detailed instructions about how to configure WinZip to launch your antivirus software (conduct a site search using the keyword "virus").

- **ZipCentral** (Windows freeware)
  http://zipcentral.iscool.net/
  Although it's hard to beat WinZip, the freeware ZipCentral comes very close. ZipCentral's home page is sometimes hard to access, and you might need IE to view it correctly. However, don't let the problems with the Web site scare you away. ZipCentral is robust, easy-to-use, and filled with all the most important features found in WinZip. You won't get the same level of technical support as with WinZip, but you probably won't need it because of ZipCentral's ease of use. Note: If you're having trouble configuring ZipCentral to launch your antivirus software, visit the WinZip Web site and follow the instructions for antivirus software integration. (The instructions that work for WinZip also apply to ZipCentral.)
- **Stuffit Expander** (Macintosh freeware)
  http://www.stuffit.com/mac/expander/index.html
  Stuffit Expander is freeware and a must have utility for all Mac owners. Don't confuse it with Stuffit Deluxe or Stuffit Lite. You don't need Stuffit Deluxe or Stuffit Lite unless you want to distribute your own software over the Internet.

If needed, download one of these tools from the Net, and you'll be able to handle any software file types that you encounter on the Net. Note that you would be in trouble if you needed a file utility to unpack a newly downloaded file utility. Happily, the people who distribute file utilities understand this, so they are careful to give you installers or ready-to-go executables for their software.

Another class of file download utilities that can improve the quality of your computing life is the download manager. It is especially helpful if your Internet connection tends to die in the middle of long downloads. A **download manager** is a utility that specializes in managing file downloads and offers many features not found in Web browsers. A Web browser can handle file downloads in a basic way, without enhancements or nonessential features. However, a download manager has more "bells and whistsles," like file recovery if the download is interrupted, than the one provided by your browser.

 # Software Clearinghouse

The Web makes it easy to find and obtain software—you just need to know where to look. The software clearinghouse is perfect as a source for downloadable software. Just as it pays to try different search engines before you decide on your favorites, it makes sense to visit various software clearinghouses to find those that are best for you. Each has its own combination of features and its own mix of software titles.

Many software clearinghouses index large collections of downloadable software in searchable subject trees. Most include a brief description of each software item, and some include software ratings, download counts, and e-mail newsletters to keep you on top of the best new software. Some are one component in a larger Web portal, and others are dedicated sites that concentrate only on software. Some specialize in programs for a particular population (for example, Web designers), and others focus on a specific software genre (for example, Java applets). Some are easier to navigate than others, and some have larger software collections than others.

If you have time, visit different software clearinghouses to see what they offer. Even if two clearinghouses cover much of the same software, you might like the reviews at one site better or you might enjoy a special feature that one site offers.

6.9.1 Some Popular Software Sites

- **Tucows**

  `http://www.tucows.com`

  Tucows offers a massive collection of software, as well as many special features, including the famous five-cow rating system. Check out the editorials (follow the News link from the home page) and the How-To Tutorials under HTML Stuff. Tucows has many mirror sites. If it asks you to pick a region, try one close to home—some mirror sites will be faster than others. At times, Tucows might seem difficult to navigate, but persist. Although it includes Mac products, it offers better coverage for Windows products.

- **Download.com**

  `http://download.cnet.com`

  Download.com is CNet's download site (CNet is a Web portal for technical people). Navigate it with keyword searches. Drop-down menus let you filter your search results for a specific OS, general software category, and license type (for example, freeware). Also, take a look at its list of software-related newsletters. This is an excellent site for both Windows and Mac products.

- **ZDNet**

  `http://downloads.zdnet.com/download/`

ZDNet is a Web portal for software junkies. Once you get hooked on software downloads, you might want to make this page your default home page. You can filter your searches for Windows-based PCs, Macs, Palm Pilots, or laptops. If you set the filter for "all ZDNet," your keyword search will return not only hits for software downloads but also hits for product reviews, tips and help articles, technical news, commentary, and more. Each hit list is displayed separately, so you can scan it or ignore it, as you wish. The different hit lists make this a great browsing site.

- **Macdownload**
  `http://downloads.zdnet.com/mac/`
  This is the Mac side of the ZDNet portal. It's a great place to find Mac software.

- **Jumbo!**
  `http://www.jumbo.com`
  This site is a little heavy on games, but go to the Internet link for Internet applications, and check out the Jumbo Guides for software reviews and how-to tutorials.

- **Shareware**
  `http://www.shareware.com/`
  This is CNet's meta search engine for software. Use the drop-down menu to filter your search results for a specific platform.

If you think it's fun to browse software clearinghouses, you'll want to begin your own collection of favorite software sites. The ones listed here will get you started. There are hundreds of others on the Web. Some are listed in the next two sections.

6.9.2 Windows Software Sites

Here's a list of Windows-based product sites to explore:

```
http://www.completelyfreesoftware.com/
http://www.nonags.com/
http://www.freewareweb.com/
http://www.thefreesite.com/
http://www.rocketdownload.com
http://www.sedoparking.com/happypuppy.com
http://www.galttech.com
http://cws.internet.com/software_index/
```

6.9.3 Macintosh Software Sites

If you're a Mac user in search of software sites, you might feel outnumbered by the endless parade of sites for Windows products. Not only are there fewer software sites for the Mac but also there is less software. However, this is not necessarily bad. Who needs 50 different screen shot utilities anyway? The important thing is to have two or three that do it well. And if there are only two or three to choose from, think of the time you save when deciding which one to use. You can research your options, make a decision, install what you need, and get back to the rest of your life much faster than Windows users can.

The following are some sites you can explore for some great Mac software:

```
http://www.macorchard.com/
http://www.chezmark.com/osx/
http://www.macupdate.com/
http://hyperarchive.lcs.mit.edu/HyperArchive/
http://www.apple.com/support/downloads/
http://www.versiontracker.com/
http://www.tidbits.com/iskm/iskm-soft.html
http://mirror.macupdate.com
```

TIP: Mac Users Only

Still feeling neglected? Don't forget about the **MacFixIt Forums** (see Section 4.6.1), one of the best troubleshooting sites on the Net. Also check out the reader reports at **MacInTouch** at `http://www.macintouch.com/`. Then drop by **MacCentral** at `http://www.macworld.com/news/`, pick a story that looks interesting, read it, and scroll down to check out what other readers have to say about it. You'll be quickly reassured that the Mac user community is alive and well and probably a few jumps ahead of the competition.

6.10 **FTP Software Archives and Clients**

Programmers were sharing software and maintaining software archives on the Internet long before the Web came along. How did they do it? With a service called the **File Transfer Protocol (FTP)** (see the Above & Beyond section in Chapter 1). Programmers have been visiting FTP sites to find software files since the early days of the original ARPANET. FTP sites are still around, and you may need to visit one someday, for example, to find MP3 files.

An address on an **FTP server** looks like an address on a Web server, except that the ftp:// prefix is used instead of the Web server's http:// prefix. To reach an address on an FTP server, you can use an FTP client or your Web browser. Either way, FTP servers are easy to handle once you know what to expect.

Project Gutenberg is an example of an archive stored on FTP servers. The archive is an online library of books that can be freely distributed on the Internet because their copyrights have expired and they are in the public domain. To find a specific novel at Project Gutenberg, start at its Web site (see Figure 6.31), where you can conduct a search for a specific author or title.

As an example, look for *My Antonia* by Willa Cather. This search produces one hit, with all the information you need to retrieve the book from the archive (see Figure 6.32). The Web page shown in the figure is a gateway to the FTP server, where the book is actually stored. If you roll your mouse over the links for myant10.txt and myant10.zip, you'll see that the underlying

Figure 6.31

Project Gutenberg: classic books you can download for free

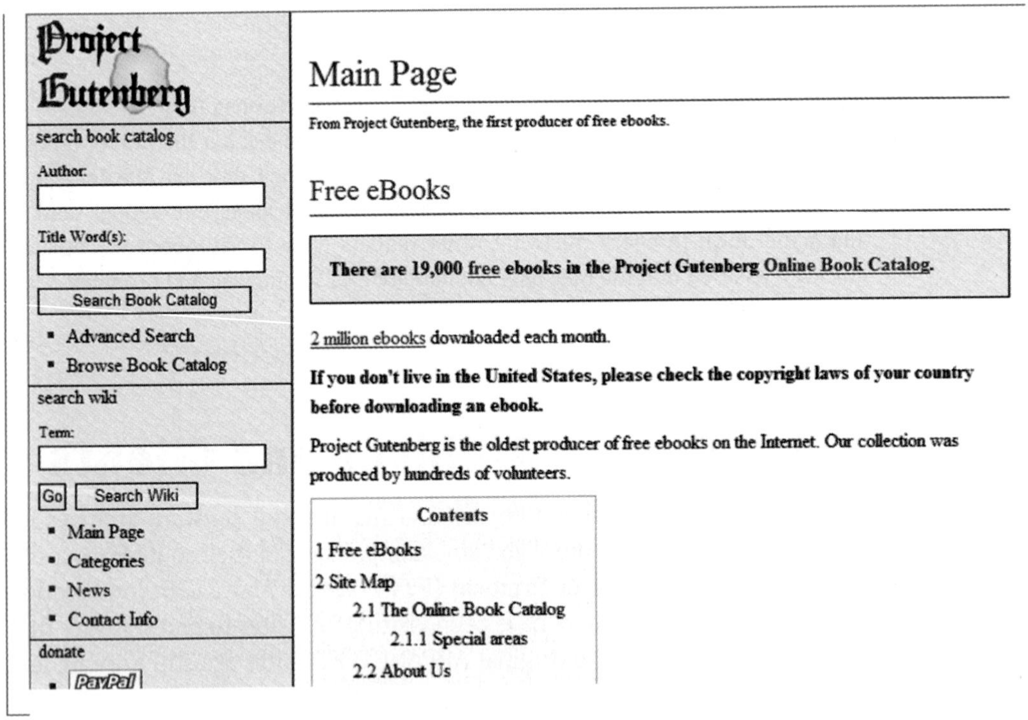

Figure 6.32

My Antonia is available at Project Gutenberg.

Bibliographic Record	
Creator	Cather, Willa Sibert, 1873-1947
Title	My Antonia
Language	English
LoC Class	PS: Language and Literatures: American literature
Subject	Frontier and pioneer life -- Nebraska -- Fiction
EText-No.	242
Release Date	1995-04-01
Copyright Status	Not copyrighted in the United States. If you live elsewhere check the laws of your country before downloading this ebook.

Formats Available For Download					
Edition	**Format**	**Encoding** [1]	**Compression**	**Size**	**Download Links**
	Plucker		none	unknown	main site
11	Plain text	us-ascii	none	455 KB	main site mirror sites P2P
11	Plain text	us-ascii	zip	177 KB	main site mirror sites P2P

TIP: I Think I Need a Map

If you're exploring a new FTP server and aren't sure where to go, watch for files named *index*, *welcome*, or *readme*, as well as subdirectories named *pub* (for public). A welcome message printed by the server at the top-level directory might say something useful to aid your navigation. You might also see directory specific welcome messages whenever you enter a new subdirectory.

When you visit an FTP site for the first time, always read everything available that could help you navigate the site, but don't be surprised if the server is not too helpful. FTP servers assume that you know where you need to go. They aren't there to help you figure out where everything is.

FYI: This Is a Busy Signal . . . Please Try Again Later

Sometimes you'll click a file's name in an FTP directory and your browser won't be able to download the file. You might be told something such as "Alert!: Unable to access document." This can happen with a heavily used server during peak periods; it doesn't necessarily mean that the file is permanently unavailable. Try again later. You might be able to get it when the server is less busy.

hyperlinks are FTP addresses instead of HTTP addresses. Because this gateway has been designed to make file downloads easy for all visitors, you can download directly from one of these two links to get a copy of *My Antonia* (use the Save Link As command on your browser's pop-up menu).

As explained, Web browsers can download files from Web servers and FTP servers. Some also allow you to upload a file to an FTP server (both Navigator and IE support file uploads using a helper application like WinSCP, an FTP client). People often find it useful to upload files when they collaborate on major projects with coworkers. For example, each chapter of this book was uploaded to an FTP server so that everyone involved in the book's production could work with those files as needed. This type of file sharing is accomplished with full-privileged FTP sessions, which are described shortly.

Many easy-to-use graphical FTP clients are available for the Mac and Windows OSs. If you need to do a lot of file transfers, you'll appreciate some of the special features that FTP clients offer and Web browsers do not. These features include the following:

- Simultaneous displays of local and remote directories
- Sorting options for directory displays
- Support for multiple FTP sessions running in parallel
- Support for multiple file transfers
- Resumable file transfers in case a transfer is interrupted
- A timer that lets you schedule large jobs to download while you're in meetings or when it's late at night or a weekend day
- Intuitive drag-and-drop file transfers
- An address book for automated logons on different servers
- File caching to speed up transfers from pokey servers
- File search facilities

When you use an FTP client to visit an FTP server, you start by specifying the DNS or IP address (see Section 1.5) of the host machine you want to contact. If you don't know which FTP server to visit, your FTP client can't help you.

Figure 6.33 shows the opening window from an FTP client named **WinSCP**. You enter the DNS address of the server you want to visit in the Host or URL: field. Enter your account name and password where requested. Some sites still support **anonymous FTP** connections (access for "guests" who do not have accounts is permitted). If you're visiting such a site, enter anonymous as your user name and use your e-mail address as the password. Because of security issues, anonymous FTP is now rare. If we select Directories in

Figure 6.33

Setting up an FTP connection with WinSCP

WinSCP Login		? X

Session
Stored sessions
Logging
Environment
Directories
SFTP
SCP
Connection
Proxy
SSH
Key exchange
Authentication
Bugs
Preferences

Session

Host name   Port number
10.0.1.2   22

User name   Password
richk   ••••••

Private key file

Protocol
○ SFTP   ⊙ SFTP (allow SCP fallback)   ○ SCP

☑ Advanced options

About...   Languages   Save...   Login   Help

TIP: Uploading Files by Using a Browser

If you don't expect to do a lot of file transfers, try using your browser for uploads. To contact an FTP server, enter an FTP address in the Location: or address field of your browser (wherever you normally enter URLs). Note that you generally need an account on the FTP server in order to upload files, so the address must contain your user ID for the account as well as the server's DNS address. For example, if your user ID is psmith and your FTP server is `atlantic.ecc.unm.edu`, then you would enter the following address:

`ftp://psmith@atlantic.ecc.unm.edu`

Your browser will prompt you for your password and then connect you to the server.

Once you are connected, your current working directory on the FTP server will be displayed in the browser window. You navigate the directories on the FTP server by clicking directory icons, and you move files between the server and your local host by dragging icons on your desktop. Treat the browser window like any other directory window on your desktop, and copy files from one location to the other by using drag-and-drop techniques.

Figure 6.33, we can specify both the starting Local and Remote directories. If we leave both fields blank, we'll go straight to the main directory on each computer. Finally, clicking Login tells WinSCP to attempt to make the connection.

With a personal account on an FTP server, you can initiate a **full-privilege** FTP session in order to move files to and from the server. To create a full-privilege session, enter your user ID in the Username field and your private password in the Password field.

Figure 6.34 shows WinSCP in action once the FTP connection has been established. Two directories are displayed: one for your computer, the local host (on the left), and one for the remote FTP server (on the right). You can navigate both by using scrolling and point-and-click operations. To download a file, select the file's name on the remote server and click the copy button in the lower toolbar. The file will be copied to the current directory (the one in the display) on the local host. To upload a file, select the file's name on the local host and click the copy button. The file will be copied to the current directory (the one in the display) on the remote host. WinSCP supports drag-

Figure 6.34

Point-and-click file transfers

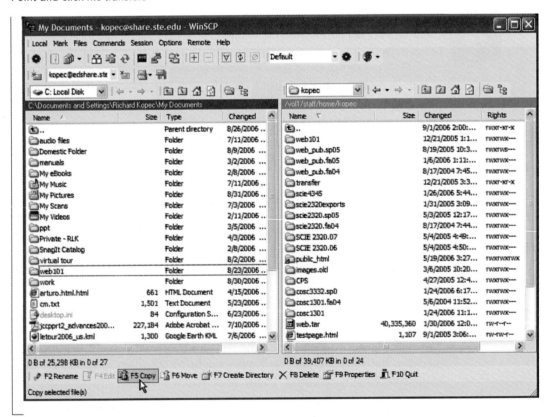

TIP: When to Use Full-Privilege FTP

If you want to set up a Web site, you will need to use full-privilege FTP. You'll be given a personal account on a Web server where you can store HTML files developed on your home computer. Then, when you've completed your pages, you'll move your HTML files from your home computer to the Web server by using FTP, which may or may not be supported by your web page editor. Uploading files to a remote host is easy with a full-privilege FTP session.

and-drop operations too, so you can move files and folders across the Internet in the same way you move files and folders on your desktop. WinSCP also allows you to edit, rename, move, and remove files; create new directories (aka folders); and even display information about new versions of itself. You can get WinSCP at `http://winscp.net` or `http://sourceforge.net/projectts/winscp/`.

Graphical FTP clients have many convenient features to make FTP fast and painless. For example, most FTP clients create a separate window for welcome messages issued by the remote server, so you can easily refer back to those messages as needed. If you need to move a lot of files at once (for example, an entire Web site), an FTP client will let you queue up entire subdirectories so you don't have to move each file individually. Some clients will let you view files on an FTP server without downloading them, and a few will let you edit text files remotely, provided that you're running a full-privilege FTP session. Remote editing is convenient if you maintain a Web site and need to make a few small corrections or updates to a Web page.

FTP servers are especially helpful when a group of people is working on a joint project and need to share files. A project directory is created on a password-protected FTP server so that project files will be available to group members only. They then can download and upload files to the FTP server via full-privilege FTP sessions. This is the easiest way to share files within a geographically dispersed workforce, especially when many files are involved or the files are very big. E-mail attachments can be used in these situations if needed, but this tends to be cumbersome when too many files, too many group members, or too many file updates are involved.

Using FTP for group projects is awkward, however. An FTP server does not provide a means to control changes made to a file. If several users modify the same file simultaneously and then upload it to the server, only the version uploaded last will persist. The other versions will be overwritten. If the documents are word processor files, Google Docs (see Section 4.5) might work

TIP: FTP Clients Now Use SFTP Protocol

You probably guessed why—SFTP is secure, while FTP is not. SFTP uses secure shell (SSH) file transfer protocol that uses public-key cryptography for authentication (see Chapter 8) to ensure confidentiality and file integrity during the transfer. Few sites still use plain FTP.

TIP: FTP Netiquette and Common Sense

Here are some tips to keep in mind when using FTP servers.

- Visit FTP servers during off hours—late evenings and early mornings are best
- Read the welcome and README files for important information
- Before you contact the FTP server technical support staff, first ask your local technical support staff for help
- If mirror sites are available use the one that is closest to you
- Anonymous FTP access is a privilege, not a right; be a courteous guest

better. Similar services for other file types are also available. Alternatively, some sort of versioning file system (such as Concurrent Versions System—CVS) can be used to check files in and out and track changes.

Managing Your Software

Now that you're ready to download tons of software from the Internet, you need to learn how to manage it all. How do you safely remove certain software from your computer? How can you determine if a new software addition is causing your machine to crash? What does it mean when two pieces of software conflict with each other? If your computer suddenly starts to freeze repeatedly, how do you return it to a stable state?

Mac users might be tempted to skip most of this section because Macs tend to be more stable and less temperamental than Windows-based machines. However, some standard maintenance routines apply to Macs and Windows-based machines. This section focuses on those.

You need to know more about caring for your computer than this section can cover. Consider purchasing a book about your particular OS (especially since the user's manual that comes with a computer is not always as comprehensive or as easy to understand as you might like or need).

6.11.1 Four Rules for All Computer Users

Here are four rules that all computer users should keep in mind, regardless of the OS used.

Restart Your Computer as Needed to Recover RAM and Speed Up Processing.   Each time you launch an application, your computer sets aside some RAM for that application to use. When you exit that application, a well-designed OS will recover that RAM for reuse. Unfortunately, some Windows implementations are not completely successful in this regard, decreasing the amount of available RAM over time, slowing things down, and possibly freezing the system. In other cases, the application itself keeps asking for more memory rather than recycling memory it already has but is no longer using, resulting in a **memory leak**. As long as the offending program is running, memory "leaks" away (to the errant program), and when all the available memory has been captured by the errant program, the system freezes.

Another Windows problem known as **Windows Rot** also causes system performance to degrade over time. Every time you install a new program, add a new user, or make other changes to your system, the Windows Registry File that tracks all these things increases in size. Windows uses the registry extensively to support OS services. As this file gets larger and larger, managing it requires more and more of the system resources causing system performance to degrade as the registry file inflates.

The memory leak problem should disappear when you quit the application, unless of course Windows itself is "leaky" or not recapturing memory freed by a quit application, in which case *your only recourse is to reboot the system*. One factor that masks this problem to some extent is the frequent need for reboots when Windows updates are installed, so it's possible that you may not notice it.

Solving the Windows Rot problem is a bit more drastic—you must reinstall the OS! This causes the registry file to be rebuilt and (hopefully) slimmed down by the elimination of useless junk that accumulates in the file over time. Manually tweaking this file is not recommended since it is crucial to system performance. Before you reinstall, you might consider installing and running

TIP: Is Your Memory *Leaking*?

One indicator of memory leaks is the Page File in Use (PF usage) indicator. Open the task manager (Ctrl + Alt + Del) and select the performance tab (see Figure 6.35). If the PF usage indicator is close to maxing out, then it may be time to reboot.

Figure 6.35

You can check PF usage in the Windows XP Task Manager performance window.

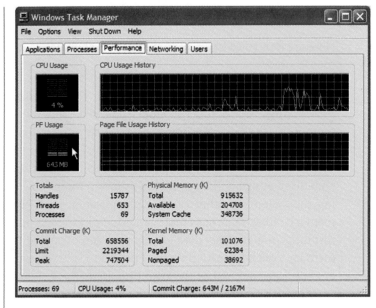

a registry cleaner program first to see if this solves the problem. But remember that any new software installation will initially make the problem *worse*.

Some people must restart their computers (usually Windows-based ones) once a day, but this is now rare. Most others can go for a week or more (usually Macs). If your computer becomes unusually sluggish or unable to open new applications, it may be time to restart. Your OS has a RAM manager that tries to free up as much RAM as possible whenever the supply looks dangerously low. You might find it instructive to watch your available RAM each time you launch a new application or exit a running application (see Available Physical Memory in Figure 6.35). A RAM monitor (part of your OS) will show you how much RAM has been allocated to existing applications and how much RAM is available to launch additional applications.

With Windows, you can also monitor your resources system (press Ctrl + Alt + Del to bring up the Task Manager and select the Performance tab, as shown in Figure 6.35). System resources generally start high (around 90%) and drop as you start up applications. Eventually, system resources could get too low. If they drop below 40%, your system is being stressed. You might or might not be able to recover system resources by exiting active applications. If resources fall to 30%, it's time to restart. If you are using a Mac, then you can launch the Activity Monitor (see Figure 6.36) found in the

Figure 6.36

The Mac Activity
Monitor

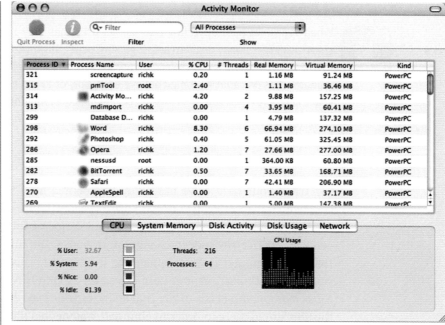

Applications→Utilities folder. The Activity Monitor presents a graphical display of CPU, memory, disk, and network usage.

Optimize Your Hard Drive.   With hard drives now measured in gigabytes, it's easy to forget that they still can get crowded (eventually). When you save a file to your hard drive, a fixed amount of space is allocated for that file. When you remove a file from your hard drive, all of the space allocated to that file becomes available for new files. The OS can retrieve a file faster if the file has been allocated a big block of contiguous space (the file is stored in one piece). When your hard drive is new and mostly empty, allocating contiguous space when a file is saved is easy. However, after you've saved and deleted a few hundred or a few thousand files (or significantly increased the size of a file you are editing), your OS will begin to have difficulty finding contiguous space for very large files. When contiguous space is not available, your system will use smaller blocks of space and spread the file across these smaller blocks. This produces a **fragmented file**, a file that does not occupy contiguous space. You'll not have a problem working with a fragmented file, but when you want to retrieve the file from the hard drive your OS will need more time to piece it together, thereby slowing the file's loading.

TIP: Is Your Hard Drive Nearly Full?

 When your boot hard drive (the one the OS uses) has only 10 percent or less free space available, it may begin to act sluggishly, especially if your drive is 40GB or less in size (with larger hard drives you can probably get by with less than 10 percent). As it approaches its capacity, it may behave erratically or even crash. Monitor your free space carefully when your disk fills up. Delete files that you don't need, or save them onto some removable storage media (like a flash drive, external drive, or CD/DVD) if you do.

When your hard drive has many fragmented files, the drive is called a **fragmented hard drive**. If your hard drive is badly fragmented, your computer will get sluggish. This happens over a long period of time, so it's likely that you won't notice any sudden changes in response. You might not even realize that your computer is not as snappy as it once was. This is why you need to run a disk optimizer on your hard drive every so often. A **disk optimizer** (aka a *disk defragmenter*) is a utility that analyzes your hard drive and reorganizes the files stored there in order to eliminate fragmented files. If your hard drive is very large and contains many files, it might take an hour or more to defragment it. Some books recommend that you defragment (defrag, for short) your hard drive once a month. How often you do this depends on how much you use your computer and the size of your hard drive. At the very least, you should defrag once or twice a year. You can find a disk defrag tool in the Windows Accessories→System Tools folder. A Mac running OS X will probably not need one. The Mac OS does this for you automatically.

Keep Your Device Drivers Up-to-Date. Computer peripherals such as printers and monitors come with special software called *device drivers*. A **device driver** creates a communication link between your computer and its peripheral device so data can flow smoothly between the two. In order to use a new peripheral, first you must install its device driver. But each time you add a new peripheral to your system, there is a chance that the new device driver will conflict with one of your old device drivers. The more peripherals you have, the more likely it is that two of them will not get along. When drivers conflict, it's not always the new peripheral that is affected.

Sometimes two devices conflict and nothing can be done about it. But you can solve or prevent many driver conflicts by keeping all your device drivers up-to-date. Hardware manufacturers periodically release new versions of their device drivers in order to keep their hardware compatible with other peripherals and newer computers. You can download device drivers for computer peripherals from manufacturers' Web sites. You are responsible for tracking these driver updates and installing them as they become available (or whenever you install a new peripheral). If you don't, you may experience what appears to be a hardware problem when you install a new peripheral. Chances are it's just a device driver conflict.

Don't Overload Your Computer with Too Many Applications Running at Once. RAM limitations determine how many applications you can run at once. Too many applications and too little RAM will lead to system crashes and freezes. If you absolutely must run your word processor, Web browser, speech recognition software, and photo editor all at the same time, and your system is crashing every two hours, you probably need to increase your RAM. Remember that lots of little applications add up to consume RAM. Included

TIP: Is it a Hardware Problem or a Software Problem?

Here are some points to keep in mind when you're trying to determine if your computer problems result from hardware or from software.

- Faulty hardware may be apparent from the start, especially the solid-state components, but hardware can and does fail at any time and without warning. Some failures are easy to troubleshoot (for example, a lack of power is probably due to the power supply). And if you don't hear the whirring of the drive motor, it might be your hard drive. One way to test memory is by using a bootable memory tester (like MemTest—http://hcidesign.com/memtest/).
- An overloaded computer is easy to spot. Watch your Windows Task Manager or Mac Activity Monitor to see if you're approaching or exceeding a RAM or disk limitation (see Figures 6.35 and 6.36). If you find yourself struggling with too little RAM or disk space (slower and slower response), shut down any open applications you can live without or install more RAM, remove files, and/or get an external hard drive.
- Software accounts for all other problems. You might need to update a device driver. You might need to reinstall a corrupt program file. You might be dealing with buggy software.
- Malware may also be causing your performance problems. Malware runs hidden in the background, consuming enough system resources to degrade the performance of your computer. Crank up your antivirus and antispyware programs to see.

TIP: So What about Those DLLs?

Windows applications use shared code libraries known as DLLs (dynamic link libraries). Sometimes, when a new application is installed, it overwrites a DLL used by other applications. The DLL will work for the new program, but it may not work for previously installed applications, causing them to crash when launched. Microsoft created the Windows File Protection (WFP) feature for Windows 2000 and Windows XP to monitor system file updates like this, keeping a cached copy of the old DLL just in case it needs to restore it when problems arise.

FYI: How to Remove Software Correctly

Sometimes you'll want to remove a program, perhaps to free space on your hard drive or to clear it of clutter. You must be careful when removing program files. If a program consists of only one executable file, you can delete that file and be done with it. However, that's not how most programs work.

Typically, Windows computer programs involve many files—sometimes dozens or hundreds. To complicate things, those files are stored in different places on your hard drive, often in places you don't know about. You can't expect to find and eliminate all of them manually: you don't know what files to look for or where to find them. A superior program always comes with an uninstaller in case you need to remove the program. An uninstaller is a utility designed to unload, safely and completely, all files associated with the program. Look for uninstallers when you select your software downloads. To uninstall a program, use the Change or Remove Programs selection in the Windows Control Panel (see Figure 6.37). It shouldn't be necessary for you to locate the specific uninstall program yourself. If you are using a Mac, you can find the files associated with some application in the Applications folder. Just drag the application and its associated files into the Trash to remove them. If you have its icon in the Dock, then remove that too.

Remember, once you have installed a piece of software, don't move any of its associated files from their original locations. If one file of the program can't find another file of the program because you've moved it from its original position, then the program might fail to launch or it might launch and crash later. If you reorganize your directories, don't touch your software directories. If you absolutely must reorganize your software directories, first uninstall any affected software (by using the uninstaller) and then reinstall it in its new location. As a rule, you should leave software files where the installer puts them.

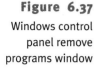

Figure 6.37

Windows control
panel remove
programs window

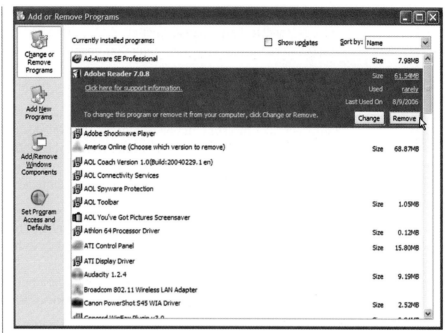

here are all those background utilities that automatically launch at startup, such as antivirus, fax, or instant messenger software, and any other programs that are in constant use on your computer.

Computers are like people: some are healthy, and some are barely alive. A computer that freezes and crashes six times a day is not healthy. If you have a sick computer, you must identify the source of the trouble. The hardware is probably working correctly but too many demands are being made of it. And sometimes the problems are in the software.

Like personal health problems, it's usually easier to prevent computer problems than to fix them. Just as you need the right tools to protect your computer from viruses, you need the right tools to protect it from software conflicts and other problems. However, if you never add new software to your computer, you can skip the rest of this section.

The more software you install, the more you should practice routine system maintenance. You'll never know before installation how a new program will interact with your computer. If all goes well, no problems result. However, in rare cases, a new software installation can interfere with older software and significantly mess up your computer. It might never happen if you use only the most popular software (there's safety in numbers). But it's always good to be prepared. Section 6.11.2 discusses various maintenance tools you can use to keep your computer operating at peak performance.

6.11.2 Maintenance Tools

If you want to explore the world of shareware and freeware, you should seriously consider investing in one or more of the available commercial software maintenance packages. You don't need a technical background to use them—in fact, the best tool suites make it easy for even nontechnical people to keep their computers in good health. A good set of maintenance tools will include the following:

- A disk scanner (for example, ScanDisk) and disk optimizer (for example, Disk Defragmenter) to keep your hard drive healthy (if you are using an older OS that lacks these tools)
- A general Windows uninstaller utility (for example, McAfee's Uninstaller) that tracks all your software installations so you can undo them as needed
- A tool for making a rescue disk (if one is not provided) to restore your system if needed
- A crash guard utility that intercepts system crashes and restores your system without restarting
- A registry scanner/cleaner (for Windows), a system utility that helps keep Windows stable
- Antivirus software

Note: Don't purchase each of these separately. Look for system utility suites that bundle all these tools.

Should you run out and buy a utility suite before you download any software? No, that's not necessary. In fact, some of these utilities might be part of your OS, for example, a disk scanner, a disk optimizer, and a tool for making a rescue disk. You might also have received in your initial software setup some form of antivirus software (at least a 30-day free-trial version of one). You probably don't need to go beyond these unless you plan to download software regularly. Everything else you can live without as long as your system is stable, you don't make many changes to your software library, and you're happy with your computer the way it is. However, if you later decide to explore other utilities, revisit this issue and think about whether your preventive maintenance routines are adequate. If a little preventive action can save you from system freezes and crashes, it's worth the extra effort.

Finding Good Software Reviews

If you're serious about making informed software decisions, start with what reviewers have to say about the products in which you are interested. Don't sweat the little choices, such as which free applet to download. However, do some homework before you purchase a big-ticket item. As mentioned previously, when you shop for your software on the Net, you can try a free-trial version before you buy. However, you probably don't want to test-drive every car on the lot. By seeing what the reviewers have to say, you should be able to limit your choices or, in some cases, learn about other solutions to your problems that might take you in a different direction altogether. Software reviews can be educational and sometimes entertaining, and they almost always save you time. You can also find out what other people think of specific software by visiting newsgroups or mailing lists. Those are good places to ask specific questions. However, if you're exploring an area in which you have little or no experience, a good software review is usually the best place to start.

As you might expect, the Net offers plenty of software reviews, in newsletters, "zines," and at some software clearinghouses, as well as at sites that specialize in the software industry or focus on particular professions. For example, in the latter case, sites for teachers might review educational software, sites for artists might review photo editors and drawing programs, and sites for interior designers might review house layout software. As you browse the Net, note any sites you see that run software reviews.

Not all software is reviewed (for example, many applets and JavaScript programs) because they are so numerous. Undoubtedly, many good freeware and shareware programs never get enough attention to earn a review. If you enjoy searching software archives and looking for undiscovered gems, you don't have to restrict yourself to reviewers' recommendations. If you want to save time, read a review or two and go from there. Your main concern should be getting what you need and getting on with your life. If you restrict yourself to software that has been reviewed, you're much less likely to be victimized by malicious code.

The following are some sites where you can find reviews for mainstream software:

- **Software reviews for all Operating Systems**
  ZDNet Reviews `http://review.zdnet.com/`
  CNET `http://www.cnet.com/`

■ **Software reviews for Windows**
Win Planet Reviews `http://www.winplanet.com/` or
`http://cws.internet.com/`
PC Magazine `http://www.pcmag.com/`

■ **Software reviews for the Macintosh**
MacReview Zone `http://macreviewzone.com/index.php`
MacDirectory `http://macdirectory.com/newmd/mac/`
`homepage.html`
Macs Only `http://www.macsonly.com/`
MacHome Journal Online Reviews `http://www.machome.com/`
`reviews/index.lasso`

If you think that a software purchase from your friendly local software retail store is safer than one purchased from the Net, remember that no computer is ever free from risk. Software obtained over the Internet is no riskier than shrink-wrapped software from a brick-and-mortar retail store as long as you remember to take the following reasonable precautions:

■ Scan all new files with antivirus software, and keep your antivirus software up-to-date
■ Don't download executable files from obscure Web sites
■ Don't accept a file if your browser warns you about an Authenticode signature failure

If you're still concerned, purchase mainstream items only. Alternatively, take advantage of software reviews, Web search engines, and Usenet newsgroups to learn everything anybody ever said about the software you're considering. If there's a problem with it, you're bound to hear about it. Remember, you're plugged into the world's largest grapevine. Listen to the buzz, use your common sense, and see how long it takes to fill that 40GB hard drive. This is one place where you can have lots of fun with your computer.

Things to Remember

■ Scan all executable downloads after you complete the download and before you run the file
■ For Windows downloads, `.exe` and `.zip` are standard file formats
■ For Mac downloads, `.sea`, `.hqx`, `.sit`, and `.bin` are standard file formats

- Before you begin a software installation, turn off any other applications that are running
- If instructed to turn off your antivirus software during a software installation, take precautions and then turn antivirus protection back on when the installation is completed
- If you don't understand a question asked by a software installer, take the default setting and continue with the installation
- You can delete an installer file after the installation is complete
- Read all the informational screens displayed by an installer, along with any README files
- If you download a lot of software, invest in some good system utilities

Important Concepts

adware any software application that displays advertisements

anonymous ftp a method used to access an FTP server. This method does not require you to have an account on the server. Public FTP servers may allow anonymous FTP logons, but restricted (private) FTP servers require a user ID and a valid password.

antivirus software a program that checks a file to see whether it is infected with a computer virus. Running antivirus software is an important precaution to take before installing any software.

file archive a single file that can be unpacked (unzipped) to produce the multiple files it contains. Software files are often packed in a file archive for easy downloading

File Transfer Protocol (FTP) the protocol that governs a means of moving files over the Internet

freeware executable software that is distributed free of charge

FTP client software designed to access FTP servers and facilitate FTP file transfers

FTP server a server that acts as a distribution site for files, for example, a software archive. On many FTP servers, anyone is allowed to download files (via anonymous FTP), but only privileged users with accounts on the server are allowed to upload files (privileged FTP).

P2P protocol a file transfer protocol that relies on the user computers as both file uploaders (file sources) and downloaders, often coordinated by a central server computer

shareware (aka **nagware, special-** or **limited-edition software**) software made available free often for a limited time or with some features disabled with the assumption that users will be so enamored of the product they will want to purchase it. Users may be nagged for payment, the software may self destruct if not purchased during the trial period, or the vendor may rely entirely on the honor system.

software downloads the process of transferring software files or software archives from a remote host to the local host

software installation the process of setting up data files, executable files, and other support files needed to run a piece of software on a computer

spyware any software application that surreptitiously collects data about your computing activities and sends it back to a data broker

Where Can I Learn More?

BitTorrent FAQ and Guide
http://www.dessent.net/btfaq/
download.com guide for downloading
http://www.download.com/1200-20-985144.html
Downloading Files: Frequently Asked Questions
http://www.pcshareware.com/download.htm
Attacks from the Inside: The Spyware Threat
http://www.homenethelp.com/Web/explain/spyware.asp
Get That Spyware Off My Computer!
http://www.pcworld.com/howto/article/0,aid,78052,00.asp
CounterExploitation
http://www.cexx.org/
The PC Magazine Ultimate Utility Guide
http://www.pcmag.com/category2/0,4148,1466,00.asp
WinPlanet's Internet Apps: FTP Client
http://cws.internet.com/ftp.html
File Formats and Extensions
http://www.learnthenet.com/english/html/34filext.htm

Problems and Exercises

1. Explain how a special edition or demo software distribution differs from freeware.

2. Why is it less expensive for a software manufacturer to distribute software over the Internet than through traditional retail stores? What are the pros and cons of these two distribution systems for the consumer? For the manufacturer?

3. Suppose you check your e-mail and find a message from someone at Microsoft.com. The message body is as follows:

   As a user of Microsoft Internet Explorer, Microsoft Corporation provides you with this upgrade for your Web browser. It will fix some bugs found in your Internet Explorer. To install the upgrade, please save the attached file (ie0199.exe) in some folder and run it.

   What should you do? Explain your answer.

4. Suppose that you download an executable file that contains a virus. Can you catch the virus by simply downloading the file? Explain your answer.

5. What is an installer, and when does it make sense to package a computer program inside of an installer? How often do you need to run the same installer? Why might you want to save an installer after you have used it? Explain why and when some software downloads contain digital signatures. Is the use of digital signatures a foolproof system? Explain your answer.

6. Suppose you have a friend who has read that surfing the Web can be dangerous. She says that according to an article she read, a person can wipe out his or her entire hard drive by clicking the wrong link. Is this true? Describe the circumstances that would have to be in place for something like this to happen. What can you do to make sure it never happens to you?

7. WinZip is the most popular file archive utility for Windows. Suppose you install this utility but when you try to run your antivirus software from inside it, the Run antivirus software command is grayed out. What is wrong, and how can you fix it?

8. Name three things that an FTP client can do that a Web browser cannot.

9. What is a fragmented hard drive? How does a hard drive become fragmented? Can it be fixed? Explain your answer.

10. What is an uninstaller, and why do you need to use one?

11. **[FIND IT ONLINE]** Visit the Tucows clearinghouse to find a color picker utility (similar to EyeDropper or ColorFinder) that gives you

the closest Web-safe color when you select a color on your desktop. Find one utility for the Mac and another for Windows-based machines. For each, list the utility's name, its home page URL, and its price. Don't download any software to complete this exercise— only read the software descriptions at Tucows.

12. **[FIND IT ONLINE]** Search some software clearinghouses to locate programs that generate fractal images. How many programs can you find? For each, list its name and the OS for which it was designed. Which is the most popular freeware fractal designer? Which is the most popular shareware fractal designer? (Hint: Go to CDNet's Download.com, conduct a keyword search on "fractal," and sort the results by clicking Downloads in the Re-sort bar at the top of the results list.)

13. **[FIND IT ONLINE]** How many Web browsers are available at CNet's Download.com? (Hint: go to the subject tree and look under Internet/Browsers). Sort the resulting list by the number of downloads to find the top five alternative browsers.

14. **[FIND IT ONLINE]** The Opera Web browser is available for both Windows-based PCs and Macs. Read some software reviews for Opera, and then explain why you think that many people choose to pay for Opera instead of opting for one of the two better known freebies (IE and Navigator).

15. **[HANDS-ON: For Windows Users Only]** Section 9.9 will describe a graphics utility called EyeDropper. You can find this utility at `http://www.inetia.com/eyedropper_eng.php`, which distributes EyeDropper as a zipped file archive. Visit this site and download the latest version of EyeDropper. Scan the software for viruses, and then install it. Did you have any difficulties with the installation? How many files are inside the zipped archive? What are their names? Use the program to find the hexadecimal color codes for the Vizija logo at the bottom of the download page.

How long did it take you to complete this exercise?

16. **[HANDS-ON: For Mac Users Only]** The EyeDropper program described in Section 9.9 does not run on a Mac, but similar programs are available for Mac users. Go to Tucows (`http://www.tucows.com`), and conduct a search by using the keyword "ColorFinder"—this will take you to a freeware color sampler utility for the Mac. This file is an `.hqx` file, which can be opened with Stuffit Expander. Scan the software for viruses, and then install it. Did you have any difficulties with the installation? How many files are inside the file archive? What are their names? Use the program to find the hexadecimal color codes for the bird at the top of `http://www-edlab.cs.umass.edu/cs120/`.

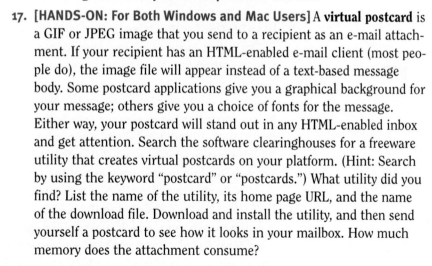

How long did it take you to complete this exercise?

17. **[HANDS-ON: For Both Windows and Mac Users]** A **virtual postcard** is a GIF or JPEG image that you send to a recipient as an e-mail attachment. If your recipient has an HTML-enabled e-mail client (most people do), the image file will appear instead of a text-based message body. Some postcard applications give you a graphical background for your message; others give you a choice of fonts for the message. Either way, your postcard will stand out in any HTML-enabled inbox and get attention. Search the software clearinghouses for a freeware utility that creates virtual postcards on your platform. (Hint: Search by using the keyword "postcard" or "postcards.") What utility did you find? List the name of the utility, its home page URL, and the name of the download file. Download and install the utility, and then send yourself a postcard to see how it looks in your mailbox. How much memory does the attachment consume?

18. **[HANDS-ON: For Windows Users Only]** Use your Web browser to visit AllTheWeb at `http://www.alltheweb.com/` and click FTP FILES on the navigation bar. This is a search engine for FTP sites. To receive any hits, you need to match your query against a filename or a directory name on some FTP server on the Net. Try conducting a search for the virus test file `eicar.com` (see Section 2.5 for a description of this file). You should get about a dozen hits on various FTP servers. Which server is closest to you? (Use the sort options to rank the hits.) Try downloading the file from one of the servers to see whether your antivirus software will catch it. If it doesn't, your antivirus software isn't turned on and running in the background. If you aren't running it in the background, scan the `eicar.com` file manually after it has been downloaded. (If you can't get an alert on this file one way or the other, your computer is a target for computer viruses.)

19. **[HANDS-ON: For Both Windows and Mac Users]** Visit Project Gutenberg at `http://www.gutenberg.org/` and download a copy of *The Lumley Autograph* by Susan F. Cooper. When was this document captured and by whom? How large is the zipped archive file? How large is the plain text file?

20. **[FIND IT ONLINE: For Both Windows and Mac Users]** Suppose you want to get an FTP client for your computer but you aren't sure which one to buy. Find three popular FTP clients (for your platform) and at least two software reviews for each. For each, list its home page URL, the URLs for its software reviews, and its price. What special features distinguish these three clients? Is there a consensus among the reviewers about which is the best choice? Which one would you choose? Why?

21. **[HANDS-ON: For Both Windows and Mac Users]** Open your Task Manager (Windows) or Activity Monitor (Macs) and examine the information found there. Do you see any potential problems on the horizon? What can you do to deal with them? If you see something you don't understand, find out about it on the Web.

22. **[FIND IT ONLINE]** Conduct an online search to find out about the Moldova scam. When did this scam take place? What were the names of the Web sites involved? How did it work? What happened to the victims? Who was behind the scam, and what was their punishment? What piece of advice in this chapter would have prevented people from getting caught by the Moldova scam?

23. **[TAKE A STAND]** How do you feel about spyware? Do you think this is a fundamentally unfair business practice, or do you think it's the consumer's responsibility to research software using resources like **SpyChecker**? Do you think spyware is in the same category as cookies? Explain why or why not. How hard do you think consumers should work to protect their online privacy?

24. Which is more effective in protecting you from spyware: antivirus software or a firewall? Explain your answer. Is either precaution completely effective? Why or why not?

25. **[HANDS-ON]** Download and install Ad-aware from `http://www.lavasoftusa.com`. Run it and find out how many spyware programs are on your computer. How many did you find? Ad-aware needs to be updated periodically in order to keep it maximally effective. How is this done?

26. **[FIND IT ONLINE]** What is "drug dealer ware"?

27. **[FIND IT ONLINE]** Visit SpyChecker at `http://www.spychecker.com/` and search the database for software titles using each of the following keywords (three separate searches):

- Cursor
- Player
- Magic

What are the names of the software companies identified in each search? How many different companies did you find altogether?

28. **[FIND IT ONLINE]** Visit the spyware forum at `http://www.cexx.org/` and peruse some of the messages (no registration required). How active is this forum? What do you think of the quality of the information being exchanged?

29. Examine the BitTorrent download window in Figure 6.10. Explain each statistic that appears in the figure.

30. The text mentions that there are several ways to acquire a BitTorrent file. Find a few. Explain how each way is different.

31. **[FIND IT ONLINE]** Search the web for BitTorrent sites. Examine the list of files available. How many of these files *appear* to be copyrighted material?

32. **[HANDS-ON]** Download and install BitTorrent software (or the Opera browser). Go to a BitTorrent site and select a file with many seeds for download. Examine the download as it progresses. How long did the transfer take? Find another file to download of approximately the same size, but fewer seeds. Now how long did the download take?

Software on the Internet

Software Licenses

Whenever you obtain new software, it's your responsibility to know what the licensing agreement says. Reading this agreement isn't much fun, and if you routinely ignore it, you're not alone. The language is stiff, the restrictions predictable, and the disclaimers unsettling. How many products are accompanied by contractual agreements in which the manufacturer disavows all responsibility for any catastrophic consequences associated with the use of its product? Still, these much maligned and traditionally ignored documents are the only weapons that stand between software manufacturers and financial ruin.

Software piracy is the bane of commercial software, and software licenses are notoriously difficult to enforce. If you install a piece of software on two computers when the license restricts you to one, the police are not likely show up at your door with a search warrant even though you *are* violating the copyright agreement. However, using a CD-burner to create a few hundred pirated copies of the same software is different.

Software licenses can test the ethics of even the straightest arrows among us. Consider the following scenarios.

The Desktop–Laptop Dilemma

The license says that you're allowed to install the software on one computer at one time. You can't install it on two computers simultaneously. You have a desktop computer you use most of the time and a laptop you use when you travel. You want to use the same software on both machines. However, to comply with the licensing agreement, you would have to uninstall and install the software each time you travel. This seems crazy, especially since you don't intend to use both installations simultaneously. You think that simultaneous usage must be what the license is trying to prohibit. Do you have the right to take liberties with the license's restrictions, as long as you adhere to their intent? One way around this problem is to use portable media like a flash drive. Install the software on the flash drive and simply plug it into the computer that needs it. Be sure to close the application properly and save all necessary files before you remove the drive from your system.

The Seven-Year-Old Software Pirate

Your seven-year old daughter spent the day at a friend's house playing a computer game. She comes home with the CD-ROM for the game and asks you to install it for her so she can play it at home. You know this can't be legal, but your daughter wants it now, and she's not going to be happy if you tell her she has to wait until you can purchase a copy of the software. The whole issue is further complicated by the fact that all of her friends routinely share their computer games with one another and you're the only parent who is uneasy about the practice. Do you have the right to install the bootlegged software now, as long as you intend to purchase your own copy at the next possible opportunity? What if your daughter loses interest in the game and forgets all about it after two days? Do you handle this situation differently if the software costs $5 or $50? Should the price of the software enter into your reasoning? This is a good opportunity to teach your daughter about ethics.

The Garage Sale Software Deal

You've been browsing a garage sale (or a flea market or eBay) and discover that someone is offering a popular piece of commercial software at a bargain price. It's used software, but it comes with all the original documentation and packaging. Is it legal to resell commercial software like this? What if the current owner has burned a backup CD of the original CD and is still using it? How can you know if the person is breaking the licensing agreement by selling the software? Can you be liable for entering into an illegal transaction if you don't know that it's illegal?

Many computer owners face such ethical and legal conundrums. In many cases, software manufacturers have acknowledged the difficulty of some licensing restrictions. For example, some licensing agreements have clarified the use of the software for desktops and laptops, loosening the restrictions to accommodate consumers who need to travel and take the software with them. However, other dilemmas remain. In particular, software CDs are frequently passed from person to person on eBay, resold as "almost new" each time they change hands. If the software's original packaging and registration forms are passed along with each sale, this is perfectly legal (assuming no backup CDs are being retained for continued use). Of course, there is no way to know if backup CDs are being burned by each buyer/seller as the software makes the rounds.

Software piracy is a serious and pervasive problem for software manufacturers. One way to solve the problem is for manufacturers to remove all unreasonable and unenforceable restrictions and give the users the right to use and redistribute software freely. Although this strategy might sound radical and incapable of supporting the people who write software for a living, it's an alternative model for commercial software and one that actually is being

FYI: Used Software: When Can You Sell It? When Can You Buy It?

Used software can be legally resold as long as the seller does not retain a copy of the software and includes all the original documentation. Stores that buy and sell used software are generally adept at spotting pirated software, so anything you buy in a store is probably being transferred legally. There is a large secondary market for computer games and a somewhat less robust market for business software. If you find software at a flea market, look for CDs (or floppies) with the manufacturer's label and complete documentation. Handwritten labels on CDs are a sure sign of pirated software, as are CDs without documentation.

used by advocates for open source software, which is discussed later in this section.

A typical freeware license includes some standard legal disclaimers and a few restrictions on secondary distributions. For example, passing on the program to friends might be all right but only if the executable is bundled with a README document or if specific comments are left intact in a source code file. If you're new to the world of freeware and shareware, you'll be pleased to know that not all licensing agreements are written by lawyers. Some are written by people (in many cases, the programmer who wrote the software) who have no training in legalese. These agreements are often written with humor, humility, and honest originality. Reading one of these just might be the highpoint of your day. For example, some freeware licenses add a quirky twist to the usual conditions and restrictions. Many programmers just want to hear from their users, so they ask only for a quick e-mail message in return for their software. Enough people are doing this that the practice now has a name: postcardware. If you look at enough freeware licenses, you might see variations on the postcard idea. For example, Jilles Groenendijk, the author of PhonConv, requests an item or postcard related to Garfield (a cartoon character) in return for his software.

Computer programmers who write their own software licenses often produce traditional-sounding legalistic licenses. However, sometimes they write something unexpected. When you download freeware and shareware from the Net, be sure to read the licensing agreements so you won't miss any idiosyncratic licenses.

Open Source Software

Although the media focuses on all of the wealth and millionaires that have resulted from the Internet, the Internet has also inspired new models of personal freedom and community that are equally deserving of attention. Prime examples are freeware and the open source software movement. The concept of free software seems surprising to many people because they think of software as a commercial product, a means for generating profits. If you give your software away at no cost, it's hard to view it as a traditional product. It becomes a means to a different end.

Proponents of free software usually explain their concept of software in terms of two ultimate goals: total personal freedom (for the end users) and an open, cooperative development community (for the programmers). For them, the term *free* really means *nonproprietary*. In the world of software, anyone can develop nonproprietary software in a commercial setting and still charge users who use it. That is consistent with the open source concept of free software. The big catch is that you can't stop other people from giving away that software at no cost. That makes software different from other commodities.

The open source software idea has some obvious advantages. A programmer who releases open source software must release not only the actual executable program files but also all the source code files that make the software work. This enables other programmers—thousands worldwide—to see how the software works. If the software is good, some might like it enough to fix it up a little—correct a bug or add a feature they think people should have. The original author then has the option of accepting those fixes and enhancements, changing the original source code, and releasing a new version of the program. If a hundred programmers suggest changes to the software, many improvements can be made before the next release, possibly a lot more than could have been accomplished by a small number of in-house programmers (who might not have much personal interest in it). People who volunteer their services on a software project are probably maximally interested and maximally motivated to work with the software. If they are also competent programmers, the benefits of their involvement can be significant.

From a programmer's perspective, free (that is, nonproprietary) software represents personal freedom and cooperative communities. Open source software allows anyone to join a community of people drawn together by their common interest in a particular piece of software. Technical problems can be identified, discussed, and solved within this cooperative working group; communication is greatly enhanced by the Internet. Files can be shared, ideas can be discussed, and anyone can listen in. It helps to have a strong supervisor—someone who can make the call on which changes to accept and which to reject. However, that's as much control as anyone can hope to have in an open source software project. A project volunteer who disagrees with a supervisory

FYI: Some Popular Open Source Software Projects

The following are some popular open source projects under way:

- Apache, the world's most popular Web server
- Mozilla Firefox, the second most popular Web browser
- Gimp, a digital imaging program similar to Adobe's Photoshop
- Linux, an open source version of the Unix OS
- PHP, the most popular programming language for server-side scripts
- Samba, an implementation of the file-sharing protocol used by Microsoft Windows products

decision is free to use the code as the basis of an alternative open source project. However, most disagreements in the open source world are discussed and resolved within one working community, so defections and splinter groups are not as common as one might expect. If someone has a bad idea, others will explain why it's bad. If someone has a good idea, others will support it. When enough people debating a design decision bring intelligence and experience to the table and set aside economic self-interest, good decisions tend to result.

This process of software design through a cooperative community of qualified volunteers works well. People unqualified to contribute tend to watch, learn, and stay out of the way. There is no input from marketing because there is no marketing department, and there's no input from some executive in the corner office because there is no corner office. The open source system optimizes intellectual competence. Rapid communication via the Internet speeds key discussions. Programmers are free to discuss any aspect of the project with other programmers, and no restrictions apply regarding what someone can do with the software. This is the sense in which open source software is free. Many believe it's the best way to design large, complicated computer systems.

It might be wonderful to be free, but you might wonder how open source programmers are expected to put bread on the table. Do they need day jobs to subsidize their contributions to open source software? Richard M. Stallman, the president of the Free Software Association and a leader in the open source software movement, claims that better working communities for programmers and total freedom for users are not incompatible with the notion of commercial software as a product that generates revenue and profits. This perspective requires a conceptual shift from a marketplace built on suspicion and mistrust (you pay first and then you receive your goods) to an economic system in which people treat each other with trust and goodwill (you receive your goods first and then you pay). If this sounds idealistic, consider that Mr. Stallman has been living off the proceeds of freeware and goodwill for more than 15 years. He fervently believes that if people are given the opportunity to do the right thing—in this case, to pay for their freeware with a voluntary donation—they will do it. A college student strapped for cash might not get around to it for a few years, but eventually, people who are financially able to pay for something that is of value to them will pay. This is not a novel idea. Many charitable organizations rely on goodwill and the passage of time. If it works for college alumni donations, why not for software? A system of voluntary payments can create some challenging cash-flow problems, but for someone who can wait out economic downturns and the occasional slow year, it just might work.

Not convinced? You don't think there's enough goodwill out there to keep afloat an economy based on "pay if you want to pay"? It's too early to tell, but some strong evidence suggests that some people will act altruistically, even when no one is holding a gun to their heads. Consider *InfoWorld*'s Best Technical Support Award for 1997. This award is usually given to the software vendor that receives the most votes from *InfoWorld* readers. Although software support might not be one of the computer industry's more shining achievements, at least a few companies always manage to do it well, and their grateful users speak up to cast nominations and votes for the *InfoWorld* award. In 1997, the Best Technical Support Award went to the Linux user community. The Linux OS, as open source software, doesn't come with commercial technical support. Users who have questions and problems must rely on the kindness of strangers in newsgroups and chat rooms for help. This altruistic system for customer support apparently works quite well. While perhaps difficult to believe, in the Linux community free support from other users is apparently as good as, if not better than, paid commercial support that accompanies purchased software.

We can also look to Microsoft for additional evidence that open source software deserves to be taken seriously. Consider the following excerpts from "the Halloween Documents" (internal Microsoft memos leaked to the public in 1998).

> *OSS [open source software] poses a direct, short-term revenue and platform threat to Microsoft, particularly in server space. Additionally, the intrinsic parallelism and free idea exchange in OSS has benefits that are not replicable with our current licensing model and therefore present a long term developer mindshare threat.*

Linux has been deployed in mission critical, commercial environments with an excellent pool of public testimonials. . . . Linux outperforms many other UNIXes. . . . Linux is on track to eventually own the x86 UNIX market. . . .

Linux and other OSS advocates are making a progressively more credible argument that OSS software is at least as robust—if not more—than commercial alternatives. The Internet provides an ideal, high-visibility showcase for the OSS world.

The ability of the OSS process to collect and harness the collective IQ of thousands of individuals across the Internet is simply amazing. More importantly, OSS evangelization scales with the size of the Internet much faster than our own evangelization efforts appear to scale.

Open source software probably won't make anyone a billionaire, but it's a surprising and noteworthy phenomenon brought about by the Internet and the programmers who use it. The next time someone claims that the Internet is all about greed and opportunism, tell that person about open source software.

Problems and Exercises

A1. Under what conditions is it legal to resell used commercial software?

A2. When you buy used software, what two signs are tip-offs that the software is pirated?

A3. **[HANDS-ON]** Go to the Business Software Alliance site at `http://www.bsa.org/`, and scroll down to the Anti-Piracy Quiz. Take the quiz as a consumer (you will have to allow the site to run an ActiveX control). How many answers did you get right? Which ones didn't you know?

A4. **[HANDS-ON]** Sometimes commercial software is sold at a discounted rate to students. If you have one or more of these software titles, examine the software license(s). Under the terms of the license(s), are users permitted to continue to use the software after they graduate? Which software did you examine?

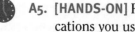 **A5.** **[HANDS-ON]** Read the licensing agreements for three software applications you use regularly. Have you unknowingly violated any of the terms of these agreements? (Your instructor must agree not to disclose any incriminating information when assigning this exercise.)

A6. **[TAKE A STAND]** Can you point to a restriction in a software license that you think is unreasonable? Do you think it's right when people violate an "unreasonable" restriction in a software license? Have you knowingly violated any such restrictions yourself? (Your instructor must agree not to disclose any incriminating information when assigning this exercise.)

A7. When Richard Stallman talks about "free" software, he is not necessarily talking about freeware. Explain what he means.

A8. Suppose you rely on open source software and you run into a problem you can't handle. Where can you go for help?

A9. What is an E.T. application? Give three examples of such applications.

A10. **[FIND IT ONLINE]** Visit `http://counter.li.org/` and find out how many Linux users have registered at that site. Then visit the link "My guess at the number of Linux users," and explain why it's so difficult to know how many people use Linux.

A11. **[FIND IT ONLINE]** A detailed definition of open source software is presented at `http://www.perens.com/OSD.html`. Review this document in order to answer the following questions:
   a. How does open source software differ from software in the public domain?
   b. Can a program be distributed under both an open source license and a commercial license?
   c. If anyone can modify and redistribute open source software, how can you know what version you're getting?
   d. Can someone make a trivial modification to an open source program and then market the slightly modified program under a commercial license?

A12. **[FIND IT ONLINE]** Search the Net and find out what UCITA is. Then read "Why You Must Fight UCITA" by Richard Stallman at `http://www.gnu.org/ philosophy/ucita.html`. Explain briefly what UCITA is and why it's a threat to the open source software movement.

A13. **[FIND IT ONLINE]** Peruse the Halloween documents at `http://www.opensource.org/halloween/` to find out what Microsoft was saying about open source software in general and Linux in particular in 1998. Then answer the following questions:

a. When were the Halloween documents written?

b. Who published the Halloween documents, and how were they obtained?

c. What two claims did Microsoft publicly advance to counter the general public's interest in Linux? (Hint: See Halloween V for an interview with Microsoft spokesperson Ed Muth.)

d. What does FUD mean, and what companies are in a position to exploit FUD?

A14. [FIND IT ONLINE] Visit `http://www.lugod.org/microsoft/ ?filter=edu` to find out how Microsoft software licenses affected public school districts in Washington and Oregon in 2002. How did the schools respond and what did Microsoft say after the story was reported?

A15. [TAKE A STAND] Read about the auditing requirements in Microsoft's Campus Agreement in `http://www.theregister.co.uk/content/ 4/25179.html`. Do you think a software license should be allowed to require an inventory of all computers regardless of the software they run, as well as a headcount of all the staff who may or may not come into contact with these computers? Are there any legal restrictions on what a software company can put into their licensing agreement? (see also `http://www.usdoj.gov/opa/pr/Pre_96/July94/ 94387.txt.html`)

E-Commerce

7.1 Taking Charge

When retail operations went high-tech, there was little for the consumer to do but sit back and watch the big guys duke it out. At first, online shopping sounded like a dream come true for retailers: no rent, no sales staff, no storefront maintenance, and minimal inventory. Just set up some software and go. But then they discovered the first rule of online retail: if another e-store undercuts your prices, you're dead. Amazon.com started in 1995 by offering 30 percent off the listed price of best-selling books. Then Barnes & Noble went online in 1997 and offered 40 percent off its bestsellers' list. Wal-Mart created its online storefront with a 45 percent discount off its bestsellers, and then Buy.com joined the circus with 50 percent discounts. The **shopping bots** (programs that search the web for you to find the best price for products you wish to buy) are in the consumer's corner, and big e-stores have to stay on top of the marketing game in order to stay in business. Profit margins are low; most online operations don't turn a profit. Brick-and-mortar stores that go online often see their traditional profits eaten up by their new online storefronts.

Chapter Goals

- Understand what you can do to protect yourself when you make purchases online
- Find out how to ensure that sensitive data is encrypted before you send it over the Net
- Learn how to check a digital certificate for an e-commerce business
- Find out how to check a secure Web server to see how strong its encryption is
- Understand what it means for commercial sites to be self-regulating
- Learn about different kinds of online auctions

Amazon.com is a major e-store success story, and it didn't turn a profit until 2001. Even so, few retailers are willing to sit on the sidelines without some sort of "Web presence." Over 100,000 e-commerce businesses were operating at the end of 1999, and online sales have soared since then (see Figure 7.1) in spite of the big dot-com crash in 2000, when many high-tech startups went under for lack of profits.

7.1.1 Buying Cars

Consider the act of buying a car. This is no longer a matter of who blinks first on the sales floor. It has been replaced by an exercise in Web research. A pre-pared buyer can go into a dealership today armed with crucial knowledge that used to be the dealership's secret weapon. For example, the buyer can know what the dealership paid for the car and with how much profit margin the dealership can work. Further, it takes only a minute or so to know what the competition has to offer on the exact same model and whether it makes sense to shop a little farther afield in order to get a better deal.

Figure 7.1

Online sales are increasing every year.

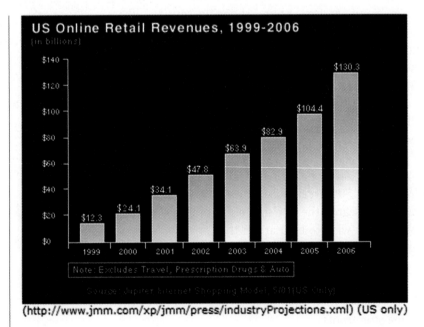

(http://www.jmm.com/xp/jmm/press/industryProjections.xml) (US only)

7.1.2 Buying Books

Suppose you want to buy a book and you want it right now. You can visit your local bookstore and pay a little more for the privilege of taking it home today. However, what if the local retail store is out of that book? What do you do? Wait one week or more for them to place a special order for the book and call you when it arrives? Or visit Amazon.com and get the book in two days—and probably for a lower price? Knowing that you have other options, you might forgo a visit to the local store altogether and just give it a call to find out about the book in question. If the book you want is out of stock, the store loses not only a sale but also the opportunity to tempt you with its aisles of specials and impulse buys. Browsing online is not the same as browsing in a retail bookstore. However, if the retail bookstore can't get you in the door, everything else is moot.

7.1.3 Buying Unusual Items

Sometimes you have to cope with an unusual one-time purchase. For example, suppose your teenage son wants an air hockey table for Christmas—it's one of those non-negotiable teenager fixations. You've probably never seen an air hockey table outside of a recreational center, and you've certainly never seen one in a store. You have no idea what they cost, what's wrong with the lower-priced models, or how hard it's going to be to find one in stock in a local store. You know that shipping costs will probably prohibit an online sale (air hockey tables are big and heavy). However, that shouldn't stop you from doing a little online research on the Web, where you can learn all you need to know about the leading manufacturers, their product lines, and their relative merits. With a little surfing, you can learn that air hockey tables typically are sold by stores that sell pool tables, and that it's easier to find local retail stores that sell them if you conduct a search for "pool tables" instead of "air hockey." If you're very lucky, you might even find a deal on a used air hockey table at eBay, a well-known auction site. In any case, you can research the situation in one day, possibly during your lunch hour, before you even make your first telephone call.

7.1.4 Shopping for Supplies

Then there are the routine shopping trips for items you need regularly. Everyone purchases certain items periodically: office supplies, disposable contact lenses, pet food, and vitamins (especially that hard-to-find kind for the iguana). You can probably buy most of these items locally. However, consider the advantages of using an online supplier:

1. You can comparison shop to find the best prices and discounts. (Be sure to take shipping costs into consideration.)

2. You can use sites that let you create a personal account. With a personal account, you can maintain a list of the items you need periodically so you don't have to track them down at the site each time you place an order.

3. After your first order, all the information for your account will have been collected, so you can probably choose **one-click shopping**, which allows you to order items without going through a registration page and without having to reenter credit card account information you entered previously on the same site (thus bypassing all possible hurdles between you and a fast impulse buy). When all goes well (no overloaded servers or Net congestion), you can place a standing order at an e-store in about two or three minutes over a slow modem connection and in less than a minute over a broadband connection. You might have to wait two to seven days for the selected items to reach you, but that's not likely to be a problem with recurring purchases because most people stock up on items they need to purchase frequently; with a little planning, you can place an order a week before you actually need the items.

Whereas e-commerce might not be as simple for the e-stores to manage, it's hard to imagine a better world for consumers. Brick-and-mortar stores are still an option and will continue to be available for traditional shopping trips—the shopping mall will not disappear anytime soon. However, the Web offers additional options and information to make consumers better educated, more aware of their choices, and better prepared to spend wisely. Marketing experts are studying the buying patterns of consumers online to understand what it takes for a business to succeed online. The data is relatively easy to collect, since every consumer leaves a digital trail (see Figure 7.2).

Online shopping can be wonderful. However, it has some risks. If you understand how things can go wrong, you'll find it easier to protect yourself. All consumers need to learn a few basics for safe shopping online.

Figure 7.2

Collecting
e-commerce data
is a business all
its own.

Nielsen//NetRatings

A global leader in Internet media and
market research

**United States: Top 10 Parent Companies
Week ending August 21, 2006
Home Panel**

Parent Name	Unique Audience (000)	Reach %	Time Per Person
Microsoft	60,445	52.48	00:33:13
Yahoo!	55,875	48.51	00:53:31
Time Warner	51,742	44.93	01:17:20
Google	48,477	42.09	00:14:58
News Corp. Online	26,176	22.73	00:44:35
eBay	22,911	19.89	00:36:50
InterActiveCorp	17,544	15.23	00:10:23
Amazon	12,628	10.96	00:10:42
RealNetworks, Inc.	11,950	10.38	00:27:25
Walt Disney Internet Group	11,882	10.32	00:18:14

Online Shopping Risks and Safeguards

Purchasing merchandise online does pose some risks, but you can take precautions to protect yourself. For example, using credit cards is safer than using personal checks and money orders. When you send someone a check or money order as payment, you might have no recourse if your order is damaged, not as requested, or lost in transit. When you use a credit card, you can always complain to the credit card issuer for help with an unresolved dispute with the vendor. Credit card issuers are required by the federal Fair Credit Billing Act to limit your potential loss to $50 when disputed charges are made on your credit card, provided that you report such charges in a timely manner. (Note: At the time of this writing, the major credit card companies all offer zero liability—no charges for credit card thefts.) Retailers and credit card issuers absorb the bulk of any losses resulting from theft of a credit card or its account number.

Note that bank cards and debit cards do not afford you the same protections as do credit cards. Be careful not to confuse the two. Credit cards are much safer than debit cards for online transactions.

If you want to buy something online, make sure that the address of the page on which you enter your credit card account information begins with `https://` Note the addition of an "s" before the colon; the "s" means that the page is secure, that is, protected by the **Secure Sockets Layer (SSL)** encryption protocol—an effective safeguard against anyone who might want to steal your card information in transit. SSL and encryption are discussed in detail in this chapter and the next.

In addition, your browser should display a special icon to indicate whether the Web page is secure, either a key or a padlock. Look in the upper right corner of your IE browser window adjacent to the location bar, for this icon. (Other browsers may display the padlock in the lower-left or lower-right-hand corner, directly in the address bar, and/or in the tab for that window.) A locked padlock indicates that the page is secure. Figure 7.3 shows a locked padlock—the page is secure.

Although you can examine a Web page to see if it is secure, you unfortunately have no way of knowing how secure the computers are that store your order history and billing data. If your order is encrypted during transit but then stored without encryption on a public server that is not properly maintained, your order history and billing data could be at risk long after your transaction has been completed.

Maintaining a secure server and monitoring network activity for possible security breaches requires the services of a professional system administrator. If an e-store outsources its storefront operation to a reputable, professionally managed e-commerce service, the e-store is paying that service to manage its storefront security. But some e-stores try to handle their storefront operations in-house. In that case, a full-time professional system administrator represents a nontrivial payroll expenditure, and many small business operators may not realize that this is a necessary business expense. Smaller companies that cannot afford experienced system administrators pose the greatest risk. However, even large corporations with no prior experience in e-commerce will go through a settling-in period during which mistakes may be made. Most companies try to cut corners wherever possible, and some view the costs asso-

Figure 7.3

The padlock icon indicates whether a Web page is secure or unsecure.

Locked—Secure

RISKS ARE EVERYWHERE

Over the past four years, there has been an enormous amount of publicity about the dangers of credit card fraud on the Net. . . . Yet, as many savvy Internet shoppers now know, the reality is that it's actually much safer to enter your credit card number on a secure online order form than it is to give your credit card to a waiter at a restaurant. After all, what's to stop the waiter from writing down your credit card number and placing orders on the phone with it later? And research shows that the rate of fraudulent purchases made by cell phones is much higher than credit card fraud on the Net.

— Internet ScamBusters

ciated with top-rate system security as unnecessary. Unfortunately, consumers can't know if any given e-store operation is being managed by professionals who are knowledgeable about computer security. A large corporation with a thriving e-commerce operation is more likely to hire the necessary technical personnel to keep its servers safe from cyberattacks. A small or medium-sized company that is trying out Web-based sales for the first time may be much less secure. But before you get too caught up in risk assessments, remember to put these risks in their proper perspective. Whenever you use a credit card in a restaurant or over the phone, you are subjecting yourself to comparable risks. The only difference is that you are probably not worrying about it in those more familiar contexts.

If you do a lot of shopping online, you'll end up with accounts at different sites so that you can track your orders and you'll probably take advantage of one-click shopping if offered. Most people pick the same user ID and the same password for each new e-commerce site with which they do business. This is like using the same key for your home, your office, your car, and your safe deposit box. It might be more convenient, but you stand to lose a lot if someone steals that key. You should always select a new password for each site. This can be cumbersome, but all browsers include password managers.

Your browser will probably offer, in a pop-up window, to remember your logon password to a particular site (see Figure 7.4). If you click the Yes button, IE (in this example) will automatically enter that password for you the next time you visit that particular site. As long as your computer is secure and no one else can ever visit that site on your computer without your knowledge, this is fine.

However, consider what could happen if your computer were stolen (a plausible scenario, particularly for a laptop). Anyone using your computer could stumble on the sites for which you've set up automatic password entries along with one-click shopping: with a little luck, all he or she has to do is visit your browser's history list. If you told your computer to remember your ISP password along with your one-click shopping passwords, a thief could be charging items to your online accounts in less than a minute. Once someone gets past the password protection for an e-store, he or she can change your

Figure 7.4
Be careful how
you answer this
question.

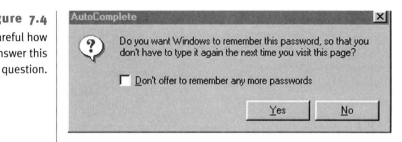

shipping address, buy all sorts of things, and charge it all to you. If you use one-click shopping, you must vigilantly protect the passwords that protect your information. With a bit of bad luck, those passwords might be all that stand between you and credit card fraud. If the possibility of theft exists, activate password protection for your computer if provided (and most do, especially laptops). If so secured, a user must enter a password before the system can be used. While not perfect, securing your computer with password protection can certainly help to limit your losses.

The technology that protects sensitive information on the Internet is discussed in Section 7.3 and Chapter 8. This section concentrates on practical advice.

If you follow these safeguards habitually, you'll probably never have a bad e-store encounter as far as the electronic end of things is concerned. Do take the time to read the policy statements for each e-store with which you're considering doing business. They are not all the same; after you've seen a few, you'll get a feel for what's typical. Figure 7.5 shows a policy page from Priceless-Inkjet.com that goes into more detail than most do. For example, this e-store says it deletes all credit card account information from its system once received, since onsite security breeches are the most common cause of credit card data theft online. This policy indicates that this company cares about its customers—good news for consumers concerned about security.

TIP: Acceptable Levels of Risk

Before you enter your credit card account number on a Web page, check whether the Web page is secure. If it is, your risk is very small. If you feel safe placing a credit card order over the telephone or if you allow store clerks to discard credit card impression carbons without tearing them up in front of you first, you have no reason to worry about making online credit card transactions. All these scenarios carry some amount of risk, but most people live with such risks in exchange for the convenience of fast transactions.

TIP: When You Shop Online, Remember These Tips

- Use a credit card instead of checks, money orders, bank cards, or debit cards.
- Examine the URL for the `https://` prefix, and check for a locked padlock or unbroken key icon before entering any credit card account information.
- Do business with reputable companies that have been selling online for at least a year.
- Do not use the same password for all of your e-commerce accounts.
- Shop with merchants whom you know and trust.
- Look for and read each site's delivery, return, and privacy policies.
- Be careful not to press the ORDER NOW button more than once.
- Never send credit card account information via e-mail.
- Keep a record of your transactions, and save all online receipts until your shipment arrives with all the items you ordered in good condition.
- Use a shopping bot (`http://www.botspot.com/BOTSPOT/Windows/Shopping_Bots/m/`) to comparison shop for big-ticket items.

Unfortunately, many things can go wrong even when people do their jobs well and all the support technology is working correctly. The e-store might ship the wrong item, and you'll have to exchange it. You might order the wrong item and want to return it. You might get what you ordered, but it might be defective or otherwise unacceptable. This is when you'll be glad you read the return policy before placing your order. As with any business, serious customer service begins when something goes wrong. So listen to friends who've had experience with e-stores. You might want to avoid any site that has a tale of woe associated with it.

Some sites give you onsite updates regarding your order (see Figure 7.6). If an e-store ships its orders via UPS, you can track your shipment by using the UPS Package Tracker (`http://www.ups.com/tracking/tracking.html`). E-tailers often integrate this technology directly into their shopping site. UPS's package tracking is especially nice if you must wait more than a day or two for something (see Figure 7.7). At the very least, the e-store should confirm your order via e-mail within 24 hours of receipt. It should also send you a note to let you know when your item has left its warehouse.

If you want to take online security one step further, you can check certain additional information about the e-store before you place an order. A Web server that is set up to protect sensitive data being sent over the Internet is assigned a digital certificate. A **digital certificate** makes it possible to keep sensitive information sent over the Internet safe from prying eyes. Your browser

Figure 7.5

A reassuring security policy

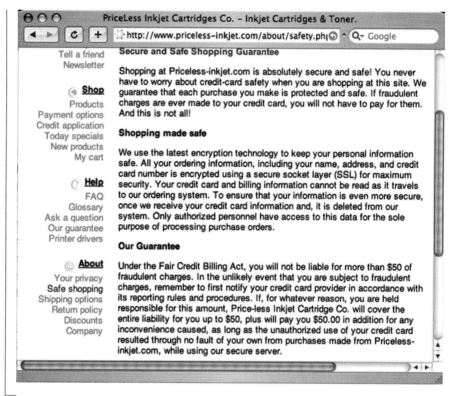

Figure 7.6

People like to track the status of their online orders.

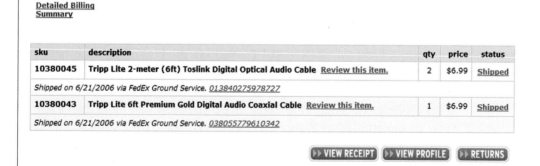

watches for a digital certificate whenever a Web server asks for a secure connection. The browser needs the digital certificate in order to encrypt your personal data. Unencrypted data sent over the Internet is *in the open*. This is like sending a message on the back of a postcard—anyone along the way can read

Figure 7.7
UPS online tracking keeps you informed while you wait.

All rights in the article and photograph above are owned by United Parcel Service of America, Inc. Copyright 1994–2006.

it. Sensitive information should always be encrypted before it goes out over the Net. Encrypted data is safer on the Internet than unencrypted data. If a server has a digital certificate, all data headed for that server can be encrypted for safe passage. If no certificate is available, the data cannot be encrypted.

TIP: Rating the E-Stores—and Everything Else

If you're considering buying from an e-store you don't know, first check out what other shoppers have to say about their experiences. Here are some sites that rate e-stores for you.

BizRate.com   `http://www.bizrate.com/`
Gomez.com   `http://gomez.com/`
Epinions.com   `http://www.epinions.com/`

You can also find sites at which consumers sound off about the products they've bought (online and off). For example, Amazon.com displays book reviews by readers, and CNet.com collects user reviews for computer software and hardware. Check out Epinions.com for a massive collection of consumer reviews on everything that's ever been bought or sold.

Consumer product reviews can be instructive and might alert you to various pros and cons you'll want to consider when researching your options. People love to talk about their experiences with beloved (or cursed) consumer products on the Internet—it seems that everyone wants to be a reviewer for something in their lives.

(Encryption on the Internet is discussed in detail in Chapter 8.) Servers that use encryption to prevent unauthorized people from reading transmitted messages are considered to be **secure Web sites**. Pages hosted at these sites are considered to be **secure Web pages**.

Your Web browser is prepared to accept a digital certificate issued by a recognized certificate authority. A **certificate authority (CA)** is an organization that can certify the identity of a certificate holder, much as a notary public vouches for the legitimacy of a notarized signature. From time to time, your browser might need to update its database of recognized CAs. If the CA database is not up to date, your browser might not recognize an otherwise legitimate CA and would therefore reject (or at least warn you about) any certificates signed by that CA. You can always examine the database of trusted CAs recognized by your browser (see Figure 7.8).

Your browser can show you everything you need to know to check an e-store's digital certificate. If you're running IE, click the closed padlock at the bottom of your browser window. You'll see a window that displays the following (see Figure 7.9):

- The name of the site that owns the certificate (in this case, `secure.buy.com`)
- The name of the CA that issued the certificate for the site (VeriSign)
- The time period for which the certificate is valid (from 10/20/2004 to 11/4/2006)

Figure 7.8
Your browser
trusts the CAs in
its CA database.

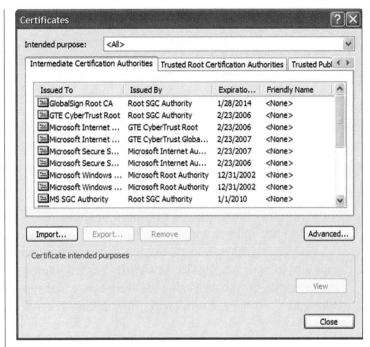

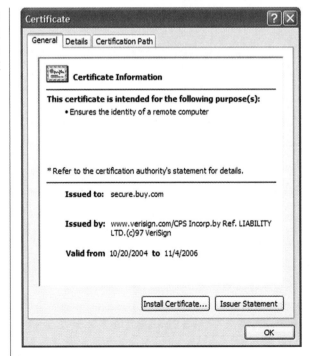

Figure 7.9
A digital
certificate viewed
with IE

TIP: How to Find Your Browser's Trusted CAs

In IE 7.0, select Internet Options from the Tools menu and go to the Content tab. Click Certificates and then select either the Intermediate Certification Authorities tab or the Trusted Root Certification Authorities tab. All the CAs known to IE are listed under these two tabs.

In Navigator 8.1, select Options from the Tools menu and select Advanced from the Options panel. In the Options panel, scroll down to Certificates and click the check box to its left. Then click the Manage Certificates button and select the Authorities tab.

With other browsers, you may need to click on a "View Certificate" button to see this information.

Navigator makes it very easy to access security information about a page/site you are viewing. To see security-related information, click the green shield next to the tab displaying the secure page. A display like the one shown in Figure 7.10 appears displaying information regarding the "trustworthi-

Figure 7.10

Trust settings viewed with Navigator.

ness" of that site. You can change the trust settings (allow/disallow cookies, pop-ups, etc.) for this site by clicking in the Advanced tab (see Figure 7.11).

Before you send your credit card account information to an e-store, pull up the certificate for the Web site (you must be on a secure Web page at the site to see it), and check the following three safeguards:

1. The domain for the current Web page's URL matches the domain listed on the certificate.
2. The CA listed on the certificate is one of the CAs in your browser's CA database.
3. The certificate's expiration date has not passed.

If you do a lot of online shopping, you may someday encounter a problem with a site certificate. Unless you've changed some security preference settings, your browser should be configured to warn you about possible problems with site certificates before you transmit any sensitive data. For example, your browser may not recognize the CA behind a site certificate (see Figure 7.12).

Figure 7.11

Changing the trust settings for a specific Web site

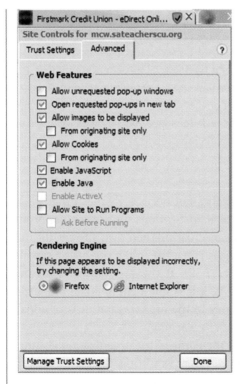

Figure 7.12

What if the browser doesn't recognize a CA?

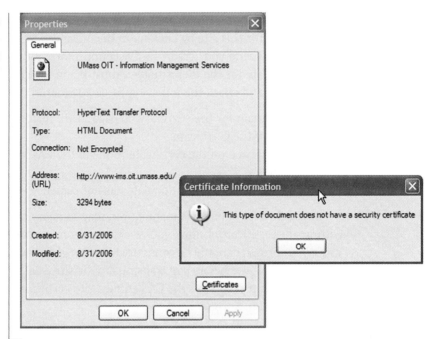

FYI: Isn't My Browser Checking These Certificates for Me?

Yes, your browser should be doing all this checking for you. But checking a site certificate yourself will give you some extra peace of mind. Plus, it's not a bad idea even if you aren't looking for peace of mind. It takes less than a minute to check a site certificate, and a manual check does give you a little extra added protection, just in case your browser isn't doing its job properly.

An unknown CA does not necessarily mean that the site is run by criminals. Some educational institutions and other nonprofit organizations are simply saving money by creating their own site certificates. (Commercial CAs charge for their services.) Or a site might not have a certificate because it's not necessary (see Figure 7.12). If you are familiar with the Web site and the organization behind it, if it is not a commercial organization, and if you are not transferring money to the organization, it is reasonable to enter the site in spite of your browser's warning.

If you recognize the name of the organization issuing the certificate, and it's the organization you were expecting, the certificate is probably legitimate.

And remember: If no money is changing hands, there is less to worry about anyway.

If you are at a commercial Web site and your browser issues a warning about the site certificate, that's another story. This happened to me several years ago when I was shopping at a computer hardware store named Egghead.com, which has since gone out of business (see Figure 7.13).

Clicking the More Info button (shown in Figure 7.13) displays the actual certificate being used by reno.onsale.com (see Figure 7.14). The dates were valid (I encountered this certificate while shopping online in December 1999), and the CA (RSA Data Security) was well known. However, the domain names didn't match. The Web server was named reno.onsale.com, but the certificate was issued to a server named reno.egghead.com. *These names should have been identical.* Something was wrong with this site certificate.

As a rule, avoid any site that doesn't have its site certificate in order. A problem with a digital certificate might be the result of an administrative error (similar in severity to someone forgetting to send in a bill payment on time), but a solid e-store operation should be attending to details like this with the utmost care. In this particular case, a little online research shed some light on the reno.onsale.com site certificate. According to an Egghead press release, Egghead and OnSale merged on November 3, 1999, and integrated their online sales operations. The original Egghead server was

Figure 7.13

A warning about a possible problem at a commercial site

Figure 7.14

Checking the site
certificate

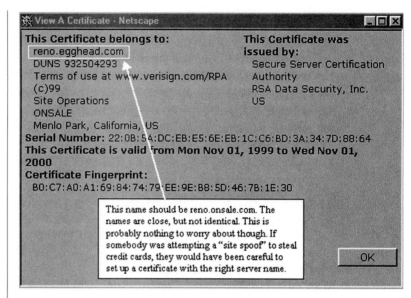

probably named `reno.egghead.com` (the one listed on the certificate). After
the merger, we might conjecture that the e-store either renamed its server or
started using a new server named `reno.onsale.com`. Note that this certificate
was created November 1, 1999, very near the time of the merger. The host
name mix-up probably happened when the newly reorganized operations staff
forgot to worry about the new server names and the old site certificate.

If you enjoy puzzles and guessing games, you can try to investigate dis-
crepancies like this and decide for yourself whether the risk is worth taking.
(For the record, I completed my online transaction with Egghead without any
problems.) For people with better things to do, the easy solution is to simply
back out of any transaction if your browser issues a warning about the site
certificate.

Chapter 8 revisits CAs and site certificates in greater detail. For now,
remember the following:

- Each e-store should send a site certificate to your browser.
- View this certificate before you send sensitive information to the site
  with your browser.
- Before sending your credit card account number to a site, check the
  site's current digital certificate.
- The name of the certificate owner should match the domain name of
  the current URL.

- The name of the CA on the certificate should be a trusted CA.
- The certificate should not have expired.

TIP: Craigslist.com

Craigslist, founded in 1999, is an online service that provides many of the services originally provided by your local newspaper. On Craigslist you can look for a job, housing, goods and services, social activities, a date, community information, and just about anything else, all in a relatively commercial-free environment, and all for free (see Figure 7.15). This is a particularly good place to sell items like furniture that are too difficult to sell on eBay because of the shipping complications. A local flavor of Craigslist is available in over 300 sites in all 50 states and over 50 countries.

Figure 7.15
Austin, Texas
Craigslist.com
Web site

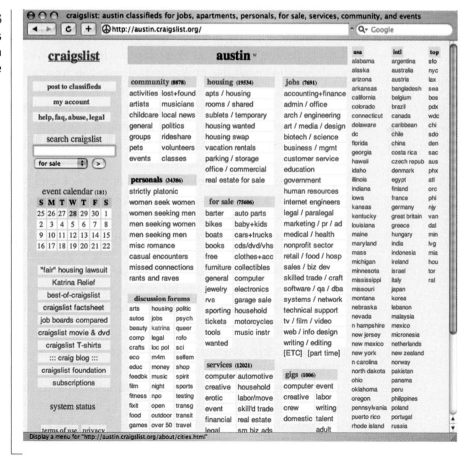

Your browser will also be looking for problems with digital certificates, so a transaction that doesn't prompt a browser alert is probably safe. But it never hurts to run a manual check yourself, and if you ever do see a browser warning about a site certificate, it is wise to back out of the transaction for safety's sake.

7.3 Secure Servers and Secure Web Pages

In 1995, Netscape introduced the Secure Sockets Layer (SSL) protocol for transmitting private documents securely via the Internet. SSL has been instrumental in the growth of e-commerce on the Web and is now an industry standard. The installation of SSL on an e-commerce site eliminates a number of potential security problems.

- **Site spoofing** is the deceptive art of setting up a counterfeit Web site that looks identical to some other legitimate Web site. Anyone with a basic knowledge of Web page design can spoof a site. Even the site's URL can be engineered to look familiar, if only at a glance. A wary user, however, might notice what appears to be (but isn't) a typographical error in the URL. If unwary consumers can be routed to the counterfeit Web site, many credit card account numbers could conceivably be collected before anyone recognizes and reports a problem.
- **Unauthorized disclosure** is the practice of sending unencrypted data from a browser to a Web server, thereby enabling hackers to intercept the transmission and obtain sensitive information.
- **Unauthorized action** is an intrusion associated with unauthorized access to and modification of the pages on a Web server in subtle and destructive or obvious and embarrassing ways.
- **Data alteration** is the interception of unencrypted data sent from a browser to a Web server and alteration of that data en route, either maliciously or accidentally.

All modern Web browsers support SSL, so users don't have to use Navigator in order to benefit from the protocol. A Web page URL that begins with the prefix https:// (note the addition of the "s" before the colon) indicates that the Web server is prepared to offer a secure connection to your browser. Recall that if your browser is SSL-enabled, a closed padlock in the

padlock (or no padlock at all) indicates that the connection is not secure. You might also see an alert box like that shown in Figure 7.16, but alert boxes pop up only if your browser is configured to display one each time you access a secure Web site (see Figure 7.17).

Figure 7.16

Optional alert boxes help you stay safe.

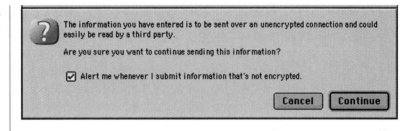

Figure 7.17

You decide which alert boxes you want to see.

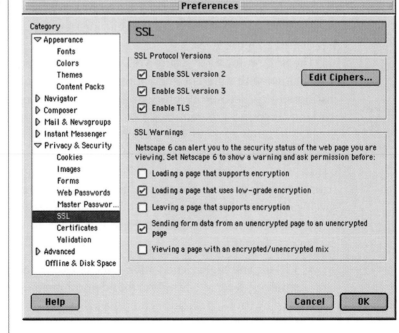

A secure SSL connection guarantees the following operations:

- **Authentication** Users can verify the actual owner of the Web site by checking the site digital certificate (as described in Section 7.2).

- **Message privacy** SSL encrypts all information moving between a Web server and a browser by using public-key encryption and unique session keys (see Chapter 8).
- **Message integrity** When a message is sent, the sending computer generates a signature code based on the message's content and sends that code along with the message. The receiving computer generates its own signature code for the file content just received. If the message was not altered en route, these two signature codes agree. If even a single character in the message was altered, the receiving computer generates a different code and sounds an alert—the software responsible for decrypting the message issues a warning about the legitimacy of the document. When the two codes agree, the result is message integrity and both parties can be confident they are working with unaltered messages.

The mechanisms underlying message privacy and message integrity are explained in more detail in Chapter 8. For now, you need to understand only that SSL is the right protocol for moving sensitive information via the Internet (see Figure 7.18).

The SSL protocol for secure Web-based communications can be used in combination with different encryption algorithms. An **algorithm** is a set of instructions spelled out in sufficient detail so that a programmer can write a working computer program based on those instructions. As you will see in Chapter 8, some encryption algorithms are harder to break than others. If you're curious about the strength of the encryption algorithms a specific e-store uses, you can always check the digital certificate to find out how strong the encryption is. Encryption strength is measured by bit counts. More specifically, these bit counts refer to the length of a session key (see the Above & Beyond section in Chapter 8). Here is a guide to the relative levels of encryption strength.

- **128-bit and higher encryption (strong encryption):** This is the strongest level of encryption found in commercial Web sites. Always used by banks, insurance companies, health delivery services, and most e-store operations nowadays. No one in the world can break this level of encryption.
- **64-bit encryption (medium-level encryption):** Not the best, but still quite secure. Only the U.S. National Security Agency (NSA) can break this level of encryption. (The NSA doesn't disclose its code-cracking

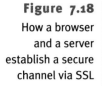

Figure 7.18

How a browser and a server establish a secure channel via SSL

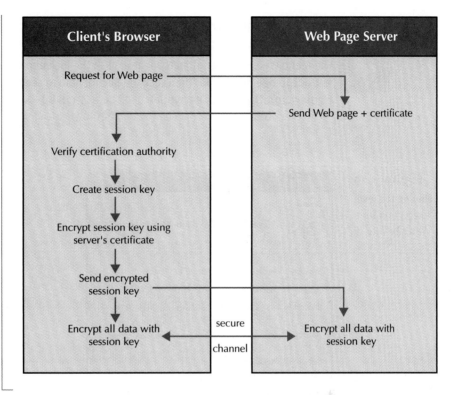

capabilities, but cryptography experts believe that the NSA must have this capability.)

- **56-bit encryption (medium-level encryption):** Somewhat safe—but probably not for long. A crime ring might be able to crack a 56-bit key today, but only with the help of a very expensive code-breaking computer. In a few more years, this level of encryption will be too weak to be of any use on the Internet.

- **40-bit encryption (weak encryption):** At one time, 40-bit encryption was the industry standard for safe commercial transactions online. However, 40-bit encryption is no longer adequate for commercial purposes.

If you want to feel nervous about something, think about all of the nondigital transfers of your credit card account information. It makes no sense to worry about giving out your credit card account information over the Net if you aren't at least a little worried about doing so everywhere else.

TIP: Checking the Strength of a Site's Encryption

To use IE to discover how strongly encrypted a site is, select "Properties" from the File Menu (see Figure 7.19). In Navigator, click the locked padlock icon on the lower left side to open Page Info. Then click the Security tab to see the encryption type (see Figure 7.20). The level of encryption used here is 128-bit—strong.

Figure 7.19

Finding the level of encryption for a Web site with IE

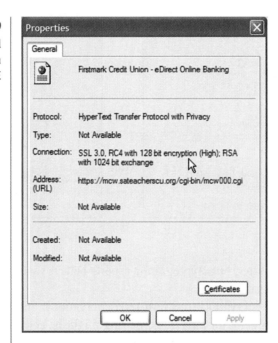

TIP: Where Are You Taking Risks?

Before you read this chapter, you might have felt safe about using your credit card on the Web, but now the idea might be making you nervous. You really shouldn't worry. Sending your credit card account number over an SSL connection is safer than sending it over a telephone line to a mail-order catalog, giving it to a waitress in a restaurant, or giving it to a clerk in an upscale retail store. The chances of it being stolen in those more traditional scenarios are much greater than during an SSL transfer.

Figure 7.20

Netscape Page Info, Security tab information

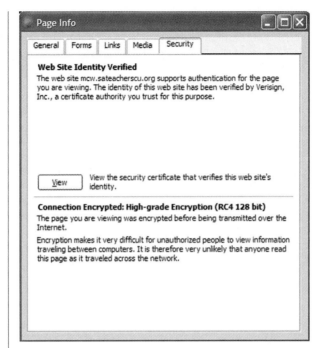

7.4 Commercial Sites and Self-Regulation

The world of e-commerce is advancing at a breakneck pace. Although security, privacy, and taxation raise many difficult questions, the U.S. government has been very reluctant to intervene in the evolution of e-commerce. The No-Electronic Theft Act was passed in 1997, and the Digital Millennium Copyright Act took effect in 1998. The Children's Online Privacy Protection Act and the Electronic Signatures in Global and National Commerce Act went into effect in 2000, and the government issued new, less stringent encryption export regulations in 2000 as well. The Cyber Security Enhancement Act was signed into law in 2002, and the Online Privacy Protection Act was moving through Congress at the time of this writing. These are all federal laws that shape the behavior of U.S. citizens and institutions online. This may seem like a lot of laws, but Congress has debated and rejected many more.

Why is the federal government so cautious about passing laws to regulate online businesses and business practices? What is the rationale for this hands-off attitude toward the Internet? The answer seems to be based on a commitment by federal legislators best described as "less is more." Many politicians believe that U.S. citizens want less interference from big government and more freedom to let businesses regulate themselves. Washington thinks that businesses know better than anyone what American consumers want, and that the businesses will not engage in business practices that are offensive or otherwise unwanted by the general population. It is, after all, in the best interests of businesses to give consumers what they want. Government has no business regulating American businesses. But is this right? Can businesses be trusted to regulate their own behaviors on behalf of consumers? Is what's best for business really what's best for consumers?

The Federal Trade Commission (FTC) acknowledged in 1997 the concerns about the adequacy of self-regulation on the Internet. In that year, the FTC held a hearing to explore the problem of privacy on the Internet and to determine whether government regulation was needed. There were arguments both pro and con. At the close of the hearings, FTC Chairman Robert Pitofsky commented:

> *There has been some talk, especially in the last hour or so, about whether voluntary guidelines ever work. . . . Believe it or not, there are some people who think government regulation doesn't work all that well either. And in an era in which all of government must do more with less, you cannot afford to ignore the possibility that cooperation and collaboration will lead to the appropriate result.*

People who view government regulations as intrusive prefer to see industry adopt self-regulating standards. Indeed, the desire to avoid federal privacy regulation was so great that Microsoft Corp. and Netscape Communications Corp., bitter rivals in the Internet market, pledged to work together on voluntary industry standards.

Advocates for self-regulation point to some notable instances in which industry has demonstrated that it can be responsive to public opinion. For example, in 1990 Lotus Development Corp. teamed with the consumer credit bureau Equifax to produce a database, called *Marketplace*, of 120 million consumer profiles consisting of names, marital status, estimated income, and purchasing habits. Lotus planned to market the data on a CD-ROM for $700. Word of this got out on the Internet, and privacy rights advocates initiated a letter-writing campaign to stop the project. In a short time, Lotus received

30,000 letters from angry Internet users who objected to the project. Sensing a public relations disaster, the company quietly dropped the project.

More recently, AOL in 1997 reversed itself regarding a plan to sell subscriber telephone numbers. AOL reserves the right to sell personal information about its subscribers to direct marketers, and it was about to add telephone numbers to its data sales. Word got out, the media voiced widespread criticism of the plan, and AOL backed down.

This shows that at least some companies are sensitive to public opinion and want to comply with emerging industry standards on a voluntary basis. On the other hand, voluntary self-regulation could be easily side-stepped by smaller companies that struggle to survive, larger companies that maintain a low public profile, or very large corporations that are simply not worried about public opinion. Whenever an industry relies on voluntary compliance, inevitably some of its members violate the guidelines to gain a competitive advantage.

Privacy policies are an interesting case study of the effectiveness of self-regulation on the Internet, if only because the goals of commercial marketing departments are at odds with the privacy rights of consumers. Consider the case of DoubleClick, Inc., the largest ad server and consumer profiling operation on the Internet. In 1999, a proposed merger between DoubleClick and Abacus Direct Corp., a marketing firm that maintains databases on consumer buying habits, attracted media attention and opposition from many privacy advocacy groups, including the Electronic Privacy Information Center, Junkbusters, and Privacy International. At issue were the potential privacy violations that such a merger would enable, violations that would not be tolerated in many European countries in which nonconsensual data collection is illegal. DoubleClick argued that it offers consumers an opt-out option and that only 10 people, out of 75 million ad viewers, choose to opt out each month. The obvious explanation for this is that perhaps only 10 people in 75 million know enough about what's going on to track down the opt-out page

TIP: Personal Privacy Is Respected in Europe

Personal privacy rights are well established in Europe. Within the European Union, businesses accept the dictum that personal data released to one organization, for one purpose, should not be distributed to other organizations without the permission of the individual being described. This is a simple rule of conduct that gives Europeans much more control over their personal information than we have in the United States.

at DoubleClick's Web site. Moreover, DoubleClick claimed that it is in compliance with the self-regulation policies promoted by the marketing industry (this presumably consists of offering notice and consent to users). The proposed merger between DoubleClick and Abacus was completed at the end of 1999 without government interference. DoubleClick is unlikely to alter its extremely successful consumer-profiling operation for the sake of placating a few privacy advocates.

When consumer interests and business interests collide, the best weapon for the consumer is a widespread boycott. A boycott backed up by a visible public protest is one way to promote stronger self-regulation and voluntary controls. However, in the case of the Internet, many business practices are embedded in the technologies of the Web (for example, banner ads), and people can't boycott DoubleClick unless they know what cookies are and how to block them. It takes time to educate consumers. DoubleClick retains the upper hand, thanks to a largely ignorant user population.

On the other hand, self-regulation does seem to work admirably when the best interests of business and consumers do not collide. The widespread adoption of data encryption for sensitive online communications is a good example of industry self-regulation that is in step with basic economic survival. No one had to pass a law requiring e-commerce sites to use encryption for credit card transactions, and the adoption of SSL by commercial Web sites is an obvious win for both businesses and consumers.

7.5 Online Auctions

Online auctions link buyers with sellers who might never find each other any other way. Hard-to-find items might be no further away than the right search query, and prices are subject to the simple rules of supply and demand. When all goes well, the seller is happy, the buyer is happy, and everyone will tell you how a particular online auction site, such as eBay (see Figure 7.21), has changed their lives. Millions of transactions take place at online auctions every day.

Participating in online auctions also involves risk. Online auction sites have topped Internet Fraud Watch's (`http://www.fraud.org/`) list of popular Internet scams since its inception in 1997. In 2005, the Federal Trade Commission (FTC) received more than 70,000 complaints about Internet auctions, three times more than the number received four years earlier. The FTC, Justice Department, U.S. Postal Inspection Service, and other federal agencies

Figure 7.21

All sorts of things are sold on eBay.

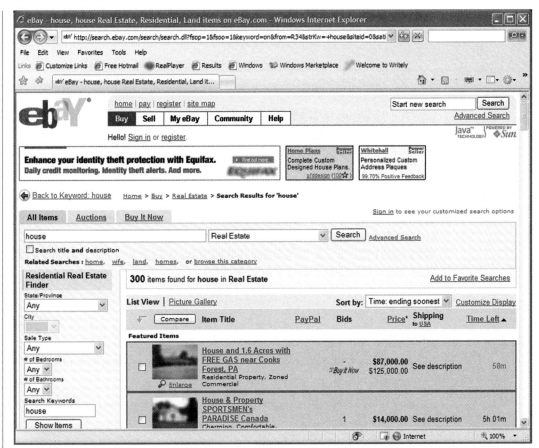

These materials have been reproduced with the permission of eBay, Inc. 2006 EBAY INC. ALL RIGHTS RESERVED.

have filed dozens of law enforcement actions concerning online auction fraud. At the same time, the number of complaints is probably growing no faster than the number of people who use eBay, the largest online auction site on the Net. According to eBay, only 1 in 25,000 eBay transactions is reported as fraudulent. Indeed, 212 million people used eBay in the third quarter, 2006, exchanging $12.6 billion worth of goods. eBay could never be this successful if people were getting burned left and right.

Before buying an item at an online auction, do some homework and proceed with caution. On your first visit to an auction site, look around to find

FYI: eBay Ceases Reporting Fraud Statistics

In the fall of 2003, eBay removed the link from its Web site to the National Consumer's League fraud center. eBay now claims that 0.01 percent to 0.001 percent of its auctions involve fraud.

FYI: eBay Has Ethics

eBay is a trading post for almost everything under the sun, but not quite everything. eBay does not allow people to post auctions from a long list of prohibited items including animals, firearms, prescription drugs, surveillance equipment, and tobacco products. eBay actively monitors its auctions to make sure sellers follow the rules, and eBay also employs full-time fraud investigators to handle complaints from buyers. Over 100,000 people run successful full-time businesses based on eBay auctions, and eBay has sponsored a number of charity auctions, including the Auction for America, during which eBay raised $7 million for the victims of September 11, 2001. eBay operates on the premise that most people can be trusted to do the right thing, and it looks like plenty of people agree.

out how it operates. Most sites are just fancy bulletin boards for public notices. The site assumes no responsibility for the accuracy of its posts or the integrity of its sellers. Look for sites that post fraud warnings and offer the following features:

- Escrow services for expensive items (see the description later in this section)
- Feedback areas
- Easy-to-follow complaint procedures
- A policy for removing problem vendors

If you see an item that interests you, find out anything you can about the seller. If it's a company, contact the Better Business Bureau (BBB) (http://www.bbb.org) and see if any complaints have been filed. Be aware, however, that not all legitimate companies are members of the BBB. Also, no record at the BBB means only that no one has filed a complaint against a company; it doesn't mean the company is perfect. Having said that, a clean record with the BBB should at least reassure you that thousands of customers are not clamoring for legal action or restitution. If the auction site offers online feedback from other customers, check out what they say. Of course, feedback com-

FYI: How Does eBay Work?

A seller pays $.25 to post an item. The listing is created when the seller fills out a simple form on the eBay Web site. A file that contains a photograph of the item can also be uploaded to eBay for inclusion in the listing. If the seller wishes, the listing can appear in boldface type for an extra $2 or be listed under Featured Auctions at the top of eBay's homepage for $99.

Buyers find items by browsing the categories or conducting keyword searches. A fixed amount of time (usually 5 to 12 days) is set for each auction, and the highest bidder at the end of that time period wins the auction. The buyer and seller mutually arrange for payment and shipping. The buyer can expect to receive the purchase in a week or two.

ments are not completely above suspicion either; for example, a seller might post bogus messages to bolster his or her image. Furthermore, an upstanding seller who is just getting started will have no track record.

Sales transactions with private sellers are riskier than transactions with commercial retailers. Consumer protection laws apply only to commercial businesses, so if you have problems with a private seller, you are on your own. A legitimate private seller should be happy to provide you with his or her name, street address (don't accept a P.O. box address), and telephone number. Avoid transactions that can't be backed up with this much information.

Never pay for an item in cash unless you can first examine the item. Paying with a credit card gives you the greatest protection should you need to return the item. However, many sellers at online auctions are not merchants and therefore can't process a credit card transaction. In this case, a good alternative is payment via PayPal (`http://www.paypal.com`). And for more expensive items, always use an **escrow service**, which will withhold your payment from the seller until you've received your item and deemed it acceptable. In some cases you might be able to arrange for a COD shipment (although that option is very risky for the seller).

Until you become better educated about how online auctions work, follow these tips:

- Start with inexpensive items.
- Work with large, well-known auction sites. (eBay is the largest.)
- Deal with sellers who are willing to give you their telephone numbers.
- For expensive items, always use an escrow service.

If you have trouble with a transaction, report the incident to the National Fraud Information Center (`http://www.fraud.org/`) , which will relay the report to the appropriate federal, state, or local law enforcement agencies.

Although there are hundreds, possibly thousands, of online auction sites at this time, eBay is the largest and most visible. At any given time, it lists over 7 million items in more than 18,000 categories. It draws over 4 million visitors each week and actually turns a profit (unlike so many Internet companies that depend on venture capital and air to get by). eBay seems to have struck a chord in a commercial world dominated by shopping malls, brand recognition, and ubiquitous advertising by offering its visitors a completely different shopping experience. The variety of products is there, but not the stores. Detailed information is available, but not the sales personnel. Convenience is clearly a factor, although most purchases have to be delivered, and delivery costs can add up if you do a lot of online shopping. Impulse buys are tempered by the fact that each item remains "on the block" for some fixed period, during which time other people can bid up the price. Whatever the appeal of the online auction is, it's definitely unlike anything else in the world of commerce.

In general, there are three types of e-commerce:

1. Customer-to-customer (C2C) interactions
2. Business-to-customer (B2C) interactions
3. Business-to-business (B2B) interactions

eBay is primarily a C2C operation, although a few small businesses appear on eBay for B2C contacts. For a small B2C business getting off the ground or testing the waters for a new product, eBay makes product marketing and pricing experiments possible.

The site uBid.com (`http://www.ubid.com`) is an interesting counterpoint to eBay and a good representative of a C2C online auction Web site. Unlike eBay, on which goods pass directly from sellers to buyers, uBid.com either purchases its goods outright or attains the rights to sell them for the manufacturer on a percentage basis. This is a much more costly model for an auction site because the site must handle all the product shipping and storage, as well as assume liability for unsatisfactory products. However, buyers can be confident that the merchandise will meet a fixed set of standards. Therefore, buyers likely place more trust in a uBid.com auction.

Things to Remember

- Keep a record of all your online transactions.
- Use credit cards on the Internet; never use debit cards.
- Do not send sensitive information over the Internet to a nonsecure Web page. (Look for `https://` and the locked padlock to confirm that a site is secure.)
- Check an e-store's digital certificate before you send sensitive data to that e-store site.
- If you're unsure about a digital certificate for any reason, proceed with caution or don't buy from that site.
- SSL is the industry standard for secure communications on the Web.
- Don't worry about what type of encryption you have. Do make sure that all your transactions are being encrypted.
- Online auctions are the number-one source of Internet-related consumer fraud complaints (by a landslide).

Important Concepts

digital certificate a document on a Web server that can be checked to verify the identity of the server

online auction a popular way for individuals to buy and sell items of all kinds

secure sockets layer (SSL) a protocol for establishing secure (encrypted) communications between a Web browser and a Web server

secure Web page a Web page where it is safe to enter sensitive data such as credit card account numbers

shopping bot, shopbot a program that searches the web for the best price of some product you wish to purchase

40-bit encryption weak encryption no longer adequate for e-commerce

56-bit encryption medium-level encryption still good for e-commerce but rarely seen anymore

64-bit encryption medium-level encryption approved by the U.S. government (as of January 2000) for e-commerce in the United States

128-bit encryption strong encryption used by commercial sites in the United States

Where Can I Learn More?

A Framework for Global Electronic Commerce
http://www.technology.gov/digeconomy/framewrk.htm
Digital Certificates: What Are They?
http://www.entrust.net/ssl-resources/pdf/
    understanding_ssl.pdf
E-Commerce Times
http://www.ecommercetimes.com/
Ecommerce-Guide.Com
http://www.ecommerce-guide.com/
Articles on E Business
http://onlinebusiness.about.com/cs/startingup/a/101.htm
Shopping bots (and others)
http://www.botspot.com/

Problems and Exercises

1. How much did e-store sales increase between 1998 and 2006?

2. List three ways that e-stores give consumers the upper hand when a sale depends on negotiation. (Hint: Consider the process of buying a car.)

3. Why is it reasonable for e-stores to want your e-mail address? What do they do with it?

4. [HANDS ON] Find the list of CAs recognized by your browser. How many are there?

5. What could happen if you never update your browser's CA database?

6. Why should a consumer check the site certificate for an e-store?

7. What three things should you look for when you examine a site certificate?

8. **[HANDS ON]** Visit a Web site where you have conducted business and examine its site certificate. Which Web site did you visit? Who is the CA?

9. Is it always unwise to visit a Web site if that site uses a certificate issued by an unknown CA? Explain your answer.

10. How can you tell whether you have an SSL connection to a Web site?

11. Will your browser always show an alert box when you establish or break an SSL connection? Explain your answer.

12. How does SSL ensure that the data you send to a Web server is not altered en route?

13. What is site spoofing? How does it differ from pharming (see Section 2.4.1)?

14. What is one-click shopping? Where is personal information stored for one-click shopping?

15. Why is it a bad idea to let your computer remember all your e-store passwords inside cookies?

 16. **[TAKE A STAND]** Research the Children's Online Privacy Protection Act and summarize its contents. Do you think this law is accomplishing what it set out to accomplish? Try to find some statistics to back up your arguments.

17. What types of companies are likely to ignore industry guidelines when an industry is self-regulating?

18. Why do privacy advocates object to the business practices of DoubleClick?

19. Why is it difficult to mount a consumer protest against DoubleClick?

20. What simple guideline for privacy rights has the European Union adopted?

21. Why isn't the practice of notice and consent by itself an adequate policy for protecting personal privacy online?

22. Which is safer to use online: a check, a credit card, or a money order? Explain your answer.

23. According to Internet Fraud Watch (`http://www.fraud.org/`), what online activity is responsible for the largest number of consumer complaints?

24. If you are thinking of participating in an online auction, what four safeguards should you look for at the auction site?

25. How are online auction sites useful to small businesses?

26. **[FIND IT ONLINE]** Visit `http://www.paypal.com/` and find out how PayPal works. What do you need to set up a PayPal account? How many members does PayPal have?

27. Explain how eBay differs from uBid.com.

28. **[FIND IT ONLINE]** Visit Nielsen/NetRatings at `http://www.nielsen-net ratings.com/`, and find its most recent list of the top 10 advertisers on the Net. Which of those companies are also present in the list in Figure 7.2?

29. **[FIND IT ONLINE]** eBay imposes some restrictions on the items that people can sell. In particular, restrictions apply to the sale of concert tickets. Describe those restrictions.

30. **[FIND IT ONLINE]** Excepting the "Buy it now" option, eBay auctions run for a fixed period of time. When that time is up, the highest bidder wins. What is the shortest possible time period for an eBay auction? What is the longest possible time? How do proxy bids work at eBay?

31. **[FIND IT ONLINE]** Some auctions at eBay are "Dutch" auctions. What is a Dutch auction? Explain how it differs from a regular auction, and describe how it works.

32. **[FIND IT ONLINE]** PayPal (`http://www.paypal.com`) is a service that many eBay users rely on for electronic funds transfers (EFTs). If both the buyer and the seller have PayPal accounts, the buyer can use a credit card to send a payment to the seller's PayPal account. The seller then can confirm the receipt of the payment in minutes and immediately dispatch the purchased item. Without EFTs, the seller would have to wait for the buyer's check to arrive in the mail and then wait for the check to clear the buyer's bank, a process that can take a week or more. How much does PayPal charge users for its service? How do PayPal users convert money in their PayPal accounts into cash? How long does it take to get cash back from PayPal? How does PayPal turn a profit?

33. **[FIND IT ONLINE]** Visit `http://www.securityfocus.com/news/573` and read about a Windows/IE SSL failure discovered by security researcher Mike Benham. For more details, see `http://www.thoughtcrime.org/ie-ssl-chain.txt`. What was the nature of the failure and how long had it been a problem? Benham posted his discovery to a mailing list on August 5, 2002, and Reuters released its story on August 13, 2002. When did Microsoft release a patch to fix the problem? Were any browsers other than IE affected?

34. **[FIND IT ONLINE]** Find out the current status of the Online Privacy Protection Act at `http://www.thomas.gov`. Are there other similar laws also being considered?

E-Commerce

E-Commerce, National Security, and Hackers

The Above & Beyond section in Chapter 2 explored the origins and evolution of the hacker culture. In particular, you saw that although the media tend to portray all computer hackers as brilliant, alienated, and potentially dangerous, no monolithic stereotype fits all hackers. Of course, the media have a vested interest in stories that sell, so you can't be too shocked if reporters tend to emphasize the "weird kid with frightening powers" angle. Similarly, Hollywood would have little interest in hackers if the hacker stereotype were closer to reality: a bored teenager of average intelligence dabbling in activities that are no more threatening than trespassing or shoplifting.

When the Internet was primarily a tool for programmers and researchers, hackers were accepted as an inevitable annoyance and a good reason to take system security seriously. In those days, no one equated hacker attacks with billion-dollar losses. Today, when many people hear the word *hacker* they think of credit card theft and extortion. They worry about the security of their personal information on the Web. The expanded use of the Internet has elevated the hacker problem to new heights. But how real is this threat to the nascent world of e-commerce? Could hackers pull down the global economy like a house of cards? Should hackers be handled like any other criminal element, even if they are minors? Or is the whole business of computer hackers primarily media hype, with no more real impact on society than the older and more traditional methods of corporate theft?

As always, the media shape public perceptions for events that most people don't experience firsthand. Stories in the press can be written to cause a stir or create low-level anxiety, and a single incident can galvanize public opinion. For example, a writer could either tell people that there are 16,000

FYI: What Is CERT?

The Department of Defense set up a tracking center for computer security problems (CERT) in 1988 after Robert Morris, Jr., a graduate student in Computer Science at Cornell University, released a network worm that crippled thousands of computers connected to the Internet. The purpose of CERT is to research and compile information about the technology behind hacker attacks. CERT is not an acronym, it's a name and service mark registered to Carnegie Mellon University, where CERT is based.

HACKERS AND THE WORLD ECONOMY

The very same means that the cyber vandals used a few weeks ago [in the denial-of-service cyber attacks on several major Web sites in February 2000] could also be used on a much more massive scale at the nation-state level to generate truly damaging interruptions to the national economy and infrastructure.

—Daniel Kuehl,
National Defense University

If there's one lesson both the government and the private sector can learn from the world's continuing million-dollar bout with various strains of the "Love Bug"—as the "I LOVE YOU" virus is known alternatively—it is that a group of teenage students and fresh college graduates can pose a threat to a nation's economic well-being.

—Fidel R. Anonuevo, Jr.,
National Security Council

known computer viruses or explain that only 300 different computer viruses are active "in the wild" (making the rounds outside of research laboratories). Both statements are true. However, the first is much more effective if you want to frighten people.

Regarding the subject of computer hackers and their impact on e-commerce, you can find pronouncements by many people with a professional stake in hackers and hacking. To fully understand the truth of the matter, you need to look at some hard facts, which are sometimes buried beneath the rhetoric. Consider the adjoining and following quotations.

Are these statements of fact? Or is this simply arresting rhetoric designed to shape a political agenda?

Let's check the facts. The Federal Bureau of Investigation (FBI) estimated that the denial-of-service attacks in February 2000 cost the affected businesses hundreds of millions of dollars. The LoveLetter virus released in May 2000 was estimated to cost $2.6 billion worldwide. If attacks of this kind were leveled at essential businesses and communication backbones (for example, airlines and telephone companies) on a nonstop basis, the economic loss would qualify as a national emergency.

Should we expect to see more of these types of high-profile attacks? Has there been a general increase in overall hacking activities in recent years? Or is the press simply reporting more of them now because so many people depend on the Internet? CERT says that the number of reported attacks is increasing explosively. In 1988, that organization logged 6 attacks. In 2003, the last year documented, 137,529 attacks were reported. Because of the increasingly automated nature of the attacks, CERT discontinued reporting them, arguing that the attacks are becoming too commonplace and that the incident count does not reflect the nature or scope of the attacks.

For a blow-by-blow account of what hackers are up to daily, drop by InfoWar.com and read about the latest security breaches, software alerts, and reports from the front lines. Then keep in mind that most security breeches are not reported.

According to the FBI, only 210 Fortune 1000 companies reported attacks on their computer networks during 1999. However, an estimated 65 percent of all corporate cybercrime victims don't report their attacks out of a fear of negative publicity. The FBI also estimates that 85 to 95 percent of all intrusions into corporate and private networks are never detected.

Hackers who target military and government operations pose a different type of risk. Shutting down e-commerce sites can cost millions of dollars. However, hacker attacks designed to damage military security or halt infrastructure operations can cost more than money. They could cost lives.

What are the chances that a serious cyberterrorism attack will someday result in death and destruction? Once again, let's look at some facts. In 1997, the NSA hired 35 hackers and launched simulated attacks on the U.S. electronic infrastructure. The exercise was called "Eligible Receiver," and the hired hackers managed to achieve privileged access to 36 of the Department of Defense's 40,000 networks. The simulated attack also turned off sections of the U.S. power grid, shut down parts of the 911 network in several cities, including Washington, D.C., and gained access to systems aboard a Navy cruiser at sea. Later that same year, Senator Jon Kyl (R-Arizona), chairman of the U.S. Senate Subcommittee on Technology, Terrorism, and Government Information, reported that nearly two-thirds of U.S. government computer systems have security holes.

In the Fall of 2000, a Middle East cyberwar broke out when Lebanese Shiite fighters captured three Israeli soldiers on patrol along the Lebanese border. The Shiite Hizbullah Web site was bombarded with 9 million Internet "pings" (short messages used to see if a server is awake) which caused it to crash. Several other sites linked to Hamas, the Palestinian resistance group, were similarly attacked. Pro-Palestinian hackers launched a counterattack against as many Israeli sites as they could locate, eventually reaching targets in the United States. These facts suggest that we're living on borrowed time, although the

HACKERS AND MILITARY OPERATIONS

During the Gulf War (1990–91), Dutch hackers stole information about U.S. troop movements from U.S. Defense Department computers and tried to sell it to the Iraqis, who thought it was a hoax and turned it down.

—John Christensen, CNN Interactive

We are detecting, with increasing frequency, the appearance of doctrine and dedicated offensive cyber warfare programs in other countries. We have identified several [countries], based on all-source intelligence information, that are pursuing government-sponsored offensive cyber programs.

—John Serabian, Central Intelligence Agency

threat has been somewhat over-hyped in the press. But the threat is very real nonetheless.

NO WONDER SO MANY KIDS ARE HACKERS NOWADAYS

A few years ago, hacking took a lot of time and study. While expert hackers still abound, the Internet has entered a new era. Using almost any search engine, average Internet users can quickly find information describing how to break into systems by simply searching for keywords like hacking, password cracking, and Internet security. Thousands of sites publish step-by-step instructions for breaking into or disrupting service to Windows NT systems, Web servers, UNIX systems, etc. The sites often include tools that automate the hacking process. In many cases, the tools have easy-to-use graphical interfaces.

—Robert A. Clyde,
AXENT Technologies, Inc.

Today, it's all too easy to exploit known vulnerabilities. The Internet has placed the best cracker tools within easy reach of anyone who knows how to use the World Wide Web. The tools can be found using any common, free search engine.

—ITATF Security Working Group,
University of California at Berkeley

I think that these attacks [the denial-of-service cyberattacks on several major Web sites] have been inevitable. The Internet is totally vulnerable to this kind of thing. It was just a matter of time before the automated attacking tools became so easy and widespread that everyone started using them.

—Avi Rubin, AT&T Laboratories

Why is there so much cybercrime, and what can we do about it? Do we need more laws? Stronger law enforcement? Are we digging our own grave by protecting hacker sites under the First Amendment? An estimated 30,000 Web sites are written for hackers by hackers, on which software tools can be found along with mini-tutorials on topics such as denial-of-service attacks and encryption cracking. These tools of destruction are distributed freely, like recipes for cheesecake, in the name of free speech and intellectual inquiry. Anyone can learn the tools of the trade.

How hard is it to be a hacker? Does it require superior intelligence? A technical background? Extensive programming expertise? Widespread agreement exists among security experts regarding these questions.

This situation seems to resemble the problem of children with guns. When guns are easily available in many households, some number of children invariably handle one. Once in a while, the outcome is tragic. Adults also pick up guns and kill people. However, in those cases, the intent is usually criminal, and the legal system holds adults accountable for their actions. As the hacker/gun analogy suggests, we must address several different problems. How should we punish a minor for an intentional act of destruction and mayhem? How should we punish an adult for committing an act of destruction if the adult did not fully comprehend or intend the consequences of that act? How can we prevent these acts of destruction from occurring in the first place? Should we hold the software (gun) manufacturers responsible for making their software (guns) too easy to use? Should we sue a software (gun) manufacturer for the monetary losses associated with its products?

Should we blame our schools and places of work for not maintaining secure environments in which people are safe from cybercrimes (violence)? Should we blame parents or teachers or television for not teaching our children to stay away from hacking software (guns)? Should we blame society for producing people who see cybercrime (violence) as the solution to their problems? For both software and guns, the problems are thorny and not prone to quick fixes.

Like many analogies, the hacker/gun analogy breaks down if you examine it closely. In the case of guns, you're dealing with physical objects. Gun production can be regulated, and gun distribution can be limited. In the case of hackers, the weapons are intellectual property. Software and algorithms cannot be regulated, and their distribution cannot be controlled, at least not in a free society. In addition, we would never blame the victims of shooting incidents for not defending themselves better. But that is exactly what proponents of better system security do when corporations and institutions are hurt by hackers. They blame the victims' software for being poorly designed, and they blame the victims for not being vigilant enough about system security.

Consider the case of ProMobility Interactive, a wireless telephone merchant in Ontario, Canada. ProMobility was one of nine e-commerce sites in the United States, the United Kingdom, Canada, Thailand, and Japan attacked by two 18-year-olds in Wales. The hackers infiltrated the sites and stole credit card account records for more than 26,000 accounts. The teens then posted the credit card account data on a Web site; credit card losses were estimated to exceed $3 million.

ProMobility said the hackers had infiltrated its site through a two-year-old security hole in a Microsoft e-commerce software package. Microsoft posted a patch for the problem in July 1998 on its security update site. It issued a sec-

TIP: Security through Obscurity Doesn't Work

 Eric Geiler, Vice President of Information Systems at ProMobility Interactive, was puzzled as to why the hackers went after ProMobility. "How the hell did he even find us? We are nobody. Why did he pick us?" Sensitive data at small e-commerce sites often is at risk. Thus small e-commerce sites have become very popular targets for hackers because they are less likely to have up-to-date security software and adequate maintenance routines. "In a lot of companies, you have one system/admin guy who goes around and fixes computers, and you can't keep up to date with all of the patches," explained Geiler. (See `http://archives.cnn.com/2000/TECH/computing/03/24/hackers.wales/index.html`.)

BACK TO THE FUTURE

Selwyn Gerber, a managing partner with the offshore banking firm PrimeGlobal USA, said his company considers the Internet so insecure that it won't use it to transmit sensitive customer data.

"We're back to using faxes, and we find that much more secure. We use FedEx [Federal Express]. In fact, if there were ponies still traveling across Europe we'd probably use those, too."

E-COMMERCE, SECURITY, AND THE BOTTOM LINE

Often times they're going for the money-maker, that's getting the product out there, getting the site up. And security is often an afterthought.

—Elinor Abreau, The Industry Standard

If you have a choice of spending a million dollars on getting 250,000 new customers, or a million dollars on serving the ones you already have, better, that's a difficult value proposition.

—William P. Crowell, Chief Executive Officer, Cylink Corp.

You wouldn't build a swimming pool in the center of town and not put a fence around it, and I think that's what the software companies are doing.

—Glenn Tenney, Pilot Network Services

ond warning on the site in July 1999. ProMobility failed to install this patch and was attacked in February 2000.

Many e-commerce sites don't realize how vulnerable they are—even less, how much work is required to secure an e-commerce site. Those that do might decide that it's more cost-effective to move some of their most sensitive operations offline rather than attempt to maintain good security on their computers.

Why not hold the software manufacturers responsible for software that does not better protect private data? Servers, routers, firewalls, and database programs all can be susceptible to attack. Disclaimers protect software manufacturers from legal liability. However, why can't those manufacturers produce better software and thereby close security gaps at the source? Buyers would certainly pay more for software that didn't require patches and updates in order to stay one jump ahead of hackers.

Unfortunately, software manufacturers are under at least as much pressure to produce and release products as are the e-commerce sites that rely on those products. The e-commerce sites often are racing to establish an online presence before their competition does. Along the way, they suffer from a relentless sense that everything must be done as fast as possible. In this rush to be first, concerns about security are often set aside.

Easy access to hacking tools, inadequate resources on the part of e-commerce sites, pressure on software manufacturers to cut corners, and people with criminal intent as well as kids looking for thrills—all conspire to keep hacking a major problem for e-commerce. Eliminating hackers is probably impossible without a major overhauling of the Internet's underlying architecture. Some Net observers accept hackers as an inevitable and compelling force in the Internet's evolution.

HACKERS AND THE EVOLUTIONARY PROCESS

Technology advances. In the process you get a little lax about security. Hackers come in and remind us about the problem. Companies respond appropriately and the system gets tighter.

—Paul Saffo, Institute for the Future (describing the "safety cycle" that becomes the Internet's learning curve)

In an arms race, there are two sides. Each side is constantly building up its forces to try to outdo the other side. We typically see this with the nuclear capabilities of various countries. On the Internet, there's a similar situation. The attackers move several steps forward by coming up with new ways of penetrating systems, and the protectors come up with new things, such as firewalls, to counter that. Unlike a typical arms race, however, the security specialists can only respond to the new attacks. There's very little you can do proactively.

—Avi Rubin, AT&T Laboratories

Meanwhile, the problems are very real, the potential for disaster is great, and the situation will probably get worse before it gets better. New concerns for national security in the United States have increased public awareness of many security problems, including Internet security. The Antiterrorism Act of 2001 was signed into law immediately after the terrorist attacks on September 11, 2001, in an effort to strengthen U.S. intelligence gathering and law enforcement powers in President Bush's War against Terrorism. The Antiterrorism Act of 2001 defines terrorism so broadly that any malicious activities on the Internet could conceivably fall under its jurisdiction. Follow-up legislation, the Cyber Security Enhancement Act of 2002, makes the connection more clear, specifying life sentences for computer intrusions that put lives at risk. A similar law passed in the United Kingdom (the Terrorism Act 2000) says that any interference with or disruption of an electronic system will be viewed as an act of terrorism. Before September 11, hacker attacks were viewed primarily as expensive disruptions for the business world. Since September 11, hackers are now viewed as potential terrorists as well. In the United States the stakes are now higher, and public opinion has visibly shifted on all matters that threaten public welfare. Any activities that maliciously interfere with the lives of other people are a focal point for law enforcement agencies, and the general public has been reexamining the balance between homeland security and civil liberties. Many fear that the Internet will be instrumental in another terrorist attack. Anyone who breaks into a computer or releases a virus in this climate cannot hope to be treated with tolerance.

Where Can I Learn More?

CERT http://www.cert.org/

InfoWar.com http://www.infowar.com/

Problems and Exercises

A1. What is CERT and why was it created?

A2. [FIND IT ONLINE] What percentage of all retail sales in the United States occur online? If the entire Internet were somehow rendered inoperable for one week, how much impact do you think that would have on the retail establishment?

A3. Is the number of hacker attacks increasing each year, or are we just hearing about them more because the media are reporting them more?

A4. According to the FBI, what percentage of hacker attacks and intrusions are never reported?

A5. [FIND IT ONLINE] Find a current estimate for how much hacker attacks are costing the global economy. (Hint: Visit `http://www.ecommercetimes.com/`, and conduct a site search.)

A6. [FIND IT ONLINE] Software manufacturers have enjoyed strong legal protection from lawsuits associated with software failures. Are any organizations or politicians working to create a law that would force software manufacturers to assume more responsibility for product failures? Report on any effort you can find along these lines and its current status.

A7. [FIND IT ONLINE] The music industry is looking for new business models that involve digital technologies. Find a proposed business model supported by the major record labels. Describe it in detail, and evaluate it from the consumer's perspective.

A8. [FIND IT ONLINE] Can companies buy insurance to cover losses in the event of a hacker attack? (Hint: Visit `http://www.ecommercetimes.com/`, and conduct a site search.) Explain your answer.

A9. [FIND IT ONLINE] Research the Cyber Security Enhancement Act of 2002 and summarize its major points.

A10. [TAKE A STAND] How do you feel about the Cyber Security Enhancement Act of 2002? Do you think it infringes on your Constitutional rights in any way? Do you think we are better off or worse off with this legislation?

A11. **[TAKE A STAND]** Visit `http://www.infosyssec.com`, and read the headlines in the news ticker box. Do you think it's wise to publicize all these software vulnerabilities? Explain your reasoning.

A12. **[TAKE A STAND]** The architecture of the Internet is robust because its functionality is distributed across many different sites, as opposed to being organized in a centralized hierarchy. Do you think the Internet would be safer or less safe if the administration of the Internet were strongly centralized? Explain your reasoning.

A13. **[TAKE A STAND]** About 97 percent of all home computers run some version of Microsoft Windows, Microsoft Internet Explorer, Microsoft Word, and Microsoft Outlook Express. What implications does this have for safety online? Would the Internet be safer if there were four or five popular OS platforms and no one OS had more than 25 percent of the home computer market? Explain your reasoning.

A14. **[TAKE A STAND]** Do you think stricter laws would be an effective way to reduce the damage caused by hackers? Do you think stricter gun control laws would be an effective deterrent to violent crime? Discuss the hackers/guns analogy. Is this a useful analogy or does it break down in important places?

A15. **[FIND IT ONLINE]** Are there any laws being considered in the current congress covering hackers and hacker-related crime? Consult `http://www.thomas.gov/`.

Encryption and the Internet

8.1 | Taking Charge

Most of us never encounter the word *cryptography* outside spy movies and espionage novels. **Cryptography** is the study of secret codes associated with classified information and intelligence gathering. You might know something about the important role of cryptography in World War II, but chances are you know about cryptography only if you went out of your way to read a book about it. Even though everyone has probably heard of clandestine operations associated with the Central Intelligence Agency (CIA), many Americans have never heard of the National Security Agency (NSA). The NSA is responsible for developing and applying secure communication technologies in the service of national security. Cryptography used to be a science whose applications were of interest only to the military. Now, as we move into a new era of digital communication, cryptography and government interest in cryptography are touching all our lives.

Cryptography is of great interest to client/server software developers, anyone interested in digital commerce, and all Internet users who want to keep their personal communications private. In the absence of special safeguards, such com-

Chapter Goals

- Understand how private-key and public-key encryption work
- Learn how digital signatures protect document integrity
- Understand why key authentication is needed to protect people from counterfeit keys
- See how the web-of-trust approach to key authentication works
- Find out how digital certificates and certificate authorities solve the problem of key authentication
- Understand the difference between strong and weak encryption

munications as sensitive personal e-mails, legal contracts, valuable data, proprietary documents, insurance records, digital monetary transfers, and medical records are all at risk on the Internet and on any digital medium. Cryptography offers us good options for protecting this information. Cryptographic methods have become increasingly commonplace in business environments and will eventually permeate all digital media as we come to appreciate the importance of secure communications.

When TCP/IP (see page 72) was adopted as the standard communication protocol for global networked communication, secure communication was not a high priority. Open software design, open resource sharing, and public information were the forces driving early network research. The Internet has succeeded as a highly accessible and expandable public network, but our priorities are slowly shifting. As the Internet becomes more commercialized, vendors need to conduct secure business transactions to allay the fears of consumers who are nervous about the risks of online shopping. We have yet to see a high-profile scandal unfold as the result of an Internet "wiretap," but it's probably just a matter of time before some technically inclined investigator figures out how to surreptitiously tap into the e-mail of some unsuspecting individual. Private investigators and lawyers are already examining backup files as a potential source of legal evidence, but the general public is just beginning to ask about legal protections that pertain to privacy rights.

Companies must insist that sensitive information is not up for grabs just because it is stored on a computer, and citizens should feel reassured that tax returns and other private documents are not available to random individuals for recreational browsing. Online medical records must be handled with care so that employers and insurance companies can't review sensitive information without authorization. Credit records should be safe from the prying eyes of newspaper reporters and private investigators.

With so much public information going online, we've been a little slow to appreciate just how much sensitive personal information has also been going online. The technologies that promote public access were never designed to protect private data. The public has embraced the Internet without fully understanding exactly how it differs from relatively private communication channels, where safeguards for privacy are taken for granted.

The military has always understood that security is a big problem on computer networks. Sensitive military computers are carefully shielded from potentially invasive network connections. Large corporations followed suit by opting for intranet connectivity as an alternative to Internet access. An

intranet is an internal computer network carefully segregated from all external computer networks such as the Internet.

Internet access from an intranet is possible, but only through a secure gateway called a **firewall** (see Section 2.8) that is designed to keep sensitive data within organizational walls. A firewall is like a wall around a castle. As long as the wall works, everyone feels safe and sound. But a wall that is not carefully designed and maintained might be breached, so constant vigilance is needed. A castle wall without sentries is no better than a wall with a gaping hole in it.

Intranets and firewalls afford good protection and work well for large organizations, but many of our communications are not circumscribed by institutional boundaries. We also want privacy safeguards when we contact friends, acquaintances, and business contacts all over the world. Today's Internet does not have any privacy safeguards built into it. However, as time goes on we will see more and more applications incorporating privacy measures. It is not necessary to understand all the technical foundations that enable digital privacy, but some understanding of the basic ideas will help you evaluate the available choices.

As we explain how encryption algorithms work, we demonstrate key concepts with screen shots of encryption software in action. In particular, we show some software traces from a command-mode version (running under UNIX) of an encryption program called **Pretty Good Privacy** (**PGP**). Later we present screen shots of PGP working in a point-and-click environment (under Windows). The command-mode traces actually offer a better picture of what's going on because there is a lot of explanatory text in these traces. Once you understand what the software is doing, the point-and-click environment is quicker and easier to work with. But the explanatory text in the command-mode version is very nice for beginners, which is why we've chosen to include some older PGP traces in this chapter.

 # Private-Key Encryption

There was a time in the 1950s when it seemed as if every kid in America wore a big purple plastic ring with white and yellow lightning bolts on it. It had a large dial on top covered in letters and symbols. Captain Midnight Decoder Rings were hot, and countless seven-year-olds deftly used these coveted artifacts to unscramble secret messages issued straight from Captain Midnight through the magic of television.

A key for a simple substitution code is just a map that tells you how to substitute one character for another. When you receive a coded message, you trade each character for a new one according to the instructions in the key. For example, suppose your coded message says this:

IUUJ IU JNIN66N/ KJ C2I ?95U6 JAU IK23U J6UUL

Applying the key in Figure 8.1 to each symbol in the encoded message gives you the unencoded message:

MEET ME TOMORROW AT 4PM UNDER THE MAPLE TREE.

The process of creating a coded message is called **encoding** (or **encrypting**). The process of unscrambling a coded message using a key is called **decoding** (aka **decrypting**). To encode a message, you can use the same key you use for decoding, but you have to reverse the key (that is, think of all the arrows in Figure 8.1 going in the opposite direction). When the same key is used for both encoding and decoding, the code is called **private-key encryption** (aka **single-key encryption** or **symmetric encryption**). See Figure 8.2.

Figure 8.1
Substitution code key

A → H	F → 7	K → A	P → 5	U → E	Z → ?	5 → D	/ → W
B → C	G → 0	L → .	Q → F	V → S	1 → X	6 → R	. → Q
C → 4	H → B	M → V	R → 1	W → Z	2 → P	7 → K	! → G
D → I	I → M	N → 0	S → !	X → J	3 → L	8 → Y	? → U
E → 6	J → T	0 → 3	T → 9	Y → 2	4 → 8	9 → N	

Figure 8.2
Private-key (single-key) encryption

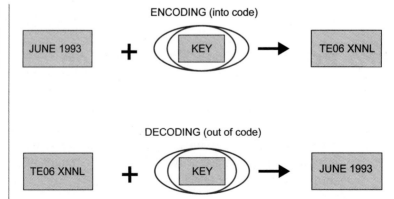

ENCODING (into code)

JUNE 1993   +   KEY   →   TE06 XNNL

DECODING (out of code)

TE06 XNNL   +   KEY   →   JUNE 1993

If you have the key for a code, it is easy to decode messages. If you don't have the key, you can try to break the code, but it requires some work. If you have enough encoded messages, you can study them and try to figure out the key. You start by identifying the most frequently used characters and character sequences in the encoded messages. Then you need to know some helpful facts about the English language. For example, the letter *e* is the most frequently used letter in the English alphabet. Chances are, one of the frequently used characters in the encoded messages is the code for *e*. The most frequently used three-letter word is *the*. If you see the same three-letter character sequence over and over again, it might be *the*. These sorts of observations make it possible to break simple substitution codes.

An effective code is one that transmits messages to its intended recipients—and only its intended recipients. No one else should be able to decode the messages. However, you should always assume that coded messages will be intercepted by people who will try to break the code. Every effort must be made to confound the code breakers. A substitution code is one of the easiest ones to break and is never used for serious applications of cryptography. Many other methods are far more satisfactory, but we won't pursue them here. (See the Where Can I Learn More? section for resources about cryptography.)

A very important problem associated with private-key encryption is the problem of ensuring key security. If a code breaker can somehow steal the key for a code, the code is broken. To keep your diary safe from your snoopy big brother, you can use Captain Midnight's decoder ring to encode your diary entries. But then you have to make sure your ring is safely hidden where big brother can't find it. The most sophisticated code in the world is of no use if the key cannot be held securely. Every precaution must be taken to keep code keys out of the wrong hands.

Private-key encryption methods are potentially risky because the same keys have to be shared by too many people. At the very least, the sender needs the key to encode messages, and the receiver needs the key to decode messages. Even when just two people share a key, you could have a problem because the key must be passed from one person to the other person. Each time a key is transferred, you take a chance that it might be intercepted. How can you make sure that no one intercepts the key? Should you trust the U.S. mail? Federal Express? A telephone call? An e-mail message? A military courier? Some options are safer than others, but they all entail some risk.

If the information you want to encode is not a matter of life and death, you might decide that the risks associated with private-key encryption are acceptable (it was good enough for Captain Midnight, after all). But some applications for cryptography are very sensitive and require the best possible safeguards. To convince a few million consumers that they can safely use their credit card numbers on the Internet, we need the best safeguards available. Indeed, concerns about the security of digital funds have been a major stumbling block in the commercialization of the Internet. No one wants to broadcast his or her credit card number to the world. The solution to this dilemma is called **public-key encryption** (aka **double-key encryption** or **asymmetric encryption**).

The next section explains how public-key encryption works, but private-key encryption has its place. Private-key encryption algorithms tend to run much faster (about 1,000 times faster) than public-key encryption algorithms. If you encrypt a lot of documents (or Web forms or e-mail), this is a significant slowdown. So while public-key encryption is superior to private-key encryption in key safety, private-key encryption is superior to public-key encryption in speed. When public-key encryption is used for practical applications, a little trickery makes it possible to combine private-key encryption with public-key encryption and end up with the best of both worlds. We won't digress to explain this cleverness right now, but we will cover it in the Above & Beyond section. Right now, it's more important to understand how public-key encryption works.

 # 8.3 Public-Key Encryption

The major weakness in private-key encryption is the problem of key security. Public-key encryption is an alternative to private-key encryption that addresses the problem of key security. The trick is to use two keys instead of one: one key for encoding and one key for decoding. These two keys are generated as a special key pair that can work only together. If one key is lost, the other key is useless by itself. One of the two keys is designated as the public key. A **public key** can be freely distributed to anyone and everyone. The remaining key becomes the private key. A **private key** is held by only the owner of the key pair. Now here's the really clever part. Although the two keys are uniquely connected to one another, having the public key doesn't make it possible to deduce the private key.

Let's see how public-key encryption works by looking at an example. If you want me to send you an encrypted message, you first need to create a pair of keys that will enable me to encode the message. You give me a copy of your public key, and you keep your private key to yourself. I can then use your pub-

Public-key encryption was first proposed in 1976 by Martin Hellman and Whitfield Diffie. In 1977 three computer scientists (Ronald Rivest, Adi Shamir, and Leonard Adleman) published a specific public-key encryption scheme known as the RSA Public Key Cryptosystem. At the heart of RSA is a patented method for generating secure asymmetric key pairs. RSA key pairs exploit the fact that although it is relatively easy to multiply two large prime numbers, it is much harder to take the product and find its prime factors. Although no one can prove that RSA key pairs are unbreakable, the method has been studied extensively since 1977, and thus far no efficient factorization algorithms have been found for very large numbers. (We are talking about *very* large numbers here.) RSA is one of the most widely used public-key algorithms today, and it is embedded inside many encryption programs used on the Internet.

lic key to encode the message, and you can use your private key to decode it. This system is very secure because your private key is the only key that can decode messages encoded by your public key.

Then if you are the only person with access to your private key, you are the only person who can read messages encoded for you. It doesn't matter how many people hold the public key because it is used only for encoding messages. Figure 8.3 shows the basic idea behind public-key encryption.

For you to send me an encoded message, we need another pair of keys. I need to create my own pair of keys: a public key I can distribute to anyone and

Figure 8.3

Public-key (double-key) encryption

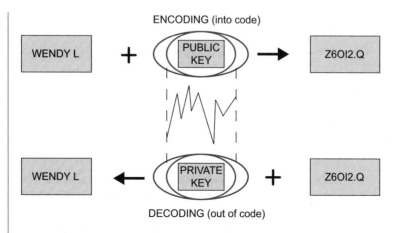

a private key only I can access. I give you a copy of my public key so that you can encode messages for me. Then when I get an encoded message from you, I use my private key to decode it. You and I can now exchange messages back and forth, using our public keys for all the encoding and our private keys for all the decoding.

Let's consider the implications of public-key encryption a little further. If everyone on the Internet wanted to communicate with everyone else using public-key encryption, we would all need to own a personal key pair, and we would all need to access everyone else's public keys. This may not sound very practical, but all this key management and key-related bookkeeping could be automated by communications software. For example, a central directory for public keys could be created for the distribution of public keys. Once your public key goes into the directory, anyone could look it up and make a copy for their personal use. Even better, your software could go out on the Net and do the directory lookups for you automatically. If you wanted to send e-mail to someone, your mail program could look up the required key in the public-

FYI: How Hard Is It to Crack a Private Key?

A key is just a string of ones and zeros (a bit string). If someone can figure out the bit string, they've cracked the key. Assuming that no one can deduce private keys from public keys (so far so good for RSA), there is not much left to do but try a brute-force search. In a brute-force search, you simply generate and test each of the possible strings of ones and zeros until you find the right string. A shorter string is easier to crack than a longer one because there are fewer possibilities. Keys become much harder to crack as they get bigger:

10-bit keys: 1,024 possibilities
20-bit keys: 1,048,576 possibilities
40-bit keys: 1,099,511,627,776 possibilities
56-bit keys: 72,057,594,037,927,936 possibilities

In 1995 a programmer in France with access to 120 workstations cracked a 40-bit key in eight days. (Note that a 600MHz Pentium III PC can crack a 40-bit key in four days—a more current 3GHz Pentium D could probably do it in a few hours.) In 1998, a special-purpose computer built by the Electronic Frontier Foundation (EFF) for $250,000 demonstrated that it could crack a 56-bit key in less than a week. Although 64-bit keys are still reasonably secure, they are slipping into reach for cracking. It would take the EFF computer a year or two to crack a 64-bit key. By comparison, 128-bit keys are extremely safe. The EFF computer would need about 1,971,693,055,818,000,000,000 years to crack a 128-bit key.

TIP: PGP Freeware

At the time of writing, there is one free version of PGP that runs safely under Windows XP. Gpg 4wind 1.0.6 was released in August 2006. You can download it at `http://www.pgp4win.org/`. Mac users can get PGP8 at `http://www.pgpi.org/products/pgp/versions/freeware/mac/8.0/`.

key directory. Then the program would use that key to encrypt your mail message before sending. The key could be saved to a virtual key ring of useful public keys for future reference, just as e-mail addresses are saved in virtual address books. At the receiving end, your mail program could be smart enough to recognize an encoded message when it sees one, in which case the program would apply your private key and decode the message for you automatically.

Growing communities of Internet users use PGP for secure e-mail communications today, and many mail clients can be configured to use a PGP plug-in that makes all the encoding, decoding, and PGP key management quite painless. Reading a PGP-encoded e-mail message requires the correct passphrase for your private key. Outgoing mail messages can usually be encrypted with a single mouse click using the proper tools.

The phrase **public-key infrastructure (PKI)** refers to the business of establishing and maintaining a system of public-key servers (a problem not unlike the challenge of maintaining domain-name servers for the entire Internet). All the overhead associated with locating public keys and encoding outgoing e-mail can be handled by PKI software running quietly behind the scenes, requiring no extra effort on the part of the user. Everything needed to realize this scenario exists today, including mail programs that automate message encryption and decryption. All the technical know-how is there to secure our e-mail from prying eyes. Privacy-enhanced e-mail is available right now to anyone who installs the PGP plug-in, and encrypted e-mail will be commonplace in a few more years.

8.4 Digital Signatures

Signatures of one kind or another are probably as old as written language. When a document is signed, we know who wrote it and who should be given credit for its contents. In the case of legal contracts, signatures are backed up by laws. Signatures are routinely written on receipts, prescriptions, grade transcripts, business correspondence, certificates of achievement, works of art, bank checks, income tax forms, loan applications, traffic tickets, photographs, notarized documents, fishing licenses, and hall passes. It's hard to get through a day without crossing paths with a signature of some kind. Sometimes a signature is forged, and when a forgery goes undetected, the outcome is rarely good.

As we move into a digital millennium we can now add a new kind of signature to the list: the **digital signature**. At first glance, it may seem that a digital signature would be especially vulnerable to forgery. If we have to use a keyboard instead of freehand writing, how can we possibly create distinctive signatures that offer some resistance to forgery?

In fact, digital signatures are even more distinctive than a traditional handwritten signature, but we have to use public-key encryption to make digital signatures unique and forgery-resistant. Encryption is not only important for maintaining privacy online, it is also the only way to know for sure just who is on the receiving end of your outgoing communications and who is behind each incoming communication. Safe digital signatures are crucial for e-commerce and other sensitive communications online, so digital signatures are important to everyone who intends to conduct business online.

If you understand how public-key encryption works with public and private keys, you will be able to understand how digital signatures are generated and verified. Consider the following scenario. You want to post a document on the Web and you don't care who reads it, but you do want everyone to know that you are the original author. You don't need an encoded document—just add a digital signature to a plain-text document. You can create a digital signature with the private half of a public cryptography key pair and some special software designed to generate digital signatures. When you launch the software, it asks for the file you want signed and the private key you are signing it with. The signature program identifies you as the source of this signature because you are using your private key to create the signature.

Suppose you post your document and someone else wants to make sure your signature is legitimate. To verify the signature, he or she will need the public key of your key pair and some special software designed to verify digital signatures. He or she can retrieve your public key (perhaps from a public-key library) and use encryption software to see if the public key from the library and the key that signed the document are a valid key pair. The software can tell whether the keys are paired by trying to use the public key to decode the signature block generated by your private key (see Figure 8.4).

Figure 8.4

Digital signature
verification

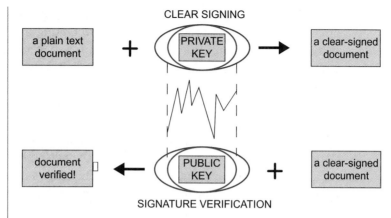

Digital signatures can be found on Web pages, in mailing list archives, and in Usenet newsgroups. People have been using the PGP encryption program ever since it was first distributed online in 1991 (see the Above & Beyond section at the end of this chapter). In Figure 8.5 we can see the encrypted PGP signature block at the bottom of a short plain-text document. A digital signature attached to a plain-text file is called a **clear signature**, and a document signed with a clear signature is called a **clear-signed document**. Digital signatures can also be added to encrypted documents, in which case the document is referred to as *encrypted and signed*.

Figure 8.5

Plain-text
document with a
digital signature

```
-----BEGIN PGP SIGNED MESSAGE-----

5/12/97 voting results

Smith   27
Jones   23
Fox     16
Webb    12


-----BEGIN PGP SIGNATURE-----

Version: 2.6.2
iQBVAwUBM3en5sY2EipHoMxpAQGLXgH/ahfFSW/7uwBGHslozlDiLQWC23gNm2S7
B6kIusLnYH2v/BkIAKUu5+ULTLb3QBRMNmLC1DD3ld1FxslsYYuyHQ==
=p1dn
-----END PGP SIGNATURE-----
```

Notice how the process of generating and verifying a digital signature is similar to the process of encrypting and decrypting a file. In the case of encryption, other people use your public key to encrypt a file for you, and then you use a private key to decrypt it. But for a digital signature, you use your private key to sign the file, and then other people use your public key to verify the signature.

Digital signatures differ from handwritten ones in one very important way: a digital signature changes from document to document. A digital signature contains information not only about the person behind the signature but also about the document being signed. This makes it impossible to forge a digital signature by copying a signature from one document and inserting it into a different document. A digital signature cannot fit any document other than its original one.

Let's look more carefully at the example document in Figure 8.5. The body of the text that was present at the time of the signing is marked "BEGIN PGP SIGNED MESSAGE"; the digital signature appears at the end of the text body and is marked by the lines "BEGIN PGP SIGNATURE" and "END PGP SIGNATURE." If this clear-signed document went out via e-mail to 100 people, each recipient could (if he or she chose to) verify the authenticity of the message contents by running a PGP signature check on the document using PGP software and the author's public PGP key.

Let's see how someone on the receiving end could verify this message by checking the signature. Assume that the receiver already has a copy of the author's public PGP key. If the signed message resides in a file called comm.txt.asc, a single PGP command can check the signature and verify the message. We can see this verification process in Figure 8.6, which shows a trace of an old command-line version of PGP running on a UNIX platform.

PGP not only identifies the signature as legitimate but also guarantees that the body of the message was not altered after the signing. Let's see what would happen if we edit comm.txt.asc and then try to verify the altered document. After making a minor edit (changing the vote count for Smith from 27 to 20—changing nothing in the file but the 7 in 27), let's try to verify the document to see if everything is still OK. Figure 8.7 shows the resulting trace.

PGP warns us that the signature on this file does not match the file's contents. This tells us that the file we're looking at is not the file the author signed. Clear signatures are a good way to make sure that information moves across the Internet untouched and unscathed.

Note that a clear signature is created by one person with the expectation that anyone should be able to verify it. An encrypted document can be created

Figure 8.6

Verifying a digital signature

```
el19:~/.pgp> pgp comm.txt.asc
No configuration file found.
Pretty Good Privacy (tm) 2.6.2 - Public-key encryption for the masses.
(c) 1990-1994 Philip Zimmermann, Phil's Pretty Good Software. 11 Oct 94
Uses the RSAREF (tm) Toolkit, which is copyright RSA Data Security, Inc.
Distributed by the Massachusetts Institute of Technology.
Export of this software may be restricted by the U.S. government.
Current time: 1997/05/12 23:32 GMT


File has signature. Public key is required to check signature.
Good signature from user "Prof. Lehnert <lehnert@elux3.cs.univ.edu>".
Signature made 1997/05/12 23:30 GMT
```

Figure 8.7

Failed signature verification

```
el19:~/.pgp> pgp comm.txt.asc
No configuration file found.
Pretty Good Privacy (tm) 2.6.2 - Public-key encryption for the masses.
(c) 1990-1994 Philip Zimmermann, Phil's Pretty Good Software. 11 Oct 94
Uses the RSAREF(tm) Toolkit, which is copyright RSA Data Security, Inc.
Distributed by the Massachusetts Institute of Technology.
Export of this software may be restricted by the U.S. government.
Current time: 1997/05/12 23:36 GMT


File has signature. Public key is required to check signature.
WARNING: Bad signature, doesn't match file contents!

Bad signature from user "Prof. Lehnert <lehnert@elux3.cs.univ.edu>".
Signature made 1997/05/12 23:30 GMT
```

by anyone with the expectation that only one person can read it. Clear-signed documents are like an inverse of encrypted documents. You use a private key to create a signature and a public key to verify it. You use a public key to create an encrypted document and a private key to decode it. Note that with RSA key pairs, either key can be used to unravel an encoding created by the other key. It's just convenient to encode with one key (the public key) all the time and decode with the other (the private key) because that makes the most sense. If the owner of the key pair wanted to encode something with the private key, she could do that. Then anyone with the public key could decode it. But that scenario is a little silly: Why encrypt a document that could be decrypted by anyone? On the other hand, the duality of the key pair is very handy when we want to add a digital signature to a document. Signature generation with the private key and signature verification with the public key is exactly what we want for public documents. This makes RSA an elegant solution to the dual demands of document encryption and digital signatures.

When you place a clear signature on a document, your PGP tool will ask you for a passphrase before it allows you to use your private key. As long as you are the only person who knows the passphrase, your PGP signature is secure. No one else will be able to generate PGP signatures using your private key, even if they somehow get their hands on your private key. For maximal security, you could clear-sign a document and then encode it using your recipient's public key. Then your recipient would use her private key to decode the message and a copy of your public key to verify your signature. A communication that is both signed and encrypted using PGP is very secure.

Since clear signatures can't be copied and moved to different documents, digitally signed documents are even more secure than handwritten signatures, which are relatively easy to forge. In 2000, the Electronic Signatures in Global and National Commerce Act was signed into law, recognizing the crucial role of digital signatures in e-commerce, digital communications, and legal documents in a digital environment. Digital signatures may be implemented with the use of "smart cards" or other devices, but public-key encryption is always at the heart of the enterprise. Digital signatures can now be used for legal purposes and will gradually become more commonplace as people begin to trust and accept the technology.

 # Key Management

Public-key encryption makes it easier to keep a private key private, but safeguards must still be taken. If you store a private key on your computer, you must have a way to protect it if someone breaks your computer's security. If your private key is stolen, encrypted documents intended for you would be compromised, and your digital signatures could be forged. Although public-key encryption is generally safer than private-key encryption, the whole system still hinges on the security of the private keys.

What could prevent someone from stealing your laptop computer and rooting around all your files in search of your private key? The answer is very simple: private keys are password-protected. When you generate a key pair for yourself, you are asked to enter a password—actually a passphrase. Then whenever you need to use your private key to decode a document or generate a digital signature, you are asked to enter your passphrase. If you forget your passphrase or don't know it (because the key isn't your key), you won't be able to use that private key.

Any hackers who want to use your private key will have to get past two hurdles: (1) they need the file that contains your private key, and (2) they need the passphrase for your private key. The problem of keeping your file secure is the same problem you face whenever you have anything sensitive or private on a computer (see Section 2.6). Some people store their private keys on a flash drive or other removable medium in case of an attack over the Net. This is a good idea because it thwarts hacker attacks, and you can hide a flash drive in any number of unlikely places (or even store it in a safe-deposit box for maximal security).

But let's assume for the moment that you didn't take such safeguards and your private key has been appropriated by an unknown party. How hard is it to crack your passphrase? Once again, we can only hope that you have taken to heart the advice in Section 2.3 about password security. If you have never written your passphrase down anywhere and never told it to anyone, your passphrase will be very hard to crack. Brute-force attacks won't work on long passphrases because the number of possibilities is too large. However, someone could conceivably watch you at your computer and hope to see you enter your passphrase. This is why computers never echo passwords when you enter them. But even if no one is standing over your shoulder to study your every keystroke or bugging your work area with a video camera, a Trojan horse could be recording every key you press (including the ones for your passphrase) if someone were really out to get you. So good computer security is, once again, your best line of defense.

If all else fails, a wily hacker might still hope to get your passphrase directly from your computer. After all, your passphrase must be stored on your computer so that the encryption software can check your passphrase when you enter it. Of course, the people who design encryption software have thought of this too. So when your encryption program stores your passphrase, the system is careful not to store your original passphrase at all. Instead, it stores a coded version of your passphrase. It uses a special type of code for this called a **hash code**, an encoding algorithm that converts an input string into a numerical signature for that string. (It's the same idea as a parity bit, but the possible output values are more complicated.) Then when you type in your passphrase, the same hash code is applied to what you've typed. If the resulting hash code matches the one stored in memory, your passphrase is accepted. If hackers managed to steal the hash code for your passphrase, they would still be locked out because they wouldn't be able to deduce the original password from the hash code for the password. Whenever passwords are stored on a computer, the actual passwords should never be stored directly; it is much safer to store only hash codes for passwords.

In the end, the whole business relies on passphrase security, and everything that can be done to keep your passphrase secure is already being done for you by your software. All you have to do is keep your passphrase to yourself.

 # 8.6 Counterfeit Keys

Public-key encryption has a lot going for it. We've seen how key pairs make public-key encryption safer than private-key encryption. We've seen how digital signatures cannot be forged and signed documents are impervious to tampering as long as private keys are held securely. But there is still one soft spot in the system that needs to be addressed. A hacker could generate a key pair under your name and then intercept messages intended for you using the bogus key pair. How can we stop people from generating and using counterfeit keys?

This problem is called the man-in-the-middle attack, and you have to think like a criminal to grasp it. So let's pretend to be hackers for the sake of understanding the problem. Imagine for a moment that you have no scruples and you want to read John's e-mail. Intercepting John's e-mail is fairly easy for you if you know your way around computers, so while we're at it, let's pretend you also know all about packet sniffers (see Section 2.15). With a packet sniffer you could grab all of John's incoming mail before it ever gets to him. All you need is access to John's mail server or any of the hosts that feed mail to his mail server. You probably have to access one of these machines illegally, but that won't deter someone with criminal tendencies. So let's suppose you've got access to an appropriate host machine and you've got the software needed to intercept John's e-mail. If John's e-mail is not encrypted, you can read it, of course. But suppose the e-mail you want to read is encrypted with John's public key. Then you need to work a little harder.

It's probably too hard to break the code once a message has been encrypted, so you'll have to find a way to stop people from using John's public key in the first place. It might sound impossible, but this is where a devious imagination comes in handy. All you need to do is plant a counterfeit key wherever John's key has been posted for public consumption. For example, suppose John has posted his public key in a public directory. You have to break into that directory and replace John's public key with a counterfeit public key that is actually part of a key pair you own. Putting aside the question of exactly how you might do this, let's assume that you somehow manage to plant your counterfeit key under John's name in the key directory. Then anyone looking up John's key will have no way of knowing that a counterfeit key has been substituted for his legitimate key. Hang on to a copy of John's real public key—you'll need it later.

Now suppose someone decides to send John an encoded message. She (and/or her mail client) looks up John in the key directory and unknowingly grabs a copy of the counterfeit key. She uses the counterfeit key to encode a message, and then she mails the message to John. You are intercepting all of John's incoming e-mail, so you get this message before it reaches John. Since you have the private key that decodes messages encoded by the counterfeit key, you can decode the message and see what it says. If that's all you care about, then you're done.

But chances are you really want to monitor a steady stream of incoming mail, and you know John is going to become suspicious if he gets no mail for one or two days. You need to make sure John thinks everything is normal. In particular, you have to ensure that John gets all his mail. Here's how you do so. You take the decoded message that was intended for John and encode it using John's real public key (this is why you saved a copy of his key). Now all you have to do is send the newly encoded message to John with a forged e-mail header so that it looks as if it came from the original sender. When John finally receives the message, he will decode it with his private key, and everything will appear to be as it should. John won't have a clue that his e-mail has been tampered with. Figure 8.8 illustrates how all this is done.

You can now monitor all John's incoming e-mail and never cause any suspicion. Once the packet sniffer has been set up and the counterfeit key has been planted, everything else you need to do can be totally automated so that no significant delays slow down the delivery of John's incoming mail. John will have no way of knowing that his privacy has been violated unless he realizes that the key in the public directory has been altered. In the meantime, you are getting a copy of everything John gets at the same time he gets it

Figure 8.8

Man-in-the-middle
attack

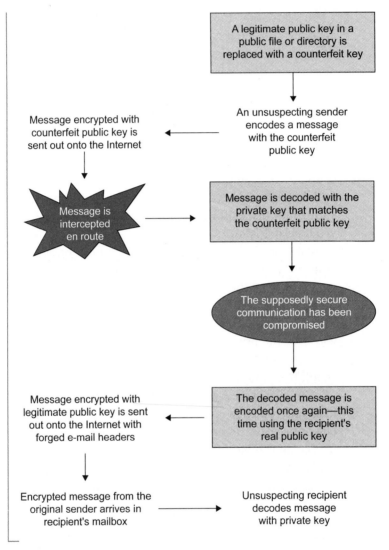

(although you could program a little delay into John's mail stream if it's important to know about something before John knows about it).

The interception of encrypted e-mail is no small undertaking. It requires technical expertise as well as a willingness to break a host of state and federal laws. So the scenario described here is highly unlikely. But it can happen. If secure communications are crucial to the operation of a business or a military operation, there can be no room for sabotage. Organizations like CERT (originally named for the Computer Emergency Response Team) that monitor computer viruses and other security threats on the Internet require reliable communication channels to minimize misinformation and disinformation. CERT uses PGP for secure communications and places its digital signature on all official announcements, warnings, and alerts (see Figure 8.9).

The solution to this problem lies in the integrity of the public keys. All public keys must be subject to careful scrutiny. You need to know who really owns all the keys. If you can't determine with a high degree of reliability the actual owner of a public key, the key may be a security hazard, and you should not use it. A public key is said to be a **trusted key** when you are certain it cannot be a counterfeit key.

The process of identifying a person as the legitimate owner of a public key is called **key authentication**. A lot of thought has gone into this process. Different levels of authentication have been identified, ranging from risky (unprotected) digital distributions to highly secure distributions made at public meetings in the presence of colleagues and associates who are willing to vouch for the identity of anyone distributing a public key. Many rituals have been proposed for secure key exchanges (see Section 8.7).

Figure 8.9

Counterfeit keys can compromise secure communications.

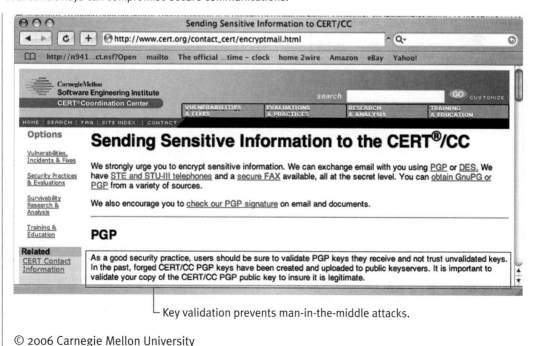

└ Key validation prevents man-in-the-middle attacks.

Key authentication is a special case of a more general problem related to the concept of signatures. When you pen a written signature on paper, your signature should be recognizable to at least those correspondents who know you well enough to know your signature. Your written signature is actually quite useless in the hands of someone who has never seen you sign anything in person. How could anyone know if the signature before them is really yours without having seen the genuine article? It is an imperfect system, but it does offer some degree of security, at least among friends. If more security is needed, you can sign papers in the presence of a notary public, who stamps the paper with a unique impression and signs off on the document as a trusted agent. The notary public's signed stamp tells the world that whoever signed this document at least had a copy of something that looked like a legitimate driver's license complete with an ID photograph when presenting the document to be notarized. This is a good system as long as no one steals the notary's stamp or tricks the notary with a false ID. Most reasonable systems can be breached if someone really wants to.

When people accept a public key and use it for encoding a message, they need to understand the level of risk associated with the key. If the level of risk is too great, they shouldn't use the key. Each person should decide individually how much risk is acceptable. As you will see in the next section, steps have been taken to make that decision as easy as possible for the general public.

 # 8.7 Key Certification

In the previous section we explained how counterfeit keys could be used to break a seemingly secure communication channel if people are too quick to trust the public keys available to them. A system of key authentication is needed to help people decide how much risk is associated with any given public key. Let's start by imagining the safest key authentication possible. Suppose you want to use a public key that belongs to your best friend. Your friend hands you a disk with a public key on it and says, "Here. This is my public key." You can imagine your friend making a mistake or having his disks switched on him by a malicious elf, but if you trust your friend at his word, this key transfer is as secure as it gets. You can take the disk, add it to the virtual key ring on your computer, and feel confident that this is a legitimate public key. If everyone could collect all their public keys this way, the world would be a very safe place. In fact, PGP keys used to be traded in just this way, between friends in person. If your world is relatively small and you never need to communicate with anyone outside a close circle of friends, this is a good system.

Now let's extend this world beyond a close circle of friends to a world that includes friends of friends. Suppose you want a key for someone you don't know but who is a friend of your best friend. Suppose your best friend handed you a disk and said, "Here. This is George's public key." Chances are you would feel pretty safe about it. You are one step away from getting the key from George directly, but your best friend is the step in the middle, and you trust your best friend to give you a legitimate public key for George. In the jargon of key authentication, we would say that George's public key was *certified* for you by your best friend. If you trust your best friend to give you a legitimate key, this certification is quite trustworthy. It may not be quite as good as getting the key from George directly, but it's still pretty good.

Key certification refers to a process through which someone can vouch for the legitimacy of a public key. When a key is certified by a trusted friend, that person can add his or her digital signature to the public key being certified. Then if the key is sent to you over the Net, you can verify the digital signature and feel confident that the certification is legitimate. Public keys can be certified by anyone who uses them. That way, if you receive a public key for someone you don't know, you could look at all the key certifications and see if anyone you trust has certified the key. If you can find and verify a trustworthy certification, you can feel safe about the key. If no trusted friends have certified the key, the key is a security risk.

The model for key certification based on friends and friends of friends is called a **web of trust**. Public keys get passed along from friend to friend, accumulating certifications as they go. When you receive a key you can assess the certifications on the key and make a decision for yourself about the authenticity of the key based on whom you know and how well you trust them. The web-of-trust model works well in small worlds or highly interconnected worlds. But what if you receive a public key for someone you don't know? There are no trusted certifications on the key, and you really need to determine the authenticity of the key as quickly as possible. That's where digital fingerprints come in.

A **digital fingerprint** for a key pair is a unique sequence of integers associated with the key pair. Digital fingerprints are generated when a key pair is created, based on random conditions that cannot be manipulated by the key's owner (much like a biological fingerprint). The fingerprint is built into the key and cannot be tampered with (using digital signatures). If a key owner knows the fingerprint for his or her key pair, then you can check a key's authenticity by contacting the (alleged) owner and asking him or her for the key's fingerprint. Fingerprints for public keys can be confirmed with a phone call, which is a safe and convenient substitute for handing off disks in person. So even if a key is not certified by anyone, you can still trust it by confirming its fingerprint. If you were to accept a key's authenticity based on its fingerprint, then you might also choose to certify it yourself to start a web of trust for that particular key.

PGP relies on the web of trust, key certifications, and fingerprints to help people assess the authenticity of public keys. Whenever you add a public key to your public key ring, you need to guard against counterfeit keys. So PGP asks a lot of questions whenever you add a new key to your key ring. The following example shows a trace of PGP accepting a new public key. Let's assume that Lee Cunningham has acquired a public key for Ann Rodak and stored the key in a file named arodak.key.pgp. The key may have come from a public directory or an e-mail message sent (supposedly) by Ann herself. Here is what happens when Lee adds this new key to his key ring.

```
el18:~> pgp -ka arodak.key.pgp
No configuration file found.
Pretty Good Privacy(tm) 2.6.2 - Public-key encryption for the masses.
(c) 1990-1994 Philip Zimmermann, Phil's Pretty Good Software. 11 Oct 94
Uses the RSAREF(tm) Toolkit, which is copyright RSA Data Security, Inc.
Distributed by the Massachusetts Institute of Technology.
Export of this software may be restricted by the U.S. government.
Current time: 1997/05/16 13:02 GMT
Looking for new keys...
pub 512/80B7AF61 1996/12/03 Ann Rodak <arodak@edlab.cs.univ.edu>
Checking signatures...

...
Keyfile contains:
1 new key(s)
One or more of the new keys are not fully certified.
Do you want to certify any of these keys yourself (y/N)? y
Key for user ID: Ann Rodak <arodak@edlab.cs.univ.edu>
512-bit key, Key ID 80B7AF61, created 1996/12/03
Key fingerprint = 38 57 B7 43 D8 46 FB 33 76 44 13 11 CE 72 FA A0
This key/userID association is not certified.
```

At this point Lee could call Ann on the phone and verify the key's fingerprint to make sure this is a valid key. A counterfeit key won't have the same fingerprint as Ann's real key. If Lee doesn't want to go to that much trouble, he can just accept the key and take his chances.

```
Do you want to certify this key yourself (y/N)? y
Looking for key for user 'Ann Rodak':
Key for user ID: Ann Rodak <arodak@edlab.cs.univ.edu>
512-bit key, Key ID 80B7AF61, created 1996/12/03
Key fingerprint = 38 57 B7 43 D8 46 FB 33 76 44 13 11 CE 72 FA A0
READ CAREFULLY: Based on your own direct first-hand knowledge, are
you absolutely certain that you are prepared to solemnly certify that
the above public key actually belongs to the user specified by the
above user ID (y/N)? y
```

When Lee answers yes, he is indicating his willingness to certify this key and put his own PGP signature on it. Lee's signature has now been added to this copy of Ann's key and will be there if Lee ever passes the key to someone else. Lee should think carefully before putting his signature on the key. His good reputation as a trustworthy key certifier is on the line. If he has any doubts about the key, he should not certify it. (He can still use it if he feels confident enough about the key for his own purposes.) Whenever you are asked to certify a key, you are being asked to act as a notary public; take that responsibility very seriously. If people certify public keys too casually, the web of trust breaks apart.

In this scenario, Lee says that he is willing to certify Ann's key. That means he is going to place his digital signature on the key. He is "signing off" on the validity of the key.

Lee's private PGP key is used to generate Lee's signature. So Lee needs to enter his password or phrase before his signature can go on the key.

Now Lee has to decide how meaningful Ann's signature is when it appears on other public keys. If Lee ever acquires another public key signed by Ann, PGP will check to see if Lee considers Ann a trustworthy key certifier and then remind him about how he answered this question when he certified her key.

All this care is taken because key integrity and the web of trust is a potential weak spot in PGP. As long as all the public keys we use are valid, PGP keys will be impossible to crack. If a security failure ever occurs, it is likely to happen as a breach in key authentication.

You need a passphrase to unlock your RSA secret key.

```
Key for user ID "Lee Cunningham <lcunning@elux3.cs.univ.edu>"
Enter passphrase: Passphrase is good. Just a moment....
Key signature certificate added.
Make a determination in your own mind whether this key actually
belongs to the person whom you think it belongs to, based on available
```

```
evidence. If you think it does, then based on your estimate of
that person's integrity and competence in key management, answer
the following question:
Would you trust "Ann Rodak"
to act as an introducer and certify other people's public keys to you?
(1=I don't know. 2=No. 3=Usually. 4=Yes, always.) ? 1
el18:~> pgp -kc
No configuration file found.
Pretty Good Privacy(tm) 2.6.2 - Public-key encryption for the masses.
(c) 1990-1994 Philip Zimmermann, Phil's Pretty Good Software. 11 Oct 94
Uses the RSAREF(tm) Toolkit, which is copyright RSA Data Security, Inc.
Distributed by the Massachusetts Institute of Technology.
Export of this software may be restricted by the U.S. government.
Current time: 1997/05/16 13:05 GMT
Key ring: '/users/users3/fac/lehnert/.pgp/pubring.pgp'
Type        bits/keyID  Date        User ID
pub         512/80B7AF61 1996/12/03 Ann Rodak <arodak@edlab.cs.univ.edu>
sig! C2309975 1997/05/16 Lee Cunningham <lcunning@elux3.cs.univ.edu>
pub 768/C2309975 1997/05/16 Lee Cunningham <lcunning@elux3.cs.univ.edu>
 KeyID      Trust       Validity    User ID
 80B7AF61   unknown     complete    Ann Rodak <arodak@edlab.cs.univ.edu>
 c          ultimate    Lee Cunningham <lcunning@elux3.cs.univ.edu>
* C2309975  ultimate    complete    Lee Cunningham
lcunning@elux3.cs.univ.edu
```

When you view the contents of a key ring, you can see all the signatures
associated with each key and the level of security that applies to each signature (in the opinion of the key ring owner). An ultimate level of trust is given
to any keys signed by the owner of the key ring.

The web-of-trust model is used successfully by communities of people
who sign each other's keys with due care. Unfortunately, this model does not
scale well when we need a web of trust for millions of Internet users who want

FYI: The Web of Trust Is Delicate

Never certify a PGP key unless you are absolutely confident the key is valid. If you
transfer your copy of the key with your signature validating the key, your reputation
for credibility automatically goes with it. A PGP key that passes through many hands
can accumulate a number of signatures with different authentication values. Each
new user can examine the available signatures and decide whether the key seems to
be a good risk. One trusted certification that is not based on proper precautions can
sink the whole system.

to conduct safe e-commerce transactions with trusted keys. All you need is one counterfeit key with trusted certifications on it and the whole system falls apart. As the Internet evolved into a foundation for a global economy, a new system for key authentication was created, and the web of trust became institutionalized through the use of "trusted agents" or "certificate authorities." We explain this model in the next section.

 # Digital Certificates

The problem of key authentication had to be solved before public-key encryption could be used for e-commerce on the Internet. Without a system for certifying valid public keys, counterfeit Web pages could masquerade as legitimate e-stores and dupe visitors into placing credit card orders with bogus operations. It was not enough to add encryption to the Web. Digital signatures also had to be used to validate the identity of any operation collecting credit card orders.

A digital certificate is a digital signature attached to a public key, just like the digital signatures attached to a public key in the web-of-trust model. The purpose of the certificate is to reassure users that the public key they are about to accept is an authentic key and not a counterfeit key. But now we use the certificate-authority (CA) model of key authentication instead of the web-of-trust model. In the CA model, there are only a few trusted institutions that can generate digital certificates, and any key carrying a certificate generated by a trusted CA can be immediately trusted without question. All the user has to do is decide which CAs can be trusted.

If you have ever placed a credit card order on the Web, your browser was probably checking server certificates for you and you never even knew it. That's because your Web browser already has a list of trusted CAs built into it, and it will accept any public key certified by a recognized CA. You can intervene in this process if you wish, but most people just want to be reassured that everything is under control. If you want to see the CAs recognized by your browser, however, you'll have to hunt around under the security settings. In Netscape Communicator, go to the Communicator menu, click Tools, Options, Advanced, scroll down to the Certificates heading and Manage Certificates. Select the Authorities tab to see the certificate authorities recognized by your browser. You'll see a list of CAs that looks something like the one in Figure 8.10. Internet Explorer has a similar list of CAs you can examine (see Exercise 21).

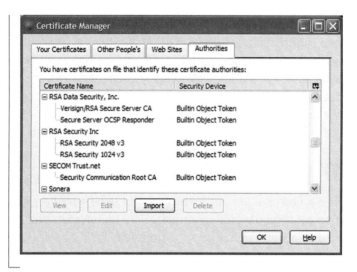

In the context of the Web, you are sending sensitive information to the Web server, so you need to encrypt only data going from your browser to the Web server. That's fine, because a secure Web page offers your browser a pub-

FYI: Is My Credit Card Number Safe on the Internet?

Chances are your credit card is safer in transit than it is once it reaches its final destination. If 128-bit encryption is used to move your credit card information across the Net and nothing goes out without a trusted CA check, that transmission is safer than any other available mode of communication. If your credit card is stolen online, it will probably be the result of an onsite security breech. For example, the database that stores customer information might not have been adequately secured against security breaks and cybertheft. It is impossible to know which sites are handling their in-house security correctly and which are not. In general, a large, established operation should have the resources to maintain good onsite computer security. Smaller businesses and start-ups may not have the resources to take care of computer security correctly. It is not really possible to assess all the risks associated with e-commerce transactions because you can't know what's going on inside an e-store operation. But keep in mind that traditional credit card transactions (those occurring off the Net) are not 100% safe either. If you feel safe placing a credit card order over the phone or if you allow store clerks to discard your credit card carbons without tearing them up in front of you, then you have no reason to worry about credit card transactions over the Internet. There is some amount of risk in all these scenarios, but most of us live with a reasonable level of risk as a fact of modern life.

lic key to use to encrypt the data. But your browser is going to be careful about using any public keys it finds on the Web. Your browser will examine the key and look for a certificate from one of its trusted CAs. Figure 8.11 shows the security information window in Netscape that will take you to a view of the public key associated with a secure Web page at Amazon.com. If the Amazon.com server presents a certificate from a recognized CA, then communication can commence. In Figure 8.11 we can see the public key from the Amazon.com server, and we can also see that this key was certified by RSA's Secure Server CA. If we check the list of recognized CAs in Figure 8.10,

Figure 8.11

Your browser can show you the site certificate for any secure Web page.

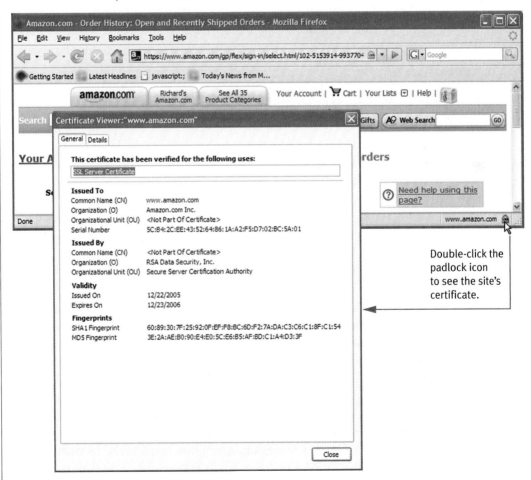

we can see an entry for "VeriSign/RSA Secure Server CA." This means that the browser recognizes the CA that signed the public key, and the browser will therefore accept this key as an authentic public key for Amazon.com. If this certificate had not been recognized or was somehow inconsistent with the server under consideration, your browser would notify you of a problem. You will probably have to do a lot of online shopping before you are likely to see any such notification. Most of the time, the certificate checks out, your browser accepts the public key, and you can send encrypted data on to the approved server with confidence. It's reassuring to know that all this work is going on inside your browser to keep your credit card transactions secure.

Casual users will normally never need to see the CAs shown in Figure 8.10. But the list is there in case you ever have reason to remove a trusted CA. (Make sure you have a good reason before you do so since it will limit the number of e-commerce sites you can use.) If you add a new CA to the list, again, be careful. Make sure you know what you are doing before you decide to trust a new CA.

 # Strong and Weak Encryption

When people worry about whether they can trust encryption, they generally are concerned about how hard it is to break the code. If someone can crack the code that's being used to protect credit cards online, that's a catastrophic failure. We know that 40-bit keys can be broken by run-of-the-mill personal computers in a matter of minutes. The amount of time needed to crack a code is important. Any key that can stand up to thousands of years of computing time on the world's fastest computers is safe enough. The term **strong encryption** refers to encryption methods that are safe in this practical sense. A code that can be broken in a practical time frame is called **weak encryption**.

Anything that can be done using a large number of conventional computers over a period of weeks or months is reproducible using special-purpose hardware within a period of minutes or hours, so the question of practical time frames should always be approached by asking what could be done with a special-purpose computer? A casual hacker with a $3,000 PC is in no position to pick off credit card numbers encoded with 56-bit keys. But if someone starts to sell black market "black boxes" designed to crack 56-bit keys, then any transactions relying on 56-bit keys are in trouble.

Strong encryption steadily becomes weaker over time. According to Moore's law, computer processors double in speed every 18 months. Each time a processor doubles in speed, it can take on one more bit in an encryption key and break the key in the same amount of time. In 1997, 56-bit encryption was cracked, so according to Moore's law, 64-bit encryption will be weak by the year 2011, and 128-bit encryption will be weak by 2107. It is, of course, impossible to predict these milestones with any real confidence. Moore's law might stop working, or a dramatic breakthrough in microchip technologies could change everything. It is simply impossible to say anything about the limitations of future computer technologies with any real certainty.

Although much is made of the line between weak and strong encryption, security breeches are rarely the fault of inadequate technologies. More often, the most exploitable link in the chain is a weak link caused by human error. Someone failed to secure a database correctly or failed to monitor ongoing network activities or neglected to secure a backup file or failed to do some other task. You can learn all you want about weak and strong encryption in an effort to reassure yourself about the relative merits of 64-bit or 128-bit encryption, but security will still be at the mercy of humans in the loop. If they all do their jobs correctly, the system will work. But if there is a slip-up anywhere along the line, that's when disaster can occur.

Things to Remember

- Public-key encryption is safer than private-key encryption.
- Public keys are used to encrypt; private keys are used to decrypt.
- Private keys are used to create digital signatures; public keys are used to verify digital signatures.
- Digital signatures are verified when a public key is used to check the authenticity of the signature.
- Public keys (and certificates) are validated (also said to be authenticated) when a signature on the key is verified with a trusted public key.
- A public key is trusted when you are confident that it cannot be a counterfeit key.
- A public key is certified when someone places their digital signature on the key.
- Digital signatures are safer than traditional signatures if a reliable model of key authentication is in place and people are careful to validate the signatures.

- Never certify a public key unless you are absolutely sure the key is authentic. The web of trust depends on cautious key certification.

- A certificate authority can be trusted to authenticate public keys for e-commerce.

- Your browser does not accept any public keys for encrypted communications unless the key has been certified by a recognized certificate authority.

- In a few years 64-bit keys may not be very secure, but 128-bit keys are very secure and will remain secure for the foreseeable future.

- Strong encryption becomes weaker over time.

Important Concepts

certificate authority (CA) trusted agent that certifies public keys for general use (typically a corporation or a bank)

counterfeit key public key that does not belong to the person it says it belongs to

digital signature encoding of a document with a private key to preserve document integrity and document ownership

document integrity in the context of document transfers, the retaining of the original form of the document, free from subsequent alterations during transit

encrypted document encoded document created and decoded in one of two ways: (1) encoded with a private key and decoded only with that same private key or (2) encoded with a public key and decoded only with a private key

key authentication general process of verifying the owner of a public key

key certification process of placing a digital signature on a public key in order to vouch for its authenticity (a form of key authentication)

private-key encryption encryption strategy based on a single key

public-key encryption encryption strategy based on a pair of keys

strong encryption encryption that cannot be cracked by brute-force means within a reasonable period of time

weak encryption encryption that can be cracked by brute-force means within a reasonable period of time

web of trust key-authentication model based on key certification by friends and friends of friends

Where Can I Learn More?

Basic Cryptography in a Nutshell `http://www.itsc.state.md.us/oldsite/info/internetsecurity/crypto/cryptointro.htm`

Certificate Authorities: How Valuable Are They?
`http://www.networkcomputing.com/806/806f1.html`

Crypto-Gram Newsletter
`http://www.counterpane.com/crypto-gram.html`

Public Key Encryption for Dummies
`http://www.networkworld.com/news/64452_05-17-1999.html`

The Metaphor Is the Key: Cryptography, the Clipper Chip, and the Constitution `http://www-swiss.ai.mit.edu/6095/articles/froomkin-metaphor/text.html`

Problems and Exercises

1. **[FIND IT ONLINE]** Cryptographers distinguish codes and ciphers. What is the difference?

2. **[FIND IT ONLINE]** When one substitution key (such as the one in Figure 8.1) is used, the resulting system is called *monoalphabetic*. When two or more keys are used with some system for moving from one key to another, the system is called *polyalphabetic*. The most commonly used polyalphabetic cipher is called Vigenere's system. Vigenere's system was the main cryptographic method used by the Confederates during the American Civil War. Find out how the standard Vigenere system works and find three Vigenere key phrases used by the Confederates during the Civil War.

3. **[FIND IT ONLINE]** Substitution keys sometimes use *homophones*. What is a homophone?

4. Explain the difference between private-key and public-key encryption. Is one better than the other? Explain your answer.

5. What does it mean to crack a key by brute force? Explain the process and why it can take a long time.

6. Do you think you'll ever see an e-commerce site with an encryption level greater than 128 bits? Why or why not?

7. If you want to send me an encrypted message, do you need your own key pair? Do you use my public key or your own private key?

8. If you want to place a digital signature on a document meant for me, do you need your own key pair? Do you use my public key or your own private key?

9. If you want to verify a digital signature on a document from me, do you need your own key pair? Do you use my public key or your own private key?

10. If you want to certify my public key by adding your own digital signature to my key, do you need your own key pair? Do you use my public key or your own private key?

11. Suppose you've generated a key pair for yourself but you use it only for signing documents—you never use it to encrypt anything. Does the strength of your private key matter? Why or why not?

12. **[FIND IT ONLINE]** Does the Electronic Signatures in Global and National Commerce Act specify any technological requirements (for example, specific encryption algorithms) for a digital signature to be recognized under law?

13. Describe a method of key authentication that does not rely on certificate authorities.

14. Explain how hash codes are used to protect passwords and passphrases.

15. Explain how a man-in-the-middle attack works. Is it possible to set up a man-in-the-middle attack without breaking the law?

16. Explain how people use digital fingerprints in connection with public keys. When are they useful?

17. **[HANDS-ON]** Visit `https://www.hushmail.com/` and examine the certificate for this secure Web page. When does this certificate expire? What is its fingerprint? (Note: IE calls it a "thumbprint.")

18. In 1995, 40-bit keys were first cracked. Given this fact and Moore's Law, when would you have expected 56-bit keys to be first cracked? Did Moore's law give you an accurate prediction? Can you draw any conclusions about encryption predictions from this exercise?

19. Explain how the web of trust works to solve the problem of key authentication.

20. What is a certificate authority (CA)? Explain why a system of CAs is better than the web of trust for e-commerce. When is the web of trust still a useful model of key authentication?

21. **[HANDS-ON]** Examine your Web browser's list of CAs and look for one called the "Thawte Server CA." When does it expire? (If you have IE, select Internet Options from the Tools menu, click the Content tab, and then click Certificates. You will find CA lists under the tabs labeled Certification Authorities.)

22. If your credit card information is stolen on the Net, is the reason likely to be that someone broke a weak encryption code or something else? Explain your answer.

23. Suppose your browser rejects a digital certificate found on a Web server, but the same certificate is accepted on your friend's computer. Suppose you are both running the exact same browser (same version, same platform). What could explain the difference?

24. What is the difference between weak encryption and strong encryption? Why does the dividing line between them change over time? Where is the line being drawn today? (Note: You may have to research this question on the Web to see if the information given in this chapter is outdated.)

25. **[FIND IT ONLINE]** Visit `http://www.netsurf.com/nsf/v01/03/nsf.01.03.html` and find out what steganography is. Is this technique better suited to military applications or e-commerce? Explain your reasoning.

26. **[FIND IT ONLINE]** Companies periodically announce a "cryptochallenge," complete with a prize for the winner, in order to see how long it takes the public sector to break a key of a certain length. Look to see if there is an outstanding cryptochallenge going on right now. If so, describe who is sponsoring it, how long it has been running, and the length of the key to be cracked.

27. **[FIND IT ONLINE]** Visit a secure Web site and examine the digital certificate for that site. If you have a Web-based e-mail account, use the server that handles your mail. If you frequent a particular e-store, use its server. List the URL of the secure server, the owner of the server's certificate, the CA that issued the certificate, the certificate's expiration date, and its fingerprint.

28. **[FIND IT ONLINE]** DES is a 56-bit private key encryption system used extensively by government and business. It was first cracked in 1997 by the DESCHALL project. Visit `http://www.interhack.net/pubs/des-key-crack/` and find out how many computers were used by DESCHALL. How long did it take them to crack the key? How many keys could be tested by a 3GHz Pentium D system in one second?

29. **[FIND IT ONLINE]** The Diffie-Hellman algorithm was published in 1976 in a paper titled "New Directions in Cryptography." This algorithm explains how two parties can communicate with each other in public and produce a secret key that will be known to both parties but cannot be deduced by anyone else who has been listening in on their conversation. Diffie-Hellman is one of the main components in modern public-key encryption. The major contribution of Diffie-Hellman is something called a *one-way function*. What is a one-way function?

Encryption and the Internet

Fighting Spam with Encryption

In the Above & Beyond section in Chapter 4 we looked at some attempts to control spam on Usenet newsgroups. The basic idea was to identify offending articles and filter them out, but great care was needed to avoid censorship. Since the line between legitimate filtering and unwanted censorship may be drawn differently by different people, filters on Usenet must be designed and managed with care. Although the connection between spam filters and strong encryption may not be immediately obvious, encryption has made it possible to fight spam without infringing on anyone's right to read what someone else might consider to be unwanted spam. If spam is in the eye of the beholder, then everyone must have the right to make that distinction for himself or herself. The trick is to minimize the number of people who have to make those judgment calls so that others can benefit from the efforts of a few. Suppose, for example, that one person could be trusted to identify spam for one segment of the Usenet community. Then it should not be necessary for everyone in that group to reproduce the same judgment calls individually: it would be better to broadcast the decisions of the one trusted person and let others accept (or not) the filtering decisions. This is something like having different CAs for key authentication. But here we are talking about trusted agents for spam filtering.

Trusted agents for spam filtering are at work right now battling spam on Usenet. **NoCeM** (pronounced "No see 'em") is a Usenet client that can be installed by end users or applied by a Usenet administrator on a Usenet server. Here's how it works. People watch for spam on Usenet. When somebody sees spam, he or she can post a notice describing the offending article on a special newsgroup called news.lists.filters (see Figure 8.12). Anyone can post to news.lists.filters, but posts from unrecognized agents will be ignored. When someone launches a NoCeM-enabled news reader, it checks news.lists.filters for spam notices and kills off any targeted articles it is authorized to kill. Authorization is needed lest censors place notices on news.lists.filters in an effort to kill random articles.

To authorize a NoCeM action, each NoCeM user creates a file of authorized signatures representing individuals whom the user trusts to issue spam notifications. Then the NoCeM software acts on only the notices posted with

Zimmermann often explains PGP via an analogy involving letters and postcards. He argues that encrypted e-mail is like a letter in an envelope. A letter in an envelope is a private communication, and everyone takes its privacy for granted. An e-mail message that is not encrypted is like a message on a postcard. Anyone can read what you write on the back of a postcard, so people don't put a lot of sensitive personal information on postcards.

No one needs to defend their right to put a letter in an envelope. No one assumes that you are engaged in an illegal activity just because you choose to put a letter in an envelope. In the same way, no one should assume that you are up to something suspect if you prefer to encrypt your e-mail. You are just asking for the same level of privacy that an envelope affords you. If someone denies you that level of privacy, he or she is effectively saying that you must put everything you write on postcards for all the world to see.

The letter/postcard analogy is provocative for anyone who thought e-mail communications were private or secure. Zimmermann is right about the lack of security inherent in unencrypted e-mail. If you wouldn't want to write something on a postcard, you shouldn't put it in unencrypted e-mail. But the postcard analogy is not quite accurate when you consider that the Postmaster General can open envelopes containing letters when authorized by a court order. PGP is not like a letter in an envelope because no one can inspect a PGP file unless he or she holds the one and only private key that can decode the file.

The encryption war is fundamentally a battle between centralized control and distributed control. As we will see in the following sections, key escrow schemes and export restrictions depend on centralized power and institutional controls. Throughout the ages, governments have feared transforming communication technologies. Literacy was restricted to the ruling classes in the Middle Ages, and the invention of the printing press represented a serious threat to the status quo. The very concept of public education is a democratizing force that enables upward mobility and lessens the advantages of social class distinctions. Special interests have always resisted certain technologies out of self-interest and a legitimate desire to maintain social stability. When a technology promises profound social change, the status quo will be affected. For better or for worse, encryption threatens our status quo today, and many social forces are stumbling and colliding over the question of unregulated encryption technologies.

Strong Encryption and Law Enforcement

Suppose that strong encryption is available for general use. Anyone can generate his or her own pair of keys, post a public key in a public directory, and exchange encrypted e-mail with anyone else. The codes for the keys cannot be cracked. This means that terrorists can safely communicate with one another and say anything without fear of discovery. Criminals can plan robberies and plot murders. Right-wing militia leaders can debate the best way to retaliate for the attack on the Branch Davidians in Waco, Texas. Religious extremists can talk about which abortion clinic to bomb next. Al-Qaeda members all over the world can communicate freely with one another. In short, communications that used to require face-to-face meetings in very private settings can now be conducted with blinding speed over unimaginable distances. Material that wouldn't be trusted to a phone conversation or a mail service is perfectly safe on the Internet because powerful encryption is available to anyone who wants it.

Before the advent of computer-based communications, law enforcement agencies had technological capabilities that enabled them to eavesdrop on certain conversations. With a court order, the police can tap a phone line or a local postmaster can open a piece of mail. The FBI has a variety of surveillance techniques used to listen in on private conversations. Although these powers can and have been abused on occasion, they also provide law enforcement personnel with legitimate weapons for combating crime and terrorism. Some people believe that the loss of these powers would be tantamount to pulling the plug on law enforcement.

Powerful encryption on the Internet pulls the law enforcement plug in a big way. As long as the codes can't be cracked, there is no way for the FBI to monitor an encrypted e-mail conversation between suspected criminals. Encrypted communications would make it much harder for the police to collect evidence in a criminal investigation. Drug dealers, organized crime, terrorist organizations, and random criminals can all use strong encryption to great advantage. So the government has a strong vested interest in cryptography. Digital communications and strong encryption open the door for problems unlike anything seen before. The distribution of PGP over the Internet has brought strong encryption into the hands of the masses, good and bad alike. People who use PGP today routinely create 1,024-bit keys, thereby ensuring a level of security like that of top-secret military communications.

What can the government hope to do about this technology? At one time, the best strategy was to outlaw the use of strong encryption. Encryption software would be restricted and distributed only to authorized personnel, probably through some sort of government licensing. The good guys could have it, but the bad guys couldn't.

The U.S. government did attempt to limit the spread of strong encryption by making it illegal to export it outside the United States and Canada. For many years encryption software was categorized as a "munition." The unregulated export of encryption programs was therefore prohibited under the Arms Export Control Act and International Traffic in Arms Regulations (ITAR), a set of laws dating from 1976 that are usually used against illegal arms dealers. Commercial software vendors claimed that the ITAR export restrictions tied their hands with respect to all software development involving encryption. Other countries were selling products with strong encryption (128 bits and more), but U.S. companies could sell only products that used inferior encryption (the limit prior to 2000 was 64 bits). The Clinton administration gradually lifted these export restrictions on strong encryption to keep the U.S. software industry on par with that of the rest of the world.

Since U.S. export restrictions on strong encryption could not prevent the spread of the technology to other countries, other containment strategies have been pursued by law enforcement agencies. The most visible and controversial plan addresses the problem of digital wiretapping through key escrow legislation (for example, the "Clipper Chip" idea). Here's how the key escrow plan would work.

Public-key encryption would be hard-wired into all computer chips inserted into modems, cable boxes, and other network communication devices. Then all communications going out onto the Internet would have to pass through a government-approved encryption chip. Packets going to the Net would automatically be encoded using strong encryption approved by the government, and files coming off the Internet would be automatically decoded using the same technology. Everything would be handled behind the scenes by ubiquitous encryption chips. The casual user wouldn't have to know anything about it.

Each embedded encryption chip would be programmed with its own unique key pair. To give law enforcement the power to monitor encrypted communications, the government must be able to access all the private keys in all these embedded encryption chips. Access would be accomplished with a key escrow system. Whenever an encryption chip was manufactured, a copy of its private key would be indexed by its serial number and handed to the government for safekeeping. No one would have access to any of the private keys except by a court order (the legal authorization for a digital wiretap). Then the serial numbers of the relevant devices would be collected and used to retrieve the necessary private keys for the proper authorities, effectively giving law enforcement personnel a "backdoor" into all Internet communications.

A key escrow system is the government's best bet for digital wiretapping. Unfortunately, anyone who wants to thwart all wiretaps (authorized or otherwise) could get their hands on their own encryption software and encode messages using keys that aren't held in escrow. The use of unauthorized key pairs would sabotage the whole key escrow system. So the government's backdoor can work only if powerful encryption software is not available to the general public. But there's the rub. Powerful encryption software has been distributed freely over the Internet for more than a decade, and passing a law to make it illegal now won't have much effect on its general availability. As encryption advocates say, "When privacy is outlawed, only outlaws will have privacy."

A war on unauthorized encryption seems unlikely to stem the tide of PGP users and other software hobbyists who cannot resist the urge to tinker with their own software implementations of published encryption algorithms. And now that PGP has been given permission to be exported freely, it seems highly unlikely that U.S. citizens could ever be legally prohibited from using PGP. In spite of persistent lobbying efforts and renewed soul searching in the wake of the terrorist attacks of September 11, 2001, it appears that law enforcement has lost its bid for centralized control over strong encryption.

U.S. Export Restrictions

In 1992, the U.S. government placed an export restriction on encryption software so that U.S. software vendors could not incorporate encryption keys stronger than 40 bits in their products. Strong encryption was added to the list of munitions covered by ITAR, placing it in the same category as nuclear missiles and other weapons of mass destruction.

Privacy advocates have strongly objected to any governmental restrictions on encryption on the grounds that citizens have a right to protect personal materials on personal computers and private communications on the Internet. Although the ITAR restrictions did not affect most U.S. citizens at home, it did make it illegal to take a laptop computer out of the country if it had PGP installed on it. Computer science professors could not post course notes describing strong encryption on the Internet without violating ITAR restrictions. Protesters pointed out how impossible it was to enforce the ITAR restrictions and how pointless it all was since the rest of the world already had strong encryption anyway.

However persuasive many arguments against ITAR might seem, the only protests that made their mark in Washington came from the business sector. U.S. companies couldn't add strong encryption to products destined overseas, while European manufacturers were free to use strong encryption technologies (many of which came from the United States) without restriction. ITAR had tied the hands of American software manufacturers, and they lobbied hard in Washington to change that. The voice of American business was loud and clear on the subject of ITAR, and Washington was responsive, albeit slowly.

In 1996, ITAR software restrictions were relaxed under certain conditions so that selected vendors could receive permission to go up to 56 bits. (This meant that DES-based encryption could be exported.) Although a step in the right direction, this measure was not much help to U.S. software companies. They were still competing with European manufacturers that were free to incorporate 128-bit encryption in all of their products. Eventually, the software lobbyists began to gain ground.

In 1997, the U.S. Department of Commerce granted Netscape permission to export a strong (128-bit encryption) version of Netscape Navigator. At the same time, permission was also given to VeriSign Inc., a leading CA, to issue 128-bit certificates to banks and large-scale e-commerce operations. Ever since 1997, Netscape Navigator has been establishing 128-bit communication channels with sites bearing a VeriSign certificate. Sites without the VeriSign certificate were still restricted to 40-bit encryption. Internet Explorer upgraded to 128-bit encryption in 1999.

In 1999, as the Clinton administration struggled to meet international standards for privacy protection and to address controversial issues in intellectual property rights, Washington observers began to sense a shift in Congress over the encryption debate. At the end of 1999, Network Associates, Inc., was given permission to distribute industrial-strength PGP worldwide with 1,024-bit session keys. Shortly afterward, U.S. software manufacturers were allowed to add 64-bit encryption to all software products without restriction. Although 64-bit encryption is not as good as 128-bit encryption, the government had at least admitted that the old boundary line between weak and strong encryption had shifted since 1992 and that export restrictions had to move with it. Then changes in European Union export regulations prompted the United States to relax export restrictions once again. U.S. export restrictions on strong encryption were effectively lifted on October 19, 2000, to expedite software trade with other industrialized nations.

With browsers handling e-commerce transactions with strong encryption and a growing community of individuals using strong encryption for personal and professional communications, the Internet is gradually moving in the direction of a heavily encrypted medium. It's only a matter of time before encryption becomes the norm for all private and sensitive communications over the Net.

Problems and Exercises

A1. [FIND IT ONLINE] Is there a version of PGP that runs on a Palm Pilot? List five OS platforms on which you can run PGP.

A2. [FIND IT ONLINE] U.S. Senator Joseph Biden inadvertently encouraged Phil Zimmermann to move PGP into the public sector with the release of Senate Bill 266 (S266) on January 24, 1991. Which statement in S266 prompted Zimmermann to act? What world events in 1990–1991 prompted Biden to include in S266 statements with implications for encrypted communications?

A3. Explain how a key escrow system would make it possible for the government to conduct digital wiretaps on the Internet.

A4. Explain what is meant by the saying "When privacy is outlawed, only outlaws will have privacy."

A5. [FIND IT ONLINE] Read "Jackboots on the Infobahn: Clipping the Wings of Freedom" by John Perry Barlow (`http://www.eff.org/Misc/Publications/John_Perry_Barlow/ HTML/infobahn_jackboots.html`) and "Crime and Crypto on the Information Superhighway" by Dorothy E. Denning (`http://www.cs.georgetown.edu/~denning/crypto/ Crime-and-Crypto.txt`). Describe three concerns raised by Barlow and explain how Denning would respond to them. Who presents the most compelling arguments? Do you think this controversy can ever be resolved in a way that will satisfy everyone?

A6. [TAKE A STAND] Suppose you had a time machine and you could go back to January 1, 1991, and talk to Phil Zimmermann. At this time Phil was planning to release PGP, but PGP was not yet ready for public consumption. If you could go back in time and talk to Zimmermann about PGP, would you encourage him to go ahead with his plans or would you discourage him? What facts about our world today could you tell him to strengthen your argument? Do you think the world would be a better place or a worse place without PGP?

A7. [FIND IT ONLINE] Visit the ITAR Civil Disobedience page at `http://online.offshore.com.ai/arms-trafficker/` and read about the button that ships a strong encryption program to Anguilla. At the time this site was created, the act of pushing this button violated ITAR's munitions export law, and anyone who clicked the button became an illegal arms dealer (a felony offense). Export laws on strong encryption have since been relaxed. Is it still illegal to press this button? Or is this Web site out-of-date?

A8. **[FIND IT ONLINE]** Recently relaxed export laws on strong encryption still place restrictions on exports to terrorist countries. Which countries are terrorist countries with respect to U.S. export restrictions?

A9. **[FIND IT ONLINE]** Find out what the FBI's Magic Lantern program is. Explain how this relates to law enforcement and strong encryption.

A10. **[TAKE A STAND]** (Do this exercise after Exercise A9.) Do you think the events of September 11, 2001, have changed the way the general public views projects like the Magic Lantern? Do you think Magic Lantern could help stop a terrorist attack? Why do some people object to Magic Lantern? How do you feel about the Magic Lantern project?

A11. **[FIND IT ONLINE]** What restrictions on the use of encryption apply to organizations and individuals in the People's Republic of China?

A12. **[HANDS-ON]** Install PGP on your personal computer. Visit http://www.cert.org/reporting/incident_form.txt and verify the digital signature for this Web page. You will need to download a copy of CERT's public key first. (See http://www.cert.org/contact_cert/encryptmail.html for a link to its public key: you can download the key directly from a hyperlink named "PGP public key" on this page. When the download box asks you if you want to open it or save it, select Open and PGP will take it from there.) To verify the signature, go to the Web page, choose Select All from the Edit menu, and then copy the text to the clipboard. Launch the PGP toolbar, click the Decrypt/Verify icon, and when PGP asks you for a file, click the Clipboard button. When was CERT's Web page signed? Examine the CERT public key to find out when this key was created. When does it expire? Check the fingerprint on the key to make sure it matches the fingerprint posted at http://www.cert.org/contact_cert/encryptmail.html. How strong is this key?

A13. **[HANDS-ON]** Install a PGP tool on your personal computer. Visit the public PGP key server at http://www.keyserver.net/ and download my public key (search for "Wendy G. Lehnert"). Send me an encrypted mail message. Send it to lehnert@cs.umass.edu with the subject header "Chapter 8, A13." Ask me a question, tell me about a great Web site, let me know what you think of this book, or just say hello. I will send you a reply. Plus, if you tell me where to find your public PGP key, I'll encrypt my reply to you.

Basic Web Page Construction

9.1 Taking Charge

Anyone with access to the Internet can publish a Web page. Moreover, it doesn't take much expertise to do so. A neophyte using the right resources can put up a decent Web page in about an hour. More than a few college students bring in a little extra income as freelance Web page designers; some will turn this sideline into a full-time career after graduation. Professional seminars are available for people who want to stay on top of the latest developments in Web design. Beginners, however, can get started right here.

You don't need to major in computer science to master Web page design, although professionals do need to know something about computer programming. Creating sophisticated Web pages is becoming more possible for nontechnical users, thanks to increasingly powerful software tools. This chapter reviews the basics of Web page design and construction using two different Web page editors. Chapter 10 covers advanced topics, including style sheets, basic HTML code, and ways to add dynamic elements to your Web pages.

To create a Web page, you can get by with just a text editor and a browser. However, you can make the process easier and faster with software designed to expedite Web page devel-

Chapter Goals

- Review the basics about copyright law and the Web
- Learn the fundamentals of Web page design
- Learn how to use Mozilla Composer to build Web pages
- Learn how to add absolute links, relative links, mail links and internal links using named anchors to your Web pages
- Learn how to add pictures and colors to a Web page
- Find out how to use tables to format your Web pages
- Learn how to publish a Web page
- Find out about browser-safe colors and valid image file formats

opment. Many Web page construction tools are available, and some are designed specifically for beginners. All of them are easy to use once you understand the basics. In this chapter we will focus first on using tools to build Web pages the quick and easy way. In the next chapter we will look "under the skin" of the Web page to see how things work. This will be especially helpful if you are using Mozilla Composer to build your Web page. While Composer has all the basic tools needed to insert popular Web page elements, it lacks the tools needed to create more sophisticated features. Composer users will need to learn a little **Hypertext Markup Language (HTML)** to edit the page source and create features that Composer cannot build directly.

 # Copyright Basics

Before you begin building Web pages, there are a few things you need to know about copyright laws. As you may be aware, it's very easy to "capture" content from the Web. Virtually every line of text, picture, video clip, animation, and sound file can be downloaded from the server where this material resides onto your personal computer. This same material can then be inserted into your own Web pages. Unless explicitly stated otherwise, this is generally illegal, especially if your Web page is to be published on the Web—and you almost certainly will be doing so. There would be no reason to create the Web page otherwise!

The relevant details of copyright law are explained further in Appendix D. Some very important points to note right away—*everything* you see, read, or hear from any source (electronic or otherwise) is copyrighted, even if it does not explicitly say so! This includes the Web pages that you create—then *you* are the copyright holder. You can only use content from another source if you have explicit permission to do so.

Resources obtained from a government source are generally *not* copyright protected, so you can use these resources without fear of penalty. But even at government Web sites, some material may still be copyrighted if it was created under a contract awarded to a private business. Under certain conditions (here's where the gray area appears!) you *may* be able use portions of copyright-protected material. These "gray areas" are described in detail in Appendix D.

One recommendation that you should consider when using material obtained from another source: Always acknowledge the source of any materials you place on your Web page that you did not create. At the very least it is a courtesy to the author of the material to assign credit where due.

TIP: Copyleft and Copyright

You may also encounter the term **copyleft** ☺ when you are examining sites to find material. Copyleft is a play on the word *copyright* and is used to *remove* typical **copyright restrictions** associated with intellectual property. A copyleft may be implemented in terms of a **license** that gives the user specific permission to study, use, modify, and redistribute the original or modified work *as long as the same license terms apply to the redistributed version*. You are also expected to attribute the author when you use copylefted material, something that you should do in any case. The most common license associated with copyleft is the GNU General Public License (GPL) or the GNU Free Documentation License (GFPL), designed by the Free Software Foundation (`http://www.fsf.org`).

9.3 Planning Your Web Page

Now that you have considered the legal aspects associated with Web page authoring, you're ready to begin designing your Web page. Keep in mind that, once properly published on a Web server, your Web page is viewable by *anybody in the world* with a browser and Internet access. You certainly want to make sure that page presents a favorable reflection of you and the message you are intending to communicate. You also want to make sure that you have not violated any copyright laws! Consequently, it's a good idea to do some planning before you actually build your Web page. The goal should be to create a Web page that is not only functional but also attractive to your viewers. If you plan to use copyrighted materials on your Web page, you can contact the copyright holders and secure their permission to use the materials. Remember that *everybody*, including the copyright holder, will be able to view your Web page. If you have not secured copyright permission, then you might be facing legal action should the copyright holder happen to view your page!

The first thing you need to do is to decide what you hope to communicate using your Web page. Will this be a page dedicated to your favorite charity? Are you creating a Web page to support your favorite candidate for elective office? Are you creating a page that shows the viewer how to build a canoe? The purpose will become the overall guiding theme to your Web page, and all the content you insert should be consistent with your chosen theme.

Once you have selected your theme, you need to decide exactly what you want to place on your page and where you want to place it. In other words, how will your page content be *organized*? The best way to do this is to create a storyboard using paper and pencil. A **storyboard** is a graphical representation of the layout of your Web page that describes the basic content of each component of your Web site, including descriptions of pictures, links, and text, and how these components will be arranged with respect to each other. You don't need a computer to do this—a piece of paper and a pencil is best for this task. Figure 9.1 shows a storyboard for a typical Web page layout.

Figure 9.1

A sample storyboard

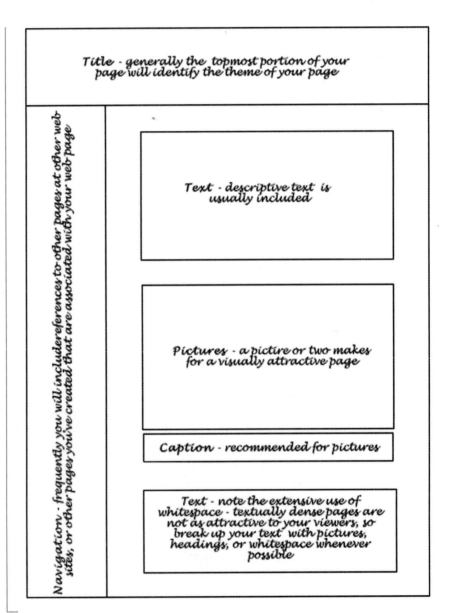

TIP: **Review the Web Content and Accessibility Guidelines**

As you plan your Web page, there are some general guidelines you should consider. These guidelines are not intended to be exhaustive; they are just recommendations that you should consider when building any Web page. As is usually the case, some of these guidelines will not apply in every circumstance, and other guidelines might be more appropriate than these in specific cases.

The ultimate authority regarding the design and implementation of Web pages are the Web Content Accessibility Guidelines (WCAG). It is especially important to observe these guidelines when designing business Web content to ensure that the pages you create appeal to the broadest segment of the market. The guidelines presented here form a subset of a more comprehensive and professionally oriented set of documentation provided by the World Wide Web Consortium (`http://www.w3.org`). These guidelines are published at `http://www.w3.org/WAI/intro/wcag.php`.

9.3.1 Guidelines: Basic Elements

Most themed Web pages will typically include a set of basic elements. These elements appear so frequently on Web pages that they can be considered essential in many respects to the successful implementation of the page. As you proceed through this chapter, you will learn how to create each of these elements using Mozilla Composer. Use this list as a guide for reviewing the common essential elements.

1. **Include a descriptive title.** There is a specific HTML element, `title`, that displays the page's title in the title bar of the Web page window (so it's technically not *on* the Web page). The title should be short and capture the purpose of your Web page as succinctly as possible. Some search engines index Web pages by the words used in the title. If you use imprecise or inaccurate terms, then the search engine may not categorize your page correctly, reducing the number of hits your page receives. A title should always be present, even though your page is OK without it.

TIP: **A Page with No Name**

Have you ever seen the word "Untitled" in the title bar of a Web page window? That page lacks a title!

2. **Include the author's name and contact information.** Viewers of your Web page may want further information about the page's topic, they might want to let you know of factual or functional errors, or they might just want to know more about you or the topic of your page. You can use the mail link feature to facilitate communication between you and your viewers. One caveat: avoid providing personal contact information such as telephone numbers and addresses. It's much easier to ignore unwanted e-mails than it is to ignore someone knocking at your door!

3. **Indicate the creation/modification date.** Web pages are intended to be dynamic—their content can and should be changed when new information becomes available. When publishing a Web page for the first time, it is helpful to list a modification date. This helps the viewer to decide if there is new content that should be examined. You might also add a "What's New" section to your page if there are significant changes from one version to the next.

4. **Use pictures to highlight and emphasize the purpose of the page.** Remember the old adage: *A picture is worth a thousand words.* On the other hand, don't get too carried away with them either! Image files tend to be much larger than the Web page file itself. If your page is viewed over a dial-up connection, then it may take some time for the images to appear. Some viewers may not want to wait and move on before the page has completely loaded.

5. **Provide navigational content.** If you will be creating more than one page, then you will also need to provide navigational content to help your viewers find their way around the set of pages you create. Every page should have a clearly labeled link to every other page in the set, or if there is an expected sequence that should be followed when viewing your pages, then previous and next links should be provided. Even if there is only a single page, navigation is often used to direct the viewer to related content at other Web sites.

9.3.2 Guidelines: General Design and Organization Recommendations

A common use of a Web page is to communicate some useful information to a targeted audience. Consequently, you don't want the message to be obscured by garish colors, busy type fonts, or excessive graphics. You also want to avoid having the text clash with the background color or image (if used). And you especially want to be sure that there are no grammar or spelling errors! A Web page that is well executed will be more successful at communicating its message than one that is hastily assembled with little forethought. Use the following list as a general style guide and content reference when you plan and implement your Web page. Table 9.1 summarizes the critical style and content guidelines presented here.

1. **Put the most interesting and important information at the top of the page.** When your Web page appears on the screen, viewers will see it from the top. Viewers should find something here that is engaging, which will hopefully encourage them to continue examining your page. Because text loads much faster than pictures, the top of your page should be mostly text. Ideally, text should appear before any images placed near the top of the page.

2. **Keep your image files small and few.** When pictures are included, these files can be very large—how many of you own digital cameras that create images that are 3 million pixels in size or larger? Large files can take a noticeable amount of time to transfer from the server to the browser, and the browser cannot display some files unless the entire file has been received. Even on a broadband connection, if the files are very large, it may take minutes for the page to load completely if there are several pictures and/or the pictures themselves are very large. A good rule of thumb is to keep your image files 15KB to 40KB. Photo editing programs (such as Adobe Photoshop) can often be used to safely reduce the image file size without a significant loss of resolution, because most displays have a resolution of 72 pixels per inch (ppi), and many images have significantly higher resolution than this. A reduction in the image resolution to 72 ppi with a corresponding reduction in image size will be transparent to the viewer. If this is not possible, create a "thumbnail" of your image (see the Above & Beyond section at the end of this chapter), which can be used as a link to the larger image file as desired by the viewer. The thumbnail file itself is usually very small.

TIP: Resolution and Images

Screen resolution is usually expressed in **ppi** (pixels per inch) or, somewhat inaccurately, **dpi** (dots per inch), which specifically refers to printed images created dot by dot by a printer. The higher the ppi/dpi for an image, the greater the level of detail can be rendered by the display device. Most computer screens have a fixed maximum resolution between 72 and 96 ppi.

Criteria	Recommendation
Readability	Put the most important information at the top of each page, and avoid using multiple fonts and unnecessary text. Use headings to organize your text, and be sure to check spelling and grammar.
Color	Choice of color should be coordinated with text and images throughout the site. Avoid bright clashing colors. Use of browser-safe colors is recommended.
Navigation	If there are multiple pages, all the pages should be linked together in a simple and intuitive fashion.
Page size	Each page should only be as large as it needs to be and should focus on a single topic. Use a separate page for each logically distinct topic.
Downloading speed	Ensure that the page size is kept to a minimum to keep download times as short as possible—especially the first page if there are additional pages!
Graphics	Graphics should be used only if they convey a message, because they can significantly increase the download time of your page. *Do* use small graphics files to improve the appearance and appeal of your page and alternate text with all pictures.
Multimedia content	Too many multimedia files (audio, video, etc.) put a heavy overhead on the page. Use links instead of embedded content.
Page currency	The page/site should be updated as needed. Put "Last modified" date on the page.
Contact information	A page/site should include easy-to-find author contact information including telephone, e-mail, and fax numbers.
Portability	Ideally the page should display the same information in different browsers, although there will inevitably be differences from one browser to the next due to implementation issues. Preview and test your page in several browsers before you publish it.

3. **Add alternate text to your images.** Note that some of the viewers of your Web page may not be sighted. As a courtesy, include alternate text with every image that describes the content of the picture being dis-

played. Alternate text will also display when the browser cannot display the image for some reason, so your sighted viewers will also appreciate this information. You will learn how to do this later in this chapter.

4. **Avoid excessive use of embedded multimedia content.** You may have visited a Web page that takes some time to load because it includes a very sexy video display embedded into the page, forcing the viewer to wait for the file to load in order to see the page. The video may be really impressive, but it also results in a longer load time for the page. It's better to keep the initial page small, simple, and multimedia-free. Instead, put links to the sexy multimedia stuff on the page with warnings about download times. Then your viewer can choose which content to look at.

5. **Use the so-called "browser-safe" colors.** Later we will examine the color palette issue. What you need to be aware of now is that there is a set of colors known as the *browser-safe palette* that generally ensures that colors seen by your viewers are the intended ones. Using other color choices could result in totally different shades or colors than those intended by the author. The browser-safe colors are discussed in Section 9.7.

6. **Use only the default fonts.** The fonts available on different computers can vary greatly. When you choose uncommon fonts, be aware that the appearance of your Web page will be noticeably different if the viewer's computer lacks the font you chose. The only way to guarantee that the appearance of the fonts will be the same from one computer to the next is to change all your text to an image using graphics software. If you do this, bear in mind that the text will no longer adjust itself to the margins when you resize the page window.

7. **Use only a few fonts.** Web pages with multiple fonts can also be distracting, especially if the chosen fonts are substantially different from each other. A different type font can be used when it is desirable to draw attention to significant text passages. Generally you should keep the bulk of your text in a single font and use perhaps one other font for contrast when needed.

8. **Use a style sheet.** It is possible to separate the content data from appearance data on a Web page if you use a style sheet. When you study advanced Web page topics in Chapter 10, you will learn about style sheets and how to use them.

9. **Break up your content with subtitles using headings.** A solid block of text is hard to read regardless of the media used to present it. Placing

subtitles at logical breaks in the text make your page more viewer friendly. Be sure to use the built-in `Heading` feature available in HTML for your subtitles.

10. **Use the spell checker!** Nothing is more distracting than trying to read a Web page that has numerous spelling and grammar errors. If your Web page editor lacks the capability to perform spelling and grammar checks, write your text using a word processor that does, then cut and paste the text into the Web page.

11. **Preview/test your page.** As you add new features that do not display or function in edit mode, and also when you have completed your Web page, use the preview capability to see how the browser will display your page. While most editors will display a "What You See Is What You Get" (WYSIWYG) view of your Web page, links don't work, invisible borders will be visible, and interactive elements are inactive. The only way you can be sure that your page appears and functions as expected is to preview *and test it* in the browser. You should also check it one more time after you've finally "published" your Web page. I can remember numerous times when my students had everything working in preview mode, but then failed to confirm it after publishing the page. When I checked the Web page later, I often would find missing elements or defective links.

Creating Web Pages with a WYSIWYG Editor

As you will see in the next chapter, a Web page file is simply a text file with the *.htm* or *.html* extension appended to the file name. As such, this file could be created with a text editor like Notepad (if you are a PC user) or TextEdit (if you are a Mac user). Creating a Web page using a text editor is an extremely tedious and error-prone process, so in this chapter we will use a commonly available Web page editor instead that greatly simplifies the process of Web page authoring by providing a "What You See Is What You Get" (WYSIWYG— pronounced "whizzy wig") graphic-based interface. When in "Edit" mode, the window is not quite WYSIWYG, but it's much better than viewing a text file filled with HTML!

The Web page editor used here is Mozilla Composer, part of the Mozilla suite. Composer includes the fundamental tools needed to create basic "plain vanilla" Web pages, although many of the "bells and whistles" can be added if

TIP: Collect All Your Page Components First

Regardless of how you build your Web page, it's a good idea to gather the components you plan to use first, based on the storyboard you created. Any pictures, sound files, video clips, and other external components you wish to place on your page should be placed into a single folder (aka directory) on your hard drive. Remember where everything is located, because that's where you will want to save your Web file. Even though it appears that elements like pictures are placed into the Web page file we will create, you will see later that we are only placing the *name of the file* that contains the picture (or other media content) into the Web page file, not the file itself!

you know how to edit the HTML (you will see how to do this in the next chapter). Composer also has a tool to publish your Web pages. The best thing about Composer is that it's free! It comes packaged with Mozilla Web browser (also available as SeaMonkey), which also includes an advanced mail and IRC (see Section 4.7) chat client for both PC and Macintosh users. The Mozilla Suite can be downloaded from `http://www.mozilla.org/`. For those of you familiar with Netscape, this Composer editor is the same one provided with the Netscape suite for the PC, up to and including version 7.2. Beginning with Netscape 8, Composer is no longer included.

In this section we will describe the tools needed to build basic Web pages. We will begin by proposing some recommended preference settings, then we will create a simple Web page with elementary features like headings, formatted text, horizontal lines, and the ubiquitous hyperlinks. Then we will move on to more sophisticated features like lists, images, and tables. In a later section we will show you how to publish your page. In the next chapter, we will look at how more sophisticated elements can be added by editing the HTML source code directly using Composer tools.

9.4.1 Setting Preferences

Before you begin building a Web page, it's a good idea to examine the default preferences that have been established by the product's provider. There may be some changes you might wish to make from the typical behavior or appearance associated with the editors you will be using. At some point the preferences we will review in the following two sections could make your life a little easier later on when you begin to attempt more sophisticated pages.

When you launch Mozilla, like most browsers, it opens a browser window rather than a Web page authoring window. This is, of course, why browsers were designed in the first place! Before beginning to create a Web page, set the

Composer preferences to optimize the Web page creation task. Figure 9.2 shows a picture of the Composer Preferences dialog box found under the Edit menu option in Mozilla (or the Mozilla menu on a Macintosh running OS X).

The maximum number of pages listed refers to the number of pages that will appear when the "Recent Pages" selection under the File menu is chosen. The next two buttons under the "When Saving or Publishing Pages" section refer to the way the HTML source code will display. The Retain button will display the source as you type it, while the Reformat button will reorder the source in an attempt to make it easier to read. For now the second choice is recommended, but when you alter the source code directly, you may wish to revisit this selection again to preserve the code as you type it. Neither of these two options will affect how the page appears in browser or normal edit view, however.

The Save checkbox in this section causes Composer to save the HTML file along with any other files included on your Web page *in the same place* on your hard drive when the page is saved for the first time, or when it is saved to a new location. If you are new to Web page construction, then you should be aware that Web pages are frequently constructed from several different files, only one of which is the HTML file you create with an editor. For example, each picture on your Web page lives in a distinct and separate file from the HTML file, and each picture file must be "published" along with the HTML

Figure 9.2

The Composer Preferences dialog box

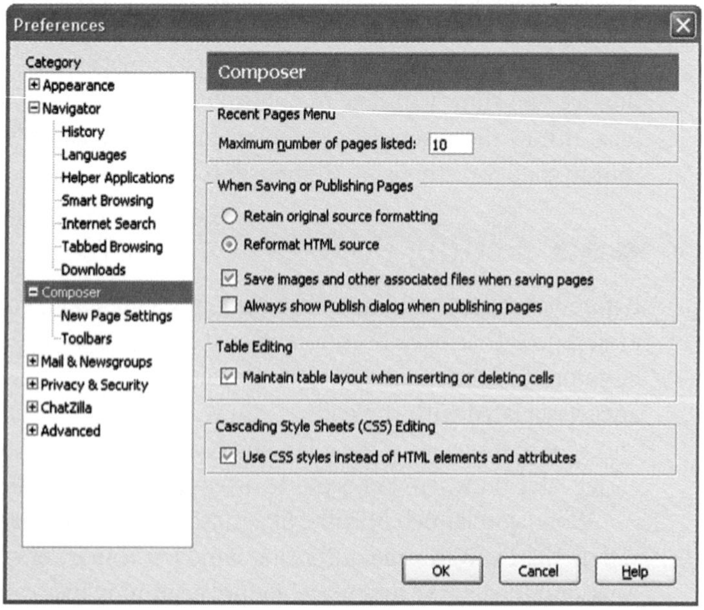

file if you wish to view it successfully on the Internet. If you are a novice, your editing experience will be less challenging if you always *put all the files included in your Web page in the same place on your hard drive*. This will make it easier for you to "publish" your page when finished and save yourself a lot of aggravation.

Selecting the table editing option maintains the rectangular shape of a table element (when used) if cells are deleted. If not selected, deleted cells appear as blank spots in the table (borders are also removed), or the table will have an irregular shape if the deleted cells are on the table edges. We recommend selecting this option.

The **Cascading Style Sheet** (**CSS**) style checkbox determines how your page elements will appear in browser mode. The significance of this selection will not become apparent until the next chapter, but we recommend that you select this checkbox. With CSS formatting, your page will be more compatible with other browsers and easier to maintain. If you edit a document that does not use CSS formatting, then Composer will substitute CSS style information for non-CSS style information in any edited element found in the document. Additionally, with this checkbox selected, you can set the background color of individual page elements (rather than the entire page), and you can also highlight sections of text in the color of your choice. Unfortunately, the various browsers you can use to view Web pages (Netscape, Internet Explorer, Opera, Mozilla, etc.) each have their own quirks, which can cause subtle to glaring differences in the way a Web page displays. Using CSS will minimize this problem when a CSS-compliant browser is used.

New Page Preferences. The New Page Settings Preferences dialog box (see Figure 9.3) allows you to specify in advance the background color or image to be used automatically on all your Web pages, as well as selecting normal text and link colors. For now, we recommend the default selections for these choices (as shown in Figure 9.3). You can also enter the name of the Web page author. If this text box is completed, then the author's name will appear in the HTML code automatically—but it will not appear in the browser window! You must view the page source to see the name of the author. We recommend that you complete this text box if you are using your own computer. If you insert your name as the author on a public computer, anybody else who uses the editor to create a web will have you listed as the author. Your instructor might get the wrong idea if the new author fails to change it!

Toolbars Preferences. The Toolbars Preferences dialog box (see Figure 9.4) is used to specify which tools should have a button in the Composition and

Figure 9.3
Composer New
Page Settings
Preferences
dialog box

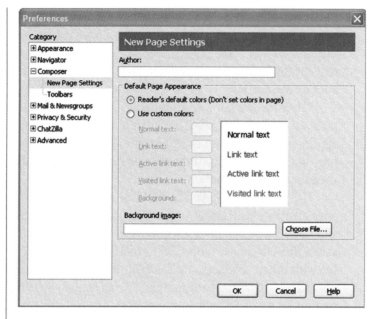

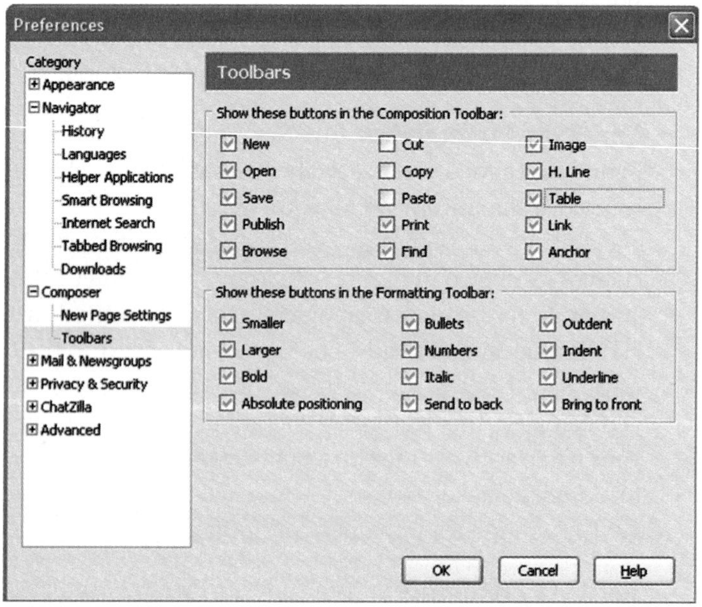

Figure 9.4
Composer
Toolbars
Preferences
dialog box

Formatting toolbars. You use the composition tools to place various elements on your page, and the formatting tools are used primarily to alter the appearance and placement of text. Two tools are omitted from the default list of selected preferences in the Composition toolbar: the horizontal line (H. Line) and the anchor. We recommend that these two boxes be checked, although these elements can still be inserted using the Insert menu option (as can any element) if these tools are not selected for toolbar inclusion. Because cut, copy, and paste can be done using keyboard shortcuts (Ctrl + X, Ctrl + C, and Ctrl + V on a PC or ⌘ + X, ⌘ + C, and ⌘ + V on a Mac), we are not recommending these tools for placement in the toolbar to keep the toolbar length manageable.

Click the OK button to save your preferences and you are ready to go!

9.4.2 Creating a New Web Page

We're finally ready to build a Web page. Our first Web page will be devoted to apples, and we will use the storyboard shown in Figure 9.5 as a guide, adding elements one by one to construct the various components of our page until completed.

Open Mozilla and select Composer from the Window menu. You will see a window like the one shown in Figure 9.6. The blue bar at the top of the window is known as the *title bar*. All new Web pages get the ubiquitous title: untitled. Notice that after the current title is the name Composer. As you begin to accumulate several open windows while running Mozilla, it's useful to be aware of what you are looking at—sometimes it's hard to distinguish a Composer edit window from a browser view window. (You can't edit the browser window!) All edit windows will have the word Composer in their title bars. A Mozilla browser will display "Mozilla" in the title bar.

You will save yourself a great deal of trouble if you *immediately save the file*. Saving the file will do several things that will be helpful as you construct your Web page, in addition to saving the file. The first time a file is saved, Composer prompts for a title for the page as shown in Figure 9.7.

Enter a descriptive title into the dialog box as shown in Figure 9.7. When you click OK, Composer will then display a save dialog box with a suggested file name based on the title you entered in the dialog box, as shown in Figure 9.8. It is *not* necessary to use the suggested name, but it's a good idea to give the file a name that suggests its theme. Note also that there is *no* connection between the page title and the name of the file that contains it. They can (and probably should) be different. In this example, we named the file *apples*, and Composer automatically adds the appropriate file extension (.html). The

Figure 9.5

Apple Web page
storyboard

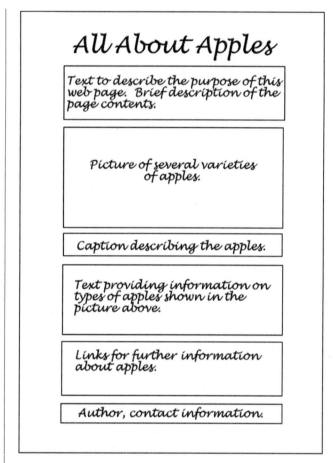

Composer-recommended file name is taken from the page title entered in Figure 9.7— All About Apples—which includes space characters. We changed it to "apples" to remove the space characters. You can choose to name this something different if you'd prefer.

Notice that the title you've assigned will now appear in the title bar, as shown in Figure 9.9. The name of the file that contains this Web page is also shown in brackets after the file name. If it's not too long, the *path* to this file (its location on the hard drive) is also shown. As you may have both a browser window and Composer window for this file, it's useful to know how to tell them apart. A Composer window always includes the word Composer in its title. A browser window will replace Composer with Mozilla, so they should be easy to distinguish from each other.

Figure 9.6

New page window in Composer

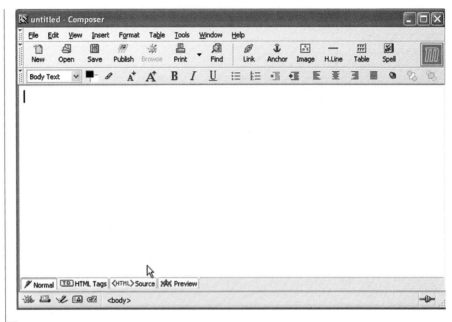

Figure 9.7

Saving a new Composer file

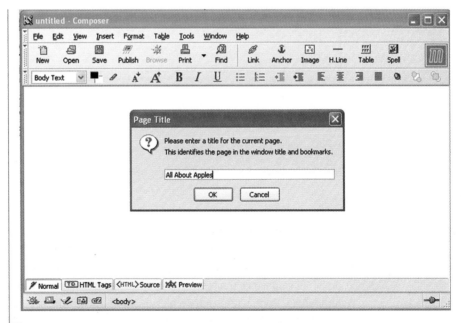

Figure 9.8

Composer Save
Page As dialog
box using the
page title for the
file name

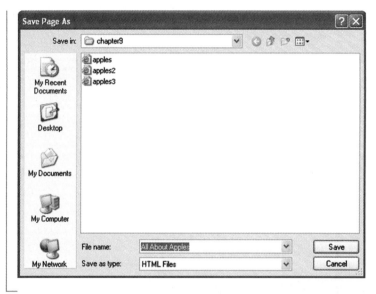

Figure 9.9

A saved
Composer window
displaying the
new title

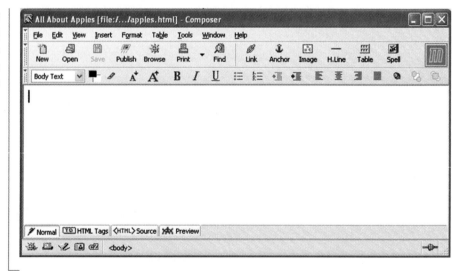

TIP: Avoid Space Characters in Your File Names

When you name a file, avoid using any characters other than letters and digits.
Especially avoid using *space characters* in your file names! Some Web page servers
do not like space characters as part of the file name. Use the underscore (_) character instead. Composer is not so picky—it will put space characters in the file names
it recommends for you, but be sure to change the file name to remove them.

9.4.3 Headings

Headings are very useful on Web pages. They serve to organize the text into logical segments and they are helpful in breaking up large sections of text. Headings are comparable to chapter, section, and subsection titles in a textbook. Although it may appear that headings are nothing more than ordinary text rendered in bold style and a larger font size, in fact they are coded differently from regular text. When we look at cascading style sheets, you will find that the use of headings for titles can be very helpful when you wish to make style changes.

As shown in Figure 9.9, Composer features a typical menu bar below the title bar, stacked above the two toolbars: the Composition toolbar and the Formatting toolbar. At the far left side of the Formatting toolbar there is a drop-down menu (see Figure 9.10). The heading choices represent different sizes of headers, with Heading 1 being the largest and Heading 6 the smallest. The first three heading choices will appear in a text font size larger than the default (like the section headings in this book) and the next three are smaller. All appear in a bold text style. We will choose a Heading 1 for the main page title. When you press the [Enter] or [Return] key after typing your heading, Composer automatically skips a line and resets this menu choice to "Body Text" (the default), which is the choice for ordinary text.

Figure 9.10

Adding a heading in Composer

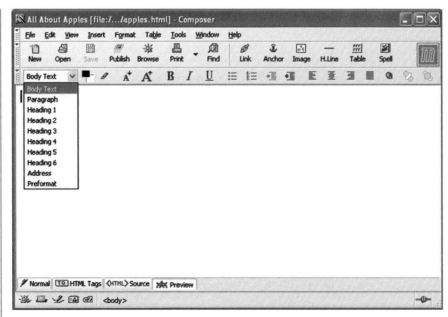

We will also center this heading on our Web page using the text alignment buttons, as demonstrated in Figure 9.11. The button selected in the figure is used to center text. The button to the left of this sets left alignment (the default), the button to the right sets right alignment, and the button adjacent to the right alignment button is used to *justify* text (both the right and left margins of a body of text are aligned to the border of the page or element in which the aligned component is placed). Although we usually think about text when considering alignment, pictures and other page elements can be aligned using these tools as well.

Headings can be placed anywhere they are needed, using any size that is desired. You can also change heading sizes later if you want to. Just place the cursor anywhere in the heading and use the drop-down menu on the left hand side of the formatting toolbar to select the desired new heading value. Changing the heading size also resets alignment to the default setting (left justified), so it may be necessary to reset this too.

9.4.4 Adding and Formatting Text

Text is added in much the same way you would add text in a typical word processor document, and the formatting is applied to text in a similar fashion. Simply highlight the text to be formatted (as bold, italic, highlighted, etc.),

Figure 9.11

Centering the
heading

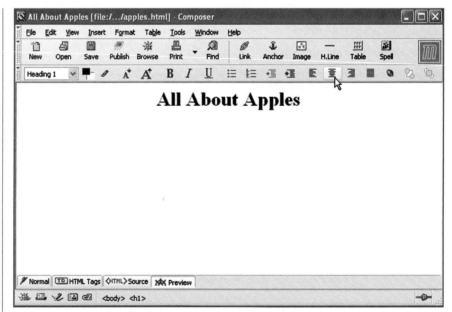

then select the appropriate button in the Formatting toolbar. The buttons adjacent to the drop-down menu in Figure 9.10 are used to adjust the visual appearance of typed text (color, highlighting, smaller, larger, bold, italic, underline). In the Formatting toolbar, text formatting and alignment are accomplished using the buttons labeled **B** (bold), *I* (italic), <u>U</u>, and the previously seen alignment buttons for left, centered (selected here), right, and full justification of text segments. Like a word processor, text formatting can be applied at any time. It's probably easiest to type your text first and apply formatting later. In the Composer Composition toolbar, note also the last button labeled *Spell*. Use this tool often—it will (hopefully) catch your spelling errors!

Don't use your Tab key to indent! Composer uses instead the Indent buttons ⬚ ⬚ found to the left of the text alignment buttons. The button pointing to the left removes a tab; the button pointing to the right adds a tab.

Text color can be changed by selecting the section of text to be colored, then choosing the button immediately to the right of the Heading drop-down menu. The Text Color dialog box shown in Figure 9.12 will appear. Click a color square to choose it. Composer will display a six-character code preceded by a pound sign (#) that represents the color chosen. The Default button can be used to set colored text back to the default color if desired. We will learn more about color codes in Section 9.7.

In general, the default font is recommended. In the next chapter you will learn an easy way to change the text font for the entire document. Remember that the fonts available differ from computer to computer. The upshot of this

Figure 9.12

Composer Text Color selection dialog box

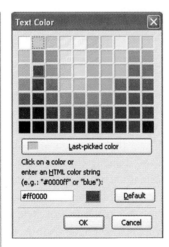

is that a page may look totally different from one computer to the next. Consequently, the default font is probably the safest choice. Many fonts, especially exotic ones, may not be available on many computers. Figure 9.13 shows our page so far as viewed in Composer. Notice the different text formats used on this page.

Figure 9.13 Text formatting

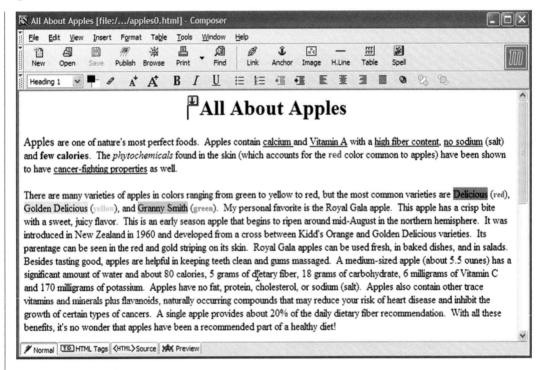

TIP: Use Preformatted Text to Preserve Original Formatting

Occasionally it may be necessary to insert text that has already been formatted for printing by another application, or text that relies on whitespace for special visual arrangements of the words and lines. Usually copying this preformatted text into your Web page will mess up the formatting. Composer provides a special selection, Preformat, found at the bottom of the drop-down menu on the left side of the Formatting toolbar (see Figure 9.10). Avoid the use of style elements to alter the properties of preformatted text if you include it (see Chapter 10).

9.4.5 Adding Lists

There are two types of lists that can be placed onto a Web page: an unordered (or bulleted) list and an ordered (or numbered) list. The tools used to add lists are to the right of the underline tool in the Composition toolbar. The first button places an unordered list at the location of the insertion cursor. An indented bullet will appear automatically to mark the list origin. Simply type your values and press Enter or Return to add a new item to the list. Press the Enter or Return key twice to terminate the list. Figure 9.14 illustrates an unordered list. An ordered list is created with the second list tool. By default these list items are marked by digits rather than bullets, but otherwise the list is created the same way as a bulleted list. The list buttons (like most of the text tools) have a **toggle** feature. To remove a list but preserve the text, highlight the list and press the appropriate list button again. The bulleting (or numbering) will disappear along with the indentation, leaving only normal text. Press it again and the list reappears.

Further customization of the list is possible by using special dialog boxes. To specify the list's appearance in Composer, select the list items and then select the Format > List Properties menu option as shown in Figure 9.15. The

Figure 9.14
Unordered list

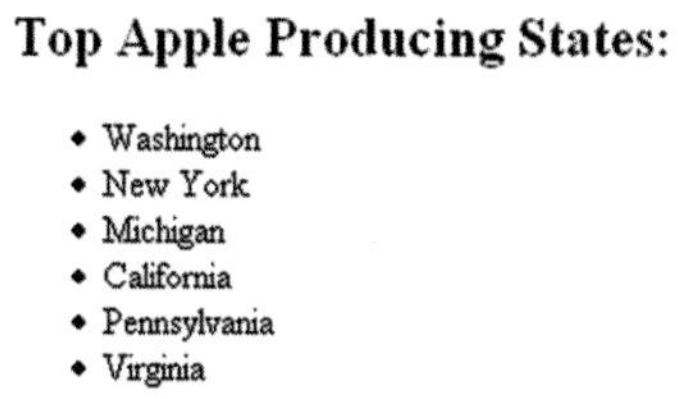

Top Apple Producing States:

- Washington
- New York
- Michigan
- California
- Pennsylvania
- Virginia

Figure 9.15
Modifying list properties in Composer

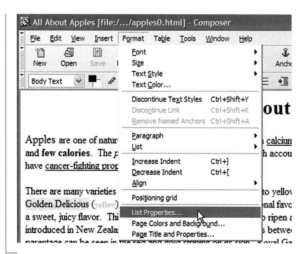

dialog box shown in Figure 9.16 will appear. This dialog box can be used to change the list type, the bullet style (see Figure 9.17), and the number style (see Figure 9.18).

Figure 9.16

Changing the list type in Composer

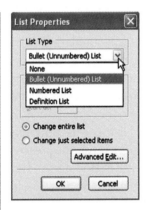

Figure 9.17

Changing the bullet style in Composer

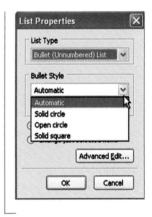

Figure 9.18

Changing the numbered list style in Composer

CHECKLIST: Web Page Construction Checklist 1

Now you try it!

1. Create a new page using your editor of choice and immediately name and save your Web page.
2. Add a heading at the top of the Web page.
3. Add text using the default text type, changing sections of the text to show colored, bold, italic, underlined, undersized, and oversized text.
4. Add a numbered list using lowercase Roman numerals.
5. Save your page, then view it in a browser using the File ·····⟩ Open menu option.

9.4.6 Adding Links

One of the most powerful features that can be included on a Web page is a **hyperlink**, or **link** for short. A link is also known as a *Uniform Resource Locator* (URL). Links can be used to change the display to any of the following:

- Another location on the same Web page (an internal link or named anchor)
- Another page at the same Web site (a relative link or URL)
- Another page at a different Web site (an absolute link or URL)

Links can also be used to play a sound or video file, to display a picture file, or to open a mail window. All of these links use the same link tool. Alternatively, links can be created by using the appropriate menu option in the menu bar.

Internal Links. Internal links require the use of an additional Web object known as a **named anchor** that will serve as the target location. This named anchor must be created first with the provided **Anchor tool**. A frequent use of internal links is to move the display from the bottom of the page to the top of the page. This is the link we will create in this example. The first step is to move the cursor to the top of the page, and then place the anchor by clicking on the anchor button in the Composition toolbar ⚓. The dialog box shown in Figure 9.19 will appear, requesting that you name this anchor. Names should reflect something about the purpose of the anchor. Later when you use an anchor to make links, you will appreciate having used meaningful names when there is more than one anchor on the page. In this case, because we are using the anchor to mark the top of the page, the name *top* seems to be most appropriate.

An anchor is an example of a Web page element that does not cause anything to display in the *browser view* of the Web page. It merely serves as a target location for resetting the page display location. It is very helpful to know

Figure 9.19

Named Anchor
Properties dialog
box in Composer

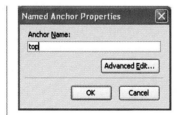

TIP: Name Your Anchors Wisely

Anchor names should be simple, descriptive, and limited to one word if possible. Names should be constructed using letters and digits only, avoiding special characters (anything other than a letter or digit, except for the *underscore_character*) and especially avoiding the use of the *space character*. When referencing a named anchor, the spelling and capitalization must be reproduced *exactly*, as these names are *case-sensitive*.

where anchors have been placed, and when viewing the page in a Web page editor, you will see an anchor icon where an anchor has been placed, as shown in Figure 9.20. To edit the anchor name, simply double-click its icon and the dialog box shown in Figure 9.19 will reappear. Changes can be made here. Remember that the anchor icon will not appear when the page is viewed in browser mode.

Now we are ready to place our internal page link. We will create a "Go to top of page" link. When we move the cursor to the bottom of the page and click the Composer Link button 🖊, the dialog box shown in Figure 9.21 will appear. There are two text boxes to be completed. The first text box is used to enter the link text, text that will display as a link (in color and underlined) on your Web page. Because the purpose of the link is to move to the top of the page, it makes sense to use "Go to Top of Page" as the link text. In the second text box we can either type the name of the anchor we created previously *preceded by the pound sign character* (#), or we can use the drop-down menu as shown in Figure 9.21 to select the desired anchor.

When there are several anchors on the same page, it's useful to name them according to the location being marked. We recommend using the drop-down menu to select an anchor for internal links, because internal links won't work unless the anchor name is typed correctly (case is important too) and the pound sign is present. Sometimes Composer gets a little cranky when creating internal links. If you are having a problem adding this link using the drop-down list, enter the link location value manually.

When creating an **internal page link**, there must be some *length* to your Web page in order for the link to function as expected. If, for example, you can view the entire page in the browser window (there will be no scrollbar), click-

Figure 9.20
Composer anchor
icon

Figure 9.21
Creating an
internal link using
Composer

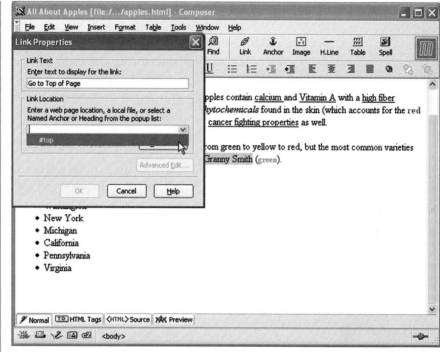

TIP: Minimize Errors—Let the Editor Do the Work

When a Web page displays or behaves incorrectly, typing errors are frequently the cause, so whenever you can get your Web page editor to do the typing for you, then let it!

ing on an internal link at the bottom of the page that is intended to shift the view to the top of the page will cause no *visible* change to the display. On the other hand, if you are at the bottom of the page and can no longer see the top because the window is not deep enough to show it, then clicking on the link *will* cause a visible shift to the display. Consequently, internal links are only useful if your page is longer than the depth of the window.

Relative and Absolute Links. When you have multiple Web pages in the same directory on your Web server, you can insert links to your own pages without specifying the full URL (although the full URL will also work). You can use a shortcut address that consists of only the file's name and its location relative to the current directory. This is called a **relative URL** or **relative link**.

Relative URLs work only when the destination page is on the same Web server as the page that contains the link. If you see a relative URL on someone else's Web page, you cannot simply copy that link and expect it to work on your Web page on a different server. You must convert the relative URL to an absolute URL in order to make it operational on your own Web page.

You can't know when you might need to move your Web site to a new server, so plan for an uncertain future and opt for relative URLs whenever possible.

If your Web pages are stored in a different directory, you will need to include a directory path to the file name in the relative URL. If you are familiar with directory paths, you know what to do. If you are not, avoid the added complication of trying to use them by keeping all your Web files in the *same directory*.

A relative link is created exactly the same way we created the internal link except that the name of the file to be displayed is placed where the anchor

TIP: Use Relative URLs Whenever You Can

When you create a link to another Web page *on your own site*, you can use either a relative URL or an absolute URL. It's best to choose relative URLs. Doing this will make your Web pages portable if you need to move them from your current Web server to a different Web server. When a Web page is *portable*, you can relocate the page on a new Web server and all its links will still be operational. People do switch Web servers for various reasons. When you move your Web pages, you want to install them on the new server with a minimal amount of work and adjustment. If your internal links are all absolute URLs, you will have to edit each one to replace the old DNS name (see Section 1.5) with the new DNS name. If the links are all relative URLs, they will continue to work on the new Web server (unless you change your directory structure).

TIP: So What's in a URL?

A URL specifies the DNS name of the server where a given web page resides, path information needed to locate that file on the server (depending on where the file is located this part may not appear), and the name of the file to be located. The text between the first pair of slash characters is the DNS name, and the text after the last slash is the name of the desired file. The text in between these two items is the path to that file from a default starting point on the server. In the example URL shown, the DNS name is in blue, the path is in red, and the file desired is displayed in green.

```
http://www.myserver.org/produce/domestic/bananas.html
```

name was placed (see Figure 9.22). In this example we are assuming that the Web page file "cherries.html" exists and is stored in exactly the same place that the "apples.html" Web page file has been stored. If this condition is not satisfied, then the link will not work when selected in the browser.

If a complete URL (`http://` + the Web server name + the path to the file from the base Web directory) is placed in the second text box instead of a simple file name, then you have created an **absolute URL** or **absolute link**. Figure 9.23 shows an example of an absolute link, presumably pointing to some remote Web site, although a link to your own Web site is considered absolute if the full URL is specified (including the `http://`). You can place as many links of any type as you wish on your Web page.

To edit a URL, double-click the link in the editor to reopen the dialog box shown in Figure 9.23, then edit the link location appropriately. The link text can also be edited in the document window just like you would edit normal text.

Figure 9.22

A relative link in Composer

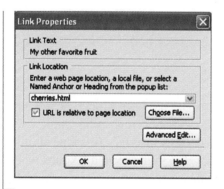

TIP: Drag and Drop Links

To minimize the chances of typographical errors when creating links in Composer, a quick and easy way to add an absolute link to your page is to grab the icon immediately to the left of the URL (shown in Figure 9.24) in the navigation bar in a Mozilla or Netscape browser window displaying the desired page and drag it to the desired location in your Composer window. A link will be created automatically that uses the browser page URL as both the Link Text and Link Location. You do not need to use the Link button to do this. If you don't want to use the URL as the link text, you can always edit the link text in the Web editor to change it. If you are using Internet Explorer, this process will only capture the URL, pasting it into your Composer Web page as ordinary text. You will need to use the link button in the Web page editor to change it into a link.

Figure 9.24

Quick links using the browser link icon

Mail Links. If your browser has been properly configured, then clicking on a mail link will open a message composition window with a predetermined recipient address automatically inserted. This type of link is created the same way as the others, except that in the second text box type the text *mailto:* followed by the fully qualified e-mail address, as shown in Figure 9.25.

Figure 9.25

Composer mail link

TIP: *mailto:* Is Written as One Word with *No* Spaces!

A common error is to separate the words "mail" and "to" with a space character, or forget the colon character. If you do this, then the link won't work!

Horizontal Lines (aka Rules). The Composer view of our Web page with the links we've added is shown in Figure 9.26. We also added a horizontal line to serve as a separator. The horizontal line is added using the H. Line button ▭ in the Composition toolbar. First place the cursor where you wish to have

Figure 9.26

Composer Web page with text and links

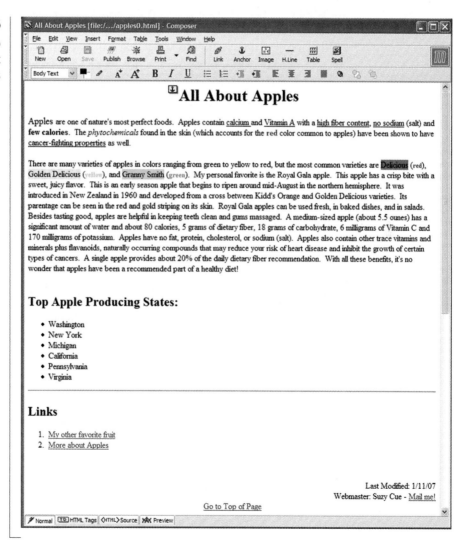

a horizontal line inserted, and then click the horizontal line tool. Double-clicking on a horizontal line opens a dialog box that lets you change the height (thickness) of the line, its length either in pixels or as a percentage of the window, and its alignment (if it does not occupy the entire window width).

One final piece we added is a "Last Modified" date. This lets your viewers know how recent your page is. Some pages "degrade" quickly. A modification date helps the viewer assess the reliability of the page content.

That's all there is to it. If the URL is current and you insert it into your HTML file without typos, it should be operational. Always check each link you add to a Web page to be sure it works. Visitors get frustrated by broken (non-functional) links, so keep your Web page in good operating condition. To maintain your Web page properly, periodically check it to verify that all links still work. It is not enough to know that a link was working when you created it. A link that works today might not work tomorrow if the page's author renames some files or directories. Ongoing maintenance is needed to ensure an operational Web page next week, next month, and next year. This is one of the hidden costs associated with publishing pages on the Web. It's fun to create new Web pages, but most people find it tedious to maintain them.

Testing Your Hyperlinks.   Links will definitely *not* work in editor view. The only way to be sure links work as expected is to test your page. We can do this using the Browse tool in the Composition toolbar. After you add new elements, especially links, to your Web page, use the Browse tool to examine the new version to ensure that it displays properly and that links work. Watch out for the following scenario:

1. You view one of your Web pages and find a problem with one of the links.
2. You replace the faulty link with an updated link and save the modified file.
3. You view the new Web page to check it, but the problem is still there.

TIP: About the Preview Tool

Mozilla Composer has a tab at the bottom of the window labeled *Preview*. Selecting this tab will only display the page the same as a browser would by hiding "invisible" table borders, anchor icons, and other normally visible editor features. You are still in a Composer window and your page remains editable. Links will *not* work, so to test your page links and get a true preview of how the browser will display your page, use the Composer tool labeled *Browse* for previewing.

CHECKLIST: Web Page Construction Checklist 2

Now you try it!

1. Explain the difference between an absolute URL and a relative URL.
2. Explain why using relative URLs is better than using absolute URLs (given a choice).
3. Add an absolute URL to a Web page and then test it.
4. Add a relative URL to a Web page and then test it (you'll need a second Web page for this).
5. Create a named anchor, and then create an internal that links to this anchor.
6. Add a centered horizontal line that occupies 80 percent of the window width with a height of 5 pixels to your Web page.
7. Test your page in the browser to make sure that all your links work.

To avoid this, be sure that you're viewing the newly updated Web page and not a previously opened browser window still displaying the old page. If you close the browser window after you complete reviewing it (recommended to avoid window clutter), then this should not be a problem.

9.4.7 Graphics for Web Pages

A Web page without color or graphics is rather dull. The addition of just one or two colored or graphical elements can make a big difference. A lot of artistry can go into the design of graphical elements for the Web. If you aren't an artist, don't despair. Everyone can brighten up a Web page with a touch of color, a photograph, or some simple artwork. Working with graphics is fun—that's one of the reasons why so many people want to create their own Web pages. We will start by explaining how graphical images are inserted into Web pages. In subsequent sections, we will take a look at using colors and background patterns on Web pages and briefly discuss image-processing utilities.

In Section 9.2 we discussed copyright law and how it applies to Web page authors. To make a long story short, the upshot with respect to artwork and photography can be summarized fairly simply: If an image does not belong to you, you have no right to place it on your page and publish it on the Web. Free clip art libraries on the Net are one big exception to this rule. If you absolutely must have, for example, a penguin balancing on a soccer ball, you just might be able to find it in a clip art library. In fact, the Web offers all sorts of resources and tool archives for Web page designers that go far beyond the realm of clip art. Just be sure that any materials you obtain from these

Web sites are used in accordance with the specific permissions granted by the copyright holders. For example, many materials can be used for most academic purposes, but commercial use may be totally disallowed.

All artwork and photographs found on the Web are stored in binary files on a Web server, along with the HTML files that refer to them. This is important—when you place an image on your Web page, what you are actually placing is a reference (a link) to the file that has the image information in it. Your Web page file and the images it contains are each stored in separate files. There are many ways to obtain graphics you can use on your Web pages, including clip art, digital cameras, scanners, and software for artists (or adventurous amateurs).

Regardless of the source of your image, the only file types that will reliably display your images in a browser are **JPG** (*jay-peg*), **GIF** (*jif*), and **PNG** (*ping*) formats. JPG is a common file format for photographs, GIF is usually used for images created with a software paint program (like Microsoft Paint), and the PNG format is the newest image format, which was designed to replace and improve on the old GIF format. When a choice is possible, the PNG format is preferred over GIF, although this format does not directly support animation (only the GIF format supports animation). See Section 9.6 for more details about these image file formats.

Adding an Image.   Be sure to acquire the image files in advance and save them in the same place that your Web page is stored. To insert an image into your Web page, place the cursor at the place on your page where you wish to insert the image, as if you were planning to add text there. Then move the cursor to the Image button in the Composition toolbar and press the mouse button. A dialog box like that shown in Figure 9.27 will appear, requesting information about the image you want to place on your page.

By default the Location tab is selected. The other three tabs are used to make changes to the appearance and behavior of the image on the page. If you know the name of the image file *and* the image file is stored in the same directory as the Web page, simply type the file name into the Image Location text box. The Web server is usually case sensitive, so be sure to type the name *exactly* as it appears in a listing of your files on the disk where it's stored! Most of the time it's easier to use the Choose File button. When selected, a list of files in the current directory will appear, from which you can select the correct file.

The text box labeled "Alternate text" should always be completed and its radio button selected (the default). Alternate text will display if the image file

Figure 9.27

Composer Image Properties dialog box

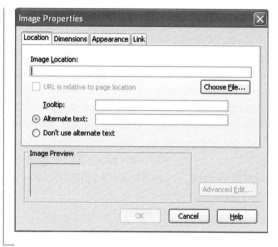

is corrupted or otherwise unavailable, and it will also be read to viewers of your page who are visually challenged by a Web page reading device. The alternate text should impart the same information that the picture would have given had it been viewed. Sometimes this may be satisfied by a simple description of the picture; other times an explanation of the purpose of the image might be more appropriate. When the image is used purely for decoration (like a floral border) or spacing (to separate Web page elements) rather than communication of information, then alternate text should be omitted. If so, select the "Don't use alternate text button" before closing the dialog box. Figure 9.28 shows a completed Image Properties dialog box.

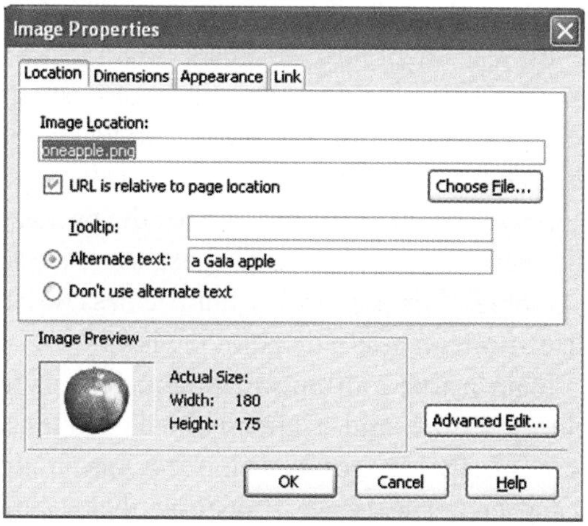

Figure 9.28

Completed Composer Image Properties dialog box

Image Properties

Location | Dimensions | Appearance | Link

Image Location:

`oneapple.png`

☑ URL is relative to page location   Choose File...

Tooltip:

⊙ Alternate text: a Gala apple

○ Don't use alternate text

Image Preview

Actual Size:
Width: 180
Height: 175

Advanced Edit...

OK   Cancel   Help

TIP: Keep Your Image Files and Web Page Files in the Same Folder

When you develop your Web page locally, keep your image files in the same directory as the Web page files that refer to them. If both files are in the same directory, you can specify just the name of the image file. However, if you are comfortable working with directory paths, you can use different directories, as long as you specify the correct directory path for the Image Location value relative to the location of the Web page that contains the picture. If you do use images in different directories, then you must replicate this same directory structure on the Web server or the image will not be found. If you are not familiar with directory path notations, don't worry about it. Just be sure to keep all your files in the same directory as your Web page and your life will be a lot simpler!

As mentioned earlier, the image is assumed to be a file residing in the same directory as the Web page that references it. If the file is stored on a *remote* Web server, then the box "URL is relative to page location" should be unchecked, and the full URL should be typed for the Image Location text entry box.

Aligning Images with Text. The Image tool creates an inline image on the Web page. An **inline image** is an image treated as if it were a single alphanumeric character (created by a key on the keyboard) similar to the inline images of editor tools used in the text in this chapter. If you place an image between two words, the image will be inserted on the Web page as if it were another typed character. The main difference is its size—the image you insert is usually larger than the characters on the page. This forces the Web browser to rework the text placement near the image. Figure 9.29 shows what happens when an inline image is placed in the middle of a paragraph. Note that this new "character" is treated as an extra large single character. By default, the text that follows aligns itself with the baseline of the inserted image.

The Web browser needs to make room for the oversized inline graphic, so it increases the vertical and horizontal space set aside for the text line that contains the graphic. This is probably not the best way to combine text and graphics, at least from an aesthetic point of view.

You can obtain a more attractive combination of text and graphics by alternating left-justified and right-justified images, with text flowing down and alongside the images by using the Appearance tab in the Image Properties dialog box. The Image Properties dialog box will appear if you

Figure 9.29 Text with an inserted image

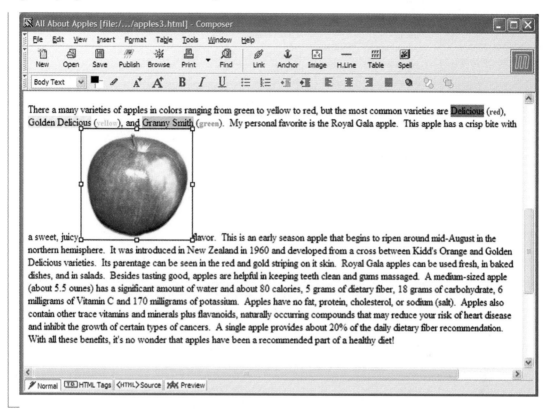

double-click the image. The image appearance can be adjusted so that any text near that image will automatically flow around the image, which is almost always what you want it to do. Alternatively, you can control the vertical alignment of an image relative to its text baseline to "bottom," "top," or "middle." The default appearance is to have text align itself with the bottom of the image as shown in Figure 9.29. Figure 9.30 shows the Composer setting needed to cause text to "flow" to the right of the image (Wrap to the right), selected from the drop-down menu found in the "Align Text to Image" section of the dialog box. Figure 9.31 shows how the text now flows around the image when the settings shown in Figure 9.30 are selected. Text can also be set to flow to the left of the image, which would place the image on the opposite side of the page. The best way to learn what these various settings accomplish is to experiment!

Figure 9.30
Appearance tab in
the Composer
Image Properties
dialog box

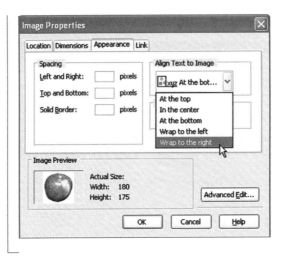

Figure 9.31 Text wrapped to the right of an image

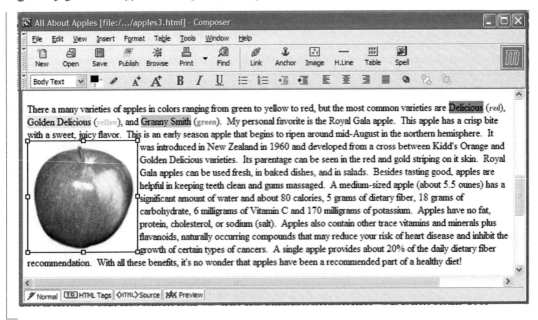

Image Dimensions. Two important attributes for the image element are HEIGHT and WIDTH. Each image has vertical and horizontal dimensions that should be specified in the image element. If the browser knows the dimensions to expect, it can work out the page layout and print the text without hav-

TIP: Finding an Image's Dimensions

If you have an image file but have no idea what its dimensions are, open it up using your Web browser. You will either see the height and width in the browser window's title bar, or you will be able to see both by choosing View→Page Info. Let your browser tell you what you need to know. In Composer, you can double-click the image to open the Image Properties dialog box. Select the Dimensions tab to see the width and height of the image (see Figure 9.32).

ing to wait for each image to download. Without this information, the browser will still display the page properly, but it will take longer because the browser will have to wait for each image to download in order to find out how much space should be set aside for it. A Web page that can display its text while it waits for the images is easier on users, especially those with slow Internet connections.

Scaling Images. Sometimes an image is not the right size for your Web page. It might be too big, or perhaps you don't think it's big enough. In these cases, you need to **scale** the image, that is, resize it by increasing or decreasing its dimensions on the Web page. It's easy to adjust the amount of space allocated for an image in Composer by changing its HEIGHT and WIDTH attributes using the Dimensions tab in the Image Properties window, as shown in Figure 9.32. If you want a larger image, increase the attributes' values; if you want a smaller image, decrease them.

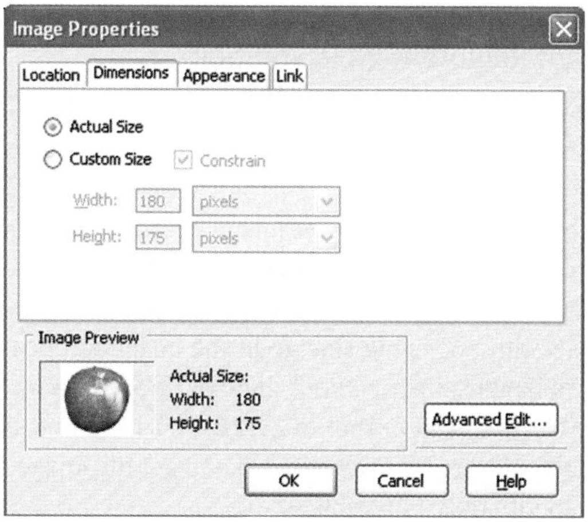

Figure 9.32

Dimensions tab in the Composer Image Properties dialog box

Image Properties
Location   Dimensions   Appearance   Link
⊙ Actual Size
○ Custom Size   ☑ Constrain
Width: 180   pixels
Height: 175   pixels
Image Preview
Actual Size: Width: 180   Height: 175   Advanced Edit...
OK   Cancel   Help

You can also change the image size by using the "handles" that appear on the image's borders when it is selected, as shown in Figure 9.33. Place the cursor on one of the handles, hold the mouse button down, and drag the handle appropriately to resize the image.

When you resize an image, be careful to preserve the original *scale* (the height-to-width ratio) using the corner handles only so that the resized image is not distorted (compressed or stretched). Also, keep in mind that shrinking an image by scaling it does not reduce its memory or bandwidth requirements. Scaling should only be used to make minor changes in the image size, especially if you are increasing the image size. To decrease the image file size to reduce download times, or to make significant changes in

Figure 9.33
Composer image handles, with the right handle selected

Handle

This handle is selected.

TIP: Web Images Do Not Require High Resolution

Most methods of creating digitally recorded images result in files with resolution far greater than most computer monitors can display. My digital camera produces images with a resolution of 180 pixels per inch (ppi), but a typical computer monitor displays images at 72 ppi. Most of the image information in the file is not needed by a computer displaying this image. A single photo requires about 11.1MB of storage at this resolution. Decreasing the resolution to 72 ppi decreases the storage requirement to 1.77MB with no visible change in the image's appearance. Decreasing the original image's dimensions by about one-half (from 12.6 inches to 6 inches wide) decreases the file size even further to 410KB. This is quite a significant change from the original file size! Note that we would like to get the image size even smaller, ideally less than about 40KB if possible.

the dimensions of your image, image processing software such as Adobe Photoshop is recommended.

Image Links. It is also possible to make an image behave like a link. The Composer "Link" tab in the Image Properties dialog box can be used to accomplish this. A picture can be converted into any of the four types of links discussed earlier: internal, relative, absolute, and mail links. Figure 9.34 shows the dialog box used to transform an ordinary image into a link using the Composer editor. To open the Image Properties dialog box, just double-click the image in Composer.

Figure 9.34

Link tab in the Composer Image Properties dialog box

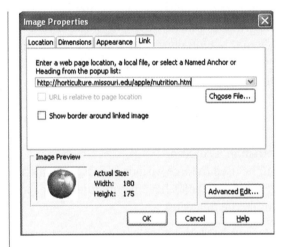

CHECKLIST: Web Page Construction Checklist 3

Now you try it!

1. Create a Web page with a paragraph of black text on a plain yellow background.
2. Download three image files from `http://www.grsites.com/` and add them to your page as inline images.
3. Align your images on the left side of the Web page with your text wrapping around them to the right.
4. Resize the middle image so it is three times as wide as the other two images (but the same height).
5. Convert one of your images into a link to the URL cited in Figure 9.34 (or some other absolute URL).
6. Test your page in the browser to make sure that your image link works.

9.4.8 Page Layouts Using Tables

If your Web pages are mostly text, you can skip this section. However, if you want your Web pages to grab attention and show off your content in style, you'll want to use tables to control the layout of your graphical elements. Note that in the absence of something like a table element, the arrangement of text, graphics, lists, and other page elements are not fixed; the browser will arrange elements in the window in order to minimize *clipping* due to the window borders.

You may have noticed that when you resize a Web browser window, the objects on your page sometimes rearrange themselves to accommodate the change. The most frequent change that occurs is the rearrangement of lines of text. If the window widens, then the lines of text will correspondingly lengthen. This may potentially reduce the number of lines of text in the window (but no text is lost, of course!). Likewise if the window is narrowed, then the lines of text will get shorter, with one or more words being moved to successive lines, potentially resulting in more lines of text. This same effect also occurs with images and other Web page objects. This can be annoying, especially when you have several small images that are intended to be displayed in a row rather than in a column.

Tables can be used to force various Web page elements to align with each other in specific ways. Tables have many other uses too. For example, with tables you can do the following:

- Change your background colors for different areas of the same page
- Add margins around your text so there is more room between the text and the edge of the browser's display window
- Create a two-column text display to make a Web page look more like a newsletter
- Override a busy background color or pattern with regions of contrasting solid colors to make text segments easier to read
- Add a three-dimensional frame around a picture to give your Web page a look of depth
- Center an image on a Web page no matter how the browser window is resized
- Display a table of data

Tables are powerful tools because they can adjust to any browser window and give the Web page author a lot of control over the layout of different visual elements.

All tables contain rows and columns, and distinct column elements for each column are placed in each row. The simplest possible table is a table that has one row and one column. If you have ever studied arrays or matrices in a mathematics class, a table may look like an array to you. The basic idea is the same, but with tables, the rows and columns are not indexed, so you can't refer to them with subscripts.

Adding a Table with a Caption. To add a table, put the cursor at the location where you want the table to be placed relative to the other page elements and click the Table button in the Composer Composition toolbar . A dialog box will appear, as shown in Figure 9.35, requesting basic information about the nature of the table to be inserted.

We will use a table to place the list and the links alongside each other rather than sequentially, as they now appear on the Apples page (last shown in Figure 9.26). The browser will not normally place these two elements side by side without some special work on our part using a table.

We will use a table size of 2 rows by 2 columns, with a border of 0 to make the table boundaries invisible when viewed by a browser. The table boundaries *will* be visible in the editor. If they weren't, you couldn't edit them! The first row of our table will hold the headings for the list and the links, and the next row will contain the values. The resultant Composer view of the table (only) is shown in Figure 9.36, and the Mozilla browser view is shown in Figure 9.37. Notice that the table borders are invisible when viewed by a browser.

Regardless of how the window is resized, the placement of the two lists and headings relative to each other will be maintained. In this way, we can create tables to coerce the Web page elements to appear in a specific relationship in respect to each other. For example, if we have four images we wish to display side by side, we can create a table with one row and four columns, and

Figure 9.35

Composer Insert Table dialog box

Figure 9.36

Composer view of
a table

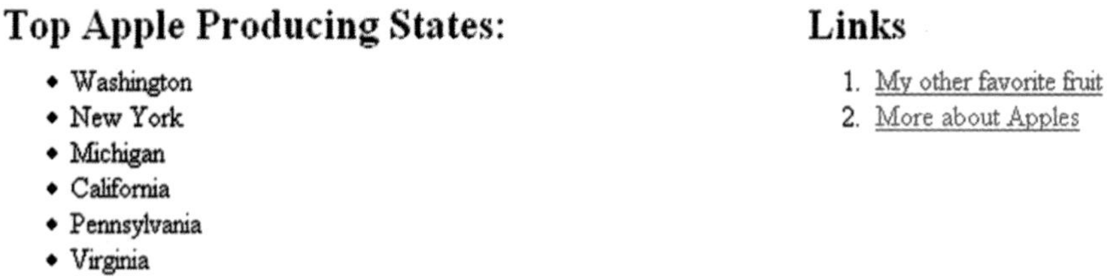

Top Apple Producing States:	Links
• Washington • New York • Michigan • California • Pennsylvania • Virginia	1. My other favorite fruit 2. More about Apples

Figure 9.37

Mozilla browser
view of a table

Top Apple Producing States: ## Links

• Washington
• New York
• Michigan
• California
• Pennsylvania
• Virginia

1. My other favorite fruit
2. More about Apples

place one picture in each column. This will force the browser to display the images side by side, regardless of the width of the window.

Curiously enough, double-clicking on the table border in Composer will cause a different Table Properties dialog box to open, as shown in Figure 9.38, with the Table tab selected. This dialog box provides a wider array of table formatting choices than those found in the Insert Table dialog box (displayed

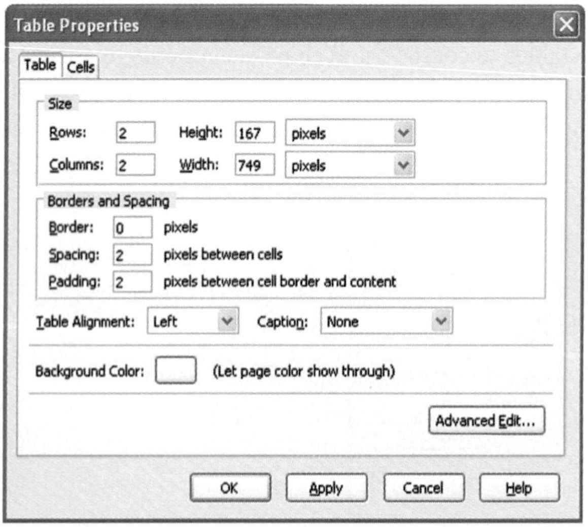

Figure 9.38

Composer Table
Properties dialog
box

Table Properties

Table | Cells

Size
Rows: 2   Height: 167   pixels
Columns: 2   Width: 749   pixels

Borders and Spacing
Border: 0   pixels
Spacing: 2   pixels between cells
Padding: 2   pixels between cell border and content

Table Alignment: Left   Caption: None

Background Color: [ ]   (Let page color show through)

Advanced Edit...

OK   Apply   Cancel   Help

when you click the Table button). We can change the alignment of the table relative to the left border of the page (the default value is left alignment), and we can assign a background color to the table using the background color button. Figure 9.39 shows a background color applied to the table in this way. We can also add or remove rows and columns, adjust the table alignment, change the border size, and change the spacing between separate cells in the table and the spacing between the cell border and its contents.

Selecting the Cell tab in this dialog box displays a different set of choices that will be applied only to the selected cell (see Figure 9.40). Among the things we can do here is change the color, size, and content alignment in the selected cell.

A caption that remains "attached" to the table but appears outside the table borders can also be placed using the Caption button (see Figure 9.38). In Composer, caption text can be placed by closing the Table Properties dialog

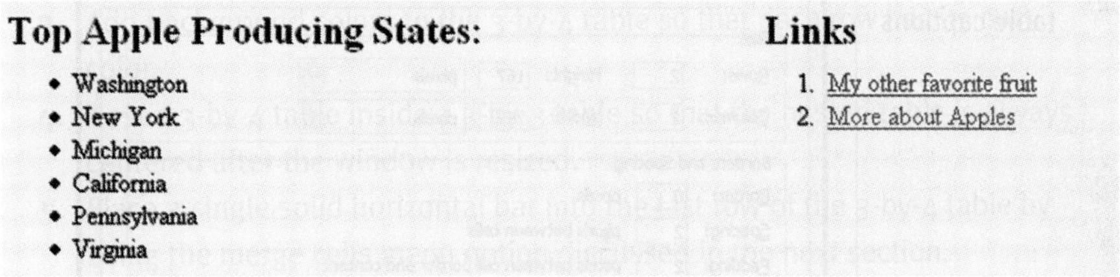

Figure 9.39

Browser view of a table with a background color

Top Apple Producing States:

- Washington
- New York
- Michigan
- California
- Pennsylvania
- Virginia

Links

1. My other favorite fruit
2. More about Apples

Figure 9.40

Cells tab in the Composer Table Properties dialog box

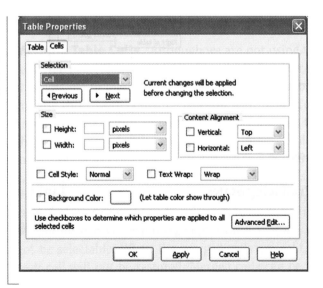

Figure 9.48 The complete Web page displayed in Mozilla

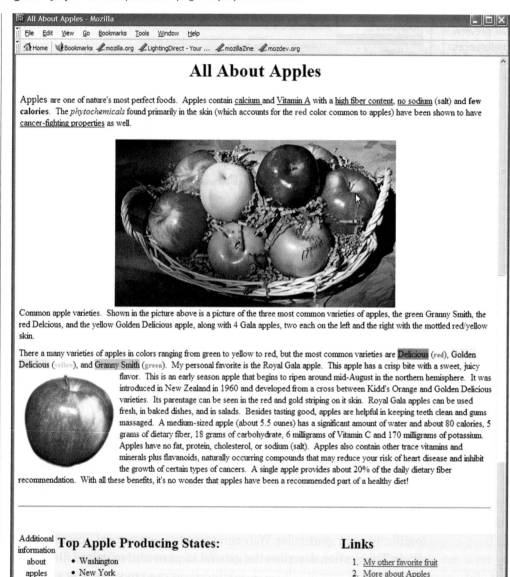

have a commercial banner ad appear in the browser window each time someone visits your site. If you pay for your Web server access by subscribing to a commercial ISP, you may be able to publish Web pages without the ads.

To install your pages on a server, you need to upload (copy) your files onto the server and make sure they go to the right place on the server. Some people run into trouble because they have the name of their Web server but are not clear about where their Web pages have to go on the server. Locations for files on Web servers are specified by directory paths. However, there can be more than one directory path. The path you see in a URL may not be the path that you need to use when you upload your files to the server. This can be a cause of much confusion.

Once you've uploaded your pages to the server, you are almost home free. However, there are still some snags that can get you. First, you need to know the URL that will allow you to view your pages with a Web browser. If you don't know this URL, you won't be able to tell people how to get to your site. Second, if your pages are on the server but the general public can't see them, you might need to fuss with file protection codes on the Web server. Problems with file protection codes should never occur on a commercial site, but it can in educational environments where the computer administrators might not be bending over backward to make your online activities as easy as possible.

Here is a summary of the six steps involved in publishing a Web page.

1. **Acquire access to a Web server.**
   You must do this before you do anything else. You need to know your user ID and password for your personal account on the Web server.

2. **Determine the DNS address of your Web server.**
   You might be able to find your Web server's DNS address in online documentation for your computer account. Look for a Frequently Asked Questions document. This address might have either an `ftp://` or

---

TIP: **Use the Refresh/Reload Button to Get the Latest Version**

When you update a Web page and upload it again to the Web server, you may find your browser still displaying an older version of the page just uploaded. This occurs because all browsers maintain a *cache* (aka *browser cache*) of recently viewed pages to save time, since the expectation is that you will want to see these pages again soon. If this happens, click the Refresh or Reload button in the browser you are using to force the browser to get the updated copy. Sometimes you need to hold down the Ctrl or ⌘ key (on a Mac) when you do this.

`http://` prefix. These represent the two different protocols that Web servers can support. If you can't find the DNS address in the online documentation, ask the staff members of the Help Desk for your computer account; they will be able to tell you the correct host name for your Web server.

TIP: You Probably Won't Be Able to Guess the DNS Address You Need

The DNS address might be the same address that appears in URL addresses for the server, or it might be something different. Chances are, it's something different.

3. **Determine the pathname needed when you upload files to the server.**
   This step is very similar to Step 2. Typically there will be a special directory or folder on the server where all Web files must be placed for publishing. You may be able to find this information online, or you may need to ask the Help Desk staff.

TIP: Don't Try to Guess at This Directory Path

It is probably not the same directory path that appears in the URL for your home page.

4. **Upload your Web files to the Web server.**
   Do this by using an FTP client or a Web page construction tool such as Mozilla Composer. As long as you have the correct information from steps 2 and 3, you should be able to complete this step. (For more discussion on this step, see Sections 9.5.1 and 9.5.2.)

5. **Determine the URL to use to view your home page.**
   While working on steps 2 and 3, ask about this URL. Anyone who knows the answer to the other questions should be able to answer this one.

6. **Fix any file protection codes that need fixing.**
   (With luck you won't need to do this.)
   This step applies only if you've successfully completed steps 1 through 5 and you still cannot view your home page on the Web server. If you visit your page and the browser displays an error message that says you are not authorized ("Forbidden") to view the page (it may say something about access permission), then you need to adjust some settings on the Web server that control which files can be viewed by the public

and which cannot. If you visit your page and the browser returns a "404 Not Found" error message, then your Web page has not been installed correctly. To fix this problem, you'll need to repeat one of the earlier steps.

9.5.1 Uploading Your Pages

You can upload files with Netscape, Mozilla, or Internet Explorer. (See the Tip "Uploading Files by Using a Browser" in Section 6.10 for more details.) You can also upload files with an FTP client (see Section 6.10). In this section, we illustrate the process of uploading your pages using Mozilla; other software will operate similarly.

Even if you created your Web pages without using Composer, you can use Composer to upload them to a Web server. Follow these steps.

1. From the File menu, select Open File and then use the dialog box to locate an HTML file you are ready to upload.
2. From the File menu, select Publish. Figure 9.49 shows the window that pops up at this time.
3. Complete the fields in the pop-up window. If you are not using subdirectories, you can leave the site subdirectory field blank. If the page you want to publish has been saved and titled, and is open, then the first three fields will be filled-in automatically.
4. Click the Settings tab. Figure 9.50 shows this window.

Figure 9.49
Composer Publish tab

Figure 9.50

Composer
Settings tab

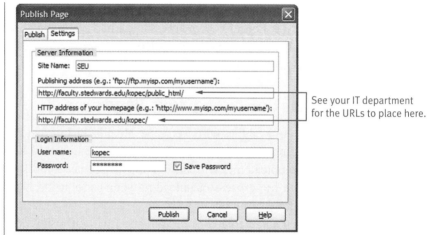

See your IT department
for the URLs to place here.

5. The first field, the site name, is your choice. The remaining two fields will be specific to your Web site provider; you will need to contact your provider for the correct values for these fields. Once you've entered this information, it becomes the default. Composer will fill it in for you automatically the next time you need to upload a Web page.

6. In the remaining two fields, your user name and password are those for your account on the Web server. If you are working on your own personal computer, you can check the "Save Password" checkbox so that these entries will be saved for you. If you are working in a public computer lab, you should *never* allow any software applications to save passwords for you.

7. Click Publish. A dialog box will appear indicating success or failure. If the page fails to publish, contact the help desk for advice.

TIP: File Uploads Cannot Be Undone

Be careful! If your directory on the Web server already contains a file with the same file name as one of the files you are uploading, the file being uploaded will overwrite the file on the server. You will probably not see any warnings, and you will not be asked if you want to overwrite the file. It will just happen. Once the original file has been overwritten, you won't be able to recover it if you decide you've made a mistake. Once you upload a file and overwrite an existing file, you can't undo the file upload.

9.5.2 Using an FTP Client to Upload Pages

If you have an **FTP client**, for example, WinSCP (see Section 6.10) for Windows or Fetch for the Mac, you can upload your files to a Web server using that client. You will need the same information just discussed in the previous section, but you will be able to find your way to the correct Web page directory by clicking each subdirectory along the way. This might seem easier than typing in the complete path as shown in Figure 9.50. However, it also might be slower if any of the intermediate subdirectories contain a thousand or more directory entries (this may be the case on some large Web servers that have many user accounts). Either way, you can connect to the server and upload your files. If you get an access permission error after you've uploaded your Web pages, contact your system administrator for assistance. You can fix it yourself, but you will need a working knowledge of UNIX protection codes; most people don't want to be bothered with this. Most Web servers available for general use are programmed to save authors from having to make these protection adjustments. With a little luck, you will never have to deal with any file access protection codes.

Some FTP clients have a setting you need to check before each upload command. You might need to tell your FTP client the type of file being uploaded: text or binary. Or your client might offer an automated setting that, when checked, instructs the client to figure this out based on the file extension. If you have an automated option, take it.

All FTP clients can recognize the most common file types used for Web pages. If you have to select this setting yourself, separate your text files (.htm and .html) from your binary files (.png, .jpg, and .gif) and transfer them in different upload groups. If you pick the wrong setting for a file, the file will be transferred to the server and you won't see any warning or error message. However, the resulting file will probably be mangled and unusable. If any of your file transfers fail to produce healthy copies of your original files, try the transfer again, paying attention to any file type settings you might need to reset.

9.6 Image File Formats

In the previous sections we showed how images could be placed on pages, but we did not talk much about the characteristics of the files we use. There are three different types of image files that can be displayed by a typical browser.

Each file format has its particular advantages and disadvantages. In this section we will discuss these file formats so you can choose the correct format for the particular type of image you wish to display.

9.6.1 File Formats Used for Images

As mentioned earlier in this chapter, the two most popular file formats used for Web page graphics are the GIF and the JPEG (referred to as *JPG*) formats. The GIF (Graphics Interchange Format) format is best for line art, cartoons, and simple images. The JPEG (Joint Photographic Experts Group) format is better for photographs and artwork that include many colors or special effects. Figure 9.51 shows a GIF image acquired from a book via a scanner. A third file format that is increasing in popularity is the .PNG format. Pronounced "ping," the PNG (Portable Network Graphics) format was designed to be a royalty-free replacement, including source code and documentation, for the GIF file format and the patented compression algorithm it uses. PNG features better lossless compression (read on), and it stores information that allows variable transparency, image scaling information for display at different resolutions, and brightness data. In time, the PNG format may eventually replace the GIF format. It can also compete successfully with the TIFF format (discussed next), which it may also replace. Unlike GIF, how-

Figure 9.51

A 38KB GIF image acquired from a scanner

THE BADGER-DOG AT WORK.

Prior to the development of PNG, the GIF format was widely used for the insertion of images onto Web pages. In 1995, Unisys and CompuServe announced that they would start charging royalties for the use of the GIF file format. It turns out that Unisys held the patent on the algorithm used to compress GIF images, so royalties could legally be charged of any user of the format. PNG suddenly had a reason for being!

A variation of the PNG is the MNG (Multiple-image Network Graphics, pronounced "ming") format. The MNG format shares many of the advantages of the PNG format, plus the ability to produce animations. The MNG format has better compression and more sophisticated looping control than GIF. Unfortunately, few browsers come packaged with the capability to display a MNG image. But you may be able to find a browser add-on for your browser to view MNGs.

ever, PNG does *not* provide multiple image support (animations). However, there are other ways to add animation using PNG images.

Be careful acquiring images from books, magazines, and newspapers—they are usually subject to copyright restrictions (see Section 9.2 and Appendix D). This file is named *woodcut2.gif* (see Figure 9.51), and its size is 38KB.

The scanner originally created a **TIFF (Tagged Image File Format)** file (another graphics format) that was 100KB. Then a software tool was used to convert the TIFF file into a GIF file (see Section 9.9 for a description of graphics viewers and converters). The GIF image looks as good as the TIFF image, but it is considerably smaller (byte-wise). Keeping graphics files small is important when you are putting them on the Web because smaller files mean faster Web page downloading. As a rule of thumb, try to use image files that are no larger than 40KB. The GIF and PNG formats are very good for the Web because they can significantly reduce the size of many image files without compromising the quality of the image.

The JPG file format is better suited for high-resolution photographs and sophisticated artwork that contains many colors. Whenever an image contains a subtle spectrum of color and you want to see smooth transitions across the spectrum, you should work with the JPG format. Figure 9.52 shows

Figure 9.52
GIF images (top) and JPG images (bottom) handle color gradients differently.

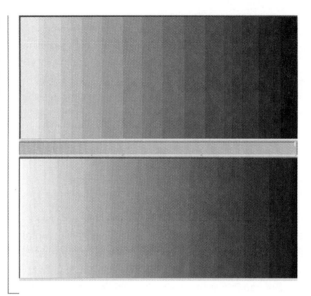

a computer-generated color spectrum saved in both GIF and JPG formats. The GIF image (on the top) shows significant "banding," which is the result of abrupt color transitions. The JPG image (on the bottom) exhibits some banding, but much less than the GIF image.

The JPG format is also very good for the Web because JPG images can be compressed using **lossy compression** techniques, which reduce the amount of memory required by an image in exchange for some degradation in the image quality. Many JPG images can be compressed to a certain point without any visible loss of quality. After that, additional attempts to compress the image result in increasingly unacceptable reductions in image quality. Some images can be greatly compressed without visible detriment, but eventually a large amount of compression causes the quality of the image to degrade. Some amount of degradation might be worth an additional reduction in file size, but eventually the image will become unacceptable. Figure 9.53 shows four different levels of compression on a JPG image that was originally 46KB. The image on the far left shows no visible signs of degradation even though it has been compressed by 59 percent into a 19KB file. The other three images show increasing levels of degradation at 7KB, 5KB, and 3KB. The 19KB version is perfectly acceptable for the Web. The PNG format is "lossless," meaning that no information is lost when the picture is compressed. However, for photographs, JPG is still better, even if it is "lossy."

Figure 9.53
Lossy
compression
trades image
quality for smaller
files.

When large images cannot be reduced effectively via compression techniques, Web page authors have other tricks they can use. One of these, the thumbnail preview, is described in the Above & Beyond section.

9.6.2 Using Transparent GIFs

There are many tools and special effects you can use to make your graphics more striking. Many of them do not require artistic talent. One technique that every Web author should know about is the effect achieved by transparent images. A **transparent GIF** or **PNG** looks as if it were drawn directly on your Web page (see Figure 9.54). To create a transparent GIF or PNG, you designate some portion of the image as the background of the image. Then, whenever that image is placed on a Web page, the image's background region behaves as if it were transparent, inheriting the background color (or pattern) of the Web page beneath it.

Transparent images work well on images that have clearly defined backgrounds, such as line art and cartoons. You can turn a photograph into a transparent image after some digital tinkering with the right graphics tools. There are many good image-editing tools available to help you doctor your images (see Section 9.9).

If you want to turn a photograph into a transparent image (see Figure 9.55), you need to edit the background of the photograph in order to make it one uniform color. (Even if a photograph appears to have a uniform background color, there are almost always a few different colors dispersed throughout that region—you can see them at the pixel level when viewed with an image editor.) Pick a color not found elsewhere in the picture. If the

Figure 9.54

A transparent GIF

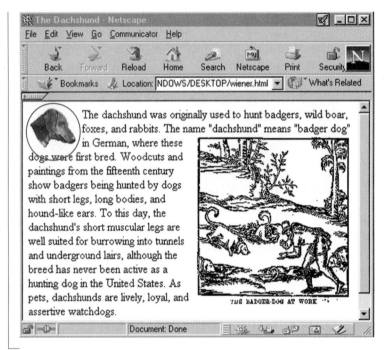

Figure 9.55

Transforming a photograph into a transparent GIF

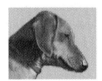

background color occurs in places other than the background, those pixels will be replaced by the Web page's background as well. Once you have prepared the image, you can convert it to a transparent image. Figure 9.56 shows a Web page service that will help you convert plain PNG or GIF files into transparent image files, as long as you can upload the image you want to convert onto a public Web server. After you have created the transparent image, you can experiment with various background colors to find one that works well with the image.

Transparent images are often used for buttons and navigational icons as well as larger pieces of artwork. A few small transparent images can dress up

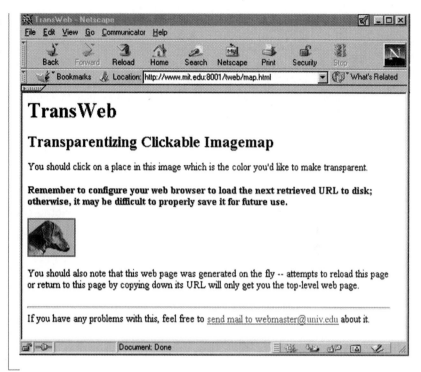

a Web site without overpowering it. You can also use transparent images in various ways to create special effects and color-coordinated page layouts (see the Above & Beyond section of this chapter for more examples).

 # All about Color

Color is an important tool to use when building a Web page. Color can appear in the background, as colored text, or color images. Without doubt, color can add a great deal of flash to your Web page. This section discusses how color selection is specified to the browser, how you can assign a background to your page, and explains true color, color palettes, and Web-safe colors.

9.7.1 Color Codes

The simplest way to dress up a page of text is with a background color or pattern. When you tell a Web browser to color the background of a Web page, you have a choice of 16,777,216 colors. If that seems too overwhelming, you

TIP: CSS and RGB Color Code

Although HTML uses a hexadecimal code to specify a color, CSS uses RGB code, so it's very useful to learn both types of color. When a Web page editor is configured to produce CSS compliant code (see Section 9.4.1), then you will see this coding scheme used in many places where hexadecimal code would otherwise appear. We will learn about CSS in Section 10.3.

can select from any of 216 **Web-safe colors**, colors that can be faithfully reproduced on any computer monitor regardless of the operating system used.

All Web browsers use a code system for describing colors in **hexadecimal notation**. Each code contains 6 characters from the 16 possible alphanumeric digits (0123456789ABCDEF) used to represent numbers in base 16 (hence the name, *hexadecimal*). You can find out which codes to use for various colors on any number of Web sites that show color wheels or charts illustrating the 216 Web-safe colors (also see the last page of this book).

The hexadecimal color code and RGB (red-green-blue) color code are two different notations for describing colors. The RGB code is based on three color dimensions: red, green, and blue. These are the colors given off by the phosphorous coating inside an RGB color monitor in order to create colored pixels on the monitor. Each dimension can have any value between 0 and 255 inclusive; a value from each of the three spectra specifies a unique color for that pixel. For example, the RGB value (0,0,255) is royal blue and the value (0,192,192) is a dark turquoise blue. All RGB decimal numbers can also be described as hexadecimals (base 16 instead of base 10). For example, (0,0,255) in decimal notation becomes (0,0,FF) in hexadecimal notation and (0,192,192) becomes (0,C0,C0).

To minimize keystrokes, hexadecimal RGB values are normally run together in one six-digit string, adding leading zeros as needed to fill up the full six digits. For example, (0,0,FF) is written as 0000FF. Given one notation, you can always convert to the other. However, because HTML requires hexadecimal notation, it's more convenient to work with software that gives you the hexadecimal color codes directly.

9.7.2 Adding a Background Color to a Web Page

To add a background color to a Web page in Composer, choose Format > Page Colors and Background to display the dialog box shown in Figure 9.57. Select the "Use custom colors" button and select the "Background" button. You can

Figure **9.57**
Composer back-
ground color
selection

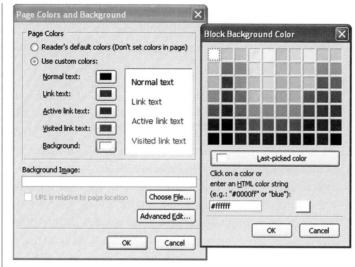

select the background color from the color palette that appears or enter the hex code (using the codes found in the inside back cover) into the text box shown in the Block Background Color dialog box, preceded by a pound sign (#). Most browsers will also recognize some number of **standard colors** based on names alone. For example, if you type "blue" into this text box (without the pound sign), the background color is set to blue. Almost all Web browsers will recognize these 16 color names: *aqua, gray, navy, silver, black, green, olive, teal, blue, lime, purple, fuchsia, maroon, red, white,* and *yellow*. These names are case-insensitive. Of course you will probably prefer to use the color picker chart display in this dialog box and let your editor do the typing for you.

Color Palettes. A **color palette** is a collection of colors. Some color palettes are larger than others, and these differences are important for certain types of image manipulations. For example, you may encounter references to 8-bit color and 24-bit color. These terms describe the size of the affiliated color palettes. All the colors in an 8-bit palette can be represented with bit strings of length 8. All the colors in a 24-bit palette can be represented with bit strings of length 24. Recall that a bit has only two possible values—0 and 1— so the number of possible bit strings with exactly 8 bits is $2 \times 2 \times 2 \times 2 \times 2 \times 2 \times 2 \times 2 = 256$. It follows that an 8-bit color palette contains exactly 256 colors. The number of possible bit strings with exactly 24 bits is the same as all the possible combinations of three 8-bit strings (place three 8-bit strings next to each other and you have one 24-bit string), or $256 \times 256 \times 256 = 16,777,216$. So a 24-bit palette contains exactly 16,777,216 colors. If you ever see a software preference setting that says "millions of colors," that means 24-bit color.

What Is True Color? The term **true color** refers to any image in which each pixel in the image is defined in terms of its actual color value. In the RGB color system, each pixel must represent one of 256 (8-bit) possible color values for each of the R, G, and B dimensions. Any 24-bit (or higher) palette based on RGB colors (or its equivalent hexadecimal notation) produces a true color image. JPG images are true color images. GIF images are not true color because they are restricted to a smaller color palette. Image formats that are limited to 256 colors or fewer produce **indexed color** images instead of true color images. All GIF images have 8-bit indexed color. TIFF images can use either true color (like a JPG image) or indexed color (like a GIF image). PNG images support up to 48-bit true color (including 24-bit true color), 16-bit grayscale (as the name suggests, images are rendered only in shades of gray), and 8-bit palette image types. As such, it is potentially superior to both GIF and JPG images; however, JPG format is still recommended for photographic images because JPG compression produces smaller files than are possible with PNG.

All JPG images use 24-bit color, although the exact set of colors in that palette may not be the same on all computer monitors or all operating systems. For example, the color palette used by Macintosh computers is a bit more subdued and less vibrant than the palette used by Windows. For color computer monitors (and therefore Web page displays), 24-bit color is more than adequate—no one needs a larger color palette for Web graphics. The GIF format can save images in relatively small files by restricting each image to 8-bit color, so the images that work well in GIF format are those that do not require millions of different colors. Indeed, if an image cannot be faithfully reproduced using a color palette of only 256 colors, then that image is not a good candidate for a GIF file. Yet a surprising number of images display very nicely with 8-bit color, including many photographs. The power of the

FYI: 32-bit Color Standard

A new color standard has been defined that uses 32 bits. The array of colors is the same as that used for 24-bit color. The extra 8 bits are used to assign an opacity value to each pixel, referred to as *alpha transparency*. The extra byte is used to represent one of 256 possible levels of transparency, ranging from completely transparent to completely opaque.

GIF (and PNG) format lies in the fact that although each image is limited to 256 colors, the color palette is customized for each image so that a different set of 256 colors is used for each image. Similar advantages can be realized with the PNG format as well, without the fear of patent infringement, primarily a concern for developers rather than casual Web page authors.

You can achieve many fanciful visual effects by manipulating color palettes. Figure 9.58 shows an undoctored photograph of a horse on the left, next to the same photograph rendered with a different color palette on the right. Two more renderings of the same image using different color palettes are shown in Figure 9.59, and this figure shows the explicit 8-bit color palettes underlying each image.

Figure 9.58
GIF color palettes revealed

Figure 9.59
The same image with two different color palettes

Color palettes used

Background Patterns

You can use any PNG, JPG, or GIF file as a background for a Web page. With Composer this can be done using the Format menu to open the Page Colors and Background dialog box shown in Figure 9.57. Use the "Choose File..." button to select the file with the desired background image. The browser will place the background file in the upper-left corner of the Web page and will repeat the graphic behind your other Web page elements in a tiling pattern from left to right and from top to bottom as needed to fill the entire browser display window (see Figure 9.60).

Although the mechanics of background files are trivial, the artistry is not. Some files work better as tiles than others. If you have any artistic inclinations, this is a good place to experiment with images and image editors. Keep your background files small (byte-wise) so that you don't slow down your page's downloading. If you cannot resist using a large file for your background pattern, you should add both a background color and a background image to the BODY element. The background color will appear immediately, giving a

Figure 9.60

Web page with a tiled pattern background

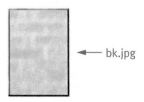

The Dachshund

The dachshund was originally bred to hunt badger, wild boar, fox, and rabbit. The dachshund comes from Germany and the name "dachshund" means "badger dog" in German. Woodcuts and paintings from the fifteenth century show badgers being hunted by dogs with short legs, long bodies, and hound-like ears.

To this day, the dachshund's short muscular legs are well suited for burrowing into tunnels and underground lairs, although the breed has never been active as a hunting dog in the United States. As pets, dachshunds are lively, loyal, and assertive watchdogs.

← bk.jpg